Mastering Java 1.1

Second Edition

Mastering™ Java™ 1.1

Second Edition

Laurence Vanhelsuwé
Ivan Phillips
Goang-Tay Hsu
Krishna Sankar
Eric Ries
Philip Heller
John McGloughlin
John Zukowski

SYBEX®

San Francisco · Paris · Düsseldorf · Soest

Associate Publisher: Amy Romanoff
Acquisitions Manager: Kristine Plachy
Acquisitions & Developmental Editor: Suzanne Rotondo
Editor: Marilyn Smith
Project Editor: Alison Moncrieff
Technical Editor: John Zukowski
Graphic Illustrators: Patrick Dintino, Inbar Berman
Desktop Publisher: Franz Baumhackl
Production Coordinator: Robin Kibby
Proofreaders: Jennifer Metzger, Theresa Gonzalez
Indexer: Ted Laux
Cover Designer: Design Site
Cover Illustrator/Photographer: Sergie Loobkoff, Mark Johann

Screen reproductions produced with Collage Complete.

Collage Complete is a trademark of Inner Media Inc.

SYBEX is a registered trademark of SYBEX Inc.
Mastering is a trademark of SYBEX Inc.

TRADEMARKS: SYBEX has attempted throughout this book to
distinguish proprietary trademarks from descriptive terms by
following the capitalization style used by the manufacturer.

Netscape Communications, the Netscape Communications logo,
Netscape, and Netscape Navigator are trademarks of Netscape
Communications Corporation.

Library of Congress Card Number: 97-65906
ISBN: 0-7821-2070-9

Manufactured in the United States of America

10 9 8 7 6 5 4 3 2 1

THE AUTHORS

Laurence Vanhelsuwé (lva@telework.demon.co.uk) is an independent software engineer. He is the typical self-taught wiz kid who, after dropping out of higher education, started his professional career writing arcade games. Soon after, he worked on such diverse technologies as X.25 WAN routers, Virtual Reality flight simulation, PostScript, and real-time digitized video-based traffic analysis. Laurence thinks Java will revolutionize computer science by leveling the computing landscape into one pan-Java playing field.

Ivan Phillips, Ph.D., is president of Pendragon Software Corporation, a software development and consulting firm specializing in Java programming and PDA applications. He is the author of the CaffeineMark applet, the industry standard Java benchmark.

Goang-Tay Hsu is a graduate of both Ohio State University and Carnegie Mellon University. He is now with Yahoo! Inc. Before that, he worked for Enterprise Integration Technologies Inc., Knight-Ridder Information Inc. (formerly Dialog), and Lexical Technologies Inc. His areas of interest include information retrieval, WWW service, user interface design, internationalization, and Java.

Krishna Sankar is the cofounder and president of US Systems & Services Inc., a San Francisco Java technology company. He has experience in designing and developing various systems ranging from real-time process control applications to client/server and groupware systems for organizations like the U.S. Air Force and Navy, Hewlett Packard, AT&T, GM, Ford, Testek, Qantas Airways, and TRW. Currently you will find him evangelizing the "information reengineering through components based on Java servlets and applets" paradigm. Occasionally you will also see him searching in vain for venture capitalists to expand his software company.

Eric Ries is a student at Yale University. Eric writes in what spare time he has left after his class work, watching Star Trek, and reading Ayn Rand.

Philip Heller is a software consultant and a Java instructor. He worked as an engineer for both Sun Microsystems and NeXT in the early years. He is the co-author of *Java 1.1 Developer's Handbook* (Sybex, 1997).

John McGloughlin is a founder of Focused Technologies, a research and development company specializing in electronic and optical sorting equipment. He teaches C and Visual Basic programming at the University of California, Davis Extension. His experience over the last 17 years includes programming in assembler, C, C++, Pascal, Delphi, Basic, VB, and Java. John's interest in Java was ignited by its platform independence, the compact JavaOS, and Java chip technologies.

John Zukowski (`j.zukowski@ieee.org`) is having fun with Java as he writes/edits books, speaks at conferences, and teaches Java for MageLang Institute. In November 1995, John founded the Mid-Atlantic Java UserGroup (MAJUG), which he coordinated until his move out of the DC area. Before Java, John was a C/X-Windows/database/network programmer for a Maryland-based consulting firm. He has a master's degree in computer science from Johns Hopkins University, with undergraduate degrees in math and computer science from Northeastern University. He is currently working on a new book, *Borland JBuilder: No experience required* (Sybex) due out in late Summer 1997.

ACKNOWLEDGMENTS

The reason there are no names on the front cover of *Mastering Java 1.1* is that listing every team member who worked on this book would obscure some of the cover artwork! It took a large group of people—working overtime and then some—to transform these chapters into a cohesive, in-depth exploration of Java technology.

In the frontline trenches, of course, were the authors:

Introduction: John Zukowski

Chapters 1–4: Ivan Phillips (revised by Eric Ries)

Chapters 5–8: Goang-Tay Hsu

Chapters 9–16: Laurence Vanhelsuwé (revised by Philip Heller)

Chapters 17: Krishna Sankar (revised by John McGloughlin)

Chapters 18–22: John Zukowski and Philip Heller

Chapter 23: John McGloughlin

Appendix A: Eric Ries

At Sybex, many people processed the authors' less-than-perfect raw manuscript. Foremost were our editors, Suzanne Rotondo, Marilyn Smith, Linda Good, and Alison Moncrieff, and our technical editor, John Zukowski. And let's not forget Sybex's Patrick Dintino and Inbar Berman, who transformed Stone Age sketches into the quality illustrations and diagrams you see in the book; Electronic Publishing Specialist Franz Baumhackl who meticulously laid out every page of this big book; Production Coordinator Robin Kibby, who, in addition to shuttling manuscript to all parts of the globe, worked to ensure these pages be error-free; and finally the CD-ROM Producers

Dale Wright and Molly Sharp, who created the high-quality CD that accompanies this book.

Last but not least, we should acknowledge that without the Internet itself (the cauldron from which Java emerged glowing and hot), this book would have been much harder to produce. The authors of this book are scattered geographically over the continent. But thanks to the Internet, the lines of communication among the team members were kept open. E-mail, World Wide Web, and IRC technologies were all exploited to meet the communication and organizational needs such a project requires.

While fascinating computer technology is both the raison d'être for and a key catalyst in creating the book you are holding, it is hoped that you—the reader and software developer—will use the knowledge presented herein to improve our world, and not just to make it smaller, faster, or cheaper.

—Laurence Vanhelsuwé

CONTENTS AT A GLANCE

Appendices

TABLE OF CONTENTS

PART III   **Advanced Topics**   **725**

17   **The Java Virtual Machine**   **727**

INTRODUCTION

Welcome to *Mastering Java 1.1, Second Edition*, the book that provides comprehensive coverage of the latest version of the Java language. This book takes you through introductory, intermediate, and advanced topics to lead you on your way to becoming a proficient Java programmer.

A Road Map

Is this book for you? Although this book was designed with a logical sequence in mind, most readers will not pick it up and read it from cover to cover. Depending on your particular background, the following should help you figure out how to make this book suit your individual needs.

For Non-C/C++ Programmers

If you are new to Java and the C/C++ style of programming, you will probably need to go through the whole book. Some concepts will be similar to those of other languages, but in order to get a grasp on how Java does things, you should work through each of the examples yourself. You might want to take a break of a few hours or days between sections to make sure you understand the material you have read.

For C/C++ Programmers

Due to the similarities between C/C++ and Java, C/C++ programmers can probably breeze through several chapters of this book.

C programmers can skim through most of Chapters 4 and 6; C++ programmers can additionally skim Chapter 3, the sections in Chapter 5 on classes, and Chapter 7 if you have dealt with exception handling. While these chapters are worth reviewing, they do not demand the attention that the completely new material in the remainder of the book requires.

For Java Programmers

If you have played with Java on your own and decided it was time to get a book to help you out, most of Part I will probably be review. Scan through it to see if there is anything you might have missed in your prior travels, paying special attention to Chapters 7 and 8, which cover exception handling and multithreading, respectively. If Java 1.1 is new to you, be sure to look through the description of inner classes in Chapter 5.

For Everyone

Once you have your bearings, use the table of contents to find the areas that interest you most. Chapters 10, 11, and 12 go together somewhat; they deal with building and using Java forms. (Some people might find reading Chapter 11 before Chapter 10 more natural.) If you are particularly interested in network programming (the subject of Chapter 16), you need to have a grasp of I/O first (covered in Chapter 15), since networking builds upon input and output streams. You can read the other chapters in almost any order.

The examples given in each chapter clarify the concepts explained, and reviewing the code provides a better understanding of the topic. All the source code is on the enclosed CD, so you do not need to type in the examples yourself.

Features and Structure of This Book

The goal of this book is simple: to make you productive with Java as quickly as possible. This book contains a great deal of information; use the table of contents in the front and/or the extensive index in the back to locate the information you need. Here are brief descriptions of what is in the book and where you can find it.

Part I: Foundations of Java

The first part of the book introduces you to Java—the history, the language, and the programming concepts. Chapter 1 starts off with a lesson on what Java is and where Java came from. Chapter 2 gets you started using the Java development environment. In Chapter 3, you learn about object-oriented programming basics. Chapter 4 describes the Java language grammar. In Chapter 5, you start to build up your understanding of Java by learning about classes, interfaces, and packages. Chapter 6 explains how Java deals with arrays and flow control. In Chapter 7, you learn about Java's exception-handling mechanisms. Finally, in Chapter 8, you learn how to create multithreaded programs in Java.

Part II: Applying Standard Java Classes

The next part of the book examines the Java libraries (or *packages* in Java-speak). Chapter 9 provides a brief overview of the different Java packages and their parts. Chapter 10 describes the windowing package and how you can position objects on the screen. In Chapter 11, you learn about the different objects a user interacts with. Chapter 12 explains how to deal with those interactions, through events. Chapter 13 provides an overview of the graphics and animation capabilities of Java. In Chapter 14, techniques from the previous four chapters are put together for more advanced programming. Chapter 15 introduces you to I/O programming through Java streams. Finally, Chapter 16 teaches you how to make your programs Internet savvy.

Part III: Advanced Topics

The third part of the book is designed for those who want to learn more about Java. Read these chapters if you are interested in taking your Java programs to the next level, and if you would like to look under the covers to see how Java works from the inside.

Chapter 17 provides the behind-the-scenes details of the Java Virtual Machine (JVM). Chapter 18 introduces Java Database Connectivity (JDBC) for access to SQL databases. In Chapter 19, you learn about applet-based shopping and Java's Electronic Commerce Framework (JECF). Chapter 20 discusses the JavaBeans API and how it stretches your software development budget. In Chapter 21, you learn about the Java Web Server and extending your Web server through servlets. In Chapter 22, Remote Method Invocation (RMI) and serialization, for distributed computing and object persistence support, are explained. Finally, Chapter 23 takes a look at JavaOS, the Java Desktop, and Network Computers, and how they will change the future of network computing.

At the Back

After the chapters, you will find two appendices and a glossary. Appendix A contains a list of deprecated methods. When Java 1.1 was released, JavaSoft decided that old method names were not good enough. Numerous methods were renamed, mostly to follow various design patterns. This appendix provides a mapping of old names to new. Although you can continue to use the old names, for now, the compiler generates a warning if you do. Appendix B includes instructions on how to install the companion CD. The glossary provides definitions of terms related to Java programming.

What Is on the CD?

The CD contains all the source code from the examples in the book, along with the appropriate HTML applet loaders. In addition, numerous third-party tools and class libraries are provided for many hours of enjoyment. See Appendix B for details.

Conventions

This book uses various conventions to help you find the information you need quickly. Tips, Notes, and Warnings, shown here, are placed throughout the book to help you locate important highlights quickly.

TIP   This is a tip. Tips contain helpful hints and information to make you more productive with Java faster.

NOTE   This is a note. Notes contain extra information related to the discussion at hand.

WARNING   This is a warning. Warnings contain information that flags potential trouble spots.

In addition, the book takes advantage of various font styles. **Bold** font in text indicates something that the user types (in a text field, for instance). A `monospaced` program font is used for program code.

The program code itself follows the standard conventions for capitalization used by the Java API. For example, in class names, each word is capitalized, and in function names, each word but the first one is capitalized. The code formatting follows standard programming conventions: a left brace is placed at the end of a line (or the start of the next line), the right brace is on its own line, and indentation is used to highlight the grouping of code.

Technical Support

When you need help, there are several sources available for technical support. Some of your options are described here.

FAQs

There is a plethora of Java-related Frequently Asked Question lists (FAQs) available online. The following are some FAQ sites:

`http://java.sun.com/sfaq/index.html`	One of the most useful lists, maintained by Sun. It answers numerous security-related Java questions.
`http://sunsite.unc.edu/javafaq/javafaq.html`	This tends to answer questions for people new to Java development.
`http://www-net.com/java/faq/`	An index that lists some other FAQs.

Product Support

Depending on the tools you are using, it may be prudent to go through the technical support channels available for a particular product. This could involve toll-free or 1-900 support (live or prerecorded), the World Wide Web, or online newsgroups, among other options.

Check the documentation provided with the tool or Web-based source you are using to see what support is available. If you are using the Java Development Kit (JDK) from Sun, the first place to look is the bug list at `http://www.javasoft.com/products/jdk/1.1/knownbugs/index.html` to see if the problem you have encountered is a product bug. Symantec Café users should start at `http://cafe.symantec.com`. Most other products maintain similar sites.

Newsgroups

When the Java hype was just beginning, there were no newsgroups, and Sun was running a handful of mailing lists to keep everyone informed and provide a question-and-answer medium. The Sun mail server quickly got bogged down due to the popularity (and cross-mailing list postings), and the newsgroup `comp.lang.java` was born (along with `alt.www.hotjava`). Over time, `comp.lang.java` became so popular (thousands of messages per week) that the signal-to-noise ratio nearly made the group useless. After much debate, conflict, and a vote, the single group split into eight:

`comp.lang.java.advocacy`

`comp.lang.java.announce` (moderated)

`comp.lang.java.api`

`comp.lang.java.misc`

`comp.lang.java.programmer`

`comp.lang.java.security`

`comp.lang.java.setup`

`comp.lang.java.tech`

Somewhere in one of those groups is either the answer to your unasked question or someone who can answer it. If the question has already been asked and answered, you can search the archives at either Digital Espresso (a digest version of the newsgroups), `http://www.mentorsoft.com/DE/`, or DejaNews (a Usenet search utility), `http://dejanews.com`. For those who are inclined not to read the news, MageLang maintains a moderated mailing list (`http://www.MageLang.com/mailing_list.html`) that is monitored by some of the members of the early development team.

User Groups

Another good source of information is area user groups. Focus tends to vary widely, but networking is almost always key. And there is usually someone in the group who can answer your question. To find a group in your area, look at JavaSoft's list at `http://www.javasoft.com/aboutJava/usrgrp.html` or the Java Special Interest Group (of the Sun User Group) list at `http://www.sug.org/Java/groups.html`. Most groups maintain a mailing list of some sort to send technical questions.

Books and Periodicals

Sybex offers many books at all levels of expertise. For more advanced questions, the *Java Developer's Handbook* (Sybex, 1997) may hold the answers. Or if you encounter a problem that is not Java related, another Sybex offering may provide the solution. For the latest catalog, write to:

Sybex Inc.

1151 Marina Village Parkway

Alameda, CA 94501

Tel: (800) 227-2346

Fax: (510) 523-2373

You can also visit the Sybex Web page at `http://www.sybex.com`, where you will find a searchable catalog and updates to this book.

On the Java side, there are also some magazines you might want to read. *JavaWorld* is an online publication at `http://www.javaworld.com`. *Java Report* is a print publication with information available from `http://www.sigs.com/java/`. Also, *Java Developers Journal* is a combined print/online publication at `http://www.JavaDevelopers-Journal.com/java/`. There are others, and more are popping up all the time from the different magazine houses.

PART 1

Foundations of Java

CHAPTER
ONE

Introducing Java

- Java and its history

- Java and the World Wide Web

- The Java architecture

Java is a technology that makes it easy to build *distributed applications*, which are programs executed by multiple computers across a network. The state of the art in network programming, Java promises to expand the Internet's role from an arena for communications to a network on which full-fledged applications can be run. Its breakthrough technology will allow businesses to deploy full-scale transaction services and real-time, interactive information on the Internet.

Java also simplifies the construction of *software agents*, which are programs that move across a network and perform functions on remote computers on behalf of the user. In the near future, users may be able to send software agents from their PCs out onto the Internet to locate specific information or make time-critical transactions anywhere in the world.

Before Java, the Internet was primarily used for information-sharing. Though the Internet was created in the 1960s, it only started to realize its business potential in the 1990s, thanks to the World Wide Web. The Web is a technology that treats Internet resources as linked documents, and it has revolutionized the way we access information. The Web has enabled Internet users to access Internet services without learning cryptic commands. Through the Web, businesses can easily create online corporate images, provide product information, and even sell merchandise directly through PCs. Java technology will take this a step further by making it possible to serve fully interactive applications via the Web. The reasons so much attention has been paid to Java are summarized in the following list of what Java allows the developer to do:

- Write robust and reliable programs.

2. • Build an application on almost any platform, and run that application on any other supported platform without recompiling the code.

3. • Distribute applications over a network in a secure fashion.

In particular, Java programs can be embedded into Web documents, turning static pages into applications that run on the user's computer. No longer is online documentation limited to articles, like a printed book. With Java, the documentation can include simulations, working models, and even specialized tools. This means that Java has the potential to *change the function of the Internet*, much as the Web has changed the way we access the Internet. In other words, not only will the network provide us with information, it will also serve as our operating system.

In this chapter, you will learn about the history and evolution of Java, see how Java is enhancing the Web, and begin to understand how Java programming language features enable developers to build robust Internet applications.

A Brief History of Java

In 1990, Sun Microsystems began a project called "Green" to develop software for use in consumer electronics. Sun is best known for its popular Unix workstations, but has also engineered several popular software packages, including the Solaris operating system and the Network File System (NFS). James Gosling, a veteran of classic network software design, was assigned to the new project.

Gosling began writing software in C++ to be embedded into such things as toasters, VCRs, and Personal Digital Assistants (PDAs). The embedded software is used to make appliances more intelligent, typically by adding digital displays or by using artificial intelligence to better control the mechanisms. However, it soon became apparent to him that C++ was the wrong tool for the job. C++ is flexible enough to control embedded systems, but it is susceptible to bugs that can crash the system. In particular, C++ uses direct references to system resources and requires the programmer to keep track of how these resources are managed, which is a significant burden on programmers. This burden of resource management is a barrier to writing reliable, portable software, and was a serious problem for consumer electronics. After all, computer users have come to expect their software to have some bugs, but no one expects their toaster to crash.

Java's Predecessor: Oak

Gosling's solution to this problem was a new language called Oak. Oak preserved the familiar syntax of C++ but omitted the potentially dangerous features like explicit resource references, pointer arithmetic, and operator overloading. Oak incorporated memory management directly into the language, freeing the programmer to concentrate on the tasks to be performed by the program. In order to be successful as an embedded systems programming language, Oak needed to be able to respond to real-world events within microseconds. It also needed to be portable; that is, it had to be able to run on a number of different microprocessor chips and environments. This hardware independence would allow a toaster manufacturer to change the chip used to run the toaster without changing the software. The manufacturer could also use some of the same code that runs the toaster to run a similar appliance, such as a toaster oven. This would cut down on development and hardware costs, as well as increase reliability.

As Oak matured, the World Wide Web was in a period of dramatic growth, and the development team at Sun realized that Oak was perfectly suited to Internet programming. In 1994, they completed work on a product known as WebRunner, an early Web viewer written in Oak. WebRunner was later renamed HotJava, and it demonstrated the power of Oak as an Internet development tool. HotJava is well known in the industry, and the HotJava project is still active, with new versions under development.

Finally, in 1995, Oak was renamed Java (for marketing purposes) and announced at SunWorld 95. Since then, Java's rise in popularity has been meteoric. Even before the first release of the Java compiler in January 1996, Java was considered an industry standard for Internet development.

Java's Arrival on the Market

In the first six months of 1996, a number of leading software and hardware companies licensed Java technology from Sun, including Adobe, Asymetrix, Borland, IBM, Macromedia, Metrowerks, Microsoft, Novell, Oracle, Spyglass, and Symantec. These, and other Java licensees, are incorporating Java into their desktop products, operating systems, and development tools.

Also in 1996, substantial new additions to the Java language were introduced. New APIs (Application Program Interfaces—libraries of functions that application developers can use to construct software), sponsored by many of the aforementioned companies, now provide advanced graphics, multimedia, networking, and security enhancements to the Java environment. The new JavaOS will bring Java to special low-end markets such as PDAs and special network computers. Also, the advent of Java 1.1, released in early 1997, has significantly improved Java's portability, security, and functionality. And more improvements are on the horizon, with new companies signing on every day.

There are also several integrated development environments now available for Java developers from Sun, Symantec, Metrowerks, Borland, and Natural Intelligence. Many major companies, like Corel, are translating their major desktop applications into Java, allowing them to be used across the Internet. Even the giant Microsoft is starting to make its applications Internet-aware and Java-compatible. (Of course, companies like Microsoft have their own agendas and are trying to lock Java into their proprietary operating systems and application architectures.) It is clear that the momentum of this technology is so great that few doubt Java's ability to transform the computer industry as we know it.

> **NOTE** Perhaps the most common question about Java's history is about the origin of the name Java. The answer is that the name Java survived the trademark search.

Java and the Web

Today, the most likely place you'll find Java is on the World Wide Web. The Web acts as a convenient transport mechanism for Java programs, and the Web's ubiquity has popularized Java as an Internet development tool.

An Introduction to the Web

This section is a brief introduction to the World Wide Web. If you are already familiar with the Web, you may want to skip this introduction and go on to the next section.

The World Wide Web is a huge collection of interconnected hypertext documents on the Internet. A *hypertext* document is a document that contains *hot links* to other documents. Hypertext links are usually visible as highlighted words in the text, but they can also be graphics. Hot links are frequently used for online help systems. Links are activated by clicking on them with a mouse.

There are many thousands of hypertext authors on the Internet, each of them free to connect their documents to anyone else's. It follows then that the Web has no beginning and no end, although groups of associated pages are usually structured hierarchically. Since organization of the Web is not enforced, finding your way around can be difficult. Fortunately, Web search engines, such as

Yahoo, Excite, and Infoseek, have alleviated much of the navigation problem by allowing users to search by keyword, name, or subject. The lack of regulation has gone a long way toward broadening the user base and enriching the content. As things stand, anyone who learns to write hypertext documents can make information available over the Internet.

The Web is based on two standards: the *HTTP* protocol and the *HTML* language. HTTP stands for HyperText Transfer Protocol, and it describes the way that hypertext documents are fetched over the Internet. HTML is the abbreviation for HyperText Markup Language, and it specifies the layout and linking commands present in the hypertext documents themselves.

NOTE   For the purposes of this book, a *protocol* is a procedure followed by all sides of an Internet conversation in order to facilitate the transfer information. The most popular application protocols on the Internet are HTTP (Hypertext Transfer Protocol), FTP (File Transfer Protocol), and SMTP (Simple Mail Transfer Protocol). Each protocol defines commands sent to the server from a program requesting services and the way the server may respond.

Resources on the Web are specified with a *Uniform Resource Locator* (URL). A URL specifies the protocol used to fetch a document as well as its location. For example, the URL for a page about the history of Sybex publishing is http://www.sybex.com:80/about/history.html. The URL can be divided into five pieces:

```
http:  //www.sybex.com  :80  /about/  history.html
```
Protocol | Server Address | Port Number | Directory | Document Name

The http: prefix indicates that the document should be fetched via HTTP. The //www.sybex.com specifies the machine that is running the Web server. The :80 refers to the port number; each protocol server on a machine is typically assigned its own port number. The default port number for HTTP is 80, and Web server administrators rarely change it. For this reason, the port number is rarely specified in HTTP URLs. The file itself is called history.html, and it is located in the directory /about. Java also uses URLs to specify the locations of network resources.

The HTTP protocol is implemented in software on the server and on the user's machine (also known as the *client machine*, or simply the *client*). The server software is called a *Web server* or *HTTP server*, and the client software is called a *Web browser*.

To open an HTML document, the Web browser sends an HTTP command to the server requesting the document by its URL. The Web server responds by sending the HTML document to the client. The client then displays the document on the user's screen. If the HTML document contains graphics, the Web browser makes additional requests for the graphics files to be sent, and then displays the graphics with the text. Figure 1.1 illustrates this process.

FIGURE 1.1

How Web documents are fetched with HTTP

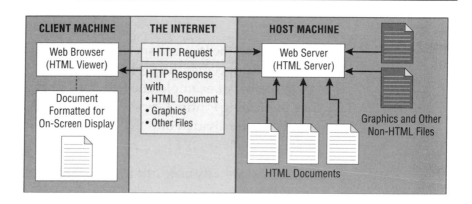

Thus, Web documents are essentially static objects. When the HTML document reaches the browser, it is in its final form.

NOTE

There are protocol extensions that allow an HTML document to be refreshed after reaching the client. These extensions are called *server-push* and *client-pull*, and are written into documents or scripts on the server. These enhancements force the HTML document that was downloaded from the server to be refreshed at regular intervals.

Server-push
client-pull

Some servers generate HTML upon request using *Common Gateway Interface* (CGI) programs. With the ability of CGI and HTML to create fill-in-the-blank forms, you can create form-based applications on the Web. Perhaps the most notable application like this was created by Federal Express for package tracking. Figure 1.2 shows an example of this application. Users can track their FedEx packages over the Internet at http://www.fedex.com.

Note that CGI is not suited to real-time display of information. Although CGI programs generate HTML upon request, the document returned to the browser is still a static document.

CGI programs are very widespread and have generally been successful, but they are prone to performance problems. When the Web server runs a CGI program to create an HTML document on the fly, it usually creates a new operating system process for that program on the Web server machine. Creating new processes is time-consuming and inefficient. Nonetheless, CGI is used on the Internet simply because it is compatible with almost every Web browser.

Another option for doing even more dynamic serving is JavaSoft's new Servlet API. This API allows for client-side programs, similar to applets, to provide dynamic content or interface with applets on the client. For more information, see Chapter 21.

FIGURE 1.2

The FedEx tracking form. The user fills in a tracking number, selects a destination, and then clicks a button to send the data to the server. This type of form is usually handled by CGI scripts on the server.

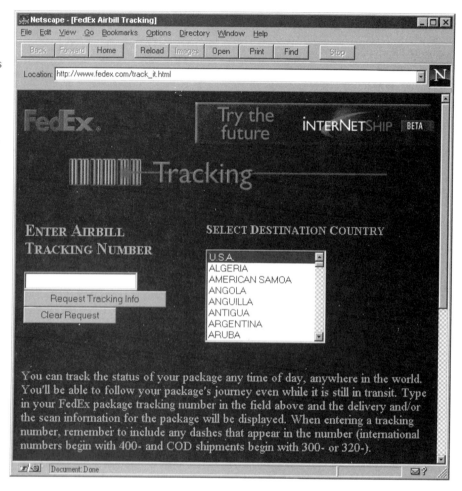

Extending Web Browser Capability

Much of the power of the World Wide Web stems from its platform independence; that is, it presents information in a way that can be viewed on almost every type of machine and operating system. It doesn't matter whether you use a PC, Macintosh, or Unix workstation—the Web is architecture-neutral, which is why so many people have access to it.

Unfortunately, being so widely accepted also has its drawbacks. It is very difficult to extend the Web protocols without leaving many Web users behind. For instance, Web content developers are constantly trying to extend the capability of the Web by integrating new types of media, like 3-D worlds and animation, but these developers then face the prospect of excluding people without those viewing capabilities, which limits their audience.

The existing Web standards permit seamless integration of graphics with text. Other forms of media, such as sound, video, and animation, are accessible via the Web, but they are not smoothly connected with normal Web content. For example, it is easy to create a link to a sound file in an HTML document; the Web browser will either play the sound or download it to a file when the user clicks on the link. However, there is no browser-independent way to create background music for a document or give audio feedback when a button is pressed. This is just one of the many creative limitations that have frustrated Web developers over the last few years.

Until now, the solution to this extensibility problem has been to create a proprietary protocol, then try to sell the solution to as many users on as many platforms as possible. This is a hard sell, and has had limited success. As a result, Web pages tend to cater to the lowest common denominator; therefore, the content has not reached its full potential in many instances.

A good example of this is Adobe's Portable Document Format (PDF). This is a cross-platform solution for creating robust documents and distributing them on the Internet. PDF provides support for documents far richer than simple HTML, allowing groups like the IRS to ship tax forms across the Web. Adobe gives the viewer away, but tries to make money on the tools used to create PDF documents. PDF's main limitation is that you need to download a special program from Adobe to view the files.

Java as a Universal Protocol

Java has begun to address the protocol problem by using Java applets. An *applet* is a Java program that appears embedded in a Web document, just as graphics would be. The Java applet runs when it is loaded by a Java-enabled Web browser, such as Netscape Navigator 2.0 or 3.0. The running applet then draws itself in the user's browser window according to the programmer's instructions.

Let's say you want to create a stock market ticker applet for use in a Web page (a stock market ticker is a horizontally scrolling summary of stock prices and stock price changes). The stock quotes must be sent to the user's Web browser in real-time so that users can get up-to-the-minute information. Since a continuous stream of stock quotes is needed, HTTP is not a good protocol for this application (HTTP is really a kind of file transfer protocol, not a continuous data stream protocol). Therefore, you need to design a new protocol, say the Simple Stock Quote Protocol (SSQP).

Imagine a conversation between the client and the server:

Client: GET NASDAQ

Server: OK

Server: AAA 104 3/8 - 1 1/2 ICP 80 1/4 + 1/4 ...

(Client displays data continuously as long as user requires.)

Client: STOP

This conversation is the blueprint for the SSQP. The server responds to the GET commands by acknowledging the request and then sending back a continuous stream of data. The STOP command terminates the conversation.

You can implement the SSQP server in whichever language is best for the job. This could be C, Java, or another nonportable language, because you know that it will run on your server machine. In Java, you can very easily write a stock ticker Java applet that implements the client side of the conversation and displays the returned data. When executed by the browser, the applet connects to the server using the SSQP and displays a stock ticker with live data. Thus, without any manual intervention from the user, a stock ticker can be made to appear in the browser window.

Figure 1.3 shows a Web page using a Java applet to display the latest Major League baseball scores. You'll notice that the applet integrates seamlessly with the rest of the page. The browser's functionality has been extended automatically and transparently. In this way, Java acts like a protocol for adding new protocols. It would be impractical for Web browser manufacturers to build in every new protocol that comes along. Instead, browsers can be equipped with Java and can learn new protocols on demand.

FIGURE 1.3

The image in the lower left is a Java applet that displays up-to-the-minute sports scores. The underlined text is a hypertext link.

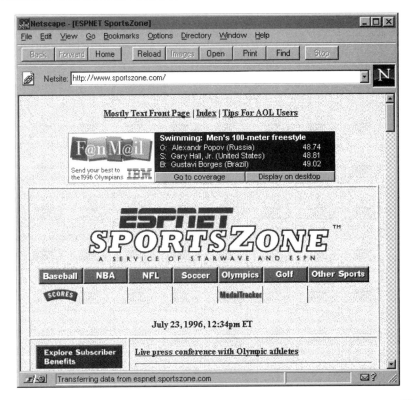

The Java Architecture

Java's strength derives from its unique architecture. The designers of Java needed a language that was, above all, simple for the programmer to use. Yet in order to create reliable network applications, Java needed to be able to run securely over a network and work on a wide range of platforms. Java fulfills all of these goals and more. The next few sections describe how Java works and the features that make Java a powerful network application development tool.

How Java Works

As with many other programming languages, Java uses a compiler to convert human-readable source code into executable programs. Traditional compilers produce code that can be executed by specific hardware; for example, a Windows 95 C++ compiler creates executable programs that work with Intel *x*86 compatible processors. In contrast, the Java compiler generates architecture-independent *bytecodes*. The bytecodes can be executed by only a Java *Virtual Machine* (VM), which is an idealized Java processor chip usually implemented in software rather than hardware.

NOTE   The VM has also been implemented as a hardware chip by Sun Microsystems, and several other electronics companies have announced plans to manufacture Java processors. These processors are expected to have significant performance advantages over VMs written in software. They will also make it easier for Java to be embedded into consumer electronics products such as toasters and TV sets. See Chapter 23 for more information about Java processors and embedded Java.

The compilation process is illustrated in Figure 1.4. Java bytecode files are called *class files* because they contain a single Java class. Classes will be described in detail in Chapter 3. For now, just think of a class as representing a group of related routines or an extended datatype. The vast majority of Java programs will be composed of more than one class file.

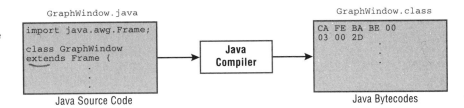

FIGURE 1.4

Java compilers produce Java bytecodes, not traditional executable files.

GraphWindow.java

```
import java.awg.Frame;

class GraphWindow
extends Frame {
        .
        .
        .
```

Java Source Code

Java Compiler

GraphWindow.class

```
CA FE BA BE 00
03 00 2D    .
            .
            .
```

Java Bytecodes

To execute Java bytecodes, the VM uses a *class loader* to fetch the bytecodes from a disk or from the network. Each class file is fed to a *bytecode verifier* that ensures that the class is formatted correctly and that the class will not corrupt memory when it is executed. The byte-code verification phase adds to the time it takes to load a class, but it actually allows the program to run faster because the class verification is performed only once, not continuously as the program runs.

The execution unit of the VM carries out the instructions specified in the bytecodes. The simplest execution unit is an *interpreter*, which is a program that reads the bytecodes, interprets their meaning, and then performs the associated function. Interpreters are generally much slower than native code compilers because they continuously need to look up the meaning of each bytecode during execution. Fortunately, there is an elegant alternative to interpreting code, called *Just-In-Time* (JIT) compilation.

The JIT compiler converts the bytecodes to native code instructions on the user's machine immediately before execution. Traditional native code compilers run on the developer's machine, are used by programmers, and produce nonportable executables. JIT compilers run on the user's machine and are transparent to the user; the result-ing native code instructions do not need to be ported because they are already at their destination. Figure 1.5 illustrates the way JIT compilers work. In the example, identical bytecodes are received by both a Macintosh and a Windows PC, and each client performs a local, JIT compilation.

FIGURE 1.5

The JIT compiler in the client system improves performance by compiling bytecodes to platform-specific instructions just before execution. The resulting machine-level instructions are executed directly.

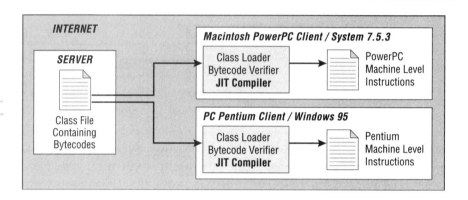

Java-Enabled Browsers

A Java-enabled Web browser contains its own VM. Web documents that have embedded Java applets must specify the location of the main applet class file. The Web browser then starts up the VM and passes the location of the applet class file to the class loader. Each class file knows the names of any additional class files that it requires. These additional class files may come from the network or from the client machine. This may require the class loader to make a number of additional class-loading operations before the applet starts. Note that supplemental classes are fetched only if they are actually going to be used or if they are necessary for the verification process of the applet.

After loading the class file, execution begins, and the applet is asked to draw itself in the browser window. Figure 1.6 shows the Java VM fetching classes.

FIGURE 1.6

The Java Virtual Machine fetches classes from a disk or from the network, and then verifies that the bytecodes are safe to be executed.

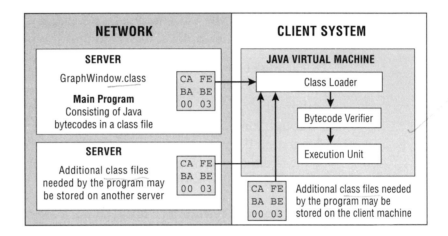

Java Features

In this section, we will look briefly at the major characteristics that make Java such a powerful development tool. These include its security features, the Core API, open standards, and memory management. Also covered are Java's distributed and dynamic, object-oriented, and multithreaded characteristics.

Security Features

Security is probably the number one problem facing Internet developers. Users are typically afraid of two things: that confidential information will be compromised, and that their computer systems are vulnerable to corruption or destruction by hackers. Java's built-in security addresses both of these concerns.

Java's security model has three primary components: the class loader, bytecode verifier, and SecurityManager. You have already learned that the bytecode verifier ensures that the Java programs have been compiled correctly, that they will obey the VM's access restrictions, and that the bytecodes will not access "private" data when they shouldn't. Without these defenses, the other security constraints within the VM could be bypassed, and there would be no limit to what the applet could do to the system.

The next layer of security is provided by the class loader. When the class loader retrieves classes from the network, it keeps classes from different servers separate from each other and from local classes. Through this separation, the class loader prevents a class that is loaded off the network from pretending to be one of the standard built-in classes, or from interfering with the operation of classes loaded from other servers.

The `SecurityManager` implements a security policy for the VM. The security policy determines which activities the VM is allowed to perform and under what circumstances. A key example is file input/output (I/O); for example, saving or loading documents in disk files. Java has the capability to read and write files, but requests to perform such an I/O pass through the `SecurityManager` first. This allows the `SecurityManager` to determine if the Java program is trusted to access the disk files without doing malicious damage to the file system.

The `SecurityManager` is generally written to err on the side of caution. In the most popular Java-enabled browser, Netscape Navigator, the security policy does not even permit file access. However, the `SecurityManager` is itself written in Java (it is a Java class file), so that it can be overridden if required. Of course, there are safeguards to prevent hostile Java programs from writing their own security policy! These safeguards prevent alternate `Security-Managers` from being added to the system while the Web browser is running.

On a private network, file access or arbitrary network access may be necessary to address business requirements. For example, when implementing a client/server database application on a private network, it may be necessary for a Java applet to establish connections with multiple servers. The standard `SecurityManager` prohibits this because it is a security risk on a public network. The application developers may therefore change the `SecurityManager` source code and recompile it into the Web browser for each PC on the network. This customizes the security policy for the private network. Custom `SecurityManagers` are more difficult to write if the private network has any gateways to public networks such as the Internet. Great care must be taken when overriding the `SecurityManager`, or hostile applets from the public network may take advantage of the relaxed internal security policy.

With the advent of Java 1.1, developers can now add another layer of security to their applets. An addition to the Core API is an extensive Security API that allows Java classes to be *signed*. A *digital signature* is used in the same way that your normal signature is used every time you write a check—it ensures that the check really came from you and not from some impostor. Digital signatures allow developers to sign the code that they write, using a nearly unbreakable public-key encryption system. The user can then use this signature to decide if he or she trusts the program being loaded. The program can be given limited access to local disk, memory, or network resources based on the level of trust. The encryption itself is rather complicated, but the entire process happens transparently to both the user and the developer, making it even easier to deliver secure content over the Web.

To summarize, Java's built-in security measures ensure that Java programs will operate within the rules of the VM and prevent untrustworthy programs from accessing system resources that might contain proprietary information or jeopardize the integrity of the client. Java also allows developers or institutions to sign the programs they create, allowing users to grant limited access to "trusted" applets or applications.

The Core API

Java's Core API (formerly known as the JavaApplet API) provides a common set of functions on all platforms.

The API is divided into *packages*, which are groups of classes that perform related functions. One of these packages includes some core language functionality, such as text handling and error processing; it is almost impossible to write a Java program without using this library. The other packages contain utilities, networking, I/O, graphical user interface tools, and interaction with Web browsers. Packages that deal with security and database access have been introduced with the latest version of Java, and new ones are in development all the time.

Open Standards

Today, Java VMs are available for more than a dozen different hardware/operating system combinations. The most exciting aspect of Java's cross-platform capability is that Java class files do not need to be compiled for each platform in advance. The same compiled Java program will work on the PC, Macintosh, and every other platform that runs a Java VM. A Java application you write on your system should run on every supported platform.

Another key to being a successful cross-platform development tool is having a common core set of functions on every platform. The Core API is the same for all implementations of Java, and it is sophisticated enough that native code does not need to be written for desktop applications.

Of course, the real world is slightly more complicated. Java is a new language, and most implementations of the Java VM and Core API have minor problems conforming to the Java specifications, especially with respect to the user interface. To combat this problem, JavaSoft, the Sun Microsystems business unit that is responsible for the development of Java products, has released an exhaustive test suite that all Java-compatible systems must pass in order to claim compatibility with the Java 1.1 API. This, along with several other industry-wide measures, should help eliminate any differences between implementations of the Java VM.

JavaSoft

Java VMs

In addition to common desktop operating systems, you can expect to see Java VMs implemented on-chip for use in embedded systems. Sun has announced plans to manufacture three Java processors, known as picoJava, microJava, and UltraJava. LG Semicon, Mitsubishi, and Samsung have also signed letters of intent for the licensing of Java processor technology. Java is on its way toward fulfilling the original goals of the Green project, and will undoubtedly be showing up in household appliances at some point in the near future.

Distributed and Dynamic

DLL

In the Windows operating system, parts of programs can be placed into dynamic link libraries (DLLs) so they can be shared and loaded dynamically; that is, when the program is running. The operating system does the final stage of linking at execution time. Using shared DLLs saves memory and improves the modularity of the software. Under Unix, this same type of dynamic linking is accomplished via shared libraries.

Shared libraries.

Distributed and Dynamic.

Java takes dynamic libraries a step further. The VM class loader fetches class files from the network, as well as from the disk, making Java applications distributed as well as dynamic. These features allow a Java-enabled browser to adapt automatically to protocols available at a new Web site. It also means that a Java application does not need to fetch parts of the program that will not be used.

Java has the potential to change the software distribution model used by the industry. Instead of buying software on disk or CD-ROM, people could "rent" just the pieces (Java classes) of the applications they need directly over the Internet, much like "renting" online time. The software would be the latest version because it came directly from the manufacturer. However, today there are three major obstacles that make this scenario all but impossible:

- The time it takes to download a real-world application is prohibitive for most users. For downloaded software to compete with today's disk-based applications, users will likely need connections that are 100 times faster than today's standard 28.8kbps modems.

- The standard security policy prevents file I/O that is required to save work on the local machine.

- There is no prevailing standard for making secure software rental payments. Without such a standard, it would be as if each software vendor had its own form of currency, requiring you to make a special arrangement with each vendor before renting the software.

Although these problems are not insurmountable, it will be some time before the network infrastructure can support this kind of distribution model. One positive first step toward this goal is the new Java Enterprise API, which includes APIs for electronic commerce and added security, as well as support for other industry standards pioneered by Netscape, Visa, and others. Also, with the advent of new distribution methods, such as Marimba's Castanet product, you should start to see commercial Java applications delivered over the Internet in the very near future.

Object-Oriented

Object-oriented programming (OOP) is a way to write software that is reusable, extensible, and maintainable. Java is an object-oriented language; that is, it has facilities for OOP incorporated into the language. The Core API is actually a collection of prefabricated OOP components, known to object-oriented programmers as a *class library*. Class libraries give programmers a big head start when it comes to developing new projects. A detailed explanation of object-oriented technology is presented in Chapter 3.

Multithreaded

A single-threaded application has one thread of execution running at all times, and such programs can do only one task at a time. If a single-threaded program needs to perform a task that will take several minutes—for example, downloading—its user interface will usually become unresponsive while the task is in progress.

A multithreaded application can have several threads of execution running independently and simultaneously. These threads may communicate and cooperate, and to the user will appear to be a single program. Multithreading is commonly used to perform the following functions:

Maintaining user interface responsiveness If your application needs to perform a time-consuming task, you can use multiple threads to prevent your user interface from becoming unresponsive while the task is in progress. If your program will be downloading information from the Internet (this is very likely), you can create a separate thread for the download routine. This will keep your user interface running at nearly full speed while a download is in progress.

Waiting for a wake-up call The best way to have a routine wait for a specified time is to place the routine in a sleeping thread. The alternative—continuously watching the time-of-day clock—is very processor-intensive. For instance, if you wanted an applet to download new data from a server every 60 seconds, you could place the download routine in a thread that sleeps for a minute between transfers.

Simple multitasking Multithreading allows you to run multiple instances of a process quite easily. The downloading routine just mentioned can be extended so that the program can transfer multiple files simultaneously and still keep the user interface well-behaved. All you need to do is create another thread for each file to download.

Building multiuser applications   Multithreading is often used when building server applications. Server applications wait for requests to arrive and then establish conversations with the requester. It is much easier to write a routine that handles a single conversation and spawns multiple copies of that routine than it is to write a piece of code that handles multiple conversations at once.

Multiprocessing   Many operating systems support machines with multiple processors. Most of these systems are unable to break a single thread of execution into multiple pieces for execution on different processors. By breaking an application into different threads, it is possible to make the best use of processing power.

Every item in this list applies to Internet and embedded-systems applications. Java implements multithreading through a part of its class library, but Java also has language constructs to make programs thread-safe. A *thread-safe* program guarantees that the different threads will not accidentally harm one another. Java's `synchronized` keyword can be used to prevent two threads from entering the same critical block of code at the same time. This is vital because some program steps need to be made together as one atomic group.

Memory Management and Garbage Collection

Memory management is the bane of all C and C++ programs. During the course of a program's execution, memory will be required for temporary operations, such as sorting lists or displaying images. In C and C++, it is the programmer's responsibility to allocate the required memory and free that memory after the task has been completed. If the memory allocations do not match memory deallocations perfectly, the program will either crash immediately or consume system resources until exhausted. In either case, the result is abnormal termination of the program, often bringing down the operating system with it.

Java overcomes this problem by using *garbage collection*. Temporary memory is automatically reclaimed after it is no longer referenced by any active part of the program. This frees the developer from much of the housekeeping that would otherwise be required.

Historically, the problem with garbage collection has been performance. The garbage collector must scan memory for objects that can be eliminated, then sweep the removable objects from memory. Taking out the trash too often is inefficient, but checking too infrequently causes the system to pause while large amounts of garbage are collected. To improve performance, Java's garbage collector runs in its own low-priority thread, providing a good balance of efficiency and real-time responsiveness.

Memory management reinforces the security of the VM. In C and C++, the programmer can access any part of the system available to an application. This can be done by using *pointers*, which are variables that reference specific memory locations. Java does not use pointers in the strict sense of the word. Java's "pointers" are actually references to VM resources, and no arithmetic is permitted with such variables, which prevents programmers from accessing system resources outside the VM. Although this eliminates some of the most advanced programming "tricks" of C++, it greatly simplifies the lives of developers and users alike. And because the Core API provides many important data structures built into the language, arbitrary pointers lose much of their usefulness anyway.

Using Java with Other Tools

Java is a unique development tool and is already a highly successful product. As an Internet development tool, Java joins several other Internet development tools vying for market acceptance. Recognizing that Java is here to stay, vendors are making their products interoperable with Java.

The following is a brief survey of Java-related Internet technologies, including native code, JavaScript, Netscape plug-ins, ActiveX, JDBC, and Java Beans.

Native Code

Native code refers to code that is native to a specific processor. On Windows 95, native code refers to code compatible with Intel $x86$ processors. Java can call native code quite easily, although such calls are not subject to the VM's security measures; this is why most Web browsers do not permit Java applets to make native calls. In Java 1.1, however, native calls are subject to at least a minimal amount of security checking.

Native code access means that Java can call upon millions of lines of existing code and can be used as a development tool for stand-alone, platform-specific applications.

JavaScript

JavaScript is a separate programming language loosely related to Java. JavaScript can be coded directly in an HTML document, which makes the JavaScript source code part of the document itself. JavaScript is less powerful than Java, but it gives the programmer a bit more control over the browser, and it is used primarily to create dialog boxes and animation on Web pages.

JavaScript does have a limited ability to call Java applet routines and alter Java applet variables. However, the Core Java API has no mechanisms for calling JavaScript code or changing JavaScript variables. Netscape has promised to provide a Java–JavaScript connectivity package, which should be available soon.

Netscape Plug-Ins

Netscape Communications has created a standard interface to its Navigator browser product line. Products adhering to the specification are called Netscape Plug-Ins. Netscape provides a Software Development Kit (SDK) so that third parties can implement plug-ins for new types of media, and it allows the new media to integrate seamlessly with the browser. Currently available Plug-Ins support a number of multimedia formats, as well as spreadsheets, AutoCAD drawings, and live news feeds.

Plug-Ins are written with native code; that is, they are platform-specific. The SDK itself changes only slightly from platform to platform, but the implementation details may be totally different between platforms. If you want to use a Plug-In, you will need to download it for your specific platform before being able to utilize the new media. The advantage of this approach is that after downloading a Plug-In to your hard disk, the new media will appear in your browser with no delay.

Netscape has announced an interface, the Java Runtime Interface, which will allow native code (including Plug-Ins) to access Java code and data. A specification of the interface is available from Netscape's Web site. Netscape has also introduced a new set of standards called the Open Networking Environment (ONE), which will provide even tighter integration between Java and Netscape's proprietary standards. With the advent of Java Beans (see Chapter 20), components like Netscape Plug-Ins and Java applets will be able to integrate seamlessly into the browser and other environments.

ActiveX

ActiveX is Microsoft's answer to the Netscape Plug-In. ActiveX (formerly known as OCXs) uses controls based on the Component Object

Model (COM). COM is used throughout Microsoft's desktop applications for communication and automation. Integrating a Web browser with ActiveX extends the Microsoft desktop across the Internet.

Like Netscape Plug-Ins, ActiveX controls are native code modules, and Microsoft intends to support ActiveX on other platforms, not just Microsoft Windows. Unlike Plug-Ins, ActiveX controls are designed to be downloaded as needed. A digital signature is used to guarantee that the ActiveX control has not been tampered with. Interestingly, Ncompass Labs has created a Netscape Plug-In that runs ActiveX controls.

Java interfaces and COM interfaces are semantically similar, and Microsoft has designed a VM that allows ActiveX and Java to communicate automatically. Sun has also announced intentions to unite Java with ActiveX through Java Beans. These bridges will make Java an excellent development tool for creating components that can be used in Windows-based development tools and applications like Word, Excel, Visual C++, Visual Basic, and Delphi. Microsoft has also proposed its own Windows-platform VM that will run both ActiveX and Java. Although this will make writing Java programs for the Windows platform much easier, it will limit Java's usefulness to platforms that support ActiveX, which will give Microsoft major control over Java.

JDBC

Java Database Connectivity (JDBC) is an API for linking Java programs to databases. JDBC is quite similar to Microsoft's Open Database Connectivity (ODBC) standard. JDBC-compliant database applications are not tied to a specific database vendor. As with ODBC, a vendor-specific driver is used to link JDBC applications to the actual database.

Suppose you write an employee database application using JDBC. There's no need to decide which vendor's database management system (for example, Oracle, Sybase, or Informix) you want to use when you write the code because your program will work with any database that has a JDBC driver.

A JDBC-ODBC bridge was released by Sun in 1996. This bridge gives JDBC the ability to interface with the large number of existing ODBC drivers. Many other vendors have released bridges of their own. JDBC is likely to be critical to industry acceptance of Java as a corporate client/server development tool. For more information about JDBC, see Chapter 18.

Java Beans

More than just yet another coffee metaphor in Java's vocabulary, JavaBeans is a powerful new API for linking Java objects with objects created in other languages, including ActiveX, Open Transport, and several other industry standards.

With Java "Beans," Java objects will be able to run within non-Java containers, such as word-processing programs, like ClarisWorks or Corel OfficePerfect. Look for more information about Java Beans in Chapter 20.

New Features in Java 1.1

Java 1.1 has finally been implemented with the advent of the new 1.1 version of the JDK (Java Development Kit). Here is a summary of the new features:

Internationalization   New classes and methods have been added to make writing programs for international users even easier. This includes support for non-English characters and text sorting, as well as a variety of time and date standards.

Security Several enhancements, including digital signing, have been incorporated into a new and improved `SecurityManager`. Also, security for native method calls has been enhanced.

Performance enhancements A new AWT model and rewrite of native code for AWT has boosted GUI performance dramatically. Also, much compiler and interpreter code has been rewritten.

Network and I/O enhancements New classes provide extra network functionality, as well as greater customization. New `reader` and `writer` classes provide high-performance, internationalized, buffered input and output.

Object reflection A special API for getting privileged information about a specific object has been added. This is especially useful for debuggers and other VM-enhancement programs.

In addition to these changes, a whole host of changes to methods, classes, and packages have provided extra functionality. These changes are documented throughout this book.

CHAPTER
TWO

Applets, Applications, and the Java Development Kit

- The difference between Java applets and applications

- The Java Development Kit (JDK)

- Java application creation with the JDK

- Java applet creation with the JDK

- New features in JDK 1.1

Java programs come in two flavors: *applets* and *applications*. Simply speaking, a Java applet is a program that appears embedded in a Web document; Java application is the term applied to all other kinds of Java programs, such as those found in network servers and consumer electronics. Much of this chapter will be devoted to the differences between these two types of programs and to the ways these differences affect the Java software development path.

The Java Development Kit (JDK) from JavaSoft contains the basic tools and libraries necessary for creating and executing both types of Java programs. It also contains a number of useful utilities for debugging and documenting Java source code, and for interfacing C to Java code. You will learn how to download, install, and apply the JDK to the construction of both applets and applications. Along the way, you will receive a primer on Hypertext Markup Language (HTML) for applets and get your first taste of Java source code.

Java Applets versus Java Applications

Traditionally, the word *applet* has come to mean any small application. In Java, an applet is any Java program that is launched from a Web document; that is, from an HTML file. Java applications, on the other hand, are programs that run from a command line, independent of a Web browser. There is no limit to the size or complexity of a Java applet. In fact, Java applets are in some ways more powerful than Java applications. However, with the Internet, where communication speed is limited and download times are long, most Java applets are necessarily small.

The technical differences between applets and applications stem from the context in which they run. A Java application runs in the simplest possible environment—its only input from the outside world is a list of command-line parameters. On the other hand, a Java applet receives a lot of information from the Web browser: It needs to know when it is initialized, when and where to draw itself in the browser window, and when it is activated or deactivated. As a consequence of these two very different execution environments, applets and applications have different minimum requirements.

The decision to write a program as an applet versus an application depends on the context of the program and its delivery mechanism. Because Java applets are always presented in the context of a Web browser's graphical user interface, Java applications are preferred over applets when graphical displays are unnecessary. For example, a Hypertext Transfer Protocol (HTTP) server written in Java needs no graphical display; it requires only file and network access.

The convenience of Web protocols for applet distribution makes applets the preferred program type for Internet applications, although applications can easily be used to perform many of the same tasks. With Java, writing Internet-based software, either as applets or applications, is extremely easy. Non-networked systems and systems with small amounts of memory are much more likely to be written as Java applications than as Java applets.

Table 2.1 summarizes the differences between the two flavors of Java programs.

TABLE 2.1   Differences between Java Applets and Applications

	Java Application	Java Applet
Uses graphics	Optional	Inherently graphical
Memory requirements	Minimal Java application equirements	Java application requirements plus Web browser requirements
Distribution	Loaded from the file system or by a custom class loading process	Linked via HTML and transported via HTTP

TABLE 2.1   Differences between Java Applets and Applications (Continued)

	Java Application	Java Applet
Environmental input	Command-line parameters	Browser client location and size; parameters embedded in the host HTML document
Method expected by the Virtual Machine	main—startup method	init—initialization method start—startup method stop—pause/deactivate method destroy—termination method paint—drawing method
Typical applications	Network server; multimedia kiosks; developer tools; appliance and consumer electronics control	Public-access order-entry systems for the Web; online multimedia presentations; Web page animation and navigation

Using the Java Development Kit (JDK)

The JDK was the original Java development environment for many of today's Java professionals. Although many programmers have moved on to third-party alternatives, the JDK is still considered to be the reference implementation of Java. If you can build and test an application with the JDK, it should run on any third-party implementations, such as those in Web browsers, development tools, or device-specific VMs. In fact, JavaSoft has recently released a whole suite of tests to ensure that third-party Java environments conform to the JDK version.

TIP The latest version of the JDK, version 1.1, is available in its entirety on the CD-ROM included with this book. You can also download it for free on the Internet from Javasoft's Web site. See the instructions for downloading and installing the JDK, coming up shortly.

The JDK can create and display fully graphical applications, but the JDK itself has a somewhat primitive command-line interface. For instance, you run the JDK programs by typing commands into a command shell window (in Windows, a DOS box; on Unix systems, a normal command shell). Do not be discouraged by the apparent complexity of the JDK commands; they are all quite easy to use after a bit of practice.

The JDK consists of a library of standard classes and a collection of utilities for building, testing, and documenting Java programs. As explained in Chapter 1, the Core API (previously called the Java-Applet API) is the library of prefabricated classes. You need these classes to access the core functionality of the Java language.

The Core API includes some important language constructs (including String datatypes and exceptions), as well as basic graphics, network, and file I/O. It is generally safe to assume that the non-I/O parts of the Core API are common to all platforms running Java, including embedded systems. The I/O parts of the API are implemented in general-purpose Java environments. A Java VM in a toaster or other household appliance is unlikely to support the graphics part of the API, but it will almost certainly implement String datatypes and other Core API language classes. A Web browser running on a desktop computer will likely implement the complete Core API (and also many of the optional Extension APIs, which are additional libraries discussed later in this book).

JDK Utilities

Version 1.1 of the JDK includes the following utilities:

javac   The Java *compiler*. Converts Java source code into bytecodes.

java   The Java *interpreter*. Executes Java application bytecodes directly from class files.

appletviewer   A Java interpreter that executes Java applet classes hosted by HTML files.

javadoc   Creates HTML documentation based on Java source code and the comments it contains.

jdb The Java *debugger*. Allows you to step through the program one line at a time, set breakpoints, and examine variables.

javah Generates C header files that can be used to make C routines that can call Java methods, or make C routines that can be called by Java programs.

javap The Java *disassembler*. Displays the accessible functions and data in a compiled class file. It also displays the meaning of the bytecodes.

rmic Creates class files that support Remote Method Invocation (RMI). See Chapter 22 for information about RMI.

rmiregistry Registry used to gain access to RMI objects on a specific machine.

serialver Another RMI utility. It gives version information about various objects.

native2ascii Special program used to convert between standard Latin-1 Unicode characters and other international encoding schemes.

jar Java Archive (JAR) file generator. JAR files allow multiple Java classes and resources to be distributed in one compressed file.

javakey Implements digital signing of JAR and class files. Allows applets to be certified by trusted authorities.

> **NOTE**
>
> Each of the JDK utilities has a companion program for debugging purposes. The companion functions have _g at the end of their names: javac_g, java_g, appletviewer_g, and so on. You should not need to use these extra utilities; just be aware that they exist.

The way these tools are applied to build and run Java applications is illustrated by the flowchart in Figure 2.1. When building applets, the flowchart looks slightly different, as you can see in Figure 2.2.

FIGURE 2.1

How Java applications are built using the JDK

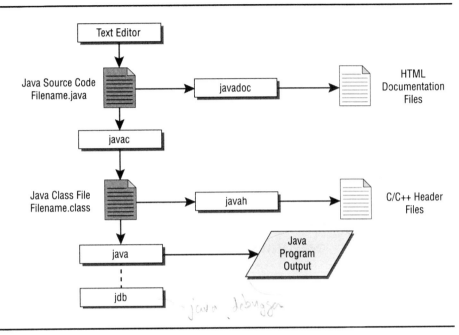

FIGURE 2.2

How Java applets are built using the JDK

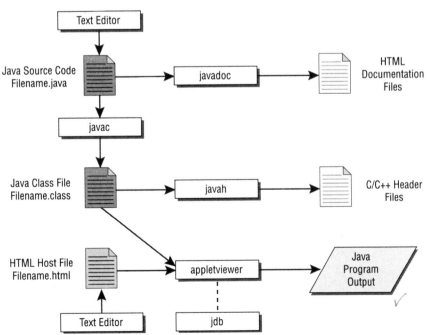

After the descriptions of how to download and install the JDK, you will see how the flowchart in Figure 2.1 applies to a sample Java application. Then you will see how to follow the flowchart in Figure 2.2 for building applets.

Downloading and Installing the JDK

To help get you started with Java, the following sections summarize the steps you need to follow to install the JDK on your machine. You need to install it before you can follow any of the exercises presented in this book.

Downloading the JDK

The latest version (1.1) of the JDK can be found on the CD-ROM accompanying this book, or it can be downloaded from JavaSoft's Web site at http://java.sun.com. The JDK is a self-extracting, compressed executable file. Version 1.1 is available for the following platforms:

- Solaris 2.4 for both SPARC and *x*86 architectures

- Windows 95 and Windows NT for *x*86 architectures

- Macintosh System 7.5 for PowerPC and 68K architectures (mid-1997)

NOTE Notice that there is no version for Windows 3.1*x*. It takes extra effort to implement Java on Windows 3.1*x* because Java requires long filenames and some other features that are not present in 16-bit versions of the operating system. Nonetheless, IBM is currently in the process of porting the JDK to Windows 3.1*x* (see the Web page http://www.alphaworks.ibm.com) and is already distributing versions for OS/2 and AIX. IBM is also working on MVS and OS/400 versions of the JDK. Other firms have ported Java to several types of Unix, including Digital Unix and Linux. Although some of these projects have successfully ported Java 1.0, Java 1.1 ports may not be available for a while.

The first step is to locate the correct binary files at JavaSoft's Web site or FTP server, or from the appropriate site if you are using a platform other than those supported by JavaSoft. The complete JDK is distributed as a single file approximately 7 (Windows 95) to 14 (Solaris) megabytes in size. The download may take 90 minutes with a 28.8kbps modem, or about half that much time with a single-channel ISDN connection, assuming that the server is not busy. It may help to try downloading the file early in the morning or late in the evening when the server is not so busy.

JavaSoft also has a separate distribution binary file for the JDK documentation. This includes release notes, help files, and documentation for all of the classes and tools distributed with the JDK. It is strongly recommended that you download this as well. It is about 2 megabytes compressed, and is well worth the download time. You can also access this documentation online on JavaSoft's Web page.

Installing the JDK

The JDK installation process is straightforward but generally takes a little manual setup to finish off. Be sure to obtain the complete set of instructions from JavaSoft's Web pages, and have them handy during installation. To give you a head start, Table 2.2 summarizes the installation procedure for JDK 1.1 for each platform supported by Sun.

TIP

Don't forget to obtain the latest documentation and troubleshooting tips for your platform from JavaSoft's Web site: http://java.sun.com/products/JDK/1.1/.

TABLE 2.2   JDK Installation Instructions for Windows, Solaris, and Macintosh
Platforms

Installation Procedures	Windows 95 & Windows NT	Sun Solaris*	Macintosh System 7.5
Downloaded file type	Self-extracting executable (.exe)	Compressed archive (.tar.gz)	Compressed MacBinary HQX (.sea.bin)
Where to install the JDK	Usually installed in c:\java, by the self-extracting executable.	Can be installed anywhere, preferably a new directory.	The installer will create the folder for you. The default folder name is JDK-1.1.
If you have already installed a previous version of the JDK	Save any files you have changed or created in the original Java directory tree in a separate directory, then delete the original installation.	Rename the old Java directory if there are any files you would like to keep.	Make a backup folder if you have files you want to keep.
Decompression procedure	If this is a new installation, simply run the executable and then run the install batch file.	Use gzip and tar to decompress and then run the install script.	Use Stuffit to decompress the MacBinary file, then use BinHex4 or DeHQX to decompress the installer. Or use Stuffit Expander to decompress everything.
Additional setup	Add the java/bin directory to your path.	Add the java/bin directory to your path.	
If you have already installed a previous version of the JDK	Check that the CLASSPATH environment variable points to the new version of the JDK.	Check that the CLASSPATH environment variable points to the new version of the JDK.	

*Versions 2.3, 2.4, and 2.5 on SPARC-based machines; version 2.5 on x86 based machines.

Building Applications with the JDK

Now that you have installed the JDK, it's time to take it for a test drive. To smooth the ride, this section describes how to create a small Java application, applying each JDK utility to the code. You will see the same code compiled, executed, disassembled, documented, and interfaced to the C language.

Java Application Source Code

Java source code can be written with a simple text editor. In Unix, vi or emacs will do; in Windows or System 7.5, you can use Notepad, EDIT, or SimpleText. Many programmers have a preferred text editor or use the editor shipped with third-party integrated development environments (IDEs). For your convenience, the source code examples are included on the CD-ROM accompanying this book.

The first example is a little Java program that you can use to play with the JDK:

```
public class TestDrive {

    public static void main(String[] argv) {

        System.out.println("JDK Test Drive");

    }

}
```

This is a rework of the classic HelloWorld program, which simply prints the words "JDK Test Drive." It is the simplest Java program you can write, but to the uninitiated, it may still look rather cryptic. For the purposes of this chapter, there is no need to understand it all perfectly; don't worry too much about what each keyword means.

The code defines a Java class called `TestDrive`, which contains a single method called `main`. When the Java interpreter tries to execute the `TestDrive` class, it will look for a method called `main`. The `public`, `static`, and `void` keywords will be explained in detail in later chapters; for now, you just need to know that they are required for the `main` method to behave correctly.

In fact, every Java application must define a function called `main` as:

```
public static void main(String[] argv)
```

The VM will execute this function to run the program. Here, `argv` is an array of `String` (text) variables. When you run the program, the array will be filled with the values of any arguments it was given on the command line.

If you know how to program in C, the main function will look familiar. The C equivalent:

```
int main(char *argv[], int argc)
```

includes `argc`, an integer variable that tells you how many arguments are in the array. In Java, this is unnecessary because arrays know how many elements they contain. Another difference between Java and C is that in C, the first element in the array, `argv[0]`, contains the name of the program itself. In Java, `argv[0]` is the first parameter on the command line.

Type the Java source code for the `TestDrive` class into your text editor and save it under the name TestDrive.java.

> **NOTE**
> The name of the Java source file is not arbitrary; it must be the same as the name of the public class defined in the .java file. Consequently, there can be only one public class defined in each source file, although there can be additional nonpublic classes defined in each file. If there is no public class defined in the Java source file, the name of the file can be anything you wish.

You are now ready to compile your first Java program.

Using javac

The javac compiler converts Java source code into Java bytecodes, which can then be executed by java (the Java interpreter), the appletviewer, or any other Java VM, such as Netscape.

You can compile your TestDrive program by entering the following at the shell prompt:

javac TestDrive.java

If the Java code is acceptable to the compiler, the file TestDrive.class will be created (no messages will be displayed).

If you are curious and would like to see the details of the compilation, you can use the `verbose` option. The `verbose` option is rarely used, but it is instructive to see it at least once. The `verbose` option will cause the javac compiler to tell you which other Java classes the compiler needs to create the compiled class file and how long it took to do the compilation. When you enter:

javac -verbose TestDrive.java

it produces something like this (your times and locations may vary):

```
[parsed TestDrive.java in 667ms]
[loaded c:\java\lib\classes.zip(java/lang/Object.class) in 187ms]
[checking class TestDrive]
[loaded c:\java\lib\classes.zip(java/lang/String.class) in 180ms]
[loaded c:\java\lib\classes.zip(java/lang/System.class) in 118ms]
[loaded c:\java\lib\classes.zip(java/io/PrintStream.class) in 82ms]
[loaded c:\java\lib\classes.zip(java/io/Serializable.class) in 19ms]
[loaded c:\java\lib\classes.zip(java/io/FilterOutputStream.class) in 24
    ms]
[loaded c:\java\lib\classes.zip(java/io/OutputStream.class) in 19ms]
[wrote TestDrive.class]
[done in 4210ms]
```

Behind the scenes, the compiler must check that the TestDrive program is consistent with any other classes it uses. `String`, `System`, `PrintStream`, `FilterOutputStream`, `OutputStream`, and `Serializable` are included in Java's standard class library, the Core API. All of these classes are essential to print a string to the standard output.

TIP

In version 1.1 of the JDK, there are about 600 classes in the standard class library, and about 800 supplementary classes provided as a tools and debugging class library. This class library contains a wealth of ready-to-use functionality and will save you a great deal of development time. These classes are stored in a compressed zip file in the java/lib directory. Do not remove the classes.zip file, because the Java compiler and VM access the library classes from this file directly. If you want to see the source code for the library classes, you can unzip the src.zip file, which is stored in the java directory.

bytecodes

After running javac to compile TestDrive.java, the file TestDrive.class contains bytecodes that can be executed by any Java VM on any platform. The class file format is an open standard, and a detailed specification for it can be found at JavaSoft's Web site. If you use a binary file viewer to analyze the file, you will notice that there is text as well as binary data in the file. The names of classes and methods used by the class file must be stored in the bytecodes in order to access those classes and methods on the destination system.

Using java

After compiling TestDrive, you can run the program with the Java interpreter by entering the following command:

java TestDrive

The output will be the words "JDK Test Drive," as shown in Figure 2.3.

FIGURE 2.3

A sample Windows 95 command-line session that compiles and executes TestDrive.java

The interpreter has many command-line options, most of which are functions likely to be used only by advanced Java programmers. Nevertheless, it is worth your while to take a look at a useful, relatively simple feature built into the interpreter: a *profiler*. A profiler is used to analyze how much time a program spends in each part of the code. You can use this information to determine which parts of a program to optimize. If you use the `prof` option of the interpreter, with the command:

java -prof TextDrive.java

a file called java.prof will be created. This file shows how many times each method was called and how many milliseconds were spent executing each one. An excerpt of the profile for TestDrive.class is shown here:

```
count callee caller time

3 java/io/FileDescriptor.initSystemFD(Ljava/io/FileDescriptor;I)Ljava/io/
FileDescriptor; java/io/FileDescriptor.<clinit>()V 1

1 java/lang/Class.getPrimitiveClass(Ljava/lang/String;)Ljava/lang/Class;
java/lang/Integer.<clinit>()V 11

1 java/lang/System.currentTimeMillis()J java/lang/System.nullPrintStream()
Ljava/io/PrintStream; 0

1 java/lang/System.arraycopy(Ljava/lang/Object;ILjava/lang/Object;II)V
java/lang/StringBuffer.ensureCapacity(I)V 0

1 java/lang/System.currentTimeMillis()J java/lang/System.nullInputStream()
Ljava/io/InputStream; 15
```

```
1 java/lang/Class.newInstance()Ljava/lang/Object; java/io/CharToByteConverter
.getConverter(Ljava/lang/String;)Ljava/io/CharToByteConverter; 0

...

handles_used: 831, handles_free: 26214, heap-used: 100400, heap-free: 738456
sig   count   bytes   indx
[C      130     19286      5
[B        5     19200      8
*** tab[796] p=6ef5a0 cb=a602e8 cnt=191 ac=2 al=802
   Ljava/util/HashtableEntry; 191 3056
  [Ljava/util/HashtableEntry; 2 3208
*** tab[786] p=6ef500 cb=a602c0 cnt=1 ac=0 al=0
   Ljava/util/Hashtable; 1 16
*** tab[782] p=6ef4c0 cb=a602b0 cnt=1 ac=0 al=0
   Ljava/util/Properties; 1 20
*** tab[696] p=6eef60 cb=a60158 cnt=2 ac=1 al=4
   Ljava/lang/ThreadGroup; 2 80
  [Ljava/lang/ThreadGroup; 1 16
*** tab[620] p=6eeaa0 cb=a60028 cnt=480 ac=0 al=0
   Ljava/lang/String; 480 5760
*** tab[610] p=6eea00 cb=a60000 cnt=3 ac=2 al=8
   Ljava/lang/Thread; 3 132
  [Ljava/lang/Thread; 2 32

...
```

The first section of the file shows which methods were called in order of decreasing frequency. The next section shows how much memory was used, providing handles and heap information. The third section lists the types of variables that were created and how many bytes were used to store them. There is also plenty of other information stored in this output; most of it is too complicated to go into here.

As you learn more about Java, you will be able to put this information to good use. It is particularly helpful for deciding how to optimize your software. Programs often follow an 80/20 rule: 80 percent of the execution time is spent in 20 percent of the code. The profiler points out which methods are using up the most time, so you can optimize the most time-consuming parts of the code.

Using javadoc

By adding a few comments to your Java source code, you make it possible for javadoc to automatically generate HTML documentation for your code. Add the following few comments to your TestDrive.java file:

```
/** TestDrive — A test file for demonstration of the JDK. */
public class TestDrive {

    /** This method is called first by the Java interpreter.
        It prints a message to the console. */
    //  javadoc will ignore this comment
public static void main(String[] argv) {

        /* javadoc will also ignore this comment */
        System.out.println("JDK Test Drive");

    }

}
```

C and C++ programmers will immediately notice the similarities between Java and C syntax. The curly braces ({}) group code together into blocks. As in C, line indentation is unnecessary, but it helps make the code more readable.

Java also uses the same kind of comments as C++, but a comment beginning with multiple asterisks has a special meaning for javadoc. It signifies the start of a *documentation comment* block, which is a comment block that will be used by javadoc to create documentation. Given our newly commented TestDrive.java, javadoc will produce the files AllNames.html, tree.html, packages.html, and TestDrive.html, all of which can easily be viewed using a standard Web browser, as shown in Figure 2.4. To run javadoc, simply enter the following command:

javadoc TestDrive.java

FIGURE 2.4

Viewing source code documentation in HTML format produced by javadoc

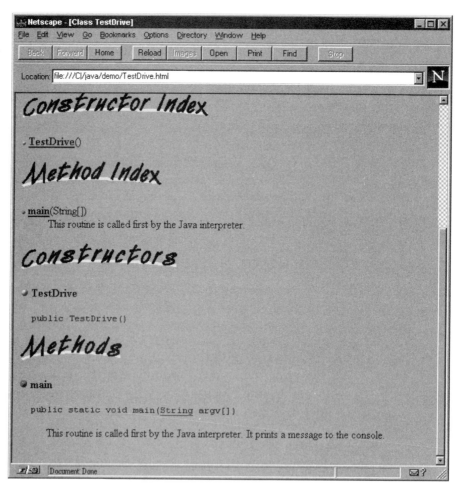

The graphical titles and bullets shown in Figure 2.4 are provided with the HTML documentation for Java API. To see the HTML with the graphics displayed correctly, you must copy the image directory to the directory that contains your documentation. The relationship between the graphics and the HTML will be clearer after you have read the HTML primer in the next section.

Using javah

In order for Java to be applied to platform-specific or performance-critical problems, Java needs the ability to call native code written in C or other languages. Embedded applications are prime examples of where a Java program would need to access platform-specific information, such as LED displays, relays, and sensors. Similarly, rendering complex 3-D graphics in real-time is an application that demands the raw speed of C. Because Java was originally based on an embedded systems language, Java has built-in support for calling native routines.

To help you write C code that interfaces with Java, the JDK includes javah, a utility that, given a class file, generates the C header files needed by C programs to access the class's data.

Using jdb

The Java debugger, jdb, is used to monitor and control the execution of a Java program so that bugs can be found. With jdb, a running program can be stopped at any point so that the variables and internal operation of the program can be examined.

NOTE   Many programmers prefer third-party debuggers, like the ones included with Symantec Café and Borland's jBuilder development environments, because they have all of the features of jdb and also allow you to set breakpoints directly in the code, and view the program internals with separate windows for variables, threads, and function calls.

Although jdb may seem difficult to use and is poorly documented, it can still be a useful tool. It is worthwhile to take a few moments to learn how to use some of the more basic features of jdb. Once you get started, learning more advanced techniques is much easier. Also, Unix C programmers who are used to using tools such as dbx and gdb will probably find jdb very easy to use.

Here is the procedure to use jdb on TestDrive.class, performing only a few basic functions:

1. Load TestDrive class into jdb, and set a *breakpoint*. When the debugger hits a breakpoint in the code, it stops executing the program and allows the user to *inspect* the state of the program. Tell the debugger to stop when it reaches the main() method.

2. Take a look at the source code for TestDrive. The debugger lists the code and also shows where it is about to execute a new instruction (it uses a => to indicate its current position). If there were many lines of code, you could also have jdb *step* through the code one line at a time.

3. Clear the breakpoint and allow jdb to finish executing the program.

Here's the output of the jdb session just described:

```
C:\internet\MasteringJava\ch02>jdb TestDrive
Initializing jdb...
0xa50198:class(TestDrive)

> stop in TestDrive.main
Breakpoint set in TestDrive.main

> run
run TestDrive
running ...
main[1]
Breakpoint hit: TestDrive.main (TestDrive:10)

main[1] list
```

```
6
7                 public static void main(String[] argv) {
8
9                     /* javadoc will ignore this comment */
10      =>           System.out.println("JDK Test Drive");
11
12             }
13
14         }
```

```
main[1] clear TestDrive.main
Breakpoint cleared at TestDrive.main

main[1] cont
main[1] JDK Test Drive

main[1] exit
```

Note that this debugger can connect to a VM that is running in another process, even on a remote machine. This could be especially useful when debugging VMs running on remote servers, appliances, or consumer electronics. To learn more about jdb, type **?** at the prompt.

Using javap

It is possible to examine the bytecodes of a compiled class file and identify its accessible variables and functions. The javap utility creates a report that shows not only what functions and variables are available, but what the code actually does, albeit at a very low level. If you run javap with no command-line arguments:

javap TestDrive

the output shows from which file the class was compiled and the accessible functions and variables:

```
Compiled from TestDrive.java
public class TestDrive extends java.lang.Object {
    public static void main(java.lang.String []);
    public TestDrive();
}
```

In this case, we have no "public" variables, so only the `main` and `TestDrive` functions are displayed. The `TestDrive()` function is a *default constructor*, a special function that is automatically created by the compiler if you do not write one. You will learn more about default constructors in the next chapter.

If you use javap with the -c option to display the meaning of the bytecodes in the file:

javap -c TestDrive

the output shows each step that will be taken by the VM to execute the class.

```
Compiled from TestDrive.java
public class TestDrive extends java.lang.Object {
    public static void main(java.lang.String []);
    public TestDrive();

Method void main(java.lang.String [])
    0 getstatic #7 <Field java.lang.System.out
Ljava/io/PrintStream;>
    3 ldc #1 <String "JDK Test Drive
">
    5 invokevirtual #8 <Method
java.io.PrintStream.println(Ljava/lang/String;)V>
    8 return

Method TestDrive()
    0 aload_0
    1 invokenonvirtual #6 <Method java.lang.Object.<init>()V>
    4 return

}
```

This is much more complicated than the original TestDrive.java file, but it shows each step that the VM will take when executing the program. As you can see, javap is a tool for advanced Java programmers.

Building Applets with the JDK

So far, you have seen the process by which Java applications are built using the JDK. In this section, you will learn about creating Java applets and the HTML documents in which they are hosted.

This section presents a sample Java applet called FilledBox.java, whose only function is to display a filled rectangle in the HTML document. The HTML document can control the color of the rectangle by passing a parameter to the applet, which illustrates the relationship of HTML to Java applets.

Before going any further, you may find it helpful to take a minute to understand the following short lesson in HTML. After a brief introduction to HTML, you will be up and running with Java applets in no time. If you're already familiar with HTML, feel free to skip this section.

HTML for Java Applets

HTML files are text files with special character sequences that specify the document-formatting characteristics. The special character sequences are called *tags*, and they consist of words placed between left and right angle brackets, as shown in the following excerpt:

```
Here is some normal text. <I>Here is some italic text.</I>
```

The <I> tag sets the italic attribute, and the closing </I> tag resets it. A Web browser or HTML viewer interprets the HTML file and produces the corresponding output. This excerpt of HTML produces the following output:

```
Here is some normal text. Here is some italic text.
```

Most HTML tags use the *<tag>* and *</tag>* sequences to set and reset their relevant properties. For example, <B> turns on bold, and </B> turns it off. Other tags, such as the start new paragraph tag, may not require a closing tag; Web browsers tend to be very forgiving about missing tags, as long as the document can be displayed unambiguously.

A complete HTML file has both formatting and structure tags:

```
<HTML>
 <HEAD>
  <TITLE>Sample HTML Document</TITLE>
 </HEAD>
 <BODY>
  <H1>HTML Demo</H1>
  This document is a sample of HTML.
 </BODY>
</HTML>
```

The <HTML> tag indicates that the file is an HTML document. The <HEAD> tag marks the start of an invisible header section that is normally used for recording the title and author of the document. The phrase between the <TITLE> and </TITLE> tags is the name of this document. The BODY of the document contains all the displayed information, in this case, a level one heading and a line of normal text. The output generated by this HTML file is shown in Figure 2.5.

To include an image in an HTML file, use the <IMG> tag and specify the name and location of the image you wish to load. You can use the full URL of the image; a simpler relative reference can be used if the graphic is located on the same server as the HTML file itself.

```
<HTML>
 <HEAD>
  <TITLE>Sample HTML Document</TITLE>
 </HEAD>
 <BODY>
  <IMG SRC="sybex.gif">       add image
  <H1>HTML Demo</H1>
  This document is a sample of HTML.
 </BODY>
</HTML>
```

The resulting display is shown in Figure 2.6.

FIGURE 2.5

A sample HTML file
displayed in Netscape
Navigator

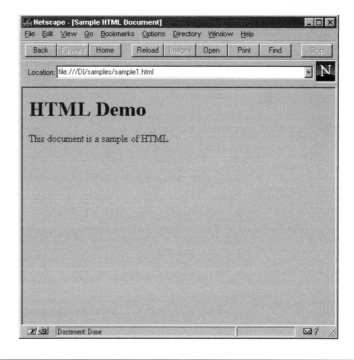

FIGURE 2.6

An HTML document with
an embedded image

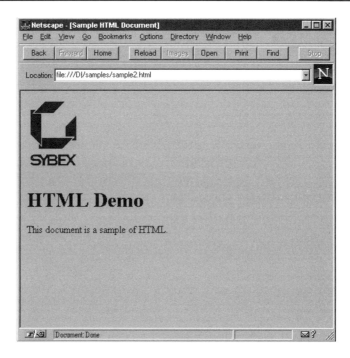

> **NOTE**
> Web browsers can display image files formatted in GIF (Compu-Serve Graphics Interchange Format) and JPEG image formats automatically. Most browsers also support animated and transparent GIF images (also known as GIF89a format). Both of these formats are supported by the Core API. In the future, other graphics formats will probably be supported via Extension APIs.

If you want to connect this page to another document via a hypertext link, you must insert an *anchor* tag (<A>). Everything between the anchor tag and the closing anchor tag will be highlighted, so the user knows that the highlighted text or graphics can be clicked on. The following will build a hypertext link to JavaSoft's home page in the sample document.

```
<HTML>
 <HEAD>
  <TITLE>Sample HTML Document</TITLE>
 </HEAD>
 <BODY>
  <IMG SRC="sybex.gif">
  <H1>HTML Demo</H1>
  This document is a sample of HTML.
  <P>
  You can get the Java Development Kit from the
  <A HREF="http://java.sun.com">JavaSoft Home Page</A>.
 </BODY>
</HTML>
```

The paragraph tag (<P>) makes the text easier to read. A Web browser ignores excess spaces and new lines when displaying a document, so if you need to break a line or begin a new paragraph, you must insert <BR> or <P> tags as necessary. Now the HTML document has text, graphics, and a link, as shown in Figure 2.7.

FIGURE 2.7

A sample HTML document including text, an image, and a hypertext link

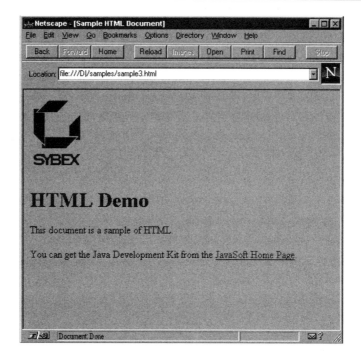

Adding a Java applet to an HTML document is quite straightforward. There is an <APPLET> tag that specifies the location of the class file and the display area allocated to the applet. Suppose you want to add a Clock applet that will display the current time in hours, minutes, and seconds. A compiled Clock applet, called Clock.class, is included on the CD-ROM accompanying this book. Here is a simple example of an <APPLET> tag that loads the clock applet:

```
<APPLET CODE="Clock.class" WIDTH=200 HEIGHT=60> </APPLET>
```

When it encounters these tags, a browser will start the VM and ask it to load Clock.class. It also tells the VM that the applet may draw in a region that is 200 x 60 pixels. The coordinate of the top left of the applet's display area is determined by the location of the <APPLET>

tag in the document. Add the line to load the Clock applet to the HTML file:

```
<HTML>
 <HEAD>
  <TITLE>Sample HTML Document</TITLE>
 </HEAD>
 <BODY>
  <IMG SRC="sybex.gif">
  <H1>HTML Demo</H1>
  This document is a sample of HTML.
  <P>
  You can get the Java Development Kit from the
  <A HREF="http://java.sun.com">JavaSoft Home Page</A>.
  <P>
  <APPLET CODE="Clock.class" WIDTH=200 HEIGHT=60> </APPLET>
 </BODY>
</HTML>
```

The output should look like the document in Figure 2.8.

FIGURE 2.8

The Clock applet embedded in an HTML document

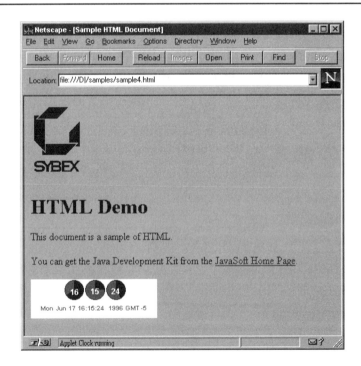

As you can see, embedding applets into Web pages is very simple. Java is able to create plug-in components that can be used by novices as well as experts. For this component strategy to work, the HTML author must be able to customize the properties and behavior of the applet via HTML. The Java programmer decides which parameters will have meaning for the applet, and the HTML author uses <PARAM> tags to pass initial parameters to the applet.

The Clock applet needs no parameters; telling the time is a universal function. On the other hand, the sample FilledBox applet needs to know what color to make the box. You can write the FilledBox applet to expect a parameter called color to be present in the HTML using the <PARAM> tag:

```
<APPLET CODE="FilledBox.class" WIDTH=50 HEIGHT=50>
<PARAM NAME=color VALUE="blue">
</APPLET>
```

The <PARAM> tag accepts two arguments: NAME and VALUE. The NAME argument is used to specify the name of the parameter, and the VALUE argument defines its value. As far as Java is concerned, all parameters are Strings, although they can be converted to any other Java datatype quite easily. The output of the FilledBox applet is shown in Figure 2.9. Notice that only the applet is displayed.

FIGURE 2.9

The appletviewer running the FilledBox applet from FilledBox.html

appletloader.started

If the Web browser includes a Java VM, it will display the applet and ignore everything but the <PARAM> tags, which lie between <APPLET> and </APPLET>. Web browsers that are not Java-enabled will ignore the <APPLET> and <PARAM> tags and display any valid

HTML between the <APPLET> and </APPLET> tags. This allows you to provide an alternative for non-Java-enabled browsers, which is important because some users cannot (or choose not to) run Java applets. If you want your Web page to be accessible to everyone, you need to make it readable by non-Java platforms.

Web Browser Applet Processing

A Java-enabled Web browser follows a specific series of steps when it encounters an <APPLET> tag in an HTML document:

1. The browser reserves space in the document for displaying the applet. The WIDTH and HEIGHT parameters of the <APPLET> tag determine the amount of space used by the applet.

2. The browser reads the parameters from the <PARAM> tags.

3. The VM starts and is asked to load and initialize the applet. The applet has access to the names and values in the <PARAM> tags.

4. The VM creates a running copy of the applet based on the class file.

5. The browser calls the applet's init method so the applet will initialize itself.

6. The VM calls the start method of the applet when it is ready for the applet to start processing. It also calls paint to draw the applet in the browser window.

7. Whenever the applet needs to be redrawn (for example, when the user scrolls the applet into view), the browser calls the applet's paint method.

8. The browser calls the stop method when the user moves on to another HTML document.

9. The browser calls the destroy method when it clears the applet out of memory.

do not have main method

Java Applet Source Code

Java applet source code is written in the same way as Java application source code—with a text editor. The difference is that Java applets do not have a main method. Instead, they have several other methods that are called by the VM when requested by the browser. Here is the source code for the simple FilledBox applet:

```java
import java.awt.*;
import java.applet.Applet;

/** FilledBox displays a filled, colored box in the browser window
*/
public class FilledBox extends Applet {

    // This variable stores the color specified in the HTML document
    Color boxColor;

    /** Get the box color from the host HTML file
    */
    public void init() {

        String s;

        s = getParameter("color");

        // The default color is gray
        boxColor = Color.gray;


        // We expect a parameter called color, which will have
        // the value red, white, or blue. If the parameter
        // is missing, s will be null
        if (s != null) {
        if (s.equals("red")) boxColor = Color.red;
        if (s.equals("white")) boxColor = Color.white;
        if (s.equals("blue")) boxColor = Color.blue;
        }

    }
```

```
/** Paint the box in region assigned to the applet.
    Use the color specified in the HTML document
*/
public void paint(Graphics g) {
   g.setColor(boxColor);
   g.fillRect(0, 0, size().width, size().height);
}

}
```

It's a little more complicated than the Java application example, but that is because it does more. You will recall that a `main` method is required by all Java applications; it is conspicuously absent in this applet. In fact, Java applets do not have any required methods at all. However, there are five methods that the VM may call when requested by the Web browser (or appletviewer):

`public void init()`   Initializes the applet. Called only once.

`public void start()`   Called when the browser is ready to start executing the initialized applet. Can be called multiple times if user keeps leaving and returning to the Web page.

`public void stop()`   Called when the browser wishes to stop executing the applet. Called whenever the user leaves the Web page.

`public void destroy()`   Called when the browser clears the applet out of memory.

`public void paint(Graphics g)`   Called whenever the browser needs to redraw the applet.

If the applet does not implement any of these methods, the applet will have no functionality at all. In the example, `init` and `paint` are implemented. The `init` function obtains the desired box color from a parameter in the host document (applet parameters are explained in the previous section, "HTML for Java Applets"). The `paint` method draws the filled box in the browser window.

Save this Java applet as FilledBox.java.

Using javac

The javac compiler works the same on applets as it does on Java applications:

javac FilledBox.java

Here are a few tips that may help you get started. First, applet classes must always be declared public or they will not get compiled. Also, remember that Java is case-sensitive; filledbox.java is *not* the same as FilledBox.java, and will not be compiled.

If the Java code is acceptable to the compiler, no messages will be displayed, and the file FilledBox.class will be created. If there were error messages, you need to go back and fix your code. There are many different types of warning and error messages that the compiler may generate when given a source file. The simplest to fix are syntax errors, such as a missing semicolon or closing brace. Other messages will highlight incorrect use of variable types, invalid expressions, or violation access restrictions. Getting your source code to compile is only the first part of the debugging process; error-free compilation does not guarantee that your program will do what you want it to. But don't worry about debugging just yet; this example is simple enough that it should run without any problems.

Before you can run your applet, you must create an HTML document to host it.

Creating an HTML File

Now that you know a little about HTML, it is easy to create a simple HTML file to host your applet:

```
<HTML>
 <HEAD>
  <TITLE>Sample HTML Document With Filled Box</TITLE>
 </HEAD>
 <BODY>
  <H1>FilledBox Demo</H1>
```

```
<P>
<APPLET CODE="FilledBox.class" WIDTH=200 HEIGHT=60>
<PARAM NAME=color VALUE="blue">
</APPLET>
</BODY>
</HTML>
```

You can create this file by simply typing it into a text editor. Save the file as FilledBox.html. HTML files can be named anything you like, although it is common practice to name them after the applets they host.

Using appletviewer

The appletviewer utility is used to display the applet as it would be seen by the browser without displaying any of the HTML document itself. In the case of FilledBox.html, appletviewer will display a filled box in its own window:

appletviewer FilledBox.html

Refer back to Figure 2.9 to see the output. For comparison, you can open the file FilledBox.html using a Java-enabled Web browser: Figure 2.10 shows the output as it would be seen by Netscape Navigator. Both the applet and the text are displayed.

If there is more than one applet in a page, appletviewer will open a separate window for each applet; a Web browser will show them in their respective locations within the same Web page. One rather nice feature of appletviewer is that it can load classes from across the network, not just from files. Just give appletviewer the URL of the HTML document containing one or more applets, and it will load the applets as if they were on your local disk. Note, however, that the SecurityManager for the appletviewer may expose your system to greater risks from network-loaded applets than would a Web browser like Netscape Navigator.

FIGURE 2.10

Netscape Navigator
displaying the file
FilledBox.html

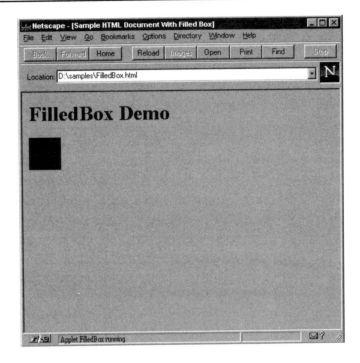

Appletviewer makes it possible to distribute and run Java applets without the aid of a Web browser, so the choice between writing applets versus applications becomes less critical. Most applets are easy to convert into applications and vice versa. The key to this convertibility is to avoid placing a lot of code directly in the `main`, `init`, `start`, `stop`, `destroy`, and `paint` methods, and use calls to generic methods instead.

Using javadoc and javah

The javadoc and javah utilities work on applet source code, too. The command lines are just like the application command lines:

javadoc FilledBox.java

and

javah FilledBox.class

> **TIP**
>
> Because we commented this example code well, javadoc will produce useful results, which make it easier to keep track of what all of the code does. Although this is not critical for a simple applet like this, it is a valuable lesson to remember as you go on to more complicated applets.

What's New in JDK 1.1

If you're already used to writing programs with JDK 1.0.2, you may have noticed some of the changes introduced with the 1.1 release. Here we present a brief list of these changes, most of which will be dealt with in greater detail in later chapters. This list consists of changes that affect the JDK tools; it is not meant to be a comprehensive list of the features of Java 1.1:

(appletviewer) `<APPLET>` **tag changes**   The tag used to load Java applets has been modified. You can now specify resources and other objects to be loaded along with the applet.

(javac) @deprecated tag   The javac compiler will now warn you if you use methods that were supported in previous releases of the JDK but are not the preferred ones in the 1.1 release. See Appendix A for a complete list of deprecated methods and an explanation of how they work.

(jar) Java archives   Java classes and resources, such as images and sounds, can now be bundled into compressed archives called JAR files. This facilitates digital signing and reduces download time.

(javah) New native method interface   The interface for calling native methods has been reworked and standardized across all platforms.

(javakey) Java key generator   The program used to digitally sign class and JAR files so that they can be authenticated.

Summary

This chapter explained the differences between Java applets and Java applications. Although their initialization processes and context differ, you will find that the nuts and bolts of Java programming do not change. Indeed, it is usually easy to convert an applet into an application and vice versa (as long as the applet does not require services built into the browser).

After downloading and installing the JDK, and following the examples presented in this chapter, you should have no problem running demos and examples provided with the JDK and the CD-ROM. Several third-party compilers and development environments (such as Symantec's Café, MOJO, and Metrowerks CodeWarrior Java) are also available.

Working with Java Objects

- Object-oriented programming (OOP) data structures and classes

- Simplifying code with polymorphism

- Defining constructors for classes

- Using finalizers for cleanup before garbage collection

The object-oriented programming (OOP) paradigm has swept through the software industry over the last decade, bringing with it advances in programmer productivity, software reuse, and maintainability. OOP is now considered "best practice" in the development business. Java is a fully object-oriented language, and a thorough understanding of object-orientation is required to make effective use of the Java programming language. To that end, this chapter begins with an introduction to OOP.

An Introduction to OOP

At its core, OOP is simply a way of thinking about problems and their solutions. Instead of tackling programs in a top-down, linear fashion (as with traditional Pascal or C), OOP attempts to break a problem into its component parts. The solution focuses on these independent *objects* and their relationships to other objects. This approach is better-suited to most tasks, because most problems are complex and multifaceted, and do not conform easily to a linear approach.

Classes of objects closely resemble structures and record types in non-OOP languages, so this section starts by reviewing simple data structures and by looking at the software development problems inherent in structures. To maintain continuity with the sample code presented here, as well as to provide an illustrative example of OOP, these concepts will be applied to the design of an air traffic control system.

> **NOTE**
>
> Although C++ is an OOP language, it also supports non-object-oriented techniques. Because C++ and Java syntax are so similar, the examples of non-object-oriented code are in C++.

Data Structures

In almost all programming languages, data is stored in variables that have a specific *datatype*; for example, integer datatypes hold whole numbers, character datatypes hold individual alphanumeric characters, and string datatypes hold groups of alphanumeric characters. Many languages also allow you to create your own datatypes by grouping several simple datatypes together. In C++, these "compound" datatypes are called *structures*; in Pascal, they are called *record types*. Here is a sample structure written in C++ that represents an aircraft:

```
struct Flight {
    int     altitude;
    int     heading;
    int     speed;
    float   latitude;
    float   longitude;
}
```

members

The `Flight` structure is a new datatype made up of built-in C types, namely integers and floating-point numbers. The components of a structure are called *members*. The `Flight` structure could also contain members for the destination of the flight, the type of aircraft, and other pieces of information, but the members listed here are sufficient for the examples.

The structure itself stores no information; it is only a pattern for creating new `Flight` variables. To declare a new `Flight` variable called `incomingFlight`, you would use the following code:

```
struct Flight incomingFlight;
```

You access the members of `incomingFlight` by using the name of the `Flight` variable followed by a period and the name of the member:

```
incomingFlight.altitude = 3000;

if (incomingFlight.heading < 180) {… }
```

In Pascal or Visual Basic, similar code would be used to create the `Flight` structure and to access member variables.

In non-OOP (structure-specific programming, referred to here as *structure-oriented* code), the code that accesses the `Flight` variables is separate and specific to the datatype. For example, a C++ routine that represents a turn of an aircraft might be declared as follows:

```
void turnFlight(Flight &aFlight, int angle) {

  aFlight.heading = (aFlight.heading + angle) % 360;

  // make sure angle is in the range 0-359 degrees
  if (aFlight.heading < 0) aFlight.heading = aFlight.heading
     + 360;
}
```

The `turnFlight` routine expects to be given variables that are `Flight` and `int` datatypes, respectively. Turning an incoming flight 90 degrees to the right is now achieved with the following code:

```
turnFlight(incomingFlight, 90);
```

Similar routines would be written to descend the aircraft and display it on the computer screen. A schematic representation of this code and data structure is shown in Figure 3.1.

FIGURE 3.1

A schematic view of the Flight data structure and the code that references it

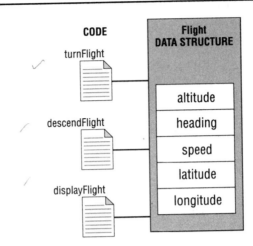

The next step is to model commercial flights. You create a new structure called CommercialFlight that includes everything that the Flight structure included, plus the flight number and number of passengers:

```
struct CommercialFlight {

    // extra members in CommercialFlight
    int     flightNumber;
    int     passengers;

    // members in Flight
    int     altitude;
    int     heading;
    int     speed;
    float   latitude;
    float   longitude;
}
```

Again, to create a CommercialFlight variable called incoming-CommercialFlight, you could simply type:

```
struct CommercialFlight incomingCommercialFlight;
```

However, the routines written for generic flights will not work with `CommercialFlight` variables. For example, the compiler will not allow you to use the `turnFlight` routine with a `CommercialFlight` variable. Therefore, the following call is illegal:

```
turnFlight(incomingCommercialFlight, 90);
```

A schematic representation of the `CommercialFlight` datatype and its functions is shown in Figure 3.2.

FIGURE 3.2

The Flight and CommercialFlight data structures and associated routines

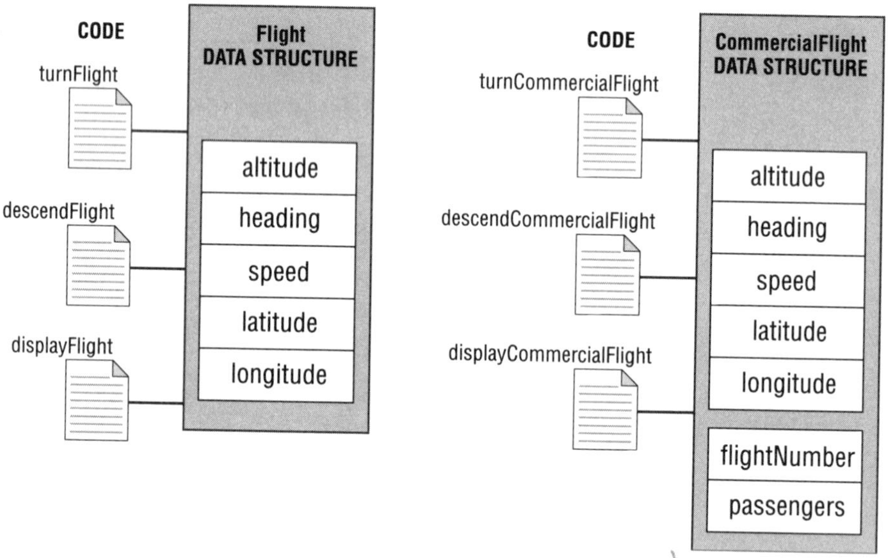

Although there are tricks that can be used to circumvent the datatype problem, the tricks make the code harder to read, more complex, and less reliable. The only safe alternative is to create a new routine for commercial flights called `turnCommercialFlight`:

```
void turnCommercialFlight(CommercialFlight &aFlight, int
                          angle) {

    aFlight.heading = (aFlight.heading + angle) % 360;
```

```
// make sure angle is in the range 0-359 degrees
if (aFlight.heading < 0) aFlight.heading = aFlight.heading
    + 360;
}
```

However, this kind of code duplication presents a maintenance problem. If changes need to be made for ten different structures, ten different routines need to be modified. Not only is this hard work, but it is also an opportunity to introduce additional defects into the code.

Maintenance is only one of several problems with non-OOP structures. Traditional structures are also difficult to use more than once. Structures and their associated routines can quickly become entangled, making it difficult for someone to extract the required code for reuse in a new program. In effect, these entanglements force programmers to look at every detail of the original code in order to use it as part of a new piece of program. To avoid this, developers must exercise a lot of discipline to keep the interface of a structure and its routines—in other words, the parts that need to be used by future applications—separate from the details of their implementation.

Finally, structure-oriented code has some inherent safety flaws. In the previous examples, routines were created to turn aircraft by any angle. These routines guaranteed that the angle would always be between 0 and 359 degrees, inclusive. However, with structures, there is nothing to stop a programmer who is unfamiliar with the class from bypassing the turnFlight routine and entering the following code:

```
// right turn 90 degrees
incomingFlight.heading = incomingFlight.heading + 90;
```

Although the code may be essentially correct, it may lead to headings greater than 359 degrees. This, in turn, may break some other part of the code that assumes all angles will be in the range 0–359 degrees. This lack of data protection also contributes to the fragility of source code.

NOTE   From this point forward, Java source code, not C++ source code, is used. But note that in many cases, the two may appear similar.

From Structures to Classes: Encapsulation

In OOP, the routines for a structure and the structure itself are combined, or *encapsulated*, into a single entity called a *class*. Here is the Java source code for a `Flight` class, an object-oriented version of the `Flight` structure:

```java
class Flight {
    int     altitude;
    int     heading;
    int     speed;
    float   latitude;
    float   longitude;

    // change the flight's heading by angle degrees
    void turnFlight(int angle) {

        heading = (heading + angle) % 360;

        // make sure angle is in the range 0-359 degrees
        if (heading < 0) heading = heading + 360;

    }

    // print information about the flight
    void printFlight() {

        System.out.println(altitude + "/" + heading + "/" + speed);

    }

}
```

The turnFlight routine is now a *member function* of the class; that is, the routine is part of the structure itself. You will notice that the code for the function is actually a little cleaner because you no longer need to refer to the heading as a member of a dummy variable—the variable aFlight has been eliminated altogether. The routine now also includes a member function called printFlight that prints some flight information on the console.

> **NOTE** Member functions are more properly referred to as *methods*, although other terms are often used.

Just as with the structure definition, this class definition is a pattern, or template, for variables to be created with the Flight class datatype. Variables with the Flight class datatype are called Flight *objects* (hence the name object-oriented programming). An object is a storage variable that is created based on a class. Objects are said to be an *instance* of a class. Classes define the variables and routines that are members of all objects of that class. This may sound confusing if you've never worked with objects before, but a look at how the sample Flight class is applied will help you get a feel for using objects.

The next step is to create a Flight object variable based on the Flight class (this process is often referred to as *instantiation*). An *object variable* is a reference to an object; creating a reference to an object and creating the object itself are two separate steps. To create the object variable, use:

```
Flight incomingFlight;
```

The Flight variable can have two possible kinds of values: null or a Flight object. The default value of incomingFlight above is null; it is simply a name and does not yet refer to any object. To create an object referenced by incomingFlight, use the new operator:

```
incomingFlight = new Flight();
```

Now `incomingFlight` refers to a new `Flight` object, and you can access its member variables:

```
incomingFlight.altitude = 2500;

if (incomingFlight.heading < 180) {…}
```

Member functions are called in an analogous way:

```
incomingFlight.turnFlight(90);
```

To understand how this works, imagine that `incomingFlight` points to an object that understands how to turn itself, and that you are sending a message to the object, asking it to turn right by 90 degrees. In fact, in OOP systems, all objects interact by sending messages to each other. The object-oriented equivalent of Figure 3.1 now looks like Figure 3.3.

FIGURE 3.3

The Flight data structure and associated routines as an encapsulated class

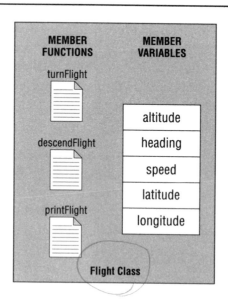

Encapsulation also allows you to use *data hiding*, which is a way to prevent direct access to the variables in an object. This can force other objects to use member functions to alter or read data in member variables, rather than accessing them directly. This is a key strength of

encapsulation: It separates the interface to the class from its implementation, so you do not need to know the implementation details of
the class to safely reuse the code. You can modify the `Flight` class to
hide the `heading` member variable by using the `private` keyword:

```
class Flight {
    int     altitude;
    private int    heading;
    int     speed;
    float   latitude;
    float   longitude;

    void turnFlight(int angle) {
        heading = (heading + angle) % 360;

        // make sure angle is in the range 0-359 degrees
        if (heading < 0) heading = heading + 360;
    }


    void setHeading(int angle) {
        heading = angle % 360;

        // make sure angle is in the range 0-359 degrees
        if (heading < 0) heading = heading + 360;
    }


    int getHeading() {
        return heading;
    }

    void printFlight() {
        System.out.println(altitude + "/" + heading + "/" + speed);
    }

}
```

Now that the `heading` variable is private and hidden to code outside
the class, two additional functions are needed: `setHeading`, in order
to set the heading, and `getHeading`, to obtain the current heading.

It is generally good practice to hide as many variables as possible. This separates the implementation of your class from its interface and makes it more difficult for another programmer to break your code by bypassing the safety measures in your member functions.

Class Inheritance

Using classes instead of structures also solves the problem of code duplication. Recall that for extended structures, such as Commercial-Flight, you need to create a new copy of each function that acts on the original structure (Flight). With classes, you can inherit both the data members and member functions when creating a new class:

```
class CommercialFlight extends Flight {

    // extra members in CommercialFlight
    int    flightNumber;
    int    passengers;

}
```

The CommercialFlight class, a *subclass* of Flight, automatically inherits all the data members and member functions of the Flight class, so you can write:

```
CommercialFlight incomingCommercialFlight;

incomingCommercialFlight = new CommercialFlight();

incomingCommercialFlight.altitude = 2500;
incomingCommercialFlight.setHeading(45);
incomingCommercialFlight.flightNumber = 101;
incomingCommercialFlight.passengers = 24;
```

As you can see, inheritance makes life much easier. It also makes code more maintainable, because the code to alter the heading of both a Flight and a CommercialFlight is all in one place, namely in the definition of the parent or *base class*. A schematic for the relationship of class and subclass is shown in Figure 3.4.

FIGURE 3.4

The CommercialFlight class inherits member variables and functions from Flight and then adds its own member variables.

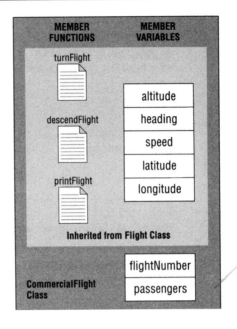

In many cases, you will want a subclass to override one or more member functions of the parent class. Continuing with the example, you may want a commercial flight to print in a special way on the console, displaying the flight number in addition to other information. You can easily override the `printFlight` routine of the `Flight` class by reimplementing it in the `CommercialFlight` class:

```
class Flight {
    int     altitude;
    private int    heading;
    int     speed;
    float   latitude;
    float   longitude;

    void turnFlight(int angle) {
        heading = (heading + angle) % 360;

        // make sure angle is in the range 0-359 degrees
        if (heading < 0) heading = heading + 360;
    }
```

```
void setHeading(int angle) {
    heading = angle % 360;

    // make sure angle is in the range 0-359 degrees
    if (heading < 0) heading = heading + 360;
}


int getHeading() {
    return heading;
}

// print the flight's altitude, heading and speed on the console
void printFlight() {
    System.out.println(altitude + " ft / " + heading
                                + " degrees/" + speed + " knots");
}

}

class CommercialFlight extends Flight {

    // extra members in CommercialFlight
    int     flightNumber;
    int     passengers;

    // reimplement the printFlight routine to
    // override the previous definition
    void printFlight() {
        System.out.print("Flight " + flightNumber + " ");
        super.printFlight();
    }

}
```

Notice that the new `printFlight` member function calls `super.printFlight()`. The super keyword refers to the *superclass* of `CommercialFlight` (in this case, the `Flight` class) and so `super.printFlight()` is a call to the original `printFlight` function as defined in the `Flight` class. You will often see the `super` keyword used when overriding member functions because the overriding function usually implements supplementary processing—it does all its parent class did and more.

If you call a `Flight` object's `printFlight` function:

```
incomingFlight.printFlight();
```

you will get output like the following:

```
2500 ft / 270 degrees / 240 knots
```

If you call a commercial flight's `printFlight` routine:

```
incomingCommercialFlight.printFlight();
```

the output might look like the following:

```
Flight 101 3000 ft / 185 degrees / 350 knots
```

Figure 3.5 shows how the `CommercialFlight` class reimplements the `printFlight` function.

reimplement

FIGURE 3.5

The CommercialFlight class inherits member variables and functions from Flight, adds its own member variables, and overrides the printFlight function.

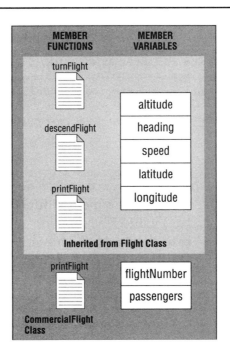

It is sometimes advantageous to use inheritance even when the base class is so generic that it cannot be implemented. This can be done using the concept of abstract classes.

Abstract Classes

This section describes how to incorporate air traffic control facilities into the example by including classes for flight control towers (for aircraft flying, landing, and taking off) and ground control towers (for taxiing aircraft). To begin, you create `ControlFacility` as a parent class, and then create `FlightControlTower` and `Ground-ControlTower` as subclasses. Then create a member function called `getClearance`, which is called to see if a facility will clear a flight for landing, take-off, taxiing, and so on. However, you cannot create a generic `ControlFacility` object because you could not implement `getClearance` without knowing whether you control space on the ground or in the air. On the other hand, you still want to insist that every subclass of `ControlFacility` implements the `getClearance` member function.

The solution to this dilemma is provided by Java's ability to define *abstract classes*. The code for the `ControlFacility` class illustrates how abstract classes work:

```
abstract class ControlFacility {

    abstract boolean getClearance(FlightAction request);

}
```

In this piece of code, you declare your new class and the `getClearance` method function that returns a boolean (`true` or `false`) value. The function will accept an object of a class named `FlightAction` (which is not defined here; it is just part of the illustration). However, the function is defined as `abstract`, and it has no implementation. Any class that has such abstract functions is said to be an *abstract class*, and no objects of such classes can ever be created.

The FlightControlTower and GroundControlTower subclasses must implement the getClearance function so you can create objects that represent such facilities:

```
class FlightControlTower extends ControlFacility {

    boolean getClearance(FlightAction request) {

        // implementation of the getClearance function for
        // flight control towers
        .
        .
        .

    }

}


class GroundControlTower extends ControlFacility {

    boolean getClearance(FlightAction request) {

        // implementation of the getClearance function for
        // ground control towers
        .
        .
        .

    }
}
```

Since both these subclasses—FlightControlTower and GroundControlTower—implement the abstract functions defined in the parent class, they are not abstract classes and can both be instantiated. In addition to formalizing the interface, abstract classes give the programmer other advantages, which are discussed in the next section.

Polymorphism

Polymorphic functions are functions that do not care which variable types are passed to them. The PRINT statement in BASIC and the writeln statement in Pascal are examples of polymorphic routines because you can pass any type of variable to them and they always act appropriately. Standard BASIC does not need a PRINTINTEGER or PRINTSTRING statement because PRINT is smart enough to take care of any datatype. However, the PRINT statement has this ability specially coded into the BASIC interpreter, and its ability does not extend to user-defined structures. BASIC also has no provision for creating user-defined polymorphic routines.

Java make it possible for programmers to simplify their code with polymorphism in three ways:

Inheritance   Allowing subclasses to automatically inherit member functions from their parent classes. Also, any function that accepts a particular class as an argument will also accept any subclass of that class as an argument.

Overloading   Implementing identically named member functions that take different arguments within the same class.

Interfacing   Implementing identically named member functions that take identical arguments in different classes.

Let's look at these three cases in turn.

Inheritance

Inheritance is the simplest kind of polymorphism, as well as one you have already encountered. In the air traffic control example, you can ask any Flight object or Flight-subclassed object to turn left by calling the member function turnFlight(-90). This means that instead of requiring a multitude of function names like turnFlight, turnCommercialFlight, or turnMilitaryFlight (for a MilitaryFlight class), you can use turnFlight consistently:

```
incomingFlight.turnFlight(-90);
incomingCommercialFlight.turnFlight(-90);
incomingMilitaryFlight.turnFlight(-90);
```

Better still, you can easily write code that works with the Flight class and all subclasses of the Flight. For example, you can create a new class called Airport that has a member function called aircraftInbound; in turn, this adds a flight to the list of inbound flights:

```
class Airport {
   String airportName;
   Flights[] inboundFlights, outboundFlights;

   void aircraftInbound(Flight aFlight) {

      //implementation of aircraftInbound function
      .
      .
      .

   }
}
```

An Airport object will now accept any Flight object and any object that is a subclass of Flight. For example, you could write:

```
Airport CityAirport;

CityAirport = new Airport();

CityAirport.airportName = "City National Airport";
CityAirport.aircraftInbound(incomingFlight);
CityAirport.aircraftInbound(incomingCommercialFlight);
CityAirport.aircraftInbound(incomingMilitaryFlight);
```

Polymorphism by inheritance also allows you to take full advantage of abstract classes. Inheriting from a generic abstract class allows you to group together classes that share common functions but not common implementation. Having created the abstract class `Control-Facility` in the previous section, you can now write code that refers to `ControlFacility` objects and works with all subclasses of `ControlFacility`, even though `ControlFacility` objects themselves can never be created.

Overloading

Another way to add polymorphic functions is known as *function overloading*. In Java, C++ and other languages that support function overloading, it is possible to define the same function twice while using different parameters for each definition. For example, in the previous listing, the `aircraftInbound` function does the same thing no matter which subclass of `Flight` is passed to it. Suppose you want to add inbound aircraft to the `Airport` class's list of the inbound flights with different priorities according to the type of flight. By overloading the `aircraftInbound` function, you can customize its behavior for each kind of `Flight` object:

```
class Airport {
   String airportName;
   Flight[] inboundFlights, outboundFlights;

   // aircraftInbound function accepting Flight objects
   void aircraftInbound(Flight aFlight) {

      // implementation of aircraftInbound function for
      // generic flights
      .
      .
      .

   }

   // aircraftInbound function accepting CommercialFlight objects
   void aircraftInbound(CommercialFlight aFlight) {
```

```
    // implementation of aircraftInbound function for commercial
    // flights
        .
        .
        .

}

// aircraftInbound function accepting MilitaryFlight objects
void aircraftInbound(MilitaryFlight aFlight) {

    // implementation of aircraftInbound function for
    // military flights
        .
        .
        .
    }
}
```

Just as before, you call the function identically, no matter which type of `Flight` object is passed to the function:

```
Airport CityAirport;

CityAirport = new Airport();

CityAirport.aircraftInbound(incomingFlight);
CityAirport.aircraftInbound(incomingCommercialFlight);
CityAirport.aircraftInbound(incomingMilitaryFlight);
```

Polymorphism can be achieved by implementing the same member functions in different classes, a technique called *interfacing*. Note that the method signature for polymorphic methods does not include return type.

> **NOTE** Overloading is not a feature of object-oriented languages per se, although it is most commonly implemented in object-oriented languages.

Interfacing

Suppose you need to create a report that lists both airports and all their incoming and outgoing flights. You could do this by writing a `printOnReport` function for both the `Airport` and `Flight` class:

```java
class Airport {
    String airportName;
    Flight[] inboundFlights, outboundFlights;

    // printOnReport function prints an Airport entry on the report
    void printOnReport() {
        System.out.println("Airport: " + airportName);
    }
}

class Flight {
    int     altitude;
    private int     heading;
    int     speed;
    float   latitude;
    float   longitude;

    // print the flight's altitude, heading, and speed on the console
    void printOnReport() {
        System.out.println("Flight: " + altitude + " ft / " + heading
                                + " degrees/" + speed + " knots");
    }

}
```

You can call these new functions in the following way:

```java
incomingFlight.printOnReport();
CityAirport.printOnReport();
```

Informally speaking, these classes now have a common interface as far as printing reports is concerned. Java allows you to formalize the interface so that you can guarantee that a class will support all the functions (there may be more than one) that make up an interface. By using formal interfaces, you can write a function that will accept an argument of any class that implements a particular interface.

Let's define a formal interface for the report printing example. Java's `interface` keyword is used just like the `class` keyword:

```
interface ReportPrintable {
    void printOnReport();
}
```

Note that `ReportPrintable` is not a class and cannot be instantiated; essentially, the member functions declared in an interface are abstract. To tell the compiler that the `Airport` and `Flight` classes implement the `ReportPrintable` interface, add an `implements` clause to the class declarations:

```
class Airport implements ReportPrintable {

        .
        .
        .

}

class Flight implements ReportPrintable {

        .
        .
        .

}
```

Next, you can create a `ReportGenerator` class that creates reports from any object that implements the `ReportPrintable` interface:

```
class ReportGenerator {
    void addToReport(ReportPrintable anObject) {
        anObject.printOnReport();
    }
}
```

The `addToReport` function of `ReportGenerator` will accept *any* class that implements the `ReportPrintable` interface.

As you can see, polymorphism greatly simplifies writing code, especially when modeling complex, real-world situations. The programmer does not need to remember as many function names, and the source code becomes much more readable.

Constructors and Finalizers

You can define two special kinds of member functions:

Constructors   Member functions that return new instances of the class. If you do not write a constructor, a default constructor can be used to create instances of the class.

Finalizers   Functions that are called just before an object is garbage-collected.

These member functions, as well as garbage collection, are described in the following sections.

Constructors

Going back to the `Airport` class, you will recall that you created and initialized the code as follows:

```
Airport CityAirport;

CityAirport = new Airport();

CityAirport.airportName = "City National Airport";
```

After the first line, `CityAirport` has been defined as an object variable. After the second line, an object is created and `CityAirport` refers to the object. The third line initializes the name of the `Airport` object. The function `Airport()` is the *default constructor* for the `Airport` class.

The default constructor is inherited from `Airport`'s parent class, `Object`, and it is automatically added to the class by the Java compiler. The `Object`'s constructor allocates storage for any member variables that are declared as one of Java's built-in datatypes. In this case, none of the `Airport`'s member variables are allocated because neither the `String` variable nor the `Flight` datatypes are built-in (the built-in datatypes will be discussed in the next chapter). For example, the `airportName` member object variable is null until you allocate space for the corresponding `String` or assign an object to it.

To simplify the object creation process, and to protect yourself from uninitialized object variables, you can create your own constructor for the `Airport` class:

```
class Airport {
    String airportName;
    Flight[] inboundFlights, outboundFlights;

    // a new constructor that takes no arguments
    Airport() {

        super();
        airportName = "Unknown";
    }

        .
        .
        .


}
```

A constructor is defined in the same way as an ordinary member function, but it must have the same name as the class and it has no return datatype. In this example, the constructor calls `super()`, which is a reference to the constructor in the parent class, `Object`. Writing the call to `super()` is optional because the compiler will implicitly call the parent class's constructor if you do not call it. You can call the new constructor exactly as you called it earlier:

```
Airport CityAirport = new Airport();

CityAirport.airportName = "City National Airport";
```

Now, after calling the new constructor, `CityAirport.airport-Name` will default to "Unknown". However, because you will always change the airport name, you can save a step by writing another constructor that creates the `Airport` object and sets the `airportName` to the caller's choice, as follows:

```
class Airport {
    String airportName;
    Flight[] inboundFlights, outboundFlights;

    // a new constructor that takes no arguments
    Airport() {

        super();
        airportName = "Unknown";
    }

    // a new constructor that takes the new airport's name as
    // an argument
    Airport(String newName) {

        super();
        airportName = newName;
    }

    .
    .
    .

}
```

This is an example of overloading: The two constructors have the same name, but accept different parameters. Now you can write the following:

```
Airport CityAirport = new Airport("City National Airport");
```

Constructors can call other constructors. You can rewrite the `Airport()` constructor so that it calls the `Airport(String newName)` constructor by using the `this` keyword:

```
// a new constructor that takes no arguments
Airport() {

    this("Unknown");

}
```

The keyword `this` followed by parentheses (and arguments, if any) refers to a constructor for this class. In this case, the compiler knows that you are referring to the `Airport(String newName)` constructor because it is the only constructor that takes a `String` as an argument. Since the different constructors of a class typically perform common tasks, you will find the ability to call other constructors very useful.

Garbage Collection

What happens when an object is no longer needed by the system? The following code and Figures 3.6 and 3.7 illustrate what "no longer needed" means:

```
CityAirport = new Airport("City National Airport");
CityAirport = new Airport("Potter's Field");
```

FIGURE 3.6

The object variable CityAirport initially references the object representing City National Airport.

99

The object variable then references a new object representing Potter's Field. Since there are no references to the first object, it will be automatically discarded by the garbage collector.

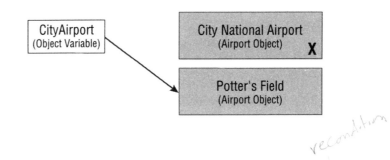

Two objects are created in this code, but there is only one object variable here. After the first statement, `CityAirport` points to the object representing City National Airport. After the second statement, `CityAirport` points to the other object representing Potter's Field, and nothing points to the first object. Just as you would expect, the original object is lost from the system. Java automatically reclaims memory used by an object when no object variables refer to that object, a process known as *garbage collection*. Consider the following assignments and the corresponding Figures 3.8 and 3.9:

```
LocalAirport = new Airport("City National Airport");
CityAirport = LocalAirport;
CityAirport = new Airport("Potter's Field");
```

In this instance, the object representing City National Airport is not garbage-collected because `LocalAirport` still refers to it.

The object variables LocalAirport and City-Airport initially reference the new object representing City National Airport.

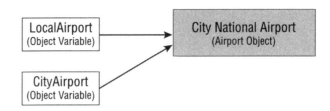

FIGURE 3.9

Next the object variable CityAirport is used to refer to the new object representing Potter's Field. Since there is still a reference to the first object (LocalAirport), the original object will not be discarded by the system.

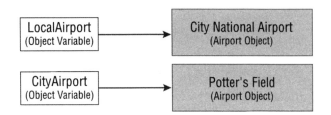

Finalizers

There are a few situations in which a class needs to clean itself up before garbage collection. It can do this by implementing a finalizer member function. Finalizers are called just before a class is garbage-collected. They are typically used to close open files or connections, or to ensure that related tasks are completed before the object is forgotten.

To create a finalizer, simply define a member function called finalize:

```
protected void finalize() {
    System.out.println("This object is about to be garbage collected");
    }
```

The protected keyword will be explained in the next chapter (it limits the classes that may call the finalizer function).

Finalizers are rather tricky to write because it is impossible to determine exactly when an object will be garbage-collected; it could be within microseconds or, if the program is terminated, may never occur. This means that a finalizer should rely as little as possible on the existence of other objects, because there is no guarantee that the other objects were not garbage-collected first. It is also possible for an object to avert its own garbage collection by creating a new reference to itself in the finalizer. Therefore, if your class must perform some shutdown or cleanup operation before being garbage-collected, you should write a non-finalizer function to take care of the operation, and call that function explicitly before discarding the object.

101

For example, suppose you write a class called ComLink that handles network communications and a member function called close that closes the network channel. You know you need to close the network channel before discarding any ComLink objects, so the simplest solution might appear to be calling close from ComLink's finalize method. However, it is possible that close will not be called for an extended period of time, or perhaps not at all. This could cause the system to run out of network channels because channels have not been freed by discarded ComLink objects in a timely manner. The only reliable solution in such cases is to make sure you call the close function explicitly, before any objects are discarded.

Summary

OOP languages support encapsulation, inheritance, and polymorphism. Encapsulation separates the interface from the implementation by hiding data within the object and making that data accessible via member functions. Subclasses inherit the member functions and variables of their parent classes, making it very easy to reuse the functionality in the parent class. Polymorphism allows you to create generic, reusable code that will work with a wide range of different class datatypes. Because Java supports all these features, Java code is reusable and reliable.

The Java Core API contains about 600 prefabricated classes you can use to do everything from graphics to network programming to database access. You can use Java's object-oriented features to inherit functionality from the class library as you write your own programs. In fact, most interface-related classes will inherit much of their capability from the class library.

The next chapter provides a detailed discussion of the Java language datatypes, keywords, and expressions, as well as the finer points of data hiding.

CHAPTER

FOUR

4

Datatypes, Modifiers, and Expressions

- Java syntax

- Basic datatypes

- Inner classes

- Datatypes and method modifiers

Java's program structure and syntax is quite similar to that of C++. The first part of this chapter describes basic Java syntax and Java keywords. You will learn a standard way to choose variable, class, and function names, and how to enter data values into your code.

Java datatypes come in three varieties: basic built-in (or primitive) datatypes, system classes that have been defined in Java's Core API, and user-defined classes. The built-in datatypes hold atomic units of information, such as individual characters, numbers, or true/false values. The built-in datatypes themselves are not classes, so they do not have member methods. The API includes a language package (java.lang), which has class equivalents of the basic datatypes and other commonly used datatypes, such as the String class for storing strings of characters and the Thread class for multithreading.

In the previous chapter, you learned how to create your own user-defined classes. In this chapter, you will learn how to define your own classes with more advanced data hiding.

Using Java Syntax

A language *syntax*, or *grammar*, defines how and when words can be used, as well as the punctuation required. Java's syntax specifies the way the following are written:

Comments Remarks added by the programmer for documentation purposes.

Statements A single "line" of the program.

Code blocks A set of statements grouped together as a unit.

4 **File structure**   The components of a Java source file, and the order in which they are defined.

5 **Keywords**   Words that are predefined in the Java language (not to be used as identifiers).

6 **Identifiers**   The names you give to classes, variables, and methods. Identifiers have restrictions on length and leading characters. There are also some optional, yet widely used, conventions for identifiers.

7 **Literals**   Constant values are written differently, depending on the datatype—for example, to distinguish the characters "123" from the number 123.

8 **Expressions**   A combination of terms that evaluate to a single data value.

9 **Operators**   Operators perform addition, subtraction, multiplication, and other operations.

Each one of these concepts will be described in the following sections.

Comments

Comments can be added to Java source code in the same two ways as they are added in C++. The first type of comment begins with / * and ends with * /, and allows you to add comments that extend across several lines of text:

```
a = b + c;
/* Here is a comment which
   extends across two lines */
```

Generally, you cannot *nest* comments (that is, place comments within comments):

```
a = b + c;
/* Here is a comment which /* a comment within a comment */
   extends across two lines */
```

In this example, the first comment ends at the first * /, leaving the second line of text without a starting comment marker. This results in a compile-time error.

As mentioned in Chapter 2, multiple-line comments have special meaning for the javadoc utility when the first character inside the comment is an asterisk; that is, when the comment begins with /** (/* is not a javadoc comment; the slash must be followed by two or more asterisks):

```
a = b + c;
/** This comment has special meaning for the javadoc utility.
    It will be part of documentation automatically generated
    by the javadoc program. */
```

The second type of comment extends from the comment marker // to the end of the line of text:

```
a = b + c; // this comment extends to end of this line of text
```

These comments can be embedded within comments that begin with /* and end with */.

Statements

A *statement* is a single "line" of Java code. There is not a one-to-one correspondence between lines of code and lines of text in a Java source file. Java uses the semicolon to indicate the end of a line of code. This line:

```
a = b + c + d + e + f + g;
```

is the same as as this one:

```
a = b + c + d +
    e + f
+ g;
```

The spaces between terms in a statement can consist of any number of *whitespace* characters. Whitespace characters are spaces, tabs, line-feeds, and carriage returns.

NOTE On Unix and Macintosh systems, a carriage return character (ASCII code 13) usually terminates each line of text. In Windows, lines of text are usually delimited by carriage return and linefeed characters (CR/LF or ASCII code 13 followed by ASCII code 10). Java compilers see all these characters as whitespace, and they do not care how lines of text are terminated. For more information about ASCII, see the section on character datatypes, later in this chapter.

Code Blocks

Statements can be grouped together into blocks so that a single statement can easily control the execution of many other statements. Java code blocks are delimited with braces ({ and }). You have already seen code blocks used to group the statements belonging to a class, as well as code blocks nested within other blocks, as in this example from Chapter 3:

```
class Flight {
    int     altitude;
    int     heading;
    int     speed;
    float   latitude;
    float   longitude;

    // change the flight's heading by angle degrees
    void turnFlight(int angle) {

        heading = (heading + angle) % 360;

        // make sure angle is in the range 0-359 degrees
        if (heading < 0) heading = heading + 360;

    }
}
```

The amount of whitespace between braces and statements is arbitrary, but conventionally, a left brace is placed at the end of a line (or the start of the next line), the right brace on its own line, and indentation is used to highlight the grouping of code. Of course, code style is a matter of individual choice, and every programmer has his or her own method of formatting code. Ultimately, it does not matter which style you choose, as long as you are consistent throughout your source code files.

Source File Structure

Java source files may contain only three types of statements that are not contained within code blocks:

1. `package` Defines the package to which the classes in the file will belong.

2. `import` Establishes a shorthand for referring to existing classes (such as those in the API) by class name only, without specifying the full package name.

3. `class` Defines your top-level classes.

The `package` and `import` statements are both optional. A *package* is a group of related classes. Classes in the same package have freer access to each other's member variables and methods, and they need to be stored in a predefined location on the server or on the client machine. In addition, classes that are immediately contained within a package are said to be *top-level* classes. This distinguishes them from *inner classes*, which are defined within other classes. (See Chapter 5 for more information about Java packages.)

Note that the statements in a source file must appear in the order listed (`package`, `import`, then `class`).

Here is a sample Java source file with all three types of components:

```
package com.sybex.examples;

import java.awt.Panel;
import java.awt.Color;

class ColorPanel extends Panel {

    ColorPanel        .
    .
    .
}
```

This code fragment defines a new class called `ColorPanel` that belongs to a package called `com.sybex.examples`. Another program referring to this class would refer to the class as `com.sybex.examples.ColorPanel`.

The `import` statements make it easier to refer to classes in an existing package called `java.awt`. The `java.awt` package is the AWT (Abstract Window Toolkit) package, part of the Core API. The first `import` statement allows you to refer to the class `java.awt.Panel` from class `java.awt` as simply `Panel`. Similarly, the second `import` statement allows you to refer to the `Color` class in the same package by its class name, `Color`, rather the package and class name, `java.awt.Color`.

The last statement in the file is a class definition. It is a compound statement; that is, it is a statement containing a block of other statements. Additional class definitions may follow this one.

Keywords

A *keyword* is a word that has a special meaning for the Java compiler, such as a datatype name or a program construct name. The complete list of Java keywords is shown in Table 4.1.

TABLE 4.1   Java Keywords

abstract	double	int	static
boolean	else	interface	super
break	extends	long	switch
byte	final	native	synchronized
case	finally	new	this
catch	float	null	throw
char	for	package	throws
class	goto*	private	transient
const*	if	protected	try
continue	implements	public	void
default	import	return	volatile
do	instanceof	short	while

* Reserved but currently not used by the language.

Identifiers

An *identifier* is a name given to a variable, class, or method. You can choose identifiers to be anything you wish, as long as the identifier begins with a letter and is not spelled the same as a keyword.

You may have noticed a pattern in the way the identifiers in this book are capitalized. The capitalization follows the identifier conventions used in the Java Core API, and it is recommended that you follow the same convention to keep your code more readable. Familiarity with these conventions will also make it easier to read the sample code provided. Table 4.2 lists these identifier conventions. Although their use is recommended, the compiler will not complain if you do not follow these conventions.

Identifiers are not restricted to ASCII characters. If your editor supports it, you can have Unicode characters in variable names. Also, there is no limit to the number of characters in an identifier. If you have two variables that differ at the 512th position (or beyond), the compiler will detect this, and treat them as separate. Of course, most humans reading your code probably won't be that accurate, so be careful.

TABLE 4.2 Conventions for Naming Identifiers

Type of Identifier	Convention	Examples
Class names	Capitalize each word within the identifier	`Flight`, `CommercialFlight`
Function names	Capitalize every word within the identifier except the first	`printFlight`, `turnFlight`
Variable names	Capitalize every word within the identifier except the first	`altitude`, `flightNumber`
Constant variable names	Capitalize every letter; underscores between words.	`MAX_INBOUND_FLIGHTS`

Literals

Whereas an identifier is a symbol for a value, a *literal* is an actual value such as 35, or "Hello". Table 4.3 summarizes the formats for literals for each datatype. As you can see, a datatype may have more than one format for a literal.

By default, integer literals are of type `int`, but you can override this by adding the letter L to the end of the number to make it a `long`. Similarly, a floating-point literal represents a double-precision number unless the F suffix is used to mark it as `float`.

For the `char` datatype, you can use predefined escape sequences. These are listed in Table 4.4.

TABLE 4.3   Formats for Literals of Each Datatype

Datatype	Literal

`byte`
`short`
`int`
	Decimal digits (not starting with 0)
	`0x` followed by hexadecimal digits, e.g., `0xFF`
	`0` followed by octal digits, e.g., `0726`

`long`	Same as for `int` datatype but followed by the character `1` or `L`, e.g., `1234L`, `0x12FABL`, `043543212L`, `12341`
`float`	Digits with a decimal point and/or exponent, followed by the character f or F, e.g., `1.234f`, `1.234E+5F` ($1.234 \times 10^5 = 123400$), `.1234F`
`double`	Same as for `float` datatype but without the f or F suffix and with an optional d or D suffix, e.g., `1.234D`, `1.234`, `1.234E-5` ($1.234 \times 10^{-5} = 0.00001234$), `.1234`
`boolean`	`true` or `false`
`char`	Unicode (or ASCII) character within single quotation marks, e.g., `'a'` or `'B'` (if your editor supports input of Unicode characters, these can go right into the single quotation marks), a predefined escape sequence within single quotation marks, e.g., `'\t'`, `'\012'`, `'\u000A'` (see Table 4.4)
`String`	A sequence of characters or escape sequences within double quotation marks, e.g., `"Hello World\n"`

TABLE 4.4   Character Escape Sequences

Escape Sequence Type	Escape Sequence	Character Represented
Special	\b \t \n \f \r \" \' \\	Backspace Horizontal tab Linefeed Form feed Carriage return Double quotation mark (") Single quotation mark (') Backslash
Octal	\DDD	Character with ASCII code DDD octal, where DDD is a sequence of three octal digits (0-7), e.g., \071 is ASCII character 71 octal, 57 decimal
Unicode	\uHHHH	Character with Unicode value HHHH hex, where HHHH is a sequence of four hexadecimal digits (0-9, A-F, a-f), e.g., \u0041 is Unicode character 41 hex, 65 decimal

Expressions and Operators

Expressions are combinations of variables, keywords, or symbols that evaluate to a value of some type. The value may be a number, string, or any other class or datatype. You might think of an expression as something that could be written on the right side of an assignment statement.

The simplest expressions are simply variables or literals, as in 15, a, or "Hello". These expressions may be found on the right side of an assignment statement such as the following one, which assigns the string "Hello" to the variable s:

```
s = "Hello";
```

As in C, an assignment has a value of its own; namely, the value of the assignment is the value of the right-hand side of the assignment itself:

```
b = a = 15;
```

In this example, the value 15 is assigned to a, and the value of the assignment "a = 15" is itself 15, so 15 is also assigned to b.

Method Calls

Another type of expression is the *method call*. As you have seen, methods can evaluate to a datatype, so they can appear on the right side of an assignment:

```
a = incomingFlight.getHeading();
b = weatherStation.getCelsius(fahrenheit);
```

The generic structure of a member function or variable reference is:

```
object.membervariable
object.memberfunction ( arguments )
```

or in the case of static member functions and variables (see the section "Storage and Lifetime Modifiers," later in this chapter):

```
class.membervariable
class.memberfunction( arguments )
```

Object Allocation

Object allocation is just a special kind of function call. You can use the new keyword to call the constructor for the class you are instantiating:

```
new classname( arguments )
```

Here are three different examples:

```
Flight f;
f = new Flight();

Airport f;
f = new Airport("City National Airport");

Airport f = new Airport("City National Airport");
```

If you do not provide a constructor for your class, a default constructor that accepts no arguments is created. However, if you provide only a constructor that requires arguments/parameters, there will not be a constructor that accepts no parameters. Note that a class cannot be instantiated if the class is abstract.

The this and super Reserved Words

There are two special reserved words that can also be used to form expressions. If you want to refer to the current instance of the class in which the code is written, you can use the this keyword. The super keyword refers to the superclass of the class in which the code is written. Note that static methods may not use these keywords, because they do not have an instantiated object to refer to.

Using the `this` keyword, you can have an object print itself on the console when you call its `print` method, by adding the following code to any class:

```
public void print() {
    System.out.println(this);
}
```

If, for example, this code were added to the `Flight` class, you could write:

```
Flight incomingFlight = new Flight();

incomingFlight.setHeading(140);
incomingFlight.print();
```

In the `print()` method, `this` points to `incomingFlight`, so the last line of this listing is equivalent to:

```
System.out.println(incomingFlight);
```

As shown in Chapter 3, `this` is also used when referring to a constructor from within another constructor. In this case, the reference appears as a method call:

```
public Flight(int heading) {
    setHeading(heading);
}

public Flight(int heading, int newAltitude) {
    this(heading);
    altitude = newAltitude;
}
```

The call to `this(heading)` in the second constructor calls the first constructor.

The `super` keyword is used to refer to the methods or member variables of the superclass. If a subclass defines a member variable with the same name as its parent's member variable, you can use the super keyword to reference the parent's variable from the sub-class. super is also used to refer to the methods of the parent class:

```java
class Parent {
    String name;

    void print () {
        System.out.println("Parent " + name);
    }
    .
    .
    .
}

class Child extends Parent {
    String name;

    String childName() {
        return name;
    }

    String parentName() {
        // return the name of the parent
        return super.name;
    }

    void print() {
        System.out.println("Child " + name + " is child of");
        super.print();
    }
    .
    .
    .
}
```

Operator Expressions

The other types of expressions involve combinations of variables, literals, function calls, and operators. An *operator* is a symbol that trans-forms a variable or combines it in some way with another variable or literal. The multiplication operator, *, combines two numbers to form a third number:

```
a = b * c;
```

The expressions on which an operator acts are called *operands*. The multiplication operator is an example of a *binary operator*—it takes two operands and creates a new result.

Other operators act on a single variable to produce another value:

```
a = - b;
```

Here, the negation operator (-) transforms a single variable b into another quantity that is then assigned to a. An operator that creates output from a single operand is called a *unary operator*. Another type of unary operator automatically assigns a new value to the operand; the auto-increment (++) and auto-decrement (- -) operators add and subtract one from the operand, respectively:

```
a = 10;
a++; // add one to a (a is now 11)
a--; // subtract one from a (a is now 10)
```

Operator Precedence

When several operators are used in a single expression, it is important to know in which order the operators will be applied. If you use addition and multiplication as shown here:

```
a = 4 + 5 * 6;
```

do you get 34 or 54? The answer depends on *operator precedence* (that is, the order in which the operators will be applied). As with normal math, multiplication (*) has higher precedence than addition (+), so the multiplication is done first, and the answer is 34. If you want to do the addition before the multiplication, use parentheses to group parts of the calculation together:

```
a = (4 + 5) * 6; // the number 54 will be assigned to a
```

Java will evaluate expressions in parentheses as a single unit before proceeding with the rest of the calculation. You can take advantage of parentheses to program defensively. Use parentheses to group parts of the calculation together whenever possible, even when they are not needed:

```
a = 4 + (5 * 6);
```

This is unambiguous and helps you, and the reader of your programs, know what is going on. It also means you won't need to remember the precedence of the operators.

If two operators have the same precedence, there is a well-defined order in which the computations will be performed: from left to right or right to left. This property of an operator is known as the operator's *associativity*. The multiplication operator is left associative, so when evaluating the product 2 * 3 * 4, the leftmost product will be evaluated first to get 6 * 4, before finally performing the last product and arriving at the result of 24.

Arithmetic Operators

Java's *arithmetic operators* are summarized in Table 4.5. These operators accept integer or floating-point operands and produce integer or floating-point results. The auto-increment and auto-decrement operators are included as arithmetic operators.

TABLE 4.5   Arithmetic Operators

Operator	Purpose	Precedence (1 = highest)	Associativity
++ , --	Auto-increment, auto-decrement	1 (2 if it precedes an expression, i.e., ++j)	Right
+ , -	Unary plus, unary minus	2	Right
*	Multiplication	4	Left
/	Division	4	Left
%	Remainder (modulo division)	4	Left
+ , -	Addition, subtraction	5	Left

The remainder operator (%) returns the remainder of dividing the first operand by the second, so 24 % 10 is the remainder left over after dividing 24 by 10, namely 4. This operator also works with floating-point operands.

Relational Operators

Relational operators compare two quantities to determine if they are equal or if one is greater than the other. The operator that tests for equality is the == operator. If the operands are built-in types (arithmetic, character, or boolean), the equality operator returns the boolean value true if the operands have the same value or false if they do not. If the operands are object variables, the equality operator returns true if the object variables refer to the same object (or are both null). If the object variables refer to different objects, or if one refers to an object and the other is null, the equality operator returns false.

When the operands are built-in types, the equality operator works as you would expect:

```
boolean a, b;
a = (2 == 2);  // a will be true
b = (2 == 3);  // b will be false
```

In contrast, if two objects are compared for equality:

```
boolean a, b;
Flight f1, f2;

// f1 and f2 will be two separate Flight objects
// with the same default values
f1 = new Flight();
f2 = new Flight();

a = (f1 == f2); // a will be false because f1 and f2 refer
                // to different instances, even though they
                // contain exactly the same data

f1 = f2;
b = (f1 == f2); // b will be true because f1 and f2 now refer
                // to the identical instance
```

TIP Because you often need to check to see if the *contents* of two objects are equal, most objects implement the `equals()` method, which allows you to check the equality of objects in the same way that you would with primitives.

*equals()
method*

The inequality operator (`!=`) does the exact opposite of the equality operator: It returns `true` when the operands are not equal.

Numeric operands can be compared with each other using the greater than (`>`), less than (`<`), greater than or equal (`>=`), and less than or equal (`<=`) operators:

```
boolean a, b, c, d;

a = (1 > 2);  // a is false
b = (1 < 2);  // b is true
c = (1 <= 2); // c is true
d = (1 >= 0); // d is true
```

Java has kept C's question mark/colon, or conditional, operator that takes three operands (it is a *ternary operator*). The first operand is boolean, and the two other operands may be of any type. If the boolean operand is true, the result is the second operand; if it is false, the result is the third operand:

```
boolean b;
int c;

b = true;
c = (b ? 1 : 2); // 1 will be assigned to c because b is true
b = false;
c = (b ? 1 : 2); // 2 will be assigned to c because b is false.
```

WARNING Be wary of this particular conditional operation. Although it is useful, it makes your code less readable.

These comparison operators are usually used in conjunction with conditional statements (these are covered in Chapter 6). The relational operators are summarized in Table 4.6.

TABLE 4.6   Relational Operators

Operator	Purpose	Precedence	Associativity
>, <, >=, <=	Tests relative magnitude	7	Left
==	Tests equality	8	Left
!=	Tests inequality	8	Left
? :	Conditional—returns one of two operands based on a third	14	Left

Boolean Operators

Boolean operators act on boolean operands and return a boolean result. They implement the standard boolean algebraic operations: AND, OR, NOT, and XOR (eXclusive OR).

The AND operator returns `true` if both operands are true. The OR operator returns `true` if either operand is true. Java has two versions of each of these operators. The first version (& for AND; | for OR) forces evaluation of both operands. The second version (&& for AND; | | for OR) will not evaluate the second operand if it can determine the result after evaluating the first. Here is an example to illustrate the difference between these two versions of the OR operation:

```
boolean b;

// to compute the following, the VM will evaluate both expressions
// and, therefore, will perform both multiplications
b = ( 100 > ( 5 * 6 ) )  | ( 100 > (8 * 8));  // b will be true

// to compute the following, the VM will evaluate only the
// expressionon the left, and, therefore, will perform only
// one multiplication (7 * 9)
b = ( 100 > ( 7 * 9 ) )  || ( 100 > (4 * 5));  // b will be true
```

The two AND operators work analogously.

There are occasions when you want the VM to evaluate both sides, whether or not the result of the AND/OR operation can be deduced by evaluating only one operand. In other situations, you do not want the VM to continue because it will result in needless comparisons or exceptions, if you are assuming previous conditions succeeded.

The XOR operator returns `true` if the operands are not the same—one operand is true, and the other is false (`true ^ false == true`). The NOT operator is a unary operator that returns the opposite of its operand (`!false == true`).

The boolean operators are summarized in Table 4.7.

TABLE 4.7 Boolean Operators

Operator	Purpose	Precedence	Associativity
!	NOT	2 (++/-- first)	Right
&	Boolean AND	9	Left
^	XOR	10	Left
|	Boolean OR	11	Left
&&	Conditional AND	12	Left
||	Conditional OR	13	Left

Bitwise Operators

The integral types (`byte`, `short`, `int`, and `long`) are represented in the computer's memory as a sequence of bits (binary digits). Just like decimal numbers, binary numbers have their most significant digits to the left. In decimal, the most significant digit in the number 325 is the 3 because it represents 300, and the least significant digit is the 5. Written as a binary number, 325 is 101000101. The leftmost digit represents 100000000 binary (256 decimal) and is the most significant digit.

Java's integers are signed numbers, so Java must use the leftmost bit of storage to represent the sign of the integer. For Java's integer datatypes, the high bit is used to represent the sign of the number, as shown in Figure 4.1. If the high bit is 1, the number is negative.

FIGURE 4.1

Java's integral datatypes use the high bit to indicate the sign of the number. If the high bit is 1, the number is negative.

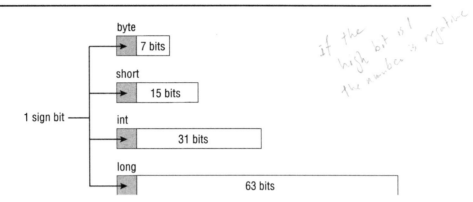

if the high bit is 1 the number is negative

bitwise operators

Java uses the same operators as the C language to manipulate the bits of integers. Because all of Java's integral datatypes are signed, Java supplements the C operators with an additional operator. Bit-manipulation operators are referred to as *bitwise* operators. The bitwise operators perform the same sorts of functions as the boolean operators, as well as bit shifts.

The bitwise AND operator applies the AND operation to the corresponding bits of each operand. The bitwise OR, XOR, and NOT operators work in a similar fashion. The bitwise operators are illustrated in Figure 4.2.

The shift operators shift all the bits in an integral type to the left or the right, as shown in Figure 4.3. The shift operators are binary operators. The second operand is an integer that determines the number of bits to shift. The standard C shift operators act slightly differently in Java. In Java, all numbers are signed, and the sign bit is preserved through all shifts. Even though this sign bit is shifted, it is also copied, so that the resulting number will have the same sign as the original. Java adds the >>> operator, which shifts all bits to the right as if the integer were unsigned.

FIGURE 4.2

Boolean bitwise operators

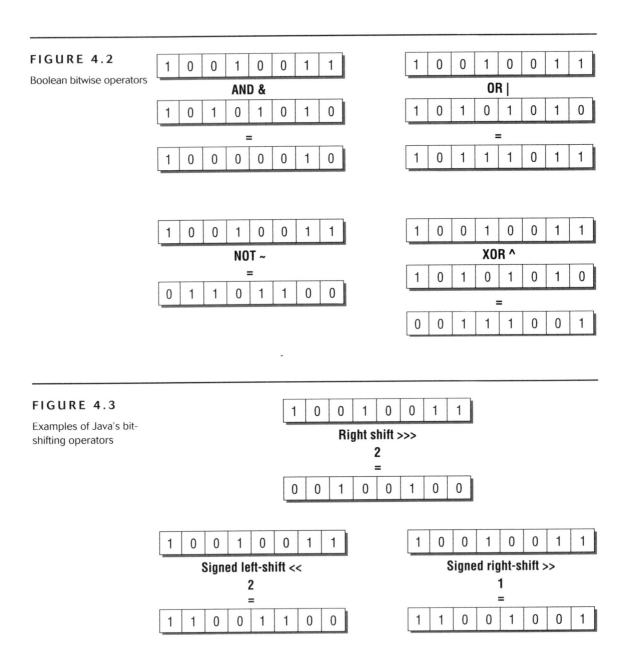

FIGURE 4.3

Examples of Java's bit-shifting operators

NOTE
For simplicity, Figure 4.3 uses signed 8-bit bytes. However, you should be aware that Java's shift operators work with `int` and `long` datatypes only. If you shift a negative `short` to the right using the `>>` operator, you may end up with a larger number than you started with. This is because the left operand is cast (converted) into an `int` before being shifted.

The bitwise operators are summarized in Table 4.8.

TABLE 4.8 Bitwise Operators

Operator	Purpose	Precedence	Associativity
~	NOT (bitwise complement)	2	Right
<<, >>	Left shift, Right shift	6	Left
>>>	Right shift as if unsigned	6	Left
&	Bitwise AND	9	Left
^	Bitwise XOR	10	Left
|	Bitwise OR	11	Left

String Operators

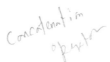

The concatenation operator (+) is the only operator that applies to strings in particular. It glues two strings together to form a third:

```
String s;

s = "Hello" + " " + "World"; // "Hello World" is assigned to s
```

If only one operand is a string, the other operand is converted to a string automatically:

```
String s;

s = "5 * 6 =" + (5 * 6); // "5 * 6 = 30" is assigned to s
```

method

If the operand that is not a string is an object, Java uses the `toString()` member function to obtain a string equivalent of the object. The `toString()` method is inherited by all classes, because it is implemented by the `Object` class. The default behavior of `toString()` is to return the name of the class of the object along with an @ and the *hashcode* of the object. The hashcode is a unique number calculated by the `hashCode()` method. All objects can call this method since it is defined in class `Object`. The following code illustrates the implicit use of `toString()`:

```
String s;
SomeObject m;

s = "m is " + m; // "m is a SomeObject@1393870" assigned to s
```

The concatenation operator, like the addition operator, has a precedence of 5 and is left-associative.

Assignment Operators

As was mentioned earlier, the assignment operator is an operator that assigns the second operand to the first and returns the second operand as a result.

Other assignment operators serve as shorthand for combined operation and assignment. If you wanted to add 5 to a number, you could write:

```
int i;
i = i + 5;
```

You could also use the assignment operator +=:

```
int i;
i += 5; // this is the same as i = i + 5
```

Assignment operators exist for most of the operators already mentioned. They are summarized in Table 4.9.

TABLE 4.9 Assignment Operators

Operator	Purpose	Precedence	Associativity
=	Assignment	15	Right
*=	Assignment with operation	15	Right
/=	Assignment with operation	15	Right
%=	Assignment with operation	15	Right
+=	Assignment with operation	15	Right
-=	Assignment with operation	15	Right
>>=	Assignment with operation	15	Right
<<=	Assignment with operation	15	Right
>>>=	Assignment with operation	15	Right
^=	Assignment with operation	15	Right
|=	Assignment with operation	15	Right
&=	Assignment with operation	15	Right

Special Operators

The *cast* operator converts from one datatype into another. A cast is written as the name of the type into which you are casting the operand within parentheses:

```
int i;
long l;

l = 1 << 40; // l is a very large number
l--;
i = (int) l; // l is being cast into an integer
```

If you are assigning a value of lower precision to a variable of higher precision, no cast is necessary. For example, no cast is needed to assign an `int` to a `long`, or a `float` to a `double`.

WARNING C/C++ programmers need to be careful here. In C, typecasting is automatic for related datatypes. Java, however, requires that you explicitly specify any cast that might alter the contents (or precision) of a variable. Java objects can also be cast into any superclass of the same object.

Typecast operators have a precedence of 3 and are right-associative.

The `instanceof` operator is used to test the class of an object:

```
boolean b;
Flight f;
CommercialFlight cf; //CommercialFlight is a subclass of
                     //Flight

f = new Flight();
cf = new CommercialFlight();

b = f instanceof Flight; // b will be true
b = f instanceof String; // b will be false
b = cf instanceof Flight;// b will be true because cf is a
                         //subclass of Flight
```

The `instanceof` operator has a precedence of 7 and is left-associative.

TIP Here's an easy way to remember associativity: Only unary, assignment, and conditional operators are right-associative; all others are left-associative.

Java's Built-in Datatypes

Java's built-in datatypes are understood by the compiler itself, without reference to any libraries or the Core API. These types can be classified into numeric, boolean, and character datatypes.

Before using any variable, it must first be declared. A variable declaration specifies the datatype, the variable name and, optionally, the default value for the variable. The following sections describe variable declarations, each of the basic datatypes, and class declarations.

Variable Declarations

A general variable declaration looks like the following:

```
datatype identifier [ = defaultvalue ] {, identifier [ = defaultvalue ] }  ;
```

Identifiers are just symbols; in this case, they are the names of the variables being defined. To define integer variables i, j, and k, and initialize them to 1, 2, and 3, respectively, you can enter:

```
int i;
int j;
int k;
i = 1;
j = 2;
k = 3;
```

or in an abbreviated form:

```
int i = 1, j = 2, k = 3;
```

Variable declarations can be placed anywhere in your code, as long as they precede the first use of the variable. However, it is common practice to place the declarations at the top of each block of code. This makes your code easier to read, especially for those programmers who are used to older languages that required you to declare your variables at the beginning of functions. Later in this chapter, you will see how to limit access to a variable in its declaration.

The Numeric Datatypes

Java has six numeric datatypes that differ in the size and precision of the numbers they can hold. The basic numeric datatypes are listed in Table 4.10.

TABLE 4.10   Java's Built-in Numeric Datatypes

Type	Description	Size	Minimum Value	Maximum Value
byte	Tiny signed integer	8 bits	-128	127
short	Short signed integer	16 bits	-32768	32767
int	Signed integer	32 bits	-2147483648	2147483647
long	Long signed integer	64 bits	-9223372036854775808	9223372036854775807
float	Floating-point number	32 bits	Positive: $1.40239846 \times 10^{-45}$ Negative: $-3.40282347 \times 10^{38}$	Positive: $-3.40282347 \times 10^{38}$ Negative: $-1.40239846 \times 10^{-45}$
double	Double precision floating-point	64 bits	Positive: $4.9406564584124654 \times 10^{-324}$ Negative: $-1.797693134862315 70 \times 10^{308}$	Positive: $1.797693134862315 70 \times 10^{308}$ Negative: $-4.9406564584124654 \times 10^{-324}$

Generally, when choosing a datatype for a variable, you will want to use the smallest datatype that holds the largest number you will work with, either now or in the foreseeable future. This saves memory yet provides room for expansion should your code require modifications. For example, suppose a company carries 6000 items in its catalog, and you need to choose a datatype to represent each item's number. You might select a short integer to save space, but if the company catalog grows to more than 32,767 items, the company will need to rewrite the software. Choosing a standard integer datatype will give your code greater longevity.

Choosing the right floating-point datatype is a little trickier, because the decision depends on both the size and precision of the numbers you will be working with. For example, if you are converting Celsius to Fahrenheit, you probably need only four digits of precision and a range of temperatures between ±150 degrees, so you should use a float. Scientific applications, which involve a large number of computations—for example, orbital trajectories—require higher precision to reduce rounding errors, even if the results themselves will not exceed single-precision magnitudes.

A new feature of Java 1.1 is a pair special object classes, called `BigDecimal` and `BigInteger`, which can be used to create arbitrary precision numbers apart from those available to primitive datatypes. This can be useful if you need more precision or a larger range than `double` can offer.

The Java VM initializes every numeric variable to zero before it is used. This is in contrast to most other programming languages where uninitialized variables contain random values. This issue generally does not arise, because the use of uninitialized variables is detected and prevented by most Java compilers.

Not-a-Number and Infinity

Java's floating-point datatypes have special values for "Not-a-Number," positive infinity, and negative infinity. Not-a-Number, or NaN, is the result of an invalid mathematical operation, such as dividing zero by zero or multiplying an infinity by zero. Positive infinity is the result of dividing a positive number by zero. Negative infinity is the result of dividing a finite negative number by zero. This is only true of high-precision IEEE-standard datatypes (like `float` and `double`); integer division by zero is not allowed.

The Boolean Datatype

Boolean variables hold true or false values. Many older languages treated integers as boolean variables, regarding zero as false and nonzero as true. However, like Pascal, Java has its own boolean datatype, separate from any numeric datatype. Although it requires a slightly more verbose programming style, it is considerably safer than using integers as boolean types, because integers will never accidentally be treated as boolean variables. Uninitialized boolean variables are initialized to `false`.

The Character Datatype

The character datatype, char, holds a single character. Each character is a number or character code that refers to a *character set*, an indexed list of symbols. For example, in the ASCII (American Standard Code for Information Interchange, pronounced "as-key") character set, the character code 65 corresponds to the letter *A*, and the character code 33 refers to the digit 1.

Most PC character sets use an extended form of the ASCII character set with 256 character codes, so each character can be stored in a byte. The first 127 characters of such character sets are standard across character sets (except for the currency symbol); the last 128 characters vary from set to set, and are used for special characters, such as foreign alphabetic characters or currency symbols.

Java's creators designed Java with expandability and internationalization in mind. The Java char datatype is 16 bits wide and holds a Unicode symbol rather than an ASCII character. The initial value of a char variable is '\u0000'.

NOTE Unicode is an extended version of the ASCII character set, designed for handling multiple languages. Fortunately, Unicode corresponds to a standard extended ASCII character set (ISO-LATIN-1) for the first 127 characters. It is possible to write Java programs and not know you are using Unicode. Unicode also gives Java the ability to use other encoding schemes than the simple ISO-LATIN-1, including character codes for non-Latin-based languages like Japanese, Chinese, and Hebrew. For more information about Unicode, refer to this Web page: http://www.stonehand.com/unicode.html.

The String Datatype

rather than

A string is a sequence of characters. The String datatype is actually a class of the Core API (java.lang.String), rather than a built-in type, but it is used so frequently that it is appropriate to cover here. The String class has special status in Java, because the compiler recognizes String constants; the compiler recognizes characters within double quotation marks as String literals.

Strings can contain as many characters as you wish; there is no maximum string length specified in the Java language specification. However, most implementations will probably limit you to about two billion characters, which is plenty for almost any application.

Strings are immutable in Java; that is, you cannot change the contents of a string, although you can redefine a String object variable. For instance, the string message is initially defined as

```
String message = "Hello World";
```

There is no way to change the contents of the object pointed to by message by, say, passing it to another method:

```
changeString(s); // impossible to change object pointed to by s
```

However, you can make the string variable message refer to a new string object:

```
message = message + "!!";
```

This is a rather subtle point, and the key to understanding it is to keep the concept of an object variable and the object itself distinct. There is an additional string-handling class in the API called StringBuffer. A StringBuffer is like the String datatype, but it has methods for modifying the contents of the StringBuffer. When the Java compiler encounters the code in the preceding example, it rewrites it as follows:

```
message = new StringBuffer(message).append("!!").toString();
```

The compiler converts the original `message` into a `StringBuffer`, appends the exclamation points to the `StringBuffer`, and then converts the `StringBuffer` back into a `String`.

Class Declarations

As explained in Chapter 3, a class declaration begins with the keyword `class`, then specifies the name of the class, the name of the superclass (if different from `Object`), and any interfaces supported by the class:

```
class classname extends parentclassname implements
interfacename {

  member-variable-declarations

  member-function-declarations

  class-initializer

}
```

Member variable declarations are just like other variable declarations, but they may have modifier keywords that alter their visibility outside the class:

```
modifier(s) datatype-specifier identifier = initial-value ;
```

(Modifiers are described in the next section.)

Sample member functions were shown in Chapter 3. Their general structure is:

```
modifier(s) datatype-specifier identifier( argument-list ) {
    code-block
}
```

The *datatype-specifier* can be any datatype or the keyword `void`, which means no datatype. Functions can be declared to return `void`, meaning that they return no value. The *argument-list* specifies the parameters that will be accepted by the function:

```
datatype identifier , datatype identifier, datatype identifier
```

Finally, the *code-block* consists of one or more statements (refer to earlier sample code for examples).

The *class-initializer* contains code that will be executed once when the class is loaded by the VM. The structure of the class initializer is as follows:

```
static { code-block }
```

An example of the use of the class initializer appears later in this chapter, in the section on the static modifier.

Scope Rules

In early programming languages such as COBOL, all variables were considered global variables. A *global variable* is a variable that can be accessed from any part of a program, and, consequently, global variables must have unique names. Since all variables in COBOL were global, every variable in a COBOL program needed to be unique. This led to the practice of using a single variable for different purposes in different parts of the program.

Keeping track of global variables is a difficult task, and makes such programs prone to bugs. In particular, a change in one small part of the code can adversely affect a completely different part of the program.

The solution to the problem of global variables is to use *local* variables, which are variables that have a limited life span and relate to only a single part of the code. You can use two local variables with identical names as long as they are in different parts of the program.

The rules that dictate which parts of the program can see which variables are called *scope rules*.

Variables defined within a member function are local to that member function, so you can use the same variable name in several member functions, as shown in this example:

```
class MyClass {

    int i; // member variable


    int First() {
        int j; // local variable

        // both i and j are accessible from this point

        return 1;

    }

    int Second() {
        int j; // local variable

        // both i and j are accessible from this point

        return 2;
    }

}
```

The variable j defined in the function First() is created when it is declared as the function is called, and it is destroyed when then function exits. The same is true for the local variable j in the function Second(). With multithreading, it is possible for the interpreter to be in both functions simultaneously, but this causes no conflict, because the two local variables are completely independent of each other. Another way to think of these local variables is to imagine that the compiler renames them uniquely (for example, j1 and j2).

Java's Inner Classes

A new feature in Java 1.1 is support for inner classes. *Inner classes* are classes that are defined within other classes, much in the way other types of variables are defined within those classes. These inner classes have the same scope and access as other variables and methods defined within the same class. Here is an example:

```
class PrivateAirport extends Airport {
   String owner;

   PrivateAirport(String str) {
      owner = str;
   }

   class PrivateFlight extends Flight {
      String flightOwner;
      PrivateFlight() {
         flightOwner = owner;
      }
   }

   Flight getFlight() {
      return new PrivateFlight();
   }
}
```

This example uses the classes presented in Chapter 3, which define classes for `Airport` and `Flight` objects. In this example, there is a top-level class, called `PrivateAirport`, which represents an airport owned by some individual. This `Airport` can create `Flight` objects that cannot be created by any other class, because no other class knows the name of the owner of the `Airport`. However, other objects can ask the `Airport` to create a new `Flight` object for them, which in this case is `PrivateFlight`, an inner class. Other objects do not have access to the name of the owner of `Flight`, because they do not know about the `PrivateFlight` class. Nevertheless, a `PrivateFlight` object can use this information internally.

Java's Datatype and Method Modifiers

A *modifier* is a keyword that affects either the lifetime or the accessibility of a class, a variable, or a member function. Table 4.11 shows the applicability of each modifier to classes, functions, member variables, and local variables.

TABLE 4.11   Applicability of Modifiers to Classes, Member Functions, Member Variables, and Local Variables

Modifier	Classes	Member Functions	Member Variables	Local Variables
abstract	✓	✓	—	—
static		✓	✓	—
public	✓	✓	✓	—
protected	✓	✓	✓	—
private	—	✓	✓	—
private protected	—	✓	✓	—
synchronized	—	✓	—	—
native	—	✓	—	—
transient	—	—	✓	—
volatile	—	—	✓	—
final	✓	✓	✓	✓

Storage and Lifetime Modifiers

The following sections describe the storage and lifetime modifiers: `abstract`, `static`, `synchronized`, `native`, `volatile`, `transient`, and `final`.

The abstract Modifier

When applied to a class, the `abstract` modifier indicates that the class has not been fully implemented and that it should not be instantiated. If applied to a member function declaration, the `abstract` modifier means that the function will be implemented in a subclass. Since the function has no implementation, the class cannot be instantiated and must be declared as abstract. Interfaces are abstract by default.

The static Modifier

Ordinarily, each instance of a class has its own copy of any member variables. However, it is possible to designate a member variable as belonging to the class itself, independent of any objects of that class. Such member variables are called *static* members and are declared with the `static` modifier keyword. Static member variables are often used when tracking global information about the instances of a class. The following class tracks the number of instances of itself using a static member variable called `instanceCount`:

```
public class MyClass {
    public static int instanceCount;

    public MyClass() {
        // each time this constructor is called,
        // increment the instance counter
        instanceCount++;
    }

    static {
        instanceCount = 0;
    }
}
```

Notice that a static initializer is used to initialize the static variable.

Methods can also be declared as static. For example, a static method called `resetCounter()` can reset the `instanceCounter` for `MyClass`:

```
public class MyClass {
    public static int instanceCount;
```

```
public MyClass() {
    // each time this constructor is called,
    // increment the instance counter
    instanceCount++;
}

public static void resetCounter() {
    instanceCount = 0;
}

static {
    instanceCount = 0;
}

}
```

The resetCounter() method can be called via the class MyClass or via an instance of MyClass:

```
MyClass m, n;

m = new MyClass(); // instanceCount will equal 1 after this constructor call
n = new MyClass(); // instanceCount will equal 2 after this constructor call
System.out.println(MyClass.instanceCount + " instances have been created");

m.resetCounter();       // reset the counter
MyClass.resetCounter(); // another way to reset the counter
```

The System class that is in the java.lang package of the API defines all its public methods and variables as static. All variables and functions are accessed via the class directly, not via an instance of the System class. In fact, the constructor for the System class is private, so you cannot create a new System object with the usual code:

```
System MySystem = new System(); // this is illegal
```

Instead, all variables and functions of the System class are accessed via the class itself. Recall from previous examples that you can print information on the console with the following code:

```
System.out.println("Hello World");
```

The member variable `out` is a static member variable of type `PrintStream`. It is defined in the API as:

```
public static PrintStream out;
```

Because the `System` class defines its functions as static, you can call the function `currentTimeMillis()` to get the current time, with the following expression:

```
long timeNow = System.currentTimeMillis();
```

`currentTimeMillis()` is defined in the `System` class as:

```
public static long currentTimeMillis()
```

Use totally static classes (classes in which all members are static) when you want to model a unique entity. Use static member variables when you want only a single unique copy of a variable, such as when you want to track the number of times that instances have been created.

The synchronized Modifier

A *synchronized* member function allows only one thread to execute the function at a time. This prevents two threads of execution from undoing each other's work. (For details about threads, see Chapter 8.)

Suppose you have two threads that are responsible for updating a bank balance, here called threads A and B. Suppose also that the account has $100 in it. Now, simultaneously, thread A tries to deposit $50 in the account, while thread B tries to deposit $75. Both threads proceed to query the account balance. They both find it to be $100. Each of them, independently, adds its deposit to the old sum and sets the new balance accordingly. If thread A finishes last, the account contains $150. If thread B finishes last, the account balance is $175. Of course, neither of these new figures is correct! The account should have $225 in it (100 + 50 + 75). The problem is that both threads tried to execute the same code (querying and changing the balance) at the same time. This is exactly the scenario that the `synchronized` keyword can prevent.

Synchronized methods are not static by default, but they may be declared as static.

The `synchronized` modifier does not apply to classes or member variables.

The native Modifier

Native methods are implemented in other languages, such as C, so they have no code block. Many of the classes in the Core API are native because they need to access operating-system-specific routines, such as those for drawing graphics on the screen. Here is an excerpt from the API's `Math` class:

```
/**
 * Returns the trigonometric sine of an angle.
 * @param a an assigned angle that is measured in radians
 */
public static native double sin(double a);
```

This declaration calls a function in a native code library that calculates the sine of the angle a. On an Intel *x*86 platform, the native code would call the sine function in the *x*86 processor's floating-point unit or coprocessor. On other platforms, the native code function may do the computation with software instead. This function happens to be declared with the `public` and `static` modifiers also.

The `native` modifier applies to functions only.

The volatile Modifier

A *volatile* variable is one whose value may change independent of the Java program itself. Typically, *volatile* variables represent input from the outside world, such as a variable that denotes the time of day. They are also used to flag variables that could be changed by other threads of execution. The `volatile` keyword will prevent the compiler from attempting to track changes to the variable. The variable will always be assumed by the compiler to have a (potentially) new value each time it is accessed by Java code. Use of this modifier is rare, because building a class with volatile storage usually requires a special VM.

The transient Modifier

One of the changes introduced with JDK is the `transient` modifier, which is used in conjunction with serialization to provide for persistent objects. These objects can be saved to disk and restored on another machine or on the same machine. For more information about serialization, see Chapter 22.

The final Modifier

Most languages have a way to declare a variable as constant (that is, unchangeable), which is true of Java as well. The `final` keyword indicates that a local variable or member variable cannot be altered. The main use of `final` variables is as symbolic constants. You can refer to a constant by name, and define that name in a single location in your code. If you later need to change the number in your code, you need only make the change at the point your `final` variable is defined.

Note that if you declare a variable as `final`, you must also initialize it at the same time:

```
final int MAX_PAGES = 23;
```

(The use of all caps for final variables is in accordance with the naming conventions used here, listed in Table 4.2.)

Member functions and classes can also be declared as `final`. A `final` member function cannot be overridden, and a `final` class cannot be subclassed.

When anything is declared `final`, the compiler/optimizer can make many assumptions that can dramatically increase performance.

Accessibility Modifiers

Java has other modifiers that are used to change the accessibility of classes and their members to other classes. By default, a class and its member functions and variables are known only to other classes in the same package. For simple applets, this means that a class is accessible only to other classes in the same directory.

The effects of the modifiers are listed here and shown in Figure 4.4. In the figure, there are three bars for each type of member modifier. The first bar represents the ability of a subclass to inherit a member variable or function. The second bar indicates the ability of a subclass to access a member in instances of the original class. The third bar denotes the accessibility of a member by non-subclasses.

For example, the figure shows that member functions or variables that are declared as `private protected` have the following characteristics:

- Will be inherited by subclasses, whether the subclasses are in the same package or not. This allows a subclass to access these members in instances of the subclass only.

- Can be accessed by subclasses in the same package; that is, subclasses can access these members in instances of the original class.

- Cannot be accessed by non-subclasses at all.

A public class can be accessed by any other class. When a VM is asked to execute a new applet, the class for the applet must be public. However, any other classes required by the applet need not be public, as long as they are accessible.

FIGURE 4.4

The accessibility of classes and their member functions and variables depends on the modifier used when the class or member was declared public.

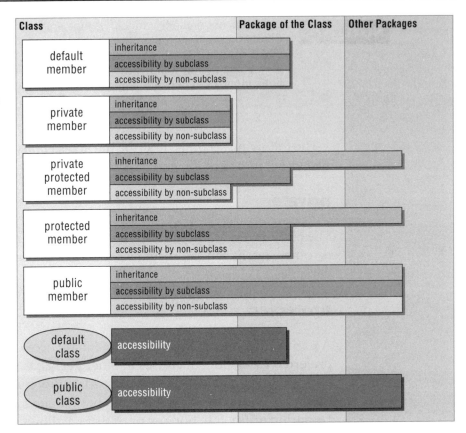

Methods and member variables of public classes that are declared themselves as public can be accessed by code from other classes. Public members can also be accessed by JavaScript, VBScript, and ActiveX controls operating outside the VM. If members of a nonpublic (default) class are declared as public, those members will be accessible to all other classes within the same package. As a guideline, avoid defining functions and variables as public unless it is necessary.

If no modifier is specified, the default accessibility for the class, variable, or function is assumed.

NOTE   Default is not actually a modifier; that is, there is no keyword for default accessibility. Don't be misled by the `default` keyword that is used in `switch` statements (see Chapter 6); it is not a modifier. Some people call the default behavior "friendly," but that is not a modifier either (although there is a `friend` modifier in C++).

The following sections describe the accessibility modifers: `private`, `protected`, and `private protected`.

private

The `private` modifier restricts access to members of a class, so that no other classes can call member functions or directly access member variables.

protected

A `protected` member is similar to default access, but gives preferred access for subclasses in other packages. Member functions are sometimes created within a class for utility purposes (that is, to be used only within the class itself and not for general consumption). Declaring utility functions as `protected` allows them to be used not only by the class itself, but by its subclasses as well.

Suppose you create a class called `Chicken`, which knows how to cross the road. The public member function `crossRoad()` has two steps: (1) check for oncoming traffic and (2) walk across the road. These steps would be written as two utility member functions called `checkTraffic()` and `walkAcrossRoad()`. The utility functions should not be public because you wouldn't want a programmer who is simply using the class to call `walkAcrossRoad()` without first calling `checkTraffic()`; this could have adverse consequences for `Chicken`. However, if you make the utility functions private, you will not be able to reuse these functions yourself when you write the subclass `SmarterChicken`. Ideally, the `SmarterChicken` class can override the `crossRoad()` function to check for a traffic light, then call `checkTraffic()` and `walkAcrossRoad()` as required. By declaring the utility functions as `protected`, they will be available to programmers such as yourself who will be creating subclasses of `Chicken`, and who should, therefore, understand the dangers inherent in crossing roads.

private protected

A `private protected` member is similar to a `protected` member, but it cannot be accessed by any non-subclass, whether in the same package or not.

The choice between `private protected` and `protected` depends on how the classes within the same package will be cooperating. If the `Chicken` class will be part of a `Farm` package, and the `Farmer` class will need to be able to escort a `Chicken` across the road without the `Chicken` calling `checkTraffic()`, the utility functions of `Chicken` class should be declared as `protected`. On the other hand, if the `Chicken` class will always check traffic before crossing the road, there is no need to make the utility functions available to other classes in the `Farm` package, and the functions should be declared as `private protected`.

Summary

The datatypes, modifiers, and expressions described in this chapter make up the essential building blocks of the Java language. Although some of the information in this chapter is reference material, you should now have a basic understanding of how to define your own datatypes for best use of storage space, ease of use, and interaction with other classes.

The next chapter describes interfaces and packages and will help you understand the finer points of class design. It also explains how to use existing Java packages.

CHAPTER
FIVE

5

Java Classes, Interfaces, and Packages

- Casting between datatypes

- Keywords for member and constructor references

- Java's object memory model

- Interfaces for multiple inheritance and callback functions

- Java's packages of classes and interfaces

This chapter introduces some important elements in Java programming. In particular, you will learn about *casting*, or explicitly converting a value from one datatype to another. And you will learn about using `this` and `super` to refer to the otherwise hidden data members, hidden method members, and constructors of a class and its superclass.

This chapter also covers the object memory model, showing you how the memory of an object is handled, and interfaces, Java's solution for multiple inheritance and callback functions. Finally, packages are introduced for grouping classes and interfaces to achieve better organization and minimize naming conflicts.

Casting for Converting Datatypes

The general form of a casting operation is:

```
(datatype) expression
```

where the datatype can be either a reference type or a primitive one. As a unary operator, casting has the highest operator precedence of the unary operators like ++ and -- (negative). For example, casting is used in the following expression to make sure floating-point division, rather than integer division, is performed:

```
(float) 5 / 2
```

Since (`float`) has higher operator precedence than the division operator (`/`), the integer 5 will be converted into a floating number before the division. When one of the operands of a division is a floating number, the other operand will be converted into a floating number, and the division will be performed as a floating-number operation. If the expression is changed into:

```
(float) 3 + 5 / 2
```

an integer division followed by a floating-point addition will be performed, because the division operator has higher operator precedence than the addition operator.

Rule number one in casting is that you cannot cast a primitive type to a reference type, nor can you cast the other way around. The compiler will check for all violations on casting rules. However, when dealing with object references, there are still cases where the correctness of casting can be checked only at runtime. If a casting violation is detected at runtime, the exception `ClassCastException` will be thrown. (You will learn more about exception handling in Chapter 7.) The next sections cover the rules for casting between primitive types and reference types in more detail.

Casting between Primitive Types

As explained in Chapter 4, the primitive datatypes can be divided into the boolean type and the numeric type. The boolean type cannot be cast from or to any other datatype.

Casting from any numeric type—`byte`, `char`, `short`, `int`, `long`, `float`, or `double`—to any other numeric type is allowed. Casting from one numeric type to another may cause loss of information, however. Casting from a wider type (like `int`) to a narrower one (like `byte`) will cause the higher-order bits to be discarded. For a signed number, the sign of the number may be changed after the conversion. For example, the result of `(byte) 256` is 0, and the result of `(byte) 255` is -1, because the `byte` type can hold only numbers ranging from –128 to 127.

If you are casting in a way that does not present the possibility of information loss, such as from `byte` to `int` or from `int` to `float`, the casting is automatic, and you do not need to manually cast. If the possibility of information loss exists, you must cast yourself.

Assignment of a primitive value to a variable of primitive type is allowed only if the assignment will not cause any loss of information. Otherwise, explicit casting is needed. The same rule applies to arguments of method calls. Automatic widening of the data will be performed if the value of the argument is of a numeric type narrower than the argument type prescribed for the method. For example, in the second statement of the following program fragment, a variable of float type is passed into method sqrt(), which requires an argument of double type. The value of the variable f will be converted into double type before the method (remember, a *method* is the same thing as a *member function*) is called.

```
float f = 4;
double d = Math.sqrt(f);
int  i = 1;
byte b = i;
```

Also, the last statement is not a legitimate one, because conversion of an int type to a byte type could lose information. The compiler will produce an error message similar to this one:

```
CastTest.java:6: Incompatible type for Identifier. Explicit
cast needed to convert int to byte.
      byte b = i;
               ^
```

To make it pass compiler checking, the statement must be changed as follows:

```
byte b = (byte) i;
```

Casting between Reference Types

The first rule of casting between reference types is that one of the class types involved must be the same class as, or a subclass of, the other class type. Assignment to different class type is allowed only if a value of the class type is assigned to a variable of its superclass type. Assignment to a variable of the subclass type needs explicit casting. For example, the second statement of the following program fragment is not a legitimate one, because class String is a subclass of class Object:

```
Object o = new Object();
String s = o;
```

The compiler will issue an error message similar to this one:

```
CastTest.java:12: Incompatible type for Identifier. Explicit
cast needed to convert java.lang.Object to java.lang.String.
    String s = o;
            ^
```

An explicit casting is needed:

```
String s = (String) o;
```

If the casting turns out to be illegal at runtime, a ClassCast-Exception will be thrown. This can happen because explicit casting can fool the compiler to allow an object to access the data or method members of its subclass. The attempt at runtime to make such a method or data reference will fail, and an exception will be thrown. For example, adding either one of the following two statements to the previous program fragment will incur a runtime exception, because both s and o refer to an object of Object type at runtime, and the method length() is defined in class String:

```
int i = s.length();
int j = ((String) o).length();
```

If the exception is not handled, the execution will be terminated, and an error message similar to the following will be displayed:

```
java.lang.ClassCastException: java.lang.Object
at CastTest.main(CastTest.java:12)
```

Using this and super for Member and Constructor References

The use of this and super keywords is twofold:

- To override the scope rules so that the otherwise hidden data and method members of a class and its superclass can be referred to

- To act as method names representing the constructor methods of the current class and its superclass

Both of these uses are discussed in the following sections.

this and super for Member References

Local variables in a method can share the same names as instance variables or class variables. Subclasses can define their own instance variables to shadow those defined in the superclasses. Subclasses can also define methods to override the methods defined in their superclasses. Two special references are available inside any instance method to allow for access to the shadowed variables or overridden methods of that instance:

this   Used to refer to the object the method is called upon.

super   sed to access the methods or data members defined in the superclass.

For example, the constructor of a Point2D class to hold the x- and y-coordinates of a two-dimensional point can be defined as follows:

```
public class Point2D {
    int x, y;
```

```
Point2D() {
   x = 0;
   y = 0;
}

Point2D(int x, int y) {
   this.x = x;
   this.y = y;
}

double length() {
   return Math.sqrt(x * x + y * y);
}

}
```

Here, `this.x` on the left side of the assignment statement refers to the instance variable `x`, whereas the `x` on the right side refers to the argument variable. `sqrt()` is a method defined in class `Math` of package `java.lang` to calculate the square root of the input argument.

You may define a subclass of the `Point2D` class with the same set of instance variables:

```
public class MyPoint extends Point2D {
   int x, y;
   MyPoint(int x, int y) {
      this.x = super.x = x;
      this.y = super.y = y;
   }
   double length() {
      return Math.sqrt(x * x + y * y);
   }

   double distance() {
      return Math.abs(this.length() - super.length());
   }
}
```

Here, `this.x` refers to the instance variable x defined in class `MyPoint`, and `super.x` refers to the instance variable x defined in class `Point2D`. The `abs()` method is defined in class `Math` of package `java.lang` to calculate the absolute value of its argument. The `this.length()` and `super.length()` methods are defined in classes `MyPoint` and `Point2D`, respectively.

> **NOTE**   It is necessary to override the `length()` method defined in class `Point2D`, because the one defined in class `Point2D` can access only data members defined in class `Point2D`, not those defined in its subclass, `MyPoint`.

this and super for Constructor References

In constructors, there is an implied first statement; the superclass constructor with no parameters is automatically called. If you do not like this default behavior, you can override it by using a different `this()` or `super()` method call in the first statement to refer to other constructors of the object and its superclass, respectively. For example, to make the constructor of the `Point2D` class defined earlier more polymorphic, another constructor can be added with only the x-coordinate as the argument:

```
Point2D(int x) {
    this(x, 0);
}
```

Here, the y-coordinate is set to a default value of zero when not specified. Or you can define a constructor with no argument to set the coordinates to default values, as follows:

```
Point2D() {
    this(0, 0);
}
```

Also, the constructor of class `MyPoint` can be rewritten as follows:

```
MyPoint(int x, int y) {
    super(x, y);
    this.x = x;
    this.y = y;
}
```

Here, `super` refers to the constructor with two integer arguments defined in class `Point2D`.

Accessing Superclass Members from Outside the Class Definition

Data references are resolved at compile time. If a data member is defined in both a class and its superclass, the data member referred to is decided syntactically by the class type the object is declared to be. Therefore, you can cast an object to its superclass so that you can access the otherwise hidden data member. For example, assume three variables are declared as follows:

```
Point2D p  = new Point2D(11,0);
MyPoint mp = new MyPoint(4,5);
Point2D q  = mp;
```

`p.x`, `mp.x`, and `q.x` refer to the data member defined in classes `Point2D`, `MyPoint`, and `Point2D`, respectively. On the other hand, `((Point2D) mp).x` and `((MyPoint) q).x` refer to the data member defined in classes `Point2D` and `MyPoint`, respectively.

Method references are resolved at runtime. The class type an object belongs to when it is first created will determine which method will be called. Casting the object to its superclass, or assigning the object to a variable declared as its superclass type, will not change where the called method is from. For example, both `mp.length()` and `q.length()` refer to the `length()` method defined in class `MyPoint`, whereas `p.length()` refers to the method defined in class `Point2D`. The following code is added to the definition of classes `Point2D` and `MyPoint` to demonstrate this example:

```
class PointTest {
   public static void main(String[] args) {
      PrintWriter out = new PrintWriter(System.out, true);
      MyPoint mp = new MyPoint(4,3);
      Point2D p  = new Point2D(11);
      Point2D q  = mp;

      mp.x = 5; mp.y = 12;

      out.println("\n\tData Member Access Test:\n");
      out.println("mp = (" + mp.x + ", " + mp.y + ")");
      out.println(" p = (" +  p.x + ", " +  p.y + ")");
      out.println(" q = (" +  q.x + ", " +  q.y + ")");

      out.println("\n\tCasting Test:\n");
      out.println("(Point2D) mp = (" + ((Point2D) mp).x + ", " + ((Point2D) mp).y + ")");
      out.println("(MyPoint) q = (" + ((MyPoint) q).x + ", " + ((MyPoint) q).y + ")");

      out.println("\n\tMethod Member Access Test:\n");
      out.println("mp.length() = " + mp.length());
      out.println(" p.length() = " +  p.length());
      out.println(" q.length() = " +  q.length());
      out.println("mp.difference() = " + mp.difference());

      out.println("\n\tCasting Test:\n");
      out.println("((Point2D) mp).length() = " + ((Point2D) mp).length());
      out.println("((Point2D)  q).length() = " + ((Point2D) q).length());
      out.println("((MyPoint)q).difference() = " + ((MyPoint) q).difference());
   }
}
```

> **NOTE** `PrintWriter` is a class contained in the `java.io` package, which is concerned with output. See Chapter 15 for details.

The class definition for classes Point2D and MyPoint is restated as follows:

```
class Point2D {
    int x;
    int y;

    Point2D(int x, int y) {
        this.x = x;
        this.y = y;
    }

    Point2D(int x) {
        this(x, 0);
    }

    Point2D() {
        this(0, 0);
    }

    double length() {
        return Math.sqrt(x * x + y * y);
    }
}

class MyPoint extends Point2D {
    int x;
    int y;

    MyPoint(int x, int y) {
        this.x = super.x = x;
        this.y = super.y = y;
    }

    double length() {
        return Math.sqrt(x * x + y * y);
    }

    double difference() {
        return Math.abs(length() - super.length());
    }
}
```

The output of the above program is shown here:

```
C:\MasteringJava\Ch05>java PointTest

Data Member Access Test:

mp = (5, 12)
 p = (11, 0)
 q = (4, 3)

        Casting Test:

(Point2D)mp = (4, 3)
(MyPoint) q = (5, 12)

        Method Member Access Test:

mp.length() = 13.0
 p.length() = 11.0
 q.length() = 13.0
mp.difference() = 8

        Casting Test:

((Point2D)mp).length() = 13.0
((Point2D)q).length() = 13.0
((MyPoint)q).difference() = 8.0
```

The Object Memory Model

The dynamically changing part of program memory can be divided into two areas:

- A stack memory area, which is used to store the local variables declared in methods or blocks. The stack memory will always grow in one direction and shrink in the opposite direction. The memory grows as the declaration of local variables (including argument variables in method calls) is encountered. These variables are popped out of the stack upon exit from the enclosing methods or blocks.

2. • A heap memory area, which is used to store the memory for objects. References to the objects can be put in the stack area, but the space for data members of the objects must reside in the heap area. A heap is a huge table of memory cells. Small blocks of memory cells are reserved or allocated from time to time when new objects are created by the new statements. And whenever a block of memory cells is no longer referred to by any existing variables, these unused cells can be freed, or garbage-collected.

> **NOTE**
>
> The term *heap* is also used to mean a complete binary tree where each node is at least as large as the values at its children, as in *heap sort*. These two usages of heap represent two totally different concepts and happen to have the same name for historical reasons.

As an example, assume that you have two methods defined as follows, where class Point2D is defined to hold the x- and y-coordinates of a two-dimensional point (as in the earlier example of this and super):

```
void m1() {
    int    a1 = 1;
    Point2D p1;                 // checkpoint #1

    p1 = new Point2D(2,3);  // checkpoint #2
    m2(a1, p1);
    a1 = 8;                     // checkpoint #5
}

void m2(int a2, Point p2) {
    int    a3 = 4;
    Point2D p3;                 // checkpoint #3

    p3 = new Point2D(5,6);
    a2 = 7;                     // checkpoint #4
}
```

When method m1() is called, and its local variable declaration is executed—that is, when checkpoint #1 is reached—the two local variables, a1 and p1, will be put on the stack memory area with values 1 and null, respectively. The memory model at this point is shown in Figure 5.1.

FIGURE 5.1

The memory model after checkpoint #1

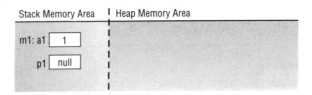

A new object of Point type is then created at checkpoint #2. The newly created object is put in the heap area, and a reference to the object is stored in local variable p1 on the stack. The memory model at this point is shown in Figure 5.2.

FIGURE 5.2

The memory model after checkpoint #2

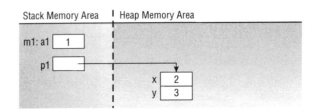

Next, method m2() is called with two arguments. Java basically calls by values for arguments of primitive datatypes; that is, in a method call, the arguments are passed by their values if they are of primitive datatypes. If the arguments are objects, the values are references to the objects, and the effect is call-by-reference. Therefore, the argument variable p2 refers to the same object as the local variable p1 of method m1(). At checkpoint #3, where the local variables a3 and p3 are declared, the memory model after the declaration looks like Figure 5.3.

FIGURE 5.3

The memory model after
checkpoint #3

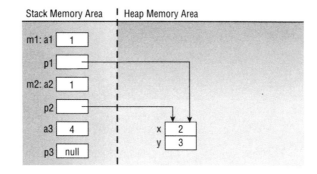

Next, a new object is created by a new statement and assigned to
local variable p3. Again, the newly created object is put on the heap
area. Then the argument variable a2 is assigned a new value. Since it
is call-by-value, the value of the local variable a1 of method m1() is
not affected. The memory model at this point is shown in Figure 5.4.

FIGURE 5.4

The memory model after
checkpoint #4

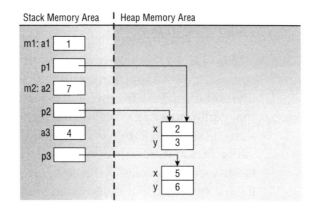

Finally, method m2() is exited, and the memory for the local and
argument variables is popped out of the stack area. This leaves the
object memory originally allocated for the local variable p3 hanging
freely in the heap area with no reference to the block of memory cells.
This free-hanging object will be reclaimed later by the garbage collector when needed. At checkpoint #5, an assignment statement is executed; the memory model after the execution is shown in Figure 5.5.

FIGURE 5.5

The memory model after
checkpoint #5

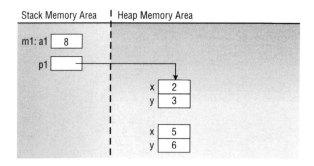

Using Java Interfaces

In Java, a class can have only one immediate superclass. Multiple inheritance, where a class has more than one superclass (as used by C++), is not allowed in Java. Problems may arise when you want to have different implementations of a method in different classes and delay the decision on which implementation of a method to execute until runtime.

In Java, the class where the method is defined must be present at compile time so that the compiler can check the signature of the method to make sure the method call is legitimate. All the classes that could possibly be called for the aforementioned method need to share a common superclass, so that the method can be defined in the superclass and overridden by the individual subclasses. If you want to force every subclass to have its own implementation of the method, the method can be defined as an abstract one. Chances are you will want to move the method definition higher and higher up the inheritance hierarchy, so that more and more classes can override the same method. And—guess what—you will find yourself pondering how you can add a few new methods to the Object class, the root of all classes, so that these methods can be implemented in many otherwise unrelated classes.

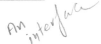

Java's interfaces come to the rescue here. An *interface* is a collection of constants and abstract methods. A class can implement an interface by adding the interface to the class's `implements` clause and overriding the abstract methods defined in the interface. A variable can be declared as an interface type, and all the constants and methods declared in the interface can be accessed from this variable. All objects whose class types implement the interface can then be assigned to this variable. Therefore, to solve the problem of how to decide which method implementation to execute at runtime, you can define an interface with the method to be shared among classes. All these classes will declare to implement the interface and create their own implementation of the method. Instances of these classes can then be assigned to a variable of the interface type. Reference to this commonly implemented method from the interface variable will then be resolved at runtime.

Defining an Interface

Defining an interface is just like defining a class, except the `class` keyword is replaced with the `interface` keyword, and only constants and abstract methods are allowed in an interface. Every interface is by default abstract. All the methods declared in an interface are by default abstract and public, so you do not need to explicitly put the `abstract` or `public` modifiers before them. Similarly, all the data members declared in an interface are by default public constants, and you do not need to explicitly insert the `final`, `static`, or `public` modifiers before them. For example, the `java.lang` package has a `Runnable` interface defined as follows:

```
public interface Runnable {
    void run();
}
```

Interfaces can form hierarchies just like classes. An interface uses the `extends` clause to inherit the methods and constants defined in the superinterface. An interface can never extend a normal class, however.

Additionally, the major difference between extending classes and extending interfaces is that you can allow for multiple inheritance in an interface by putting a list of interfaces, separated by commas, in the extends clause. For example, the following program fragment shows that the declaration of an interface, Operable, inherits two other interfaces, Openable and Closeable:

```
interface Operable extends Openable, Closeable {
    . . .
}
```

The implements Clause

A class declares all of the interfaces it is implementing in its implements clause of the class declaration. The implements clause consists of the keyword implements followed by a list of interfaces separated by commas, and it must be put after the extends clause (if there is one).

A class can implement more than one interface. A class implementing an interface will need to override all the methods declared in the interface and all its superinterfaces. Otherwise, the class must be declared as an abstract one. For example, the following class definition fragment implements the Runnable interface declared earlier:

```
class MyClass extends MySuperClass implements Runnable {
    . . .
    public void run() {
        . . .
    }
}
```

Since all the methods defined in an interface are inherently public, the overriding methods implemented in the class need to be declared public, too. In Java, methods cannot be overridden to be more private.

If you try to declare an overriding method without the `public` modifier, the compiler will issue an error message similar to this one:

```
InterfaceTest.java:51: Methods can't be overridden to be more
private. Method void method() is public in interface
MyInterface.
   void method() {}
     ^
```

If you forget to override one of the methods in an interface and do not declare your class to be abstract, the compiler will issue an error message as follows:

```
ErrorExample.java:1: class OneError must be declared abstract.
It does not define void run() from interface java.lang.
Runnable.class OneError implements Runnable {
     ^
```

Using an Interface to Implement Callback Functions

A *callback function* in C or C++ is a pointer to a function or function object provided by a service requester for a server to execute when some previously specified event happens. Callback functions are frequently used in event handling, where event handlers are registered as callback functions to be called when events happen.

In Java, references to methods cannot be passed around. Instead, an object is passed to the server, and the method defined for the object is called from the server. If the clients are instantiated from otherwise unrelated classes, an interface needs to be created to define the method the server is calling. And all the classes whose instances are requesting service from the server class must implement the interface. A client can then pass itself as an argument to the server, so that the server can execute the method defined in the client class.

In the next example, a message server is created to call the method, `printMessage()`, to be implemented by the client in regular intervals. The length of the interval and the number of times the method is called is provided by the client when the server instance is created. The server will create a new thread running concurrently with the client when the constructor is called (see Chapter 8 for details on threads). The client repeatedly increments a counter after some computation until the counter reaches some preset value. The program listing is as follows:

```java
class CallbackTest {
   public static void main(String[] args) {
      LoopingClient client = new LoopingClient();
      new MessageServer(5, 100, client); // create a new server
      client.run();                      // run the client
   }
}

class LoopingClient implements MessagePrintable {
   int counter = 0;
   PrintWriter out = new PrintWriter(System.out, true);
   void run() {
      while (counter++ < 200000)
         int dummy = counter * counter / (counter + 1);
   }

   public void printMessage() {
      out.println("The counter value is now: " + counter);
   }
}

class MessageServer extends Thread {
   int times;
   int interval;
   MessagePrintable object;

   MessageServer(int times, int interval, MessagePrintable object) {
      this.times    = times;
      this.interval = interval;
      this.object   = object;
      this.setPriority(Thread.NORM_PRIORITY + 2); // let server get higher
                                                  // priority
      this.start();            // start running the new thread
   }

   public void run() {
```

```
    // repeat sleep-printMessage several times

    for (int i = 0; i < times; i++) {
       try { // try-catch is for exception handling
          sleep(interval);
       } catch (InterruptedException e) {}
       object.printMessage();
    }
  }
}

interface MessagePrintable {
   void printMessage();
}
```

The `try-catch` statement is for exception handling (the topic of Chapter 7). The output of the above program is as follows:

```
C:\MasteringJava\Ch05>java CallbackTest
The counter value is now: 29750
The counter value is now: 57739
The counter value is now: 87719
The counter value is now: 122998
The counter value is now: 149327
```

Using Java Packages

A *package* is a collection of related classes and interfaces. As the first noncomment statement of a file, you can use a `package` statement to specify to which package the classes and interfaces defined in the program file belong. You can then use `import` statements to specify the packages whose classes are going to be referred to in the rest of the program.

A package is a grouping mechanism with two main purposes:

- Reduce the problems in name conflicts.
- Control the visibility of classes, interfaces, and the methods and data defined within them.

Resolving Class Names

Classes can share the same name only if they belong to different packages. When a class is referred to in a program, the compiler will check all the imported packages to find out where the class is defined.

If there is only one imported package in which the named class is defined, the definition of the class in that package will be used. If more than one imported package contains the definition of the named class, you must use the package name as a prefixing qualifier so that there is no ambiguity regarding the referred class. You use a period as the separator between the class name and the package name. For example, you may define a Point class to hold the x-, y-, and z-coordinates of a three-dimensional point in a user-defined three_d package, and another Point class to hold the x- and y-coordinates of a two-dimensional point in a two_d package. If both the three_d and two_d packages are imported to the program, you will need to use three_d.Point and two_d.Point to refer to the Point class of three- and two-dimensional points, respectively.

Packages can be nested to form a nice hierarchy. This nesting capability can help further in grouping classes, just like the hierarchy of directories can help you to organize your files. To refer to a class of a nested package, you can use a fully qualified name with all the containing package names prefixing the class name. For example, to refer to the Point class of the awt package under the java package, use the fully qualified class name, java.awt.Point. However, if java.awt is imported and the class name will not conflict with the class names of other imported packages, you can use Point without any qualifier to refer to the class.

All classes and interfaces in a package are accessible to all other classes and interfaces in that package. All the data and method members of a class can be accessed from any method of any class under the same package, except when the data and method members are declared private.

Packages and Directories

Every package must be mapped to a subdirectory of the same name in the file system. Nested packages will be reflected as a hierarchy of directories in the file system. For example, the class files of package `java.awt.image` must be stored under the directory java/awt/image in a Unix file system and java\awt\image in a Windows file system.

You can put package directories anywhere in the file system as long as the users have read access to them. The `CLASSPATH` environment variable is used by both the Java compiler and Java runtime to locate the packages. The list of directories is separated with semicolons on Windows systems, and by colons on Unix systems. With Windows, for example, a command line similar to the following is placed in the autoexec.bat file:

```
SET CLASSPATH=.;C:\java\lib;C:\myprog\classes
```

And with Unix, the following command line might be used under C-shell:

```
setenv CLASSPATH .:/java/lib:/users/hsu/classes
```

When a class reference like `java.util.Date` is encountered, the directory list is searched from start to end, and the `Date` class of the first directory containing java\util\Date.class (or java/util/Date .class on Unix) will be used. Therefore, if you define your `CLASS-PATH` variable as above and there is a subdirectory .\java\util (or ./java/util on Unix) with Date.java defined as in the following program fragment, your own `Date` class will be used instead of the one defined under the Java Core API:

```
package java.util;
public class Date {
    . . .
}
```

TIP

You should try to avoid having the fully qualified package name confict with the names of other publicly available packages, such as `java.util`. Other people running your program with the `CLASSPATH` environment variable set differently may get different behavior or may not be able to run your program at all.

All of the Java built-in classes (that is, the Java Core API) are put under the java package. Ten subpackages are defined under the java package, as listed in Table 5.1. These packages are discussed in later chapters.

TABLE 5.1   Subpackages under the java Package

Package	Description
java.lang	Essential classes, like `String`, `Object`, and `Thread`
java.awt	Graphic user interface components
java.io	Input/output streams and files
java.net	Networking-related classes
java.applet	Applet creation, including an audio clip interface
java.util	Utility classes for special data structures, like `vector`, `hashtable`, and `date`
java.rmi	Classes for remote method invocation (RMI)
java.security	Classes for security-related operations, such as digital signatures, data encryption, key management, and access control
java.sql	Classes for sending SQL statements to relational databases
java.text	Classes related to text handling for internationalization

The package Statement

The general form of a `package` statement is:

```
package name;
```

where *name* is either a single package name or a list of package names separated by commas. For example, the following two statements are both legitimate package statements:

```
package my_package;
package java.awt.image;
```

Only one package statement is allowed in a program file, and it must be the first noncomment statement in the file. If the package statement is omitted from the program file, the classes generated will be put under an unnamed default package that is always imported.

The import Statement

The import statement allows classes and interfaces defined in packages to be referred to solely by the class names instead of the fully qualified names. There are two forms of import statements:

```
import package_name.class_name;
import package_name.*;
```

where *package_name* is a single package name or a list of nested package names separated by periods.

In the first form, only the specified class of the named package is imported. In the second form, all the classes and interfaces in the named package are directly accessible by simple names. You must put import statements at the beginning of a program file. The only noncomment statement allowed before an import statement is a package statement. In the following program fragment, class Vector of the java.util package is imported, as are all the classes and interfaces of the java.awt package, but not those defined in the subpackage java.awt.image . Therefore, Vector can be directly referred to by a simple name, as are the classes (like Label and Button) defined in the java.awt package. However, neither the java.io package nor the PrintStream class defined in the package is imported, and `PrintStream` must be referred to by its fully qualified name.

```
import java.util.Vector;
import java.awt.*;

class ImportTest {
    Vector v;                    // in java.util package
    Label  label;                // in java.awt package
    Button button;               // in java.awt package
    java.io.PrintStream out;     // fully qualified class name
                                 // required
}
```

TIP

> Having a class or package imported does not mean the class or classes inside the package will necessarily be loaded at runtime. The `import` statement is used only to give the Java compiler hints on resolving class names. The classes or packages mentioned in the `import` statements may never be referred to in the program body.

Summary

Casting is used to convert a value from one datatype to another type. It can only be done between two primitive types or reference types. If an assignment statement causes loss of information or extension of the datatype, an explicit casting is necessary.

The `this` and `super` keywords can be used as method names referring to the constructors in the current class and the superclass, respectively. They also can be used to refer to the current object and members in the superclass, respectively.

An interface is a collection of constants and abstract methods. Interfaces are Java's solution to multiple inheritance and callback functions. A class implements an interface by adding the interface to the `implements` clause and overriding the abstract methods defined in the interface and its superinterfaces.

A package is a collection of classes and interfaces. Packages can be nested to form a tree-like hierarchy. A package is reflected as a directory of the same name in the file system. A class defines the package it belongs to with a `package` statement. And `import` statements allow classes and interfaces defined in packages to be referred to by their simple names.

This chapter provided information about objects and classes that, together with the information presented in previous chapters, is the key to creating Java programs in an object-oriented way. Combine this with arrays, flow-control statements, exceptions, and threading (the topics of the following chapters), and you have the core of the Java language.

CHAPTER
SIX

6

Arrays and Flow-Control Statements

- Arrays in Java

- Conditional statements

- Loop statements

- Flow-breaking statements

Up to this point, you have seen examples of programs that use variables of a single object type or primitive datatype only. Also in these programs, the line of execution is sequential, from the first line to the last one, with occasional excursions to execute linearly the code segments in methods. The tasks that can be accomplished using these language constructs are limited, and inevitably, you will need to execute portions of the code repeatedly or selectively, as well as handle a group of similar objects as a whole. In this chapter, you will learn to manipulate groups of objects and to use conditional, loop, and flow-breaking statements. Together, these program constructs will allow you to do much more complicated tasks.

Using Arrays

This section describes basic array operations, including accessing array elements and declaring, creating, and copying arrays. But first, you should understand just what an array is.

What Is an Array?

An array is a group of variables of the same type that can be referred to by a common name. The type can be either a primitive datatype like int, or an object type like String. For example, you can define an array of integers to hold the daily high temperature in a month as:

```
int[] dailyHigh;
```

Or, using the Point class defined in the java.awt package, you can define an array to hold a list of two-dimensional points as:

```
Point[] points;
```

An array is an object; that is, it is handled by reference. When you pass an array to a method, only the reference to the array is passed, rather than the whole array of elements. Declaring an array variable creates only a place holder for the reference to the array, not the memory holding the array of elements per se. Also, the actual memory used by the array elements is dynamically allocated either by a new statement or an array initializer. The memory referenced by the array variable will be automatically garbage-collected when it is no longer referred to. Every array object has a public instance variable length to hold the size of the array.

The following example gives you a close look at the memory model of an array. First, a class to hold a point in two-dimensional graphics is defined as follows:

```
class Point {
    int    x;
    int    y;
    Point(int x, int y)    // constructor
        {
        this.x = x;
        this.y = y;
        }
}
```

After declaring the array to hold a list of points, the memory model looks like Figure 6.1.

FIGURE 6.1

The memory model after adding an array declaration: Point []
points;

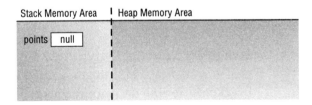

You can then use the following new statement to allocate memory space for holding two references to the Point object:

```
points = new Point[2];
```

After the allocation, you can access the size of the array as `points.length`. The memory model is shown in Figure 6.2.

FIGURE 6.2

The memory model after allocating space for array elements: `points = new Points [2] ;`

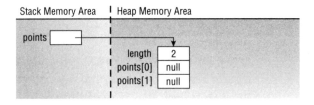

The first element of the array can be filled by:

```
points[0] = new Point(1,2);
```

Figure 6.3 shows the memory model after the above statement is added.

FIGURE 6.3

The memory model after the first element of the array is assigned: `points [0] = new point (1,2) ;`

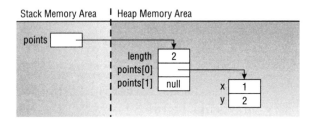

Accessing Array Elements

Java follows normal C-style indexing for accessing an array element; that is, you attach an integer-valued expression between square brackets after the name of the array. The array index starts with zero. Therefore, to get the daily high temperature of the second day of the month, you can use the following code fragment:

```
daily_high[1]
```

All subscript accesses will be checked to make sure they are in the legal range—greater than or equal to zero and less than the array length. If the value is out of bounds, the exception `ArrayIndexOut-OfBoundsException` is thrown. See Chapter 7 for details on what exceptions are and how to handle them.

Declaring and Creating an Array

Square brackets are used to declare an array type. There are two formats for declaring an array:

- Put the brackets after the datatype.
- Put the brackets after the array name.

For example:

```
int[] a;
```

is equivalent to:

```
int a[];
```

The former format is preferred by the authors of this book, because it shows clearly that an array is an object reference to a list of instances of a certain datatype.

A new statement is used to allocate the space needed for either holding the actual values of the array elements (if the elements are of primitive datatype) or holding the references to array elements (if they are of object type). For example, to create an array to hold the daily high temperature for the month of January, you can use the following statement:

```
int[] daily_high = new int[31];
```

To create an array to hold the coordinates of the three vertices of a triangle, you can declare an array as:

```
Point[] triangle = new Point[3];
```

An array created by a `new` statement will have the elements automatically initialized to the default value of the element types. For example, elements of `int` or `double` type will be initialized to zeros, and elements of object type will be set to null.

An array initializer may be used to create an array with preset values. A list of comma-separated expressions that will each be evaluated to the array's element type is enclosed in curly braces. For example, to initialize an array to hold the number of days in each month of a leap year, you can declare the array as:

```
int[] month_days = {31, 29, 31, 30, 31, 30, 31, 31, 30, 31, 30, 31};
```

> **NOTE** Array initializers can be used only in array declaration statements; they cannot be used as the right-hand side of normal assignment statements.

Copying an Array

Because an array is an object, assigning the value of an array variable to another array variable will copy only the reference to that array. For example, you can assign the value of the `points` array described in previous examples to the new array variable `points2` as:

```
Point[] points2 = points;
```

The memory model for these two variables is shown in Figure 6.4.

FIGURE 6.4

The memory model after assignment: `Point[] points2 = points;`

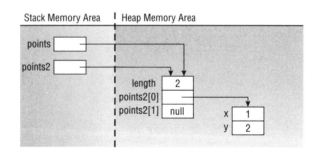

To actually copy the values or a portion of the values stored in an array into another array, the arraycopy() method of the System class under the java.lang package can be used. The synopsis of that method is:

```
void arraycopy(Object source_array,
    int source_start_position,
    Object destination_array,
    int destination_start_ position,
    int number_of_elements_to_be_copied);
```

For example, to copy all the values in points into points2, you can use:

```
System.arraycopy(points, 0, points2, 0, points.length);
```

Be aware that the memory space for the destination array must be allocated before calling the arraycopy() method. For the above example, points2 may first need to be created as:

```
points2 = new Point[points.length];
```

The memory model after copying the array is shown in Figure 6.5.

FIGURE 6.5

The memory model after array copy:
System.arraycopy
(points, 0,points2,
0,points.length);

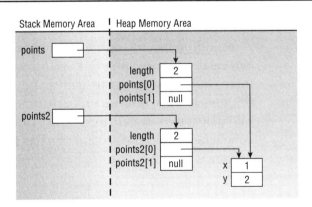

For an array of objects, the values stored in an array are references to the objects. To duplicate an array with its component object elements, you can use the clone() method of the Object class (the root of all objects) in conjunction with the `arraycopy()` method. Only classes implementing the `Cloneable` interface may be cloned. They include the `Vector`, `Hashtable`, and `BitSet` classes defined in the `java.util` package. See Part 2 for more details about these classes.

For example, if `val` is already declared and created as an array of `Vector`, the following code fragment can be used to duplicate `val` as `va2`:

```
Vector[] va2 = new Vector[val.length];

System.arraycopy(val, 0, va2, 0, val.length);
for (int i = 0; i < val.length; i++)
    va2[i] = (Vector) val[i].clone();
```

If there is no `clone()` or similar method available, you will need to explicitly create a new copy of each element in the array. For example, the following code segment can be added to the earlier example so that `points2` is a full duplicate of `points`:

```
points2[0] = new Point(points[0].x, points[0].y);
```

Multidimensional Arrays

A multidimensional array is implemented as an array of arrays. You can create a nonrectangular multidimensional array by having elements of an array refer to arrays of different sizes. To initialize a multidimensional array, nested curly braces are used. For example, to initialize a two-dimensional array of which the first element has two subelements and the second one has three subelements, you can declare it as:

```
int[][] a = {{1,2}, {3,4,5}};
```

To create a three-by-three matrix of integers, you can say:

```
int[][] matrix = new int[3][3];
```

The earlier statement for declaring and initializing a can be rewritten as:

```
int[]  a0 = {1,2}, a1 = {3,4,5};
int[][] a = {a1, a2};
```

Or even lengthier, as:

```
int[]  a0 = {1,2};
int[]  a1 = {3,4,5};
int[][] a = new int[2][];
a[0] = a0;
a[1] = a1;
```

The memory model for this example is shown in Figure 6.6.

FIGURE 6.6

The memory model for a multidimensional array:
`int [] [] a +`
`{{1,2}, {3,4,5}};`

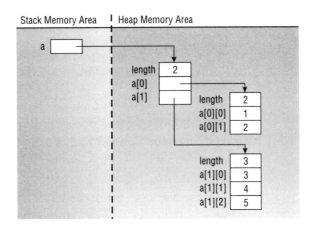

You should be careful when you are declaring a list of multidimensional arrays with different dimensionalities. In the following code fragment, b is declared as a one-dimensional array, and c as a two-dimensional array:

```
int[] b, c[];
```

The above statement can be legitimately rewritten as:

```
int b[], c[][];
```

> **TIP**
>
> This can be a little bit confusing to C/C++ programmers. It might help if you treat the set of square brackets after the datatype as a modifier to the datatype rather than to the array name(s).

Using Flow-Control Statements

Java's flow-control statements are basically modeled after those of C/C++:

- `if` and `switch` statements are used for selective execution of code segments.

- `for`, `while`, and `do` statements are used for repeated execution of code segments.

- `break`, `continue`, and `return` statements are used for breaking the flow.

There are two major differences in Java, however. First, the conditional expressions used in `if`, `for`, `while`, or `do` statements must be valid boolean expressions that will be evaluated to values of either `true` or `false`. In Java, the values `0` or `null` cannot be a substitute for `false`. Neither can nonzero or non-null values be used in place of `true`. Furthermore, you cannot explicitly cast an `int` type into a `boolean` type. The other difference is that there is no `goto` statement in Java; labeled `break` and `continue` statements are provided as better solutions where the use of `goto` statements may be justified.

Conditional Statements

Conditional statements allow for the selective execution of portions of the program according to the value of some expressions. Java supports two types of conditional statements: `if` and `switch` statements. In addition, the tertiary ? : operators can sometimes be used as alternatives to if-else statements.

if Statements

The general form of an if statement is:

```
if (conditional_expression)
    if_statement
else
    else_statement
```

An if statement will first test its conditional expression. If it is evaluated to true, the statement or block of statements immediately after the conditional expression will be executed. Otherwise, the statement or block of statements after else will be executed. The else part is optional. For example, the following code fragment will test if a character is a digit, a whitespace, or another type of character, and set the appropriate boolean variable to true:

```
char ch = 'a';
boolean is_digit = false, is_space = false, is_other = false;
if (Character.isDigit(ch))
    is_digit = true;
else if (Character.isWhitespace(ch))
    is_space = true;
else
    is_other = true;
```

isDigit() and isWhitespace() are class methods of the Character class defined in the java.lang package; they are used to determine if the character argument passed in belongs to a certain character type.

As another example, the following code fragment will assign a character grade according to the score in a 100-point system:

```
int score = 65;
char grade;
if (score >= 90)
    grade = 'A';
```

```
else if (score >= 80)
   grade = 'B';
else if (score >= 70)
   grade = 'C';
else if (score >= 60)
   grade = 'D';
else
   grade = 'F';
```

Using nested ? : operators, the above example can be succinctly rewritten as:

```
int score = 65;
char grade = (score >= 90) ? 'A' :
             (score >= 80) ? 'B' :
             (score >= 70) ? 'C' :
             (score >= 60) ? 'D' : 'F';
```

> **TIP** Although if (score = 70) is valid in C/C++, it will result in a compilation error in Java, because score = 70 is an assignment operation evaluated to an integer value of 70, not a conditional expression that will be evaluated to a boolean value of true or false.

switch Statements

The general form of a switch statement is:

```
switch (expression) {
   case value1:
      code_segment_1
   case value2:
      code_segment_2
   . . .
   case valueN:
      code_segment_N
   default:
      default_code_segment
}
```

A `switch` statement is used for multiple-way selection that will branch to different code segments based on the value of a variable or an expression. The optional default label is used to specify the code segment to be executed when the value of the variable or expression cannot match any of the `case` values. If there is no `break` statement as the last statement in the code segment for a certain `case`, the execution will continue on into the code segment for the next `case` clause without checking the `case` value. `break` statements are discussed later in this chapter.

TIP

It is a common programming error to forget to have a `break` statement as the last statement of a code segment for a `case` clause of a `switch` statement.

The expression used in a `switch` statement must be an integral expression or one whose evaluated result can be implicitly cast into an `int` type without losing information. Datatypes that can be cast into an `int` type without losing information include `byte`, `char`, and `short`. For datatypes like `long`, `float`, and `double`, explicit casting is required. The `case` values must be constant expressions that can be evaluated to or later implicitly cast to a constant value of `int` type at compile time.

Similar to the earlier example of `if` statements, the following code fragment will set the appropriate boolean variable according to the character type of the character variable `ch` . This `switch` statement will recognize only digits and whitespaces defined in ASCII; the `if` statement shown earlier can handle digits and whitespaces defined in other languages or code sets covered by Unicode.

```
switch (ch) {
   case '0': case '1': case '2': case '3': case '4':
   case '5': case '6': case '7': case '8': case '9':
      is_digit = true;
      break;
```

```
            case ' ':
            case '\t':
            case '\n':
                is_space = true;
                break;
            default:
                is_other = true;
        }
```

If the break statement after is_digit = true is missing, both is_space and is_digit will be set to true for characters of digit type.

Loop Statements

Loop statements allow for the repeated execution of blocks of statements. There are three types of loop statements: for, while, and do loops. for and while loops test the loop condition at the top of the loop, before the loop body is executed. do loops check the condition at the bottom of the loop, after the loop body is executed.

for Statements

The general form of a for statement is:

```
for (initialization_statement; conditional_expression;
        increment_statement)
    loop_body
```

To execute a for statement, the initialization statement is first executed. The conditional expression is then evaluated. If it is evaluated to true, the loop body is executed, followed by the increment statement. The evaluation of the conditional expression and the execution of the loop body and the increment statement are repeated until the conditional expression is evaluated to false. Multiple initialization or increment statements are allowed if separated by commas.

As in C++, local loop variables can be declared in the initialization section of a `for` loop. The scope of the loop variables is just the loop itself. These loop variables follow the general rules for declaring variables inside a block delimited by curly braces: They cannot have the same names as any variables declared in an outer scope and they cannot be referred to outside the loop.

For example, the following code fragment can be used to prepare a two-dimensional array for holding a full year's daily high temperatures, grouped by months:

```
int[] month_days = {31, 28, 31, 30, 31, 30, 31, 31, 30, 31, 30, 31};
int[][] daily_high = new int[month_days.length][];
for (int i = 0; i < month_days.length; i++) {
   daily_high[i] = new int[month_days[i]];
 }
```

And the following method can be defined to return the highest temperature in a year:

```
int getYearlyHigh(int[][] daily_high) {
   int yearly_high = Integer.MIN_VALUE;
   for (int i = 0; i < month_days.length; i++)
      for (int j = 0; j < daily_high[i].length; j++)
         if (yearly_high < daily_high[i][j])
            yearly_high = daily_high[i][j];
   return yearly_high;
 }
```

MIN_VALUE is a class variable (a constant, in fact) of the `Integer` class under the `java.lang` package defined as the smallest possible value of type `int`.

while Statements

The general form of a `while` statement is:

```
while (conditional_expression)
    loop_body
```

To execute a `while` statement, the conditional expression will first be evaluated. If it is evaluated to `true`, the loop body is executed. Otherwise, program control passes to the line after the loop body. The testing of the conditional expression and the execution of the loop body is repeated until the conditional expression is evaluated to `false`. For example, the following code fragment will calculate the sum of the numbers from 1 through 100:

```
int i = 1, sum = 0;
while (i <= 100)
      sum += i++;
```

do Statements

The general form of a do statement is:

```
do
      loop_body
while (conditional_expression);
```

The only difference between a `do` statement and a `while` statement is in the order of execution. In a `do` statement, the loop body will be executed before the conditional expression is evaluated. Therefore, the loop body will be executed at least once in a `do` statement; the loop body in a `while` statement may never be executed. For example, the following code fragment will repeatedly prompt the user until the user enters **exit**:

```
String buffer;
BufferedReader my_in =
   new BufferedReader(new InputStreamReader(System.in));
PrintWriter out = new PrintWriter(System.out);
do {
      out.print("Enter a command: ");
      out.flush();
      buffer = my_in.readLine();
} while (! buffer.equals("exit"));
```

BufferedReader is a class defined in the java.io package with methods allowing you to read text lines from an underlying character-input stream, which, in the above example, is the byte stream of standard input, System.in, translated into a character stream by the InputStreamReader class.

Flow-Breaking Statements

Three types of flow-breaking statements are supported in Java:

- break statements are used to exit from switch statements, loop statements, and labeled blocks.

- continue statements are used to jump to the end of the loop body just past the last line of the statement.

- return statements are used to exit from a method or a constructor.

Statements and blocks of statements delimited by curly braces can be labeled and later referred to by the enclosed break statements. However, only labels of enclosing loop statements can be referred to by continue statements.

break Statements

The general form of a break statement is:

```
break label;
```

where the label is optional. Without a label, the break statement will transfer the program control to the statement just after the innermost enclosing loop or switch statement. With a label, it will transfer the program control to the statement just after the enclosing statement or block of statements carrying the same label. For example, the following code fragment will print the third day in a year with a daily high of above 70 degrees:

```
PrintWriter out = new PrintWriter(System.out);

outer_loop:
    for (int i = 0, count = 0; i < daily_high.length; i++)
        for (int j = 0; j < daily_high[i].length; j++)
            if ((daily_high[i][j] > 70) & (++count == 3)) {
                out.println("The date is: month = " + (i + 1) +
                    ", day = " + (j + 1));
                break outer_loop;
            }
// break outer_loop, if executed, will reach here
```

continue Statements

The general form of a `continue` statement is:

```
continue label;
```

where the label is optional. Without a label, it behaves exactly the same as in C/C++. The program control is transferred to the point right after the last statement in the enclosing loop body. In `while` and `do` statements, the conditional expressions will now be retested. In `for` loops, the increment statements will be executed next. With a label, the program control will be transferred to the end of the enclosing loop body with the same label, instead of the innermost one.

For example, the following code segment defines a method to return the offset position of the first occurrence of one string, `str2`, in the other string, `str1`:

```
int indexOf(String str1, String str2)
{
        int len1 = str1.length();
        int len2 = str2.length();
        char str2_first_char = str2.charAt(0);
    advance_one_char_at_str1:
```

```
for (int i = 0; i + len2 <= len1; i++)
    if (str1.charAt(i) == str2_first_char) {
        for (int j = 1; j < len2; j++)
            if (str1.charAt(i + j) != str2.charAt(j))
                continue advance_one_char_at_str1;
        return i;
    }
return -1;
}
```

return Statements

The general form of a `return` statement is:

```
return expression;
```

A `return` statement is used to return control to the caller from within a method or constructor. If the method is defined to return a value, the expression must be evaluated to the return type of that method. Otherwise, only an unlabeled `return` statement can be used.

An Example: The Daily High

This section presents an example that demonstrates the use of one- and two-dimensional arrays and various flow-control statements. Three arrays are used in the example:

- `month_days`, a one-dimensional array of `int` type to hold the number of days in each month

- `month_names`, a one-dimensional array of `String` type to hold the names of the months

- `daily_high`, a two-dimensional array of `int` type to hold a full year's daily high temperatures, grouped by months

The program first initializes the `daily_high` array with random numbers between 10 and 100. `random()` is a class method defined in the `Math` class of the package `java.lang`. This method will return a random number between 0 and 1 of `double` type. The program then prints a year's daily high grouped by months. It continues on to print the third day in the year with a daily high above 76 degrees. At last, it reports the number of months with monthly highs less than or equal to 96 degrees. The whole program is listed here:

```java
import java.io.PrintWriter;

class DailyHigh
{
   static int[] month_days={31,28,31,30,31,30,31,31,30,31,30,31};
   static String[] month_names=
      {"Jan", "Feb", "Mar", "Apr", "May", "Jun",
       "Jul", "Aug", "Sep", "Oct", "Nov", "Dec"};
   int[][] daily_high;
   PrintWriter out;
   // constructor
   DailyHigh(PrintWriter out)
      {
         daily_high = new int[12][];
         this.out = out;
         for (int i = 0; i < 12; i++)
            daily_high[i] = new int[month_days[i]];
      }
   // fill in the 2-D array with random temperatures between 10 and 100
   void init()
      {
         for (int i = 0; i < 12; i++)
            for (int j = 0; j < month_days[i]; j++)
               daily_high[i][j] = (int) ( Math.random() * 90.0
                                          + 10.0);
      }
   // print the daily_high array
   void print()
      {
         out.println("\nDaily High:\n");
         for (int i = 0; i < 12; i++)
            {
```

```
                out.print(month_names[i] + ":");
                for (int j = 0; j < month_days[i]; j++)
                  {
                    if ((j != 0) && (j % 7 == 0))
                      out.print(j % 14 == 0 ? "\n     " : "  ");
                    out.print(" " + daily_high[i][j]);
                      }
          out.println();
      }
    }
}
// the number of months with monthly high less than or equal to
// certain number; a demonstration of usage of labeled continue
int monthlyHighNotMoreThan(int reference)
    {
        int count = 0;
    outer_loop:
        for (int i = 0; i < daily_high.length; i++) {
            for (int j = 0; j < daily_high[i].length; j++)
                if (daily_high[i][j] > reference)
                    continue outer_loop;
            count++;
        }
        return count;
    }
public static void main(String[] args)
    {
        PrintWriter out = new PrintWriter(System.out, true);
        DailyHigh t = new DailyHigh(out);
        t.init();
        t.print();
    // find the third day in the year with daily high above 76
    // a demonstration of use of labeled break
    out:
        {
          out.print("\nThe third day with daily high above 76 is: ");
        for (int i = 0, count = 0; i < t.daily_high.length; i++)
          for (int j = 0; j < month_days[i]; j++)
              if ((t.daily_high[i][j] > 76) && (++count == 3)) {
                  out.println(month_names[i] + " " + (j + 1));
            break out;
              }
```

```
        // reach here only when the 3rd date cannot be found
        out.println("no such date");
    }

    int reference = 96;
    out.println("The number of months with monthly high <= " +
                      reference + " is " +
                      t.monthlyHighNotMoreThan(reference));
    }
}
```

Here is an output of the program (your output may be different
due to the random numbers):

```
C:\MasteringJava\Ch06>java DailyHigh

Daily High:

Jan:  81  16  30  35  60  37  38     25  11  59  72  68  23  86
      94  72  85  24  59  95  32     46  37  30  54  29  28  72
      89  56  36
Feb:  90  24  14  44  92  21  66     64  37  71  40  52  40  68
      33  99  10  37  28  26  69     19  74  48  53  63  59  95
Mar:  26  95  64  61  17  62  20     16  68  52  26  62  71  81
      25  25  87  24  26  40  25     45  93  77  77  65  65  48
      14  21  10
Apr:  84  71  74  84  62  55  42     62  84  36  76  70  46  21
      56  10  53  27  58  67  59     76  92  14  18  28  23  36
      70  34
May:  49  22  63  18  34  46  85     65  86  16  38  85  62  58
      35  79  62  28  26  12  82     14  61  80  28  17  98  88
      10  74  62
Jun:  38  21  91  78  81  57  53     99  92  15  59  58  89  56
      17  13  19  33  73  98  43     96  45  83  12  83  58  60
      14  78
Jul:  88  38  36  32  14  54  42     20  53  13  24  37  74  47
      47  43  88  88  27  77  45     61  38  20  70  54  24  43
      51  95  46
Aug:  97  37  67  69  77  59  86     49  70  69  83  87  36  62
      56  82  23  40  46  35  70     82  96  21  81  61  32  47
      72  15  23
Sep:  14  16  85  22  87  24  51     27  97  35  90  78  97  38
      41  16  10  10  74  14  56     96  14  16  57  59  51  13
      51  27
```

```
Oct:  80 28 94 55 64 67 29    58 97 96 64 26 82 85
      86 80 55 32 19 58 20    50 94 84 92 61 33 84
      59 26 46
Nov:  51 54 61 52 26 38 85    21 66 66 59 43 81 16
      86 51 95 23 72 13 42    94 43 88 26 43 92 91
      13 40
Dec:  81 27 24 95 75 41 18    76 37 46 42 93 61 68
      86 96 86 88 93 67 32    61 83 58 72 38 19 24
      73 90 90
The third day with daily high above 76 is: Jan 15
The number of months with monthly high <= 96 is 6
```

Summary

This chapter introduced the use of Java arrays and control statements. An array is a group of variables of the same type that can be referred to by a common name. An array is an object. Declaring an array variable creates only a place holder for the reference to the array. You need to use either a new statement or an array initializer to allocate the space for the array. A multidimensional array is implemented as an array of arrays, and therefore can be nonrectangular.

Java's flow-control statements are similar to those in C/C++: if and switch statements are used for selective execution of code segments; for, while, and do statements are used for repeated execution of code segments; and break, continue, and return statements are used for breaking the flow. There is no goto statement in Java, but labeled break and continue statements are usually good solutions in places where you would want to use a goto statement.

Arrays allow you to handle similar data objects as groups. Flow-control statements allow you to selectively and/or repeatedly execute program fragments. Together with exception handling for handling abnormal conditions and multithreading for concurrent execution of programs, they allow you to manage complicated program control for your applications.

CHAPTER
SEVEN

Exception Handling

7

- Exception handling basics

- The hierarchy of exception classes

- Constructs for exception handling

- Customized exception classes

As programs become more complicated, making them robust is a much more difficult task. Traditional programming languages like C rely on the heavy use of `if` statements to detect abnormal conditions, `goto` statements to branch to the error handlers, and `return` codes for propagating the abnormal conditions back to the calling methods. Thus, normal program flow is either buried in the web of exception detection and handling statements or robustness is sacrificed for the sake of clarity.

Using an exception-handling mechanism similar to that of C++, Java provides an elegant way to build programs that are both robust and clear. In this chapter, you will learn to use this cleaner mechanism to handle errors and unusual conditions.

Overview of Exception Handling

An *exception* is an abnormal condition that disrupts normal program flow. There are many cases where abnormal conditions happen during program execution, such as the following:

- The file you try to open may not exist.

- The class file you want to load may be missing or in the wrong format.

- The other end of your network connection may be nonexistent.

- The network connection may be disrupted for some mysterious reason.

- An operand is not in the legal range prescribed for operations or methods. For example, an array element index cannot exceed the size of the array, and a divisor in a division operation cannot be zero.

If these abnormal conditions are not prevented or at least handled properly, either the program will be aborted abruptly or the incorrect results or status will be carried on, causing more and more abnormal conditions. Imagine a program that reads from an unopened file and does computations based on those input values!

The Basic Model

Java basically follows C++ syntax for exception handling. First, you try to execute a block of statements. If an abnormal condition occurs, something will throw an exception that you can catch with a handler. And, finally, there may be a block of statements you always want executed—no matter whether an exception occurred, and no matter whether the exception is handled if it does occur.

Throwing an exception is more friendly than terminating the program because it provides the programmer with the option of writing a handler to deal with the abnormal condition. For example, the following program fragment causes the program to sleep for ten seconds (10,000 milliseconds) by calling the sleep() class method defined in class Thread of the java.lang package. If the sleep is interrupted before the time expires, a message is printed and the execution continues with the statement following this try-catch construct.

```
PrintWriter out = new PrintWriter(System.out, true);
try {
    Thread.sleep(10000);
} catch (InterruptedException e) {
    out.println("Sleeping interrupted.");
}
// reaches here after try-block finished or exception handled
```

The next program, which copies the contents of one file to another, demonstrates exception handling in a more practical setting. The program first takes filenames from the command-line arguments. Then it opens the files and copies data in 512-byte block increments. The number of bytes copied is tracked, and the byte count is reported once the operation is completed. The program fragment to carry out these operations is as follows:

```
int     byte_count = 0;
byte[] buffer = new byte[512];
String input_file  = null;
String output_file = null;
PrintWriter out = new PrintWriter(System.out, true);
FileInputStream  fin;
FileOutputStream fout;

input_file  = args[0];
output_file = args[1];
fin  = new FileInputStream(input_file);
fout = new FileOutputStream(output_file);
int bytes_in_one_read;

while ((bytes_in_one_read = fin.read(buffer)) != -1) {
   fout.write(buffer, 0, bytes_in_one_read);
   byte_count += bytes_in_one_read;
}

out.println(byte_count + " written");
```

The FileInputStream and FileOutputStream classes are defined in the java.io package. Their constructors allow you to open files by name, and their methods let you read data from or write data into a single byte or a byte array.

But what if the user does not provide the input and output filenames? Or what if the user provides a nonexistent input file? In Java, these abnormal conditions are system-defined exceptions that will be thrown by the system as they occur. Accessing an array with an index larger than or equal to the array size will cause an

ArrayIndexOutOfBoundsException to be thrown. The constructor of the FileInputStream class will throw a FileNotFound-Exception exception if the file cannot be located. The constructor for FileOutputStream and the read() and write() methods will throw an IOException exception for an I/O error.

Furthermore, exception handlers can be located together. A catch clause is constructed for each exception handler to identify the abnormal condition the handler is attending to. Three handlers are added to the previous program to attend to the abnormal conditions mentioned above:

- One handler will print the usage of the program when the user does not provide both the input and output filenames.

- The next handler will notify the user when the input file does not exist.

- Another handler will print an error message when other I/O exceptions occur.

The program to print the number of bytes copied is moved to the finally clause so that it will always be executed even if some abnormal condition disrupts the normal program flow. Here is the full program:

```java
import java.io.*;

public class MyCopy {

    public static void main (String[] args) {

        int     byte_count = 0;
        byte[] buffer = new byte[512];
        String input_file  = null;
        String output_file = null;
        PrintWriter out = new PrintWriter(System.out, true);
        FileInputStream  fin;
        FileOutputStream fout;
```

```
        try {
            input_file  = args[0];
            output_file = args[1];
            fin  = new FileInputStream(input_file);
            fout = new FileOutputStream(output_file);
            int bytes_in_one_read;

            while ((bytes_in_one_read = fin.read(buffer)) != -1)
            {
                fout.write(buffer, 0, bytes_in_one_read);
                byte_count += bytes_in_one_read;
            }
        }
        catch (ArrayIndexOutOfBoundsException e) {
            out.println(
                "Usage: java MyCopy [input_file] [output_file]");
        }
        catch (FileNotFoundException e) {
            out.println("Cannot open input file: " + input_file);
        }
        catch (IOException e) {
            out.println("I/O exception occurs!");
        }
        finally {
            if (byte_count > 0)
                out.println(byte_count + " bytes written");
        }
    }
}
```

Here is a sample output of the previous program run under different conditions:

```
C:\MasteringJava\Ch07>java MyCopy
Usage: java MyCopy [input_file] [output_file]

C:\MasteringJava\Ch07>java MyCopy MyCopy.java temp.java
1273 bytes written

C:\MasteringJava\Ch07>java MyCopy NoSuchFile.java temp.java
Cannot open input file: NoSuchFile.java
```

Why Use Exception Handling?

There are several good reasons why you should use exception handling. One is that error-handling code is separated from normal program flow to increase the readability and maintainability of the program.

Imagine how you would rewrite the example from the previous section in C-style if exception handling were not available. You would need an `if` statement after every I/O operation to make sure of the successful completion of the I/O operation. You would also need to use an `if` statement to check whether the user provided enough filenames. To handle these abnormal conditions, you would either add more code in place or use `goto` statements to branch to the code fragment that handles common failures. Add a few more I/O calls, and even you, the author of the program, will not be able to easily recognize what the program was originally intended to accomplish. With Java, there is no need to test if an exception condition happens. Adding more handlers requires adding more `catch` clauses, but the original program flow need not be touched.

Another benefit of using exception handling is that you can easily say where the exception will be handled. Exceptions propagate up the call stack at runtime—first up the enclosing `try` blocks and then back to the calling method—until they are caught by an exception handler. For example, the previous example can be rewritten as a method with input and output filenames as the arguments. The synopsis of this new method is as follows:

```
int copyFile(String input_file, String output_file)
```

The caller of this method may want to handle the abnormal condition by itself. For example, an application with a GUI may want to display a dialog box prompting the user for another filename when the input file does not exist. In this case, the error handler for an I/O exception is removed from the method and a `throws` clause is added to the method declaration. The caller can then have its own error-handling routines for these abnormal conditions. Here is the modified method definition:

```
int copyFile(String input_file, String output_file) throws IOException
{
    int     bytes_in_one_read, byte_count = 0;
    byte[] buffer = new byte[512];
    FileInputStream  fin = new FileInputStream(input_file);
    FileOutputStream fout= new FileOutputStream(output_file);

    while ((bytes_in_one_read = fin.read(buffer)) != -1) {
        fout.write(buffer, 0, bytes_in_one_read);
        byte_count += bytes_in_one_read;
    }

    return byte_count;
}
```

Here is a code fragment to call this method and handle the abnormal conditions by itself:

```
int byte_count = 0
String input_file, output_file;
PrintWriter out = new PrintWriter(System.out, true);
try {
    input_file  = args[0];
    output_file = args[1];
    byte_count = copyFile(input_file, output_file);
}
catch (ArrayIndexOutOfBoundsException e) {
    out.println(
        "Usage: java MyCopy [input_file] [output_file]");
}
catch (FileNotFoundException e) {
    out.println("Cannot open input file: " + input_file);
}
catch (IOException e) {
    out.println("I/O exception occurs!");
}
finally {
    if (byte_count > 0)
        out.println(byte_count + " bytes written");
}
```

Exceptions are objects with hierarchical relationships. You can create a single exception handler to catch all exceptions from a class and its subclasses or a series of exception handlers, each handling exceptions from individual subclasses. The `MyCopy` example demonstrates another option. The second `catch` clause deals with `FileNotFoundException`, and the next one catches any other `IOExceptions`. `FileNotFoundException` is a subclass of `IOException`, so you can check for both subclass and superclass exceptions.

Hierarchy of Exception Classes

Just like nearly everything else in Java, exceptions are objects or class instances. Exception classes form their own class hierarchy. The root class of all the exception classes is the `Throwable` class, which is an immediate subclass of the `Object` class. Methods are defined in the `Throwable` class to retrieve the error message associated with the exception and to print the stack trace showing where the exception occurs (see the next section for more details).

There are two immediate subclasses of class `Throwable`: class `Error` and class `Exception`. Subclasses of class `Exception` have the suffix `Exception`. Subclasses of class `Error` have the suffix `Error` (and then there is `ThreadDeath`, a subclass of `Error`). The subclasses of `Error` are basically used for signaling abnormal system conditions. For example, an `OutOfMemoryError` signals that the Java VM (Virtual Machine) has run out of memory and that the garbage collector is unable to claim any more free memory. A `StackOverflowError` signals a stack overflow in the interpreter. These `Error` exceptions are, in general, unrecoverable and should not be handled.

The subclasses of the `Exception` class are, in general, recoverable. For example, an `EOFException` signals that a file you have opened has no more data for reading. A `FileNotFoundException` signals that a file you want to open does not exist in the file system. You can choose to handle the exceptions by using a `try-catch` block to enclose the statements whose exceptional conditions will be handled.

Figure 7.1 illustrates the hierarchical relationships among some of the more common errors and exceptions.

FIGURE 7.1

Hierarchy of common exceptions

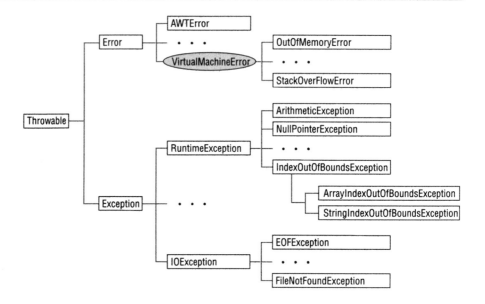

The following example loops through four pathological cases in which the system throws four types of `RunTimeException`:

`ArithmeticException`   For exceptional arithmetic conditions like integer division by zero.

`NullPointerException`   For accessing a field or invoking a method of a null object.

`ArrayIndexOutOfBoundsException`   For accessing an array element by providing an index value less than zero or greater than or equal to the array size.

`StringIndexOutOfBoundsException`   For accessing a character of a `String` or `StringBuffer` with an index less than zero or greater than or equal to the length of the string.

Here is the test program:

```java
import java.io.*;

class ExceptionTest
{
    public static void main(String[] args)
        {
        PrintWriter out = new PrintWriter(System.out, true);

        for (int i = 0; i < 4; i++) {
            int k;

            try {
                switch (i) {
                    case 0:      // divided by zero
                        int zero = 0;
                        k = 911 / zero;
                        break;

                    case 1:      // null pointer
                        int[] b = null;
                        k = b[0];
                        break;

                    case 2:      // array index out of bound
                        int[] c = new int[2];
                        k = c[9];
                        break;

                    case 3:      // string index out of bound
                        char ch = "abc".charAt(99);
                        break;
                }
            }
            catch (Exception e) {
                out.println("\nTest case #" + i + "\n");
                out.println(e);
            }
        }
    }
}
```

The output of the previous test program is shown here:

```
C:\MasteringJava\Ch07>java ExceptionTest

Test case #0

java.lang.ArithmeticException: / by zero

Test case #1

java.lang.NullPointerException:

Test case #2

java.lang.ArrayIndexOutOfBoundsException:

Test case #3

java.lang.StringIndexOutOfBoundsException: String index out of range: 99
```

Exception-Handling Constructs

The general form of an exception-handling construct (the `try` statement) is:

```
try {
    normal_program_body
}
catch (exception_class_1 exception_variable_1) {
    exception_handler_program_body_1
}
catch (exception_class_2 exception_variable_2) {
    exception_handler_program_body_2
. . .

}
finally {
    exit_program_body
}
```

TIP

Early versions of the JDK (before 1.0.2) did not require the use of curly braces in the body of a `try-catch-finally` construct if the program body consisted of only a single statement. However, curly braces are always required in JDK versions 1.0.2 and later.

The `try` keyword is used to specify a block of statements whose exceptions will be handled by the succeeding `catch` clauses. There can be any number of `catch` clauses. When an exception condition occurs, the body of the first exception handler whose exception class type is the same class as or is a superclass of the thrown exception will be executed.

Since exception matching is done sequentially, an exception handler may never be reached if its `catch` clause is after the `catch` clause for its superclass exception handler. For example, in an earlier example, the handler for `FileNotFoundException` needed to be placed before the handler for `IOException`, the immediate superclass of `FileNotFoundException`. The compiler checks to ensure all exception handlers are reachable. If you exchange the order of the handlers for `FileNotFoundException` and `IOException`, the compiler will issue the following error message:

```
MyCopy.java:33: catch not reached.
     catch (FileNotFoundException e) {
     ^
1 error
```

The exit program block after the `finally` keyword will be executed before the program control is transferred outside the programming construct. This will eventually happen when the execution of the program body or the exception handler is finished, a flow-breaking statement—a `break`, `continue`, or `return` statement—is encountered, or an exception is thrown with no handler inside the construct capable of catching it.

The catch clause is optional, as is the finally clause. However, at least one of the catch or finally clauses must exist in a try-catch-finally construct. The exit program body comes in handy for freeing resources like the file handles allocated in the normal program body.

The following example demonstrates the effects of break and continue statements on a finally clause. Inside the nested for loop, labeled and unlabeled break and continue statements are executed and the flow is traced.

```java
import java.io.*;

class FinallyTest {
    public static void main(String[] args) {
        PrintWriter out = new PrintWriter(System.out,
            true);
    outer_loop:
        for (int i = 0; i < 3; i++)
            for (int j = 0; j < 3; j++)
                try {
                    out.println("try before if: i=" + i + ", j=" + j);

                    if ((i == 0) && (j == 1))
                        continue;
                    else if ((i == 0) && (j == 2))
                        continue outer_loop;
                    else if ((i == 1) && (j == 0))
                        break;
                    else if ((i == 2) && (j == 1))
                        break outer_loop;

                    out.println("try after  if: i=" + i + ", j=" + j);
                }
                finally {
                    out.println("finally:       i=" + i + ", j=" + j + "\n");
                }
    }
}
```

The output of the program is shown next. You can see that the finally clause is always executed once the try block is entered.

```
C:\MasteringJava\Ch07>java FinallyTest
try before if: i=0, j=0
try after   if: i=0, j=0
finally:        i=0, j=0

try before if: i=0, j=1
finally:        i=0, j=1

try before if: i=0, j=2
finally:        i=0, j=2

try before if: i=1, j=0
finally:        i=1, j=0

try before if: i=2, j=0
try after   if: i=2, j=0
finally:        i=2, j=0

try before if: i=2, j=1
finally:        i=2, j=1
```

If the exception is not caught in the current try-catch-finally construct, it will be propagated up the program stack. The same exception-matching process will be repeated for all the enclosing try-catch-finally constructs, from the innermost construct to the outermost one, until a matching exception handler can be found. If no match can be found in the current method, the same process will be repeated for all the try-catch-finally constructs of the calling method, again from the innermost construct to the outermost one, until a match is found.

As the system tries to find a handler for the exception, from innermost to outermost, it executes the finally clauses of the try-catch-finally construct, from the innermost to the outermost. When the program runs out of try-catch-finally constructs and does not find a matching exception handler, it will print the message associated with the exception and a stack trace showing where the exception occurred; then it will terminate.

Here is a sample output of a program with an uncaught exception:

```
java.lang.ArithmeticException: / by zero
        at NoHandler.inner(NoHandler.java:6)
        at NoHandler.outer(NoHandler.java:11)
        at NoHandler.main(NoHandler.java:15)
```

Even if an exception is caught, the handler can rethrow the exception or throw another exception, and the exception-matching process will continue. The next example generates three different exceptions in the `for` loop of the `method()` method. The first exception, `ArithmeticException`, is caught in the inner `try-catch-finally` construct because of an exact match in exception type. The second exception, `ArrayIndexOutOfBoundsException`, is caught in the inner `try-catch-finally` construct, because it is a subclass of `IndexOutOfBoundsException`, but then it is rethrown and caught by the outer `try-catch-finally` construct. The last exception, `StringIndexOutOfBoundsException`, is caught in the inner `try-catch-finally` construct, because it is also a subclass of `IndexOutOfBoundsException`. It is then rethrown, but no handler in the outer `try-catch-finally` construct can catch it. It is thus propagated to the calling method and caught because it is a subclass of `RuntimeException`.

```
import java.io.*;

class NestedException {

    static PrintWriter out = new PrintWriter(System.out, true);
    public static void method()
    {
        for (int i = 0; i < 3; i++) {
            int k;

            try {
                out.println("\nOuter try block; Test Case #" + i);

                try {
                    out.println("Inner try block");
```

```
            switch (i) {
                case 0:       // divided by zero
                    int zero = 0;
                    k = 911 / zero;
                    break;

                case 1:       // array index out of bound
                    int[] c = new int[2];
                    k = c[9];
                    break;

                case 2:       // string index out of bound
                    char ch = "abc".charAt(99);
                    break;
                }
            }
            catch (ArithmeticException e) {
                out.println("Inner ArithmeticException>" + e);
            }
            catch (IndexOutOfBoundsException e) {
             out.println("Inner IndexOutOfBoundsException>" + e);
             throw e;
            }
            finally {
             out.println("Inner finally block");
            }
         }
        catch (ArrayIndexOutOfBoundsException e) {
            out.println("Outer ArrayIndexOutOfBound>" + e);
        }
        finally {
            out.println("Outer finally block");
        }
    }
  }

public static void main(String[] args)
{
    try {
        method();
    } catch (RuntimeException e) {
        out.println("main() RuntimeException>" + e);
```

```
      } finally {
          out.println("\nmain() finally block");
      }
   }
}
```

Here is the output of the program:

```
C:\MasteringJava\Ch07>java NestedException

Outer try block; Test Case #0
Inner try block
Inner ArithmeticException>java.lang.ArithmeticException: / by
zero
Inner finally block
Outer finally block

Outer try block; Test Case #1
Inner try block
Inner
IndexOutOfBoundsException>java.lang.ArrayIndexOutOfBounds
Exception:
Inner finally block
Outer
ArrayIndexOutOfBound>java.lang.ArrayIndexOutOfBoundsException:
Outer finally block

Outer try block; Test Case #2
Inner try block
Inner
IndexOutOfBoundsException>java.lang.StringIndexOutOfBounds
Exception: String index out of range: 99
Inner finally block
Outer finally block
main()
RuntimeException>java.lang.StringIndexOutOfBoundsException:
String index out of range: 99

main() finally block
```

Methods Available to Exceptions

All errors and exceptions are subclasses of class `Throwable` and thus can access the methods defined in it. Of them, the following are the most commonly used:

`getMessage()`   To obtain the error message associated with the exception or error.

`printStackTrace()`   To print a stack trace showing where the exception occurs.

`toString()`   To show the exception name along with the message returned by `getMessage()`.

Most exception classes have two constructors: one with a `String` argument to set the error message that can later be fetched through the `getMessage()` method; the other with no argument. In the second case, the `getMessage()` method will return null. The same error message will be embedded in the return of the `toString()` method or be a part of the stack trace output by the `printStack-Trace()` method. An example of output or return from these methods is listed here:

```
*** example of return from getMessage() ***
/ by zero

*** example of return from toString() ***
java.lang.ArithmeticException: / by zero

*** example of output by printStackTrace() ***
java.lang.ArithmeticException: / by zero
        at NoHandler.inner(NoHandler.java:6)
        at NoHandler.outer(NoHandler.java:11)
        at NoHandler.main(NoHandler.java:16)
```

The throw Statement

A `throw` statement causes an exception to be thrown. The synopsis of a `throw` statement is:

```
throw expression;
```

where the expression must be evaluated to an instance of class `Throwable` or its many subclasses.

In the most common usage, a `new` statement is used to create an instance in the expression. For example, the following statement will throw an I/O exception with "cannot find the directory" as the error message:

```
throw new IOException("cannot find the directory");
```

The throws Clause

A method that throws an exception within it must catch that exception or have that exception declared in its `throws` clause unless the exception is a subclass of either the `Error` class or `RuntimeException` class. When multiple exceptions are to be put in one `throws` clause, use commas to separate them. For example, the following program segment declares a method that propagates out `IOException` and `InterruptedException`:

```
int ReadModel(String filename) throws IOException,
InterruptedException
```

There are three reasons why exceptions that are subclasses of the `Error` or `RuntimeException` class need not be declared or handled in a method:

- If you need to catch or declare a `throws` clause for every such exception that might occur in the method, the program will look very cumbersome.

- It is difficult to check at compile time whether such exceptions will occur. For example, every reference to an object potentially can throw a `NullPointerException`. It is a formidable task for a compiler to make sure that every object referred to will be non-null at runtime, especially when the object is passed in as an argument of the method.

- Most of the errors can occur beyond the programmer's control. It does not make much sense to ask the programmer to be responsible for handling these errors.

The compiler relies on the declaration of `throws` clauses to determine if an exception may occur in an expression, a statement, or a method. The exceptions that may occur in a method are derived as the union of all the exceptions that can be generated by the `throw` statements within the method and all the exceptions contained in the `throws` clauses of the methods that might be called within the method. The compiler issues an error message for any method that does not declare all (non-error/non-runtime) exceptions in its `throws` clause. A sample output for such an error message is shown here:

```
DontCompile.java:8: Exception java.io.FileNotFoundException must be
caught, or it must be declared in the throws clause of this method.
        FileInputStream fin = new FileInputStream("BasicException.java");
                                 ^
```

Creating Your Own Exception Classes

When writing a method, there are two ways to report abnormal conditions to the calling method: use a predefined error code as the return value or throw an exception.

If an exception is thrown, the calling method is automatically handed the convenience and power of the whole exception-handling mechanism to respond to the abnormal conditions. It will also be possible for the compiler to check if these abnormal conditions are dealt with properly, since these abnormal conditions are declared in the `throws` clause of the method.

When throwing an exception, you can create an instance from an exception class already defined in the language or from one you define on your own. It may be difficult to find a predefined exception that is designed for your particular situation. By using an exception already prescribed for other conditions, you may complicate the exception handler's task. The reason is that the exception handler may need to differentiate your abnormal condition from the ones the exception class is originally prescribed for, if they can both occur in the method.

The common practice in creating a customized exception class is to subclass the `Exception` class. This ensures the compiler checks if it is dealt with properly. However, if you are writing system- or hardware-related utilities, you may be justified in creating subclasses from either `Error` or `RuntimeException` classes. You should not subclass `Error` or `RuntimeException` just so you do not need to create `throws` clauses for your methods.

Because exception classes are class objects, they can have data members and methods defined within them. As an example, `InterruptedIOException,` defined in the `java.io` package, has a public instance variable, `bytesTransferred`, to hold the number of bytes read or written before the operation is interrupted. You may choose to create customized exception classes in a hierarchy so that the handler has the options of handling the superclass as a whole, handling the subclasses individually, or handling both classes simultaneously.

An Example:
Age Exceptions

The example presented in this section demonstrates how to create a hierarchy of user-defined exception classes for abnormal conditions and how to write a program using these user-defined exceptions for abnormal condition handling. In the first part of the example, a hierarchy of exception classes to report age-related anomalies is constructed, as shown in Figure 7.2.

FIGURE 7.2

The class hierarchy for
the AgeException class

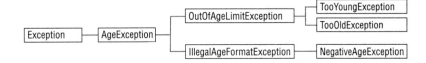

The root of this hierarchy is the AgeException class. It has a data
member, age, to hold the age causing the occurrence of the exception. It has two subclasses: class OutOfAgeLimitException for
cases where the age given is too young or too old to perform a certain
activity and class IllegalAgeFormatException for cases where
the age given is out of the legal age range or in the wrong format.
The former class has a data member, age_limit, to hold the limit
being violated. The program for defining these classes is listed here:

```
class AgeException extends Exception
{
    int age;

    AgeException(String message) {
        super(message);
    }
    AgeException() {
        super();
    }
}

class OutOfAgeLimitException extends AgeException
{
    int age_limit;

    OutOfAgeLimitException(int age_limit, String message) {
        super(message);
        this.age_limit = age_limit;
    }
    OutOfAgeLimitException(String message) {
        super(message);
    }
}
```

```
class TooYoungException extends OutOfAgeLimitException
{
   TooYoungException(int age, int age_limit, String message) {
      super(age_limit, "You are too young to " + message + ".");
      this.age = age;
   }
   TooYoungException() {
      super("too young");
   }
}

class TooOldException extends OutOfAgeLimitException
{
   TooOldException(int age, int age_limit, String message) {
      super(age_limit, "You are too old to " + message + ".");
      this.age = age;
   }
   TooOldException() {
      super("too old");
   }
}

class IllegalAgeFormatException extends AgeException
{
   IllegalAgeFormatException(String message) {
      super(message);
   }
   IllegalAgeFormatException() {
      super("Illegal age format");
   }
}

class NegativeAgeException extends IllegalAgeFormatException
{
   NegativeAgeException(String message) {
      super(message);
   }
   NegativeAgeException(int age) {
      super("Age must be nonnegative.");
      this.age = age;
   }
}
```

The second part of the example is a program to use the previous exception hierarchy. The program will loop through different ages to see if people in the age specified can ride a roller coaster. The method `RideRollerCoasterAtAge()` will throw `TooYoungException`, `TooOldException`, or `NegativeAgeException` if it finds an age that is too young, too old, or negative, respectively. The program listing is as follows:

```
import java.io.*;

class AgeExceptionTest
{
   static PrintWriter out = new PrintWriter(System.out, true);
   static void RideRollerCoasterAtAge(int age)
        throws NegativeAgeException, OutOfAgeLimitException
   {
      out.println("Trying to ride a roller coaster at age " +
                age + "...");

      if (age < 0)
         throw new NegativeAgeException(age);
      else if (age < 5)
         throw new TooYoungException(age, 5,
                         "ride a roller coaster");
      else if (age > 45)
         throw new TooOldException(age, 45,
                         "ride a roller coaster");

      out.println("Riding the roller coaster....");
   }

   public static void main(String[] argc)
   {
      int ages[] = {-3, 2, 10, 35, 65};

      for (int i = 0; i < ages.length; i++)
         try {
            RideRollerCoasterAtAge(ages[i]);
            out.println("Wow! What an experience!");
         }
         catch (OutOfAgeLimitException e) {
```

```
                    out.println(e.getMessage());
                    if (ages[i] < e.age_limit)
                       out.println((e.age_limit - ages[i]) +
                          " more years and you'll be able to try it.");
                    else
                       out.println((ages[i] - e.age_limit) +
                          " years ago riding it was like a piece of cake.");
                 }
                 catch (NegativeAgeException e) {
                    out.println(e.getMessage());
                 }
                 finally {
                    out.println();
                 }
          }
   }
```

The output of the sample program is listed here:

```
C:\MasteringJava\Ch07>java AgeExceptionTest

Trying to ride a roller coaster at age -3...
Age must be nonnegative.

Trying to ride a roller coaster at age 2...
You are too young to ride a roller coaster.
3 more years and you'll be able to try it.

Trying to ride a roller coaster at age 10...
Riding the roller coaster....
Wow! What an experience!

Trying to ride a roller coaster at age 35...
Riding the roller coaster....
Wow! What an experience!

Trying to ride a roller coaster at age 65...
You are too old to ride a roller coaster.
20 years ago riding it was like a piece of cake.
```

Summary

Java provides a clean and robust mechanism for handling abnormal conditions. First, you try to execute a block of statements. If an abnormal condition occurs, an exception is thrown and you can catch the exception. And, finally, there can be a code fragment you always want to execute, whether or not an exception happens and is handled.

Exceptions are objects, and exception classes form their own class hierarchy. The root of all error and exception classes is the `Throwable` class. You can create your own exception classes as subclasses of the `Exception` class. The whole exception-handling mechanism is then at your disposal. You can even create a hierarchy of exception classes so that the handler has more flexibility in handling the exceptions.

A method that may cause an exception to be thrown must catch that exception or have that exception defined in its `throws` clause, unless the exception is a subclass of either the `Error` or `RuntimeException` class. Checking of this rule is done at compile time.

It is always unpleasant for a user to encounter errors in your application. How you deal with these errors will make a difference to the user, and will be an important factor in your application's success. The clean and robust exception-handling capability provided with Java makes writing a friendly program an easier task.

Threads and Multithreading

- Thread creation and execution

- Methods for controlling threads

- Thread synchronization

- Communications between threads

- Thread priorities and scheduling

Up to now, all of our sample programs have been single-threaded; that is, they have had only one line of execution. If the program execution is blocked waiting for the completion of some I/O operation, no other portion of the program can proceed. However, users of today's modern operating systems are accustomed to starting multiple programs and watching them work concurrently, even if there is only a single CPU available to run all the applications. Multithreading allows multiple processes to execute concurrently within a single program.

The advantage of multithreading is twofold. First, programs with multiple threads will, in general, result in better utilization of system resources, including the CPU, because another line of execution can grab the CPU when one line of execution is blocked. Second, there are a lot of problems better solved by multiple threads. For example, how would you write a single-threaded program to show animation, play music, display documents, and download files from the network at the same time?

Java was designed from the beginning with multithreading in mind. Not only does the language itself have multithreading support built in, allowing for easy creation of robust, multithreaded applications, but also the runtime environment relies on multithreading to concurrently provide multiple services—like garbage collection—to the application. In this chapter, you will learn to use multiple threads in your Java programs.

Overview of Multithreading

A thread is a single flow of control within a program. It is sometimes called the *execution context,* because each thread must have its own resources—like the program counter and the execution stack—as the context for execution. However, all threads in a program still share many resources, such as memory space and opened files. Therefore, a thread may also be called a *lightweight process.* It is a single flow of control like a process (or a running program), but it is easier to create and destroy than a process because less resource management is involved.

NOTE   The terms *parallel* and *concurrent* occur frequently in computer literature, and the difference between them can be confusing. When two threads run in parallel, they are both being executed at the same time on different CPUs. However, two concurrent threads are both in progress, or trying to get some CPU time for execution at the same time, but are not necessarily being executed simultaneously on different CPUs.

A program may spend a big portion of its execution time just waiting. For example, it may wait for some resource to become accessible in an I/O operation, or it may wait for some timeout to occur to start drawing the next scene of an animation. To improve CPU utilization, all the tasks with potentially long waits can be run as separate threads. Once a task starts waiting for something to happen, Java runtime can choose another runnable task for execution.

The first example demonstrates the difference between a single-threaded program and its multithreaded counterpart. In the first program, a `run()` method in the `NoThreadPseudoIO` class is created to simulate a ten-second I/O operation. The main program will first perform the simulated I/O operation, then start another task. The method showElapsedTime() is defined to print the elapsed time in seconds since the program started, together with a user-supplied message. The currentTimeMillis() method of the System class in the java.lang package will return a long integer for the time difference, measured in milliseconds, between the current time and 00:00:00 GMT on January 1, 1970. The single-threaded program is listed here:

```java
import java.io.*;

class WithoutThread {
    static PrintWriter out = new PrintWriter(System.out, true);

    public static void main(String[] args) {

        //  first task: some pseudo-I/O operation

        NoThreadPseudoIO pseudo = new NoThreadPseudoIO();
        pseudo.run();

        //  second task: some random task

        showElapsedTime("Another task starts");
    }

    static long base_time = System.currentTimeMillis();

    // show the time elapsed since the program started

    static void showElapsedTime(String message) {
        long elapsed_time = System.currentTimeMillis() - base_time;

        out.println(message + " at " +
                        (elapsed_time / 1000.0) + " seconds");
    }
}

// pseudo-I/O operation run in caller's thread

class NoThreadPseudoIO {
    int data = -1;
```

```
NoThreadPseudoIO() {    // constructor
   WithoutThread.showElapsedTime("NoThreadPseudoIO created");
}

public void run() {
   WithoutThread.showElapsedTime("NoThreadPseudoIO starts");

   try {
      Thread.sleep(10000);    // 10 seconds
      data = 999;             // the data is ready

      WithoutThread.showElapsedTime("NoThreadPseudoIO finishes");
   }
   catch (InterruptedException e) {}
}
}
```

Even if the second task does not refer to any data generated or modified by the pseudo-I/O operation, the task cannot be started until the I/O operation is finished. For most real I/O operations, the CPU will be sitting idle most of the time waiting for a response from the peripheral device, which is really a waste of precious CPU cycles. A sample output of the above program is shown here:

```
C:\MasteringJava\Ch08>java WithoutThread
NoThreadPseudoIO created at 0.0040 seconds
NoThreadPseudoIO starts at 0.035 seconds
NoThreadPseudoIO finishes at 10.037 seconds
Another task starts at 10.039 seconds
```

The multithreaded second program declares the class for the pseudo-I/O operation as a subclass of the Thread class:

```
class ThreadedPseudoIO extends Thread {
```

After the thread is created, it uses the start() method of the Thread class to start the I/O operation:

```
ThreadedPseudoIO pseudo = new ThreadedPseudoIO();
pseudo.start();
```

The thread's start() method in turn calls the run() method of the subclass.

235

TIP

Up to JDK version 1.0.2, there is a bug in the code for running multiple threads under Windows 95 and NT: Programs that start multiple threads will not automatically exit. The workaround is to either have the last running thread call the `System.exit()` method or have a thread monitor other threads by calling the `join()` methods of the monitored threads. `exit()` is a class method defined in the `System` class of the `java.lang` package for terminating Java runtime. For security reasons, an applet is not allowed to call `exit()`. Forcibly calling `exit()` from an applet will cause a `SecurityException` to be thrown. The workaround is not necessary for other platforms.

A full listing of this multithreaded program is as follows:

```java
import java.io.*;

class WithThread {
    static PrintWriter out = new PrintWriter(System.out, true);

    public static void main(String[] args) {

    // first task: some pseudo-I/O operation

    ThreadedPseudoIO pseudo = new ThreadedPseudoIO();
    pseudo.start();

    // second task: some random task
    showElapsedTime("Another task starts");


    }

    static long base_time = System.currentTimeMillis();

    // show the time elapsed since the program started

    static void showElapsedTime(String message) {
        long elapsed_time = System.currentTimeMillis() - base_time;
```

```
        out.println(message + " at " +
                      (elapsed_time / 1000.0) + " seconds");
   }
}


//  pseudo-I/O operation run in a separate thread

class ThreadedPseudoIO extends Thread {
   int data = -1;

   ThreadedPseudoIO() {    // constructor
      WithThread.showElapsedTime("ThreadedPseudoIO created");
   }

   public void run() {
      WithThread.showElapsedTime("ThreadedPseudoIO starts");

      try {
         Thread.sleep(10000);   // 10 seconds
         data = 999;            // data ready

         WithThread.showElapsedTime("ThreadedPseudoIO finishes");
      }
      catch (InterruptedException e) {}
   }
}
```

Here is the output of the multithreaded program. You will notice that the second task starts even before the pseudo-I/O operation starts; this is natural when you have only one CPU running two threads. The run() method of the newly created thread will not be executed until the currently running thread relinquishes program control.

```
C:\MasteringJava\Ch08>java WithThread
ThreadedPseudoIO created at 0.0030 seconds
Another task starts at 0.07 seconds
ThreadedPseudoIO starts at 0.075 seconds
ThreadedPseudoIO finishes at 10.096 seconds
```

Thread Basics

The following sections introduce the basics of working with threads, including how to create and run threads, use the thread-control methods defined in the Thread class, and how to get information about threads and thread groups. You will also learn about the life cycle of a thread and thread groups.

Creating and Running a Thread

When you have a task that you want to be run concurrently with other tasks, there are two ways to create the new thread: create a new class as a subclass of the Thread class or declare a class implementing the Runnable interface.

Using a Subclass of the Thread Class

When you create a subclass of the Thread class, this subclass should define its own run() method to override the run() method of the Thread class. This run() method is where the task is performed.

Just as the main() method is the first user-defined method the Java runtime calls to start an application, the run() method is the first user-defined method the Java runtime calls to start a thread. An instance of this subclass is then created by a new statement, followed by a call to the thread's start() method to have the run() method executed. This is exactly what has been done with the Threaded-PseudoIO class in the previous example.

Implementing the Runnable Interface

The Runnable interface requires only one method to be implemented—the run() method. You first create an instance of this class with a new statement, followed by the creation of a Thread instance with another new statement, and finally a call to this thread instance's start() method to start performing the task defined in the run() method. A class instance with the run() method defined within it must be passed in as an argument in creating the Thread instance so that when the start() method of this Thread instance is called, Java runtime knows which run() method to execute.

This alternative way of creating a thread comes in handy when the class defining the run() method needs to be a subclass of other classes. The class can inherit all the data and methods of the superclasses, and the Thread instance just created can be used for thread control.

The previous multithreaded example can be reimplemented using the Runnable interface by first changing the class definition to implement the Runnable interface instead of subclassing the Thread class:

```
class RunnablePseudoIO implements Runnable {
```

Then, an instance of the class is created and passed to a newly created Thread instance, followed by a call to the start() method to start the execution of the run() method as follows:

```
RunnablePseudoIO pseudo = new RunnablePseudoIO();
Thread thread = new Thread(pseudo);
thread.start();
```

A full listing of the program is included here:

```
import java.io.*;
class RunnableThread {
    static PrintWriter out = new PrintWriter(System.out, true);

    public static void main(String[] args) {

        // first task: some pseudo-I/O operation

        RunnablePseudoIO pseudo = new RunnablePseudoIO();
        Thread thread = new Thread(pseudo);
        thread.start();

        // second task: some random task

        showElapsedTime("Another task starts");
```

```
      }

      static long base_time = System.currentTimeMillis();

      // show the time elapsed since the program started

      static void showElapsedTime(String message) {
         long elapsed_time = System.currentTimeMillis() - base_time;

         out.println(message + " at " +
                        (elapsed_time / 1000.0) + " seconds");
      }
   }

// pseudo I/O operation run in a separate thread

class RunnablePseudoIO implements Runnable {
   int data = -1;

   RunnablePseudoIO() {    // constructor
      RunnableThread.showElapsedTime("RunnablePseudoIO created");
   }

   public void run() {
      RunnableThread.showElapsedTime("RunnablePseudoIO starts");

      try {
         Thread.sleep(10000);    // 10 seconds
         data = 999;             // data ready

         RunnableThread.showElapsedTime("RunnablePseudoIO finishes");
      }
      catch (InterruptedException e) {}            }
   }
```

The output of the program is similar to that of the earlier program:

```
C:\MasteringJava\Ch08>java RunnableThread
RunnablePseudoIO created at 0.02 seconds
Another task starts at 0.044 seconds
RunnablePseudoIO starts at 0.046 seconds
RunnablePseudoIO finishes at 10.05 seconds
```

The Thread-Control Methods

There are many methods defined in the `Thread` class to control the running of a thread. Here are some of the ones that are most commonly used:

`start()`   Used to start the execution of the thread body defined in the `run()` method. Program control will be immediately returned to the caller, and a new thread will be scheduled to execute the `run()` method concurrently with the caller's thread.

`stop()`   Used to stop the execution of the thread no matter what the thread is doing. The thread is then considered dead, the internal states of the thread are cleared, and the resources allocated are reclaimed.

`suspend()`   Used to temporarily stop the execution of the thread. All the states and resources of the thread are retained. The thread can later be restarted by another thread calling the `resume()` method.

`resume()`   Used to resume the execution of a suspended thread. The suspended thread will be scheduled to run. If it has a higher priority than the running thread, the running thread will be preempted; otherwise, the just-resumed thread will wait in the queue for its turn to run.

`sleep(long `*`sleep_time_in_milliseconds`*`)`   A class method that causes the Java runtime to put the caller thread to sleep for a specified time period. The exception, `Interrupted-Exception`, may be thrown while a thread is sleeping. Either a `try-catch-finally` statement needs to be defined to handle this exception or the enclosing method needs to have this exception in the `throws` clause.

`join()`   Used for the caller's thread to wait for this thread to die—for example, by coming to the end of the `run()` method.

`yield()` A class method that temporarily stops the caller's thread and puts it at the end of the queue to wait for another turn to be executed. It is used to make sure other threads of the same priority have the chance to run.

NOTE All the class methods defined in the `Thread` class, such as `sleep()` and `yield()`, will act on the caller's thread. That is, it is the caller's thread that will sleep for a while or yield to others. The reason is that a class method can never access an instance's data or method members unless the instance is passed in as an argument, created inside the method or stored in a class variable visible to the method.

The following example shows how some of the above methods are used. The main thread creates two threads, then waits for the first thread to finish by calling the first thread's `join()` method. The first thread calls the `sleep()` method to be asleep for ten seconds. Meanwhile, the second thread calls its own `suspend()` method to suspend itself until the main thread calls its `resume()` method. After the first thread comes to an end, the main thread will resume its execution, wake up the second thread by calling the second thread's `resume()` method, and wait until the second thread also comes to an end by calling the second thread's `join()` method. The program is as follows:

```
import java.io.*;
public class MethodTest {

    static PrintWriter out = new PrintWriter(System.out, true);

    public static void main(String args[]) {
        FirstThread  first  = new FirstThread();
        SecondThread second = new SecondThread();

        first.start();
        second.start();
```

```
        try {
            out.println("Waiting for first thread to finish...");
            first.join();
            out.println("It's a long wait!");

            out.println("Waking up second thread...");
            second.resume();

            out.println("Waiting for second thread to finish...");
            second.join();
            } catch (InterruptedException e) {}

        out.println("I'm ready to finish too.");
    }
}

class FirstThread extends Thread
{
    public void run() {
        try {
            MethodTest.out.println("  First thread starts running.");
            sleep(10000);
            MethodTest.out.println("  First thread finishes running.");
        }
        catch (InterruptedException e) {}
    }
}

class SecondThread extends Thread
{
  public void run() {
   MethodTest.out.println("  Second thread starts running.");
   MethodTest.out.println("  Second thread suspends itself.");
   suspend();
   MethodTest.out.println("  Second thread runs again and finishes.");
  }
}
```

The output of this program is shown here:

```
C:\MasteringJava\Ch08>java MethodTest
Waiting for 1st thread to finish...
   First thread starts running.
   Second thread starts running.
   Second thread suspends itself.
   First thread finishes running.
It's a long wait!
Waking up second thread...
Waiting for second thread to finish...
   Second thread runs again and finishes.
I'm ready to finish too.
```

The Thread Life Cycle

Every thread, after creation and before destruction, will always be in one of four states: newly created, runnable, blocked, or dead. These states are illustrated in Figure 8.1 and described in the following sections.

FIGURE 8.1

The thread life cycle

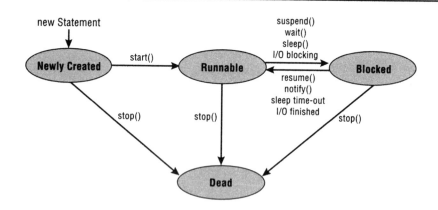

Newly Created Threads

A thread enters the newly created state immediately after creation; that is, right after the thread-creating new statement is executed. In this state, the local data members are allocated and initialized, but execution of the run() method will not begin until its start() method is called. After the start() method is called, the thread will be put into the runnable state.

Runnable Threads

When a thread is in the runnable state, the execution context exists and the thread can be scheduled to run at any time; that is, the thread is not waiting for any event to happen.

For the sake of explanation, this state can be subdivided into two substates: the running and queued states. When a thread is in the running state, it is assigned CPU cycles and is actually running. When a thread is in the queued state, it is waiting in the queue and competing for its turn to spend CPU cycles. The transition between these two substates is controlled by the runtime scheduler. However, a thread can call the yield() method to voluntarily move itself to the queued state from the running state.

Blocked Threads

The blocked state is entered when one of the following events occurs:

- The thread itself or another thread calls the suspend() method.

- The thread calls an object's wait() method.

- The thread itself calls the sleep() method.

- The thread is waiting for some I/O operation to complete.

A thread in a blocked state will not be scheduled for running. It will go back to the runnable state, competing for CPU cycles, when the counter-event for the blocking event occurs:

- If the thread is suspended, another thread calls its resume() method.

- If the thread is blocked by calling an object's wait() method, the object's notify() or notifyAll() method is called.

- If the thread is put to sleep, the specified sleeping time elapses.
- If the thread is blocked on I/O, the specified I/O operation completes.

Dead Threads

The dead state is entered when a thread finishes its execution or is stopped by another thread calling its `stop()` method.

NOTE Under the JDK 1.1 and earlier implementations of the Java runtime on Windows 95 and Solaris 2, `stop()` will be ignored if a thread is created but not yet started.

To find out whether a thread is alive—that is, currently runnable or blocked—use the thread's `isAlive()` method. It will return `true` if the thread is alive. If a thread is alive, it does not mean it is running, just that it can.

Thread Groups

Every thread instance is a member of exactly one thread group. A thread group can have both threads and other thread groups as its members. In fact, every thread group, except the system thread group, is a member of some other thread group. All the threads and thread groups in an application form a tree, with the system thread group as the root.

When a Java application is started, the Java runtime creates the main thread group as a member of the system thread group. A main thread is created in this main thread group to run the `main()` method of the application. By default, all new user-created threads and thread groups will become the members of this main thread group unless another thread group is passed as the first argument of the new statement's constructor method. A new thread group is created by instantiating the ThreadGroup class. For example, the following statements create a thread group named MyThreadGroup as a member of the default main thread group, and then create a thread named MyThread as a member of the newly created thread group:

```
ThreadGroup group = new ThreadGroup("MyThreadGroup");

Thread thread = new Thread(group, "MyThread");
```

Three methods are defined in the ThreadGroup class to manipulate all the threads in the Thread class group and its subthread groups at once: stop(), suspend(), and resume(). These methods have the same functionality as their Thread class method counterparts. They come in handy when you need to, say, suspend all your animation or multimedia threads at a time.

Getting Information about Threads and Thread Groups

There are many methods defined in Thread and ThreadGroup for getting information about threads and thread groups.

Thread Information

The following are some of the most commonly used methods for getting information about threads:

currentThread()   A class method that returns the caller's thread.

getName()   Returns the current name of the thread.

getThreadGroup()   Returns the parent thread group of the thread.

getPriority()   Returns the current priority of the thread.

`isAlive()` Returns `true` if the thread is started but not dead yet.

`isDaemon()` Returns true if the thread is a daemon thread.

Thread Group Information

The following are some of the most commonly used methods for getting information about thread groups:

`getName()` Returns the name of the thread group.

`getParent()` Returns the parent thread group of the thread group.

`getMaxPriority()` Returns the current maximum priority of the thread group.

`activeCount()` Returns the number of active threads in the thread group.

`activeGroupCount()` Returns the number of active thread groups in the thread group.

`enumerate(Thread[] list, boolean recursive)` Adds all the active threads in this thread group into the `list` array. If `recursive` is `true`, all the threads in the subthread groups will be copied over as well. This method will return the number of threads copied. The `activeCount()` method is often used to size the list when the space of this thread array is to be allocated.

`enumerate(ThreadGroup[] list, boolean recursive)` Adds all the active thread groups in this thread group into the `list` array. If `recursive` is `true`, all the thread groups in the subthread groups will be copied over as well. This method will return the number of thread groups copied. The `activeGroupCount()` method is often used to size the list when the space of this thread group array is to be allocated.

Thread priorities and daemon threads will be discussed in later sections.

A Program to Get and Print Thread Information

This section presents an example that uses the methods described in the previous sections to show information about all the threads and thread groups in an application. The program creates a thread group named MyThreadGroup and creates four threads in the thread group. It then continues on to print all the information by calling the printAllThreadInfo() method.

The printAllThreadInfo() method first locates the root thread group of all the running threads and thread groups. It then prints the information about the underlying threads and thread groups recursively from the root. The output is indented to show the depth of individual threads or thread groups in the tree. The full program is as follows:

```java
import java.io.*;
public class ThreadInfo
{
    static PrintWriter out = new PrintWriter(System.out, true);
    public static void main(String[] args) {
        Thread[] threads = new Thread[4];
        ThreadGroup group = new ThreadGroup("MyThreadGroup");

        if (args.length > 0) {
            Thread thread = Thread.currentThread();
            thread.setName(args[0]);
        }

        for (int i = 0; i < 4; i++)
            threads[i] = new Thread(group, "MyThread#" + i);

        ThreadInfo.printAllThreadInfo();
    }

    // list information about all the threads and thread groups
    // in the application

    public static void printAllThreadInfo() {
        ThreadGroup parent, root;
```

```
    // find the root of all running threads

    root = parent = Thread.currentThread().getThreadGroup();
    while ((parent = parent.getParent()) != null)
        root = parent;

    // print information recursively from the root

    out.println();
    printThreadGroupInfo("", root);
}

// print information about a thread group

public static void printThreadGroupInfo(
        String indent, ThreadGroup group)
{
    if (group == null) return;

    out.println(indent +
        "THREAD GROUP: " + group.getName() +
        "; Max Priority: " + group.getMaxPriority() +
        (group.isDaemon() ? " [Daemon]" : ""));

    // print information about component threads

    int no_of_threads = group.activeCount();
    Thread[] threads   = new Thread[no_of_threads];

    no_of_threads = group.enumerate(threads, false);
    for (int i = 0; i < no_of_threads; i++)
        printThreadInfo(indent + "   ", threads[i]);

    // print information about component thread groups

    int no_of_groups   = group.activeGroupCount();
    ThreadGroup[] groups = new ThreadGroup[no_of_groups];

    no_of_groups = group.enumerate(groups, false);
    for (int i = 0; i < no_of_groups; i++)
        printThreadGroupInfo(indent + "   ", groups[i]);
}
```

```
// print information about a single thread

public static void printThreadInfo(String indent,
                                   Thread thread)
{
    if (thread == null) return;

    out.println(indent +
        "THREAD: " + thread.getName() +
        "; Priority: " + thread.getPriority() +
        (thread.isDaemon() ? " [Daemon]" : "") +
        (thread.isAlive() ? " [Alive]" : " [NotAlive]") +
        ((Thread.currentThread() == thread) ? " <== current"
            ""));
}
}
```

The output of the previous program run under Windows 95 is as
follows:

```
C:\MasteringJava\Ch08>java ThreadInfo

THREAD GROUP: system; Max Priority: 10
   THREAD: Finalizer thread; Priority: 1 [Daemon] [Alive]
   THREAD GROUP: main; Max Priority: 10
      THREAD: main; Priority: 5 [Alive] <== current
      THREAD GROUP: MyThreadGroup; Max Priority: 10
         THREAD: MyThread#0; Priority: 5 [NotAlive]
         THREAD: MyThread#1; Priority: 5 [NotAlive]
         THREAD: MyThread#2; Priority: 5 [NotAlive]
         THREAD: MyThread#3; Priority: 5 [NotAlive]
```

The same program run under Solaris 2.5 produces similar output,
as follows:

```
harpoon:/users/hsu/java/examples/ch8> java ThreadInfo

THREAD GROUP: system; Max Priority: 10
   THREAD: clock handler; Priority: 11 [Daemon] [Alive]
   THREAD: Idle thread; Priority: 0 [Daemon] [Alive]
   THREAD: Async Garbage Collector; Priority: 1 [Daemon] [Alive]
   THREAD: Finalizer thread; Priority: 1 [Daemon] [Alive]
```

```
THREAD GROUP: main; Max Priority: 10
   THREAD: main; Priority: 5 [Alive] <== current
   THREAD GROUP: MyThreadGroup; Max Priority: 10
      THREAD: MyThread#0; Priority: 5 [NotAlive]
      THREAD: MyThread#1; Priority: 5 [NotAlive]
      THREAD: MyThread#2; Priority: 5 [NotAlive]
      THREAD: MyThread#3; Priority: 5 [NotAlive]
```

Advanced Multithreading

The following sections introduce some advanced multithreading topics: thread synchronization, interthread communications, thread priorities and scheduling, and daemon threads.

Thread Synchronization

Synchronization is the way to avoid data corruption caused by simultaneous access to the same data. Because all the threads in a program share the same memory space, it is possible for two threads to access the same variable or run the same method of the same object at the same time. Problems may occur when multiple threads are accessing the same data concurrently. Threads may race each other, and one thread may overwrite the data just written by another thread. Or one thread may work on another thread's intermediate result and break the consistency of the data. Some mechanism is needed to block one thread's access to the critical data, if the data is being worked on by another thread.

For example, suppose that you have a program to handle a user's bank account. There are three subtasks in making a deposit for the user:

- Get the current balance from some remote server, which may take as long as five seconds.

- Add the newly deposited amount into the just-acquired balance.

- Send the new balance back to the same remote server, which again may take as long as five seconds to complete.

If two depositing threads, each making a $1,000 deposit, are started roughly at the same time on a current balance of $1,000, the final balance of these two deposits may reflect the result of only one deposit. A possible scenario is depicted in Table 8.1.

TABLE 8.1   Two Depositing Threads Running Concurrently

Time	Thread #1	Thread #2	Balance in Remote Server
a	Getting balance		$1,000
b	Waiting...	Getting balance	$1,000
c	Get balance = $1,000	Waiting...	$1,000
d	Compute new balance = $2,000	Waiting...	$1,000
e	Setting new balance	Waiting...	$1,000
f	Waiting...	Get balance = $1,000	$1,000
g	Waiting...	Compute new balance = $2,000	$1,000
h	Waiting...	Setting new balance	$1,000
i	New balance set	Waiting...	$2,000
j		New balance set	$2,000

The balance stored in the remote server increases by only one deposit amount!

The following sample program simulates the scenario in Table 8.1. An Account class is defined with three methods: getBalance() to fetch the current balance from some pseudo server, with a simulated five-second delay; setBalance() to write back the new balance to the same pseudo-server, with (again) a simulated five-second delay; and deposit() to use the other two methods to complete a deposit transaction. A DepositThread class is declared to start the deposit operation on the account passed in. The main program creates an account instance and then starts two threads to make a deposit of $1,000 each to that account. The full program listing is as follows:

```java
import java.io.*;

class Deposit {
    static int balance = 1000; // simulate balance kept remotely

    public static void main(String[] args) {PrintWriter out =
    new PrintWriter(System.out, true);
        Account account = new Account(out);
        DepositThread first, second;
        first  = new DepositThread(account, 1000, "#1");
        second = new DepositThread(account, 1000, "\t\t\t\t#2");

        // start the transactions

        first.start();
        second.start();

        // wait for both transactions to finish

        try {
            first.join();
            second.join();
        } catch (InterruptedException e) {}

        // print the final balance

        out.println("*** Final balance is " + balance);
    }
}

class Account {

    PrintWriter out;

    Account(PrintWriter out) {
```

```
         this.out = out;
      }

      void deposit(int amount, String name) {
         int balance;

         out.println(name + " trying to deposit " + amount);

         out.println(name + " getting balance...");
         balance = getBalance();
         out.println(name + " balance got is " + balance);

         balance += amount;

         out.println(name + " setting balance...");
         setBalance(balance);
         out.println(name + " new balance set to " +
                        Deposit.balance);
      }

      int getBalance() {
         try {   // simulate the delay in getting balance remotely
            Thread.sleep(5000);
         } catch (InterruptedException e) {}

         return Deposit.balance;
      }

      void setBalance(int balance) {
         try {   // simulate the delay in setting new balance remotely
            Thread.sleep(5000);
         } catch (InterruptedException e) {}

         Deposit.balance = balance;
      }
}
class DepositThread extends Thread {

   Account account;
   int    deposit_amount;
   String  message;
```

```
DepositThread(Account account, int amount, String message)
{
    this.message    = message;
    this.account    = account;
    this.deposit_amount = amount;
}

public void run() {
    account.deposit(deposit_amount, message);
}
}
```

An example of the output of the above program is as follows:

```
C:\MasteringJava\Ch08>java Deposit
#1 trying to deposit 1000
#1 getting balance...
                                    #2 trying to deposit 1000
                                    #2 getting balance...

#1 balance got is 1000
#1 setting balance...
                                    #2 balance got is 1000
                                    #2 setting balance...

#1 new balance set to 2000
                                    #2 new balance set to 2000

*** Final balance is 2000
```

Java's Monitor Model for Synchronization

Java uses the idea of monitors to synchronize access to data. A *monitor* is like a guarded place where all the protected resources have the same locks on them. There is only a single key to all the locks inside a monitor, and a thread must get the key to enter the monitor and access these protected resources. If many threads want to enter the monitor at the same time, only one thread is handed the key; the others must wait outside until the key-holding thread finishes its use of the resources and hands back the key to Java runtime.

Once a thread gets a monitor's key, the thread can access any of the resources controlled by that monitor countless times, as long as the thread still owns the key. However, if this key-holding thread wants to access the resources controlled by another monitor, the thread must get that particular monitor's key. At any time, a thread can hold many monitors' keys. Different threads can hold keys for different monitors at the same time. Deadlock may occur if threads are waiting for each other's key to proceed.

In Java, the resources protected by monitors are program fragments in the form of methods or blocks of statements enclosed in curly braces. If some data can be accessed only through methods or blocks protected by the same monitor, access to the data is indirectly synchronized. The keyword `synchronized` is used to indicate that the following method or block of statements is to be synchronized by a monitor. When a block of statements is to be synchronized, an object instance enclosed in parentheses immediately following the `synchronized` keyword is required so Java runtime knows which monitor to check with.

You can think of a monitor as a guarded parking lot, where all the synchronized methods or blocks are just like cars you can drive (or execute, if you are a thread). All the cars share the same key. You need to get this unique key to enter the parking lot and drive any of the cars until you hand back the key. At that time, one of the persons waiting to get in will get the key and be able to drive the car(s) of his or her choice. This concept is illustrated in Figure 8.2.

FIGURE 8.2

Threads need a unique key to access resources protected by a Java monitor.

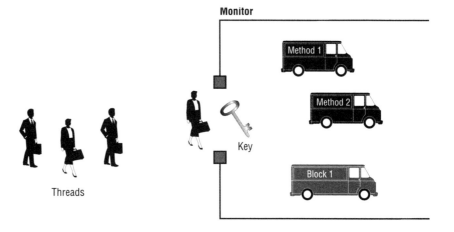

For example, the `deposit()` method in the previous example can be synchronized to allow only one thread to run at a time. The only change needed is a `synchronized` keyword before the method definition, as follows:

```
synchronized void deposit(int amount, String name) {
```

A sample output of the modified program is as follows:

```
#1 trying to deposit 1000
#1 getting balance...
#1 balance got is 1000
#1 setting balance...
#1 new balance set to 2000
                                    #2 trying to deposit 1000
                                    #2 getting balance...
                                    #2 balance got is 2000
                                    #2 setting balance...
                                    #2 new balance set to 3000
*** Final balance is 3000
```

Alternatively, a block of statements in the `deposit()` method can be synchronized on the called object, as follows:

```
void deposit(int amount, String name) {
    int balance;

    out.println(name + " trying to deposit " + amount);

    synchronized (this) {
        out.println(name + " getting balance...");
        balance = getBalance();
        out.println(name + " gets balance = " + balance);

        balance += amount;

        out.println(name + " setting balance...");
        setBalance(balance);
    }

    out.println(name + " set new balance = " + balance);
}
```

The output of this program is almost the same as the previous one, except the first message from the second thread will be interleaved in the messages from the first thread, because the first `println()` method is not inside the synchronized block. Here is an example of the output:

```
#1 trying to deposit 1000
#1 getting balance...
                                 #2 trying to deposit 1000

#1 balance got is 1000
#1 setting balance...
#1 new balance set to 2000
                                 #2 getting balance...
                                 #2 balance got is 2000
                                 #2 setting balance...
                                 #2 new balance set to 3000
*** Final balance is 3000
```

One unique key will be issued to every object containing any synchronized instance method or being referred by any synchronized block. For synchronized class methods, the key is issued to the class because the method may be called before any class instances exist. This means that every object and every class can have a monitor if there are any synchronized methods or blocks of statements associated with it. Furthermore, a class monitor's key is different from any of the keys of its class instance monitors.

Differences in Synchronization Techniques

The next example demonstrates the difference between a synchronized method and a synchronized block and the difference between class-based synchronization and object-based synchronization. Class `SyncToken` contains three methods, all synchronized differently and all calling the `ticker()` method to print out three ticks in random intervals. Class `SyncTestRunner` is a thread class that will choose different methods of class `SyncToken` to run based on the ID given.

The main() method of the SyncTest class will generate ten threads running the tickers with different synchronization schemes so the comparison can be made. The program listing is as follows:

```java
import java.io.*;

class SyncTest {

    static public void main(String[] args) {
        SyncToken token = new SyncToken();
        SyncTestRunner[] runners = new SyncTestRunner[10];

        for (int i = 0; i < 10; i++) {
            runners[i] = new SyncTestRunner(token, i);
            runners[i].start();
        }
    }
}

class SyncTestRunner extends Thread {

    SyncToken token;
    int       id;

    SyncTestRunner(SyncToken token, int id) {
        this.token = token;
        this.id    = id;
    }

    public void run() {
        switch (id % 3) {
            case 0:
                SyncToken.class_ticker("\t\t\tClass #" + id, token);
                break;
            case 1:
                token.method_ticker("Method #" + id);
                break;
            case 2:
                token.block_ticker ("Block  #" + id);
                break;
        }
    }
}
```

```
        }
    }

class SyncToken {
    PrintWriter out = new PrintWriter(System.out, true);


    //  the ticker method: give three ticks in random interval

    void ticker(String message) {
        for (int i = 0; i < 3; i++) {
            try {
                Thread.sleep((int) (800 * Math.random()));
            } catch (InterruptedException e) {}
            out.println(message + ", tick #" + i);
        }
    }

    // class-based synchronization

    static synchronized void class_ticker(String message,
                              SyncToken token) {
        token.ticker(message);
    }

    // object-based synchronization: synchronized block

    void block_ticker(String message) {
        synchronized(this) {
            ticker(message);
        }
    }

    // object-based synchronization: synchronized method

    synchronized void method_ticker(String message) {
        ticker(message);
    }
}
```

The output of this program is as follows:

```
Method #1, tick #0
                          Class #0, tick #0
Method #1, tick #1
Method #1, tick #2
Block   #2, tick #0
                          Class #0, tick #1
                          Class #0, tick #2
Block   #2, tick #1
                          Class #3, tick #0
Block   #2, tick #2
                          Class #3, tick #1
Method #4, tick #0
                          Class #3, tick #2
Method #4, tick #1
                          Class #6, tick #0
                          Class #6, tick #1
Method #4, tick #2
                          Class #6, tick #2
Block   #5, tick #0
                          Class #9, tick #0
Block   #5, tick #1
Block   #5, tick #2
                          Class #9, tick #1
Block   #8, tick #0
Block   #8, tick #1
                          Class #9, tick #2
Block   #8, tick #2
Method #7, tick #0
Method #7, tick #1
Method #7, tick #2
```

You can see that object-based synchronized methods and synchronized blocks share the same monitor key if they are for the same object. Also, class-based synchronization and object-based synchronization do use different keys, because their output interleaves each other.

Synchronization is an expensive operation, and the use of it should be kept to a minimum, especially for frequently executed methods or blocks of statements. However, synchronization can help reduce the interference among different threads. Good use of it will definitely improve the stability and robustness of the program.

Interthread Communications

Interthread communications allow threads to talk to or wait for each other. You can have threads communicate with each other through shared data or by using thread-control methods to have threads wait for each other.

Threads Sharing Data

All the threads in the same program share the same memory space. If the reference to an object is visible to different threads by the syntactic rules of scopes, or explicitly passed to different threads, these threads share access to that object's data members. As explained in the previous section, synchronization is sometimes needed to enforce exclusive access to the data to avoid racing conditions and data corruption.

Threads Waiting for Other Threads

By using thread-control methods, you can have threads communicate by waiting for each other. For example, the `join()` method can be used for the caller thread to wait for the completion of the called thread. Also, a thread can suspend itself and wait at a rendezvous point using the `suspend()` method; another thread can wake it up through the waiting thread's `resume()` method, and both threads can run concurrently thereafter.

Deadlock may occur when a thread holding the key to a monitor is suspended or waiting for another thread's completion. If the other thread it is waiting for needs to get into the same monitor, both threads will be waiting forever. The `wait()`, `notify()`, and `notifyAll()` methods defined in class `Object` of the `java.lang` package can be used to solve this problem.

The `wait()` method will make the calling thread wait until either a timeout occurs or another thread calls the same object's `notify()` or `notifyAll()` method. The synopsis of the `wait()` method is:

```
wait()
```

or

```
wait(long timeout_period_in_milliseconds)
```

The former will wait until the thread is notified. The latter will wait until either the specified timeout expires or the thread is notified, whichever comes first.

When a thread calls the `wait()` method, the key it is holding will be released for another waiting thread to enter the monitor. The `notify()` method will wake up only one waiting thread, if any. The `notifyAll()` method will wake up all the threads that have been waiting in the monitor. After being notified, the thread will try to reenter the monitor by requesting the key again and may need to wait for another thread to release the key.

Note that these methods can be called only within a monitor. The thread calling an object's `notify()` or `notifyAll()` method needs to own the key to that object's monitor; otherwise, `IllegalMonitor-StateException`, a type of `RuntimeException`, will be thrown.

The next example demonstrates the use of the `wait()` and `notify()` methods to solve the classical producer and consumer problem. In this problem, the producer will generate data for the consumer to consume. However, if the producer produces data faster than the consumer can consume, the newly created data may be overwritten before it is consumed. On the other hand, if the consumer consumes faster than the producer can produce, the consumer may keep using already processed data. Synchronization alone will not solve the problem, because it only guarantees exclusive access to the data, not availability.

The first implementation uses a monitor, an instance of the NoWaitMonitor class, to control the access to the data, token. The producer and consumer will set and get, respectively, the token value in random intervals, with the maximum interval length regulated by the speed argument passed to their constructors. The main program accepts up to two command-line arguments for setting the producing and consuming speed, creates an instance of the monitor, creates a producer and a consumer, and watches them run for ten seconds. The program is listed as follows:

```java
import java.io.*;

class NoWaitPandC {

    static int produce_speed = 200;
    static int consume_speed = 200;

    public static void main(String[] args) {
        if (args.length > 0)
            produce_speed = Integer.parseInt(args[0]);
        if (args.length > 1)
            consume_speed = Integer.parseInt(args[1]);

        NoWaitMonitor monitor = new NoWaitMonitor();
        new NoWaitProducer(monitor, produce_speed);
        new NoWaitConsumer(monitor, consume_speed);

        try {
            Thread.sleep(1000);
        } catch (InterruptedException e) { }

        System.exit(0);
    }
}
class NoWaitMonitor
{
    int token = -1;
    PrintWriter out = new
        PrintWriter(System.out, true);
```

```java
      // get token value

      synchronized int get () {
         out.println("Got: " + token);

         return token;
      }

      // put token value

      synchronized void set(int value) {
         token = value;

         out.println("Set: " + token);
      }
   }
class NoWaitProducer implements Runnable {

   NoWaitMonitor monitor;
   int    speed;

   NoWaitProducer(NoWaitMonitor monitor, int speed) {
      this.monitor = monitor;
      this.speed = speed;
      new Thread(this, "Producer").start();
   }

   public void run() {
      int i = 0;

      while (true) {
         monitor.set(i++);
         try {
           Thread.sleep((int) (Math.random() * speed));
         } catch (InterruptedException e) {}
      }
   }
}


class NoWaitConsumer implements Runnable {
```

```
NoWaitMonitor monitor;
int    speed;

NoWaitConsumer(NoWaitMonitor monitor, int speed) {
    this.monitor = monitor;
    this.speed = speed;
    new Thread(this, "Consumer").start();
}

public void run() {
    while (true) {
        monitor.get();
        try {
            Thread.sleep((int) (Math.random() * speed));
        } catch (InterruptedException e) {}
    }
}
}
```

Here is an example of the output of the program where the producer outpaces the consumer:

```
C:\MasteringJava\Ch08>java NoWaitPandC 100 400
Set: 0
Got: 0
Set: 1
Set: 2
Set: 3
Set: 4
Got: 4
Set: 5
Set: 6
Set: 7
Set: 8
Set: 9
Set: 10
Got: 10
Set: 11
Set: 12
```

You can see there is a lot of data generated (shown as Set) but overwritten before it is processed (shown as Got).

Here is an example of the program's output where the consumer is faster than the producer:

```
C:\MasteringJava\Ch08>java NoWaitPandC 400 100
Set: 0
Got: 0
Got: 0
Got: 0
Got: 0
Got: 0
Got: 0
Set: 1
Set: 2
Got: 2
Set: 3
Got: 3
Got: 3
Got: 3
Got: 3
Got: 3
Set: 4
Got: 4
Got: 4
Got: 4
Got: 4
Got: 4
```

This time, some of the data is processed multiple times.

The second implementation of the sample program uses the wait() and notify() methods to make sure all data is created and used exactly once. The program is the same as the previous one, except for the implementation of the monitor. A boolean variable, value_set, is added to indicate whether the data is ready for consumption or already used. The get() method will first test if the data is ready for consumption. If not, the calling thread will wait until some other thread sets the data and notifies the current thread. The boolean variable is then set to indicate that the data is consumed. Any thread waiting to produce new data will then be notified to start the production. If there is no thread waiting to produce, the `notify()` method will be ignored. The `get()` method is shown here:

```
synchronized int get() {
    if (! value_set)
        try {
            wait();
        } catch (InterruptedException e) { }

    value_set = false;

    out.println("Got: " + token);

    notify();

    return token;
}
```

Symmetrically, the `set()` method will first test whether the data is already used. If not, the calling thread will wait until some other thread uses the data and notifies the current thread. The boolean variable is then set to indicate that the data is ready for consumption. Any thread waiting to consume the data will then be notified to start the consumption. If there is no thread waiting, the `notify()` method will be ignored. The `set()` method is shown here:

```
synchronized void set(int value) {
    if (value_set)
        try {
            wait();
        } catch (InterruptedException e) { }

    value_set = true;

    token = value;

    out.println("Set: " + token);

    notify();
}
```

The full program listing is shown here:

```java
import java.io.*;

class PandC {

    static int produce_speed = 200;
    static int consume_speed = 200;

    public static void main(String[] args) {
        if (args.length > 0)
            produce_speed = Integer.parseInt(args[0]);
        if (args.length > 1)
            consume_speed = Integer.parseInt(args[1]);

        Monitor monitor = new Monitor();
        new Producer(monitor, produce_speed);
        new Consumer(monitor, consume_speed);

        try {
            Thread.sleep(1000);
        } catch (InterruptedException e) { }

        System.exit(0);
    }
}

class Monitor
{
    PrintWriter out =
        new PrintWriter(System.out, true);
    int token;
    boolean value_set = false;

    //    get token value

    synchronized int get () {
        if (! value_set)
            try {
                wait();
            } catch (InterruptedException e) { }

        value_set = false;
```

```
        out.println("Got: " + token);

        notify();

        return token;
    }

    // set token value

    synchronized void set(int value) {
        if (value_set)
            try {
                wait();
            } catch (InterruptedException e) { }

        value_set = true;

        token = value;

        out.println("Set: " + token);

        notify();
    }
}

class Producer implements Runnable {

    Monitor monitor;
    int   speed;

    Producer(Monitor monitor, int speed) {
        this.monitor = monitor;
        this.speed = speed;
        new Thread(this, "Producer").start();
    }

    public void run() {
        int i = 0;

        while (true) {
            monitor.set(i++);
            try {
```

```
                    Thread.sleep((int) (Math.random() * speed));
            } catch (InterruptedException e) {}
        }
    }
}

class Consumer implements Runnable {

    Monitor monitor;
    int   speed;

    Consumer(Monitor monitor, int speed) {
        this.monitor = monitor;
        this.speed = speed;
        new Thread(this, "Consumer").start();
    }

    public void run() {
        while (true) {
            monitor.get();
            try {
                Thread.sleep((int) (Math.random() * speed));
            } catch (InterruptedException e) {}
        }
    }
}
```

Here is an example of the output of this program:

```
C:\MasteringJava\Ch08>java PandC 400 100
Set: 0
Got: 0
Set: 1
Got: 1
Set: 2
Got: 2
Set: 3
Got: 3
Set: 4
Got: 4
```

This time, every piece of data generated is consumed exactly once.

Priorities and Scheduling

Priorities are the way to make sure important or time-critical threads are executed frequently or immediately. *Scheduling* is the means to make sure priorities and fairness are enforced.

If you have only one CPU, all of the runnable threads must take turns being executed. Scheduling is the activity of determining the execution order of multiple threads.

Thread Priority Values

Every thread in Java is assigned a priority value. When more than one thread is competing for CPU time, the thread with the highest priority value is given preference. Thread priority values that can be assigned to user-created threads are simple integers ranging between `Thread.MIN_PRIORITY` and `Thread.MAX_PRIORITY`. User applications are normally run with the priority value of `Thread.NORM_PRIORITY`. Up to JDK 1.1, these constants—MIN_ PRIORITY, MAX_PRIORITY, and NORM_PRIORITY—of the `Thread` class have the values of 1, 10, and 5, respectively. Every thread group has a maximum priority value assigned. This is a cap to the priority values of member threads and thread groups when they are created or want to change their priority values.

When a thread is created, it will inherit the priority value of the creating thread if the priority value doesn't exceed the limit imposed by its parent thread group. The `setPriority()` method of `Thread` class can be used to set the priority value of a thread. If the value to be set is outside the legal range, an `IllegalArgumentException` will be thrown. If the value is larger than the maximum priority value of its parent thread group, the maximum priority value will be used.

The `setMaxPriority()` method of class `ThreadGroup` can be used to set the maximum priority value of a thread group. For security reasons (so that a user-created thread will not monopolize the CPU), a Web browser may not allow an applet to change its priority.

Preemptive Scheduling and Time-Slicing

Java's scheduling is *preemptive*; that is, if a thread with a higher priority than the currently running thread becomes runnable, the higher priority thread will be executed immediately, pushing the currently running thread back to the queue to wait for its next turn. A thread can voluntarily pass the CPU execution privilege to waiting threads of the same priority by calling the `yield()` method.

In some implementations, thread execution is *time-sliced*; that is, threads with equal priority values will have equal opportunities to run in a round-robin manner. Even threads with lower priority will still get a small portion of the execution time slots, roughly proportional to their priority values. Therefore, no threads will be starving in the long run.

Other implementations do not have time-slicing. A thread will relinquish its control only when it finishes its execution, is preempted by a higher-priority thread, or is blocked by I/O operations or the `sleep()`, `wait()`, or `suspend()` method calls. For computation-intensive threads, it is a good idea to occasionally call the `yield()` method to give other threads a chance to run. It may improve the overall interactive responsiveness of graphical user interfaces.

NOTE Up to JDK 1.1, Java runtime for Windows 95 and NT is time-sliced; Java runtime for Solaris 2 is not time-sliced.

Scheduling Threads with Different Priorities

The next example demonstrates the effect of scheduling on threads with different priorities. The main program will accept an optional command-line argument to indicate whether the threads created will yield to each other regularly.

The main program starts four threads with priority values of 1, 2, 4, and 4, respectively. Each thread will increment its counter 600,001 times and optionally yield to threads with equal priority on every three-thousandth increment. Because the main thread has a higher priority value, 5, than these computation-intensive threads, the main thread may grab the CPU every 0.3 second to print the counter values of these four computing threads. The program is listed as follows:

```java
import java.io.*;

class PriorityTest {

    static int    NO_OF_THREADS = 4;
    static boolean yield = true;
    static int[]   counter = new int[NO_OF_THREADS];

    public static void main(String[] args) {
        PrintWriter out =
            new PrintWriter(System.out, true);
        int no_of_intervals = 10;

        if (args.length > 0)
            yield = false;

        out.println("Using yield()? " + (yield ? "YES" : "NO"));

        for (int i = 0; i < NO_OF_THREADS; i++)
            (new PrTestThread((i > 1) ? 4 : (i + 1), i)).start();

        ThreadInfo.printAllThreadInfo();
        out.println();

        //   repeatedly print out the counter values
        int step = 0;
        while (true) {
            boolean all_done = true;
```

```
        try {
           Thread.sleep(300);
        }
        catch (InterruptedException e) {}

        out.print("Step " + (step++) + ": COUNTERS:");
        for (int j = 0; j < NO_OF_THREADS; j++) {
           out.print(" " + counter[j]);
           if (counter[j] < 600000)
              all_done = false;
        }
        out.println();

        if (all_done)
           break;
     }

     System.exit(0);
  }
}

class PrTestThread extends Thread {

   int  id;

   PrTestThread(int priority, int id) {
      super("PrTestThread#" + id);
         this.id = id;
         setPriority(priority);
   }

   public void run() {
      for (int i = 0; i < 600001; i++) {
         if (((i % 3000) == 0) && PriorityTest.yield)
            yield();
         PriorityTest.counter[id] = i;
      }
   }
}
```

Here is an example of the output when the program is run on a time-sliced system (Windows 95), with the computing threads frequently yielding to each other:

```
C:\MasteringJava\Ch08>java PriorityTest
Using yield()? YES

THREAD GROUP: system; Max Priority: 10
    THREAD: Finalizer thread; Priority: 1 [Daemon] [Alive]
    THREAD GROUP: main; Max Priority: 10
        THREAD: main; Priority: 5 [Alive] <== current
        THREAD: PrTestThread#0; Priority: 1 [Alive]
        THREAD: PrTestThread#1; Priority: 2 [Alive]
        THREAD: PrTestThread#0; Priority: 4 [Alive]
        THREAD: PrTestThread#1; Priority: 4 [Alive]

Step 0: COUNTERS: 0 2999 98999 89999
Step 1: COUNTERS: 2999 8999 224999 221999
Step 2: COUNTERS: 11999 17999 347999 347999
Step 3: COUNTERS: 14999 26999 473999 476999
Step 4: COUNTERS: 20999 43011 600000 600000
Step 5: COUNTERS: 38999 289258 600000 600000
Step 6: COUNTERS: 56999 535929 600000 600000
Step 7: COUNTERS: 256657 600000 600000 600000
Step 8: COUNTERS: 522386 600000 600000 600000
Step 9: COUNTERS: 600000 600000 600000 600000
```

From the output, you can see that threads with lower-priority values still get small portions of CPU time, and the two threads with the highest priority get roughly equal portions of CPU time.

Here is an example of the output when the same program is run on Java runtime, with no time-slicing and, again, the threads yielding to each other regularly.

```
harpoon:/users/hsu/java/examples/ch8> java PriorityTest
Using yield()? YES

THREAD GROUP: system; Max Priority: 10
    THREAD: clock handler; Priority: 11 [Daemon] [Alive]
```

```
THREAD: Idle thread; Priority: 0 [Daemon] [Alive]
THREAD: Async Garbage Collector; Priority: 1 [Daemon]
        [Alive]
THREAD: Finalizer thread; Priority: 1 [Daemon] [Alive]
THREAD GROUP: main; Max Priority: 10
    THREAD: main; Priority: 5 [Alive] <== current
    THREAD: PrTestThread#0; Priority: 1 [Alive]
    THREAD: PrTestThread#1; Priority: 2 [Alive]
    THREAD: PrTestThread#0; Priority: 4 [Alive]
    THREAD: PrTestThread#1; Priority: 4 [Alive]

Step 0: COUNTERS: 0 0 103563 101999
Step 1: COUNTERS: 0 0 206999 208476
Step 2: COUNTERS: 0 0 314999 312189
Step 3: COUNTERS: 0 0 419999 416889
Step 4: COUNTERS: 0 0 527999 520335
Step 5: COUNTERS: 0 67070 600000 600000
Step 6: COUNTERS: 0 295645 600000 600000
Step 7: COUNTERS: 0 521522 600000 600000
Step 8: COUNTERS: 145375 600000 600000 600000
Step 9: COUNTERS: 374097 600000 600000 600000
Step 10: COUNTERS: 515023 600000 600000 600000
Step 11: COUNTERS: 600000 600000 600000 600000
```

From the output, it is obvious that lower-priority threads do not have any chance to run until all the higher-priority threads finish their execution.

Here is the output when the same program is run on a time-sliced system with no yielding:

```
C:\MasteringJava\Ch08>java PriorityTest 0
Using yield()? NO

THREAD GROUP: system; Max Priority: 10
    THREAD: Finalizer thread; Priority: 1 [Daemon] [Alive]
    THREAD GROUP: main; Max Priority: 10
        THREAD: main; Priority: 5 [Alive] <== current
        THREAD: PrTestThread#0; Priority: 1 [Alive]
        THREAD: PrTestThread#1; Priority: 2 [Alive]
        THREAD: PrTestThread#0; Priority: 4 [Alive]
        THREAD: PrTestThread#1; Priority: 4 [Alive]
```

```
Step 0: COUNTERS: 15236 37419 282994 213847
Step 1: COUNTERS: 26765 54548 375313 299946
Step 2: COUNTERS: 30711 72722 501015 416601
Step 3: COUNTERS: 49419 99759 600000 533904
Step 4: COUNTERS: 74398 267193 600000 600000
Step 5: COUNTERS: 110608 497597 600000 600000
Step 6: COUNTERS: 272488 600000 600000 600000
Step 7: COUNTERS: 539175 600000 600000 600000
Step 8: COUNTERS: 600000 600000 600000 600000
```

NOTE Running the program on a different operating system may generate a different pattern of output. You are at the mercy of the scheduling algorithm of either the operating system and/or the particular porting of the JDK.

Interestingly, the lower-priority threads get more chances to run than in the previous run with yielding. This is probably because yielding disturbs the scheduler's original plan to execute lower-priority threads by forcing the scheduler to look for threads with equal priority first. With no yielding, all the schedules for lower-priority threads can be smoothly exercised.

Finally, the program is run with no yielding on an implementation with no time-slicing:

```
harpoon:/users/hsu/java/examples/ch8> java PriorityTest 0
Using yield()? NO

THREAD GROUP: system; Max Priority: 10
    THREAD: clock handler; Priority: 11 [Daemon] [Alive]
    THREAD: Idle thread; Priority: 0 [Daemon] [Alive]
    THREAD: Async Garbage Collector; Priority: 1 [Daemon]
           [Alive]
    THREAD: Finalizer thread; Priority: 1 [Daemon] [Alive]
    THREAD GROUP: main; Max Priority: 10
        THREAD: main; Priority: 5 [Alive] <== current
        THREAD: PrTestThread#0; Priority: 1 [Alive]
```

```
THREAD: PrTestThread#1; Priority: 2 [Alive]
THREAD: PrTestThread#2; Priority: 4 [Alive]
THREAD: PrTestThread#3; Priority: 4 [Alive]

Step 0: COUNTERS: 0 0 203552 0
Step 1: COUNTERS: 0 0 203552 210978
Step 2: COUNTERS: 0 0 413376 210978
Step 3: COUNTERS: 0 0 413376 422790
Step 4: COUNTERS: 0 0 600000 444539
Step 5: COUNTERS: 0 57353 600000 600000
Step 6: COUNTERS: 0 272848 600000 600000
Step 7: COUNTERS: 0 488745 600000 600000
Step 8: COUNTERS: 100596 600000 600000 600000
Step 9: COUNTERS: 314749 600000 600000 600000
Step 10: COUNTERS: 587513 600000 600000 600000
Step 11: COUNTERS: 600000 600000 600000 600000
```

The lower-priority threads have no chance to run until all the higher-priority threads finish. Even threads with equal priority values do not have the chance to run until the main thread preempts the running thread. When a thread is preempted, it will be put to the end of the waiting queue. When the main thread relinquishes program control after printing the counter values, the previously waiting thread that is ahead in the queue will get the chance to run. You can see proof of this in the output listing—only one of the highest-priority threads advances its counter between each printing.

Daemon Threads

Daemon threads are service threads. They exist to provide services to other threads. They normally enter an endless loop waiting for clients requesting services. When all the active threads remaining are daemon threads, Java runtime will exit.

For example, a timer thread that wakes up in regular intervals is a good candidate for daemon threads. This timer thread can notify other threads regularly about the timeouts. When no other thread is running, there is no need for the timer thread's existence.

To create a daemon thread, call the `setDaemon()` method immediately after the thread's creation and before the execution is started. The constructor of the thread is a good candidate for making this method call. By default, all the threads created by a daemon thread are also daemon threads. The synopsis of the `setDaemon()` method is:

```
setDaemon(boolean is_daemon)
```

When *is_daemon* is `true`, the thread is marked as a daemon thread; otherwise, it is marked as a non-daemon thread.

Summary

A thread is a single line of execution within a program. Multiple threads can run concurrently in a single program. A thread is created by either subclassing the `Thread` class or implementing the `Runnable` interface. In either case, a public `run()` method is defined as the thread body to be run in the newly created execution context when the thread's `start()` method is called. In addition to the `start()` method, there are `stop()`, `suspend()`, `resume()`, `join()`, `yield()`, and `sleep()` methods defined in the `Thread` class to control the execution of a thread.

Any thread that has not been destroyed yet is always in one of four states: newly created, runnable, blocked, or dead. When the state of a thread is changed into the blocked state by I/O blocking or a call to the `suspend()`, `wait()`, or `sleep()` method, a counter-event of the event putting the thread into the blocked state will move the thread back to the runnable state. These counter-events are I/O being finished for I/O blocking, the `resume()` method being called for a `suspend()` method call, the `notify()` or `notifyAll()` method being called for the `wait()` method call, and a timeout occurring for the `sleep()` method call.

Every thread is the member of exactly one thread group. Thread groups can be nested. All the threads and thread groups in a program form a tree with the system thread group as the root. The `stop()`, `suspend()`, and `resume()` methods are defined in class `ThreadGroup` to allow for manipulating all the threads inside a thread group by a single method call. There are abundant methods defined in the `Thread` and `ThreadGroup` classes to get the information about a thread or a thread group.

Synchronization is a way of avoiding data corruption caused by simultaneous access to the same data. In Java, synchronization is implemented by the monitor model. A monitor is a guarded place for methods and blocks of statements. Only one thread is allowed in a monitor at a time. Every object can become a monitor if there are synchronized instance methods defined in the class the object is instantiated from, or synchronized blocks of statements that refer to the object. The `wait()` method is used inside a monitor for a thread to wait for another thread to call the called object's `notify()` or `notifyAll()` method.

Every thread has a priority value associated with it. In the event of multiple threads competing for execution, the thread with the highest priority is preferred. Java's scheduling is preemptive; that is, a higher-priority thread will preempt the lower-priority running thread and be executed immediately.

A daemon thread is a service thread. When all the active threads remaining are daemon threads, Java runtime will exit. A thread is marked as a daemon thread by calling the `setDaemon()` method.

Multithreading allows for multiple lines of execution at the same time. Multiple threads running concurrently can not only improve the utilization of resources, but also open the door for easier and creative programming of multimedia or animation effects. Having the threading capability defined in the language will definitely encourage the creation of multithreaded programs. You can expect to see more and more multithreaded applets on the Web, enriching your Web-surfing experiences.

PART II

Applying Standard
Java Classes

C H A P T E R

N I N E

9

Standard Java Packages

- ■ **Package** `java.lang`

- ■ **Package** `java.util`

- ■ **Package** `java.io`

- ■ **Package** `java.awt`

- ■ **Package** `java.awt.image`

- ■ **Package** `java.net`

- ■ **Package** `java.applet`

- ■ **Advanced programming packages**

This chapter introduces the Java packages, focusing on the seven that are most commonly used. But before learning about the individual packages, you will see how these package relate to Java's class hierarchy.

Java Packages and the Class Hierarchy

Java has been object-oriented from day one. And as befits real object-oriented languages, as opposed to object-oriented procedural hybrids like C++, it comes with a standard set of support classes. These classes are very different from the familiar libraries that accompanied procedural languages like C or Pascal. Java's support classes transcend simple libraries, because they exploit the full potential of every object-oriented language. Class inheritance is by far the most common and most powerful feature used. (See Chapters 3 and 5 for more informaton about class inheritance.)

The entire Java hierarchy can be viewed from two organizational angles: as an object-oriented inheritance hierarchy and as groups of classes in packages. The inheritance hierarchy groups classes that share common implementation aspects (that is, code and/or variables). Java packages simply collect classes on a more pragmatic basis: Classes with related functionality are bundled together in the same package, whether they share code or data or not. In addition to their obvious structuring benefits, packages use namespace partitioning, which means that every class contained in a package has a unique name that cannot conflict (collide) with class names defined elsewhere.For example, two companies could safely sell code for classes with identical names. A bubble-sorting class from Mango Macrosystems might be called `mango.utilities.Bubble`, while a similar product from Sun-So-Soft Inc. might be called `sosoft.utils.Bubble`. The class names are the same, but Java uses the package names and sub-package names to distinguish one class from another.

The language's strict single inheritance scheme determines the way Java's standard classes relate to one another in terms of object-oriented inheritance. The resulting inheritance tree is, therefore, a pure tree, and not a graph, as is the case with multiple inheritance object-oriented hierarchies. Multiple inheritance of sorts is employed within the Java classes by using the language's powerful interface mechanism (discussed in Chapter 5).

Since packages give you an easy handle on the entire hierarchy, they will now be your guides as you explore the Java class hierarchy. There are 23 packages in the Java 1.1 release. This chapter examines the 7 most commonly used packages:

- Package `java.lang` contains the main language support classes. These deal with object wrappers, strings, multithreading, and related areas.

- Package `java.util` contains language support classes of a more utilitarian nature. These include linked list, stack, and hashtable classes, as well as some useful abstract designs codified by the interfaces `Enumeration` and `Observer`.

- Package `java.io` provides device-independent file and stream input and output services.

- Package `java.awt` hides the bulk of all standard classes. Because it contains Java's Abstract Window Toolkit (AWT), the package should really be considered as the heart of the entire hierarchy.

- Package `java.awt.image` contains classes related to image processing.

- Package `java.net` combines the classes supporting low-level Internet programming plus World Wide Web/HTML support.

- Package `java.applet` contains a single class with support for HTML embedded Java applets.

Multiple Inheritance versus Single Inheritance

Multiple inheritance is a mechanism that allows one class to inherit from more than one superclass. This has the net effect of mixing the characteristics of those classes into the new class.

Multiple inheritance was introduced to solve single inheritance's straightjacket effect. For example, say that you have a single inheritance hierarchy branching into two fundamental subtrees, `Living` and `InAnimate`. From `Living` grows the successive subclass branch `Plant–FruitTree–Banana`. The `InAnimate` branch could have a `Valuable–Food` subbranch. Now `Food` might quite understandably want to have `Banana` as its subclass as well. Single inheritance does not let you have both. Class `Banana` is either a `FruitTree` or a `Food`; it can inherit from only one superclass hierarchy, not two (or more). The single inheritance tree shown below illustrates the limitations of pure single inheritance.

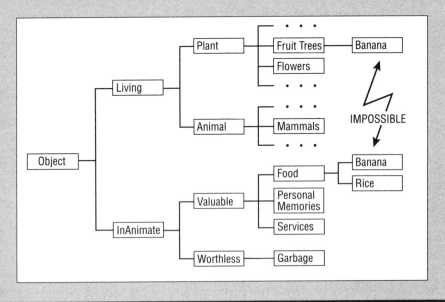

Package java.lang—Main Language Support

The java.lang package inheritance tree is shown in Figure 9.1. As you can judge from the shape of the tree, this collection of classes is flat and shallow. Apart from the Number subhierarchy, all classes are equals within this hierarchy. The majority of java.lang classes extend class Object directly, which is the root for the entire Java class hierarchy, not just the root for java.lang.

NOTE
In Figure 9.1 and the other inheritance hierarchy diagrams shown for packages in this chapter, rectangular boxes denote ordinary classes, and shaded ellipses denote abstract superclasses. A class that implements an interface is marked with an "is a" tag. Each tree is arranged by complexity and frequency of use. The topmost classes are easy to use and/or frequently used.

FIGURE 9.1

Package java.lang inheritance tree

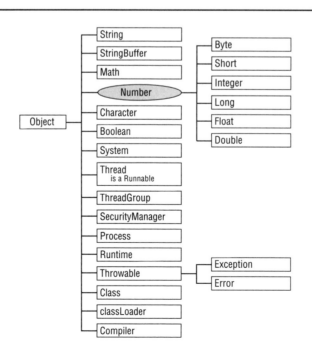

The Number subhierarchy is a good example of how object-oriented inheritance works and when to apply it. Classes Byte, Short, Integer, Long, Float, and Double have things in common, so a superclass was created to hold (encapsulate) these shared traits. Note that class Number is also declared abstract. You cannot make (instantiate) objects directly from an abstract class—you can do this from only concrete classes. Although having an abstract parent class (superclass) is common, it is by no means necessary. Concrete classes can be the local roots of entire subhierarchies (class Object is a prime example).

Of all the packages, package java.lang is exceptional, because it is the only package that you never need to explicitly import in your programs. The compiler implicitly does so by adding the following line at the top of all your source files:

```
import java.lang.*;
```

The asterisk in this line means that all of the package's classes are imported.

Package java.lang gets special treatment because some of its classes are so low-level that they are considered part of the language proper. The dividing line between language and external libraries might be important to language designers, but to application programmers the difference is mostly academic. BASIC, for example, has its string-manipulation commands defined as part of the language definition. C, on the other hand, relies instead on an external (and internationally recognized) standard library of functions to accomplish those tasks. Since Java adheres more to the C philosophy of keeping a language core as simple as possible, it too relies on an external collection of methods for anything beyond the simplest data processing or algorithmic control.

The following types of classes are contained in package java.lang:

- Type wrapper classes

- String support classes

- A math library class

- Multithreading support classes

- A low-level system-access class

- Exrror and exception classes

The following sections look at these classes in more detail.

The Type Wrapper Classes

Java deals with two different types of entities: primitive types and true objects. Numbers, booleans, and characters behave very much like the familiar equivalents of procedural languages such as Pascal, C, or even C++. Other object-oriented languages, like Smalltalk, do not handle these primitive types in the same way. Smalltalk, for example, uses objects for everything—numbers are objects, booleans are objects, characters are objects, and so on.

NOTE Although the Smalltalk language originated in an era when the punched card ruled the world (1972), it still manages to be the reference by which new object-oriented languages are judged. Every object-oriented language since has tried to improve on Smalltalk, but most barely manage to equal it. Viewed purely as an object-oriented language, Java comes very close indeed.

Although Java is truly object-oriented, it does not use objects for the most primitive types for the usual reason: performance. Manipulating primitive types without any object-oriented overhead is quite a bit more efficient. On the other hand, a uniform and consistent playing field, made up of only objects, is simpler and can be significantly more powerful.

Java contains many subsystems that can work only with objects. With many of these subsystems, the need frequently arises to have the system handle numbers or flags (booleans) or characters. How does Java get around this dilemma? By wrapping the primitive types up in some object sugar coating. You can easily create a class, for example, for the sole purpose of encapsulating a single integer. The net effect would be to obtain an integer object, giving you the universality and power that comes with dealing with only objects (at the cost of some performance degradation).

Package `java.lang`, contains such "type wrapper" classes for every Java primitive type:

- Class `Integer` for primitive type `int`
- Class `Long` for primitive type `long`
- Class `Byte` for primitive type `byte`
- Class `Short` for primitive type `short`
- Class `Float` for primitive type `float`
- Class `Double` for primitive type `double`
- Class `Character` for primitive type `char`
- Class `Boolean` for primitive type `boolean`

Among the numeric types, classes `Integer`, `Long`, `Byte`, `Short`, `Float`, and `Double` are so similar that they all descend from an abstract superclass called `Number`. Essentially, every one of these classes allows you to create an object from the equivalent primitive type, and vice versa.

The String Classes

There are two string-support classes in `java.lang`: `String` and `StringBuffer`. Class `String` supports "read-only" strings. Class `StringBuffer` supports modifiable strings. Although both classes obviously have a few things in common, they are unrelated, in that neither inherits from a common "string" superclass.

Class `String` contains the following core functionality:

- String length function
- Substring extraction
- Substring finding and matching
- String comparison
- Uppercase and lowercase conversion
- Leading and trailing whitespace elimination
- Conversion to and from `char` arrays
- Conversion from primitive types to `String` type
- Appending strings (converted from any type, including objects)
- Inserting strings (again converted from any type)

The conversion and whitespace-stripping methods might seem contradictory in view of the read-only nature of `String` strings. This is true, but class `String` does not break its own rules. During these operations, `String` creates brand new read-only strings from the old ones, which it unceremoniously discards in the process. Class `StringBuffer`, on the other hand, concentrates on operations that typically modify the string or change its length.

The Multithreading Support Classes

Two classes, `Thread` and `ThreadGroup`, are the gateways to adding multithreaded behavior in your applications or applets. Multithreading amounts to having a multitasking operating system within your own application. Several program threads can execute in parallel and at the same time.

Similar to how a multitasking operating system is more powerful and flexible than a single-tasking operating system, users greatly benefit from multithreaded applications. For example, a printing command can be handled in the background; repaginating a long document can be done while the user carries on editing that same document; and so on. Java is one of the rarer languages that provides multithreading from within the language itself (Ada is another example; C, C++, LISP, Pascal, and BASIC all lack built-in multithreading support).

The `java.lang` class `Thread` is the more important class of the two. It provides a collection of methods that allows you to perform the following tasks:

- Create new threads. This lets your applications spread independent jobs over several internal "subprograms." Overall application performance increases when several of these threads need to do I/O operations.

- Kill a thread. When a thread has completed its job, or when a thread goes crazy due to a bug, you need to kill it. This returns the resources the thread was using back to the system.

- Start and stop threads. When a thread is initially created, it does not start running immediately. You need to start it explicitly with a `start()` command. Sometimes, it is also necessary to stop a thread (this simply freezes it, permanently) with a `stop()` method call.

- Suspend threads, or put threads to sleep for a given amount of time. When a thread has no more work to do while sitting in a loop, the thread should put itself to sleep to let other threads use more of the processor's resources.

- Change thread priority, name, or daemon status. Threads have several attributes that can be dynamically altered as the thread runs. The priority attribute in particular will affect the proportion of processing resources the thread receives from the processor. Threads can also be flagged as being daemon threads.

- Query thread attributes. Any thread can find out what its priority, name, or daemon status is. This is useful when you launch several thread clones (differentiated only by name, for example) who nevertheless need to act as individuals (like twins in real life).

Class `ThreadGroup` encapsulates methods similar to those listed for `Thread`, except that thread groups are just that—a scope for related threads to operate in. They allow a number of related threads to share attributes and be affected in bulk by thread group changes. See Chapter 8 for more information about threads and multithreading.

The Math Library Class

Class `Math` groups together a typical and quite conservative collection of mathematical functions. The functions provided can be classified as follows:

- Absolute, min, and max functions. These are suitably overloaded so that you can pass in any numeric type without having your arguments automatically cast to different types, thereby possibly losing accuracy.

- Square root, power, logarithm, and exponential functions. All of these take and return `double` values only (`double`, not `float`, is the default floating-point accuracy used by Java). You do not need to use casts when passing other numeric types like `int` or `float`, because Java's compiler will automatically convert (compatible) argument types for you.

- Trigonometric functions (sin, cos, tan, asin, acos, atan). All of these functions work with angles expressed in radians instead of degrees. A full circle in radians is 2*PI radians (as opposed to 360 degrees). Pi is conveniently defined to double precision as the `Math` class constant `Math.PI`.

- A pseudo-random number generator function. One method (`random()`) is provided as a basis for randomness in applications. Random numbers are very important in simulations, statistical analysis, and, of course, games.

The System-Access Class

Class `System` encapsulates the classic file handles `stdin` (as `System.in`), `stdout` (as `System.out`), and `stderr` (as `System.err`). These allow you to write output to or get input from the console in the usual way. In addition to these class variables, the following method types are contained in `System`:

- Platform optimized array copying

- Catastrophic exit (terminates application and the Java interpreter subsystem!)

- System properties querying

- Security policy related methods

The Error and Exception Classes

The difference between errors and exceptions is that errors signify trouble in the Java VM (Virtual Machine), and exceptions signify trouble in an executing program. There are more than 20 error classes and about 100 exception classes in the 1.1 release of the JDK. So many boxes would clutter up the class hierarchy diagrams, so only the superclasses `Error` and `Exception` are shown in Figure 9.1.

`Throwable` is the root class of all the exception classes; it is an immediate subclass of the `Object` class. The methods in class `Throwable` retrieve error messages associated with exceptions and note where exceptions occur.

The immediate subclasses of class `Throwable` are class `Error` and class `Exception`. The subclasses of `Error` are basically used for signaling abnormal system conditions, such as when the Java VM runs out of memory or when there is a stack overflow in the interpreter. In general, these error conditions are unrecoverable and should not be handled.

On the other hand, the subclasses of class `Exception` represent conditions that are potentially recoverable. For example, there is an `Exception` subclass that signals end of file input; a program that encounters this condition should not crash—it should simply cease reading from the file.

See Chapter 7 for more information about Java exceptions and exception handling.

Package java.util—
Utilitarian Language Support

Package `java.util` contains more abstract datatype (ADT) classes plus two interfaces, one of which (`Enumeration`) is used frequently within the class hierarchy and within user programs. As you can see from Figure 9.2, package `java.util` uses inheritance more than package `java.lang`. The `Properties` class, for example, is an extension (subclass) of class `Hashtable`, which itself is an extension of `Dictionary`. As you look at more packages later, you will see that the hierarchies gradually become deeper and more complex.

NOTE

Notice how `Stack` is implemented as a subclass of a `Vector`. One class you would expect to see alongside `Stack` is some form of `Queue` class. Surprisingly, there is no explicit queue support in `java.util`. Fortunately, `Vector` provides all the functionality to quickly cook up a `Queue` as a subclass of `Vector`.

FIGURE 9.2

Package java.util
inheritance tree

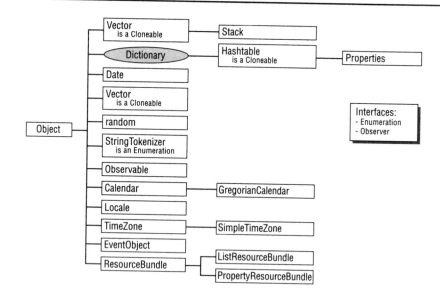

The following are the main classes contained in package java.util:

- Vector

- Hashtable

- Stack

- Date and its support classes

- BitSet

This package also includes two main interfaces:

- Enumeration

- Observer (and class Observable)

The following sections look at these classes and interfaces in more detail.

The Vector Class

Class Vector encapsulates a heterogeneous linked-list and array hybrid. It is heterogeneous because it does not insist on its elements being of a certain type—any object types can be mixed within one vector. The core Vector methods are used for the following tasks:

- Appending an element
- Finding an element
- Changing an element
- Accessing indexed elements
- Inserting elements
- Removing elements
- Getting vector information (vector size and emptiness functions)
- Enumerating vector contents

The Hashtable Class

Class Hashtable actually embodies slightly more than simple hashtable functionality; it implements a dictionary abstract datatype. Dictionaries are data structures that contain key-value pairs (the keys are the handles to the value entries).

The core methods for this class provide for the following:

- Adding a key-value pair
- Retrieving the value of a key-value entry, given its key
- Checking whether a key is already present
- Removing an entire key-value entry

- Counting the number of entries
- Enumerating all key-value pairs

The Stack Class

Class `Stack` implements that old faithful: a simple last-in–first-out (LIFO) stack. The available methods do not deviate much from the topic:

- Pushing objects
- Popping objects
- Checking for an object's presence
- Peeking at the top of stack element
- Checking whether the stack is empty

As with `Vector` and `Hashtable`, object types can be mixed freely on a `Stack`.

Despite the amount of pages invested in stack data structure examples in books, stacks are not often used in real application programs. Queue data structures (which are missing in the standard Java package), for example, are much more frequently employed.

The main use for a stack is in systems that need to "remember" things. One application where stacks are common is 2-D or 3-D graphics. Stacks can store nested coordinate system transformations in such a way that the application can easily revert to any previous coordinate system. Queues, on the other hand, are universally used to buffer objects (events, data packets, commands) so that an application can process them at its leisure and in the same arrival order. A queue structure also allows the source for these objects (the producer) to be decoupled from the system that processes the items in the queue (the consumer). This queue side effect is probably the most common reason for employing queues.

NOTE

You also may have come across the term *bag*. Other object-oriented frameworks often provide one or more `Bag` classes. The difference between a bag and a set is that bags can contain duplicates (as in real life), whereas a set contains only zero or one instance of any object type. If you want your own Java `Bag` class, a good place to start is with subclassing class `Vector`.

The Date and Support Classes

Class `Date` encapsulates the representation of an instant of time, with millisecond precision. The date support classes are `TimeZone`, `SimpleTimeZone`, `Calendar`, and `GregorianCalendar`. These provide the following types of methods for interpreting and modifying date information:

- Altering year, month, day, hour, minute, and second components

- Querying year, month, day, hour, minute, and second components

- Converting to and from strings and long integers

- Comparing date and time values (including calendar arithmetic)

- Time-zone support

The BitSet Class

Class `BitSet` implements a set of bits. Unlike many other bit set classes or language features in other languages, this bit set has no limits. You can therefore go way beyond the typical 32 or 256 bit limits imposed by other implementations. `BitSet` operations include the following:

- Setting, clearing, and getting single bits
- ANDing, ORing, and XORing bit sets together
- Comparing bit sets

The Enumeration Interface

Interface `Enumeration` is an impressive example of Java's powerful interface feature. It defines the behavior (in terms of methods to be supported) of being able to enumerate every component, element, object, or entry—in short, everything contained by any class having some "container" quality.

For example, `Vector` objects have some container quality, since they can accumulate and manipulate the objects a program hands them at runtime. So, a `Vector` should be able to enumerate all the elements it contains. And it can, by implementing the `Enumeration` interface (indirectly, through an intermediary object of type `Enumeration` returned by the `Vector` method `elements( )`). The `Enumeration` interface forces any class to implement two methods: `public boolean hasMoreElements()` and `public Object nextElement()`. These two methods mean that any object that supports enumerating its components via this standard (method) interface can be explored using the following standard Java `while` loop:

```
enum = someContainer.someMethodReturningAnEnumeration();
while (enum.hasMoreElements()) {
    containedObj = enum.nextElement();
    // process this object
}
```

This simple, clean, and, more important, standardized approach to listing or processing every element of a container class is used repeatedly throughout the class hierarchy.

The Observer Interface and Observable Class

Interface `Observer` and class `Observable` together exemplify the way Java's designers have tried to avoid reinventing the wheel, an all too common occurrence in software development. The `Observer-Observable` metaphor addresses a design obstacle slightly more abstract than the enumeration problem solved by the `Enumeration` interface.

Sometimes, within an application, it is necessary for a change in an object to trigger changes in other objects; these changes may, in turn, trigger changes in yet other objects. In short, you have a number of objects that are in some way dependent on other objects; this is called a *dependency network*. Java's class hierarchy designers developed the `Observer-Observable` duo to solve this design obstacle.

The mechanism enforced by this duo is quite simple: Any root object that needs to send some kind of notification to other objects should be subclassed from class `Observable`, and any objects that need to receive such notifications should implement interface `Observer`. The following is the sole method interface `Observer` requires:

```
public void update(Observable o, Object arg)
```

To establish the dependency, any observer objects (that is, any objects implementing interface `Observer`) are added to the observable object (that is, the object subclassed from class `Observable`). Whenever this observable object changes, it can then call its `Observable` method `notifyObservers( )`.

Package java.io—File and Stream I/O Services

Package `java.io` contains a whole arsenal of I/O related classes, as shown in Figure 9.3. A top-level classification organizes them as follows:

- Byte input and output streams
- Character readers and writers
- Stream, reader, and writer filtering
- Stream tokenization
- Class `RandomAccessFile`

As you can see from the inheritance tree, the input and output stream branches form the bulk of the tree. A *stream* is an abstract concept used frequently in the context of I/O programming. It represents a linear, sequential flow of bytes of input or output data. Streams can be "flowing toward you," in which case you have an *input stream*, or they can "flow away from you," in which case you refer to an *output stream*. You read from input streams (that is, you read the data a stream delivers to you), and you write to output streams (that is, you transfer data to a stream).

The key point about streams is that they shield you from the input or output devices you are ultimately talking to. If your code deals with these abstract objects (streams) instead, you can easily switch to different physical I/O devices without changing any of the I/O processing code in your application. This is the main raison dêtre of streams.

Readers and writers are similar to input and output streams, but their basic unit of data is a Unicode character.

FIGURE 9.3

Package java.io
inheritance tree

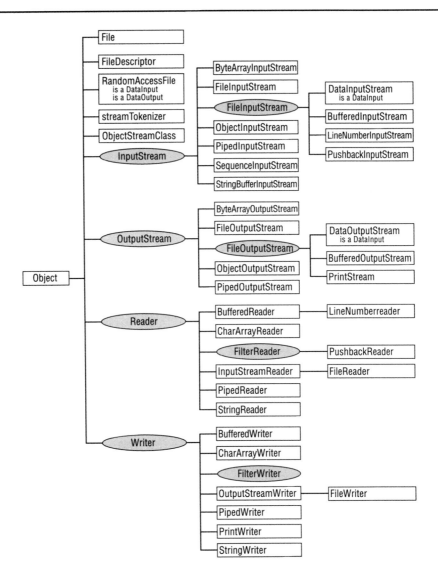

The stream, reader, and writer classes in package java.io can be classified into two types according to their main concern:

- Classes linking a stream, reader, or writer to a concrete I/O data source or destination
- Classes enhancing stream, reader, or writer functionality

The `java.io` package and its classes are discussed in detail in Chapter 15. The following sections provide an overview of the functionality of this package.

The InputStream Class

Class `InputStream` is an abstract class from which the entire input stream subhierarchy inherits. Essentially, any input stream can simply read one or more bytes (and only bytes) of data from whatever data source it supports (the mark/reset related functionality is not supported by default). Five subclasses deal with specific data sources for the input stream:

- An array of bytes

- An external file

- Another pipe stream (of type `PipedOutputStream`)

- Two or more other input streams concatenated together

- A `String` (and not a `StringBuffer` as you could be forgiven for thinking) passed as the constructor's argument

Figure 9.4 will help you visualize the relationship between an input stream and its data source. The figure depicts class `ByteArrayInput-Stream`, an input stream that lets you read from the stream, as usual, a single byte or a block of bytes at a time (as defined by class `Input-Stream`). In the case of class `ByteArrayInputStream`, the bytes read in this way originated from an array of bytes. Other classes will have other data sources; for example, class `FileInputStream` will take its data from a file.

The input streams you have seen so far read bytes from various sources of data; you might think of them as low-level input streams. The remaining input streams in the `java.io` package read bytes from low-level streams and organize the input into higher-level information. The abstract class `FilterInputStream` is the root for the subtree grouping together most of these extra classes, which perform the following functions:

- Insert a performance-enhancing input buffering mechanism between the `InputStream` class's standard reading functionality and your application.

- Add support for reading all of Java's primitive types previously saved to a stream.

- Add the option of undoing the last single-byte read operation.

- Read objects from a low-level stream.

FIGURE 9.4

Data source and input stream

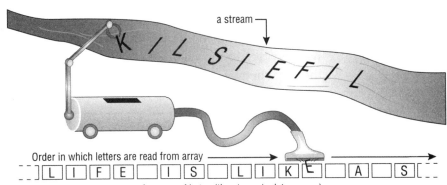

TIP

The `FilterInputStream` subclasses can be powerfully combined with other `InputStream` classes. For example, you could create a `ByteArrayDataInputStream` or a `FilePushback-InputStream`. To do this, you would pass an instance of a data source-type `InputStream` (`Byte`, `File`, `Pipe`, `Sequence`, or `String`) object as argument to the constructor of the filter-type `InputStream` (`Buffered`, `DataInput`, `LineNumber`, or `Pushback`). Because these `FilterInputStream` subclasses are themselves `InputStreams`, you could even combine several filtering types. You could therefore conceivably create a `Buffering-PushbackLineNumberingStringInputStream` (although by then you would be breaking every readability rule in the book). This same technique is possible with `OutputStreams`.

The OutputStream Class

Class OutputStream is an abstract class from which the entire output stream subhierarchy inherits. Any output stream's sole requirement is to be able to write a single byte or write an array of bytes. (Flushing and closing the stream are peripheral to what an output stream is all about.) As is the case with input streams, output streams cannot exist on their own; they need to be connected to a data destination before they become a useful stream.

OutputStream's subclasses can be similarly classified according to their main concern: choice of data destination (called *sink*) or choice of enhanced stream writing behavior. Figure 9.5 will help you visualize the relationship between an output stream and its data sink. The figure depicts the scenario for class FileOutputStream. All the bytes that were written to the stream end up stored in an external file; you specify the file when you create the output stream.

FIGURE 9.5

An output stream and a data sink

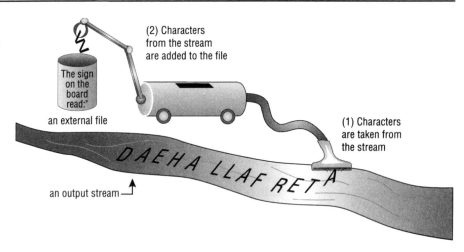

(2) Characters from the stream are added to the file

The sign on the board read:"

an external file

(1) Characters are taken from the stream

DAEHA LLAF RETA

an output stream

The output stream classes that enhance output stream behavior almost all descend from the output equivalent of FilterInput-Stream (described in the previous section): FilterOutputStream.

The Reader and Writer Classes

Class `Reader` is the abstract character-oriented counterpart of `InputStream`. There are nine subclasses of `Reader`. Like input streams, these classes fall into two categories: low-level readers that take raw character input from various sources and high-level filtering readers that organize the data delivered by low-level readers.

Class `Writer` is the abstract character-oriented counterpart of `OutputStream`. There are eight subclasses of `Writer` which also fall into the low-level and high-level categories. Low-level writers deliver character output to various destinations. High-level filtering writers convert organized input to characters that are delivered to other writers.

The RandomAccessFile Class

Class `RandomAccessFile` encapsulates full read and write access to files. This class is rather odd when compared to the other classes in the I/O hierarchy. You would expect the class to be derived from both an abstract input class and an abstract output class (plus some seeking functionality), but since `RandomAccessFile` descends directly from `Object`, a rather conventional (that is, not object-oriented) design approach was used instead.

The methods implemented by `RandomAccessFile` can be summarized into the following groups:

- Reading of primitive types and byte arrays (in binary form)
- Writing of primitive types and byte arrays (in binary form)
- Positioning of the file pointer (seeking)

The StreamTokenizer Class

Class `StreamTokenizer` extracts identifiable substrings and punctuation from an input stream according to user-defined rules. This process is called *tokenizing* because the stream is reduced to tokens. Tokens typically represent keywords, variable names, numerical constants, string literals, and syntactic punctuation (like brackets, equal signs, and so on). `StreamTokenizer` includes various methods that affect the rules for parsing the input stream into tokens. It also contains the `nextToken()` method to extract the next token from the input stream.

Text tokenizing is a common technique used to reduce the complexity of textual input. The archetypal application that uses text tokenizing is the programming-language compiler. Compilers do not analyze your source file as-is, because that would lead to an onslaught of independent characters. Instead, compilers analyze a stream of tokens representing and extracted from your source file. Keywords, identifiers, punctuation, comments, strings, and so on, are first compressed into easy-to-manipulate tokens. Only after this lexical analysis stage does a compiler start to check the complex grammar of any programming (or other) language. Class `StreamTokenizer` is used by the original Java compiler (javac) for this purpose.

Package java.awt– Heart of the Hierarchy

As you can see from Figures 9.6 and 9.7, the package `java.awt` is organized into the following main groups.

- Two GUI component branches
  - The `Component` subtree, with another important subtree, the `Container` subtree buried slightly deeper within it
  - The `MenuComponent` subtree
- Layout manager classes
  - `FlowLayout`

- BorderLayout
- CardLayout
- GridLayout
- GridBagLayout and GridBagConstraints
- Insets
- Graphics classes
  - Graphics and PrintGraphics
  - Image
  - Color and SystemColor
  - Font
  - FontMetrics
- Geometry classes
  - Point
  - Polygon
  - Dimension
  - Rectangle
- Event classes
  - Event
  - AWTEvent
  - AWEventMulticaster
  - EventQueue
- Miscellaneous classes
  - MediaTracker
  - Toolkit
  - PrintJob
  - Cursor

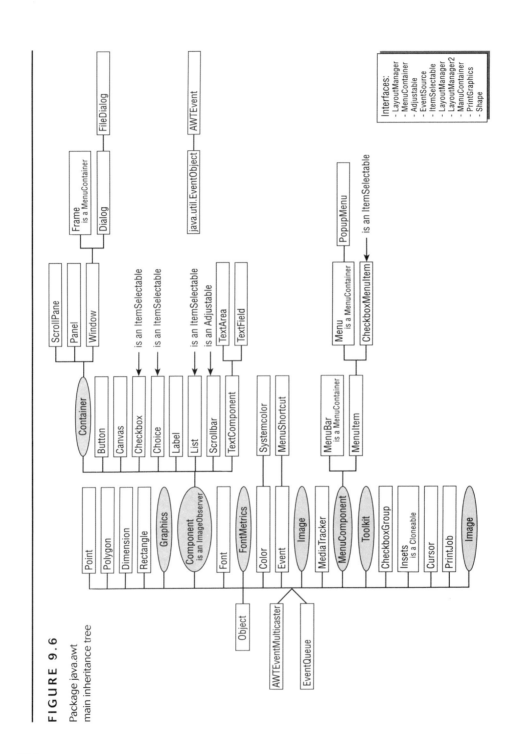

FIGURE 9.6

Package java.awt
main inheritance tree

FIGURE 9.7

Package java.awt layout
manager classes

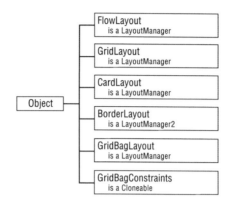

Java's AWT package is the largest and most important package of the entire hierarchy. This is what you would expect in an age when the design and implementation of application GUIs can easily consume more than a third of software development resources. The AWT aims to significantly reduce this proportion by allowing GUIs to be platform independent in a hassle-free way—a revolutionary step. The whole hierarchy is there to make the lives of application developers easier, but in particular it was meant to make GUI development quick and painless.

All the classes outlined below are 100 percent hardware and software independent. This means that your Java GUI-based applications will run on every platform that is Java-capable.

GUI Classes

The bulk of the classes within package `java.awt` relates to GUI creation and management. The classes can be classified into the following groups:

- Widget classes

- Container classes

- Widget layout classes

- Menu classes

Widget Classes

The fundamental building blocks of GUI designs are called *widgets*, *gadgets*, or *buttons*, depending on the GUI school that invented them. The most common term, and the one used in this book, is widgets (for window gadgets). Java implements quite a nice variety of them, all of which are easily deployed in your GUI designs, as you will see in later chapters.

- Class `Button` implements that bread-and-butter widget: the button. The simplest and by far most common incarnation is the labeled variety. You can also have buttons with iconic identification (not supported by class `Button`, but can be achieved by giving a `Canvas` an image and trapping mouse clicks on it).

- A `Canvas` component provides a drawable area. As such, it is invisible (it has no graphical representation) but can detect mouse click and move events, which can then be used by the application.

- Classes `Checkbox` and `CheckboxGroup` implement checkable items. The latter class forces the former into a mutually exclusive grouping, commonly known as radio buttons.

- Class `Choice` implements a multiple-choice component, typically with only a few choices (use `List` for more items). The graphical implementation for a Choice usually looks like a pop-up menu.

- The `Component` class is an abstract superclass for widgets.

- A `Label` is used to give GUI zones a title or to label other widgets. It just encapsulates a single line of read-only text.

- A `List` is a heavy-duty list display and item selection widget. It comes with a vertical scrollbar and allows selection of multiple items at the same time.

- A `Scrollbar` component is the Java slider control, which can be either horizontal or vertical. If a `List` object does not provide enough listing functionality, you could design your own custom lister by incorporating a vertical `Scrollbar` object, in a `Panel` subclass, for example. This widget represents a continuous range of values that can be "sampled" at any time by the application. Clicks on the scrollbar's arrow icons are treated as "line-increment" commands that move the scrollbar cursor according to a defined line increment. Similarly, clicks above or below the cursor are interpreted as "page-increment" commands with analogous results.

- The text-entry components start with `TextComponent`, which is the abstract superclass of `TextField` and `TextArea`. The `TextField` widget is the pillar of GUI form screens. It allows you to enter any text within a short, single-line input window. `TextArea` is a variant of the `TextField` widget. It allows multiple lines of text, such as for free-form "memo" type fields. Both `TextField` and `TextArea` allow unconstrained data entry, which often isn't what an application needs. To implement entry fields that accept only strict types of data (text only, numbers only, dates only, and so on), you need to subclass either `TextField` or `TextArea` (depending on your requirements) and enhance their behavior by validating the user's input to the type of data allowed.

Chapter 11 provides details on these GUI components.

Container Classes

An application's window typically is not just an unstructured heap of clickable or selectable components. Well-designed GUIs are highly structured to aid you in your navigation of the interface. This structuring can be in part achieved by using component containers. A window can be subdivided into areas or zones, each containing related buttons, choices, lists, and so on. When you use containers to implement these visual and logical areas, you mirror the hierarchy in your code. This is just another example of the key object-oriented principle of projecting the vocabulary and structures of the problem domain into your code. The container classes in Java's AWT are also the entities on which the layout manager classes work (see the following section).

WARNING
Do not confuse the term *container*, as used by Java's AWT, with the more general term *container class*, as used by other object-oriented frameworks. AWT containers are GUI component containers. Generic container classes, on the other hand, are abstract datatype classes that can contain other objects (for example, linked lists, stacks, bags, and vectors).

The AWT containers include the following:

- An abstract class, `Container`, which is the generic widget container on which layout managers act. All the other container classes are derived from this superclass.

- The `Panel` class is a concrete incarnation of class `Container`. It does not have a graphic representation—not even a simple outline. You typically subclass a `Panel` to define and control a logical grouping of widgets (see Chapter 14 for an example).

- Class `Frame` is the building block class for producing full-fledged windows. (There is also a `Window` class, which produces "windows" without any borders or a menu bar.) Frames have titles, background colors, optional menu bars, and layout managers.

- Class `Dialog` is used for implementing direct application-to-user feedback or questions. Typical uses include pop-up warning dialog windows, quit confirmation dialog boxes, and so on. The `Dialog` class is not a self-contained component like, for example, `Frame`. In fact, it relies on class `Frame` to provide it with a display medium in which to display itself.

- Class `FileDialog` implements the indispensable file Open/Save/Save As dialog window, complete with filename filtering capability, plus any transparent extras provided by the native operating system. On Windows 95, for example, the Java `File-Dialog` widget allows the user to create new directories on the fly, before saving a file.

- The `ScrollPane` class implements a container with scrollbars, so that a large component can be viewed through a small viewport.

Widget Layout Classes

One of Java's innovations in the field of GUI programming is its GUI component-placement strategy. With other GUI frameworks, you usually need to specify pixel coordinates for all of your components. Even with GUI building tools, you need to position your components absolutely. Java was designed to be platform independent, but since AWT still relies on the host's native windowing system to provide it with its window and button building blocks, it is not possible to specify component dimensions and placement with absolute precision. The AWT uses an automatic layout system based on layout managers instead:

- With the `FlowLayout` class, every component is positioned and sized in the same way flowing text is in a WYSIWYG word processor: from left to right, and then overflowing to the next line when the first line is filled, and so on.

- The `BorderLayout` class positions and scales components according to the conventional distribution of components around a generic window. It allows components to be laid out along the top, bottom, left, or right edges of a window and leaves one large central area for the remainder of the components. Any unassigned areas will be recovered by the other areas.

- The `GridLayout` class, as the name suggests, enforces a simple grid layout. But unlike what you would expect from a grid layout, you cannot specify the positions of your components using two-dimensional coordinates; you must use a one-dimensional index. (You can use `GridBagLayout` to avoid this annoying situation.)

- The `GridBagLayout` class extends the approach taken by class `GridLayout`. It basically allows any one component to use up more than one grid cell, in either a horizontal or vertical direction. Extra control over the precise layout process is provided by instances of a helper class: class `GridBagConstraints`. This is the most powerful layout manager of all the standard ones provided.

- Class `CardLayout` embodies the concept of a number of cards that can be flipped through, with only one card visible at any one time. This layout management style is most commonly used to implement multiple "pages" (or cards) that the user can view by selecting their "tabs." Since class `CardLayout` does not go beyond laying out the components, the trendy rendering of the card tabs themselves should be handled by another class. Unfortunately, there is currently no such standard `Component` class to do this.

- The `Insets` class encapsulates information about how close to a container's edge a component may be placed.

The layout managers are discussed in detail in Chapter 10.

Menu Classes

Drop-down or pop-up menus associated with windows are part of any modern application. Java's AWT supports quite complete menu functionality (submenus and checkable menu items are included) using a small and surprisingly easy-to-use set of menu classes:

- Class `MenuBar` acts as the anchor for the entire collection of menus connected to an application, or to be more precise, connected to a `Frame`. Every Java `Frame` can have its own menu bar with menu items responding to selections private to its context.

- The `Menu` class is the logical building block for any menu system. Menus hold logically related menu items and/or submenus. A menu is identified primarily by a simple menu title.

- The PopupMenu class implements a menu that can be popped up at any point of a GUI.

- The MenuComponent class is the abstract superclass of Menu-Item and CheckboxMenuItem, which represent the menu items that a user selects on a menu.

- The MenuShortcut class encapsulates a keyboard shortcut for a menu item.

NOTE Don't let the class hierarchy confuse you. A MenuItem (or Check-boxMenuItem) is *logically* the leaf component in a final, concrete menu system. But as far as the object-oriented hierarchy is concerned, a MenuItem must be a Menu object's parent. This is totally counterintuitive, but can be understood as follows: Wherever you have a menu item, you can in fact substitute an entire submenu for it. So, class Menu must be a subclass of MenuItem. In any case, this admittedly chicken-and-egg type situation does not in any way complicate AWT menu programming. The fact is that adding menus to applications is probably the easiest thing you can do within AWT.

You'll find more information about Java's menu-related support in Chapter 11.

The Graphics Classes

For animation or special effects, you need something very different from standard GUI classes. You need to be able to control colors and imagery without any of the window-metaphor constraints imposed by a set of GUI classes. Java provides elementary rendering classes; Graphics is the core class in this area. The Graphics classes are discussed in detail in Chapter 13, which discusses animation and images. The following sections provide an overview of the functionality of these classes.

The Graphics Class and PrintGraphics Interface

Graphics is an abstract class that supports a simple 2-D painting model with the usual rendering primitives. Specifically, the following classes of methods are provided:

- Text rendering
- Rectangular area copying (also called blitting)
- Filled and outlined rectangles, ovals, polygons, and arcs
- Lines
- Coordinate system translation
- Clipping rectangle support
- Changing current drawing color
- Various graphics state querying functions

PrintGraphics is an interface that closely resembles Graphics but renders to a printer.

The Image Class

Class Image encapsulates a platform-independent image data structure. This approach shields you from the profusion of hardware- or software-dependent bitmap "standards" (bitplane, chunky, interleaved, and so on). The methods provided by class Image allow you to perform the following tasks:

- Query the image's dimensions.
- Query the image's properties (for example, source image format, copyright information, and so on).
- Create a graphics context for the image so you can use the Graphics rendering methods on this image.

The Color and SystemColor Classes

Class `Color` encapsulates a platform-independent color data structure. As with bitmapped images, a color can be implemented in a variety of ways. The `Color` class shields you from these platform dependencies. The provided methods support the following:

- Conversion between RGB (Red, Green, Blue) and HSB (Hue, Saturation, Brightness) color models

- Accessing the red, green, and blue color components

- Increasing or decreasing the brightness of a color

The `SystemColor` class is a subclass of `Color`. It provides access to prevailing Desktop colors.

The Font and FontMetrics Classes

The `Font` and `FontMetrics` classes give you a platform-independent way of accessing and querying the platform local fonts. The methods let you do the following:

- Specify a font family, style, and point size.

- Query font attributes and metrics (family name, style, point size, character and string widths, ascender and descender lengths).

Geometry Classes

Package `java.awt` contains four geometry classes. These encapsulate the mathematical concepts point, polygon, rectangle, and dimension:

- The `Point` class represents a simple (x,y) data structure along with two methods: `move()` and `translate()`. As with all geometry classes, integers are used instead of floating-point numbers. This reflects the main use of these classes as helper classes for GUI programming (and not pure math, which assumes numbers and shapes to have infinite precision).

- The `Polygon` class represents an ordered collection of points treated as the definition of a polygon. Three methods enhance the data structure: `addPoint()` modifies the polygon to include the new point; `getBoundingBox()` calculates the smallest rectangle enclosing all points of the polygon; and `inside()` tests whether a given point lies inside or outside the polygon.

- The `Dimension` class is a pure data structure holding a width and height variable. No methods enhance the raw data structure (in other words, this is really equivalent to a C structure or a Pascal record).

- The `Rectangle` class represents a rectangle at a certain (x,y) position. The class adds several methods to manipulate rectangles (move, shrink, grow, calculate intersection with other rectangles, and test whether or not a point is inside a rectangle).

Although these classes have nothing to do with rendering or with GUI programming per se, they are used by those higher-level classes to improve code reuse, robustness, and readability. Since GUI programming constantly involves dealing with positions and rectangular component dimensions or outlines, it makes sense to localize (abstract) some representation and a set of common operations for those positions and dimensions. This way, you avoid scattering your code with bits of identical functionality with slightly differing implementations.

Miscellaneous AWT Classes

The following package `java.awt` classes do no fall neatly into any category:

- The classes that support event handling are `AWTEvent`, `AWT-MulticasterEvent`, and `EventQueue`. The `Event` class supports the earlier (before version 1.1) Java event model, which is incompatible with the more modern 1.1 model. Event handling is discussed in detail in Chapter 12.

- The Cursor class allows you to specify an appearance for the mouse cursor.

- The MediaTracker class keeps track of images that are loaded from a server.

- The PrintJob class mediates between a Java program and a printer.

- The Toolkit class allows you to bind AWT components to the underlying window system.

Package java.awt.image— Image Processing

The java.awt.image package groups together classes that deal with image generation and manipulation, plus the color models associated with bitmap-image encoding. To effectively use images, you will also need to use classes java.awt.Image and java.awt.Component.

> **WARNING** Do not confuse the package java.awt.image with the class java.awt.Image, which is a java.awt package class. The simple trick to keep them apart is to remember that package names contain only lowercase letters; class names always start with a capital.

Package java.awt.image enforces (for better or worse) a producer/consumer metaphor on all image processing. Producer classes and consumer classes need to be linked together before the image processing can begin. This approach is initially difficult to understand, but as with most of these systems, the payoff justifies the investment.

The inheritance tree for package java.awt.image is illustrated in Figure 9.8. At the heart of package java.awt.image lie three interfaces: ImageProducer, ImageConsumer, and ImageObserver.

FIGURE 9.8

Package java.awt.image inheritance tree

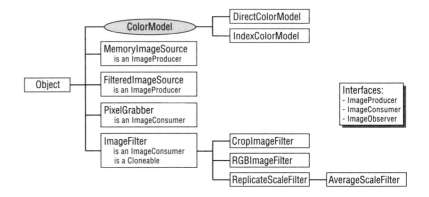

Two classes implement the ImageProducer interface:

- The MemoryImageSource class uses a simple array of bytes (for up to 8 bits per pixel) or int values (for up to 32 bits per pixel) as the source image data. MemoryImageSource allows you to construct algorithmically generated images, ranging from a simple color-gradient fill to an infinitely complex Mandelbrot fractal (see the example in Chapter 13). Since the image data is constructed in a 2-D array of pixels, this class makes any pixel manipulations easy to implement.

- The FilteredImageSource class's image data source is another ImageProducer (for example, an instance of class MemoryImageSource) that is filtered according to the filtering characteristics of an ImageFilter compliant filter (described below).

The following classes implement the ImageConsumer interface:

- Unmodified, the ImageFilter class passes through the image data without altering (filtering) it in any way. You need to subclass this class to implement useful filters. Possible useful filters include color-to-gray filters, brightness-altering filters, image noise filters, and edge-enhancement filters.

- The CropImageFilter class is a subclass of ImageFilter. It "filters" a source image by producing a new image that is a rectangular subimage of the original.

- The RGBImageFilter class is another subclass of ImageFilter. It allows you to change the color of every pixel of a source image— for example, to produce a grayscale version of the image.

- The ReplicateScaleFilter and AverageScaleFilter classes are ImageFilter subclasses that scale their source images. AverageScaleFilter is a subclass of ReplicateScaleFilter that uses a more sophisticated algorithm.

- The PixelGrabber class is used for extracting rectangular areas of another image and storing them into an array of int values for further processing.

- The ColorModel class provides support for color models. The ubiquitous RGB pixel encoding, for example, can be implemented using a variety of exact bit field assignments. There are also other color models, such as the HSB system. All of these can be supported via subclasses of ColorModel; the IndexColorModel and DirectColorModel subclasses are included as standard subclasses.

The use of the classes in the java.awt.image package is discussed in detail in Chapter 13.

Package java.net— Internet, Web, and HTML Support

The java.net package is one of the class hierarchy's other main features. It provides very high-level interfaces to the rather less high-level set of data-communication protocols (and their associated API) called TCP/IP. The java.net classes hide many of the technical quagmires inherent to low-level Internet programming. The inheritance tree for java.net is illustrated in Figure 9.9.

FIGURE 9.9

Package java.net inheritance tree

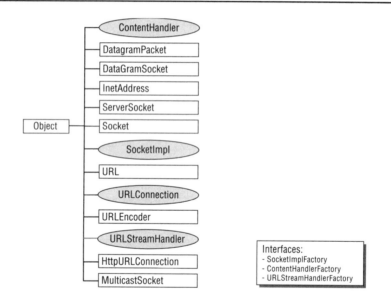

The java.net classes can be grouped according to the following responsibilities:

- Internet addressing (classes InetAddress and URL)
- UDP/IP connectionless classes (DatagramPacket and DatagramSocket)
- TCP/IP connection-oriented classes (various Socket classes)

- MIME content type handlers (`ContentHandler` and `URLStreamHandler`)

- Web-related classes (`URLConnection` and `URLStreamHandler`)

NOTE

In terms of complexity—and, therefore, ease of use—the UDP protocol lies in between the Transmission Control Protocol (TCP) protocol (the low-level protocol) and the Internet Protocol (IP) protocol (the high-level protocol). UDP is a datagram-oriented protocol, which means that data packets travel individually (like letters in the postal system), without any guarantees of delivery. This is because, unlike with TCP, UDP does not attempt to detect or correct loss of packets. This lack of protocol overhead is what makes UDP interesting for certain types of applications, such as broadcasting currency exchange rates, to gain speed at the cost of an occasional lost update. However, most Internet applications do not use the UDP protocol to achieve their functionality, but instead use the TCP protocol, which supports a guaranteed delivery end-to-end link.

The following is a brief overview of the commonly used `java.net` classes. Many of these are discussed in greater detail in Chapter 16, which covers network programming.

- The `InetAddress` class deals with Internet addresses in their mnemonic (*host.domain*) form and their 32-bit numeric form (*byte.byte.byte.byte*).

- The `URL` class encapsulates a Uniform Resource Locator (URL) specification plus associated methods, including opening a connection to the URL resource (a Web page, a file, or telnet port), retrieving the URL resource, querying URL fields (protocol, host, filenames, and port number).

- The `ServerSocket` and `Socket` classes together provide complete TCP/IP connectivity support. Each class supports one side of the client/server application model. Class `Socket` is used to implement a client; class `ServerSocket` is used to implement a server. Class `Socket` provides methods to connect any stream (as input or output) to a socket to communicate through. This way, you can essentially separate internetworking technicalities (and pitfalls!) from your application by working at the abstract stream level instead.

> **NOTE**
>
> *Sockets* are the software interfaces that connect an application to the network beyond. On the Internet, each machine has 65,536 (64K) addressable sockets it can use. All standard Internet services (like e-mail, FTP, and so on) use agreed-upon socket numbers, colloquially termed "well-known port numbers." Server programs listen to these sockets for any incoming service request. A client program needs to open a socket of its own before it can connect to a server socket at the other end.

- The `DatagramPacket` and `DatagramSocket` together provide User Datagram Protocol (UDP) Internet services. Through class `DatagramPacket`, you can specify a packet's Internet host destination (using an `InetAddress` instance), the port (or socket) to connect to on that host, and the binary contents of the packet. You can then send or receive datagrams via an instance of class `DatagramSocket`.

Package java.applet— HTML Embedded Applets

A big reason for Java's runaway success is that it's a highly efficient and easy-to-learn language for distributed software components. Java applets are nothing more or less than distributed software components. Even so, the standard class framework contains little which explicitly deals with those instrumental applets.

As you can see from Figure 9.10, package `java.applet` looks very barren compared to the other packages. Its sole contents are one class and three interfaces. Class `java.applet.Applet` is the main repository for methods supporting applet functionality.

FIGURE 9.10

Package java.applet tree hierarchy

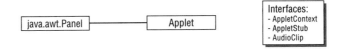

The methods it makes available can be grouped into the following categories:

- Applet initialization, restarting, and freezing
- Embedded HTML applet parameter support
- High-level image loading
- High-level audio loading and playing
- Origins querying (`getDocumentBase()` and `getCodeBase()`)
- Simple status displaying (`showStatus(String)`)

Miscellaneous Java Packages

Other Java packages support more advanced or less commonly used features. Here is a brief summary of their functionality:

`java.awt.datatransfer`   The classes in this package support clipboard data-transfer models. Clipboard data transfer is available in Java version 1.1; applets and applications may read or write the system clipboard. Drag-and-drop funtionality is not provided in version 1.1, but will be provided in a later release of the JDK. The future functionality will be based on the classes in this package.

`java.awt.event` This extensive package supports event delegation. Event delegation is covered in Chapter 12.

`java.awt.peer` This package contains classes that "glue" AWT components to the underlying window system. If you are writing Java applets or applications, you will never need to use these classes.

`java.beans` This package supports development of components, called "Beans," that are so reusable that they can interact with non-Java systems such as ActiveX, OpenDoc, and LiveConnect. Java Beans are covered in Chapter 20.

`java.lang.reflect` The classes in this package support *object reflection*. This is a feature whereby it is possible to inspect the makeup of the class of an arbitrary object.

`java.math` This package is very different from the more commonly used `java.lang.Math` class, which provides standard mathematical functions in the form of static methods. The `java.math` package contains two rarely used classes that represent decimal and integer numbers of arbitrarily high precision.

`java.rmi, java.rmi.dgc, java.rmi.registry,` and `java.rmi.server` These packages support Remote Method Invocation (RMI), which permits an object to make a method call on an object running on a different machine. RMI is covered in Chapter 22.

`java.security, java.security,` and `java.security.interfaces` The classes in these packages support secure data communication. This functionality is useful in its own right, and also supports the Java Electronic Commerce Framework, which is discussed in Chapter 19.

`java.sql`   This package provides classes and interfaces that support Java Database Connectivity (JDBC), which is discussed in Chapter 18.

`java.text`   This package provides classes that format text.

`java.util.zip`   This package provides functionality for reading and writing ZIP files. The ZIP format is used by JAR (Java Archive) files.

Summary

Java's standard class hierarchy contains a wide variety of classes which, given some time and effort to learn, should allow you to write applications within realistic time frames. The collection of classes spans a wide spectrum, with no significant gaps to obstruct real-life software development. However, as you will gradually discover, Java's classes are still a bit rough around the edges. Other class frameworks (Borland's Delphi object-oriented framework springs to mind) are significantly more mature and full-bodied. Sun is quite aware of this and will no doubt ensure that in time, Java too will be enveloped by a world-class collection of supporting classes.

CHAPTER

TEN

10

The AWT: GUI Layout Management

- The AWT environments: applets and applications

- How the layout manager classes interact with their client classes

- The five types of layout managers

- How layout managers are implemented

Java's big trump card is its AWT. It is an object-oriented GUI framework that allows you to design modern, mouse-controlled, graphical application interfaces—which isn't a revolutionary step in and of itself. But Java's AWT lets you design and implement GUIs that run unmodified (unported even) on PCs running Windows 95, Windows NT, or OS/2; Macs running MacOS; or even Unix machines running X-Windows. And that is revolutionary.

This chapter begins with a discussion of Java's approach to GUI design and then explains the differences in the applet and application environments in which the AWT can be used. The remainder of the chapter describes Java's layout managers in detail, since these are fundamental to any Java GUI implementation and, even more relevant, GUI design.

Java's GUI Approach

Ever since Xerox's pioneer work in the 1970s and Apple's subsequent mass-market introduction of mouse- and icon-driven user interfaces, developers have needed to pick competing GUI "standards" and stick to them religiously. Mastering any given GUI standard is not a trivial exercise, so it is not surprising that developers do not switch GUI APIs at the drop of a hat. Like computer languages themselves, GUIs have been thoroughly mutually incompatible. This, and the associated lack of a standard terminology, greatly helped to segregate the various GUI schools, a wasteful and divisive state of affairs. Java's GUI approach could abolish the GUI wars by supporting a functional subset of most modern GUI components and presenting them through a new platform-independent API.

NOTE

> The jargon wars will rage for a while longer. Java's AWT introduces new terms and concepts and uses some existing terms in incompatible ways (sigh). In Java land, when we talk about a "component," we mean a GUI element, a widget, a gadget, a control, or a button (depending on the GUI background you have).

At this point, you might ask yourself whether the AWT also imposes a new look and feel on our brave new (Java) world. If you are used to, for example, the Macintosh user interface, it is annoying to suddenly have an application that stubbornly thrusts upon you a GEM-style interface instead. Modern machines have personalities that they impose on us through their native and often proprietary GUI. The AWT respects these personalities by employing the underlying machine's native GUI API to construct its own universal components. Java applications built around the AWT reassuringly retain the Mac look and feel on Macs and the Windows look and feel on PCs.

Since the AWT consequently does not specify the exact look and feel—and therefore the dimensions and exact pixel rendering—of your GUI elements, how do you ensure that your GUIs will look great on every platform? The AWT answer is layout managers. These fundamental AWT classes are responsible for laying out all the visual components in aesthetically acceptable ways without requiring you to specify absolute positions. Unfortunately, this process is not yet fully automatic. Java's AWT does not have artificial intelligence or graphic design experts embedded in its layout managers. Instead, your applications give these layout managers hints as to component placement and preferred sizes. These hints vary from quite vague ("north," "center," or "third" placements) to quite specific (grid coordinates).

AWT Environments: Applets and Applications

Before embarking on your exploration of Java's novel layout system and the components it affects so thoroughly, you need to understand the two quite different contexts a Java GUI can be embedded in. Java's AWT can be used in the following two environments:

- In Java applets (mini-Web applications)
- In stand-alone applications

Both have different frameworks to respect. The AWT itself is not aware of the context you choose to deploy it in, but the chosen context means different coding techniques, possibilities, and limitations for your Java programs. The easiest context to start using is Java applets.

The Code Framework for Applets

As you've learned, an applet is a small program that runs embedded in a Web browser's HTML page. As such, any applet has a drawing or work area equal to an imaginary picture situated in the same spot, as illustrated in Figure 10.1.

FIGURE 10.1

Applets as interactive, intelligent pictures

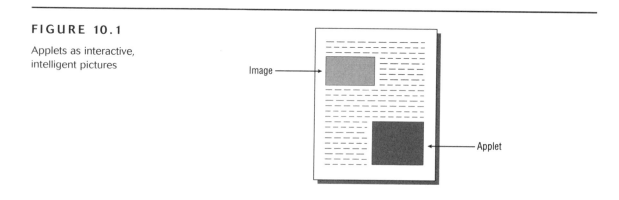

When applet code starts running, it can immediately use its applet area without any further initializations or checks. For example, the first statement in an applet could be to draw a diagonal line across its surface. The ease with which you can have an applet up and running is what makes applets easier to write than applications—in the beginning (it gets rather more complex for nontrivial applets). It is quite possible to write simple little applets without knowing much about the underlying AWT mechanisms.

Here is an example that draws the diagonal line:

```
import java.awt.Graphics;
public class Appletlet extends java.applet.Applet {

public void paint (Graphics g) {
   g.drawLine(0,0, 100,100);
}}
```

As you can see, the applet has no lengthy initializations what-soever before it starts using AWT classes. Here you use the `Graphics` class to draw a line with its `drawLine()` method (Chapter 13 discusses Java's drawing primitives and the `Graphics` class). To write an applet, you begin by extending (or subclassing) class `Applet`. That's because the browser needs your applets to be instances of the `Applet` class. Any old Java program will not do. The `paint()` method used in this example is an `Applet` method that you override.

WARNING Make sure you understand the difference between overriding a method and simply inventing a new one. *Overriding* a method means you cannot change the name or `syntax` of the method to anything else but the original method signature defined in the superclass you are extending—in our example, `public void paint(Graphics g)`. If the signature differs in any way, you are creating a brand new method, not overriding an existing one. Sometimes, subtle bugs can slip through when you meant to override a method but instead failed to use the same signature. The compiler won't generate an error, and your code will invoke the wrong method at runtime (the superclass method).

Applet Methods

Whenever the browser needs to draw the page containing this applet, it tells the applet to draw itself by calling the `paint()` method. For simplistic applets, this calling protocol between the browser and your applet might be all that you need, but for more complex applets (for example, those using animation), this approach is too limited. In fact, the browser calls many more `Applet` methods that were not over-ridden here, so only a small subset of the full browser-applet protocol was used.

For starters, there is the `init()` method that the browser calls to initialize an applet. There was not an `init()` method in the simple example because nothing needed to be initialized. But if your applet has any initialization to do (namely, code it needs to execute only once, at the start of its execution), it should put all this code in an overridden `init()` method. Here is an example that overrides the `init()` method:

```
import java.awt.Graphics;

public class Applet2 extends java.applet.Applet {

String message;

public void init () {
   message = "I was born.";
}

public void paint (Graphics g) {
   g.drawString(message, 10, 20);
}}
```

In addition to the `paint()` method responsible for the redrawing of the applet, you now have a customized `init()` method. This method will be called once by the browser before the applet is displayed. In this example, the `init()` method records the date and time at the moment the applet is initialized, and converts this to a string that the `paint()` method will use to draw this frozen time when the applet needs to be redrawn.

Graphically printing a string is done with the `Graphics draw-String()` method. It takes a string and the coordinates for the string's position.

There are three more methods that the browser invokes on an applet during an applet's life cycle:

`start()`   When the applet's HTML page comes into view

`stop()`When the applet's HTML page is left

`destroy()`   When the browser's garbage collector determines the applet is no longer necessary to keep in memory

To see the full browser-applet protocol in action, type in the following program, compile it, and tell your favorite Web browser to load a Web page with the applet embedded in it. Make sure that your browser shows "Java console output." On Netscape's Navigator browser, you enable this by selecting Show Java Console in the program's Options menu.

```java
import java.awt.Graphics;

public class AppletLife extends java.applet.Applet {

public void init () {
   System.out.println("Browser wants me to: initialize myself");
}
public void start () {
   System.out.println("Browser wants me to: start running");
}
public void stop () {
   System.out.println("Browser wants me to: stop running");
}
public void paint (Graphics g) {
   System.out.println("Browser wants me to: redraw myself");
}
public void destroy () {
   System.out.println("Browser wants me to: clean up before being removed.");
}}
```

The first time you load the HTML page, you should see the following output printed to the Java console:

```
Browser wants me to: initialize myself
Browser wants me to: start running
Browser wants me to: redraw myself
```

This means the `init()`, `start()`, and `paint()` `Applet` methods are always called when an applet is first loaded and run. The sequence can differ from what is listed above; due to asynchronous aspects of the protocol, the `paint()` method can be legally called before the `start()` method. The `init()` method, however, is guaranteed to be called before all others.

Now, whenever the browser window needs to repaint itself—for example, after having been obscured by other windows overlapping it—you should see an additional:

```
Browser wants me to: redraw myself
```

This is because the browser needed to completely redraw itself to undo the graphically inconsistent picture it was showing.

Remember that the entire GUI desktop metaphor your machine maintains is just a clever, graphical illusion. Any computer has a flat, uniform screen bitmap that doesn't enforce or care about these "overlapping" and clipping rectangular areas called "windows." The "natural behavior" of a computer screen is much more like that of a painting canvas in a painting program: The canvas has no restrictions whatsoever. In a GUI environment, then, when windows are depth-arranged in this plain bitmap environment, it means that some windows will be partially or entirely overwritten, while others will need to redraw themselves. Since your applet is part of a window, it too must play along to maintain the illusion. If not, your applet will soon become graphically corrupted, or more likely, erased completely. This is why it is important to have an applet repaint itself using the `paint()` method whenever the browser commands it to (and as quickly as possible, as always).

If you load a different Web page in your browser, you should see your applet print the following line:

```
Browser wants me to: stop running
```

You will probably wonder what this means, since your applet was not executing any code at the time anyway. Think about the kind of applications applets can be used for—animation, real-time updating of information fetched from an Internet server, general entertainment, and so on. All these types of applets are real applets, and they are very different from what has been demonstrated so far in this book. Real applets usually run constantly.

To illustrate, imagine that the `start()` method in your last applet never ended because it had to animate something all the time. Such an applet would be very wasteful of processor resources if it kept on animating even after the user switched to a different page. Yet that is exactly what it would do if you didn't take any steps to avoid this problem; the way to avoid the problem is by using threads.

In Chapter 8, you saw how threads allow you to do several things at the same time. Imagine all of an applet's core processing and functionality (the animating, for example) being run in a separate thread. This way, whenever the applet's page is displaced by a new page, you can simply freeze the thread, and when the applet's page is reloaded, you can let the thread run again; this is the real purpose of the `start()` and `stop()` `Applet` methods. They assume that all your applets are written with multithreading in the first place. In later chapters, you will learn how to actually write applets built around a thread, but for now, just keep in mind that `start()` and `stop()` are really meant to control applet threads so that they do not consume processor resources while they are not in view.

NOTE
A related use for the `start()` and `stop()` methods is to control sounds produced by your applet. Most sounds keep playing forever because they just loop round. To have a sound stop playing when the user leaves your applet's page, you need to explicitly stop that sound.

If you now click on your browser's Back button to revisit the page with our applet, you will see the console print:

```
Browser wants me to: start running
Browser wants me to: redraw myself
```

Because the browser assumed your applet thread had been put to sleep when you switched pages, it now asks your applet to wake up the thread again, immediately followed by an urgent request to repaint the applet. This is because the applet's facade was overwritten a long time ago by the previous page and its applets.

The final method (literally) that a browser can invoke on applets is the destroy() method. Just quit your browser altogether and carefully watch the console window again. What you should have seen just before the console vanished was:

```
Browser wants me to: stop running
Browser wants me to: clean up before being removed
```

The final call to destroy() gives your applet an opportunity to release any persistent and/or expensive resources it had locked while in existence. Files, I/O streams, network connections, unwritten buffers, and similar resources might need some extra closing bookkeeping operations before the applet is discarded.

WARNING Java's garbage-collection feature means that ex-Pascal/C/C++ programmers can suddenly ignore cleanup issues with a vengeance. While the language feature itself is to be applauded (buggy cleanup code has been the cause of innumerable problems in the past), developers should not be lulled into a false sense of comfort. Java's garbage collection works only on objects that have no more parts of your application referencing them. Open files, output buffers, and network connections, for example, are more than just simple objects. You should therefore remain conscious of the (old) issues of correct code termination (the opposite of code initialization). Files should still be closed, output buffers flushed, and network connections disconnected properly.

Automating the Applet Tag Process

You may find the process of modifying the $\langle$APPLET CODE= ...$\rangle$ HTML tag repetitive and a general waste of time. You can make your life easier by automating the process. The following is a shell utility written in Java that takes your applet's class name (without the .html extension) and generates a minimal HTML file with the $\langle$APPLET$\rangle$ tag pointing correctly to your applet. The program uses file and stream I/O, so you may wish to ignore its internals until you are ready for the chapter dealing exclusively with the java.io package (Chapter 15).

```
//————————————————————————————————————
// GenAppletHTML utility
//————————————————————————————————————
// Usage: GenAppletHTML <AppletName>
//
// This Java application generates an HTML file named page.html, which
// can be passed to the JDK appletviewer utility to test applets.
//————————————————————————————————————

import java.io.*;

class GenAppletHTML {

public static void main (String[] args) throws IOException {

    FileWriter      fw;
    PrintWriter     html;

    // we need the name of an applet as argument
    if (args.length == 0) {
       System.out.println("Please specify the name of the applet to view.");
       System.exit(10);
    }

    // give usage summary if user asks for it
    if ( args[0].indexOf("?") != -1 || args[0].equals("-h") ) {
       System.out.println("Usage: GenAppletHTML <AppletName>");
```

```
        System.exit(0);
    }

    // guard against illegal class names being passed (GIGO)
    if ( ! (
        Character.isLowerCase( args[0].charAt(0) ) ||
        Character.isUpperCase( args[0].charAt(0) ))
        ) {
        System.out.println("'" + args[0] + "' Is not a legal class name.");
        System.exit(10);
    }

    // enforce convention of class names starting with a capital letter
    if (Character.isLowerCase( args[0].charAt(0) )) {
        System.out.println("Class names should (by convention) start with a
                            capital letter.");
        System.out.println(args[0]);
        System.out.println('^');
        System.out.println("is lower case.");
        System.exit(10);
    }

    // open file (combining FileOutputWriter and PrintWriter)

    fw = new FileWriter ("page.html");
    html = new PrintWriter (fw);

/* Generate an HTML file with the following structure:

<HTML>
<HEAD></HEAD>
<BODY>
<HR>
<APPLET CODE= ........ WIDTH=400 HEIGHT=300>
<PARAM NAME=arg1 VALUE="val1">
<PARAM NAME=arg2 VALUE="val2">
</APPLET>
<HR>
</BODY>
</HTML>
*/

    html.print("<HTML><HEAD></HEAD><BODY><HR><APPLET CODE=");
```

```
html.print(args[0] + ".class ");

html.println("WIDTH=400 HEIGHT=300>");
html.println("<PARAM NAME=arg1 VALUE=\"val1\" >");   // note backslash esc
html.println("<PARAM NAME=arg2 VALUE=\"val2\" >");
html.println("</APPLET><HR></BODY></HTML>");
html.close();
}}
```

To run the program, you invoke it as a stand-alone application; that is, from the command line:

C:\> java GenAppletHTML MyApplet

The GenAppletHTML utility is useful mainly on non-Unix machines that lack proper batch-processing command languages. It also nicely illustrates how Java can be used as a powerful and universal batch-programming language.

You should now have a clear overview of applet internals. As you can see, the difficulties lie not in any special precautions you need to take when using AWT classes in applets. The precautions to be taken are imposed on you by the browser-applet calling protocol.

The Code Framework for Applications

Since stand-alone applications are by definition responsible for every aspect of themselves, such Java programs are free from any browser protocol and do not inherit a window or drawing area to use "straight away."

Because they do not rely on a browser protocol, anything goes for applications: They do not need to be subclasses of class `Applet` and do not consequently need any overridden `init()`, `paint()`, `start()`, or `stop()` methods. An application can be any class, as long as it has the obligatory static `main()` method as a starting point for the code.

The absence of an inherited window or drawing area is the main difference when you are writing applications instead of applets (if you are used to writing applets). Applications do not have a convenient window in which to draw or add GUI components. All this needs to be somehow acquired by the application itself, and this is how a minimal application does it:

```
import java.awt.Frame;

import java.awt.Color;
class Application {

public static void main (String[] args) {
Frame myWindow;

  myWindow = new Frame("Window !");
  myWindow.setBackground(Color.blue);
  myWindow.resize(300,300);
  myWindow.setVisible(true);
  }}
```

The program first creates a window (which initially is not visible) by constructing a new Frame object.

WARNING Java *frames* are other people's normal *windows*. This unfortunate class nomenclature is only made worse by another AWT class called `Window`. A Java `Window` is a featureless rectangular pane (no title, menu bar, close button, or resize button) from which you can construct windows that ignore any and all local GUI style conventions. As such, class `Window` is used far less than class `Frame`. Instead of `Window` and `Frame`, these classes might have been better named *Pane* and *Window*.

The Frame constructor takes a string that will be the window's title. After construction, the frame's background color is set to blue. Next, the program specifies a size for this window using the `resize()` method (the window still is not visible). And finally, it commands the window to pop open and display itself by invoking the `setVisible()` method. For simple applications of the same (trivial) complexity as the

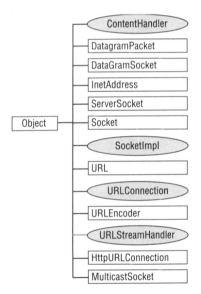

Interfaces:
- SocketImplFactory
- ContentHandlerFactory
- URLStreamHandlerFactory

you have just clobbered half of the `GridBagConstraints` parameters for button one.

Remember that Java objects are passed by reference and not by value (that is, objects are not copied). Shouldn't you therefore have needed to create a new `GridBagConstraints` object for each button? Normally, yes, but in this exceptional case, no. The reason lies hidden inside the `GridBagLayout` class itself. Method `setConstraints()` uses the `clone()` method to make a copy of the `GridBagConstraints` objects given to it. And this is why you can safely use a single `Grid-BagConstraints` object instance for any number of components.

The `clone()` method is available only on classes that implement the `Cloneable` interface. If you check back at the definition of `GridBag-Constraints`, you will see that this class does just that. Since very few classes do implement this interface, this type of object "pass-by-value" feature is rare in Java. The norm is that method arguments let your objects have full (shared) access to the passed object, and thus the programming technique used in our example would be quite incorrect. In this instance, however, it has become a Java idiom, so you can improve readability of code sections dealing with `GridBagLayout` managers by exploiting the object cloning behavior.

There is one more `GridBagConstraints` parameter to be introduced. To see its effect, recompile and run the applet with the following line removed:

```
gbc.fill = GridBagConstraints.HORIZONTAL;
```

Figure 10.14 shows an example of the resulting `GridBagLayout`.

FIGURE 10.14

A GridBagLayout with fill set to NONE

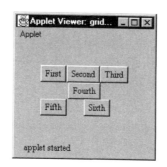

applet started

The layout suddenly looks very un-gridlike (if you look closely, the Fourth and Sixth buttons are not aligned to any grid). This is because of the other `GridBagConstraints` parameter: `anchor`. Without an explicit value for the `fill` parameter, you simply get its default: NONE. This means that any components will be sized to their preferred size (if possible). The odd-looking placement of buttons Four and Six is the result of the default `anchor` style. This default style centers components within the grid space they allocated, using `gridwidth` and `gridheight`. If you now add the following line (where you removed the fill style line), you should obtain the result shown in Figure 10.15.

```
gbc.anchor = GridBagConstraints.NORTHWEST;
```

FIGURE 10.15

A GridBagLayout with fill set to NONE and anchor set to NORTHWEST

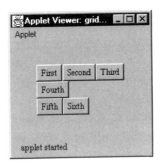

The valid values for the `anchor` parameter are CENTER, NORTH, EAST, NORTHEAST, SOUTHEAST, SOUTH, SOUTHWEST, WEST, and NORTHWEST.

In this example, the NORTH aspect of the NORTHWEST anchoring is effectively unused. Buttons Four and Six were simply pushed due WEST. This is because none of the components can move up or down within their grid size allocations (they are all one-cell tall). If you make some components taller (`gridheight` is greater than 1) and experiment with the `anchor` parameter, you will see the components move about in their "mooring" spaces according to the anchor style used.

GridBagLayout is extremely flexible, and this discussion has given only an overview of the functionality of the class. For more information, refer to the online documentation and experiment on your own. Also, the *Java Developers Handbook* (published by Sybex) contains an in-depth discussion on this and many other more advanced Java programming topics.

Now that you have been introduced to the standard AWT layout managers, you will next explore the innards of layout managers. The following section explains what all layout managers have in common.

Layout Manager Internals: Interface LayoutManager

Layout managers are powerful black boxes to help you design GUIs rapidly. But what if you want to write your own? If you look up the (online) class definition for FlowLayout, BorderLayout, CardLayout, GridLayout, or GridBagLayout, you will see that these classes all implement the same interface: LayoutManager. This interface is the key to understanding layout manager internals. Here is its definition:

```
public interface LayoutManager extends Object {
    public abstract void addLayoutComponent(String name, Component comp);
    public abstract void removeLayoutComponent(Component comp);
    public abstract Dimension preferredLayoutSize(Container parent);
    public abstract Dimension minimumLayoutSize(Container parent);
    public abstract void layoutContainer(Container parent);
}
```

The methods the interface asks you to implement can be grouped as follows:

- Adding/removing components to a container

- Calculating preferred and minimum container sizes

- Actually doing the layout operation

You might think that the addLayoutComponent() method is a direct analog of the add() container methods. However, this is only partially correct. A layout manager's addLayoutComponent() method is called only by a container's add(*String, Component*) method and not by the simpler add(*Component*) method. Layout managers FlowLayout, GridLayout, and GridBagLayout implement their addLayoutComponent() methods as follows:

```
public void addLayoutComponent(String name, Component comp) {
}
```

That's right—a void body. These managers don't manage the growing collection of components added to their associated container, because they don't need to. The container object keeps track of all the components it contains (that is its primary function, after all). And when layoutContainer() is called, the layout manager receives a handle to the container it should lay out. Via this handle, the layout manager can access all of the container's components, in sequence, with the Container methods countComponents() and get-Component(). This is how some layout managers can afford to have empty addLayoutComponent() and removeLayoutComponent() methods. But this is not universal. Layout managers BorderLayout and CardLayout have non-empty bodies for these methods, because these two layout managers use the second type of Container add() method: add(*String, Component*). While the unlabeled add() essentially just adds a component to the container's internal list, the labeled add() also tells the container's layout manager about the component.

Method layoutContainer() is the heart of any layout manager—it is where all the laying out finally takes place. Here the layout manager will use the container's insets settings and all the components' preferred sizes to determine exactly how to size and position each component.

As an example, this is the `BorderLayout` manager's `layout-Container()`:

```
public void layoutContainer(Container target) {
    Insets insets = target.getInsets();
    int top = insets.top;
    int bottom = target.height - insets.bottom;
    int left = insets.left;
    int right = target.width - insets.right;

    if ((north != null) && north.visible) {
        north.setSize(right - left, north.height);
        Dimension d = north.getPreferredSize();
        north.setBounds(left, top, right - left, d.height);
        top += d.height + vgap;
    }
    if ((south != null) && south.visible) {
        south.setSize(right - left, south.height);
        Dimension d = south.getPreferredSize();
        south.setBounds(left, bottom - d.height, right - left, d.height);
        bottom -= d.height + vgap;
    }
    if ((east != null) && east.visible) {
        east.setSize(east.width, bottom - top);
        Dimension d = east.getPreferredSize();
        east.setBounds(right - d.width, top, d.width, bottom - top);
        right -= d.width + hgap;
    }
    if ((west != null) && west.visible) {
        west.setSize(west.width, bottom - top);
        Dimension d = west.getPreferredSize();
        west.setBounds(left, top, d.width, bottom - top);
        left += d.width + hgap;
    }
    if ((center != null) && center.visible) {
        center.setBounds(left, top, right - left, bottom - top);
    }
}
```

BorderLayout starts by determining the available working area by subtracting the insets from the container's dimensions. It then proceeds to lay out its five possible components; north, south, east, west, and center, in that sequence. Remember that `BorderLayout` components must be added using the labeled `add`, `add(String, Component)`. `BorderLayout` therefore manages its "list" of components by storing each component directly into its private variables `north`, `south`, `east`, `west`, and `center` (this is done by its `add-LayoutComponent()` method). The actual layout logic is, of course, totally manager dependent. What all managers need to have in common, however, is the use of the preferred size of components to make their layout decisions. Components are eventually positioned and sized using their `reshape()` method.

These are the other two `LayoutManager` methods:

```
public abstract Dimension preferredLayoutSize(Container parent)
public abstract Dimension minimumLayoutSize(Container parent)
```

These two are in fact very similar to `layoutContainer()`, except that they do not actually lay out the components for real. Their goal is to work out what the size of the container could be set to if a layout were done honoring all components' preferred or minimum sizes. The logic for these two methods is virtually identical to that of `layout-Container()`, bar the `setSize()` and `setBounds()` calls. Additionally, method `minimumLayoutSize()` calls the `getMinimumSize()` method on components instead of calculating a size for them.

Summary

This chapter taught you the absolute basics of how to use Java's AWT. You saw that there are two fundamentally different contexts in which the AWT can be used: applets and applications. Applets are bound to the applet-browser protocol; applications need to build their GUIs from scratch, starting with a window to hold the GUI. You then studied Java's solution to platform-independent GUI designing: layout managers.

Layout managers are responsible for laying out your GUI's graphical elements in such a way that the resulting windows or screens look acceptable on all Java platforms. Layout managers interact closely with container classes (which are all descendants of class `Container`), for which they perform the layout function, and with component classes (all descendants of class `Component`), which are the objects being laid out. The AWT currently provides five different preprogrammed layout styles, that, when used in concert, offer enough layout flexibility to create modern, functional, and—last but not least—platform-independent GUIs. The preprogrammed layout managers are, in increasing order of complexity, `FlowLayout`, `GridLayout`, `BorderLayout`, `CardLayout`, and `GridBagLayout`, which relies on a helper class called `GridBagConstraints`.

For those rare occasions when the standard AWT layout managers are not sufficient for your purposes, you looked at how layout managers themselves are implemented, with a view on designing your own. Essentially, and regardless of layout approach, the sole requirement for any layout manager class is that it implements the `LayoutManager` interface.

CHAPTER

ELEVEN

11

AWT GUI Components

- The AWT GUI superclass and its methods

- Buttons, checkboxes, lists, and other standard GUI components

- Menu-support components

Modern GUIs are rich in the type of graphical elements employed to make the human-computer interface (HCI) as productive as possible. Buttons and menus are still the ubiquitous and original classics, but nowadays there is a whole collection of evolutionary descendants. The spectrum of popular buttons and menus ranges from radio buttons, pop-up menus, and slider controls to the more complex components, such as list and tree views, toolbars, and progress status windows.

Java's AWT contains a healthy mix of the simpler components. The complex components, which allow you to produce the professional-looking applications everyone has come to expect these days, have not yet been included. (Some of these are part of the Java Management API, which is an extension to the Core API.) The standard AWT components you will examine include buttons, canvases, labels, checkboxes, list-boxes, scrollbars, text, and scrollpanes. Also, the AWT's menu-related components are described.

All of the these components are accessed and used via corresponding AWT classes. Before systematically exploring the individual components, you will want to take a close look at the granddad of all components (except menus): class `Component`, itself.

NOTE Bear in mind that Java is a very recent development and that it breaks new ground in several areas, including GUI design and implementation. Therefore, the supported components and their encapsulating classes cannot be as mature and complete as, say, the Macintosh GUI toolkit, which has had more than a decade to evolve. With the current speed at which Java is evolving, the AWT's immaturity may have already been addressed by the time you read this—by Sun or by a third party establishing a de facto standard.

The Superclass of the AWT GUI Classes

Do GUI elements have anything in common? They actually have many things in common. And when classes have things in common, you immediately think "abstraction." Object-oriented methodology demands there be a superclass to any group of classes with identifiable, shared characteristics. A superclass localizes code and/or data structures that would otherwise be duplicated and scattered around your systems (negatively affecting code robustness and flexibility). The AWT GUI classes have one such superclass: class Component.

Here is what every component is supposed to have in common with every other AWT component:

```
public class Component extends Object
implements ImageObserver, MenuContainer, Serializable {

    public static final float BOTTOM_ALIGNMENT = 1.0f;
    public static final float CENTER_ALIGNMENT = 0.5f;
    public static final float LEFT_ALIGNMENT = 0.0f;
    public static final Object LOCK = new Object();
    public static final float RIGHT_ALIGNMENT = 1.0f;
    public static final float TOP_ALIGNMENT = 0.0f;

    public boolean action(Event evt, Object what);
    public synchronized void add(PopupMenu popup);
    public synchronized void addComponentListener(ComponentListener 1);
    public synchronized void addFocusListener(FocusListener 1);
    public synchronized void addKeyListener(KeyListener 1);
    public synchronized void addMouseListener(MouseListener 1);
    public synchronized void addMouseMotionListener(MouseMotionListener 1);
    public void addNotify();
    public Rectangle bounds();
    public int checkImage(Image image, ImageObserver observer);
    public int checkImage(Image image, int width, int height,
                     ImageObserver observer);
    public boolean contains(int x, int y);
    public boolean contains(Point p);
```

```
public Image createImage(ImageProducer producer);
public Image createImage(int width, int height);
public void deliverEvent(Event e);
public void disable();
public void doLayout();
public void enable();
public void enable(boolean b);
public float getAlignmentX();
public float getAlignmentY();
public Color getBackground();
public Rectangle getBounds();
public ColorModel getColorModel();
public Component getComponentAt(int x, int y);
public Component getComponentAt(Point p);
public Cursor getCursor();
public Font getFont();
public FontMetrics getFontMetrics(Font font);
public Color getForeground();
public Graphics getGraphics();
public Locale getLocale();
public Point getLocation();
public Point getLocationOnScreen();
public Dimension getMaximumSize();
public Dimension getMinimumSize();
public String getName();
public Container getParent();
public ComponentPeer getPeer();
public Dimension getPreferredSize();
public Dimension getSize();
public Toolkit getToolkit();
public final Object getTreeLock();
public boolean gotFocus(Event evt, Object what);
public boolean handleEvent(Event evt);
public void hide();
public boolean imageUpdate(Image img, int flags,
                           int x, int y, int w, int h);
public boolean inside(int x, int y);
public void invalidate();
public boolean isEnabled();
public boolean isFocusTraversable();
public boolean isShowing();
```

```
public boolean isValid();
public boolean isVisible();
public boolean keyDown(Event evt, int key);
public boolean keyUp(Event evt, int key);
public void layout();
public void list();
public void list(PrintStream out);
public void list(PrintStream out, int indent);
public void list(PrintWriter out);
public void list(PrintWriter out, int indent);
public Component locate(int x, int y);
public Point location();
public boolean lostFocus(Event evt, Object what);
public Dimension minimumSize();
public boolean mouseDown(Event evt, int x, int y);
public boolean mouseDrag(Event evt, int x, int y);
public boolean mouseEnter(Event evt, int x, int y);
public boolean mouseExit(Event evt, int x, int y);
public boolean mouseMove(Event evt, int x, int y);
public boolean mouseUp(Event evt, int x, int y);
public void move(int x, int y);
public void nextFocus();
public void paint(Graphics g);
public void paintAll(Graphics g);
public boolean postEvent(Event e);
public Dimension preferredSize();
public boolean prepareImage(Image image, ImageObserver observer);
public boolean prepareImage(Image image, int width, int height,
                            ImageObserver observer);
public void print(Graphics g);
public void printAll(Graphics g);
public synchronized void remove(MenuComponent popup);
public synchronized void removeComponentListener(ComponentListener l);
public synchronized void removeFocusListener(FocusListener l);
public synchronized void removeKeyListener(KeyListener l);
public synchronized void removeMouseListener(MouseListener l);
public synchronized void removeMouseMotionListener(MouseMotionListener l);
public void removeNotify();
public void repaint();
public void repaint(int x, int y, int width, int height);
public void repaint(long tm);
```

```
    public void repaint(long tm, int x, int y, int width, int height);
    public void requestFocus();
    public void reshape(int x, int y, int width, int height);
    public void resize(Dimension d);
    public void resize(int width, int height);
    public void setBackground(Color c);
    public void setBounds(int x, int y, int width, int height);
    public void setBounds(Rectangle r);
    public synchronized void setCursor(Cursor cursor);
    public void setEnabled(boolean b);
    public synchronized void setFont(Font f);
    public void setForeground(Color c);
    public void setLocale(Locale l);
    public void setLocation(int x, int y);
    public void setLocation(Point p);
    public void setName(String name);
    public void setSize(Dimension d);
    public void setSize(int width, int height);
    public void setVisible(boolean b);
    public void show();
    public void show(boolean b);
    public Dimension size();
    public String toString();
    public void transferFocus();
    public void update(Graphics g);
    public void validate();
}
```

Rather a long and intimidating collection of methods, isn't it? This is because the behavior of AWT components can be complex and multifaceted.

Although class Component is huge, very few of its methods are actually used frequently by the vast majority of programs. Even so, class Component is so fundamental to Java AWT programming that a study of its method groups is in order. The following sections discuss each of this class's method groups. The important thing to keep in mind is that any component (that is, all of the descendant classes of Component) can support all of these methods.

You might have noticed that class `Component` implements the interface `ImageObserver`. This interface specifies only a single method, `imageUpdate()`, to be implemented. See Chapter 13 for information about the function of this method and the relevance of all components being `ImageObservers`.

Event-Handling Methods

The most important group of `Component` methods are those relating to event handling:

```
public synchronized void
addComponentListener(ComponentListener 1);
public synchronized void addFocusListener(FocusListener 1);
public synchronized void addKeyListener(KeyListener 1);
public synchronized void addMouseListener(MouseListener 1);
public synchronized void
addMouseMotionListener(MouseMotionListener 1);
public synchronized void
removeComponentListener(ComponentListener 1);
public synchronized void removeFocusListener(FocusListener 1);
public synchronized void removeKeyListener(KeyListener 1);
public synchronized void removeMouseListener(MouseListener 1);
public synchronized void
removeMouseMotionListener(MouseMotionListener 1);
```

These methods deal with event listeners, which are part of Java's event-delegation model. This model is new in release 1.1 of the JDK and is discussed in detail in Chapter 12.

The Pre-1.1 Event Model

A number of additional methods support an almost obsolete event model that was in use before release 1.1. These methods remain in 1.1 so that pre-1.1 code will continue to work, but Sun does not guarantee that they will be part of any post-1.1 release. Code that combines the two models is not guaranteed to work, and probably will not. The new model, while slightly more complex than the old model, is more flexible and robust. The methods listed below appear for completeness, but they should not be used in new Java code.

```
public boolean handleEvent(Event evt);
public boolean action(Event evt, Object what);
public boolean mouseDown(Event evt, int x, int y);
public boolean mouseDrag(Event evt, int x, int y);
public boolean mouseUp(Event evt, int x, int y);
public boolean mouseMove(Event evt, int x, int y);
public boolean mouseEnter(Event evt, int x, int y);
public boolean mouseExit(Event evt, int x, int y);
public boolean keyDown(Event evt, int key);
public boolean keyUp(Event evt, int key);
public boolean gotFocus(Event evt, Object what);
public boolean lostFocus(Event evt, Object what);
public void requestFocus();
public void nextFocus();
```

Component Moving and Resizing Methods

The following Component methods are related to moving and resizing GUI elements:

```
public void setLocation(Point p);
public void setSize(int width, int height);
public void setSize(Dimension d);
public synchronized void setBounds(int x, int y, int width,
                                   int height);
```

As you learned in Chapter 10, the AWT is novel in its way of positioning and sizing an application's GUI elements. With Java, you always rely on a layout manager (class) to give your components their final, absolute positions and dimensions. The methods listed here are for the layout managers to use, and not for you to call. This is the general rule, although you can use these methods on class Window and its children. Layout managers have no say on where you put windows or how big or small you make them (their jurisdiction is the contents of windows). The way you position or size your application windows on a given Desktop is your business.

Position and Geometry Querying Methods

The following methods are related to querying the position and geometry of GUI components:

```
public Point getLocation();
public Dimension getSize();
public Rectangle getBounds();
public synchronized boolean contains(int x, int y);
```

Since layout managers have so much control over the final placement and size of your components, these methods allow you to find out what the layout managers finally decided upon in terms of position and size, once the layout is done.

Graphics and Rendering Methods

The following methods are related to graphics and graphical components:

```
public Graphics getGraphics();
public synchronized ColorModel getColorModel();
public Font getFont();
public FontMetrics getFontMetrics(Font font);
public Color getForeground();
public Color getBackground();
public synchronized void setFont(Font f);
public synchronized void setForeground(Color c);
public synchronized void setBackground(Color c);
public Toolkit getToolkit();
```

The most important of these methods is getGraphics(). When working with entire windows (class Frame) or with Canvas components, you can draw inside them using any of the rendering methods of class Graphics after you have obtained the graphics context for your drawing medium (see Chapter 13 for details of the Graphics class). You use getGraphics() to obtain a component's associated graphics context.

> **NOTE**
> The `getGraphics()` method is not supported by all components. Only `Frame` and `Canvas` components let you draw in them. `Buttons`, `Choices`, and other components will not let you have their `Graphics` context for you to alter their appearance.

The other methods let you query or set some graphical `Component` attributes, such as the font used for any text rendering and the foreground and background colors for the component.

Layout Manager Methods

Several `Component` methods are for layout managers:

```
public Dimension getPreferredSize();
public Dimension getMinimumSize();
public Dimension getMaximumSize();
public void doLayout();
```

Methods `getPreferredSize()` and `getMinimumSize()` have already been discussed in our study of layout managers. To briefly reiterate, these methods need to be overridden by your `Component` subclasses (`MyButton`, `ZIPCodeTextField`, and so on) to let the layout managers know how to size them under various packing conditions.

The `doLayout()` method itself forces an immediate layout for the component. You should never call this method yourself; it is called by the `validate()` method.

Self-Painting Methods

The following are the `Component` class self-painting methods:

```
public void paint(Graphics g);
public void update(Graphics g);
public void paintAll(Graphics g);
```

```
public void repaint();
public void repaint(long tm);
public void repaint(int x, int y, int width, int height);
public void repaint(long tm, int x, int y, int width, int
                    height);
public void print(Graphics g);
public void printAll(Graphics g);
```

Here, `paint()`, `update()`, and `repaint()` are the important methods. You have already seen `paint()` in action: You need to override it in order to refresh your applet. That's right—the `paint()` method is not an `Applet` method at all; it is a `Component` method. All components without visible native imagery (`Canvas`, `Panel`, `Applet`) redraw themselves via overridden `paint()` methods.

You might have wondered why we never suggested you clear your applet window by filling it to a background color, before starting to redraw it. This is because the `paint()` method starts with a clean slate each time, courtesy of method `update()`. The `update()` method does three things:

- Clears the component's visible area, using the component's background color.

- Sets the graphics object's color to the component's foreground color.

- Calls `paint()`, passing in the graphics object.

If you want to avoid this window-cleaning action, you can override the `update()` method instead of overriding `paint()` (you will see how this technique is used in Chapter 13).

The `repaint()` methods are usually called by external entities (the browser, for example) to request a `Component` redraw. The `repaint()` variant with the empty argument list is a possible exception. You can call it to force an `update()` (and, therefore, a `paint()`, too) to happen as soon as possible. See Chapter 13 for information about delayed repainting, which is explained in the discussion of asynchronous image loading and updating.

Parent/Subcomponents Methods

Two methods deal with parents and subcomponents:

```
public Container getParent();
public Component getComponentAt(int x, int y);
```

In practice, a Component is almost always part of a nested GUI hierarchy of parent containers, containers, and subcontainers. Any Component can discover whether it is part of a container by using the getparent() method (a null return value means that the Component is the topmost container).

If a Component is a Container itself, it can find out which component is located at its relative coordinates (*x*,*y*) by calling getComponentAt() on itself.

State Changing and Querying Methods

The following are the Component methods for changing and querying a component's state:

```
public void setEnabled(boolean cond);
public void setVisible(boolean cond);
public void validate();
public void invalidate();
public boolean isValid();
public boolean isVisible();
public boolean isShowing();
public boolean isEnabled();
```

Any Component can find itself in one of three boolean states: enabled/disabled, showing/hiding, or valid/invalid.

You disable components to make them unresponsive to user selections; this is sometimes called *graying out* or *ghosting*. Or you can hide a component if it is to be unavailable for prolonged periods. (Disabling a component means it is only temporarily unavailable.)

You can also invalidate components after you have modified them by adding (with add ( ))or removing (with remove ()) components. You need to call validate () to revalidate their state and have the screen updated accordingly

Image-Related Methods

The following are the image-related methods in the Component class:

```
public Image createImage(ImageProducer producer);
public Image createImage(int width, int height);
public boolean imageUpdate(Image img, int flags, int x, int y, int w, int h);
public boolean prepareImage(Image image, ImageObserver observer);
public boolean prepareImage(Image image, int width, int height, ImageObserver
                    observer);
public int checkImage(Image image, ImageObserver observer);
public int checkImage(Image image, int width, int height, ImageObserver
                    observer);
```

Components like Canvas and Frame can be used to draw images in. These are some of the methods you need in order to add images to components. Image creation and manipulation are covered in Chapter 13.

Component Peer Methods

The Component class has two methods for peer communications:

```
public void addNotify();
public synchronized void removeNotify();
```

Every component has some methods to let it communicate with its peer. Earlier you learned that the AWT relies on native components to retain the native platform's look and feel for GUIs. In reality, however, the AWT goes a step further than this: It relies on the native components for event handling, too. When a Java applet uses a Java AWT Button on a Windows 95 machine, a "peer" Windows 95 button is used to incarnate the Java AWT Button. Behind the scenes, therefore, a delicate protocol keeps the two buttons (one abstract; the other concrete) in sync with each other.

> **WARNING** Keeping two different but equivalent systems in sync is always a tricky and fragile balancing act. If the entities lose their synchronization for any reason (like a bug), the whole system breaks down. At the time of this writing, there are several problems of exactly this nature in the Windows NT/95 implementation of the AWT peers. The result is that the visible GUI, managed and presented by the peers, does not always mirror the messages addressed to the AWT components in the code.

The methods `addNotify()` and `removeNotify()` are used to force the creation and destruction, respectively, of the peer. The peer-related methods should rarely be called by application programmers. These are low-level methods used purely by the components themselves to communicate with their peers. In particular, calling `addNotify()` or `removeNotify()` could disrupt the abstract-component/concrete-component protocol, resulting in serious out-of-sync inconsistency problems.

Component Subclasses and Inheritance

You now have a general idea of the types of methods for all components. Before you explore the concrete subclasses of class `Component`, there is one more important point to highlight. As you know by now, any subclass inherits all of its parent class(es) methods. So all the AWT `Component` classes will inherit the entire list of methods discussed in the previous sections. Take class `Canvas` for example:

```
public class Canvas extends Component {
    public Canvas();
    public synchronized void addNotify();
    public void paint(Graphics g);
}
```

This much smaller class seems to consist only of its constructor and two methods, but this is not the case. Class `Canvas` extends class `Component`, so it is even larger than class `Component`. This is something to be very conscious of whenever you study a subclass definition. Never forget the functionality inherited from the parent and all its parents.

Adding Components to Your GUI

The following sections describe the standard AWT components you can add to your Java applets and applications:

Button	List
Canvas	Scrollbar
Label	TextArea
Checkbox	TextField
Choice	ScrollPane

Adding Buttons

Launch any application on any modern desktop computer, and you will see buttons all over the place. Several types of buttons are generally used to manipulate windows on every platform:

- A resizing button
- Minimize (or iconify) and maximize buttons
- A close button

Toolbars are collections of buttons. Scrollbars consist of at least three buttons: two for the up and down arrows and one stretched-out button for the scroll area. Status bars can also contain buttons camouflaged as simple labels. But whatever its exact appearance, a button always boils down to a rectangular window area that has associated with it a unique, individual behavior compared to other similar areas. From this definition, it is just a small step to graphically highlight this rectangular area by drawing its outline and adding a descriptive label or icon to identify it.

Java's idea of a button is just that: an outline, a label, and some methods for handling events. Here is its class definition:

```
public class Button extends Component {
    public Button();
    public Button(String label);
    public void AddActionListener(ActionListener al);
    public synchronized void addNotify();
    public String getActionCommand();
    public String getLabel();
    public void removeActionListener(ActionListener al);
    public void setActionCommand(String command);
    public void setLabel(String label);
    protected String paramString();
}
```

To use this class, all you need to understand is how to use the constructors. The most commonly used constructor for a Button takes a String, which will be depicted on the button as its label. Figure 11.1 shows an example of a Java Button component.

FIGURE 11.1

A Button component

Adding buttons to Java applets or applications is very easy, as you can see in the following program, which created the button shown in Figure 11.1:

```
import java.awt.*;

public class ButtonTest extends java.applet.Applet {

public void init() {
Button b;

  b = new Button("A Java Button!");
  add(b);
}}
```

This applet simple declares a variable b of type `Button`, creates a new `Button` object for it, and adds (with the `add()` method) this button to the applet. The button label `"A Java Button!"` was specified as the string argument to the `Button` constructor. As you can see in Figure 11.1, the button is centered automatically. This is because the default layout manager for applets is `FlowLayout`, which itself uses its own default alignment style: `CENTER`. The `ButtonTest` class subclasses `Applet`. This is specified with its full package name as `java.applet.Applet`.

The first `import` statement makes all `java.awt` classes available to the compilation unit (the source file). In this instance, you could have simply used the following line instead, since this is the only AWT class used in the program:

```
import java.awt.Button;
```

> **NOTE**
>
> Contrary to popular Java beliefs, importing whole packages does not increase the size of your executables. The `import` statements only make class definitions visible to other classes at compilation time. The actual linking is done at runtime, not compile time. This explains why the executables do not swell up by importing external classes, as they do with most other compiled languages.

You can change the label of a `Button` at any time using the `set-Label()` method. Similarly, you can find out which `Button` you are manipulating by asking the button what its label is with `getLabel()`.

Working with the Canvas

`Canvas` is the simplest concrete incarnation of the abstract class `Component`. Here is its class definition:

```
public class Canvas extends Component {
    public Canvas();
    public synchronized void addNotify();
    public void paint(Graphics g);
}
```

The only behavior it adds to that of `Component` is of that of the default `paint()` method, which clears the entire component (canvas) area to the component's background color. You use this class whenever you need a generic, drawable surface area that can respond to mouse and key inputs. Another possible use for class `Canvas` is as a foundation for creating your own components—for example, creating enhanced buttons that can have an icon instead of a text label.

> **TIP**
>
> Remember that the default `update()` method for `Component` also clears the component to its background area. A default `Canvas`, then, clears its background twice—first in its `update()` method, followed by its `paint()` method. Since this is clearly superfluous, you should override either the `update()` or `paint()` method to avoid this double clearing action.

Figure 11.2 shows a custom `Canvas` component drawn with an outline to highlight the canvas area. Note that the bottom line of the outline is overwritten by the "applet started" string printed by appletviewer (in other words, the code doesn't have a bug).

FIGURE 11.2

An outlined Canvas
component

Here is the demonstration program behind Figure 11.2:

```java
import java.awt.*;

public class CanvasTest extends java.applet.Applet {

    MyCanvas doodle;

    public void init() {
        doodle = new MyCanvas(getSize().width, getSize().height);
        add(doodle);
    }
}

class MyCanvas extends Canvas {

    public MyCanvas() {
        this(100,100);
    }

    public MyCanvas(int width, int height) {
        setSize(width,height);
    }

    public void paint(Graphics g) {
        g.drawRect(0, 0, getSize().width-1, getSize().height-1);
    }
}
```

In this program, you actually subclass class `Canvas` to create your own variety. Its `paint()` method draws an outline around (or, to be precise, just inside) the canvas area. Class `MyCanvas` also contains two constructors: The default constructor takes no parameters but creates a canvas area 100 × 100 pixels big. The constructor actually called from within the applet is the generic constructor that takes any dimensions.

Note how the default constructor calls the generic constructor— this is an almost universal technique among class constructors. Classes provide a small collection of overloaded constructors, of which the most flexible is the "true" constructor; the others are just convenient shorthand forms for common default cases. Since it takes very little effort to provide such collections of overloaded constructors, you should do this with your own classes.

Adding Labels to Items

A `Label` component is simply a passive (that is, completely non-interactive) and graphically unassuming single line of text. Here is its class definition:

```
public class Label extends Component {
   public final static int LEFT;
   public final static int CENTER;
   public final static int RIGHT;
   public Label();
   public Label(String label);
   public Label(String label, int alignment);
   public synchronized void addNotify();
   public int getAlignment();
   public void setAlignment(int alignment)
     throws IllegalArgumentException;
public String getText();
   public void setText(String label);
   protected String paramString();
}
```

You might use `Label` components, for example, to label areas of your GUI that are grouped together in a `Container`. Figure 11.3 illustrates three `Label` components.

FIGURE 11.3

Three Label components

Here is the demonstration program behind Figure 11.3:

```
import java.awt.*;

public class LabelTest extends java.applet.Applet {

    public void init() {
        setLayout(new GridLayout(3,1));
        add(new Label("Left label"));  // default left justify
        add(new Label("Center label", Label.CENTER));  // center
        add(new Label("Right label", Label.RIGHT));  // right justify
    }
}
```

As you can see, the only additional attribute of a `Label` is its alignment. You can choose between `LEFT`, `CENTER`, or `RIGHT`. The label's text and alignment properties can be changed or queried with the methods `getAlignment()`, `setAlignment(int alignment)`, `getText()`, and `setText(String label)`.

The alignment of a label will have a visual effect only if the layout manager that controls the `Label` component allows components to appear sized to dimensions other than their `minimumSize()`. Changing the alignment of labels within a `FlowLayout`, for example, has no effect, because `FlowLayout` always sizes components to their most compact dimensions.

Adding Checkboxes and Checkbox Groups

A `Checkbox` component is a two-state button that is typically used in GUIs containing selectable items (such as in voting forms or option preference pages). Here is its class definition:

```
public class Checkbox extends Component implements ItemSelectable {
   public Checkbox();
   public Checkbox(String label);
   public Checkbox(String label, boolean state);
   public Checkbox(String label, boolean state, CheckboxGroup group);
   public Checkbox(String label, CheckboxGroup group, boolean state);
   public void addItemListener(ItemListener l);
   public void addNotify();
   public CheckboxGroup getCheckboxGroup();
   public String getLabel();
   public Object[] getSelectedObjects();
   public boolean getState();
   public void removeItemListener(ItemListener l);
   public void setCheckboxGroup(CheckboxGroup g);
   public synchronized void setLabel(String label);
   public void setState(boolean state);
}
```

Figure 11.4 shows an example of a `Checkbox` component. Here is the demonstration program behind Figure 11.4:

```
import java.awt.*;

public class CheckboxTest extends java.applet.Applet {

   public void init() {
      Checkbox cb = new Checkbox("Black and White");
      add(cb);
   }
}
```

FIGURE 11.4

A Checkbox component

The program declares and constructs a `Checkbox` object that is labeled with the string passed as argument to the `Checkbox` constructor. The `Checkbox` component is then added, as usual, with the `add()` method. By default, a checkbox's state is initially false. You can create a checkbox with a specified initial state by calling an alternate version of the constructor: `Checkbox (String, boolean)`. The boolean parameter provides the checkbox's initial state.

Mutually Exclusive Checkboxes

If you want simple checkable buttons, all you need to do is simply construct a `Checkbox` and add it to your container. But if you want a group of checkboxes to be mutually exclusive, you will need to use the more complex constructor and associated methods.

To define a group of checkboxes to be mutually exclusive (called radio buttons in other GUI frameworks), you need one extra helper class: `CheckboxGroup`. Here is its definition:

```
public class CheckboxGroup extends Object {
    public CheckboxGroup();
    public Checkbox getSelectedCheckbox();
    public synchronized void setSelectedCheckbox(Checkbox box);
    public String toString();
}
```

The purpose of CheckboxGroup is to provide the scope for the mutually exclusive group and to manage the group's state.

Here is a demonstration program that uses a CheckboxGroup instance to define a mutually exclusive collection of checkboxes:

```
import java.awt.*;

public class MutexCheckboxTest extends java.applet.Applet {

public void init() {

CheckboxGroup checkboxFence = new CheckboxGroup();
Checkbox check1 = new Checkbox("Black and White",
checkboxFence, false);
Checkbox check2 = new Checkbox("256 Greyscale"  ,
checkboxFence, false);
Checkbox check3 = new Checkbox("True Color"     ,
checkboxFence, false);

    add(check1);
    add(check2);
    add(check3);
}}
```

As you can see, a different constructor is used to build the Checkbox instances for this program. For mutually exclusive checkboxes, you need to pass in a CheckboxGroup instance that defines the extent of the group. The third constructor argument is the initial state for the checkbox: false for deselected and true for selected. Within any group of mutually exclusive checkboxes, you can make only one of the radio buttons selected. Figure 11.5 shows the result of the above program.

Note the layout of the buttons in Figure 11.5. This format is again a result of the default FlowLayout used by applets.

To change the state of any Checkbox that is part of a mutually exclusive group, you need to use the CheckboxGroup method set-Current(Checkbox *box*) to ensure that the mutual exclusiveness is maintained (you should not use the Checkbox method setState()).

FIGURE 11.5

Mutually exclusive
checkboxes

Adding Choice (Pull-Down) Lists

The Choice class encapsulates a pull-down choice list component. It
has the following definition:

```
public class Choice extends Component implements
ItemSelectable
{
    public Choice();
    public synchronized void add(String item);
    public void addItemListener(ItemListener l);
    public void addNotify();
    public String getItem(int index);
    public int getItemCount();
    public int getSelectedIndex();
    public synchronized String getSelectedItem();
    public synchronized Object[] getSelectedObjects();
    public synchronized void insert(String item, int index);
    public synchronized void remove(int position);
    public synchronized void remove(String item);
    public synchronized void removeAll();
    public void removeItemListener(ItemListener l);
    public synchronized void select(int pos);
    public synchronized void select(String str);
}
```

The Choice component allows a user to select one of several options or items in one space-saving place. When GUI real estate becomes crowded, you can substitute a collection of mutually exclusive radio buttons with a single, compact Choice component. Figure 11.6 shows an example of a pull-down-type list created with this component.

FIGURE 11.6

A Choice component

Here is the demonstration program behind Figure 11.6:

```java
import java.awt.*;

public class ChoiceTest extends java.applet.Applet {

    public void init() {
        IcecreamChoice coolChoices = new IcecreamChoice();
        add(coolChoices);
    }
}

class IcecreamChoice extends Choice {

    public IcecreamChoice() {
        add("Chocolate");
        add("Vanilla");
        add("Strawberry");
    }
}
```

This applet uses a customized `Choice` class with a default constructor, which employs the `addItem()` method to define its list of choices. To use the `IcecreamChoice` component, you construct an instance of it and add the object to the applet container via the `add()` method.

Creating Self-Contained Software Objects

You may be wondering if it's overkill to define an entire class just for `IcecreamChoice`—it isn't. Creating compact, self-contained software objects, like `IcecreamChoice`, significantly improves your software. Here are some of the benefits of this approach:

- It reduces the complexity of your application by collapsing algorithms and/or data structures into easily manageable entities (classes, which you can then treat as "black boxes").

- It makes your code more maintainable and improves readability.

- It unambiguously draws boundaries for subsystem responsibilities.

- It helps you to view your programs as collections of interacting objects.

The advantages of properly exploiting the object-oriented class mechanism (by encapsulating chunks of code and data), are so numerous that you should consult a good book on object-oriented software engineering. The investment will repay itself a hundredfold. In the meantime, you might want to rely on the following rule of thumb: Better a class too many than one too few.

Class `Choice` provides methods that allow you to access and/or set the currently selected item in the list.

`getSelectedItem()` Returns the string of the item itself.

`getSelectedIndex()` Returns the index position of the item.

getSelectedObjects() Returns an array that contains the item.

select(int *pos*) Selects an item by index position.

select(String *str*) Selects an item by name.

Choice components are ideal for reasonably small lists of selectable items (say, from three to ten items). But if you have only two choices, it might be better to use mutually exclusive checkboxes instead (unless the list of choices is dynamic and is expected to grow beyond two). If, on the other hand, your list of choices becomes large, you should consider using a List.

Adding Lists

Consider a List component as a heavyweight analog of a Choice component. Here is its class definition:

```
public class List extends Component implements ItemSelectable
{
    public List();
    public List(int rows);
    public List(int rows, boolean multipleMode);
    public void add(String item);
    public synchronized void add(String item, int index);
    public void addActionListener(ActionListener l);
    public void addItemListener(ItemListener l);
    public void addNotify();
    public synchronized void deselect(int index);
    public String getItem(int index);
    public int getItemCount();
    public synchronized String[] getItems();
    public Dimension getMinimumSize();
    public Dimension getMinimumSize(int rows);
    public Dimension getPreferredSize();
    public Dimension getPreferredSize(int rows);
    public int getRows();
    public synchronized int getSelectedIndex();
```

```
public synchronized int[] getSelectedIndexes();
public synchronized String getSelectedItem();
public synchronized String[] getSelectedItems();
public Object[] getSelectedObjects();
public int getVisibleIndex();
public boolean isIndexSelected(int index);
public boolean isMultipleMode();
public synchronized void makeVisible(int index);
public synchronized void remove(int position);
public synchronized void remove(String item);
public void removeActionListener(ActionListener l);
public synchronized void removeAll();
public void removeItemListener(ItemListener l);
public void removeNotify();
public synchronized void replaceItem(String newValue, int index);
public synchronized void select(int index);
public synchronized void setMultipleMode(boolean b);
}
```

The following are the main differences between the `List` and `Choice` components:

- Lists are used for much longer lists of items.

- Lists are used when multiple selections are needed.

- Lists typically use up a large proportion of a GUI's real estate.

- Class `List` contains many more methods supporting its functionality.

Figure 11.7 shows an example of a `List` component. Here is the demonstration program behind Figure 11.7:

```
import java.awt.*;

public class ListTest extends java.applet.Applet {

    public void init() {

        String[] colors = { "Red", "Orange", "Yellow",
                            "Green", "Blue","Indigo", "Violet" };
```

```
        MyList colorList = new MyList(5, colors);
        add(colorList);
    }
}

class MyList extends List {

    public MyList(int numItemsToDisplayAtOnce, String[] elements)
    {

        super(numItemsToDisplayAtOnce, false);

        for (int i=0; i<elements.length; i++) {
            add(elements[i]);
        }
    }
}
```

FIGURE 11.7

A List component

If you look at the default constructors provided by a standard List, you will notice that the constructors do not let you build a fully initialized listbox in one step (you cannot do this with a Choice component either). You normally need to use the add() method to incrementally fill the list before activating it on the screen.

Since there is no good reason for not having a higher-level constructor, you can design a new List constructor in your MyList subclass that is much more programmer friendly. It can take an array of

`Strings` that provides the `List` component with its initial list of items. The numeric argument to the constructor does not specify the number of list items (since the constructor gets this information from the `array.length` field), but tells the `List` component how many lines tall it should be.

`List` components come in two interactive varieties: one that allows multiple selections (created using the second constructor and passing `true` for argument `multipleSelections`), and another that behaves like a `Choice` component in that it accepts only single (mutually exclusive) selections. To process multiple selections, the following methods are available:

`int[] getSelectedIndexes()` Returns an array of indices specifying the multiple selection.

`String[] getSelectedItems()` Similar to `getSelected-Indexes()`, except that it returns an array of selected item names.

`Object[] getSelectedObjects()` Similar to `getSelectedItems()`, except that it returns an array of objects rather than strings.

`boolean isMultipleMode()` Tells you whether or not a `List` currently accepts multiple selections.

`void setMultipleMode(boolean b)` Lets you change the multiple-selection behavior of a `List`.

WARNING You should not use `setMultipleMode()` to change list behavior after the `List` component becomes active; after that point, changing a list's response to multiple selections will surely confuse the user!

Providing Scrollbars

When you want your GUI users to enter numerical values that can range contiguously from a minimum value to a maximum value, you should provide them with slider controls to achieve this efficiently. Java's support for slider controls comes in the form of class `Scrollbar`, which is defined as follows:

```
public class Scrollbar extends Component implements Adjustable {
    public static final int HORIZONTAL;
    public static final int VERTICAL;
    public Scrollbar();
    public Scrollbar(int orientation);
    public Scrollbar(int orientation, int value, int visible,
                     int minimum, int maximum);
    public void addAdjustmentListener(AdjustmentListener 1);
    public void addNotify();
    public int getBlockIncrement();
    public int getMaximum();
    public int getMinimum();
    public int getOrientation();
    public int getUnitIncrement();
    public int getValue();
    public int getVisibleAmount();
    public void removeAdjustmentListener(AdjustmentListener 1);
    public synchronized void setBlockIncrement(int v);
    public synchronized void setMaximum(int newMaximum);
    public synchronized void setMinimum(int newMinimum);
    public synchronized void setOrientation(int orientation);
    public synchronized void setUnitIncrement(int v);
    public synchronized void setValue(int newValue);
    public synchronized void setValues(int value, int visible,
                                       int minimum, int maximum);
    public synchronized void setVisibleAmount(int newAmount);
}
```

Scrollbars are used most often when only part of an entity (document, list, picture, directory, and so on) can be displayed by the application (because either the display itself or the window is too small). The value the scrollbar depicts becomes the starting point for a scrollable "window" on the data set. The most common placement for scrollbars is to the right and bottom of the window, as shown in Figure 11.8. For this placement, you'll want to use the `BorderLayout` layout manager to accompany your `Scrollbar` component.

FIGURE 11.8

Vertical and horizontal scrollbars

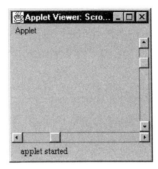

Here is the demonstration program behind Figure 11.8:

```
import java.awt.*;

public class ScrollbarTest extends java.applet.Applet {

public void init() {
Scrollbar upDown, leftRight;

   setLayout(new BorderLayout() );

   upDown    = new Scrollbar(Scrollbar.VERTICAL  , 30, 1, 0, 120);
   leftRight = new Scrollbar(Scrollbar.HORIZONTAL, 5, 2, 0, 10);

   add(upDown, "East");
   add(leftRight, "South");
}}
```

This applet begins by overriding its default layout (`FlowLayout`) and specifying `BorderLayout` instead. It then creates two

`Scrollbar` objects: one horizontal (by specifying `Scrollbar` class constant `Scrollbar.HORIZONTAL`), the other vertical (using `Scrollbar.VERTICAL`). The extra numeric arguments passed to the `Scrollbar` constructor are as follows:

value   The starting position for the slider knob (some value within the range `minimum...maximum`).

visible   The proportion of the numeric range used. For example, to indicate that your document view shows half of the document, set this value to half of maximum.

minimum and *maximum*   The minimum and maximum values this scrollbar can represent; for example, 0–100 (for percentages), 6–120 (for ages), 1–31 (for dates).

A `Scrollbar` defines two speeds at which you can alter the value represented by it: a line-increment and a page-increment speed. The easiest way to understand these concepts is to think of your favorite word processor: When you click on the vertical scrollbar's up or down arrow, you move up or down one document line at a time. When you click inside the scrollbar's slider area (but not on the slider itself), you will move a whole page up or down at a time. This behavior is supported by class `Scrollbar` through the following methods:

```
setUnitIncrement(int unitIncr)
setBlockIncrement(int blockIncr)
```

NOTE   Chapter 12 explains how to respond to slider movements and how to retrieve the value a `Scrollbar` slider is indicating.

Adding Text Fields

A `TextField` implements that old favorite: a single-line text input box. Here is its class definition:

```
public class TextField extends TextComponent {
   public TextField();
   public TextField(String text);
   public TextField(String text, int columns);
   public void addActionListener(ActionListener l);
   public void addNotify();
   public boolean echoCharIsSet();
   public int getColumns();
   public char getEchoChar();
   public Dimension getMinimumSize();
   public Dimension getMinimumSize(int columns);
   public Dimension getPreferredSize();
   public Dimension getPreferredSize(int columns);
   public void removeActionListener(ActionListener l);
   public void setColumns(int columns);
   public void setEchoChar(char c);
}
```

Text fields share behavior with a related class called `TextArea` (discussed next). Both inherit from an intermediate superclass called `TextComponent`. Here is the definition of the `TextComponent` class:

```
public class TextComponent extends Component {
   public void addTextListener(TextListener l);
   public int getCaretPosition();
   public synchronized String getSelectedText();
   public synchronized int getSelectionEnd();
   public synchronized int getSelectionStart();
   public synchronized String getText();
   public boolean isEditable();
   public void removeNotify();
   public void removeTextListener(TextListener l);
   public synchronized void select(int selectionStart, int selectionEnd);
   public synchronized void selectAll();
   public void setCaretPosition(int position);
   public synchronized void setEditable(boolean b);
```

```
   public synchronized void setSelectionEnd(int selectionEnd);
   public synchronized void setSelectionStart(int selectionStart);
   public synchronized void setText(String t);
}
```

Any text component contains some text to manage and render. The user may be allowed to edit this text, and the user can always select some part of it by click-dragging the mouse pointer over the required text. This selection ability is used in part to support the general clipboard cut/copy/paste mechanism of the host operating system. The majority of the methods defined by class TextComponent relate to these text component issues shared by the TextField and TextArea components.

Figure 11.9 shows a simple TextField component embedded in an applet. Here is the demonstration program behind Figure 11.9:

```
import java.awt.*;

public class TextFieldTest extends java.applet.Applet {

   public void init() {
      MyTextField text = new MyTextField();
      add(text);
   }
}class MyTextField extends TextField {

   public MyTextField() {
      super("Type your text", 20);
   }
}
```

Adding a TextField component is similar to adding the other simple AWT components: You call its constructor and use the add() method to place the resulting object in your container. In this example, the standard TextField was enhanced slightly by creating a subclass that initializes all blank text fields with the string "Type your text". If you refer back to the TextField class listing, you will see that the second numeric parameter specifies the width of the text input box (in characters).

FIGURE 11.9

A TextField component
with selected text

TextField components have one interesting feature that might
come in handy: You can have them accept text that is masked on the
screen to prevent bystanders from reading the text. The main application of this feature is for password entry, as shown in Figure 11.10.

FIGURE 11.10

A PasswordField as a
subclass of TextField

Here is the program that produced the applet shown in Figure 11.10:

```
import java.awt.*;

public class PasswordTest extends java.applet.Applet {

    public void init() {
        PasswordField passwordField = new PasswordField(6);
        add(new Label("Enter password:") );
        add(passwordField);
    }
```

```
        }

        class PasswordField extends TextField {

        public PasswordField() {
           this(12);
        }
        public PasswordField(int cols) {
           super("x",cols);

           setEchoCharacter('*');
        }

        } // End of class PasswordField
```

This program creates a subclass of `TextField` that, by default, sets itself in password-entry mode. This is done by setting the "echo" character used to mask the real characters on the screen. A conservative asterisk is used for that purpose. To give the user some early hint that this field takes passwords (there are no graphical changes compared to a text field in normal entry mode), the program forces the field's initial contents to be a single character (just an "x" in the program), which will appear as an asterisk.

Placing Text Areas

The `TextArea` component, as its name suggests, is used when larger amounts of text need to be input, or more often, just displayed. Here is its class definition:

```
public class TextArea extends TextComponent {
   public static final int SCROLLBARS_NONE;
   public static final int SCROLLBARS_BOTH;
   public static final int SCROLLBARS_HORIZONTAL_ONLY;
   public static final int SCROLLBARS_VERTICAL_ONLY;
   public TextArea();
   public TextArea(String text);
   public TextArea(String text, int rows, int columns);
```

```
    public TextArea(String text, int rows, int columns, int scrollbars);
    public void addNotify();
    public synchronized void append(String str);
    public int getColumns();
    public Dimension getMinimumSize();
    public Dimension getMinimumSize(int rows, int columns);
    public Dimension getPreferredSize();
    public Dimension getPreferredSize(int rows, int columns);
    public int getRows();
    public int getScrollbarVisibility();
    public synchronized void insert(String str, int pos);
    public synchronized void replaceRange(String str, int start, int end);
    public void setColumns(int columns);
    public void setRows(int rows);
}
```

Figure 11.11 shows a typical `TextArea` component. Here is the demonstration program behind Figure 11.11:

```
import java.awt.*;

public class TextAreaTest extends java.applet.Applet {

    TextArea disp;
    String multiLineText =

        "If you want to tell the story\n"
      + "of your life, you better set aside\n"
      + "a reasonable amount of space so\n"
      + "that the whole wide world can \n"
      + "read it all.\n"
      + "Otherwise, people might think you\n"
      + "are boring because they think your \n"
      + "life can be summarized in such a \n"
      + "tiny amount of text !";

public void init() {
    disp = new TextArea(multiLineText, 7, 30);

    add(disp);
}}
```

The TextArea constructor used in the program lets you specify the initial block of text and the dimensions of the TextArea box (in character rows and columns). Note how a single String composed of multiple lines is created. This is achieved by embedding new line characters in a String directly, using the standard control character escape sequence \n. A TextArea will automatically add scrollbars if the size of the text exceeds the component's visible area.

Code Style Tips

Note the formatting for the block of code creating the text string in the TextArea component example. Not only are all the string concatenation operators (the plus signs) aligned neatly and vertically to accentuate the fact that you are building a long string, but the plus signs are aligned to the left of the String constants. This combines two good coding styles in one fell swoop:

- The concatenation operators are much more conspicuous there than on the right side. This way, you can instantly spot whether one is missing (not easy to see with right-side formatting)!

- The neat alignment will not be upset the instant you change any text strings. This makes the code cheap to maintain and more robust to the introduction of bugs. Putting the concatenation plus signs on the right has no such advantages.

Adding ScrollPanes

The ScrollPane component is similar to the TextArea component. The only difference is that a ScrollPane scrolls a component
supplied by the programmer. Here is its class definition:

```
public class ScrollPane extends Container {
    public static final int SCROLLBARS_AS_NEEDED = 0;
    public static final int SCROLLBARS_ALWAYS = 1;
    public static final int SCROLLBARS_NEVER = 2;
    public ScrollPane();
    public ScrollPane(int scrollbarDisplayPolicy);
    public Component add(Component comp, int pos);
    public void addNotify();
    public void doLayout();
    public Adjustable getHAdjustable();
    public int getHScrollbarHeight();
    public int getScrollbarDisplayPolicy();
    public Point getScrollPosition();
    public Adjustable getVAdjustable();
    public Dimension getViewportSize();
    public int getVScrollbarWidth();
    public void layout();
    public String paramString();
    public void printComponents(Graphics g);
    public final void setLayout(LayoutManager mgr);
    public void setScrollPosition(int x, int y);
    public void setScrollPosition(Point p);
}
```

The following example scrolls an XCanvas, which is simply a
Canvas subclass whose paint() method draws a pair of crossed
lines. The XCanvas is larger than the ScrollPane that contains it,
so scrollbars appear automatically.

```
import java.awt.*;

public class ScrollPaneTest extends java.applet.Applet {
    public void init() {
        ScrollPane    pane;
        XCanvas       xcan;
```

```
        setLayout(new BorderLayout());
        pane = new ScrollPane();
        add("Center", pane);
        xcan = new XCanvas();
        xcan.setSize(200, 200);
        pane.add(xcan);
    }
}

class XCanvas extends Canvas {
    public void paint(Graphics g) {
        g.drawLine(0, 0, 200, 200);
        g.drawLine(0, 200, 200, 0);
    }
}
```

Figure 11.12 shows the applet produced by this demonstration program.

FIGURE 11.12

A ScrollPane within an Xcanvas

Using Menu System Components

Java menus are special AWT GUI components because they do not descend from class Component. The few menu classes descend from their own common menu superclass, called MenuComponent. You cannot add menus to applets; Frame is the only kind of container that can contain menus.

The Superclass of the Menu Classes

The root menu class, `MenuComponent`, is defined as follows:

```
public abstract class MenuComponent extends Object
implements java.io.Serializable {
    public Font getFont();
    public String getName();
    public MenuContainer getParent();
    public MenuComponentPeer getPeer();
    public boolean postEvent(Event evt);
    public void removeNotify();
    public void setFont(Font f);
    public void setName(String name);
    public String toString();
}
```

The main methods of interest are `getFont()` and `setFont()`, which allow you to query and set the font to be used for the rendering of the menu bar and items. Although this class is not abstract, it is never instantiated directly. Extending this `MenuComponent` class are the five classes that you do instantiate: classes `MenuBar`, `Menu`, `Menu-Item`, `PopupMenu`, and `CheckboxMenuItem`, which are described in the following sections.

Adding Menu Bars

The main purpose of the `MenuBar` class is to group together a collection of `Menu` instances. In this respect, its `add()` method is its core method (analogous to the `add()` methods of class `Container`). The `MenuBar` class has the following definition:

```
public class MenuBar extends MenuComponent
implements MenuContainer {
    public MenuBar();
    public synchronized Menu add(Menu m);
    public void addNotify();
    public void deleteShortcut(MenuShortcut s);
```

```
        public Menu getHelpMenu();
        public Menu getMenu(int i);
        public int getMenuCount();
        public MenuItem getShortcutMenuItem(MenuShortcut s);
        public synchronized void remove(int index);
        public synchronized void remove(MenuComponent m);
        public void removeNotify();
        public synchronized void setHelpMenu(Menu m);
        public synchronized Enumeration shortcuts();
    }
```

The MenuBar class also supports the concept of a "Help" menu. A single menu on the menu bar can be designated as being the Help menu. Its behavior, position, and rendering can then reflect this special status (this is done in platform-specific ways).

Adding Menus

The main purpose of the Menu class is to group together a collection of MenuItems and other submenus. The core Menu method is the add() method, which is used to incrementally specify the list of menu items (or menus) contained by the menu. Here is the definition of the Menu class:

```
public class Menu extends MenuItem implements MenuContainer {
    public Menu();
    public Menu(String label);
    public Menu(String label, boolean tearOff);
    public synchronized MenuItem add(MenuItem mi);
    public void add(String label);
    public void addNotify();
    public void addSeparator();
    public MenuItem getItem(int index);
    public int getItemCount();
    public synchronized void insert(MenuItem menuitem, int index);
    public void insert(String label, int index);
    public void insertSeparator(int index);
    public boolean isTearOff();
    public String paramString();
    public synchronized void remove(int index);
```

```
public synchronized void remove(MenuComponent item);
public synchronized void removeAll();
public void removeNotify();
```

The Menu class also implements a feature not universally supported on all platforms: tear-off menus. Marking a Menu as being a tear-off type menu has no effect on machines that do not support such a menu feature.

You can also add a separator to a menu at any point in the list using a call to addSeparator(). This is handy when your menus become rather long. Adding separators between groups of related items structures the menu and prevents it from becoming a messy, endless list of choices.

Adding Menu Items

The MenuItem class (and its close relative, CheckboxMenuItem) embodies the final, user-selectable menu item. Here is its definition:

```
public class MenuItem extends MenuComponent {
    public MenuItem();
    public MenuItem(String label);
    public MenuItem(String label, MenuShortcut s);
    public void addActionListener(ActionListener l);
    public void addNotify();
    public void deleteShortcut();
    public String getActionCommand();
    public String getLabel();
    public MenuShortcut getShortcut();
    public boolean isEnabled();
    public String paramString();
    public void removeActionListener(ActionListener l);
    public void setActionCommand(String command);
    public synchronized void setEnabled(boolean b);
    public synchronized void setLabel(String label);
    public void setShortcut(MenuShortcut s);
}
```

Menu items can be dynamically enabled or disabled to reflect the state of the application. For example, an Edit menu usually grays out (disables) the Cut and Copy menu items when there is no currently selected aspect of the project (text, picture, waveform, and so on). As soon as the user selects all or part of the project, the menu items become available by enabling them.

Adding Checkbox Menu Items

The `CheckboxMenuItem` class incorporates an on/off state, which is depicted graphically in a menu using a checkmark or other glyph to that effect. Here is its definition:

```
public class CheckboxMenuItem extends MenuItem implements
ItemSelectable {
    public CheckboxMenuItem();
    public CheckboxMenuItem(String label);
    public CheckboxMenuItem(String label, boolean state);
    public void addItemListener(ItemListener l);
    public void addNotify();
    public synchronized Object[] getSelectedObjects();
    public boolean getState();
    public String paramString();
    public void removeItemListener(ItemListener l);
    public synchronized void setState(boolean b);
}
```

Adding Popup Menus

The `PopupMenu` class is a subclass of `Menu`. This means that you construct and populate a pop-up menu just as you would a regular menu. The difference between regular menus and pop-up menus is that you do not attach a pop-up menu to a menu bar. Instead, you temporarily display a pop-up menu above some other component. When the user makes a selection, the pop-up menu goes away.

To display a pop-up menu, you use this method:

```
show(Component, int, int)
```

The *Component* parameter is the component above which the pop-up menu will be displayed. The two *int* parameters are the x- and y-coordinates where the pop-up menu will appear, with respect to the coordinate system of the component.

A Program to Construct a Menu Bar

The following application program uses menu classes to construct a menu bar attached to a simple window:

```
import java.awt.*;

public class MenuTest {
public static void main(String[] args) {
   MainWindow w = new MainWindow();
   w.resize(400, 300);
   w.show();
}}

class MainWindow extends Frame {

public MainWindow() {
   super("MenuTest Window");

   FileMenu fileMenu = new FileMenu();
   HelpMenu helpMenu = new HelpMenu();

   MenuBar mb = new MenuBar();

   mb.setHelpMenu(helpMenu);
   mb.add(helpMenu);

   mb.add(fileMenu);
   setMenuBar(mb);
}}

class FileMenu extends Menu {

public FileMenu() {
   super("File", true);  // tear-off menu
```

```
        add(new MenuItem("Open"));
        add(new MenuItem("Close"));
        add(new MenuItem("Exit"));
}}

class HelpMenu extends Menu {

public HelpMenu() {
    super("Help");
    add(new MenuItem("About MenuTest"));
    add(new MenuItem("Class Hierarchy"));
    addSeparator();
    add(new CheckboxMenuItem("Balloon Help"));

    Menu subMenu = new Menu("Categories");
    subMenu.add(new MenuItem("A Little Help"));
    subMenu.add(new MenuItem("A Lot of Help"));
    add(subMenu);
}}
```

Note how cleanly the program is structured to follow the main objects of its particular problem domain; the startup class MenuTest relies on a MainWindow class to create its application window. The MainWindow class in turn relies on two local classes to implement one menu each: menus FileMenu and HelpMenu. The two menu classes construct themselves privately, without encumbering the rest of the program with details of the composition of their menus. This nesting of abstraction levels is an application of the information-hiding principle made possible by object-oriented design and implementation. (The MenuTest class does not care about the structure of the menus attached to the window; it just wants to pop up the window—with or without menus.)

In class MainWindow, the menu bar is constructed by creating a new MenuBar object and then using the add() method to link the two menus to it. To attach it to the window, you call the Frame set-MenuBar() method, passing in the MenuBar instance. In class HelpMenu, you build this menu by first defining its title (by calling the standard Menu constructor and passing the menu title label as a String). Then several calls to add() create the list of menu items that the menu should contain. An `addSeparator()` invocation separates the normal items from the two special menu items at the end of this menu. The first special menu item is the "Balloon Help" `CheckboxMenuItem`, which can be toggled on or off. The second special item is an entire submenu containing two more simple menu items. Figure 11.13 shows the menu bar in action.

FIGURE 11.13

MenuBar with Menus and MenuItems (and submenu)

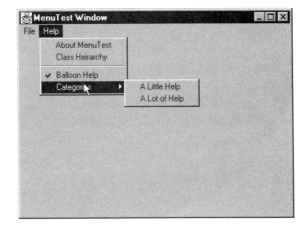

Summary

There are two concrete GUI component branches provided by the AWT hierarchy: the `Component` branch and the `MenuComponent` branch. The bulk of the AWT widgets are subclasses of the large, but abstract, superclass `Component`.

In this chapter, you explored how to use the `Canvas`, `Button`, `Label`, `Choice`, `List`, `TextField`, `TextAreas`, `ScrollBar`, `ScrollPane`, and `Checkbox` components. You rounded out your tour of AWT building blocks by looking at how menu systems are constructed and attached to application windows. In combination, all these elements can be used to construct clear, functional, and—last but not least—portable GUIs.

CHAPTER
TWELVE

Event Handling

- Event-driven applications

- Event delegation

- Java's event-class hierarchy

- Event types in the `java.awt.event` package

An *event* is an unexpected, external happening that imposes itself on you. If a fireman shouts "Fire! Everyone out of the building!" while demolishing your front door, that is an event. If you are asleep early in the morning and your alarm clock goes off, that is another event (less traumatic maybe, but equally annoying). In software systems, events have similar attributes, but programs are less flexible in dealing with the unexpected than humans. Code must be in place to recognize and handle every possible event, or else your program will be oblivious to unexpected events (it may even crash).

In the context of hardware and systems programming, events are called *interrupts*. When you press a key, the electronics inside your keyboard interrupt your desktop machine to send it the keycode of the key you pressed. Your machine responds by immediately halting whatever it was doing, receiving the key's identifying code, acknowledging the interrupt, and resuming whatever it was doing before the interrupt occurred. Within the field of GUI design and programming, user events (like a mouse click) have much the same urgency as their lower-level interrupt counterparts. Responsiveness is one of the most important attributes a GUI should have.

This chapter explains event-driven programming, your choices for handling events in your Java programs, and Java's event types.

Event-Driven Programming

Event handling lies at the very heart of GUI programming. Unlike first-generation applications, in which programs imposed a rigid sequence of program–user interaction, modern applications put the user firmly in the driver's seat. The user controls the sequence of operations that the application executes via a GUI, which waits for the user to activate a button or slider or menu. This approach is called *event-driven programming*.

An event-driven application typically constructs a GUI at initialization time, displays the GUI, and then enters a tight loop waiting for user events requesting an operation: the application's main event loop. When such an event (or trigger) occurs, a large `switch` statement determines the generated event type and invokes a corresponding action, as shown in the following pseudo-code:

```
while not quitting
|    wait for a GUI event
|    grab event
|    switch depending on event type
|    |    button click      : handle button clicks
|    |    textfield entry    : handle textfield entries
|    |    slider movement    : handle slider movements
|    |    choice selection   : handle choice selections
|    |    eventtype x        : handle events of type x
|    |    eventtype y        : handle events of type y
|    |    eventtype z        : handle events of type z
|    |    default            : beep (error)
```

In a realistic event-processing situation, the `switch` statement would typically be quite a bit longer. This central switchboard is a common scenario when the implementation language is of the older procedural kind, like Pascal or C. In object-oriented languages, the script has been modified slightly.

Java's Event-Delegation Model

In Java, events are objects. The `java.awt.event` package defines a rich hierarchy of event types, which are described later in this chapter. Through this package, instances of the various event classes are constructed when users use GUI components. It is up to the programmer to decide how to handle the event that is generated. For example, when a user clicks on a button, the system constructs an instance of class `ActionEvent`, in which it stores details about the event (when, where, and so on). At this point, the programmer has three options:

- Ignore the event.

- Have the event handled by the component (in this case a button) where the event originated.

- Delegate event handling to some other object or objects, called *listeners*.

The following sections examine each of these options.

Ignoring the Event

In the absence of any explicit event-handling code, events will be ignored. You already saw this in Chapter 11, where a sample applet was presented for each type of component. You could activate all the components (that is, you could slide the scrollbar, push the button, select from the list, and so on), and the components would respond visually, but the test programs do not do anything about your input.

Just because it is possible to respond to input from a component, it is not necessary to do so. Consider a hypothetical Java-based mail tool, with a text area for composing messages, a text field for entering a recipient, and a Send button. In the course of composing a mail message, a user types and clicks with the mouse, creating a large number of events in the text area and the text field. This hypothetical program could provide event-handling code to deal with these events, but what would that code do? The only time the program cares about the state of the text area and the text field is when the user clicks on the Send button. A clean implementation of this program would handle events from only the Send button; the event would read the contents of the other two components and build an appropriate mail message. This example shows that there are times when the best thing to do with an event is nothing at all.

Handling the Event in the Originating Component

A *self-contained* component is one that handles the events that it generates. None of the standard AWT components is self-contained; if you want a component to handle its own events, you need to create a subclass. The subclass must do two things:

- Enable receipt of events, by calling `enableEvents()`.

- Provide a `processActionEvent()` method, which will be called when the component is activated.

The following code implements a simple self-contained button:

```java
import   java.awt.*;
import   java.awt.event.*;


public class SelfButton extends Button
{
   public SelfButton(String label) {
      super(label);
      enableEvents(AWTEvent.ACTION_EVENT_MASK);
   }

   public void processActionEvent(ActionEvent e)
   {
      System.out.println("Action!");
   }
}
```

The constructor calls `enableEvents()`, passing in AWT-Event.ACTION_EVENT_MASK, which tells the button component that you are interested in action events.

When a user clicks on a `SelfButton`, the system generates an action event, and then checks whether the `SelfButton` has enabled action events. Since action events are enabled, the system calls the `processActionEvent()` method. In the example, this method just prints a brief message.

By passing in different values to `enableEvents()`, you can sensitize a component to catch many different kinds of events; all of the event handlers have names of the format `processXXXEvent()`, where *XXX* stands for the event type. (The various event types are discussed later in the chapter, in the section titled "Java's Event Types.")

You use a self-contained component just like any other component: construct one, and then add it to a container. The following code produces a very simple applet that demonstrates the use of `SelfButton`:

```
import java.applet.*;

public class SelfButtonTest extends Applet {
   public void init() {
      add (new SelfButton("Push Me"));
   }
}
```

Figure 12.1 shows the SelfButtonTest applet. The button looks like an ordinary button. This is not surprising—`SelfButton` doesn't *look* any different from a button; it just *behaves* differently when activated.

FIGURE 12.1

A self-contained button

Delegating the Event

One of the fundamental principles of object-oriented design is that a task should be performed by the object that is best suited to the task. There will be times when self-contained components are not the way to go, because the component may not be the object best suited to handling its own events.

The process of assigning a different object to handle a component's events is called *delegation*. The event-handling objects are called *listeners*. To tell a button that it should delegate handling of action events to some listener, you call the button's `addActionListener()` method, passing in a reference to the desired listener. Every component class in the AWT has one `addXXXListener()` method for each event type that the component generates.

> **NOTE**
>
> A component may have multiple listeners for an event type. If, for example, a button has five action listeners, each of the listeners will be notified when the button is activated. This is sometimes useful, but it has two drawbacks. First, there is no guarantee about the order in which listeners will be notified. Second, spreading event-handling responsibility among several objects can quickly lead to code that is difficult to maintain.

When a button with an action listener is clicked, the listener receives an `actionPerformed()` call. The listener class should implement this method to do whatever is supposed to happen. The following example has a button in an applet. The button delegates action handling to a third object, which is an instance of class `TestListener`.

```
import  java.awt.Button;
import  java.applet.Applet;
import  java.awt.event.*;


public class ButtonDelegateTest extends Applet {

    public void init() {
        Button b = new Button("I have a listener!");
        add(b);

        TestListener listener = new TestListener();
        b.addActionListener(listener);
    }
}
```

```
class TestListener implements ActionListener {

  public void actionPerformed(ActionEvent e) {
     System.out.println("Listener here: the button was
                         clicked.");
  }
}
```

There are several things to notice about this program:

- The button is a plain Button, not a subclass. When you use event delegation, your design takes on some complexity, but you are spared the necessity of subclassing.

- There is the call to addActionListener(). This is called on the button, passing in the test listener. This means that before addActionListener() can be called, the listener must be constructed.

- The declaration line for TestListener says that the class implements the ActionListener interface.

ActionListener is a simple interface that has only one method:

```
public interface ActionListener extends EventListener {
   public void actionPerformed(ActionEvent e);
}
```

The declaration for method addActionListener() requires that the listener parameter implement this interface:

```
public void addActionListener(ActionListener listener);
```

Since the listener is required to implement the interface, you know that when an action event occurs, the system can safely make an actionPerformed() call on the listener, because the listener definitely has an actionPerformed() method.

Figure 12.2 shows the ButtonDelegateTest applet.

FIGURE 12.2

A button with an action
listener

Java's Event Types

So far, you have looked at one type of event: the action event. There
are actually 11 concrete event types, which are contained in the
`java.awt.event` package. (There is also an intermediate superclass,
`InputEvent`, which is the parent of `KeyEvent` and `MouseEvent`.)
All of the event classes extend from two abstract superclasses: `java`
`.util.EventObject` and `java.awt.AWTEvent`. The event-
inheritance hierarchy is shown in Figure 12.3.

FIGURE 12.3

The Java event-class
hierarchy

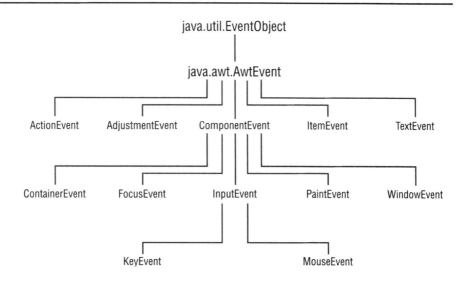

The ancestor of the hierarchy is `java.util.EventObject`, which provides a method called `getSource()`. This method returns the component in which the event took place. One level below `java.util.EventObject` is `java.awt.AWTEvent`, which provides a method called `getID()`. This method returns an `int` that describes the nature of the event. For example, calling `getID()` on an instance of `MouseEvent` results in an `int` whose value might be `MouseEvent.MOUSE_PRESSED`, `MouseEvent.MOUSE_DRAGGED`, or one of several other possible values, depending on which specific mouse activity triggered the event.

As explained earlier in the chapter, events may be handled by the originating component or they may be delegated to a listener. If your components handle their own events, you will need to know the answers to the following questions:

- For each event type, which component types can generate the event?

- For each event type, what value should a component pass to `enableEvents()`, in order to receive notification when the event happens?

- For each event type, which method is called in the component when the event occurs?

If you will be delegating component event handling to listeners, you will need to know the answers to these questions:

- For each event type, which component types can generate the event?

- For each event type, what interface should the listener implement?

- For each event type, which method in the listener is called?

Besides `ActionEvent`, which has already been discussed, there are ten non-superclass event types. These event types are explained in the following sections.

Adjustment Events

Adjustment events are sent by scrollbars. Here is the definition of the `AdjustmentEvent` class:

```
public class AdjustmentEvent extends AWTEvent  {
    public static final int BLOCK_DECREMENT;
    public static final int BLOCK_INCREMENT;
    public static final int TRACK;
    public static final int UNIT_DECREMENT;
    public static final int UNIT_INCREMENT;

    public AdjustmentEvent(Adjustable source, int id, int type,
                           int value);
    public Adjustable getAdjustable();
    public int getAdjustmentType();
    public int getValue();
    public String paramString();
}
```

If a component delegates its adjustment events, the delegate must implement the `AdjustmentListener` interface. The following is the definition of this interface:

```
public interface AdjustmentListener extends EventListener {
    public void adjustmentValueChanged(AdjustmentEvent e);
}
```

The applet code listed below constructs two scrollbars. The first is an ordinary (that is, not subclassed) scrollbar that delegates adjustment events to the applet; when the scrollbar moves, the applet writes a message to the console. The second scrollbar is a subclass called `SelfScrollbar`. This subclass handles its own adjustment events; when the `SelfScrollbar` moves, the scrollbar itself writes a message to the console.

```
import java.applet.Applet;
import java.awt.*;
import java.awt.event.*;
```

```
public class AdjustmentEventTest extends Applet
implements AdjustmentListener {

    public void init() {
        setLayout(new BorderLayout());
        // A plain scrollbar that delegates to the applet
        Scrollbar sbar1 = new Scrollbar();
        sbar1.addAdjustmentListener(this);
        add(sbar1, "West");
        // A subclass that handles its own adjustment events
        SelfScrollbar sbar2 = new SelfScrollbar();
        add(sbar2, "East");
    }

    public void adjustmentValueChanged(AdjustmentEvent e) {
        System.out.println("Scrollbar #1: " + e.getValue());
    }
}


class SelfScrollbar extends Scrollbar {

    public SelfScrollbar() {
        enableEvents(AWTEvent.ADJUSTMENT_EVENT_MASK);
    }

    public void processAdjustmentEvent(AdjustmentEvent e) {
        System.out.println("Scrollbar #2: " + e.getValue());
    }
}
```

The first scrollbar delegates adjustment events to the applet, so the
applet class must implement the AdjustmentListener interface.
The second (subclassed) scrollbar handles its own adjustment events
by calling enableEvents(AWTEvent.ADJUSTMENT_EVENT_MASK)
and providing a processAdjustmentEvent() method.

Container Events

Container events occur when a component is added to or removed from a container. Here is the definition of the `ContainerEvent` class:

```
public class ContainerEvent extends ComponentEvent {
   public static final int COMPONENT_ADDED;
   public static final int COMPONENT_REMOVED;

   public ContainerEvent(Component source, int id, Component
                         child);
   public Component getChild();
   public Container getContainer();
   public String paramString();
}
```

A container can process its own events by calling `enableEvents-(AWTEvent.CONTAINER_EVENT_MASK)` and providing a `process-ContainerEvent()` method. Alternatively, a container can delegate container events to a listener that implements the `Container-Listener` interface:

```
public interface ContainerListener extends EventListener {
   public void componentAdded(ContainerEvent e);
   public void componentRemoved(ContainerEvent e);
}
```

Typically, most programs will not need to do anything about container events.

Focus Events

Focus events are sent when a component gains or loses keyboard input focus. The following is the definition of the `FocusEvent` class:

```
public class FocusEvent extends ComponentEvent {
   public static final int FOCUS_GAINED;
   public static final int FOCUS_LOST;
```

```
        public FocusEvent(Component source, int id, boolean
                          temporary);
        public FocusEvent(Component source, int id);
        public boolean isTemporary();
        public String paramString();
}
```

A component can process its own focus events by calling enable-Events(AWTEvent.FOCUS_EVENT_MASK) and providing a processFocusEvent() method. Alternatively, you can delegate focus events to a listener that implements the FocusListener interface:

```
public interface FocusListener extends EventListener {
    public void focusGained(FocusEvent e);
    public void focusLost(FocusEvent e);
}
```

The following applet uses a BorderLayout manager to put a text field at "North" and a text area at "Center". The text field delegates its focus events to the applet, which prints a line of output when focus is gained or lost. The text area is a subclass that handles its own focus events; it too prints a line of output when focus is gained or lost.

```
import java.applet.Applet;
import java.awt.*;
import java.awt.event.*;


public class FocusEventTest extends Applet
implements FocusListener {

    public void init() {
        setLayout(new BorderLayout());
        // A text field that delegates to the applet
        TextField tf = new TextField();
        tf.addFocusListener(this);
        add(tf, "North");
        // A subclass that handles its own focus events
        SelfTextArea sta = new SelfTextArea();
        add(sta, "Center");
    }
```

```
    public void focusGained(FocusEvent e)  {
        System.out.println("Text Field gained focus");
    }

    public void focusLost(FocusEvent e)  {
        System.out.println("Text Field lost focus");
    }
}


class SelfTextArea extends TextArea {

    public SelfTextArea() {
        enableEvents(AWTEvent.FOCUS_EVENT_MASK);
    }

    public void processFocusEvent(FocusEvent e) {
        if (e.getId() == FocusEvent.FOCUS_GAINED)
            System.out.println("Text Area gained focus");
        else
            System.out.println("Text Area lost focus");
    }
}
```

The text field delegates its focus events to the applet, so the applet must implement the `FocusListener` interface. The text area handles its own focus events, so it calls `enableEvents(AWTEvent.FOCUS_EVENT_MASK)` and provides a `processFocusEvent()` method. This method inspects the `id` field of the focus event to determine whether the focus was gained or lost.

Item Events

Item events are generated by components that present users with items to choose from. The components that generate these events are `Choice`, `List`, `Checkbox`, and `CheckboxMenuItem`. The following is the definition of the `ItemEvent` class:

```
public class ItemEvent extends AWTEvent {
    public static final int DESELECTED;
```

```
        public static final int ITEM_STATE_CHANGED;
        public static final int SELECTED;

        public ItemEvent(ItemSelectable source, int id, Object item,
                          int stateChange);
        public Object getItem();
        public ItemSelectable getItemSelectable();
        public int getStateChange();
        public String paramString();
}
```

A component can process its own item events by calling `enable-Events(AWTEvent.ITEM_EVENT_MASK)` and providing a `process-ItemEvent()` method. Alternatively, a component can delegate item events to a listener that implements the `ItemListener` interface:

```
public interface ItemListener extends EventListener {
   void itemStateChanged(ItemEvent e);
}
```

The applet listed below contains a `List` component and a `Choice` component. The `List` delegates its item events to the applet. The `Choice` is a subclass that handles its own item events. Both event handlers print a message to the console.

```
import java.applet.Applet;
import java.awt.*;
import java.awt.event.*;


public class ItemEventTest extends Applet
implements ItemListener {
   List        list;
   SelfChoice  sc;

   public void init() {
      // A list that delegates to the applet.
      list = new List(5, false);
      list.addItem("Chocolate");
      list.addItem("Vanilla");
      list.addItem("Strawberry");
```

```
        list.addItem("Mocha");
        list.addItem("Peppermint Swirl");
        list.addItem("Blackberry Ripple");
        list.addItem("Butterscotch");
        list.addItem("Spumoni");
        list.addItemListener(this);
        add(list);
        // A choice subclass that handles its own item events
        sc = new SelfChoice();
        sc.addItem("Ice Cream");
        sc.addItem("Frozen Yogurt");
        sc.addItem("Sorbet");
        add(sc);
    }

    public void itemStateChanged(ItemEvent e)  {
        System.out.println("New item from list:" +
                            list.getSelectedItem());
    }
}


class SelfChoice extends Choice {

    public SelfChoice() {
        enableEvents(AWTEvent.ITEM_EVENT_MASK);
    }

    public void processItemEvent(ItemEvent e) {
        System.out.println("New item from choice: " +
                            getSelectedItem());

    }
}
```

The List delegates its item events to the applet, so the applet must implement the ItemListener interface. The Choice handles its own list events, so it calls enableEvents(AWTEvent.ITEM_ EVENT_MASK) and provides a processItemEvent() method.

NOTE   Item events are not the only kind of event created by a `List` component. If you double-click on a list element, the list will generate an `ActionEvent`.

Key Events

Key events are generated when the user presses or releases a key on the keyboard. The definition of the `KeyEvent` class is shown below. It is extensive, because there are a large number of constants. The first three constants appear in the event's `id` field, and describe the key event: `KEY_PRESSED` indicates that a key was pushed down, `KEY_RELEASED` indicates that a key was released, and `KEY_TYPED` denotes a key press followed by a key release. The remaining constants all have names that begin with `VK`, which stands for Virtual Key. The `VK` constants are values that are returned by the `getKeyCode()` method; they represent keys on the keyboard. Thus, there is a `VK_SLASH`, but no value representing a question mark, because question marks are typed by shifting the slash key.

```
public class KeyEvent extends InputEvent {
   public static final int KEY_PRESSED;
   public static final int KEY_RELEASED;
   public static final int KEY_TYPED;

   public static final int VK_0;
   public static final int VK_1;
   public static final int VK_2;
   public static final int VK_3;
   public static final int VK_4;
   public static final int VK_5;
   public static final int VK_6;
   public static final int VK_7;
   public static final int VK_8;
   public static final int VK_9;
   public static final int VK_NUMPAD0;
   public static final int VK_NUMPAD1;
```

```
public static final int VK_NUMPAD2;
public static final int VK_NUMPAD3;
public static final int VK_NUMPAD4;
public static final int VK_NUMPAD5;
public static final int VK_NUMPAD6;
public static final int VK_NUMPAD7;
public static final int VK_NUMPAD8;
public static final int VK_NUMPAD9;
public static final int VK_F1;
public static final int VK_F2;
public static final int VK_F3;
public static final int VK_F4;
public static final int VK_F5;
public static final int VK_F6;
public static final int VK_F7;
public static final int VK_F8;
public static final int VK_F9;
public static final int VK_F10;
public static final int VK_F11;
public static final int VK_F12;
public static final int VK_A;
public static final int VK_B;
public static final int VK_C;
public static final int VK_D;
public static final int VK_E;
public static final int VK_F;
public static final int VK_G;
public static final int VK_H;
public static final int VK_I;
public static final int VK_J;
public static final int VK_K;
public static final int VK_L;
public static final int VK_M;
public static final int VK_N;
public static final int VK_O;
public static final int VK_P;
public static final int VK_Q;
public static final int VK_R;
public static final int VK_S;
public static final int VK_T;
public static final int VK_U;
public static final int VK_V;
```

```
public static final int VK_W;
public static final int VK_X;
public static final int VK_Y;
public static final int VK_Z;
public static final int VK_ADD;
public static final int VK_ALT;
public static final int VK_BACK_QUOTE;
public static final int VK_BACK_SLASH;
public static final int VK_BACK_SPACE;
public static final int VK_CANCEL;
public static final int VK_CAPS_LOCK;
public static final int VK_CLEAR;
public static final int VK_CLOSE_BRACKET;
public static final int VK_COMMA;
public static final int VK_CONTROL;
public static final int VK_DECIMAL;
public static final int VK_DELETE;
public static final int VK_DIVIDE;
public static final int VK_DOWN;
public static final int VK_END;
public static final int VK_ENTER;
public static final int VK_EQUALS;
public static final int VK_ESCAPE;
public static final int VK_HELP;
public static final int VK_HOME;
public static final int VK_INSERT;
public static final int VK_LEFT;
public static final int VK_META;
public static final int VK_MULTIPLY;
public static final int VK_NUM_LOCK;
public static final int VK_OPEN_BRACKET;
public static final int VK_PAGE_DOWN;
public static final int VK_PAGE_UP;
public static final int VK_PAUSE;
public static final int VK_PERIOD;
public static final int VK_PRINTSCREEN;
public static final int VK_QUOTE;
public static final int VK_RIGHT;
public static final int VK_SCROLL_LOCK;
public static final int VK_SEMICOLON;
public static final int VK_SEPARATOR;
public static final int VK_SHIFT;
```

```
    public static final int VK_SLASH;
    public static final int VK_SPACE;
    public static final int VK_SUBTRACT;
    public static final int VK_TAB;
    public static final int VK_UNDEFINED;
    public static final int VK_UP;

    public KeyEvent(Component source, int id, long when,
                    int modifiers, int keyCode, char keyChar);
    public KeyEvent(Component source, int id, long when,
                    int modifiers, int keyCode);
    public static String getKeyModifiersText(int modifiers);
    public static String getKeyText(int keyCode);
    public char getKeyChar();
    public int getKeyCode();
    public boolean isActionKey();
    public String paramString();
    public void setKeyCode(int keyCode);
    public void setModifiers(int modifiers);
}
```

A component can process its own key events by calling `enable-Events(AWTEvent.KEY_EVENT_MASK)` and providing a `process-KeyEvent()` method. Alternatively, a component can delegate key events to a listener that implements the `KeyListener` interface:

```
public interface KeyListener extends EventListener {
    public void keyPressed(KeyEvent e);
    public void keyReleased(KeyEvent e);
    public void keyTyped(KeyEvent e);
}
```

The following applet uses a BorderLayout manager to put a text field at "North" and a text area at "Center". The text field delegates its key events to the applet, whose event handler generates a line of output. The text area is a subclass that handles its own key events; its key event handler also generates one line of output.

```
import java.applet.Applet;
import java.awt.*;
import java.awt.event.*;
```

```
public class KeyEventTest extends Applet
implements KeyListener {

   public void init() {
      setLayout(new BorderLayout());
      // A text field that delegates to the applet
      TextField tf = new TextField();
      tf.addKeyListener(this);
      add(tf, "North");
      // A text area subclass that handles its own item events
      SelfKeyTextAreasta = new SelfKeyTextArea();
      add(sta, "Center");
   }

   public void keyTyped(KeyEvent e)
   {
      System.out.println("Key typed in text field: " +
                         e.getKeyChar());
   }

   public void keyPressed(KeyEvent e)  { }
   public void keyReleased(KeyEvent e) { }
}


class SelfKeyTextAreaextends TextArea {
   public SelfKeyTextArea() {
      enableEvents(AWTEvent.KEY_EVENT_MASK);
   }

   public void processKeyEvent(KeyEvent e) {
      if (e.getId() == KeyEvent.KEY_TYPED)
         System.out.println("Key typed in text area: " +
                            e.getKeyChar());

   }
}
```

This program has a few features that have not been present in this chapter's previous examples.

First, observe the applet's two empty methods, `keyPressed()` and `keyReleased()`. These methods seem to contribute absolutely nothing to the program. They handle events that are not of interest, and the event handlers do nothing at all. The reason they appear is to appease the compiler. In order to be a key listener, the applet subclass must declare that it implements the `KeyListener` interface. This interface is listed at the beginning of this section; it contains three methods: `keyTyped()`, `keyPressed()`, and `keyReleased()`. Unless all three methods appear in the definition of the applet subclass, the compiler will not be satisfied.

NOTE The `java.awt.event` package offers a number of "adapter" classes; there is one adapter for each listener interface that has multiple methods. These adapter classes implement the corresponding interfaces, with all methods consisting of empty curly brackets. To create a listener class that cares only about a subset of an interface's methods, you can subclass the appropriate adapter and not worry about the undesired methods; you will inherit the empty stubs for them. Unfortunately, this scheme works only if your listener does not need to be a subclass of something other than the adapter. Such is the case with the example in this section, which cannot subclass `KeyAdapter` because it already subclasses `Applet`.

The second thing to notice about the example is that the `processKeyEvent()` method in class `SelfTextArea` needs to inspect the key event object to determine what type of key event has taken place. This was accomplished by calling the key event's `getId()` method.

Mouse Events

Mouse events are generated when the user clicks a mouse button or moves the mouse. There are six mouse event types, represented by the constants in the `MouseEvent` class. These constants are the possible values for a mouse event's id field. Here is the definition for the MouseEvent class:

```
public class MouseEvent extends InputEvent {
    public static final int MOUSE_DRAGGED;
    public static final int MOUSE_ENTERED;
    public static final int MOUSE_EXITED;
    public static final int MOUSE_MOVED;
    public static final int MOUSE_PRESSED;
    public static final int MOUSE_RELEASED;

    public MouseEvent(Component source, int id, long when,
                      int modifiers, int x, int y,
                      int clickCount,
                      boolean popupTrigger);
    public int getClickCount();
    public Point getPoint();
    public int getX();
    public int getY();
    public boolean isPopupTrigger();
    public String paramString();
    public synchronized void translatePoint(int x, int y);
}
```

Generally speaking, programs treat mouse-moved and mouse-dragged events very differently from the way they treat the other four event types. Java provides two mouse-event listener types and two mouse-event masks so that programs can deal separately with ordinary mouse events (pressed, released, entered, and exited) and mouse-motion events (moved and dragged).

A component can process its own ordinary mouse events by calling enableEvents(AWTEvent.MOUSE_EVENT_MASK) and providing a processMouseEvent() method. Alternatively, a component can delegate ordinary mouse events to a listener that implements the MouseListener interface:

```
public interface MouseListener extends EventListener {
    public void mouseClicked(MouseEvent e);
    public void mouseEntered(MouseEvent e);
```

```
      public void mouseExited(MouseEvent e);
      public void mousePressed(MouseEvent e);
      public void mouseReleased(MouseEvent e);
}
```

A component can process its own mouse-motion events by calling `enableEvents(AWTEvent.MOUSE_MOTION_EVENT_MASK)` and providing a `processMouseMotionEvent()` method. Alternatively, a component can delegate mouse-motion events to a listener that implements the `MouseMotionListener` interface:

```
public interface MouseMotionListener extends EventListener {
    public void mouseDragged(MouseEvent e);
    public void mouseMoved(MouseEvent e);
}
```

The following applet creates two canvases. The upper canvas is yellow; it delegates all its mouse and mouse-motion events to the applet. The lower canvas is green; it is a subclass that handles its own mouse and mouse-motion events. All four event handlers (two in the applet, two in the `Canvas` subclass) write a message to the console. The only events of interest to this applet are mouse pressed, mouse released, and mouse entered; all other mouse event types are ignored.

```
import java.applet.Applet;
import java.awt.*;
import java.awt.event.*;


public class MouseEventTest extends Applet
implements MouseListener, MouseMotionListener {

    public void init() {
        setLayout(new GridLayout(2, 1));
        // A canvas that delegates to the applet
        Canvas can1 = new Canvas();
        can1.setBackground(Color.yellow);
        can1.addMouseListener(this);
        can1.addMouseMotionListener(this);
        add(can1);
```

```
                    // A canvas subclass that handles its own item events
                    SelfMouseCanvas can2 = new SelfMouseCanvas();
                    add(can2);
                }

                public void mousePressed(MouseEvent e) {
                    System.out.println("UPPER: mouse pressed at " +
                                        e.getX() + "," + e.getY());
                }

                public void mouseReleased(MouseEvent e) {
                    System.out.println("UPPER: mouse released at " +
                                        e.getX() + "," + e.getY());
                }

                public void mouseEntered(MouseEvent e) {
                    System.out.println("UPPER: mouse entered");
                }

                public void mouseExited(MouseEvent e)    { }  // satisfy
                                                              // compiler
                public void mouseClicked(MouseEvent e)   { }  // ditto
                public void mouseMoved(MouseEvent e)     { }  // ditto
                public void mouseDragged(MouseEvent e)   { }  // ditto
            }


            class SelfMouseCanvas extends Canvas {
                public SelfMouseCanvas() {
                    setBackground(Color.green);
                    enableEvents(AWTEvent.MOUSE_EVENT_MASK |
                                 AWTEvent.MOUSE_MOTION_EVENT_MASK);
                }

                public void processMouseEvent(MouseEvent e) {
                    if (e.getId() == MouseEvent.MOUSE_PRESSED)
                        System.out.println("LOWER: mouse pressed at " +
                                            e.getX() + "," + e.getY());
                    else if (e.getId() == MouseEvent.MOUSE_RELEASED)
                        System.out.println("LOWER: mouse released at " +
                                            e.getX() + "," + e.getY());
```

```
        else if (e.getId() == MouseEvent.MOUSE_ENTERED)
            System.out.println("LOWER: mouse entered");

    }
}
```

Notice that the applet subclass declares that it implements not one but *two* interfaces. There is nothing wrong with this—Java's single inheritance concerns extending classes, and has nothing to do with implementing interfaces.

Notice also that the canvas subclass enables two event types in a single instruction:

```
enableEvents(AWTEvent.MOUSE_EVENT_MASK |
                AWTEvent.MOUSE_MOTION_EVENT_MASK);
```

The two event masks are ORed together using the | operator, which performs a bitwise OR operation on its two arguments, which are of type long.

Paint Events

A paint event is sent to a component when the component updates or paints itself. Here is the definition of the PaintEvent class:

```
public class PaintEvent extends ComponentEvent {
    public static final int PAINT;
    public static final int UPDATE;

    public PaintEvent(Component source, int id, Graphics g);
    public Graphics getGraphics();
    public String paramString();
}
```

Java programs rarely need to handle paint events.

Text Events

Text events are sent to text components (text fields and text areas) when a change occurs to the text they contain. This happens when the user types or when the program executes a method such as `setText()`. The following is the definition of the `TextEvent` class:

```
public class TextEvent extends AWTEvent {
   public static final int TEXT_VALUE_CHANGED;
   public TextEvent(Object source, int id);
   public String paramString();
}
```

A text component can process its own text events by calling `enableEvents(AWTEvent.TEXT_EVENT_MASK)` and providing a `processTEXTEvent()` method. Alternatively, a text component can delegate text events to a listener that implements the `TextListener` interface:

```
public interface TextListener extends EventListener {
   public void textValueChanged(TextEvent e);
}
```

The following applet contains two text areas: the upper one delegates text events to that applet, and the lower one handles its own text events. Both event handlers just print a message to the console.

```
import java.applet.Applet;
import java.awt.*;
import java.awt.event.*;


public class TextEventTest extends Applet
implements TextListener {

   public void init() {
      setLayout(new GridLayout(2, 1));
      // A text area that delegates to the applet
      TextArea ta1 = new TextArea();
      ta1.addTextListener(this);
      add(ta1);
```

```
      // A text area subclass that handles its own item events
      SelfTextTA ta2 = new SelfTextTA();
      add(ta2);
   }

   public void textValueChanged(TextEvent e) {
      System.out.println("UPPER get text event: " + e);
   }
}


class SelfTextTA extends TextArea {
   public SelfTextTA() {
      enableEvents(AWTEvent.TEXT_EVENT_MASK);
   }

   public void processTextEvent(TextEvent e) {
      System.out.println("LOWER get text event: " + e);

   }
}
```

Window Events

Window events are sent when a change happens to a window. Here is the definition of the WindowEvent class:

```
public class WindowEvent extends ComponentEvent {
   public static final int WINDOW_ACTIVATED;
   public static final int WINDOW_CLOSED;
   public static final int WINDOW_CLOSING;
   public static final int WINDOW_DEACTIVATED;
   public static final int WINDOW_DEICONIFIED;
   public static final int WINDOW_ICONIFIED;
   public static final int WINDOW_OPENED;

   public WindowEvent(Window source, int id);
   public Window getWindow();
   public String paramString();
}
```

Applets rarely need to be concerned with window events. Applications with GUIs are sometimes concerned with window events.

The most common use for window events has to do with a strange feature of Java's Frame class. The frame's window decoration is drawn and maintained by the underlying window system, not by Java. No matter what the underlying system may be, there is always a mechanism provided for destroying a frame. For example, in Windows 95, you can click on the little X icon in the upper-right corner. This window-destruction mechanism is not very destructive to a Java frame. All that happens is a window event is sent to the frame. The frame must explicitly respond to this event; the default behavior, if no event handler is set, is the same as the default behavior for any other Java event: The event is ignored.

Since users expect to be able to close a window (frame) from the window decoration, it is a good idea to equip all frames with a window event handler that destroys the frame on detection of a window-closing event. The code below does just that. Since there is only one frame, the event handler not only destroys the frame, it also exits the application.

```
import java.awt.*;
import java.awt.event.*;


public class KillableFrame extends Frame {

   public static void main(String args[]) {
      KillableFrame frame = new KillableFrame();
      frame.setVisible(true);
   }

   public KillableFrame() {
      setSize(250, 250);
      enableEvents(AWTEvent.WINDOW_EVENT_MASK);
   }

   public void paint(Graphics g) {
```

```
        g.drawString("Use window decoration to exit.", 20, 100);
    }

    public void processWindowEvent(WindowEvent e)
    {
        if (e.getId() == WindowEvent.WINDOW_CLOSING) {
            setVisible(false);
            dispose();

            System.exit(0);
        }
    }
}
```

Summary

This chapter began with a look at the concept of event-driven programming. You then saw the details of Java's fairly complicated event-handling infrastructure.

The most important thing to remember is that you have three choices: you can ignore an event, you can have a component handle its own event, or you can delegate an event to another object. It goes without saying that the choice you make can have a profound effect on the quality of your program. Maintenance could be a breeze or a nightmare. When choosing an event-handling strategy, the most important consideration should be the long-term robustness of the program. All other issues, including momentary convenience, are secondary.

CHAPTER

THIRTEEN

13

Animation and Images

- Basics of rendering images

- Graphics state information

- Techniques for animation

- Processing of images

Of all our senses, vision is the most high-performance, high-bandwidth input device nature has given us. No wonder there has been serious demand, ever since their earliest use in the 1950s, that computer systems evolve into systems that interact through text and pictures instead of through switches and indicator lights. No other requirement shaped the evolution of computers so dramatically as that of the need for the (bitmapped) GUI.

Graphical programming, animation, and image manipulation have become necessary skills for any modern application developer. This chapter introduces you to some of the basic techniques, set in the context of Java and its standard classes.

Java's Basic Drawing Tools

Class Graphics in the java.awt package encapsulates a small collection of rendering (that is, drawing) primitives that you can use to dynamically generate images at runtime. Here is its definition:

```
public class Graphics extends Object {
    protected Graphics();
    public abstract Graphics create();
    public Graphics create(int x, int y, int width, int height);
    public abstract void translate(int x, int y);
    public abstract Color getColor();
    public abstract void setColor(Color c);
    public abstract void setPaintMode();
    public abstract void setXORMode(Color c1);
    public abstract Font getFont();
    public abstract void setFont(Font font);
```

```
public FontMetrics getFontMetrics();
public abstract FontMetrics getFontMetrics(Font f);
public abstract Rectangle getClipRect();
public abstract Rectangle getClipBounds();
public abstract void clipRect(int x, int y, int width, int height);
public abstract void setClip(int x, int y, int width, int height);
public abstract void setClip(Shape clip);
public abstract Shape getClip();
public abstract void copyArea(int x, int y, int width, int height,
                              int dx, int dy);
public abstract void drawLine(int x1, int y1, int x2, int y2);
public abstract void drawPolyline(int xs[], int ys[], int nPoints);
public abstract void fillRect(int x, int y, int width, int height);
public void drawRect(int x, int y, int width, int height);
public abstract void clearRect(int x, int y, int width, int height);
public abstract void drawRoundRect(int x, int y, int width, int height,
                                   int arcWidth, int arcHeight);
public abstract void fillRoundRect(int x, int y, int width, int height,
                                   int arcWidth, int arcHeight);
public void draw3DRect(int x, int y, int width, int height,
                       boolean raised);
public void fill3DRect(int x, int y, int width, int height,
                       boolean raised);
public abstract void drawOval(int x, int y, int width, int height);
public abstract void fillOval(int x, int y, int width, int height);
public abstract void drawArc(int x, int y, int width, int height,
                             int startAngle, int arcAngle);
public abstract void fillArc(int x, int y, int width, int height,
                             int startAngle, int arcAngle);
public abstract void drawPolygon(int xPoints[], int yPoints[],
                                 int nPoints);
public void drawPolygon(Polygon p);
public abstract void fillPolygon(int xPoints[], int yPoints[],
                                 int nPoints);
public void fillPolygon(Polygon p);
public abstract void drawString(String str, int x, int y);
public void drawChars(char data[], int offset, int length, int x, int y);
public void drawBytes(byte data[], int offset, int length, int x, int y);
public abstract boolean drawImage(Image img, int x, int y,
                                  ImageObserver observer);
```

```
public abstract boolean drawImage(Image img, int x, int y, int width,
                                  int height, ImageObserver observer);
public abstract boolean drawImage(Image img, int x, int y,
                                  Color bgcolor, ImageObserver observer);
public abstract boolean drawImage(Image img, int x, int y, int width,
                                  int height, Color bgcolor,
                                  ImageObserver observer);
public abstract boolean drawImage(Image img, int dx1, int dy1,
                                  int dx2, int dy2, int sx1, int sy1,
                                  int sx2, int sy2,
                                  ImageObserver observer);
public abstract boolean drawImage(Image img, int dx1, int dy1, int dx2,
                                  int dy2, int sx1, int sy1, int sx2,
                                  int sy2, Color bgcolor,
                                  ImageObserver observer);
public abstract void dispose();
public void finalize();
public String toString();
}
```

Each platform that supports Java has its own (subclassed) implementation of Graphics. Class Graphics itself is abstract and cannot be instantiated. Whenever you obtain a Graphics object (called a *graphics context* or *graphics handle*), you are actually using some platform-specific subclass of Graphics.

NOTE If you look at the declaration of the Graphics **class constructor,** you will see that it declared protected. **Only subclasses can use the** Graphics **constructor.**

If you browse the methods defined by Graphics, you will quickly get a feel for what it is all about—plain 2-D rendering. The class is nothing fancy and most definitely does not support 3-D (Sun has announced a standard 3-D API for Java that the company intends to release sometime during the first half of 1997). The methods can be classified broadly into the categories listed in Table 13.1.

TABLE 13.1   Graphics Methods by Category

Category	Methods
Drawing lines	`drawLine()`
Drawing filled and outlined shapes:	
Rectangles	`drawRect()`, `clearRect()`, `fillRect()`, `drawRoundRect()`, `fillRoundRect()`, `draw3DRect()`, `fill3DRect()`
Polygons	`drawPolygon()`, `fillPolygon()`, `drawPolyline()`
Ovals	`drawOval()`, `fillOval()`
Arcs	`drawArc()`, `fillArc()`
Text rendering	`drawString()`, `drawChars()`, `drawBytes()`
Copying rectangular areas	`copyArea()`
Changing current graphics state	`setColor()`, `setPaintMode()`, `setXORMode()`, `setFont()`
Querying graphics state	`getColor()`, `getFont()`, `getFontMetrics()`, `getClipBounds()`, `getClip()`
Translating the coordinate system	`translate()`
Clipping rectangle support	`clipRect()`, `setClip()`
Image rendering	`drawImage()`

NOTE

Two notable omissions from the list in Table 13.1 are pixel-plotting and flood-fill methods. Although the need for plotting individual pixels occurs less frequently than the need for using higher primitives, not having any pixel routines is annoying. The main work-around for drawing single pixels in the AWT is to either call `fillRect()` or `drawLine()` using parameters that define 1 × 1 pixel rectangles or lines, respectively. Another (not obvious) approach to plotting single pixels is to use the `MemoryImageSource` class. See the Mandelbrot program at the end of the chapter for an example. The lack of flood-fill methods is far less dramatic since this type of rendering is quite rarely used (and when it is used, it can often lead to graphical corruption if the wrong part of an image is flood-filled). *Flood-filling*, as its name suggests, uses an algorithm that fills an enclosed area by letting pixels spread out from an initial location.

The following sections discuss most of the methods listed in Table 13.1. These are the basic tools that you will use for animation and enhancing your GUIs.

Drawing Lines and Rectangles

The following methods support basic rendering of lines and rectangles:

```
public void drawLine(int x1, int y1, int x2, int y2);
public void fillRect(int x, int y, int width, int height);
public void drawRect(int x, int y, int width, int height);
public void clearRect(int x, int y, int width, int height);
```

The artistic applet shown in Figure 13.1 demonstrates these methods for drawing lines and rectangles. Here is the code behind the output of Figure 13.1:

```
import java.awt.*;

public class Picasso extends java.applet.Applet {

public void paint (Graphics g) {
   g.fillRect(30,10,200,100);
   g.clearRect(50,30,70,50);
   g.drawRect(60,50,40,20);
   g.drawLine(10,55,250,55);
}}
```

FIGURE 13.1

Picasso applet

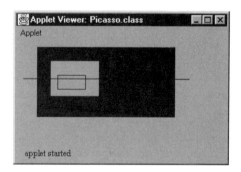

All rectangle-rendering methods take the same parameters: the coordinates of the upper-left corner of the rectangle plus the width and height of the rectangle. Note that only single-pixel-wide lines and outlines are supported. There is no method like setLineWidth() or something similar.

Rounded-Corner and 3-D Effect Rectangles

Slightly more complex than the methods above are the following rectangle-drawing methods, which support rounded corners or a 3-D lighting effect:

```
public void drawRoundRect(int x, int y, int width, int height, int arcWidth,
                          int arcHeight);
public void fillRoundRect(int x, int y, int width, int height, int arcWidth,
                          int arcHeight);
public void draw3DRect(int x, int y, int width, int height, boolean raised);
public void fill3DRect(int x, int y, int width, int height, boolean raised);
```

For the rounded-corner variants, in addition to the normal rectangle-defining arguments *x*, *y*, *width*, and *height*, you need to specify the dimensions of an imaginary rectangle acting as a bounding box for the corner. The following program illustrates the control this invisible box has by varying its size for different instances of an identical base rectangle:

```
import java.awt.*;

public class Corner extends java.applet.Applet {
final int RWIDTH = 40;
final int RHEIGHT = 30;

public void paint (Graphics g) {

    for (int i=0; i< 7; i++) {

        int cornerBoxSize = (i+1)*3;
```

```
if (i%2 == 0) {
    g.fillRoundRect(10 + i*(RWIDTH+10), 40, RWIDTH, RHEIGHT, cornerBoxSize,
                    cornerBoxSize);
} else {
    g.drawRoundRect(10 + i*(RWIDTH+10), 40, RWIDTH, RHEIGHT, cornerBoxSize,
                    cornerBoxSize);

    g.drawRect(10+ i*(RWIDTH+10)+RWIDTH-cornerBoxSize, 40, cornerBoxSize,
               cornerBoxSize);
}
}
}}
```

When run, the applet produces the output shown in Figure 13.2.

FIGURE 13.2

Rounded rectangles with
varying rounding
degrees

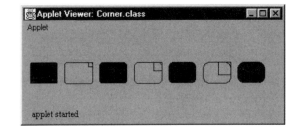

Note how the code alternates between filled and outlined rounded rectangles: It uses a modulo two (%2) function to determine if the loop's index i is odd or not. Adding 10 to the *x*-coordinates of all boxes drawn is done simply to move the string of boxes to the right a bit, away from the left edge of the applet's window.

Drawing Polygons

Outlined or filled polygons are supported by class Graphics, and there are no limitations on their concavity or self-intersection. (Many other toolkits cannot handle self-intersecting or concave polygons.) In addition to polygons, the class also supports polylines. A *polyline* is a connected series of lines. Polylines are generally not closed; the only way to close a polyline is to specify a final point that is identical to the initial point.

TIP

A concave—as opposed to convex—polygon is one whose outline has one or more indentations. (Or put mathematically, a concave polygon has one or more negative angles between successive line segments.) An easy mnemonic aid for remembering the difference between concave and convex is to associate the word *cave* with concave.

The following `Graphics` methods deal with polygon rendering:

```
public void drawPolygon(int xPoints[], int yPoints[], int nPoints);
public void drawPolygon(Polygon p);
public void fillPolygon(int xPoints[], int yPoints[], int nPoints);
public void fillPolygon(Polygon p);
public void drawPolyline(int xPoints[], int yPoints[], int nPoints);
```

Notice that `drawPolyline()` does not take a `Polygon` as an argument, but rather two arrays of coordinates. There is no `fill-Polyline()` method, since that would be functionally equivalent to `fillPolygon()`. Except for `drawPolyline()`, both the outline and filled versions come in two flavors:

- They can take a low-level (and error-prone) collection of arguments defining a polygon.

- They can take an instance of class `Polygon`, another AWT class that is useful when working with graphical polygons.

The following listing uses the latter, more readable option to demonstrate some of the polygons that you can produce. Figure 13.3 shows the output of the listing.

```
import java.awt.*;

public class Polys extends java.applet.Applet {

public void paint (Graphics g) {
```

```
Polygon convex, concave, selfintersecting;

    convex = new Polygon();
    convex.addPoint(20,20);
    convex.addPoint(60,24);
    convex.addPoint(50,50);
    convex.addPoint(21,75);
    convex.addPoint(10,30);

    concave = new Polygon();
    concave.addPoint(100+ 20,20);
    concave.addPoint(100+ 60,24);
    concave.addPoint(100+ 25,50);
    concave.addPoint(100+ 21,75);
    concave.addPoint(100+ 10,30);
    concave.addPoint(100+ 20,20);

    selfintersecting = new Polygon();
    for(int i=0; i< 10; i++) {
        selfintersecting.addPoint( 200+ (int) (Math.random()*80), 20 + (int)
                               (Math.random()*80));
    }
    g.fillPolygon(convex);
    g.drawPolygon(concave);
    g.fillPolygon(selfintersecting);
}}
```

FIGURE 13.3

Filled convex, outlined concave, and filled self-intersecting polygons

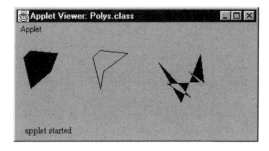

The position of the polygon is implicitly defined by the list of the polygon's vertices. The polygon-rendering methods cannot position the polygon (for example, by taking *x,y* coordinates as extra arguments), as the `drawLine()` and `drawRect()` methods do for lines and rectangles, respectively. See the discussion of `translate()`, later in the chapter, to learn how to tackle this problem.

The Polygon Class

The definition of class `Polygon` is simple:

```
public class Polygon extends Object {
   public int npoints;
   public int xpoints[];
   public int ypoints[];
   public Polygon();
   public Polygon(int xpoints[], int ypoints[], int npoints);
   public void addPoint(int x, int y);
   public Rectangle getBounds();
   public boolean contains(int x, int y);
   public boolean contains(Point p);
   public void translate(int deltaX, int deltaY);
}
```

This class cannot draw polygons itself; it is used only to define the outline of polygons. This is done with method `addPoint()`, as in the sample program.

Drawing Ovals

Ovals and circles are supported through the following two methods:

```
public void drawOval(int x, int y, int width, int height);
public void fillOval(int x, int y, int width, int height);
```

The difference between an oval and the more frequently supported ellipse shape is that the major and minor diameters of ovals are always parallel to the x- and y-axes. Ellipses usually can be rotated at will. Nevertheless, an oval is needed most of the time. Figure 13.4 shows a colorful effect obtained by drawing ever-shrinking, filled ovals. (The same result could be obtained by using outlined ovals, but using the filled variety is far more impressive at runtime.) The code that generated Figure 13.4 is listed below.

```
import java.applet.*;
import java.awt.*;

public class Ovals extends Applet {

float hue = 0.0f;
float saturation = 1.0f;
float brightness = 1.0f;

public void paint(Graphics g) {
int     w,h;
float     zeroToOne;

   w = getBounds().width; h = getBounds().height;
   g.setColor(Color.darkGray);
   g.draw3DRect(0, 0, w-1, h-1, false);

   g.translate(5,5);
   w -= 10; h -= 10;

   int squareSide = Math.min(w, h);
   for (int i=0; i < squareSide/2; i++) {
      zeroToOne = ((float) i) / (squareSide/2.0f);
      hue       = zeroToOne;
      brightness = zeroToOne;
      g.setColor(Color.getHSBColor(hue, saturation, brightness));
      g.fillOval(i,i, w - 2*i, h -2*i);
   }
}}
```

NOTE Since the oval-rendering methods take an enclosing bounding box specification, rather than center coordinates and radii (as is common in other graphics toolboxes), you "slide" a shrinking bounding box from the top-left corner toward the center of the eye to achieve your result. Using other ellipse APIs, you would normally keep the center fixed and decrease the radii instead.

FIGURE 13.4

The "Eye of Kahn" (alias drawOvals())

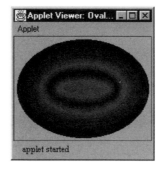

Drawing Arcs

Arcs are elliptical segments (or, more frequently, just circular segments). Two Graphics methods let you render arcs:

```
public void drawArc(int x, int y, int width, int height, int startAngle,
                    int arcAngle);
public void fillArc(int x, int y, int width, int height, int startAngle,
                    int arcAngle);
```

Filled arcs look like pieces of pie. The filled region is bounded by the arc and the two radii that join the endpoints of the arc to the center of the circle. The JDK contains an interactive ArcTest program to demonstrate the arc-rendering methods. Unfortunately, this program uses text fields to input starting angles and arc size (again in degrees). The following modified version of this program uses more user-friendly scrollbars. Figure 13.5 shows an example of the output from the improved ArcTest program.

```
/*
 * Copyright (c) 1994-1995 Sun Microsystems, Inc. All Rights Reserved.
 * Copyright (c) 1996 Laurence Vanhelsuwe.
 *
 * Permission to use, copy, modify, and distribute this software
 * and its documentation for NONCOMMERCIAL or COMMERCIAL purposes and
 * without fee is hereby granted.
 * <SEE ACCOMPANYING CD-ROM FOR FULL AND ORIGINAL COPYRIGHT INFORMATION>
```

```
 */
import java.awt.*;
import java.applet.*;

/**
 * An interactive test of the Graphics.drawArc and Graphics.fillArc
 * routines. Can be run either as a stand-alone application by
 * typing "java ArcTest" or as an applet in the appletviewer.
 */
public class ArcTest extends Applet {

ArcControls controls;

public void init() {
   setLayout(new BorderLayout());
   ArcCanvas c = new ArcCanvas();
   add("Center", c);
   add("South", controls = new ArcControls(c));
}

public void start() {
   controls.enable();
}

public void stop() {
   controls.disable();
}

public boolean handleEvent(Event e) {
   if (e.id == Event.WINDOW_DESTROY) {
      System.exit(0);
   }
   return false;
}}

class ArcCanvas extends Canvas {

int     startAngle = 0;
int     endAngle   = 45;
boolean filled     = false;
Font    font;
```

```
public Dimension minimumSize() {
   return new Dimension(100,100);
}

public void paint(Graphics g) {
Rectangle r = bounds();

   drawGrid(g);

   g.setColor(Color.red);
   if (filled) {
      g.fillArc(0, 0, r.width - 1, r.height - 1, startAngle, endAngle);
   } else {
      g.drawArc(0, 0, r.width - 1, r.height - 1, startAngle, endAngle);
   }

   g.setColor(Color.black);
   g.setFont(font);
   g.drawLine(0, r.height / 2, r.width, r.height / 2);
   g.drawLine(r.width / 2, 0, r.width / 2, r.height);
   g.drawLine(0, 0, r.width, r.height);
   g.drawLine(r.width, 0, 0, r.height);
   int sx = 10;
   int sy = r.height - 28;
   g.drawString("S = " + startAngle, sx, sy);
   g.drawString("E = " + endAngle, sx, sy + 14);
}

private void drawGrid(Graphics g) {
Rectangle r = bounds();
int hlines = r.height / 10;
int vlines = r.width / 10;

   g.setColor(Color.pink);
   for (int i = 1; i <= hlines; i++) {
      g.drawLine(0, i * 10, r.width, i * 10);
   }
   for (int i = 1; i <= vlines; i++) {
      g.drawLine(i * 10, 0, i * 10, r.height);
   }
}
```

```
public void redraw(boolean filled, int start, int end) {
   this.filled    = filled;
   this.startAngle = start;
   this.endAngle   = end;
   repaint();
}}

class ArcControls extends Panel {
Scrollbar start;
Scrollbar end;
ArcCanvas canvas;
boolean fillMode = false;

public ArcControls(ArcCanvas canvas) {
   this.canvas = canvas;
   setLayout(new GridLayout(4,1));
   add(start = new Scrollbar(Scrollbar.HORIZONTAL, 0 ,1, 0,359));
   add(end   = new Scrollbar(Scrollbar.HORIZONTAL, 45,1, 0,359));

   Panel subPanel = new Panel();        // using FlowLayout now
   subPanel.add(new Button("Fill"));
   subPanel.add(new Button("Draw"));
   add(subPanel);
}
public boolean handleEvent(Event ev) {
   if (ev.target instanceof Button) {
      String label = (String) ((Button)ev.target).getLabel();
      fillMode = label.equals("Fill");
      canvas.redraw(fillMode, start.getValue(), end.getValue());
      return true;
   }
   if (ev.target instanceof Scrollbar) {
      canvas.redraw(fillMode, start.getValue(), end.getValue());
      return true;
   }
   return false;
}}
```

FIGURE 13.5

JDK ArcTest program with an improved user interface

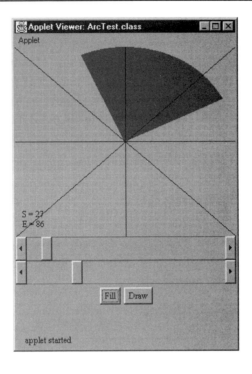

> **TIP**
>
> The starting and ending angle positions to the `drawArc` and `fill-Arc` routines start with 0 degrees at the three o'clock position and work their way counterclockwise to 90 degrees at twelve o'clock, 180 degrees at nine o'clock, 270 degrees at six o'clock, and back to 360 degrees at three o'clock.

This program consists of three classes reflecting the three main components of the applet:

- The applet itself
- The canvas area to draw the arcs (and the grid backdrop)
- The control panel at the bottom of the window

The heart of the program is the `ArcCanvas paint()` method, which invokes either the `drawArc()` or `fillArc()` method using the user-selectable starting and ending arc angles. The exact method is determined by the current drawing mode (fill or outline) used by the program. The angles that both arc methods take need to be in degrees and not radians (with 0 coding for three o'clock). The remainder of the program consists mainly of GUI code (as is so often the case with "real" applications), which applies the GUI techniques described in previous chapters.

Rendering Text

The `Graphics` class supports only simple left-to-right, horizontal text rendering. Rotated text is not supported. Three methods support text rendering:

```
public void drawString(String str, int x, int y);
public void drawChars(char data[], int offset, int length, int x, int y);
public void drawBytes(byte data[], int offset, int length, int x, int y);
```

Method `drawString()` is the usual method for drawing text strings. It just takes a string and the starting (rendering) position for the first letter of your string. The rendering position for text is always the left-most point on the text's baseline. The two other text-rendering methods use arrays of `byte` or `char` as their text source but allow a substring to be rendered. Here is a demonstration program using the latter. The output of this example is shown in Figure 13.6.

```
import java.awt.*;

public class Text extends java.applet.Applet {

public void paint (Graphics g) {

String subject = "ZigZagging Text";
char[] text;

    g.setFont(new Font("TimesRoman", Font.PLAIN, 16));
    text = subject.toCharArray();
```

```
for (int i=0; i <= text.length-3; i+=2) {
    if (i==0) {
        g.drawChars(text, 0, text.length, 20, 20);
    } else if (i == text.length-3) {
        g.drawChars(text, 0, text.length, 20, 20 + (i/2)*17);
    } else {
        g.drawChars(text, (text.length-3-i), 4,
            20+ (text.length-3-i)*7, 20+ (i/2)*17);
    }
  }
}}
```

FIGURE 13.6

Zigzag text using
drawChars()

The program uses the setFont() method to change the currently used rendering font. Method setFont() takes a Font object that can be constructed on the fly using a new Font("<fontFamily-Name>", <fontStyle>, pointSize). See the discussion of setFont(), later in the chapter, for details.

Moving Rectangular Areas

The copyArea() method is the only graphics area moving method available:

```
public void copyArea(int x, int y, int width, int height, int dx, int dy)
```

Since it does not allow any type of masking, it is most useful for scrolling areas vertically or horizontally. The *x*, *y*, *width*, and *height* arguments specify the area to move, and the *dx* and *dy* arguments specify by how many pixels and in which direction. As you can see from the method's signature, only screen-to-screen copies are supported. You cannot grab a screen area and store it for future use—for example, to copy it back to the screen at a later date.

Figure 13.7 shows one of those executive toy-type applets that relies on moving rectangular puzzle pieces horizontally and vertically. The program that follows produced the (animated) output of Figure 13.7.

NOTE You can move an image from an off-screen buffer into the screen using the `drawImage()` method; this is discussed in the "Animation Basics" section, later in this chapter.

```java
import java.awt.*;

public class Puzzle extends java.applet.Applet {

Graphics g;
Color bg;
int pieceWidth, pieceHeight;

final int PUZ_WIDTH  = 5;
final int PUZ_HEIGHT = 5;

final int MOVE_UP    = 0;  // these values are designed so that negating
final int MOVE_DOWN  = 3; // one produces the opposite direction, e.g.,
final int MOVE_RIGHT = 1; // ~MOVE_UP = MOVE_DOWN  (when ANDed with 3)
final int MOVE_LEFT  = 2;

int holeX = 0;  // starting spot for the puzzle's "hole"
int holeY = 0;

int[] xDirs={0,1,-1,0};  // dxs and dys indexable by one of the MOVE_s
int[] yDirs={-1,0,0,1};
int xDir, yDir;
int x,y;  // pixel coordinates of a puzzle piece
```

```
//─────────────────────────────────────────────────────
// Work out the size of the puzzle pieces from the available applet area.
//─────────────────────────────────────────────────────
public void init() {

    pieceWidth  = (getBounds().width-20) /PUZ_WIDTH;
    pieceHeight = (getBounds().height-20)/PUZ_HEIGHT;
}
//─────────────────────────────────────────────────────
// Draw a nice background for the puzzle. Draw the pieces and start
// animating the lot.
//─────────────────────────────────────────────────────
public void paint (Graphics g) {

    this.g = g;
    g.translate(10,10);
    bg = getBackground();

    g.setFont(new Font("TimesRoman", Font.BOLD, 85));
    g.drawString("Hey!",10,70);
    g.setColor(Color.gray);
    g.drawString("Hey!",12,72);

    drawPieces();

    while(true) {
        occupyHole();     // animate the puzzle by moving pieces
    }
}
//─────────────────────────────────────────────────────
// At init time, draw the piece outlines over the backdrop picture.
//─────────────────────────────────────────────────────
private void drawPieces() {
    for (int row=0; row < PUZ_HEIGHT; row++) {
        for (int col=0; col < PUZ_WIDTH; col++) {
            drawPieceAt(row,col);
        }
    }
}
//─────────────────────────────────────────────────────
// Pick a valid, random neighbor around the hole, then move
// that neighbor into the hole's spot. The old neighbor's
// cell becomes the new hole.
```

```
//—————————————————————————————————————————————
private void occupyHole() {
int neighborDir;      // randomly chosen neighbor cell direction
int moveDir;          // opposite direction (to move into hole cell)
int neighborX;
int neighborY;


   // choose a random neighboring direction 0..3
   do {
      neighborDir = (int) (Math.random()*4);
   } while ( cellisIllegal(neighborDir) ); // but avoid going off grid

   neighborX = holeX + xDirs[neighborDir];
   neighborY = holeY + yDirs[neighborDir];

//    System.out.println("Hole: " + holeX + "," + holeY);
//    System.out.println("Nbor: " + neighborX + "," + neighborY);

   moveDir = (~neighborDir)&3;    // opposite dir UP<->DOWN, RIGHT<->LEFT

   movePiece (neighborX, neighborY, moveDir);

   holeX = neighborX;
   holeY = neighborY;

   delay(0.5);
}
//—————————————————————————————————————————————
// Check that a tentative neighbor cell is within the puzzle.
//—————————————————————————————————————————————
private boolean cellisIllegal(int direction) {

   xDir = xDirs[direction];
   yDir = yDirs[direction];

   if (holeX + xDir < 0) return true;
   if (holeY + yDir < 0) return true;
   if (holeX + xDir >= PUZ_WIDTH) return true;
   if (holeY + yDir >= PUZ_HEIGHT) return true;

   return false;
}
```

```
//—————————————————————————————————————————————————
// Graphically move a piece in one of the four directions.
//—————————————————————————————————————————————————
private void movePiece(int row, int col, int direction) {

   xDir = xDirs[direction];
   yDir = yDirs[direction];

   x = row * pieceWidth;
   y = col * pieceHeight;

   if (xDir != 0) {
      for (int i=0; i < pieceWidth; i++) {
         g.copyArea(x+(i * xDir),y, pieceWidth, pieceHeight, xDir, 0);
         delay(0.004);
      }
   } else {
      for (int i=0; i < pieceHeight; i++) {
         g.copyArea(x,y+(i * yDir), pieceWidth, pieceHeight, 0, yDir);
         delay(0.004);
      }
   }
}
//—————————————————————————————————————————————————
// At initialization time, cut up the background into puzzle pieces.
// Each piece has an outline that is slightly inset to avoid
// smearing when copyArea() slides pieces around.
//—————————————————————————————————————————————————
private void drawPieceAt(int row, int col) {
   x = row * pieceWidth;
   y = col * pieceHeight;

   g.setColor(bg);
   g.drawRect(x,y, pieceWidth, pieceHeight);
   g.drawRect(x+1,y+1, pieceWidth-2, pieceHeight-2);

   g.setColor(Color.gray);
   g.drawRect(x+1,y+1, pieceWidth-3, pieceHeight-3);
}
//—————————————————————————————————————————————————
private void delay(double seconds) {
   try {Thread.sleep( (int) (seconds*1000));
   } catch (Exception ignored) {}
}}
```

FIGURE 13.7

Puzzle applet

> **NOTE**
>
> When you run this applet, you will see that the program does not contain any of the game's logic. Adding this is left as an exercise for the reader.

The core of the program is the `movePiece()` method. It takes the puzzle piece coordinates of the square to move and a direction in which to move the piece. The pieces are moved smoothly, one pixel at a time, using repeated calls to `copyArea()`. Note that `copyArea()` does not alter the source area at all. Therefore, when sliding a rectangular image one pixel at a time in a given direction, a graphical trace may be left behind, depending on the pixel contents of the trailing edge. To avoid this, the program draws the "outlines" for the pieces a couple of pixels on the inside of the piece, surrounded by an invisible outline of background color. This way, pieces can be slid around without leaving any traces.

Managing the Graphics State

Beyond being a collection of rendering primitives, what other function does a `Graphics` object have? Its crucial function is to allow a multitude of different graphic contexts to coexist. When the `paint()` method hands you a `Graphics` object, that object holds all graphical attributes or state for your applet's drawing area. Your applet's drawing origin (coordinates 0,0) for example, is situated in the top-left corner of the applet's drawing area, and not in the top-left corner of the browser's window or the top-left corner of the screen. A `Graphics`-controlled drawing area has several more such attributes besides the customized coordinate origin. `Graphics` objects also keep track of the following:

- The current clipping area

- The current drawing color

- The current drawing mode

- The current font to use for any text rendering

These attributes can be altered and/or queried by the `Graphics` methods discussed in the following sections.

Translating the Coordinate System

If you look back at the source code of the polygon-drawing example, you will see that the polygons were "manually" spaced apart by adding 100 to the x-coordinates of the second polygon and 200 to the x-coordinates of the third polygon. This can be avoided by using the `translate()` method:

```
public void translate(int x, int y)
```

Using this method makes the the source code much more readable. Here is how the code body could be improved with `translate()`, achieving the same result as in Figure 13.3 (shown earlier):

```
concave = new Polygon();
concave.addPoint( 20,20);
concave.addPoint( 60,24);
concave.addPoint( 25,50);
concave.addPoint( 21,75);
concave.addPoint( 10,30);
concave.addPoint( 20,20);
```

```
selfintersecting = new Polygon();
for(int i=0; i< 10; i++) {
   selfintersecting.addPoint( (int) (Math.random()*80),
                              (int) (Math.random()*80));
}
g.fillPolygon(convex);

g.translate(100,0);
g.drawPolygon(concave);

g.translate(100,20);
g.fillPolygon(selfintersecting);
```

Note that translations are cumulative. Each invocation of `translate()` translates the current coordinate system, which might already have been translated. To "undo" the last translation, you must remember the amount of the previous translation and then apply the inverse translation. This is done by translating with the previous translation values negated:

```
translate(tx,ty);
// paint stuff
translate(-tx,-ty);
// back to where we were before
```

Specifying a Clipping Area

When you specify drawing coordinates that lie outside your applet's drawing area, none of the graphics primitives complain. Instead, they simply restrict whatever they draw to be within the applet's `bounds()` and clip any rendering that would draw outside this area. This clipping rectangle can be changed to any other rectangular area located within the original applet drawing area using the `clipRect()` method. You can discover what the current clipping rectangle is set to by calling `getClipBounds()`, which returns a `Rectangle` instance. Here are the signatures for these two methods:

```
public void clipRect(int x, int y, int width, int height)
public Rectangle getClipBounds()
```

The following applet's `paint()` method proves that the initial clipping rectangle for an applet is identical to the applet's `bounds()`:

```
public void paint (Graphics g) {
    System.out.println( g.getClipBounds() );
    System.out.println( getBounds() );
}
```

If you ran this code within a minimal applet class, it would output the following:

```
java.awt.Rectangle[x=0,y=0,width=200,height=150]
java.awt.Rectangle[x=104,y=92,width=200,height=150]
```

Current Drawing Color

Every `Graphics` context has a current (foreground) drawing color. Surprisingly enough, there is no associated current background drawing color. Java does have a concept of background color, but only in the context of GUI components (via the `setBackground()` and `getBackground()` methods in class `Component`). You alter the rendering color to be used by calls to `setColor()`. Finding out which color is being used for all current rendering is done via calls to `getColor()`:

```
public void setColor(Color c)
public Color getColor()
```

The type of objects handled by both calls are instances of class `Color`. Here is its definition:

```
public final class Color extends Object {
    public Color(int r, int g, int b);
    public Color(int rgb);
    public Color(float r, float g, float b);
    public int getRed();
    public int getGreen();
    public int getBlue();
    public int getRGB();
    public Color brighter();
    public Color darker();
    public int hashCode();
```

```
public boolean equals(Object obj);
public String toString();
public static Color getColor(String nm);
public static Color getColor(String nm, Color v);
public static Color getColor(String nm, int v);
public static Color decode(String nm);
public static int HSBtoRGB(float hue, float saturation, float brightness);
public static float[] RGBtoHSB(int r, int g, int b, float hsbvals[]);
public static Color getHSBColor(float h, float s, float b);
}
```

The Color constructors should be your main focus. You can construct a new color by specifying one of the following sets:

- Red, green, and blue primary components in the integer range 0–255

- Red, green, and blue primary components in the float range 0.0F–1.0F

- A single integer encoding red, green, and blue in the standard 8-bits-per-primary format

- Hue, saturation, and brightness values in the float range 0.0F–1.0F (this is via the getHSBColor() static method, and not via a constructor)

If your color requirements can be satisfied by the basic palette, the Color class defines some class constants of type Color (itself): white, gray, lightGray, darkGray, black, red, pink, orange, yellow, green, magenta, cyan, and blue. As with all class constants, you need to prepend the name of the class to use these—for example, Color.blue.

Current Drawing Mode

All rendering can be executed in one of two modes, paint or XOR mode, using these two methods:

```
public void setPaintMode()
public void setXORMode(Color c1)
```

Paint mode simply overwrites any pixels already there, in the current drawing color. XOR mode applies a color-swapping function (reminiscent, but not equal to, bitwise exclusive ORing). The swapped colors are the color being passed as the argument to `setXORMode()` and the current drawing color. The following applet demonstrates the effect:

```java
import java.awt.*;

public class XOR extends java.applet.Applet {

public void paint (Graphics g) {

    g.setFont(new Font("TimesRoman", Font.BOLD, 32) );
    g.drawString("Java", 10, 30);
    g.drawString("Sumatra", 10, 60);

    // draw both strings on top of another in both paint and XOR mode

    g.setPaintMode();
    g.drawString("Java", 10, 100);
    g.drawString("Sumatra (Paint)", 10, 100);

    g.setXORMode(Color.white);
    g.drawString("Java", 10, 130);
    g.drawString("Sumatra (XOR)", 10, 130);
}}
```

Figure 13.8 shows paint and XOR drawing modes.

FIGURE 13.8

Paint and XOR drawing modes

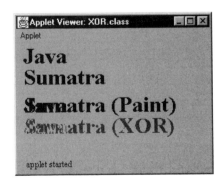

Current Font

Two methods are provided to handle font aspects:

```
public void setFont(Font font)
public Font getFont()
```

You specify the current font using the setFont() method. The argument it takes is a Font object, which is usually constructed in place, within the argument brackets of setFont(). The Font constructor has the following signature:

```
public Font(String name, int style, int size)
```

The *name* argument denotes the font family and typically can be Courier, Dialog, DialogInput, Helvetica, ZapfDingbats, or TimesRoman (on Windows and Solaris platforms). The style argument can be Font.PLAIN, Font.BOLD, or Font.ITALIC. These can be specified either alone or in combination (by ORing them together).

The *size* argument is the font-scaling in pixels. The following demo program combines Font and FontMetrics (which are explained in the next section). It determines the list of all available fonts (available to Java, that is) and renders samples of each with expanding point sizes. This example obtains the fonts at runtime on any platform.

```
import java.awt.*;

public class FontList extends java.applet.Applet {

String[]     fontList;
Font         theFont;
FontMetrics  fm;
int          fontHeight;

public void init() {
   fontList = Toolkit.getDefaultToolkit().getFontList();
}

public void paint(Graphics g) {
   for (int i = 0; i < fontList.length; i++) {
      System.out.println(fontList[i]);
```

```
    theFont = new Font(fontList[i], Font.BOLD, 16+i*4);
    g.setFont(theFont);
    fm = getFontMetrics(theFont);
    fontHeight += fm.getHeight();
    g.drawString(fontList[i] + " " + (16+i*4) + " point", 10, fontHeight);
  }
}}
```

Figure 13.9 shows the output of the program.

FIGURE 13.9

Java AWT standard fonts

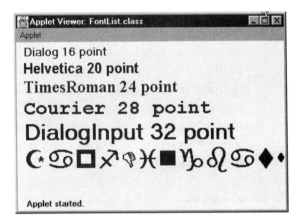

You obtain a list of available fonts by using the Toolkit class's get-FontList() method. You get a Toolkit object in the first instance (to invoke getFontList() on) by using the Toolkit class method get-DefaultToolkit() or the getToolkit() method of Component.

NOTE

This standard Java idiom for finding the list of fonts should receive the same treatment sleep() gets in the context of threads. At first, to put the current thread to sleep for some time, you use Thread.currentThread().sleep(). Because no one ever put any other threads to sleep, the sleep() instance method was "promoted" to a class method with the new semantics of always putting the current thread to sleep. The Toolkit instance method getFontList() should likewise be promoted to a class method Toolkit.getFontList(); it then takes on the meaning of producing a font list for the current Toolkit. See the JDK online documentation for details on the Toolkit class.

Accessing the Current Font's FontMetrics

Two more font-related methods are provided to access a font's set of metrics:

```
public FontMetrics getFontMetrics()
public FontMetrics getFontMetrics(Font f)
```

Whenever you render anything around rendered text, you need to know the precise dimensions of the various fonts. If you do not know these dimensions, your output will not be symmetrical or centered correctly, or worse, subsequent rendering might "collide" with parts of the text. All modern computer fonts come with a set of *metrics* that define various heights and widths for the font. Consult the JDK online documentation on class FontMetrics to learn about these font metrics. The following program demonstrates how to get a font's FontMetrics object and use it, in this case, to highlight the metrics graphically, as shown in Figure 13.10.

FIGURE 13.10

Font metrics for font TimesRoman

In addition to producing the graphical output shown in Figure 13.10, the program also dumps the following metrics to the console (for a "TimesRoman" font requested to be 100 points):

```
ascent   90
descent 24
```

```
height   118
leading  4
maxAdv   109
maxAsc   90
maxDes   24
```

The metrics listed were obtained on a Windows 95 host machine. Because font metrics vary across platforms, the program might print different values on your machine. Here is the program behind the console output and Figure 13.10:

```java
import java.awt.*;

public class FMetrics extends java.applet.Applet {

Font         theFont;
FontMetrics fm;

public void init() {
    theFont = new Font("TimesRoman", Font.PLAIN, 100);
}

public void paint(Graphics g) {
int baseline   = 100;
String testStr = "WIactiyg";

    g.setFont(theFont);
    fm = g.getFontMetrics();

int ascent  = fm.getAscent();      System.out.println("ascent  " + ascent  );
int descent = fm.getDescent();     System.out.println("descent " + descent );
int height  = fm.getHeight();      System.out.println("height  " + height  );
int leading = fm.getLeading();     System.out.println("leading " + leading );
int maxAdv  = fm.getMaxAdvance();  System.out.println("maxAdv  " + maxAdv  );
int maxAsc  = fm.getMaxAscent();   System.out.println("maxAsc  " + maxAsc  );
int maxDes  = fm.getMaxDescent();  System.out.println("maxDes  " + maxDes  );

    g.drawString(testStr, 10, baseline);

    drawHLine(baseline);
    drawHLine(baseline-ascent);
    drawHLine(baseline-maxAsc);
```

```
      drawHLine(baseline+descent);
      drawHLine(baseline+maxDes);
      drawHLine(baseline+maxDes+leading);

      int charX = 10;
      for (int i=0; i< testStr.length(); i++) {
         drawVLine(charX);
         charX += fm.charWidth(testStr.charAt(i));
      }
   }
   void drawHLine(int y) {
      getGraphics().drawLine(10,y,500,y);
   }
   void drawVLine(int x) {
      getGraphics().drawLine(x,10,x,200);
}}
```

Note that the FontMetrics object is not obtained from the font it relates to. The Graphics object is the entity that gives you a FontMetrics object for the currently selected rendering font. Note also that you can improve readability and keep the code short by writing two simple little utility-rendering functions: drawHLine() and drawVLine(). Simple methods that are only a couple of lines long can greatly improve the readability of your programs.

Animation Basics

The essence of all animation is moving pictures—a sequence of still images displayed at a fast enough rate to fool the brain into thinking the animation is continuous. Once the animation rate (the frame rate) is high enough, the discrete, static pictures merge into a constant flow of movement.

Movies use a frame rate of 24 frames per second (fps). In other words, the images are renewed at 24 hertz (Hz, or cycles per second). Normal televisions use 60Hz (for the United States NTSC broadcasting standard) or 50Hz (for the European PAL standard), although recently, newer (digital) models using 100Hz have invaded the marketplace. Multisync computer monitors can display their frames from "slow" television rates to approximately 120Hz. Faster update rates mean less image flicker and consequently more solid or realistic-looking animations.

Redrawing an entire screen or even just a sizable window in one-twenty-fourth of a second is no mean feat—especially if its content is complex and needs many computations to redraw it. Fortunately, animation effects can be achieved without needing to redraw the entire drawing canvas each time. Modifying only those areas that contain the changing parts can be just as effective.

The following applet demonstrates this technique. It draws only one new straight line for each new "frame," but it does so in such a way that the result is fascinating to watch. Figure 13.11 shows a snapshot of the Qix applet in action.

```java
import java.awt.*          ;
import java.util.Random    ;

public class Qix extends java.applet.Applet {

private Random rnd = new Random();

private Rectangle    bounceRect;
private Rectangle    colorBounce;
private BouncyPoint endPoint1,endPoint2;
private BouncyPoint R_Bouncer, G_Bouncer, B_Bouncer;
private int startx1, startx2, starty1, starty2;

public void paint (Graphics g) {

   bounceRect = this.bounds();              // applet's bbox
   bounceRect.x = 0;
   bounceRect.y = 0;

   startx1 = 4 + ((rnd.nextInt()&1023) % (bounceRect.width - 8) );
   startx2 = 4 + ((rnd.nextInt()&1023) % (bounceRect.width - 8) );
```

```
        starty1 = 4 + ((rnd.nextInt()&1023) % (bounceRect.height -8) );
        starty2 = 4 + ((rnd.nextInt()&1023) % (bounceRect.height -8) );

        endPoint1 = new BouncyPoint(bounceRect, startx1, starty1,  -1.0, 1.5);
        endPoint2 = new BouncyPoint(bounceRect, startx2, starty2,   1.0,-2.5);

        colorBounce = new Rectangle(0,0, 255,255);
        R_Bouncer = new BouncyPoint( colorBounce, 200,0, 1.0, 0.0);
        G_Bouncer = new BouncyPoint( colorBounce, 200,0, -1.0, 0.0);
        B_Bouncer = new BouncyPoint( colorBounce, 200,0, -2.0, 0.0);

        for (;;) {
            endPoint1.carryOnBouncing();    // bounce the two line endpoints around
            endPoint2.carryOnBouncing();
            R_Bouncer.carryOnBouncing();    // bounce the colors around too
            G_Bouncer.carryOnBouncing();
            B_Bouncer.carryOnBouncing();

            g.setColor(new Color(R_Bouncer.x, G_Bouncer.x, B_Bouncer.x) );
            g.drawLine(endPoint1.x, endPoint1.y,    endPoint2.x, endPoint2.y);

            try { Thread.sleep(10); } catch (Exception ignored) {}
        }
}} // End of class Qix


//─────────────────────────────────────────────────────────────────────────
// BouncyPoint class
//
// This implements a (commonly employed) bouncing "endpoint,"
// i.e., you could use 2 instances of this to animate a bouncing line
// or use 4 of these to animate a Bezier curve or a stretchy, bouncy rectangle
//─────────────────────────────────────────────────────────────────────────

class BouncyPoint extends Point {

private Rectangle boundingBox;
private double x_direction;
private double y_direction;

BouncyPoint (Rectangle limits, int startx, int starty, double dx, double dy) {
```

```
   super(startx, starty);

   boundingBox = limits;

   x_direction = dx;
   y_direction = dy;
}

public boolean carryOnBouncing () {

boolean boing=false;

     // add velocity to current position
     // if resulting position outside box, undo move and reverse speed

   x += (int) x_direction;
   if ( ! boundingBox.contains(x,y)) {
     x -= (int) x_direction;
     x_direction = - x_direction;
     boing = true;
   }

   y += (int) y_direction;
   if ( ! boundingBox.contains(x,y)) {
     y -= (int) y_direction;
     y_direction = - y_direction;
     boing = true;
   }

   return boing;
}

public String toString() {
   return super.toString() + "-Speed dx=" + x_direction +
                         " dy=" + y_direction;
}
} // End of class BouncyPoint
```

FIGURE 13.11

Qix animation applet

NOTE

Qix was one of the classic arcade games of the early 1980s. The object of the game was to gradually restrict the movements of the "Qix"—some sort of energy field—by building a fence around it. If the Qix touched you in the middle of building a fence, you died.

The applet relies on a perfectly reusable class whose sole purpose is to "bounce around" a 2-D point within a rectangular box. The Bouncy-Point class extends the java.awt.Point class (which consists mainly of an *x,y* coordinate). Two BouncyPoint instances are used to hold the moving endpoints of the animated line. The gradual color animation is also handled by more BouncyPoint instances. The program uses the numeric ping-pong functionality of a BouncyPoint to modify the red, green, and blue color components independently. Since each color primary is just a one-dimensional scalar, only the *x* part of a BouncyPoint is used for the colors.

WARNING

This Qix applet has a serious shortcoming: It never returns from its paint() method. A for(;;) loop was used to implement an infinite loop that controls the (infinite) animation. Applets that do this are useless in real-life Web pages, because they soak up CPU resources that should normally be shared among all applets. This flaw is ignored throughout this chapter's applets; the issue is addressed in detail in Chapter 14.

Working with Java Images

Animating a straight line—or any other graphics primitive—is fine for screen-saver programs or to relax a stressed-out manager, but sooner or later you will want to animate predrawn cartoons or even a large sequence of (digital) video frames. For this purpose, Java supports an Image class, along with other related classes.

Techniques for Image Manipulation

The Java API is rather confusing with regard to image manipulations. Several packages, classes, and methods deal with images in one way or another:

- The java.awt.Image class is abstract, so you cannot create Image instances from it (a bit like having a succulent apple pie behind armored glass).

- The java.awt.image package is entirely devoted to image processing.

- In package java.applet, two getImage() methods are tucked away in class Applet.

- Class Component defines two createImage() methods.

- Class Graphics contains several drawImage() methods.

Here is a sample program that draws an image inside an applet:

```java
import java.awt.*;

public class GetImage extends java.applet.Applet {

Image myimg;

public void init() {
   myimg = getImage(getDocumentBase(), "image.gif");
}

public void paint(Graphics g) {
   g.drawImage(myimg, 0, 0, this);
}}
```

This applet produces a window like that shown in Figure 13.12.

FIGURE 13.12

A GIF image displayed
by an applet

The applet's core consists of two statements: getImage() and drawImage(). This, fortunately or unfortunately (depending on your viewpoint), is the simplest aspect of using Java images; the remainder of the material is uphill all the way.

Class Image is abstract and therefore cannot be the source for Image instances itself. Other classes must create instances of Image for you. Methods that construct and return objects are sometimes called *factory methods*. In this example, the applet method getImage() is a factory method for Image objects. This method not only creates brand new Image objects, it also performs the handy function of loading an external image file and turning it into a runtime usable Image object, ready to be rendered. The image formats that are supported are mainly XBM, GIF, and JPEG; GIF and JPEG are the de facto Internet image file formats.

The signature of the getImage() method used in the example is:

```
public Image getImage(URL url, String name)
```

The URL parameter allows this method to grab image files from any willing Internet site in the world! Another Applet method, getDocumentBase(), specifies the URL origin (directory) of the picture as whatever site the applet's HTML document came from. If you run the applet on your own machine, this document base URL will have the form of a file URL, such as file:/C:/JAVA/MASTER-ING/../../page.html. If you run the applet from a Web server, the document base URL will have the form of an HTTP URL, such as http://www.sybex.com/Java/Mastering/../page.html. The name parameter is the image file's filename in the specified directory, whether local or halfway around the world.

To actually show the image on screen, you use the `drawImage()` method from class `Graphics`. Throughout Java's scattered image-support classes and methods, you can count on one thing: You always use `drawImage()` to finally render the image. The parameters it takes are the x,y coordinates for the top-left corner where the image is to be drawn and a `this` parameter:

```
g.drawImage(image, x, y, this);
```

And what about the `this` parameter? Your first clue is embedded in the online documentation description for `getImage()`: "This method returns immediately, even if the image does not exist. The actual image data is loaded when it is first needed." This means the `getImage()` statement does not actually get the image after all. The reason is the Internet: The entire image-processing and image-handling support that Java gives us takes the Internet's daily reality into account. In particular, the design reflects the unpredictable delays that occur when accessing remote Internet files and the length of time it takes to download any sizable files (image files often range between 1KB and 100KB, depending on complexity, color depth , and so on).

The `Image` subsystem deals with these issues by separating the loading of images from their actual use. The example code says "load that image and draw it," not knowing or caring about Internet response times or transfer rates, so the two (loading and using images) are completely separated. Another way of putting this is that the image loading is asynchronous, meaning that the main program does not wait for the load to finish (if it did wait, that would be a synchronous approach). What really goes on behind the scenes is not this simple, but it's all for a good purpose: to make Java applet development easier and improve performance for the user.

The exact details of the mechanisms used to fetch the image all the way from a remote site and into the `Image` object are platform dependent. In general, the `getImage()` method creates an `Image` object that, when asked to draw itself, will start the download process and render the image bit by bit, as the image data is received. This is the function of the `this` parameter in the `drawImage()` call.

Here is the method's signature:

```
public boolean drawImage(Image img, int x, int y, ImageObserver observer)
```

You can see that the last parameter must be of type `ImageObserver`. Image observers are explained in the next section.

The ImageObserver Interface

To understand why `drawImage()` needs an `ImageObserver`, you must first understand what an `ImageObserver` is. `ImageObserver` is an interface and not a class. Its definition is very short (which doesn't make it easier to understand its purpose, however):

```
public interface ImageObserver extends Object {
    public final static int WIDTH;
    public final static int HEIGHT;
    public final static int PROPERTIES;
    public final static int SOMEBITS;
    public final static int FRAMEBITS;
    public final static int ALLBITS;
    public final static int ERROR;
    public final static int ABORT;
    public abstract boolean imageUpdate(Image img, int infoflags, int x,
                                        int y, int width, int height);
}
```

Apart from the collection of constants, it defines a single method to be implemented by an `ImageObserver`: `imageUpdate()`.

The Image-Loading Chain of Events

Here is how all of the various pieces fall into place: getImage() does not actually load the image; drawImage() does. But since loading images from the Internet can be a lengthy proposition (or even worse, the loading process can fail), even it returns immediately. Method drawImage() kicks off the asynchronous loading of the image it wants to render, and returns immediately. Another invisible Java subsystem that runs in a different thread actually does all the hard work of transferring the image over the network. Each time this image-loading system has a reasonable chunk of new image data, it tells the ImageObserver for the image that some extra data is available. It does this through an invocation of the imageUpdate() method.

Again, the ImageObserver in this case is the applet. To understand its response to an imageUpdate(), you will want to sneak a peek at the API source itself. The default imageUpdate() method is found in class Component:

```
/**
 * Repaints the component when the image has changed.
 * @return true if image has changed; false otherwise.
 */
  public boolean imageUpdate(Image img, int flags,
      int x, int y, int w, int h) {
      int rate = -1;
      if ((flags & (FRAMEBITS|ALLBITS)) != 0) {
          rate = 0;
      } else if ((flags & SOMEBITS) != 0) {
          if (isInc) {
              try {
                  rate = incRate;
                      if (rate < 0)
                          rate = 0;
              } catch (Exception e) {
                  rate = 100;
              }
          }
```

```
        }
          if (rate >= 0) {
              repaint(rate, 0, 0, width, height);
        }
          return (flags & (ALLBITS|ABORT)) == 0;
        }
```

What you are looking for is that last `if` statement: `if`... `repaint()`. Most of the time, a call to `imageUpdate()` will trigger a `repaint()` of the applet, which, in turn, means the applet's familiar `paint()` method will be called. And what does the applet's `paint()` method do? `drawImage()`! And you are back to where you started. Only this time, your `drawImage()` will have a chunk of its image to render, which it does before terminating again. In the meantime, the background image-loading thread continues loading data, which it will again pass on as a stream of image chunks. This cycle continues until the entire image is loaded and displayed.

Although this long chain of cause and effect is admittedly arduous, it is a small price to pay for the advantages you gain:

- The logic of your applets does not need to be concerned with multithreaded, asynchronous loading of image data. Everything is taken care of behind the scenes (by daemon Java threads).

- The images are rendered on the screen as the data comes in. This is a handy form of user feedback, because, at any point, the user can ascertain the progress of the images being loaded.

- Multiple images can be loaded in parallel by using multiple TCP connections to exploit the bandwidth wasted by and inherent in any burst-pause-burst-pause communication link.

This last point is at least as important as the first. If image loading were left up to the thousands of applet programmers out there to program, chances are that the vast majority of applets would use very inefficient (that is, slow), "brute force" algorithms to load images. Instead, the API designers implemented a complex but high-performance system to be used by all developers.

Some aspects of this implementation are not completely hidden from the application developer. The component `repaint()` methods are a case in point. Two of the overloaded variants take a repaint timeout value. To understand what a timeout parameter has to do with refreshing a graphical display, add a simple `System.out.println()` to your applet and observe the applet's `paint()` dynamics carefully. Add the following line after the `drawImage()` statement in the `paint()` method:

```
System.out.prinln("Had to paint!");
```

If you now rerun the applet, the console should print a number of "Had to paint!" lines:

```
Had to paint!
Had to paint!
Had to paint!
Had to paint!
```

You know why `paint()` is called several times like this: Each time a new image chunk becomes available, the `imageUpdate()` method causes the applet to repaint itself. In fact, things are a little more subtle still. Suppose you have an applet with a dozen images, all loaded and displayed using the simple `getImage()`/`drawImage()` duo. Since many of the images will be loaded in parallel, new image data will become available in a fairly continuous flow, leading to an onslaught of `imageUpdate()` events. It is clear that calling the applet's `(re)paint()` method each time any of the images has more data available would be inefficient overkill. And that's where the timeout comes in: The AWT defines an incremental draw rate property that determines how long the system can buffer image data before actually physically updating it on the screen.

If you look back at the default implementation for `imageUpdate()`, this is what all the rate (redraw rate) code is about before the `if...` `repaint()` at the end. In effect, the `imageUpdate()` method is saying, "Okay, image loader, thanks very much for the new data, but let me see if the user really needs to see this data displayed right now." The method determines the refresh rate to be used and passes this on to repaint(). Internally, repaint() determines if this refresh timeout has expired or not. If not, it delays the full repaint, thereby avoiding a potentially expensive call to paint().

As you have seen, a minuscule applet can be a deceptively simple facade hiding some seriously nontrivial software activity. Fortunately, you can rely on this complex machinery to do all the hard work for you, all by using two simple methods: getImage() and drawImage().

Animation's Worst Enemy: Flicker

What if you do not need to load already stored images? Instead, you want to use the Graphics class rendering methods to construct an image from scratch and then render that image. This is possible, but you will not be able to use the applet method getImage(); images obtained via getImage() cannot be drawn into with the Graphics drawing primitives. Your Image object will need to come from another factory method in another class: createImage() in class Component.

Here is an example of an applet that creates an image of a ball and bounces it around the applet over a simple background:

```
import java.awt.*;

public class Ball extends java.applet.Applet {

final static int BALL_RADIUS = 70;

Image ball = null;

public void init() {

   ball = createImage(BALL_RADIUS, BALL_RADIUS);
   Graphics ballG = ball.getGraphics();
```

```
    for (int i=0; i<60; i++) {
        ballG.setColor(new Color((float)Math.random(),
                        (float)Math.random(),
                        (float)Math.random() ) );
        int x1 = (int)(Math.random()*BALL_RADIUS);
        int y1 = (int)(Math.random()*BALL_RADIUS);
        int x2 = (int)(Math.random()*BALL_RADIUS);
        int y2 = (int)(Math.random()*BALL_RADIUS);
        ballG.drawLine(x1,y1, x2,y2);
    }

    ballG.setColor(Color.gray);
    for (int i=-20; i<=0; i++) {
        ballG.drawOval(i,i, BALL_RADIUS + ((-i)*2),
                    BALL_RADIUS + ((-i)*2));
    }
}
public void paint(Graphics g) {

    for (int x = 0; x <400; x++) {
        double angle = ((double)x) / 20;
        int y = (int) (Math.abs( Math.sin(angle) )*80);
        g.clearRect(0,0, getBounds().width, getBounds().height);
        drawBackground(g);
        g.drawImage(ball, x, 80-y, this);
        delay(25);
    }

    System.out.println("paint() done!!");
}
private void drawBackground(Graphics g) {
    for (int i= 0; i<10; i++) {
        g.drawLine(0, i*10, 400, i*10);
    }
}
private void delay (int millis) {
    try { Thread.sleep(millis); } catch (Exception ignored) {}
}}
```

Figure 13.13 shows a snapshot frame of the animation.

FIGURE 13.13

Bouncing ball animation

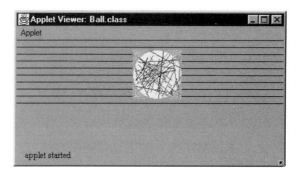

TIP

You don't need to be a latter-day Newton to breathe some gravity-like controlled motion into an object. The motion of the ball in this applet follows a sine curve whose negative lobes have been folded up using the `Math.abs()` method. It might not be an accurate modeling of physical reality, but it looks good, and that is what animation is primarily about.

This applet's `init()` method starts by creating a blank ball image, which is accomplished by invoking the `createImage()` method on itself. Applets can do this since they are descendants of `Component`. The `createImage(int width, int height)` method is actually an image constructor that creates a special type of off-screen image in which you can draw using the familiar `Graphics` drawing primitives.

To start drawing into your off-screen image, you need to obtain the `Graphics` handle associated with this image. This is done with a call to `getGraphics()`, which returns a `Graphics` object. Once you have such an object in your possession, you can use all of the graphics-rendering methods as usual. The applet draws a ball-like object consisting of random lines of random colors. The `paint()` method then proceeds by repeatedly erasing the entire applet, redrawing the background for the animation, and drawing the ball in its next position.

You probably have noticed the problem with this animation already: It flickers like mad. And Walt Disney's animations do not flicker at all, do they? Time for bouncing ball, take two.

Smooth Animation Using Double Buffering

Animation flicker occurs when animation contains sharp and repetitive discontinuities in movement and/or colors within successive frames. In the bouncing ball applet's case, the problem is the on-screen wiping of the applet area. This causes a repeated and massive color discontinuity that spoils the animation. You need to wipe the whole frame; otherwise, the bouncing ball will leave behind a trace of itself. You can see this by commenting out the g.clearRect() statement. After several frames, the applet looks like the one depicted in Figure 13.14.

FIGURE 13.14

Bouncing ball animation with wipe step removed

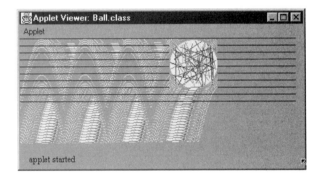

If you could only treat the entire applet drawing area as the same type of off-screen image as the ball itself, then maybe you could do all of the animation steps off-screen and display the finished frames in the applet on-screen. The following program is an enhanced version of Ball.java that does exactly that:

```java
import java.awt.*;

public class Ball2 extends java.applet.Applet {

final static int BALL_RADIUS = 70;
```

```
Image ball    = null;
Image applet = null;

Graphics appG, ballG;

public void paint(Graphics g) {

   if (ball == null) {
      applet  = createImage(getBounds().width, getBounds().height);
      ball    = createImage(BALL_RADIUS, BALL_RADIUS);

      appG    = applet.getGraphics();
      ballG   =   ball.getGraphics();

      for (int i=0; i<60; i++) {
         ballG.setColor(new Color((float)Math.random(),
                      (float)Math.random(), (float)Math.random() ) );
         int x1 = (int)(Math.random()*BALL_RADIUS);
         int y1 = (int)(Math.random()*BALL_RADIUS);
         int x2 = (int)(Math.random()*BALL_RADIUS);
         int y2 = (int)(Math.random()*BALL_RADIUS);
         ballG.drawLine(x1,y1, x2,y2);
      }

      ballG.setColor(Color.gray);
      for (int i=-20; i<=0; i++) {
         ballG.drawOval(i,i, BALL_RADIUS + ((-I)*2), BALL_RADIUS + ((-i)*2));
      }
   }

   for (int x = 0; x <400; x++) {
      double angle = ((double)x) / 20;
      int y = (int) (Math.abs( Math.sin(angle) )*80);

      appG.clearRect(0,0, getBounds().width, getBounds().height);
      drawBackground(appG);
      appG.drawImage(ball, x, 80-y, this);

      g.drawImage(applet, 0,0, this);
      delay(25);
   }
}
```

```
private void drawBackground(Graphics g) {
    for (int i= 0; i<10; i++) {
        g.drawLine(0, i*10, 400, i*10);
    }
}
private void delay (int millis) {
    try {Thread.sleep(millis);
} catch (Exception ignored) {}
}}
```

In this newer incarnation of the bouncing ball applet, create-Image() was used to obtain a second off-screen image buffer of exactly the same dimensions as the applet. This image is used to draw everything previously drawn directly into the applet. Therefore, an extra Graphics context appG is needed to provide drawing access to this new image. The rest of the code is identical, except for the use of appG instead of the usual g. Finally, you still need to use the Graphics object for the on-screen applet (g) when you draw the completed frame, in the blink of an eye, into the applet using g.drawImage().

When you run this new applet, you will see that all the flicker has magically disappeared. This technique is called *double buffering,* and it is one of the most basic computer graphics techniques for smooth animation. The technique can be summarized as follows:

1. Do all your drawing off-screen.

2. Copy the finished product (a single animation frame) to the screen.

3. Repeat the previous two steps as quickly as possible.

Since the frames displayed on-screen never differ beyond the changes intended by the animation itself, flicker is completely eliminated.

Avoiding Jerkiness in Animation

If your animation rate drops below, say, 20 fps, your animation will suffer from *jerkiness*. Home computer flight simulators are often a prime example of jerky animations. The scenery frames take so much time to generate (because of the complexity of the scenes and the expensive calculations) that the program simply can't produce a new frame every one-fiftieth of a second.

Once your animations become complex, they might also suffer from dropping frame rates. It will then be a question of optimizing the animation for speed—a subject that could fill an entire volume. Here are some pointers with which you can start:

- Draw as little as possible.
- Reduce the complexity of your animation.
- Use faster rendering algorithms.
- Reduce the dimensions of the animation (shrink the viewport).
- Use tricks like color cycling to animate parts cheaply.
- Use textures to cheaply introduce detail (or complexity).
- Use fixed-point integer math for 3-D calculations.
- Use lookup tables with precalculated results where complex math is involved.

Image Processing

Image processing is a broad term for a large collection of diverse computer graphics applications. The following list is just a sampling of what image processing is used for:

- Optical character recognition (OCR)

- Image compression and decompression

- Movie special effects

- Image interpretation (for factory robots, automated car control, surveillance, and so on)

- Image cleanup (digitally cleaning up old movie classics)

These applications all have something in common: Any real-time aspect of the application is secondary to achieving the primary goal, which is usually very expensive in terms of CPU resources. Modern full-color images easily need over 1 MB of storage alone (an 800 x 600, 24-bit-per-pixel picture requires nearly 1.4MB). Any algorithm that needs to analyze or process such a picture will almost necessarily fall short of having real-time response characteristics. But this does not mean image processing is used any less for that reason.

Java supports image processing in various ways, all of them having one feature in common: platform independence. You can manipulate colors and bitmaps extensively in hardware-independent ways, using an image pipeline metaphor, before they are output to the screen. The pipeline metaphor is analogous to the streams I/O model provided by the `java.io` package (discussed in Chapter 15). Before exploring the pipeline model, as embodied by the `ImageProducer` and `ImageConsumer` interfaces, you need to understand how color itself can be represented and manipulated.

Color Models

Color emanating from a radiating source can be decomposed into the three primary additive colors: red, green, and blue (RGB). All colors used by computers are mixtures of these three colors. The spectrum of a computer's palette will be determined by the number of different red, green, and blue shades that are available. This is, in turn, determined by the number of bits the hardware uses to encode the red, green, and blue primaries. The number of bits used has evolved historically from 1 bit each to the current norm of 8 bits each. The first systems, which used 1 bit per primary, could display eight different colors. Those eight colors are listed in Table 13.2.

TABLE 13.2   Minimal Eight-Color Palette

Color	Red Bit	Green Bit	Blue Bit
Black	0	0	0
Red	1	0	0
Green	0	1	0
Blue	0	0	1
Yellow	1	1	0
Cyan	0	1	1
Magenta	1	0	1
White	1	1	1

Modern systems use 8 bits per primary, so they can display 16.7 million colors. In between, there are numerous asymmetrical bit-assignment combinations that invariably favor green, allocating, for example, 5 bits for red and blue and 6 bits for green. (This is because the human eye is more discerning when it comes to shades of green.)

The end result is that there are a large number of incompatible color representations out there. Instead of choosing one (the most popular one, for example) and enforcing its use by all Java programmers, Java defines a software layer that shields you from these platform dependencies. The abstract class `ColorModel` is the key to this buffer layer:

```
public class ColorModel extends Object {
    protected int pixel_bits;
    public ColorModel(int bits);
    public static ColorModel getRGBdefault();
    public int getPixelSize();
    public abstract int getRed(int pixel);
```

```
    public abstract int getGreen(int pixel);
    public abstract int getBlue(int pixel);
    public abstract int getAlpha(int pixel);
    public int getRGB(int pixel);
}
```

The main feature of any `ColorModel` is that it allows you to use pixels that are encoded using almost any hardware-encoding scheme (the notable exception is bitplane-based architectures). A customized `ColorModel` should allow you to extract the universal red, green, and blue (and alpha transparency) components from any pixel encoded using any color-coding scheme. Although Java's image-processing classes support this flexible color model independence, they still define a default preferred color architecture—the popular 32-bit alpha/red/green/blue pixel format that uses the following bit assignments:

bits 0–7   blue

bits 8–15   green

bits 16–23   red

bits 24–31   alpha transparency

The `java.awt.image` package has two concrete incarnations of this abstract `ColorModel` class: classes `DirectColorModel` and `IndexColorModel`.

Class `DirectColorModel` encapsulates a `ColorModel` reflecting a True Color–style color architecture. In such a system, pixels hold the color value they represent themselves. This is in contrast to indexed architectures, in which pixels hold an index value used to index a table holding the final color values. And this is what class `IndexColorModel` models—a `ColorModel` using a color look-up table (CLUT) color architecture.

This color model independence means your applications have almost limitless flexibility in the way they encode pictures "behind the scenes."

Algorithmic Image Generation

Images are usually external files containing photographs, diagrams, or other art that was produced sometime in the past. There is one other fascinating source for images: the computer itself, or rather algorithms that generate pictures dynamically, using numerical methods. Class MemoryImageSource exists just for those types of applications needing per-pixel control over their images. Its constructor takes an array of int (or byte) representing a two-dimensional pixel map. Therefore, with this class, you can implement rendering algorithms of arbitrary complexity, since you have full and efficient access to every pixel of an image (remember that the Graphics class does not have a single-pixel-plotting method). The program below demonstrates this by generating the classic fractal: the Mandelbrot set.

```java
import java.awt.*;
import java.awt.image.*;

class Mandelbrot {

public static void main(String[] args) {
   new MandelWindow();
}}


//————————————————————————————————
class MandelWindow extends Frame {

Image    img;
int      w = 256;
int      h = 256;
int[]    pix = new int[w * h];

MandelWindow() {

int index = 0;
int iter;
double p,q, psq, qsq, pnew, qnew;
double a,b;                        // real and imaginary axis
```

```
resize(260,300);
show();
Graphics g = getGraphics();

double WIDTH_STEP = 4.0/w;
double HEIGHT_STEP = 4.0/h;

for (int y=0; y < h; y++) {        b = ((double)(y-128))/64;
   for (int x=0; x < w; x++) {     a = ((double)(x-128))/64;

      p=q=0;
      iter = 0;
      while (iter < 32) {          // see if point a,b is in the set
         psq = p*p; qsq = q*q;
         if (psq+qsq >= 4.0) break;
         pnew = psq - qsq + a;
         qnew = 2 * p*q + b;
         p = pnew;
         q = qnew;
         iter++;
      }
      if (iter == 32) {
         pix[index] = 255<<24 | 255;
      }
      index++;
   }
}

for (float i=0.0F; i< 1.0F; i+=0.01F) {  // draw a pretty background
   g.setColor(new Color(i,0,0));
   g.drawLine(0,0, (int)(300*Math.cos(i*1.5)), (int)(300*Math.sin(i*1.5))
);
}

img = createImage(new MemoryImageSource(w, h, pix, 0, w));
g.drawImage(img, 0,0, null);
}}
```

Figure 13.15 shows the applet's output (which on a 100MHz Pentium PC, using the standard Sun JDK, is generated in a very respectable time of less than five seconds).

FIGURE 13.15

Mandelbrot set generated via a MemoryImageSource

The code clearly shows the power of class `MemoryImageSource`: You simply declare any old array of `int` values (`pix` in this example) to hold the pixels you will "plot" yourself, and then generate the image using any rendering algorithm of your choice.

Now you are just a `createImage()` and `drawImage()` away from seeing the result displayed by your Java program. Plotting pixels in such arrays can be done extremely efficiently (more efficiently even than plotting individual pixels directly to the screen using some kind of `plotPixel(x,y,color)` method). The sample program does not even address the array two-dimensionally (although, logically, it is a 2-D array w pixels wide and h pixels high). Instead, it uses a most efficient linear (one-dimensional) sequential addressing (`pix[index]`). The actual plotting of a pixel is done by storing `255<<24 | 255` as its value. This, under the default RGB color model, means alpha equals 255 (completely opaque, bits 24–31) and blue equals 255; in other words, an everyday "pure blue" pixel. Since you are not plotting pixels for the points outside the Mandelbrot set, the set is surrounded by fully transparent (alpha equals 0) pixels, thus letting the background show through in those areas. (You are relying on newly allocated `int` arrays containing only zeros, which is guaranteed by the language itself.)

TIP
The mathematics behind the Mandelbrot set involve complex numbers and requires some understanding of nonlinear equations. Consult any good book on fractals if you want to know the ins and outs of the Mandelbrot (and other) fractals. A good reference is *The Beauty of Fractals*, by Peitgen and Richter (published by Springer-Verlag).

If you look at the definition of class `MemoryImageSource`, you will notice that most of its constructors allow you to specify a `ColorModel` to be used with the memory image:

```
public class MemoryImageSource extends Object implements ImageProducer {
    public MemoryImageSource(int w, int h, ColorModel cm,
                             byte pix[], int off, int scan);
    public MemoryImageSource(int w, int h, ColorModel cm,
                             byte pix[], int off, int scan, Hashtable props);
    public MemoryImageSource(int w, int h, ColorModel cm,
                             int pix[], int off, int scan);
    public MemoryImageSource(int w, int h, ColorModel cm,
                             int pix[], int off, int scan, Hashtable props);
    public MemoryImageSource(int w, int h, int pix[], int off, int scan);
    public MemoryImageSource(int w, int h, int pix[], int off, int scan,
                             Hashtable props);
    public synchronized void addConsumer(ImageConsumer ic);
    public synchronized boolean isConsumer(ImageConsumer ic);
    public synchronized void removeConsumer(ImageConsumer ic);
    public void startProduction(ImageConsumer ic);
    public void requestTopDownLeftRightResend(ImageConsumer ic);
    public void setAnimated(boolean animated);
    public void setFullBufferUpdates(boolean fullUpdates);
    public void newPixels();
    public void newPixels(int x, int y, int w, int h);
    public void newPixels(int x, int y, int w, int h, boolean notify);
    public void newPixels(byte[] pix, ColorModel model,
                          int offset, int scansize);
    public void newPixels(int[] pix, ColorModel model, int offset,
                          int scansize);
}
```

In this example, the Mandelbrot class uses the simplest constructor that conveniently avoids ColorModel issues. This means that your memory image actually uses the AWT preferred color model—the default 32-bit ARGB format (defined in the section on color models). But the image-processing flexibility of the java.awt.image package does not force you to use this. Therefore, you could ignore what Java prefers and impose a 4-bit VGA color-encoding scheme. (This is used purely for illustrative purposes and in no way suggests that VGA schemes—that is, limitations—still have a place in modern graphics applications.) The following code implements the new Mandelbrot class using a VGA color model.

```
import java.awt.*;
import java.awt.image.*;

class MandelIndex {

public static void main(String[] args) {
    new MandelWindow();
}}

//
class MandelWindow extends Frame {

final static byte[] VGAreds   = {-128,  -1,   0,   0,   0,   0,-128,  -1,
                                    0,   0, -128,  -1,   0,-128,-64,  -1};
final static byte[] VGAgreens = {  0,   0,-128,  -1,   0,   0,-128,  -1,-
                                  128,  -1,   0,   0,   0,-128,-64,  -1};
final static byte[] VGAblues  = {  0,   0,   0,   0,-128,  -1,   0,   0,-
                                  128,  -1, -128,  -1,   0,-128,-64,  -1};

Image   img;
int     w = 512;
int     h = 512;
byte[]  pix = new byte[w * h];

MandelWindow() {

int index = 0;
int iter;
```

```
double p,q, psq, qsq, pnew, qnew;
double a,b;                          // real and imaginary axis

   resize(512,400);
   show();
   Graphics g = getGraphics();

   double WIDTH_STEP = 4.0/w;
   double HEIGHT_STEP = 4.0/h;

   for (int y=0; y < h; y++) {       b = ((double)(y-256))/128;
      for (int x=0; x < w; x++) {    a = ((double)(x-256))/128;

            p=q=0;
            iter = 0;
            while (iter < 32) {        // see if point a,b is in the set
                psq = p*p; qsq = q*q;
                if (psq+qsq >= 4.0) break;
                pnew = psq - qsq + a;
                qnew = 2 * p*q + b;
                p = pnew;
                q = qnew;
                iter++;
            }

            if (iter == 32) {
                pix[index] = 15;      // VGA color 15
            } else {
                pix[index] = 4;       // VGA color 4
            }
            index++;
      }
   }

   img = createImage(new MemoryImageSource(w, h, new IndexColorModel(8, 16,
                 VGAreds, VGAgreens, VGAblues), pix, 0, w));

   g.drawImage(img, 0,0, null);
}}
```

To modify the Mandelbrot class to plot VGA-style pixels instead of expensive 32-bit pixels, start by declaring an array of bytes instead of `ints`, and then change the actual plotting . It is now much simpler to do this, of course: You store color index numbers instead of specifying the color value itself. The `if` statement colors a pixel white (VGA color 15) if it is inside the set, and colors all other pixels blue (VGA color 4) for all points outside the `Mandelbrot` set. Then, to convince `drawImage()` to use the VGA-style coloring scheme, you use an explicitly defined color model that allows Java to map your VGA pixels to its own preferred 32-bit style. (`drawImage()` doesn't know anything about VGA.) Since VGA uses a color lookup table mechanism, you create an instance of an `IndexColorModel` that defines this mapping, and tell it your pixels are only 8 bits wide and that the lookup table holds only 16 color entries. The lookup table itself is passed as three separate byte lookup arrays, one for each primary color:

```
new IndexColorModel(8, 16, VGAreds, VGAgreens, VGAblues)
```

NOTE Note the color byte arrays are filled with some bytes in the range 128–255 using negative values. The Java range for bytes is –128 through +127, because bytes are always signed numbers (like all other numerical types in Java). Literally specifying the unsigned byte value 255, for example, is not possible without using casts. And since using a cast for each item in the arrays would seriously degrade readability, we chose to go negative using the two's complement scheme. The signed byte –128 is equivalent to the unsigned byte 128. Likewise, –1 is equivalent to 255, and so on.

Since `createImage()` binds this custom color model to the image you are creating, any subsequent `drawImage()` calls will use this color model to translate the custom pixel encoding to whatever the native image subsystem implementation uses (one safe bet is that it will not be using VGA).

If you wanted to eliminate the use of the verbose `IndexColor-Model` constructor by subclassing `IndexColorModel` into a `VGA-ColorModel` class, say, to enhance readability, and using the constructor for the new class instead, something interesting happens to the program. Here is the readability enhancing VGAColorModel class:

```
import java.awt.image.IndexColorModel;
class VGAColorModel extends IndexColorModel {

final static byte[] VGAreds   = {-128, -1,   0,   0,   0,   0,-128,  -1,   0,
                                    0, -128,  -1,   0,-128,-64,  -1};
final static byte[] VGAgreens = {  0,   0,-128,  -1,   0,   0,-128,  -1,-128,
                                   -1,   0,   0,   0,-128,-64,  -1};
final static byte[] VGAblues  = {  0,   0,   0,   0,-128,  -1,   0,   0,-128,
                                   -1, -128,  -1,   0,-128,-64,  -1};

public VGAColorModel() {
    super(8, 16, VGAreds, VGAgreens, VGAblues);
            }}
```

With this new class, you can now call:

```
new MemoryImageSource(w, h, new VGAColorModel(), pix, 0, w)
```

The unexpected result comes when you run the program again using the new class—it is much slower. The drop in performance cannot have anything to do with the Mandelbrot calculations (since nothing changed here), so the slowdown must be attributed to the drawImage() method. Without the subclass, our VGA Mandelbrot appears on-screen in less than 1 second. Using the subclass, it takes 7.5 seconds!

Why the discrepancy in times? To begin, the core method of class ColorModel is getRGB(). This method is used by the image subsystem to construct in-core images in optimized formats that are native to the platform running your Java programs—for example, BMP format on Windows machines or X-Bitmaps on X-Windows machines. So, for every pixel in your images, whatever their encoding is, the image subsystem needs to invoke the getRGB() method on the associated color model being used for this image. If you now subclass IndexColorModel without overriding this getRGB() method (which you cannot do anyway, because it is declared final in IndexColorModel), Java's dynamic lookup mechanism will fail to find this method in the `VGAColorModel` class. Undeterred (this is why it is called dynamic), it will then follow the inheritance chain up to the superclass to see if the method is available there, which, sure enough, it is.

Did one paltry extra level of inheritance cause such a huge performance hit? (If it had, Java would be unusable.) The real cause lies in the declaration of the original `getRGB()` method. It was declared `final`; that is, you could not override it in subclasses. And `final` methods are very quick to call (there is no dynamic lookup whatsoever). Your first version did not subclass `IndexColorModel`, so the `getRGB()` method was called statically (that is, quickly). Then, you forced this method to be accessed via a dynamic method lookup, clearly showing the difference in the performance of static versus dynamic method binding. And that is the cause for the performance hit. Had the original method not been declared `final`, the difference would have been far less striking.

The Producer-Consumer Design Pattern

A *design pattern* is a design solution that has been proven to work time and time again. As such, you can use off-the-shelf design patterns in your software (or in construction, electronics, or architecture) with a better than even chance that the design pattern will be a solid foundation for solving the problem at hand (if you pick the right pattern for the type of problem you're dealing with). There are many kinds of design patterns out there, most of which have not yet been identified as such. The realization that the field of software also has its own design patterns is a rather recent development in computer science.

The following are some patterns that have already been identified and are used by the Java API:

Iterator Embodied by the `Enumeration` interface in package `java.util`.

Observer   Embodied by the `Observer` interface and the `Observable` class in package `java.util`.

Composite   Embodied by the AWT classes `Component` and `Container`.

The Iterator and Observer patterns are made available by Java in their most powerful forms: as interfaces. An `Enumeration` does not care what you are enumerating through it, and the `Observer/Observable` duo does not care what is being observed or who is doing the observing. Unfortunately, this generality has not been applied within the AWT, too. Classes `Component` and `Container` are an implementation of the Composite design pattern (which allows a system to handle individual objects or collections of those objects in the same way), but the design pattern itself is not made available to application programmers. It is used within the AWT, but not "exported," as are the `java.util` design patterns.

Package `java.awt.image` also relies on a common design pattern (again without making available the guts of the abstraction): the Producer-Consumer design pattern. As with so many of these patterns, the focus lies on decoupling systems. Decoupling is a powerful technique used to introduce more flexibility into a system.

NOTE   You saw a strong example of decoupling in this chapter with the `drawImage()` Graphics method. It decouples (internally) the drawing of an image from the image's data source.

The image Producer-Consumer design pattern is enforced using two interfaces: `ImageProducer` and `ImageConsumer`. Concrete classes that implement these interfaces are symbiotically linked together to form an image-generation pipeline. An `ImageProducer` is nothing without an `ImageConsumer`, and vice versa. This bidirectional dependence is defined by the methods each calls on the other.

Here are the definitions for both interfaces, since neither can be explained in isolation:

```
public interface ImageProducer {
    public abstract void addConsumer(ImageConsumer ic);
    public abstract boolean isConsumer(ImageConsumer ic);
    public abstract void removeConsumer(ImageConsumer ic);
    public abstract void startProduction(ImageConsumer ic);
    public abstract void requestTopDownLeftRightResend(ImageConsumer ic);
}
public interface ImageConsumer {
    public final static int RANDOMPIXELORDER;
    public final static int TOPDOWNLEFTRIGHT;
    public final static int COMPLETESCANLINES;
    public final static int SINGLEPASS;
    public final static int SINGLEFRAME;
    public final static int IMAGEERROR;
    public final static int SINGLEFRAMEDONE;
    public final static int STATICIMAGEDONE;
    public final static int IMAGEABORTED;
    public abstract void setDimensions(int width, int height);
    public abstract void setProperties(Hashtable props);
    public abstract void setColorModel(ColorModel model);
    public abstract void setHints(int hintflags);
    public abstract void setPixels(int x, int y, int w, int h, ColorModel model,
                                   byte pixels[], int off, int scansize);
    public abstract void setPixels(int x, int y, int w, int h, ColorModel model,
                                   int pixels[], int off, int scansize);
    public abstract void imageComplete(int status);
}
```

If you recall the Observable-Observer design pattern explained in Chapter 9, then you should have no problem understanding this pair; there is a strong similarity between the two design patterns. While the loose coupling of the Observable-Observer duo consists of a simple notification implemented by an invocation of the update() observer method, with image Producer-Consumer pairs there is actual (and substantial) data transfer of image data. This is achieved in much the same way as with the Observable-Observer pair: the

`ImageProducer` calls methods on the `ImageConsumer` to transfer image data and other information. The main method is `setPixels()`. Here is this method's signature (the types of all the `int` arguments have been stripped out to fit the whole signature on one line):

```
void setPixels(x,y, w,h, ColorModel model, byte pixels[], off, scansize)
```

> **NOTE**
>
> When an `ImageProducer` wants to transfer some image data it has produced to an `ImageConsumer`, it invokes the `setPixels()` method on that consumer. The arguments tell the consumer which subrectangle is being transferred (the *x,y* and *w,h* arguments) and what that rectangle contains as pixels. In practice, these subrectangles will almost always be complete, consecutive strips of the picture. An `ImageProducer` that produced its data as a patchwork collage of rectangles would be rather strange. (There is, however, nothing to stop a producer from having such image-production dynamics, and it would not be an error.)

This image data is specified as a one-dimensional array of pixels (`byte` or `int`), an offset into that array, and the size of a horizontal (scan) line of the image. The *scansize* argument is required by the consumer in cases when the rectangle being transferred is narrower than the width of the picture. To extract the individual lines from the subrectangle correctly, the consumer must skip bytes in the array to go to the next line of the subrectangle. The amount to skip is calculated as *scansize–w*.

How does an `ImageProducer` know which `ImageConsumer` it should hand image data to, and when? Here, the responsibility lies with the consumer. It creates the producer-consumer connection by announcing itself to an `ImageProducer` as being interested in receiving image data, by calling the `addConsumer()` method on the producer. The consumer also starts the image factory rolling by calling the `startProduction()` `ImageProducer` method.

As you can guess from the other methods in both interfaces, there is quite a bit more to the protocol between these two partners. But here is a concrete example. You have already manipulated an ImageProducer in one of the examples earlier in this chapter. Class MemoryImageSource, which was used to generate the Mandelbrot image, is an ImageProducer, because it implements the ImageProducer interface. If you look back at its definition, you will see that it has the five required interface methods. So, somewhere in the Mandelbrot program, you should have its inseparable ImageConsumer, too. While it is not stated explicitly anywhere, the image created with the createImage() method internally uses an ImageConsumer for the image data it represents. This hidden consumer will activate the producer-consumer protocol at some later point, when a drawImage() is done on an Image.

There are several benefits to having this decoupling between image data and the entities that actually use this data:

- The path between image data and image user (consumer) can be of arbitrary complexity, and therefore very flexible. If createImage() took a pointer to a pixel bitmap in memory, your options would be rather limited. But since it takes a reference to an ImageProducer instead, the data can come from anywhere.

- The image transfer from producer to consumer can be asynchronous. Although the consumer starts the image-production process, it does not control the sequence of image subrectangles produced or their timing. This is the producer's province.

- You can create image-processing pipelines. This is achieved by having classes that are both producer and consumer—consumer of some previous stage's output and producer of the next stage's input. A possible pipeline is depicted in Figure 13.16.

Each stage in an image-processing pipeline is usually called a filter. Java's `java.awt.image` package includes explicit support for such filters. The next section explores the classes that deal with image filtering.

FIGURE 13.16

An image-processing pipeline

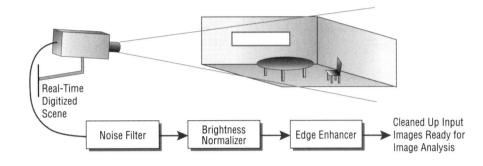

TIP The Producer-Consumer design pattern is just one of many patterns described in the excellent reference book *Design Patterns*, by Gamma, Helm, Johnson, and Vlissides (published by Addison-Wesley).

Image Filtering

The generic term image *filtering* is almost synonymous with image processing. One of the core image-processing techniques is filtering (that is, altering) an image pixel by pixel, although the term is used in the wider sense of image manipulation as well. Pixel-by-pixel processing of images is supported by several classes in `java.awt.image`.

First of all, there is class `FilteredImageSource`, which like `MemoryImageSource` is an `ImageProducer`:

```
public class FilteredImageSource extends Object implements ImageProducer {
    public FilteredImageSource(ImageProducer orig, ImageFilter imgf);
    public synchronized void addConsumer(ImageConsumer ic);
    public synchronized boolean isConsumer(ImageConsumer ic);
    public synchronized void removeConsumer(ImageConsumer ic);
    public void startProduction(ImageConsumer ic);
    public void requestTopDownLeftRightResend(ImageConsumer ic);
}
```

The key to understanding this class is its constructor: Instead of taking an array of pixels (as with `MemoryImageSource`), this class takes another `ImageProducer` plus a filter object to combine the two into a new, filtered image. The filter object must be of type `ImageFilter`, of which four concrete subclasses are provided in the `java.awt.image` package: `CropImageFilter`, `RGBImageFilter`, `ReplicateScaleFilter`, and `AverageScaleFilter`.

Using the `CropImageFilter` subclass, you can create subimages of a bigger image. With `RGBImageFilter`, you can filter the colors of an image either pixel by pixel or—if the image uses a CLUT color model—in bulk by simply modifying the image's palette. With `ReplicateScaleFilter` and `AverageScaleFilter`, you can rescale an image. (`AverageScaleFilter` is a subclass of `ReplicateScaleFilter` that uses a faster algorithm.)

The following program demonstrates the use of the `RGBImageFilter` and `CropImageFilter` filters on a color image file. The `RGBImageFilter` is used to implement a color-to-gray filter, and the `CropImageFilter` is used to cut a 40×40 pixel subimage from the original, which is then pasted back onto the original, magnified to three times its original size. The magnification is achieved simply by specifying a final image size of 120×120 pixels. Figure 13.17 shows the resulting output window.

```
import java.awt.*;
import java.awt.image.*;

//————————————————————————————————————————————————————
public class Filters extends java.applet.Applet {

Image oldImage, newImage, subImage;
ImageProducer filtered, cropped;

public void init() {
   oldImage = getImage(getDocumentBase(), "market.gif");
   filtered = new FilteredImageSource(oldImage.getSource(), new GrayFilter());
   cropped  = new FilteredImageSource(oldImage.getSource(), new CropImageFilter
                                  (300,70,40,40));

   newImage = createImage(filtered);
   subImage = createImage(cropped);
}

public void paint(Graphics g) {
   g.drawImage(newImage, 0, 0, this);
   g.clearRect(20,20,140,140);
   g.drawImage(subImage, 30, 30, 120, 120, this);

   System.out.println(".");
}}
//————————————————————————————————————————————————————
class GrayFilter extends RGBImageFilter {

public GrayFilter() {
   canFilterIndexColorModel = true;
}

public int filterRGB(int x, int y, int rgb) {

int alpha,r,g,b;
int gray;

   alpha   = rgb & (0xFF << 24);
   r       = (rgb >> 16) & 0xFF;
   g       = (rgb >>  8) & 0xFF;
   b       = (rgb >>  0) & 0xFF;
```

```
gray    = (r+g+b)/3;

return alpha | gray<<16 | gray<<8 | gray;
}}
```

FIGURE 13.17

Use of ImageFilters on an orginal color picture

This program loads the image file using a `getImage()` call and then creates two new images based on the original. Both derived images are obtained using the `FilteredImageSource` class to combine the picture with a filter. For the grayscale version of the picture, an instance of the `GrayFilter` that was subclassed from `RGBImageFilter` is used. For the subimage, an instance of a `CropImageFilter` is used (there is no need to subclass it). The two new `FilteredImageSource` objects are not yet images that can be passed to `drawImage()`. Since `FilteredImageSource` objects are only `ImageProducers`, you need to turn them into images with the two calls to `createImage()`. All of these steps should be done only once, so they are located in the applet's `init()` method. The actual drawing of the applet is done in the `paint()` method, where both processed images are drawn using `drawImage()` invocations.

The `GrayFilter` color filter has two aspects to it: the overridden `filterRGB()` method and the constructor. Method `filterRGB()` is called with individual pixels to be processed. The x and y parameters method `filterRGB()` receives are the coordinates of the pixel to be processed. Because you do not need to use these coordinates (the color filter is pixel position independent), you signal the outside world that this `RGBImageFilter` can short-circuit the bulk filtering of an image's pixels by simply filtering its palette only. This is several orders of magnitude faster than needing to process every single pixel of an `Image`, which makes the simple `canFilterIndexColor-Model = true;` assignment well worth the effort of creating the custom constructor.

Although the filtering architecture supported by the classes you have seen so far can be used for many filtering tasks, some image-filtering algorithms need to access arbitrary source-image pixels to determine the output value of any given pixel. The `ImageFilter` class cannot handle this easily. One way to solve this problem is to use yet another `java.awt.image` class: `PixelGrabber`. This class is almost the opposite of `MemoryImageSource` in that it takes an `ImageProducer` and extracts the image data from it. You can therefore use full-image-processing algorithms by using this procedure:

- Converting a source image into a simple (and fast) low-level Java array of `ints` or `bytes`, via the `PixelGrabber` class

- Applying the full-image algorithm to the array

- Reconverting the array into an image, via the `MemoryImage-Source` class

To demonstrate this approach, you will develop a class that implements the popular convolve filter. This filter is defined by a 3×3 matrix of pixel weights to be used when calculating the new value for the pixel at the center of the matrix. Different filtering effects can be obtained depending on the set of values used by the matrix. Among others, smoothing and vertical edge enhancement effects can be achieved. Here is a program that implements this filtering algorithm:

```java
import java.awt.*;
import java.awt.image.*;

//————————————————————————————————————————————————————
public class Convolve extends java.applet.Applet {

Image oldImage, newImage;
ImageProducer filtered;
double[] filter = {0.1125, 0.1125, 0.1125, 0.1125, 0.0000, 0.1125, 0.1125,
                   0.1125, 0.1125 };

public void init() {

    oldImage = getImage(getDocumentBase(), "hammock.jpg");

    MediaTracker mt = new MediaTracker(this);
    mt.addImage(oldImage, 0);
    try {
       mt.waitForID(0);
    } catch (Exception error) {
       System.out.println("Loading of image failed!");
       System.out.println(error);
       System.exit(10);
    }

    ConvFilter cv = new ConvFilter(filter);
    filtered = cv.filteredImage(oldImage);

    newImage = createImage(filtered);
}

public void paint(Graphics g) {

g.drawImage(oldImage, 0, 0, this);

g.clipRect(200,0,1000,500);
    g.drawImage(newImage, 0, 0, this);
}}
//————————————————————————————————————————————————————
```

```
class ConvFilter implements ImageObserver {

int[]   oldPixels, newPixels;  // original and result image buffers
int     w,h;  // image width and height

PixelGrabber pg;  // the way to get at the image's pixels
MemoryImageSource mis;  // the way to produce an image from result

// To process the image array we are using 1-dimensional addressing
// instead of the logical 2-D addressing. index is the main pixel
// pointer (equivalent to x,y coordinates). The collection of inn
// indices track index but address the 3x3 matrix neighbors of the
// center pixel

int     index = 0;
int     i00,i01,i02,i10,i11,i12,i20,i21,i22;    // 3x3 sliding indices into
                                                // image

int     p00,p01,p02,p10,p11,p12,p20,p21,p22;    // cached pixels
double  w00,w01,w02,w10,w11,w12,w20,w21,w22;    // cached weights


//————————————————————————————————————————————————————————————
// The CONSTRUCTOR for the class just caches (copies) the convolution
// filter's weights
//————————————————————————————————————————————————————————————

public ConvFilter (double[] matrix) {

   w00 = matrix[0]; w01 = matrix[1]; w02 = matrix[2];
   w10 = matrix[3]; w11 = matrix[4]; w12 = matrix[5];
   w20 = matrix[6]; w21 = matrix[7]; w22 = matrix[8];
}

public boolean imageUpdate(Image img, int infoflags,
                           int x, int y, int width, int height) {

   System.out.println("ImageObserver update !!!");


   w = width;
   h = height;
```

```
   System.out.println("INFO WIDTH = " + (infoflags & ImageObserver.WIDTH));
   System.out.println("INFO HEIGHT = " + (infoflags &
                        ImageObserver.HEIGHT));
   System.out.println("W,H= " + w + " " + h);

   if (w != -1 && h != -1) {
      System.out.println("GOT W & H !!");
      return false;
   }
   return true;
}


//——————————————————————————————————————————————————————————————————
// a) find out image width and height
// b) allocate original and result image pixel buffers
// c) extract pixels from image using a PixelGrabber
// d) process image
// e) convert resulting image to ImageProducer using a MemoryImageSource
//——————————————————————————————————————————————————————————————————

public ImageProducer filteredImage(Image source) {
boolean success;

   w = source.getWidth(null);
   h = source.getHeight(null);

   System.out.println("Image width = " + w + " height = " + h);

   oldPixels = new int[w*h];   // allocate image buffer for original
   newPixels = new int[w*h];   // allocate image buffer for destination

   pg = new PixelGrabber(source.getSource(), 0,0, w, h, oldPixels, 0, w);

   try {
      success = pg.grabPixels(0);      //  try to suck entire image into
   } catch (Exception e) {             //  our processing buffer
      System.out.println("Duh ! " + e);
   }

   index = w + 1;  // avoid top and left pixel edges
   for (int y=1; y < h-1; y++) {       // avoid bottom edge too
      calc3x3offsets();                // adjust all tracking offsets
      for (int x=1; x < w-1; x++) {    // and avoid right edge
```

```
        p00 = oldPixels[i00];   // cache 3x3 cluster of pixels
        p01 = oldPixels[i01];   // so we don't have to use expensive
        p02 = oldPixels[i02];   // array indexing anymore
        p10 = oldPixels[i10];
        p11 = oldPixels[i11];
        p12 = oldPixels[i12];
        p20 = oldPixels[i20];
        p21 = oldPixels[i21];
        p22 = oldPixels[i22];

           // convolution filter has to be applied to each color
           // primary individually (there's no way to treat a pixel as
           // a whole)

        int newRed  = applyWeights(16);
        int newGreen= applyWeights( 8);
        int newBlue = applyWeights( 0);
        newPixels[index++] = 255<<24 | newRed | newGreen | newBlue;

        i00++; i01++; i02++;   // slide all our tracking indices along
        i10++; i11++; i12++;
        i20++; i21++; i22++;
      }
      index += 2;
      System.out.println("Y=" + y); // give some feedback of where we're at
   }

   // we have now done all the image processing on the source image,
   // send the result back to the client as an ImageProducer.

   mis = new MemoryImageSource(w,h,newPixels,0,w);
   return mis;
}


//—————————————————————————————————————————————————————————————————————
// Convenience method to keep main loop readable. This just recalculates
// all neighbor pixel indices from index (this is done once for every
// image scanline only, within the scanline the indices are just
// incremented like index).
//—————————————————————————————————————————————————————————————————————
final void calc3x3offsets() {
```

```
    i00 = index-w-1;
    i01 = i00+1;
    i02 = i00+2;
    i10 = index-1;
    i11 = index;
    i12 = index+1;
    i20 = index+w-1;
    i21 = i20+1;
    i22 = i20+2;
}


//————————————————————————————————————————————————————————————————
// Calculate the new primary for this 3x3 pixel cluster.
// The primary is specified by the bit shift to apply to a standard 32-bit
// ARGB pixel so that the primary occupies bits 0..7
//————————————————————————————————————————————————————————————————

final int applyWeights(int shift) {
double total=0;

    total += ((p00 >> shift) & 0xFF) * w00;
    total += ((p01 >> shift) & 0xFF) * w01;
    total += ((p02 >> shift) & 0xFF) * w02;

    total += ((p10 >> shift) & 0xFF) * w10;
    total += ((p11 >> shift) & 0xFF) * w11;
    total += ((p12 >> shift) & 0xFF) * w12;

    total += ((p20 >> shift) & 0xFF) * w20;
    total += ((p21 >> shift) & 0xFF) * w21;
    total += ((p22 >> shift) & 0xFF) * w22;

    return ((int)total) << shift;

}} // End of class
```

The ConvolveFilter class takes an array of doubles specifying nine weight values. These nine values correspond to the 3 × 3 pixel cluster the filter uses to determine the central pixel's new value. The new color of a pixel is calculated by summing the weighted values of all pixels in the 3 × 3 cluster. This process needs to operate on all three color primaries separately. The actual filtering is done by the `filteredImage()` method. It relies on a `PixelGrabber` object and on a `MemoryImageSource` object to convert the image to and from the internal array representation used by the algorithm to actually do the filtering.

Much of the code is concerned with performance issues. It tries to avoid array indexing as much as possible by caching (that is, copying) values that need to be used several times. The class also avoids using loops that are considered nonfunctional overhead. Method `applyWeights()` could have been written with a loop to make it shorter and possibly more readable, but doing so would have slowed down the filtering significantly.

On the applet side of the program, there are a couple of technical points of interest. The `ConvolveFilter` requires the source image to be fully loaded and available. This is because it relies on the `Image` `getWidth()` and `getHeight()` methods to produce valid results at all times (due to the same asynchronous loading of images, width and height information might not be available until some time after the image is created using the `getImage()` method). To guarantee that `getWidth()` and `getHeight()` will not return –1 (which they do when images are not loaded yet), you use a `MediaTracker` object to wait for you until the image is completely ready and loaded. See the code and the online documentation for more information about class `java.awt.MediaTracker`.

The second interesting thing in the sample applet is the use of clipping to display part of the original image next to the processed image. For this you need to get a second (different!) `Graphics` context. This is because `clipRect()` calls, like `translate()` calls, are cumulative. You cannot just move the clipping rectangle to a new position, so you need to get a second `Graphics` object (which starts off with a `cliprect` as big as the entire applet) and specify the second clipping window in that context. The output of the program, shown in Figure 13.18, demonstrates how a smoothing filter is applied to the original image.

FIGURE 13.18

Smoothing convolution filter applied to a color image

Summary

This chapter dealt with a lot of graphics-related material, beginning with the basics: graphics-rendering primitives and how to manipulate Graphics contexts. Then you had a look at animation and the key requirements for any good animation: absence of flicker and high frame rates. You learned how double buffering can eliminate all flicker, which led to an exploration of the complex Image AWT subsystem. Although easily accessible to application programmers, asynchronous background loading of images is not entirely transparent to the application level, and might require the use of MediaTracker and other safeguards for robust implementations. You also explored the image-processing aspects of the java.awt.image package through the core metaphor of image producer-consumer pairs and the classes—MemoryImageSource, FilteredImageSource, PixelGrabber—that, in one way or other, implement the metaphor.

Advanced Applet Programming

- Simple, GUI-driven applets

- Applet pitfalls

- Well-behaved, multithreaded applets

- Tips on minimizing applet loading time

So far, the applets you have seen in this book have all been quick demonstrations of some Java class or Java method. Real-life applets, however, are usually seriously cool, functional, and/or perfectly compatible with all Java browsers.

It is a fact of life that the Web is this strange chimera of endless entertainment and serious information broadcasting. On one hand, you have an exploding population of people who use the Web as a vehicle to project their personality (through Web home pages which ooze unrestrained individuality); on the other hand, you have the world's businesses frantically trying to capture cyberspace market segments, by any means. Both groups are turning to Java to gain the edge over the competition, whether that competition is a multinational's Wall Street–listed arch rival or the guy halfway across the globe whose Web page is nearly as cool as yours. Whichever category you find yourself in, writing real-life applets will test your creative and programming skills to the fullest. But before you start dreaming of having your applet listed in the JARS (Java Applet Rating Service, http://www.jars.com) Top 30 worldwide charts, you will want to work a little bit more on the basics.

This chapter begins with simple, GUI-driven applets and progresses to real-life, functional, multithreaded applets that can please your users.

Purely GUI-Driven Applets

Using the techniques and knowledge presented so far, you can write some fairly functional applets. As long as you rely purely on a GUI to control your applet's functionality, you already have sufficient knowledge to design and implement programs like simple editors (paint programs, text editors, and so on) or even small games. To demonstrate what can be achieved with just a few buttons and a display area, you will develop a calculator. How about a scientific calculator that allows you to calculate the cosine of the logarithm of your next telephone bill?

Example: A Stack-Based Calculator

Start with some analysis first. What is the most elementary structure of any calculator? Answer: a large number of buttons and a display. These two aspects can form your top-level division of concerns for the applet you are going to write. Although modern calculator displays can plot graphics and even print text, this example is restricted to supporting simple numbers in scientific notation.

As you know, scientific notation uses a compact notation for huge and very small numbers by expressing numbers as a base number (the mantissa) raised to some power of ten. Since your calculator will have this scientific bias, you might as well make it even more so by designing it as a stack calculator. The choice of architecture is appropriate because of its simplicity compared with normal calculators. Moreover, stacks happen to be very relevant to Java: The Java VM (Virtual Machine) is a stack-based architecture with more than a passing resemblance to the calculator presented here.

The second feature of the calculator applet you will write is its display, or rather the digits it displays. Java has a number of fonts that provide a couple of digit styles, but none look like real calculator digits. Real calculators have relied (until recently) on seven-segment display elements to construct digits and numbers (first using LEDs, light-emitting diodes, then switching to LCD, liquid crystal display, technology). To give your calculator an authentic feel, you will design your own scalable, seven-segment digit character set from scratch (quite literally). Figure 14.1 shows the applet's convincing calculator appearance.

FIGURE 14.1

A scientific calculator

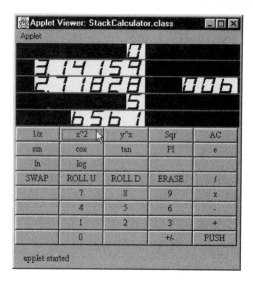

What Is a Stack Calculator?

Another name for stack calculators is *Reverse Polish Notation* (RPN) calculators. These types of calculators were used on the Apollo missions to the moon because the RPN system allows faster entry of complex calculations.

On a conventional calculator, you would add 10 and 20 by entering 10, then hitting the plus key, entering 20, and then hitting the equal key to calculate and display the result. With an RPN calculator, you would do this same addition by entering 10, then pressing the Enter key, entering 20, and finally hitting the plus key. When you press the plus key, the result is displayed; there is no need for you to press an equal key. In fact, there is no equal key on an RPN calculator (which may confuse and frustrate most people not accustomed to using them).

What Is a Stack Calculator? (Continued)

The advantage of stack calculators really becomes clear when working with complex expressions that involve prioritizing subcalculations using brackets. On RPN calculators (which do not have brackets either), the stack of the machine automatically provides for a prioritizing and remembering mechanism. It is this simple time-saving device (not having to type brackets) that prompted NASA to pick RPN calculators over the conventional type.

The applet's GUI design naturally reflects the functional and structural division of any calculator: There is a display area and a buttons panel. The StackCalculator applet program is subdivided into the following five classes:

StackCalculator   The applet framework.

KeyPanel   The customized component holding all the calculator keys and their associated functions.

LCDDigitDisplay   The customized component dealing with the numeric display.

CalcStack   A class encapsulating the calculator's stack architecture.

SevenSegmentDigits   A class encapsulating a scalable character set of calculator-style digits.

This is simply an application of the divide-and-conquer principle. These five classes cleanly subdivide the program, thus simplifying the overall problem of designing and writing a stack-based calculator applet. Although this applet can still be considered fairly trivial in terms of programming difficulty or complexity, it is already much too big to implement as one monolithic chunk of code (that is, in one class). As you have learned, breaking up problems into smaller sub-problems that you solve individually, by implementing a class for each one, is good practice as well as a good way to prevent things from going wrong.

Now take a look at each of the calculator software blocks in turn, in a top-down order:

```java
import java.applet.*;
import java.awt.*;

public class StackCalculator extends Applet {
final int STACK_DEPTH = 4;        // an N-entry stack calculator

LCDDigitDisplay LCDDisplay;       // the stack display
KeyPanel        calculatorKeys;   // the calculator buttons

//——————————————————————————————————————————————————————————
public void init() {
   setLayout(new BorderLayout());

   LCDDisplay      = new LCDDigitDisplay( STACK_DEPTH );
   calculatorKeys  = new KeyPanel( LCDDisplay );

   add(LCDDisplay, "North");
   add(calculatorKeys, "Center");
}
//——————————————————————————————————————————————————————————
public String getAppletInfo() {
   StringBuffer s = new StringBuffer();

   s.append("Stack Calculator\n");
   s.append((char) 169);                 // Copyright symbol
   s.append("1996 ORC Incorported & L. Vanhelsuwe, All Rights
         Reserved\n");
   return s.toString();
}
//——————————————————————————————————————————————————————————
```

```
public String[][] getParameterInfo() {
    String[][] result = {
        { "NONE", "NONE", "This applet takes no HTML parameters" },
    };
    return result;
}
} // End of Applet class
```

Top-level applet code does not come much cleaner than this. It is devoid of almost any application-relevant code and concentrates on its proper, prime concern—being an applet. As such, it overrides only three `Applet` methods: `init()`, `getAppletInfo()`, and `get-ParameterInfo()`.

Methods `getAppletInfo()` and `getParameterInfo()` are optional but add a touch of polish to the applet. They are there for browsers to call when users pick the browser's About Applet or Applet Info menu options (the exact menu titles differ from browser to browser). The `getAppletInfo()` method usually returns a string containing information such as author, version, and copyright (plus anything else you care to add to it). The `getParameterInfo()` method returns an array of `String` triplets describing all the parameters your applet accepts via the `<PARAM NAME=` "*parameterName*" `VALUE=`"*parameterValue*" `>` HTML parameters. Each triplet consists of the parameter's name, its type, and a short description explaining the parameter's function.

The heart of this applet is its `init()` method. It overrides the default `FlowLayout` applet component layout style and selects a `Border-Layout` instead. It then constructs two custom components: one for the calculator display (`LCDDisplay`) and one for the calculator keys panel (`calculatorKeys`). These two components are then positioned in the applet as in any real calculator, with keys below the display.

And that is it. The applet has no more concerns. It does not deal with any of the calculator logic, the display refreshing, or the button presses. This means, quite patently, that the objects the applet created manage themselves.

The Calculator Keys Panel

The KeyPanel class is the real processing heart of the calculator. Here is how it works:

```java
import java.awt.*;
import java.awt.event.*;

//─────────────────────────────────────────────────────────────
// The KeyPanel class encapsulates the entire calculator
// buttons "panel" and all the mathematical
// (and other) operations the buttons perform.
//─────────────────────────────────────────────────────────────
class KeyPanel extends Panel implements ActionListener {

int rowSize;
LCDDigitDisplay display;        // the stack display
CalcStack        stack;         // the stack within the display

// The calculator buttons are arranged as an array of 8 rows of 5 buttons

private String[] keyLabels = {
    "1/x",   "x^2",    "y^x",    "Sqr",    "AC",      // row 0
    "sin",   "cos",    "tan",    "PI",     "e",       // row 1
    "ln",    "log",    "  ",     "  ",     "  ",      // row 2
    "SWAP",  "ROLL U", "ROLL D", "ERASE",  "/",       // row 3
    "  ",    "7",      "8",      "9",      "x",       // row 4
    "  ",    "4",      "5",      "6",      "-",       // row 5
    "  ",    "1",      "2",      "3",      "+",       // row 6
    "  ",    "0",      ".",      "+/-",    "PUSH",    // row 7
};

//─────────────────────────────────────────────────────────────
public KeyPanel( int rows, int columns, LCDDigitDisplay display) {

    this.rowSize = columns;
    this.display = display;
    stack = display.getStack();

    setLayout(new GridLayout(rows,columns));

    Button[] b = new Button[ rows*columns ];
```

```
    for (int i=0; i < keyLabels.length; i++) {
       b[i] = new Button( keyLabels[i] );
       b[i].addActionListener(this);
       add( b[i] );
    }
}

//—————————————————————————————————————————————————————————
public void actionPerformed(ActionEvent e) {

       // if any of the 0..9 digit keys is pressed
    Button sender = (Button)(e.getSource());
    String label = sender.getLabel();

    if (label.equals( keyLabel(4,1) ) ||
       label.equals( keyLabel(4,2) ) ||
       label.equals( keyLabel(4,3) ) ||

       label.equals( keyLabel(5,1) ) ||
       label.equals( keyLabel(5,2) ) ||
       label.equals( keyLabel(5,3) ) ||

       label.equals( keyLabel(6,1) ) ||
       label.equals( keyLabel(6,2) ) ||
       label.equals( keyLabel(6,3) ) ||
       label.equals( keyLabel(7,1) )    ) {

           enterDigit( Integer.valueOf((String)label).intValue() );
    }

    if (label.equals( keyLabel(0,0) )) inverse();      else
    if (label.equals( keyLabel(0,1) )) square();       else
    if (label.equals( keyLabel(0,2) )) power();        else
    if (label.equals( keyLabel(0,3) )) squareRoot();   else
    if (label.equals( keyLabel(0,4) )) allClear();     else

    if (label.equals( keyLabel(1,0) )) sine();         else
    if (label.equals( keyLabel(1,1) )) cosine();       else
    if (label.equals( keyLabel(1,2) )) tan();          else
    if (label.equals( keyLabel(1,3) )) constantPI();   else
    if (label.equals( keyLabel(1,4) )) constantE();    else
```

```
      if (label.equals( keyLabel(2,0) )) ln();           else
      if (label.equals( keyLabel(2,1) )) log();          else
//    if (label.equals( keyLabel(2,2) )) FUTURE();       else
//    if (label.equals( keyLabel(2,3) )) FUTURE();       else
//    if (label.equals( keyLabel(2,4) )) FUTURE();       else

      if (label.equals( keyLabel(3,0) )) swap();          else
      if (label.equals( keyLabel(3,1) )) rollUp();        else
      if (label.equals( keyLabel(3,2) )) rollDown();      else
      if (label.equals( keyLabel(3,3) )) delDigit();      else

      if (label.equals( keyLabel(3,4) )) divide();        else
      if (label.equals( keyLabel(4,4) )) times();         else
      if (label.equals( keyLabel(5,4) )) subtract();      else
      if (label.equals( keyLabel(6,4) )) add();           else

      if (label.equals( keyLabel(7,2) )) decimal();       else
      if (label.equals( keyLabel(7,3) )) changeSign();    else
      if (label.equals( keyLabel(7,4) )) enter();         else
         ;

      System.out.println("Pressed the " + label + " key");
   }


   //------------------------------------------------------------
   // A digit was pressed; add it to the number being constructed
   //------------------------------------------------------------
   void enterDigit(int digit) {
      display.addDigit( digit );
   }
   //------------------------------------------------------------
   // The ERASE button was pressed; erase the last digit entered
   //------------------------------------------------------------
   void delDigit() {
      display.removeDigit();
   }
   //------------------------------------------------------------
   // This pushes the accumulator onto the stack
   //------------------------------------------------------------
   void enter() {
      stack.pushValue( stack.getAccumulator() );
      display.redrawStack();
   }
```

```
//————————————————————————————————————————————————————————————————
void changeSign() {
    stack.setAccumulator( - stack.getAccumulator() );
    display.redrawAccumulator();
}
//————————————————————————————————————————————————————————————————
void squareRoot() {
    if (stack.getAccumulator() >= 0.0) {
        stack.setAccumulator( Math.sqrt(stack.getAccumulator()) );
        display.redrawAccumulator();
    }
}
//————————————————————————————————————————————————————————————————
void square() {
    stack.setAccumulator( Math.pow(stack.getAccumulator() , 2) );
    display.redrawAccumulator();
}
//————————————————————————————————————————————————————————————————
// Sine, cosine and tangents all take an angle in RADIANS
//————————————————————————————————————————————————————————————————
void sine() {
    stack.setAccumulator( Math.sin(stack.getAccumulator()) );
    display.redrawAccumulator();
}
//————————————————————————————————————————————————————————————————
void cosine() {
    stack.setAccumulator( Math.cos(stack.getAccumulator()) );
    display.redrawAccumulator();
}
//————————————————————————————————————————————————————————————————
void tan() {
    stack.setAccumulator( Math.tan(stack.getAccumulator()) );
    display.redrawAccumulator();
}
//————————————————————————————————————————————————————————————————
void log() {
    if (stack.getAccumulator() > 1.0) {
        stack.setAccumulator( Math.log(stack.getAccumulator()) /
                          Math.log(10.0) );
        display.redrawAccumulator();
    }
}
```

```
//————————————————————————————————————————————————————————————
void ln() {
   if (stack.getAccumulator() > 1.0) {
      stack.setAccumulator( Math.log(stack.getAccumulator()) );
      display.redrawAccumulator();
   }
}
//————————————————————————————————————————————————————————————
// Raise next-on-stack (NOS) element to the power of top-of-stack (TOS)
//————————————————————————————————————————————————————————————
void power() {
double pow = Math.pow (stack.getStackElement(1), stack.getAccumulator());
   stack.drop(); stack.setAccumulator(pow); display.redrawStack();
}
//————————————————————————————————————————————————————————————
void constantE() {
   stack.setAccumulator( Math.E );
   display.redrawAccumulator();
}
//————————————————————————————————————————————————————————————
void constantPI() {
   stack.setAccumulator( Math.PI );
   display.redrawAccumulator();
}
//————————————————————————————————————————————————————————————
void inverse() {
   if (stack.getAccumulator() != 0.0) {
      stack.setAccumulator( 1.0/ stack.getAccumulator() );
      display.redrawAccumulator();
   }
}
//————————————————————————————————————————————————————————————
// The decimal button was pressed; tell display to go into decimals
// entry mode
//————————————————————————————————————————————————————————————
void decimal() {
   display.decimal();
}
//————————————————————————————————————————————————————————————
// Rotate the stack 1 cell up
//————————————————————————————————————————————————————————————
```

```
void rollUp() {
   stack.rollUp(1);
   display.redrawStack();
}
//————————————————————————————————————————————————————————
void rollDown() {
   stack.rollDown(1);
   display.redrawStack();
}
//————————————————————————————————————————————————————————
// Swap TOS and NOS
//————————————————————————————————————————————————————————
void swap() {
   stack.swap();
   display.redrawStack(2);
}
//————————————————————————————————————————————————————————
// Erase entire stack to zeroes (0.0)
//————————————————————————————————————————————————————————
void allClear() {
   stack.clearStack();
   display.redrawStack();
}
//————————————————————————————————————————————————————————
// Add TOS & NOS. Consumes NOS.
//————————————————————————————————————————————————————————
void add() {
double sum = stack.getAccumulator() + stack.getStackElement(1);
   stack.drop(); stack.setAccumulator(sum); display.redrawStack();
}
//————————————————————————————————————————————————————————
void times() {
double prod = stack.getAccumulator() * stack.getStackElement(1);
   stack.drop(); stack.setAccumulator(prod); display.redrawStack();
}
//————————————————————————————————————————————————————————
void subtract() {
double diff = stack.getStackElement(1) - stack.getAccumulator();
   stack.drop(); stack.setAccumulator(diff); display.redrawStack();
}
//————————————————————————————————————————————————————————
```

```
void divide() {
double div = stack.getStackElement(1) / stack.getAccumulator();
    stack.drop(); stack.setAccumulator(div); display.redrawStack();
}
//───────────────────────────────────────────────────────────────
public String keyLabel (int row, int column) {
    return keyLabels[row*rowSize + column];
}
//───────────────────────────────────────────────────────────────
public Dimension getPreferredSize() {
    return new Dimension(300,200);
}}
```

Before you focus on the application side of this class, you should see what class KeyPanel does on the Java and AWT level. To begin, KeyPanel is subclassed from Panel. This is because you need your calculator buttons to be laid out using a different layout manager from what the applet itself uses. And to specify a different layout for an area, you first need to create a new Container: the keys Panel. Since calculator keys are universally laid out in rows and columns, a natural choice for a layout manager is GridLayout. The constructor for the KeyPanel class takes a reference (read: a link) to the numeric display component that the applet created. Class KeyPanel needs to have this link so that it can call on the display to perform various functions. The design of your calculator means that the key panel is the active, controlling entity among the five classes.

The first thing the KeyPanel class does with the reference to the display object is to ask the display to hand it a reference to the numerical calculation stack embedded in the display object. As you will see, the very heart of the calculating machine (the stack) actually "belongs" to the display. This design decision is fairly arbitrary; the core calculator stack could have been created by the key panel object itself, or even by the applet. Whatever approach is taken, the key panel, the display, and the stack objects need to communicate with each other one way or another. The KeyPanel constructor then performs its main function, which is to create the panel of calculator buttons from a constant lookup array of button labels.

The next method is the event-processing heart of the applet: the `actionPerformed()` method of the `KeyPanel`. Every button has the `KeyPanel` registered as an action listener, which means that when any button is clicked, the `actionPerformed()` method is called. This method consists of a large selection of `if` constructs that try to determine the origin of the button press event. In fact, the method has only two `if` statements: one that tries to determine whether a digit key was pressed and another that tries to match a keypress to any of the other keys. The `keyLabel()` method is used to enhance program readability. This method takes two-dimensional (row,column) coordinates and returns the label for the button located at that position. This is much more readable than addressing the one-dimensional `String` `keyLabels` array directly.

If the `actionPerformed()` method traps a button press on one of the digit keys (0 to 9), it converts the digit `String` label into an equivalent integer, and tells the display to deal with it via the `enterDigit()` method (the key panel does not concern itself with the technicalities of data entry and editing—it is completely stateless). Likewise, with the remaining buttons, it matches each button up with a method that incarnates its function. For example, when the button at position row=0, column=4 is pressed, the AC (All Clear) function is executed.

Note that the large collection of `if` constructs (after the `if` determining a digit key) is a single `if-else` statement, with each `else` block as another `if-else`, and so on. The code in this (exceptional) instance just does not use consistent indentation to show the increasing depth of the `if-else-if` nesting (otherwise, you would end up in column 400 in your text editor). Could you have used a `switch` statement instead? No, because `switch` statements need cases that evaluate to integer constants, and the "cases" in the `actionPerformed()` method boil down to variables (the `Strings` the `keyLabel()` method returns).

If you now take a look at some of the methods called to respond to button presses—for example, the `cosine()` method—you will see that you have reached the inner sanctum of your calculator. These methods are where the calculator's main functions are executed.

The cosine() example shows you the general approach for all these methods: perform the calculator operation and then refresh the numeric display to show the result. Mathematical functions like cosine take only one argument, so the refresh logic is optimized to only redraw the top-of-stack (TOS) value, which is shown as the bottom-most element on the display (the TOS value is also called the *accumulator*).

Other operations (like allClear()) affect the entire stack, so at other times, the stack needs to be redrawn in its entirety. The redrawAccumulator() and redrawStack() LCDDigitDisplay methods actually do the display refreshing. The math functions the calculator provides are implemented on top of class Math methods. The exact implementation of the calculation stack itself is hidden from KeyPanel by a class that encapsulates all details: CalcStack. The cosine function shows how this separation of function and use is nevertheless reunited; the stack object provides the getAccumulator() and setAccumulator() methods to retrieve and set the current value for the TOS element. Using these two methods, it then becomes trivial to take the cosine of the TOS element and store the result back in the stack. You can now easily figure out how all the other functions are (equally trivially) implemented.

The Calculator Display

The next calculator element to examine is LCDDigitDisplay. Here is how it works:

```
import java.awt.*;
import java.util.*;

//————————————————————————————————————————————————————
//————————————————————————————————————————————————————
class LCDDigitDisplay extends Canvas {

CalcStack    stack;              // the stack of numbers
int          stackDepth;         // how many items stack holds
Dimension    displaySize,oldSize; // canvas drawing area dimension
```

```
Dimension    digitSize;
SevenSegmentDigits
   lcd = null;                    // ref to LCD-style 7-segment digits

boolean    freshNumber = true;
int        decimalPosition = 0;
Stack    undoStack;               // undo system for ERASEing digits

public LCDDigitDisplay(int stackDepth) {

   this.stackDepth = stackDepth;      // note depth
   stack = new CalcStack(stackDepth); // create calculation stack
   newNumber();                       // reset all entry modes
}
//─────────────────────────────────────────────────────────────
// Reset all number constructing/editing state
//─────────────────────────────────────────────────────────────
void newNumber() {
   freshNumber              = true;
   decimalPosition          = 0;
   undoStack                = new Stack();
}
//─────────────────────────────────────────────────────────────
// An extra digit is being entered. Depending on which
// mode we're in, this digit should be added before or
// after the decimal point.
//─────────────────────────────────────────────────────────────
public void addDigit (int digit) {
int changed = 1;        // how many lines in stack need to be redrawn

   rememberUndo();     // remember current value for possible digit erase

   if (freshNumber) {                 // brand new number ?
      stack.rollUp(1);
      stack.setAccumulator(0.0);  // clear A
      freshNumber = false;        // accumulate digits from now on
      changed = stackDepth;       // entire stack needs redrawing
   }

      // if we're not entering decimals yet, we can simply shift
      // the number up a digit by x10 and adding the digit in.
```

```
   double acu = stack.getAccumulator();
   if (decimalPosition == 0) {
      stack.setAccumulator( acu * 10.0 + digit);
   } else {

      // if we should add a decimal, we've got to add a fraction
      // scaled to the decimal place we've reached so far

      stack.setAccumulator( acu + ((float)digit)/decimalPosition);
      decimalPosition *= 10;
   }

   refreshStack( changed );   // redraw acu or the entire stack, depending
}
//————————————————————————————————————————————————————————————————————

public void removeDigit () {
   undo();                 // restore number and state to previous
   refreshStack(1);        // only acu needs redrawing
}
//————————————————————————————————————————————————————————————————————

// We're using a stack holding previous values and editing
// state so that we can cheaply revert back to a
// previous number if user erases a digit.
//————————————————————————————————————————————————————————————————————

public void rememberUndo() {
   undoStack.push(new Double( stack.getAccumulator() ) );
   undoStack.push(new Boolean( freshNumber )         );
   undoStack.push(new Integer( decimalPosition )      );
}
//————————————————————————————————————————————————————————————————————

public void undo() {

   if ( ! undoStack.empty()) {
      decimalPosition = ((Integer) undoStack.pop()).intValue();
      freshNumber     = ((Boolean) undoStack.pop()).booleanValue();
      stack.setAccumulator( ((Double) undoStack.pop()).doubleValue() );
   } else {
      newNumber();
```

```
            stack.setAccumulator(0.0);
        }
}
//─────────────────────────────────────────────────────────────
// User pressed '.'. From now on, we have to add decimals
//─────────────────────────────────────────────────────────────
public void decimal() {
    if (decimalPosition == 0) {
        decimalPosition = 10;    // tenths, hundredths, etc.
    }
}
//─────────────────────────────────────────────────────────────
public CalcStack getStack() {
    return stack;
}
//─────────────────────────────────────────────────────────────
public void redrawAccumulator() {
    redrawStack(1);
}
//─────────────────────────────────────────────────────────────
public void redrawStack() {
    redrawStack(stackDepth);
}
//─────────────────────────────────────────────────────────────
public void redrawStack(int elements) {
    refreshStack(elements);
    newNumber();
}
//─────────────────────────────────────────────────────────────
// redraw one or more lines of the stack. Starting from TOS
//─────────────────────────────────────────────────────────────
public void refreshStack(int elements) {
int y;
int LINE_GAP = 2;

        // If we haven't initialized the LCD digits class, or if
        // the size of our drawing Canvas has changed,
        // initialize LCD digits

    if (lcd == null || displaySize.width != oldSize.width ||
        displaySize.height != oldSize.height) {
```

```
        oldSize = displaySize;      // remember new size

        digitSize = new Dimension(displaySize.width/12,
                                  (displaySize.height/stackDepth) - LINE_GAP);

            // create scaled LCD digit "character set"
        lcd = new SevenSegmentDigits(this, digitSize);
    }

    for(int i=0; i < elements; i++) {
        y = (stackDepth-i-1) * (digitSize.height + LINE_GAP);

        getGraphics().fillRect(0,y,displaySize.width, digitSize.height);

        lcd.drawNumber(stack.getStackElement(i), getGraphics(), 0, y);
    }
}
//————————————————————————————————————————————————————————————————
// Repaint the LCDDisplay
//————————————————————————————————————————————————————————————————
public void paint(Graphics g) {

    displaySize = this.size();

    g.setColor(Color.gray);
    g.fillRect(0, 0, displaySize.width, displaySize.height);
    redrawStack( stackDepth );
}
//————————————————————————————————————————————————————————————————
public Dimension getPreferredSize() {
    return new Dimension(100, 120);
            }}
```

Class LCDDigitDisplay is responsible for the appearance of your calculator's numeric display. It is also a subclass of Canvas, so you can draw inside its area to your heart's content. Start with its constructor—all it does is create the numeric stack and reset the data-entry mode variables. The constructor is obviously not where all the action is hidden, in this case. The action is spread over two parts of the class: It's in the `addDigit()` and `removeDigit()` methods, and the `redrawStack()` and related display redrawing methods (including the overridden `Component paint()` method).

If you think about how a humble calculator works, you should first realize that there is more to pressing a digit key and seeing the digit appear in the display than meets the eye. If you use an accumulator to hold the current value being composed, then how do sequentially entered digits translate into a number being formed? Say the display already holds 12, and you enter an additional 7. The display then holds 127—12 and 7 were transformed into a new number, 127, by multiplying by ten and adding the new digit. But what if the display holds 3.14 and you enter an additional 1? The 3.14 multiplied by 10 is 31.4, plus 1 equals 32.4. Oops—you need to tune your algorithm a bit here.

When the decimal-point key is pressed, the data-entry algorithm should enter a new mode: decimal-entry mode. Any digits entered should be first divided by some power of ten, and then the result should be added to the current accumulator, without multiplying it beforehand by ten. The power of ten is determined by the position of the next decimal. This algorithm is implemented by the `addDigit()` method (the test for `freshNumber` is not part of this algorithm; it is used to start with 0.0 whenever a first digit is being entered).

Real calculators not only let you input numbers as just explained, they are also forgiving when it comes to little errors; they have an erase key to erase the last digits entered. The stack calculator applet also has a key for this purpose. One possible way to have implemented this would have been to undo the last digit added by somehow reversing the step using the same input data as the `addDigit()` method: the accumulator's value and the decimal-entry mode variable (`decimalPos`). But while this is possible, it is overly complex and unnecessary. Instead, you can cheat by remembering the value of the accumulator (and its associated decimal-entry state) before you change it, so that you can restore it to its original state if an "erase digit" request arrives. This remember-and-undo mechanism relies on another stack—a java.util.Stack this time—to store each undoable step. Check out rememberUndo() and undo() for the details.

Both addDigit() and removeDigit() need to update the display to reflect the change in value of the number being constructed or edited. For this, they rely on refreshStack(). This method takes the number of stack slots to redraw. This is an optimization feature that follows from the observation that many calculator operations change only the top of stack, thus allowing a fast (cheaper) redraw of only that value.

If you ignore the first if statement of refreshStack() for a moment, you will see that the method consists of a loop that simply redraws the numbers held by the stack. To render the digits of the values, you could have used drawString() and some standard Java Font. Instead, you had as an initial project requirement that you would use dynamically rendered LCD-style seven-segment digit characters. So the expected drawString() has been replaced by lcd.drawNumber(). Object lcd is an instance of class Seven-SegmentDigits. This class has the nontrivial responsibility of generating (at runtime) a character set of seven-segment style digits. Since it would be highly inefficient to generate these digit images on the fly (that is, as drawNumber() required them), the lcd object creates and caches (stores) them for later use, as part of its own initialization. And that is why the construction of the lcd object is conditional in refreshStack(). The if statement tests whether the lcd object has been created yet or if the Canvas area has changed dimensions. In both cases, the digit character set needs to be (re)generated—scaled to fit the dimensions of the Canvas.

Later, you will see what goes on when the lcd object's constructor is invoked. But first, you should return to code aspects more fundamental to the operation of the calculator.

The Calculator Stack

Class `CalcStack` is used as a front end for the calculator's numeric stack data structure. Here is the source code for it:

```
//————————————————————————————————————————————————————
// The CalcStack class encapsulates the numeric stack and all its
// nonmathematical manipulations (i.e., stack manipulations only)
//
// Class java.util.Stack was not used because the stack we need
// can't have an infinite capacity and because we only need
// doubles on our stack, not full-blown objects.
//————————————————————————————————————————————————————
class CalcStack {

double[]    stack;       // the stack at the heart of the machine
int         stackDepth;

//————————————————————————————————————————————————————
// Constructor: build a stack of capacity stackDepth
//————————————————————————————————————————————————————
public CalcStack(int stackDepth) {

   this.stackDepth = stackDepth;
   stack = new double[stackDepth];
   clearStack();
}
//————————————————————————————————————————————————————
public void pushValue(double x) {
   rollUp(1);
   setAccumulator(x);
}
//————————————————————————————————————————————————————
public void rollUp(int times) {
double lastVal;

   for (int r=0; r < times; r++) {
      lastVal = stack[stackDepth-1];
      for (int i = stackDepth-2; i >= 0; i-) {
         stack[i+1] = stack[i];
      }
      stack[0] = lastVal;
```

```
    }
  }
//————————————————————————————————————————————————————
public void rollDown(int times) {
    rollUp(stackDepth-times);
}
//————————————————————————————————————————————————————
public void swap() {
double temp;
    temp = stack[0];
    stack[0] = stack[1];
    stack[1] = temp;
}
//————————————————————————————————————————————————————
public void clearStack() {
    for (int i=0; i < stackDepth; i++) {
        stack[i] = 0.0;
    }
}
//————————————————————————————————————————————————————
public void drop() {
    rollDown(1);
    stack[stackDepth-1] = stack[stackDepth-2];
}
//————————————————————————————————————————————————————
public void setAccumulator(double x) {
    stack[0] = x;
}
//————————————————————————————————————————————————————
public double getAccumulator() {
    return stack[0];
}
//————————————————————————————————————————————————————
public double getStackElement(int n) {
    return stack[n];
}
//————————————————————————————————————————————————————
} // End of CalcStack class
```

The unassuming statement double[] stack; in the instance variables section at the top of class CalcStack is the core data structure for the entire program. The stack calculator applet relies on this array of `double` values to build all of its functionality around. Or rather, it relies on it indirectly, since class `CalcStack` mediates all access to this stack structure. This mediation is done through the methods provided by the class:

```
class CalcStack {
public CalcStack(int stackDepth)
public void pushValue(double x)
public void rollUp(int times)
public void rollDown(int times)
public void swap()
public void clearStack()
public void drop()
public void setAccumulator(double x)
public double getAccumulator()
public double getStackElement(int n)
}
```

It is clear, from the absence of a `pop()` method, that this stack has some very un-stacklike properties. This is because the characteristics of a stack have been somewhat modified to be more productive for a calculator application:

- A `CalcStack` has a fixed size. It has N slots that are always filled with numbers. Real stacks, on the other hand, can be empty, half-empty (or half-full), or full.

NOTE This example uses four number slots, but you can change the size by changing the `STACK_DEPTH` constant in the applet class and recompiling.

- A `CalcStack` can "roll" its contents "up" or "down." The best way for you to see what this means is to enter a number in the calculator applet and press the ROLL U and ROLL D buttons.

- When you remove the top-of-stack value (via a `getAccumulator()` and a `drop()`), the last slot keeps its original value (it is not cleared to 0.0).

Why not provide a pop() (which combines a getAccumulator() and drop())? You could, but the current design is more efficient. For example, to add two numbers together; the brute force solution would be to use the following algorithm (in pseudo-code):

```
a = pop()
b = pop()
sum = a + b
push(sum)
```

This code requires three full stack shuffles (two for the pop () methods and one for the push() method), but your code requires only a single stack shuffle. While this is not critical with small stacks of 4 elements, it could make a huge difference if you had a stack with 20 or 50 elements.

The Seven-Segment Digits Subsystem

The only remaining class to be dissected is SevenSegmentDigits:

```
//————————————————————————————————————————————————————
// Class SevenSegmentDigits encapsulates scalable 7-segment
// digits, which can be rendered individually or
// as full double values
//————————————————————————————————————————————————————
import java.awt.*;

//————————————————————————————————————————————————————
public class SevenSegmentDigits {

protected Image[] digits;        // holds the computed images for digits 0..9
protected Dimension scale;       // the scale user wanted the digits in
protected Component component;    // any Component so we can createImage()

final int NUM_DIGITS = 10 + 1;   // one extra for minus symbol

final int ox   = 207;
final int oy   =  53;
final int segW = 230;
final int segH = 227;
```

```
int          originalWidth;
final double italicPercent = 0.15;   // how much width to use for
                                     // italicizing
int          italicRange;
int          decimalW, decimalH, decimalXoff, decimalYoff;

   // the vertices making up a 7-seg display cell

final int[] points       = {
    207,53,  385,53,  207,280,  385,280
   ,240,75,  360,75,  240,258,  360,258
   ,207,159,385,159,240,144,  360,144,  240,176,360,176
                         };

   // each segment is a polygon composed of vertices

final int[][] segDefs  = {
    {0,1,5,4},  {0,4,10,8},  {1,5,11,9},  {8,10,11,9,13,12}
   ,{8,12,6,2},  {9,13,7,3},  {6,7,3,2}
                     };

   // each digit is a collection of "ON" segments

final String[] digitDefs= {
    "ABCEFG", "CF", "ACDEG", "ACDFG", "BCDF"
   ,"ABDFG", "BDEFG", "ACF", "ABCDEFG", "ABCDF"
   ,"D"   // minus sign is "digit 10"
                     };

//──────────────────────────────────────────────────────────────
// Constructor: note the size we've got the scale the digits
// to and dynamically render them (a la PostScript)
//──────────────────────────────────────────────────────────────
public SevenSegmentDigits( Component component, Dimension size ) {

   this.component  = component;
   this.scale      = size;

   originalWidth   = scale.width;
   scale.width = (int) (scale.width * (1.0 - italicPercent));
   italicRange = originalWidth - scale.width;
```

```
    digits = new Image[ NUM_DIGITS ];

    for(int digit=0; digit < NUM_DIGITS; digit++) {
       digits[digit] = renderDigit(digit);
    }

       // decimal point image is calculated from digit size only

    decimalW = scale.width/6;
    decimalH = scale.height/10;
    decimalXoff = scale.width - decimalW;
    decimalYoff = scale.height - decimalH;
}
//————————————————————————————————————————————————————————————
// Render a 7-segment digit from its segment list definition.
// Return as an Image to be stored.
//————————————————————————————————————————————————————————————
protected Image renderDigit(int number) {

Image digitImage;
Graphics g;
String segments;

    digitImage = component.createImage(originalWidth, scale.height);
    g = digitImage.getGraphics();

    segments = digitDefs[number];

    for(int seg=0; seg < segments.length(); seg++) {
       int segIndex = segments.charAt(seg)-'A';
       renderSegment(g, segIndex);
    }
    return digitImage;
}
//————————————————————————————————————————————————————————————
// Render a segment polygon in the given Graphics context.
// This is where all the "clever" stuff happens:
// we normalize coordinates of the segment to 0.0 .. 1.0 range
// we scale them to the sizes required
// we render the segment as a polygon
//————————————————————————————————————————————————————————————
protected void renderSegment (Graphics g, int segment) {
```

```
int[] segDef = segDefs[segment];
Polygon p = new Polygon();

    for(int vertex=0; vertex < segDef.length; vertex++) {

        int v = segDef[vertex];

        int x = points[v * 2 + 0] - ox;        // translate to origin
        int y = points[v * 2 + 1] - oy;

        double normX = ((double)x) / segW;   // normalize to 0.0..1.0
        double normY = ((double)y) / segH;

        int polyX = (int) (normX * scale.width); // scale to requested size
        int polyY = (int) (normY * scale.height);

        polyX += (1.0 - normY) * italicRange;    // italicize digits

        p.addPoint(polyX, polyY);
    }
    g.fillPolygon(p);
}
//————————————————————————————————————————————————————
// digitImage() gives clients access to the rendered digits
//————————————————————————————————————————————————————
public Image digitImage(int digit) {
    return digits[digit];
}
//————————————————————————————————————————————————————
// drawNumber() renders a double value in the given
// gfx context at (x,y)
//————————————————————————————————————————————————————
public void drawNumber( double number, Graphics g, int x, int y ) {

String doubleStr = clean(String.valueOf(number), 5);
boolean isNegative = (doubleStr.charAt(0) == '-');
int exponentPos = doubleStr.indexOf('e');
int decimalPos = doubleStr.indexOf('.');
int significantDigits = 6;  // we need valueOf() to gen 6 signif. digits
int digitIndex = 0;
int digitSlot;
int digit;
```

```
int digitX = 0 ;

   significantDigits = doubleStr.length();

      // if number is negative, render a minus in left-most slot
   if (isNegative) {
      g.drawImage(digitImage(10), x, y, component);    // draw minus
      significantDigits-;
      digitIndex = 1;
   }

   if (exponentPos != -1) {
      significantDigits -= 5;  // exponent uses 5 positions, e.g., "+e000"
   }
   if (decimalPos != -1) {
      significantDigits-;  // a decimal point isn't a digit either
   }

      // calculate the starting digit slot to align all numbers neatly
   digitSlot = 7 - significantDigits;  // slot 1 for max signif. digits

/* SOME DEBUGGING CODE HERE. YOU CAN ENABLE THIS IF YOU ENHANCE THIS CODE

   System.out.println("significantDigits " + significantDigits);
   System.out.println("digitIndex " + digitIndex);
   System.out.println("digitSlot " + digitSlot);
   System.out.println("isNeg " + isNegative);
   System.out.println("Exp " + exponentPos);
*/

      // now the mantissa rendering loop: render all signficant digits
   while (significantDigits != 0) {
      if ( (digit = doubleStr.charAt( digitIndex++ )) != '.') {
         digit -= '0';
         digitX = x + digitSlot*originalWidth;
         g.drawImage( digitImage(digit), digitX, y, component);
         significantDigits-;
         digitSlot++;
      } else {  // render decimal point in same slot as last digit
         g.fillRect(digitX + decimalXoff, y + decimalYoff,
                 decimalW, decimalH);
      }
```

```
        }
            // if number contains an exponent, render that too
        if (exponentPos != -1) {
            if (doubleStr.charAt(exponentPos + 1) == '-') {  // draw minus
                g.drawImage(digitImage(10), x + 8*originalWidth, y, component);
            }
            digitIndex = exponentPos + 2;       // skip 'e+' or 'e-'
            digitSlot = 9;
            for(int e=0; e < 3; e++) {          // render 'e+nnn'
                digit = doubleStr.charAt( digitIndex++ ) - '0';
                digitX = x + digitSlot*originalWidth;
                g.drawImage(digitImage(digit), digitX, y, component);
                digitSlot++;
            }
        }
    }
}


//————————————————————————————————————————————————————————————————————————
// Strip extraneous decimal chars from a numeric string.
//————————————————————————————————————————————————————————————————————————
private String clean(String src, int nDecimals) {
    String clean = "";
    StringTokenizer st = new StringTokenizer(src, "e.", true);
    boolean atDecimal = false;
    while (st.hasMoreTokens()) {
        String token = st.nextToken();
        if (atDecimal) {
            if (token.length() > 5 &&
                Character.isDigit(token.charAt(0))) {
                token = token.substring(0, 5);
            }
            atDecimal = false;
        }
        else if (token.equals("."))
            atDecimal = true;
        clean += token;
        System.out.println(clean);
    }
    return clean;
}}
```

Although this class only provides a more realistic looking alternative to numbers rendered using a standard AWT font and `drawString()`, class `SevenSegmentDigits` packs a lot of interesting code.

Since your goal for this subsystem is to obtain scalable digits (so the display can be sized according to the applet's dimensions), you need to reject the easy approach of storing every digit as an external GIF (or other) image file. Such inflexible bitmap fonts are not easily scalable, and even when forced, the scaled results are of poor quality. Instead, you use vector definitions for your characters. Scalable fonts can be defined in a very compact space, by storing some mathematical (vector) definition of their outline. A magnifying glass held up to any real calculator shows you how digits are usually constructed in the LCD. Figure 14.2 shows the structure of the seven-segment display building block used in every calculator.

FIGURE 14.2

Seven-segment display and a configuration for digit 3

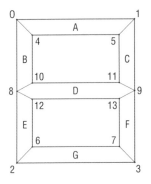

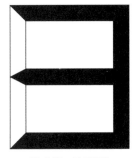

Digit '3' = "ACDFG"

If you now describe every digit as the collection of "on" segments (that is, lit segments) needed to represent it, and every segment as the list of vertices forming a polygon outline for the segment, you would have a flexible, compact definition for the entire digit character set. The `points[]`, `segDefs[]`, and `digitDefs[]` arrays together define the calculator's character set in this way.

The `points` array holds the (x,y) pairs of the nodes (or vertices) from which a seven-segment display is constructed. The exact values of these coordinates were obtained using a simple painting program, and as you will see later, these values are actually mostly irrelevant to the rest of the code. The `segDefs` array defines each segment as a list of vertices (a vertex is encoded as an index into the `points[]` array). Similarly, the `digitDefs[]` array defines digits themselves as a list of segments. Although, for readability, letters were used instead of segment array indices (later, the code simply translates the letters to numeric indices, anyway). The 3 digit, for example, is encoded as the segment list A-C-D-F-G.

> **NOTE** One thing to note at this stage is that the definitions of the digits are in regular (roman) typeface, and not italicized. If you ran the StackCalculator applet, you noticed that the digits are actually in italics. This is achieved algorithmically at the rendering stage. You will see how a bit later.

If you now have a look at the constructor for the `SevenSegment-Digits` class, you will see that it takes two arguments: a `Component` and a `Dimension`. The `Dimension` argument will be used to scale the digits to the requested size. The `Component` argument, on the other hand, is required for a very different reason, related to caching the rendered digit images. The caching mechanism you will use is to render each digit into a separate, off-screen, `Image` object. It is these `Image` objects that will simply be stored by the class, so that the `drawNumber()` method can recall them and blast them onto the screen without any further overhead. (This, by the way, is exactly the same technique used by all modern font-rendering subsystems, in laser printers, and computer operating systems.)

As you learned in Chapter 13, to create off-screen images, you need to use `createImage()`, which is called on a `Component`. Since class `SevenSegmentDigits` is not a `Component` itself (you are not extending any class, except `Object`, implicitly), you cannot just say "`createImage()`" on its own. You need the client (the class that uses class `SevenSegmentDigits`) to give you some handle to a `Component` so you can ask the `Component` to create a usable `Image` structure.

Once the constructor has taken note of the arguments it received (by making local copies), it performs a one-off calculation, which adjusts the digit dimensions to be used for the remainder of the code. The calculation has to do with the algorithmic italicizing of the digits. Figure 14.3 shows why an adjustment is required.

FIGURE 14.3

Character width adjustment necessary for italicizing digits

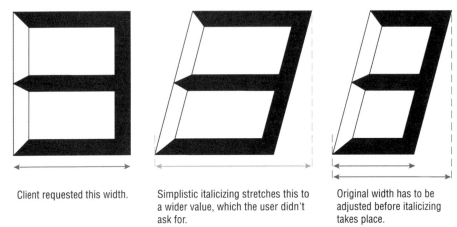

Client requested this width.

Simplistic italicizing stretches this to a wider value, which the user didn't ask for.

Original width has to be adjusted before italicizing takes place.

The constructor adjusts the requested width by -15 percent to make room for the later skewing of the digits, which must remain entirely within the bounding box dimensions requested. The difference in width between the original digits and the new digits will be the possible skewing range you will vary as a function of the character's height.

Once this initialization step has been taken, the SevenSegment-Digits object is ready to render every digit and cache them into an array of Images, called digits[] in the sample program. Note that the for loop actually renders 11 "digits." The minus sign (segment D on its own) is rendered too, as the eleventh digit.

A different approach was required for the decimal point. Since the decimal point never occupies a digit slot in the display, but instead is positioned inside the slot of the units digit, you actually render a decimal point using a simple rectFill() when needed. The alternative—overstriking the previous digit with a decimal-point image and relying on transparency—would have been considerably more complicated (although, to be honest, the `rectFill()` solution is a bit of a kludge, too).

The `renderDigit()` method called by the constructor is straightforward. It creates a new `Image` object to draw the digit in, gets the `Graphics` context from the `Image`, and proceeds by drawing every segment of the requested digit. The `renderSegment()` method, on which `renderDigit()` relies, is the method that contains all the interesting code.

Method `renderSegment()` essentially constructs a polygon, which it then renders using `fillPolygon()`. The calculation of the polygon coordinates is the heart of the vector digit-scaling and italicizing algorithm. First, original vertex coordinates had to be normalized to fit an imaginary bounding box 1.0 units wide by 1.0 units tall. This step makes it easier to scale the digits to any final, user-requested dimensions; you just multiply by those dimensions. The `ox`, `oy`, `segW`, and `segH` variables used in this process were defined as constants at the start of our class. Their values were obtained empirically by looking at the arbitrary coordinate system you used to define the digit vertices.

> **NOTE**
> There is absolutely no significance in the fact that point 0 is located at (207,53). What is important is that this point acts as the origin for all other points, and that you need to translate all points by those coordinates before you can apply the scaling.

The `polyX += (1.0 - normY) * italicRange;` statement is where the italic "style" is applied. It skews the points horizontally (by affecting their x-coordinates) as a function of the digit's height. Once all calculated coordinates have been added to the `Polygon` object used to hold them, the `renderDigit()` method just uses `fillPolygon()` to draw the scaled and italicized segment.

Finally, the `drawNumber()` method has the simple task of drawing the various digits to represent a `double` passed to it as an argument. Its internal workings are left to you, the reader, to discover.

As you can see, you can write a lot of applet code while relying purely on the GUI of your applet to activate various parts of your program. Sooner or later, however, you will write an applet that deviates from this approach, and this will be the source of a lot of problems. You will need to experiment to try and get things right. The following section will short-circuit this (painful) learning experience by highlighting the problem once, and giving you the solution to the problem without further delay.

Selfish Applets

The StackCalculator applet does not have a main loop that needs to "do" something all the time. It can afford to be fully functional by simply relying on the user activating various elements of its user interface, and on related short bursts of processing or graphical activity. But many programs are not so lucky; for example, consider an animation applet. It has a main loop that keeps on updating those animation frames. To illustrate the pitfall awaiting writers of this type of applet, Figure 14.4 shows a screen saver–like StarField applet that might go for the "cool" attribute, but fails miserably in the compatibility department.

FIGURE 14.4

StarField animation applet

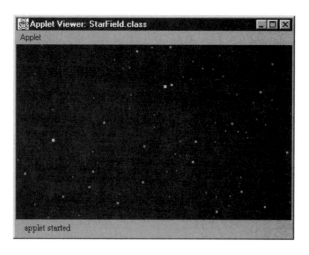

Example: Animating a Star Field

Before the simple mistake committed by this applet is explained, take a look at the things it does right. Animating a star field and creating the illusion of flying through space can be achieved in a variety of ways. This applet actually models real 3-D objects (points, actually) flying toward the observer.

The main instance variable of the `StarField` class is an array holding a large number of `Star` objects. A `Star` object has two attributes: its (x,y,z) position in 3-D space and its star temperature (which determines its color, as in reality). A `Star` has one main instance method, `draw()`, which draws the star in a window viewport. Class `Star` also has a class method `setViewPort()` that allows a client to tell class `Star` the dimensions of the viewport in which to render the stars.

The core of the program is very simple:

- Move stars toward observer (by adding a dz, for delta z, speed to their z coordinate).

- Project stars from 3-D to 2-D (using a perspective projection formula).

- Render depth-cued stars in 2-D viewport.

All of these steps are executed sequentially for each star in `Star` method `draw()`. If you refer to the listing, you will see that the code first checks whether the star has moved past (behind) the observer. If so, the star has become invisible, so it needs to be eliminated from the model. This is done by simply recycling that `Star` object by rerandomizing its 3-D position (in exactly the same way as during `Star` constructor time).

The perspective projection is achieved using these standard formulas:

screen $x = (D * x) / z$

screen $y = (D * y) / z$

The division by z is the key to understanding these equations. Objects located further away from us appear smaller; this is reflected mathematically in that if an object's z-coordinate is bigger, its size will correspondingly shrink. Figure 14.5 illustrates this relationship graphically.

FIGURE 14.5

Perspective projection

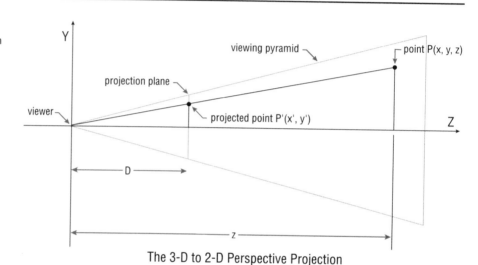

The 3-D to 2-D Perspective Projection

The z-coordinate of the stars can also be used for a simple and highly effective 3-D graphics effect—depth cueing. This is based on the physical reality that less and less light will reach an observer the further an object is located from the observer. In other words, the object becomes less bright. With modern 256-color (or more) bitmapped displays, you can easily modulate the brightness of anything you draw by multiplying each red, green, and blue primary color component by the same scaling factor.

The applet uses one final technique to improve the realism of the effect: It physically scales the infinitely small star point (in this model) depending on its distance from the viewer. To reduce flicker, a simpler technique than double buffering is used: Erase only what changes. Whenever a star draws itself, it first erases its previous position. This way, you avoid needing to wipe the whole viewport window for every star field redraw. The following code reveals the remaining nitty-gritty details of the implementation:

```java
import java.awt.*;

public class StarField extends java.applet.Applet {

// Instance variables

private final int NUM_STARS = 70;  // the more stars, the slower the
                                   // animation

private Star[] stars = new Star[NUM_STARS];  // this array holds the
                                             // StarField

private final int lensFactor = 200;

//----------------------------------------------------------------------
// Applet init()
//
// Create a cloud of random stars. Cloud is housed in an array of Star.
//----------------------------------------------------------------------
public void init() {

   for(int i=0; i< stars.length; i++) {
      stars[i] = new Star(7500);          // argument is depth Z range
   }
   System.out.println("Stars initialized!");
}


//----------------------------------------------------------------------
// Applet (Component) paint()
//
// First time only: wipe background to deep space black.
// Forever:
//   draw starfield
//----------------------------------------------------------------------
public void paint(Graphics g) {

   g.setColor(Color.black);
   g.fillRect(0,0, 10000,10000);
   Star.setViewPort( size() );       // class method !
```

```
// Now project and draw every star. Original loop was:
//
//    while(true) {
//        for(int i=0; i< stars.length; i++) {
//            stars[i].draw( g, lensFactor );
//        }
//    }
//
// ... but was changed to the faster unrolled equivalent:

    while(true) {
        int numstars = stars.length / 4;
        for(int i=0; i< numstars; i++) {
            int index = i<<2;
            stars[index++].draw( g, lensFactor );
            stars[index++].draw( g, lensFactor );
            stars[index++].draw( g, lensFactor );
            stars[index  ].draw( g, lensFactor );
        }
    }
}} // End of class StarField


//—————————————————————————————————————————————————————————————
// Class Star
//
// This class encapsulates the attributes and self-drawing
// method of a star.
//—————————————————————————————————————————————————————————————
class Star {

private static int maxDepth;
private static Dimension viewport; // applet window dimensions

private int x,y,z;   // star position
private int dz;      // star speed (parallel to z axis)

private int sx,sy;   // projected screen x,y
private int osx,osy; // old screen x,y

private int starTemperature;   // 0..100


//—————————————————————————————————————————————————————————————
// CONSTRUCTOR
```

```
//
// Randomly position a star in space by generating random (x,y,z)
// coordinates.
// Assign the star a random Z speed towards the viewer.
// Assign the star a random star color (determined by its temperature).
//————————————————————————————————————————————————————————————————
Star (int depth) {

   maxDepth = depth;    // note the maximum z distance allowed
   randomizeStar();
}


//————————————————————————————————————————————————————————————————
// Give current star a random position and a random speed
//————————————————————————————————————————————————————————————————
private final void randomizeStar() {

   x = (int) ( (Math.random()-0.5) * 10000);
   y = (int) ( (Math.random()-0.5) * 10000);
   z = (int) (  Math.random() * maxDepth);    // spread throughout volume

   dz = 70 + (int)(Math.random() * 130);       // at random speeds

   starTemperature = (int)(100*Math.random());
}
//————————————————————————————————————————————————————————————————
// draw()
//
// This method projects and clips a star from 3-D to 2-D and renders
// the depth-cued star in the viewport. To eliminate flicker, the stars
// erase their own old positions before drawing their new position.
// This eliminates the need for a global fillRect() to clear the whole
// viewport, which would create a lot of flicker.
//————————————————————————————————————————————————————————————————
final void draw (Graphics g, int D) {

float brightness;      //   0.0    ..    1.0
int starSize;          //    1     ..    5

    z -= dz;           // move stars toward us
```

```
    // recycle stars which have gone past viewer (viewer has z=0)
if (z <= 0) {
    newStar(g);
}

sx = (int) (D*x/z);    // project (x,y,z) to screen (x',y')
sy = (int) (D*y/z);

sx += viewport.width/2;    // center starfield in viewport
sy += viewport.height/2;

    // clip stars which moved outside of our viewing pyramid
if (sx < 0 || sx > viewport.width || sy < 0 || sy > viewport.height) {

    newStar(g);
}

brightness = (float) (maxDepth - z) / maxDepth; starSize = (int)
                (brightness * 5);

g.setColor(Color.black);
g.fillRect(osx, osy, starSize, starSize);

    // sprinkle sky with small amounts of colored stars
    // 85% are gray-white (equal amounts of R,G,B)
    // 10% are yellow (equal amounts of R and G only)
    // 3% are red (only R)
if (starTemperature > 15) {
    g.setColor(new Color(brightness, brightness, brightness) );
} else if (starTemperature > 5) {
    g.setColor(new Color(brightness, brightness, 0.0F) );
} else if (starTemperature > 2) {
    g.setColor(new Color(brightness, 0.0F, 0.0F) );
} else {                // remaining 2% are blue
    g.setColor(new Color(0.0F, 0.0F, brightness) );
}
    // draw star
g.fillRect(sx, sy, starSize, starSize);

osx = sx;    // remember star's position to erase it next time
osy = sy;
}
//———————————————————————————————————————————————————————————————
```

```
// newStar()
//
// When a star goes past viewer or moves out of view (above, below, left
// or right), that star should be eliminated and reused to make
// room for a new star, which is "born in the depths of space."
//----------------------------------------------------------------------
private void newStar(Graphics g) {
   randomizeStar();
   z = maxDepth;      // but start them all the way at "the far end"

   g.setColor(Color.black);     // erase old star's twinkle
   g.fillRect(osx, osy, 5,5);
}

static void setViewPort(Dimension d) {
   viewport = d;
}


// provide a toString()that summarizes a Star's state. This was
// used only during development.

public String toString() {

   return "("+ x +","+ y +","+ z +") sx=" + sx +" sy=" + sy;
}} // End of class Star
```

If you run this applet embedded within any HTML page containing other applets, you will immediately see the problem: This applet uses up all the available CPU resources and consequently prevents other applets from running.

Look at the applet's paint() method—it never returns! An infinite loop was used in a method that is called (indirectly) by the browser. Method paint() is not meant to hold an applet's main body of code (which can legally contain infinite loops). If you run the applet using the appletviewer tool, you will notice that appletviewer itself ceases to function completely, because it relies on the paint() method to return before it can continue dealing with other things (like responding to menu selections). Obviously, an applet's body code needs to go somewhere else. In fact, you need a different approach altogether to get out of this situation. The next section offers the solution.

Multithreaded Applets

To allow the StarField applet to function in a well-behaved way among other applets located on the same page as your applet, you need to refer back to Chapter 10, where the `start()` and `stop()` applet methods were explained. Remember that applets have a "life cycle" that consists of the following main events:

- Applet initialization (the `Applet init()` method is called).
- Applet gets browser's go ahead to run (the `Applet start()` method is called).
- Applet gets browser order to stop (the `Applet stop()` method is called).
- Applet is told to clean up before being killed (the `Applet destroy()` method is called).

All of these methods are imposed by the browser framework in which an applet runs. And all of them assume one important technical detail: that your applet is using a thread for all its main logic. So far, these applets have not spawned any threads for their functionality to be sidetracked into. However, for the majority of applets, this is a necessary implementation evil.

Chapter 8 explained how to create new threads and how to control these independent program flows. Here is a summary of the basics of threads:

- Any thread must be a subclass of `Thread` or must implement the `Runnable` interface.
- A newly created thread must be started by invoking its `start()` method.
- A thread will stop on the spot if its `stop()` method is called.
- A thread's code starts running with its `run()` method.

So far, all the applet examples have used the init() or paint() methods to hold the applet's main code. Neither method is the correct location for the main code of the current example. The correct place to put the main applet logic is in a thread's run() method. This way, any endless loops (like the StarField applet's while(true) endless loop) will be controllable by whoever controls the thread. And the applet is the logical choice for the controlling entity. Figure 14.6 illustrates the relationship between the browser, the applet, and its thread.

FIGURE 14.6

Time sequences between the browser, applet, and applet thread

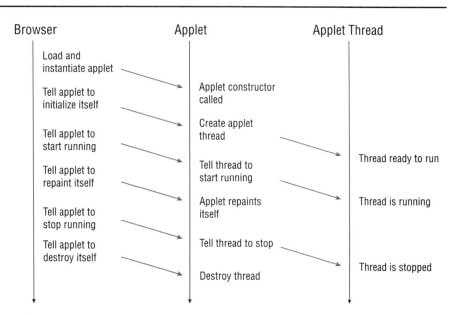

Since this browser/applet/applet thread model is the one assumed by all browsers, it is surprising that the basic java.applet.Applet class does not reflect this assumption. Fortunately, object-oriented sub-classing allows you to remedy the situation by enhancing the Applet class to mirror the model. Once you have this new, improved applet class, you can use it instead of the vanilla Applet class at very little extra cost, giving you vastly enhanced functionality.

Extending the Applet Base Class to Support Multithreading

To extend class `Applet` to support having the applet logic execute in a thread, you simply need to add the thread creation, starting, and stopping operations in the appropriate places. The `AppletTemplate` class does exactly that:

```java
import java.applet.*;
import java.awt.*;

/**
 *   Template for all good applets
 *
 *   @author Tim Rohaly
 */
public class AppletTemplate extends Applet implements Runnable {

    Thread theThread;

    /**
     * Provides a way for author to associate information with
     * an applet. Can be used for copyright, contact information, etc.
     * @return credits
     */
    public String getAppletInfo() {
        StringBuffer s = new StringBuffer();

        s.append("Applet Template\n");
        s.append((char)   169);                 // Copyright symbol
//      s.append((char)0x2122);                 // Trademark symbol
        s.append("1996 ORC Incorported, All Rights Reserved\n");

        return s.toString();
    }

    /**
     * Describes all user parameters for this Applet; their names,
     * types, and default values.
     * @return parameter name, type, description
     */
    public String[][] getParameterInfo() {
```

```
    String[][] result = {
        { "Parameter1", "int",     "Iterations (default 5)" },
        { "Parameter2", "float",   "Variation (default 2.0)" },
        { "Parameter3", "boolean", "Sea (default true)" },
    };
    return result;
}

/**
 * Called once to initialize the Applet.
 * Create Components, lay them out, and perform any
 * initializations here.
 */
public void init() {
}

/**
 * Called to start the Applet initially, and whenever Applet
 * is restarted (revisiting a page, for instance).
 * Start up threads here.
 */
public void start() {
    if (theThread == null) {
        theThread = new Thread(this);
        theThread.start();
    }
}

/**
 * Called to stop the Applet whenever it is iconified or the
 * user leaves the page. Guaranteed to be called before destroy().
 * Stop threads here.
 */
public void stop() {
    if (theThread != null) {
        theThread.stop();
        theThread = null;
    }
}

/**
 * Used to clean up system resources.
 */
```

```
public void destroy() {
}

/**
 * Used to do any drawing to screen.
 * @param g Graphic to use
 */
public void paint(Graphics g) {
}

/**
 * All work should be done here.
 */
public void run() {
}

/**
 * Used to handle action events.
 * @param e event which generated this action
 * @param arg data associated with this action
 * @return true if event was handled
 */
public boolean action(Event e, Object arg) {
    return false;
}
}
```

The main additions to `java.applet.Applet` are the `start()` and `stop()` methods. Method `start()` now turns any `Applet-Template` subclass (that is, your applets) into a thread and starts it.

Your applets can be transformed into threads because class `Applet-Template` implements the `Runnable` interface. Or to be more accurate, you will implement that interface by putting all applet main logic in an overridden `run()` method. When the browser moves to a different page, the `stop()` method will automatically kill the applet thread. This means you need to be very careful that your `run()` method does not contain any initialization code; otherwise, this code will be reexecuted each time your applet reappears. The proper place for true initialization code is the applet's usual `init()` method.

Using the AppletTemplate Class

Now that you have written the `AppletTemplate` class, you can forget almost everything about needing a thread in which to run your applets. The class will take care of everything for you. You keep using `init()`, `paint()`, and `update()` as usual, and you put your applet's main code inside the `run()` method. The following example does this, and as you'll see, it does not concern itself any further with any thread issues whatsoever (information hiding and code reuse at its best!).

To demonstrate how easy it is to work with the new `Applet-Template` class, here is a very short applet that contains a main loop (the analogue of the StarField applet's problematic infinite animation loop). This applet behaves properly, respecting the browser-applet protocol in every respect:

```
import java.awt.*;

public class Counter extends AppletTemplate {

int counter;

public void run() {
   while(true) {
      counter++;
      repaint();
   }
}

public void paint(Graphics g) {
   g.drawString(String.valueOf(counter), 10,20);
}
} // End of class implementation
```

By building on the `AppletTemplate` class, this Counter applet uses multithreading and obeys the `start()` and `stop()` orders of the browser, and yet, none of these technical details encumber its implementation. Since these technicalities serve only to obstruct your main goal of writing an applet with some required functionality, this is just as well.

> **NOTE**
>
> The Counter applet has no purpose other than to demonstrate that an applet with a main loop can be made to coexist with browsers and other applets.

Example: An Analog Clock

As an example of a much more functional, well-behaved applet that uses the `AppletTemplate` class, you will design an analog clock applet. Digital clocks, in this digital age, are not a challenge to design, because their core can simply consist of the trivial one-liner that generates a string based on the current time. Analog clocks are a bit harder, because you need to render the time by drawing a clock face and its hour, minute, and second hands. Figure 14.7 shows what you are trying to achieve.

FIGURE 14.7

GrandmotherClock applet

First, you should analyze the challenge. You can access the system's local time by constructing a `java.util.Date` object without any arguments. You must somehow convert this time into the graphical representation of Figure 14.7. The first step is to extract hour, minute, and second information from the `Date` object; this is done with another class: `GregorianCalendar`.

Designing with Radius and Angle Values

The first observation is that an analog clock can be viewed as a full 360-degree circle and that the hands can be thought of as indicating angles. Although it is 15:19:38 on this example's clock, you should think of it as that the hour hand is indicating (roughly) -12 degrees, the minute hand -24, and the second hand -138 degrees. Shifting your view of analog clocks from indicating times to indicating angles greatly simplifies the design of your program. This is because you can calculate pixel positions within circles easily if you have two values: a radius and an angle. This conversion from (radius, angle) to (x,y) coordinates is called conversion from polar coordinates to Cartesian (grid) coordinates. The formulas rely on sine and cosine for the transformation:

x = radius * cos(angle)

y = radius * sin(angle)

This set of equations produces (x,y) points located on the circle centered around the origin and having a radius *radius*. Since the clock circle is not located in the origin (0,0), you need to translate all the coordinates by adding the coordinate of the new circle origin (*ox,oy*):

x = *ox* + radius * cos(angle)

y = *oy* + radius * sin(angle)

This is all the math you will need to write any analog clock program. The angle arguments are in radians, but you will convert your degree angles into radians only at the last minute, just before plugging them into the formulas.

This clock uses several decreasing radii for the following things:

- The clock face (this is the main radius from which all others are derived)
- The second hand

- The minute hand

- The smallest hand: the hour hand

The main clock face radius is calculated from the width and height the applet was given by the `<APPLET>` `"WIDTH=.."` and `"HEIGHT=.."` HTML tag parameters.

The core of the program consists of the calculations transforming the current time in the three clock hand angles. This is done in the `draw()` method of class `AnalogClock` by transforming the 0–59 or 0–23 ranges into the 0–359 range of a full circle. Since zero seconds, minutes, or hours equal +90 degrees on a circle, you simply rotate the derived angles to compensate for this.

Once the angles are obtained, all that remains is to draw the hands. Here, an effort was made to eliminate flicker as much as possible while at the same time trying to keep the updating algorithm as simple as possible. This is done by observing that for most of the time (59 seconds out of every minute), the only movement on the clock is the second hand indicating the passage of seconds. To animate the seconds, you should not, therefore, erase the whole clock and redraw it every new second. A simple (and frequently employed) technique is to remember the second hand's last position and erase only the second hand next time round, before redrawing it in its new position. This is the same technique employed to control flicker in the StarField applet: remember old positions and erase old graphics before drawing new graphics. Only when the seconds tick over from 59 seconds to 00 seconds does the minute hand (and maybe the hour hand as well) need updating. This is when all clock hands are erased before they are repainted in their new positions.

This is the core of the program described. Peripheral to this is the main class structure for the program: The `AppletTemplate` class is being extended to hold all the applet-related aspects of the clock applet. All the analog clock aspects are encapsulated (and ready to be reused) in a separate class called `AnalogClock`.

Code Structured for Readability

When you look at the source code, note the following aspects of the code:

- Every method has a very well-defined function.

- None of the methods are too long.

- The code displays several levels of abstraction.

- The code is well-commented.

- The variable identifiers were made as readable as possible.

- Similar code lines were formatted to align features vertically, clearly highlighting their similarities.

Here is the listing for the GrandmotherClock applet:

```
//**********************************************************************
// GrandmotherClock Applet                              (C) L. Vanhelsuwe
//--------------------------------------------------------------------
//
// An analog clock with hour, minute and second hands.
// Uses APPLET PARAMETERS
//   - Timezone : Time zone from which this clock came
//   - Title    : The clock's title string beneath the clock face
//
// History:
//--------------------------------------------------------------------
// 16-JUN-96: first version.
//
//**********************************************************************

import java.awt.*;          // mainly for Graphics
import java.util.*;         // mainly for Date

public class GrandmotherClock extends AppletTemplate {

//--------------------------------------------------------------------
// GrandmotherClock instance variables. All private
//--------------------------------------------------------------------
```

```
private AnalogClock clock;  // the underlying clock we build on
private Date theTime;

private Font theFont = new Font("TimesRoman",Font.BOLD,16);
private int width;
private int height;
private int radius;

private String title;        // the text printed below the clock
private int strx = -1;
private int stry = -1;

private double hourOffset;  // the time offset for this time zone
private final long hourMillis = 1000*60*60; // no. of milliseconds in 1 hour


//————————————————————————————————————————————————————————————————
// Applet init()
//
// Work out clock size from applet dims, grab applet params, calc title
// string y coordinate (x coordinate calc needs FontMetrics which we can
// not access yet from init()).
//————————————————————————————————————————————————————————————————
public void init() {

    // set clock dimensions
    width  = bounds().width;
    height = bounds().height-20;     // leave room for clock title
    radius = Math.min(width, height)/2;

    // grab applet parameters
    // Timezone can be -12..0..12
    // Title is any reasonable string
    String TZstr = getParameter("Timezone");
    if (TZstr == null) {
        TZstr = "0";
    }
    hourOffset = Double.valueOf(TZstr).doubleValue();

    title = getParameter("Title");
    if (title == null) {
        title = "Local time";
    }
```

```
        stry = bounds().height-5;
    }
    //————————————————————————————————————————————————————————————————————
    // Applet thread body
    //
    // Forever:
    //    get local system time, adjust TZ
    //    redraw clock
    //    wait a second
    //————————————————————————————————————————————————————————————————————
    public void run() {

        while (true) {

            theTime = new Date();
            if (hourOffset != 0.0) {
                theTime.setTime(theTime.getTime() + (long)(hourOffset*hourMillis));
            }

            repaint();
            try { Thread.sleep(1000); } catch (InterruptedException ignored) {}
        }
    }
    //————————————————————————————————————————————————————————————————————
    // Applet clock time updating (called indirectly by repaint())
    //
    // If clock has never been drawn yet, create clock, redraw clock face
    // (the circular hour and minute marks).
    // Draw the clock hands to reflect the time.
    //————————————————————————————————————————————————————————————————————
    public void update(Graphics g) {

        if (clock == null) {
            clock = new AnalogClock(0,0, radius, Color.black, getBackground());
            paint(g);
        }
        clock.draw(g, theTime);
    }
    //————————————————————————————————————————————————————————————————————
    // Applet full clock repaint
    //
    // If clock already exists (paint() can be called before first update()),
```

```
//    order clock to redraw itself.
//    If title string x coordinate hasn't been calculated yet,
//    calc strx to center the title beneath the clock face.
//    Draw clock title.
//------------------------------------------------------------------
public void paint(Graphics g) {
   if (clock != null) {
      clock.drawFace(g);
      if (strx == -1) {
         strx = radius - g.getFontMetrics().stringWidth(title)/2;
      }
      g.drawString(title, strx, stry);
   }
}
//------------------------------------------------------------------
// getAppletInfo() is called by some browsers when the user requests
// the browser's "About.." or "Applet info" menu options.
// This method should always return some basic information on the
// applet.
//------------------------------------------------------------------
public String getAppletInfo() {
   return
      "Author: Laurence Vanhelsuwe\n"
    + "Title : GrandmotherClock v1.0\n"
    + "Copyright 1996 LVA";

}
//------------------------------------------------------------------
// getParameterInfo() is also called by some browsers when the user
// requests the browser's "About.." or "Applet info" menu options.
// This method should return an array of String triplets containing
// parameter name/type/description
//------------------------------------------------------------------
public String[][] getParameterInfo() {
String[][] paramDescriptions = {

   {"Timezone", "double", "Which Time Zone this clock comes from."},
   {"Title"   , "String", "Simply the title to use for this clock."}};

   return paramDescriptions;

}} // End of class GrandmotherClock
```

The heart of this applet is its `run()` method. Since the clock needs to run permanently, the method contains a forever loop (a `while(true)`) that queries the local system time, orders a repainting of the clock (just the hands!), and then goes to sleep for a second.

The `repaint()` call will eventually lead to the `update()` method being called, which is overridden to ask the underlying `clock` object to update its graphically depicted time. The `update()` method is also responsible for the creation of the `AnalogClock` instance. The `if` statement uses the fact of whether the `clock` object has already been constructed or not as its cue to trigger the first full redraw of the clock (the clock face), via a call to `paint()`. The clock face is drawn only when the applet needs to be repainted in full or at initialization time. All of the clock's rendering is the responsibility of class `AnalogClock`, listed here:

```
import java.awt.*;
import java.util.*;

//———————————————————————————————————————————————————————————
// Class AnalogClock
// This is where all analog clock matters are encapsulated, as
// opposed to applet related things, in particular, time to hand
// angles calculations and clock face and hands rendering.
//———————————————————————————————————————————————————————————
class AnalogClock {

private int radius;          // clock radius
private int ox,oy;           // clock center
private Color fg,bg;         // foreground and background colors

private int secondsAngle,secondsAngleOld;   // all angles in degrees
private int minutesAngle,minutesAngleOld;
private int hoursAngle;

private int secondsLength;
private int minutesLength,minutesLength2;
private int hoursLength,hoursLength2;

private final double toRadians = Math.PI/180.0; // to convert degrees to radians
```

```
//---------------------------------------------------------------
// CONSTRUCTOR
//   Work out hand lengths as proportions of the given radius.
//---------------------------------------------------------------
AnalogClock(int x, int y, int radius, Color fg, Color bg) {

    this.ox     = x + radius;
    this.oy     = y + radius;
    this.radius = radius;
    this.fg     = fg;
    this.bg     = bg;

        // the lengths of the hands are controlled by the percentages here
    secondsLength = (int) (0.88*radius);    // 88% of available radius
    minutesLength = (int) (0.85*radius);
    hoursLength   = (int) (0.75*radius);

        // these secondary lengths determine the diamond shape of
        // the hour and minute hands
    minutesLength2 = (int) (0.80*minutesLength);
    hoursLength2   = (int) (0.70*hoursLength);
}
//---------------------------------------------------------------
// Draw the circular marks around the clock's edge indicating
// mins and hours every five minutes, Render a bigger mark.
//---------------------------------------------------------------
void drawFace(Graphics g) {

    for (int angle=0; angle < 360; angle+= 6) {            // 6  = 1 minute
        if ((angle % 30) == 0) {                           // 30 = 5 minutes
            drawRadialLine(g, angle-1, radius-6, radius-2);
            drawRadialLine(g, angle  , radius-8, radius);
            drawRadialLine(g, angle+1, radius-6, radius-2);
        } else {
            drawRadialLine(g, angle, radius-4, radius);
        }
    }
}
//---------------------------------------------------------------
// Redraw the clock's hands to reflect the time.
// This is done in an intelligent way to avoid flicker:
//    1) calculate angles of all hands
```

```
//   2) if minutes haven't changed, erase previous second hand cheaply
//      else erase all hands
//   3) draw all hands
//   4) remember position of minute and second hands for next time
//————————————————————————————————————————————————————————————————
void draw(Graphics g, Date time) {
   GregorianCalendar calendar = new GregorianCalendar();
   calendar.setTime(time);
   int secs = calendar.get(Calendar.SECOND);
   int mins = calendar.get(Calendar.MINUTE);
   int hrs = calendar.get(Calendar.HOUR);
   secondsAngle = -90 + secs*6 ;   // 0..59 -> 0..360
   minutesAngle = -90 + mins*6 ;   // 0..59 -> 0..360
   hoursAngle   = -90 +  hrs*30;   // 0..11 -> 0..360

      // let hour hand track minutes in hour smoothly !
   hoursAngle  += (mins*6)/12;

   g.setColor(bg);
   if (minutesAngle != minutesAngleOld) {
         // erase all hands by wiping clock interior (leaving time marks)
      g.fillOval(ox-secondsLength, oy-secondsLength,
                 2*secondsLength, 2*secondsLength);
   } else {
      drawSeconds(g, secondsAngleOld);
   }

   g.setColor(fg);
   drawSeconds(g, secondsAngle);
   drawMinutes(g, minutesAngle);
   drawHours  (g, hoursAngle);

   secondsAngleOld = secondsAngle;
   minutesAngleOld = minutesAngle;
}
//————————————————————————————————————————————————————————————————
// All hand drawing routines rely on lower-level methods.
//————————————————————————————————————————————————————————————————
void drawSeconds(Graphics g, int angle) {
   drawRadialLine(g, angle, 0, secondsLength);
}
```

```
void drawMinutes(Graphics g, int angle) {
   drawHand(g, angle, 3, minutesLength, minutesLength2);
}
void drawHours(Graphics g, int angle) {
   drawHand(g, angle, 6, hoursLength, hoursLength2);
}
//———————————————————————————————————————————————————————————
// drawRadialLine is used to draw the second hand and the time
// marks around the edge of the clock face.
//———————————————————————————————————————————————————————————

void drawRadialLine(Graphics g, int angle, int innerR, int outerR) {
int x1,y1, x2,y2;

   x1 = ox + (int) (innerR*Math.cos(angle*toRadians) );
   y1 = oy + (int) (innerR*Math.sin(angle*toRadians) );

   x2 = ox + (int) (outerR*Math.cos(angle*toRadians) );
   y2 = oy + (int) (outerR*Math.sin(angle*toRadians) );
   g.drawLine(x1,y1, x2,y2);
}
//———————————————————————————————————————————————————————————
// drawHand builds a 4-point polygon to represent a clock hand
// and draws the polygon on the clock face.
//———————————————————————————————————————————————————————————
void drawHand(Graphics g, int angle, int handThickness,
              int totalLength, int intermediateLength) {
Polygon hand;
int x,y;

   hand = new Polygon();
   hand.addPoint(ox,oy);

   x = ox + (int) (intermediateLength*Math.cos((angle-handThickness)
                  *toRadians) );
   y = oy + (int) (intermediateLength*Math.sin((angle-handThickness)
                  *toRadians) );
   hand.addPoint(x,y);

   x = ox + (int) (totalLength*Math.cos(angle*toRadians) );
   y = oy + (int) (totalLength*Math.sin(angle*toRadians) );
```

```
    hand.addPoint(x,y);

    x = ox + (int)
        (intermediateLength*Math.cos((angle+handThickness)*toRadians) );
    y = oy + (int)
        (intermediateLength*Math.sin((angle+handThickness)*toRadians) );
    hand.addPoint(x,y);

    g.fillPolygon(hand);        // renders the hand on the clock
}} // End of class AnalogClock
```

Class `AnalogClock` relies heavily on the elementary trigonometry explained earlier. Read through the code, which is well-commented, to see the details of how this class works.

Minimizing Applet Loading Times

As you can see, real, functional applets are not small. This means that the more functionality you add, the longer your applet will take to load over the Internet. As applets become more popular, more and more Internet bandwidth is used up to transfer these competing applets from their server machines all the way to your client machine running your favorite Web browser. This can mean only one thing: more bandwidth pressure on the Internet and a resulting (further) slowing of response times. Therefore, in this climate of scarce bandwidth, it is important to minimize the amount of Internet resources your applet uses, as well as the response times to maintain a swift, interactive feel. You can achieve these goals in three ways:

- Minimize the size of the applet's executable.

- Minimize the number of classes used.

- Use Java Archive (JAR) files.

- Minimize the applet's initialization time.

Keeping Executables Small

Large files take longer to travel over the Internet than shorter files, and applets do not get any special treatment. If you have already looked at the sizes of the *.class files your Java compiler generates, you should be extremely impressed by their compactness. Compared to compiled C or C++ code, these Java executables are positively minute. There are two reasons for this:

- Java machine code is very compact.

- Every standard class imported by a Java program does not need to be a physical part of the program.

Nevertheless, being able to shave off a number of bytes can mean the difference between a ten-second load and a twelve-second load (and to a user, waiting always feels like an eternity). This wide discrepancy is a result of a property of Internet file transfers: packet segmentation. You must have noticed the phenomenon when surfing the Web: The progress indicator fills up burst by burst, and just before completing the load, it indicates that it is stuck waiting for just a few dozen more bytes to finish. It is at this stage that you wish your applet could have been those couple of dozen bytes shorter.

The explanation for this frequent delay, right at the end of a load, has to do with the segmentation of a transmitted file. Although the Internet (the TCP protocol to be correct) accepts data streams of arbitrary length, the networking devices (routers in particular) responsible for getting this data from point A to point B usually have strict upper limits on the size of packets they can deal with. This limit is frequently 256, 512, 1024, or 2048 bytes. Therefore, when an applet is transmitted over the network, it is segmented into N-1 packets of some fixed size plus one last tail packet containing the remaining few bytes. All of these packets travel independently and must be reassembled into the original applet executable byte stream at the client's end. When the last packet is unfortunate enough to be delayed, you can wait seconds for just a few bytes more to complete the load. And that's annoying at best.

So what can you do? Try to round down the size of your applet's classes to multiples of, say, 512 bytes? Unfortunately, it isn't that simple. The Internet is comprised of an incredibly diverse collection of networking hardware, which means that the resulting maximum transmission unit (MTU) used for any end-to-end communication might be almost anything. (The MTU is the largest packet fragment size used by the route chosen by your packets.) The best approach is to try to keep your class files as small as possible in the hope that, most of the time, those last few bytes will not need to be part of that awkward last fragmented packet. (Having said that, aiming for multiples of 256 bytes might work out well in practice.)

What techniques are available to shrink class sizes without needing to waste too much time in the process? Here are some possibilities:

- Remove debugging code.
- Shrink string literals (by editing them to be a bit shorter, reducing verbosity).
- Compile with the javac -O (optimize) option enabled.
- Remove methods that are never used.

Minimizing the Number of Classes

Few applets consist of only one class that relies exclusively on the standard Java classes for all its building blocks. Rather, the norm is that your applets will rely on classes you wrote yourself. All of these classes will need to be loaded separately by the Java VM, and here lies another inefficiency waiting to be optimized.

The problem is that, for example, loading 20 small blocks of data separately takes longer than loading one equivalent chunk 20 times the size of the small blocks. This is a result of the overhead incurred by creating network connections for each block (read: class) to be fetched. This means that you should keep a close watch on the number of extra classes your applets rely on.

One area where your project can generate lots of classes is with GUI code. As you learned in Chapter 12, you can approach the event-processing aspect of your GUI by subclassing at various levels of the GUI's container hierarchy. The lower you subclass, the more subclasses you will create. It pays to design your GUI with this issue in mind. This does not mean you should try to pack everything in one monstrous class—that would be ignoring every software engineering principle in the book. A compromise solution is always available.

Java Archive (JAR) Files

The 1.1 release of the JDK introduces JAR files. JAR files are like tar or zip files; they are aggregates of files. You create JAR files using the `jar` command.

If you aggregate all of the .class files of an applet into a single archive, a browser can read that archive from a server in a single operation. This greatly reduces the overhead of a multiple-file applet. The 1.1 class loader knows how to automatically extract classes from archives, so this technique involves no extra development on the client side. On the server side, you need to add a line to your html file. For example, if your JAR file is called myClasses.jar, you will need to add the following line to your applet tag:

```
<archives = "myClasses.jar">
```

Being Quick on Your Feet

People hate waiting, but once the waiting is over, they themselves need long seconds to process the change that has finally occurred. This means your applets should start doing something as soon as possible: Say "Hello" to the user, ask the user's name, show a progress indicator—keep the user busy. In the meantime, the applet can frantically continue to initialize itself for real, in the background. This necessitates the use of extra threads to interact with the user while the time-consuming initializations continue as the main thread. This way, you can turn an annoyingly slow applet into a lightning quick applet that entertains its viewers to boot!

The saying to remember is, "Time flies when you're having fun." The rate at which time flows can indeed vary tremendously depending on your own perception of it. You can alter your users' perception of your applets' load times by cunningly exploiting this phenomenon. The way you do this can only enhance the applet.

Summary

Applets that rely on a passive GUI to activate aspects of their functionality are the simplest types to implement. The stack calculator applet presented in this chapter is an example of this simpler type. However, the majority of real-life applets need to use multithreading. There is no way you can write a well-behaved (that is, usable) applet that contains an infinite loop (such as an animation loop) without relying on at least one dynamically created thread.

This chapter demonstrated how to add this inevitable thread and how to control it the way the browser protocol meant it to be controlled. Since the majority of applets cannot do without this thread for their main code, you learned how to extend the base `Applet` class into an `AppletTemplate` class, which gives you all the thread functionality you need, once and for all, in an easy-to-use, almost transparent way. A small, real-life clock applet was then presented to illustrate how all of the issues discussed in previous chapters come together, including the use of the new `AppletTemplate` class. Finally, you saw some techniques to make your applets load quickly and seem fast.

CHAPTER
FIFTEEN

15

Streams and Input/Output Programming

- Java's platform-independent methods for file manipulation

- Simple file I/O

- Stream input and output classes for byte manipulation

- Stream readers and writers for character manipulation

A computer's simplest model consists of a three-stage pipeline: input, processing, and output. Input and output (I/O) are therefore a fundamental aspect of computing. A computer wouldn't be much good without being able to accept data from the outside world and, as soon after as possible, present its computed results.

Computers are therefore always accompanied by built-in or peripheral I/O interfaces (called *ports*), such as a serial port, parallel port, keyboard port, audio port, video port, SCSI port, and so on. These are used to hook up actual I/O devices, such as modems, laser printers, keyboards, hi-fi systems, monitors, and hard disks, respectively.

This chapter describes how Java, through its `java.io` package, provides device- and platform-independent classes for file and stream manipulation.

I/O Software Layers

Because I/O devices are constantly being improved (and will eventually become obsolete), their programming would necessitate constant code changes to keep track of the products' evolving features. This is quite obviously an unmanageable situation, which is why the concept of a device driver was introduced.

A *device driver* shields the application (to a certain extent) from the ever-changing programming model of a given I/O device. But device drivers themselves aren't immutable over time. At some point, the physical device will have been perfected with such radically new features—or simply have evolved so much—that the driver, too, will need to change its application interface. To address this problem, an extra layer of software is needed to protect the application from this slower, but equally inevitable, evolution in device drivers. This extra device-independent I/O layer is provided by the operating system. It is device independent because the services it presents are uniform for all devices. Figure 15.1 illustrates these software layers. A layering (or buffering) approach such as this allows a very slowly evolving (or frozen, in the case of legacy systems) application to remain compatible with the very latest hardware, which evolves almost on a monthly basis.

FIGURE 15.1

Software layers that deal with different levels of evolution rate

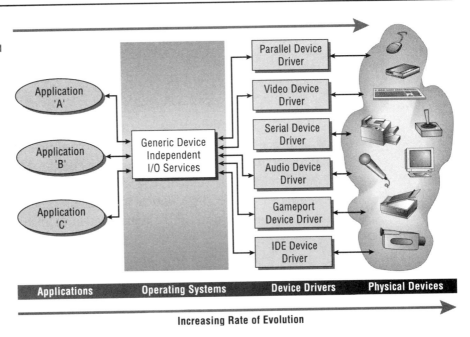

Taking the discussion one step further still, you can view different operating systems as entities that exhibit too many I/O-related differences for any one application to deal with. And that, finally, is why programming languages themselves wrap yet another layer of I/O software around the two layers depicted in Figure 15.1. Java provides this final layer in the form of an entire hierarchy of classes in package `java.io`. The classes it contains shield any application from operating-system-dependent (but nevertheless generic) I/O handling.

At the heart of the java.io package lie the concepts of streams and files. Because few applications can do without creating, processing, or managing files, we'll discuss the file classes first, and then move on to the bulk of the package: the stream classes.

Java's File-Management Methods

An operating system's filing system is one of the most basic services it provides to applications. Historically, it was one of the very first services to be developed. During the 1950s, the ability of a computer to automatically locate and load a program into its memory was not something computer programmers could take for granted.

Nowadays, all filing systems allow a hierarchical directory structure of arbitrary complexity to organize files of almost equally arbitrary length (4GB is a common limit per file). Files are identified by filenames limited in length to (usually) 32 to 256 characters. Although all filing systems are essentially identical in terms of these basic services, their exact implementations make them (as usual) mutually incompatible.

Java's File Class

To shield Java applications from this incompatibility obstacle, class File defines platform-independent methods for manipulating a file maintained by a native filing system. Here is the definition of class File:

```
public class File extends Object {
public class File extends Object implements java.io.Serializable {
    public static final String pathSeparator;
    public static final char pathSeparatorChar;
    public static final String separator;
    public static final char separatorChar;
```

```
    public File(String path);
    public File(String path, String name);
    public File(File dir, String name);
    public boolean canRead();
    public boolean canWrite();
    public boolean delete();
    public boolean equals(Object obj);
    public boolean exists();
    public String getAbsolutePath();
    public String getCanonicalPath() throws IOException;
    public String getName();
    public String getParent();
    public String getPath();
    public int hashCode();
    public native boolean isAbsolute();
    public boolean isDirectory();
    public boolean isFile();
    public long lastModified();
    public long length();
    public String[] list();
    public String[] list(FilenameFilter filter);
    public boolean mkdir();
    public boolean mkdirs();
    public boolean renameTo(File dest);
    public String toString();
}
```

As you can see from the list of supported methods, class `File` does not allow you to access the contents of the file. There are no `read()` or `write()` methods to let you do this. Class `File` is there primarily to name files, query file attributes, and manipulate directories, all in a system-independent way. Following is a description of what you can do with files without opening them.

Querying File Attributes

Class `File` provides a couple of methods for querying a minimal set of file attributes:

- Whether the file exists

- Whether the file is read protected

- Whether the file is write protected
- Whether the file is, in fact, a directory

Discovering other common file attributes, such as whether a file is a hidden, a system, or an archived file, is not supported. As with Java's AWT classes, the designers of these classes have taken the least common denominator of all filing systems as their model. If Java included features (like a hidden attribute) that aren't supported by some systems, its universal compatibility across platforms would be jeopardized.

NOTE Although the design of the Java machine code was heavily influenced (or should that be crippled?) by the requirement that Java binaries execute "efficiently" on Intel 80x86-based machines (PCs), Java was spared another possible PC anachronism: the MS-DOS pathetic 8+3 filename format. Java requires and relies heavily on the host's ability to handle proper, long filenames. Let us all rejoice if this fact helps to speed the extinction of MS-DOS from this world.

The following program shows how you use a `File` instance to query a file's attributes. The file is specified as a command-line parameter.

```
import java.io.*;

public class Attr {

public static void main (String args[]) {

File    path;

    path  = new File(args[0]);  // grab command-line argument

    String exists    = path.exists()   ? "Yes" : "No";
    String canRead   = path.canRead()  ? "Yes" : "No";
    String canWrite  = path.canWrite() ? "Yes" : "No";
    String isFile    = path.isFile()   ? "Yes" : "No";
```

```
      String isDir   =  path.isDirectory() ? "Yes" : "No";
      String isAbs   =  path.isAbsolute()  ? "Yes" : "No";

      System.out.println("File attributes for '" + args[0] + "'");

      System.out.println("Exists        : " + exists);
      if (path.exists()) {
         System.out.println("Readable      : " + canRead);
         System.out.println("Writable      : " + canWrite);
         System.out.println("Is directory  : " + isDir);
         System.out.println("Is file       : " + isFile);
         System.out.println("Absolute path : " + isAbs);
      }
}}
```

You can experiment with this program by passing it various file-names and directory names, either relative or absolute. Note the use of the ternary (?:) operator to select either a "Yes" or "No" string for variables. This approach is more compact than the logical equivalent of using if-else statements.

Manipulating Directories

A handier program would be one that could list the contents of a directory, like the dir or ls commands in most operating systems. Class File supports directory-list generation via its list() method. Here's another program that recursively (that is, calling upon itself) lists directories and their contents.

```
import java.io.*;

public class Dir {

static int indentLevel = -1;

public static void main (String args[]) {

String  names[] = new String[0];  // list of files in a directory
String  temp[]  = new String[1];  // dummy args[]
String  filename;
File    path, fpath;
```

```
        indentLevel++;                      // going down...

        path  = new File(args[0]);
        names = path.list();                // create list of files in this dir

        for (int i=0; i < names.length; i++) {
           for (int indent=0; indent < indentLevel; indent++) {
                System.out.print("     ");
           }

           filename = args[0] + File.separator + names[i];
           System.out.println(filename);

           fpath = new File(filename);
           if ( fpath.isDirectory() ) {
                temp[0] = fpath.getPath();
                Dir.main(temp);             // recursively descend dir tree
           }
        }
        indentLevel-;                       // and going up
}}
```

The program relies on a couple of interesting things. First of all, it calls itself recursively in the statement Dir.main(temp). This repeated invocation of the main() method restarts the main() with new args[] arrays, initialized to contain the full name of the deeper directory to list.

To highlight the current directory level, the contents of a directory are indented according to its nesting level in the filing hierarchy. This nesting level is, in turn, determined by the depth of the program's recursion level, which is tracked in the static class variable indentLevel. When a method exits, static variables are not destroyed as are simple method variables. The program relies on this behavior to track the recursion level across multiple invocations of main().

Static variables have one more interesting attribute: They also are not allocated anew each time a new instance of a class is made; therefore, they are also called class variables. (This aspect of variable indentLevel is not relevant in the program because it does not explicitly create instances of class `Dir`, although `Dir` is instantiated once when the program is loaded.)

Another aspect to note is the program's use of the `File.separator` class constant to display full paths using the same notation your machine uses (that is, the implementation is platform independent). This separator character could be a slash, backslash, or any other reserved character, depending on the native filing system.

Java's RandomAccessFile Class

Class `File` doesn't let you read or write files, but other classes provide this functionality. To read or write files, you can use one of two approaches. You can use the extremely powerful stream classes (which are discussed later in this chapter), or you can use class `RandomAccessFile`. The latter option is easy to use but has severe limitations if you want to start writing flexible and/or more complex applications. Class `RandomAccessFile` does I/O on only files, whereas the stream I/O classes can do I/O on almost anything, including files. So bear in mind that there is a much more powerful way to do the same things.

The definition of class `RandomAccessFile` neatly sums up its functionality:

```
public class RandomAccessFile extends Object implements DataInput, DataOutput {
    public RandomAccessFile(String name, String mode) throws IOException;
    public RandomAccessFile(File file, String mode) throws IOException;

    public native void close() throws IOException;
    public final FileDescriptor getFD() throws IOException;
    public native long getFilePointer() throws IOException;
    public native long length() throws IOException;
    public native int read() throws IOException;
    public int read(byte b[], int off, int len) throws IOException;
    public int read(byte b[]) throws IOException;
    public final boolean readBoolean() throws IOException;
    public final byte readByte() throws IOException;
    public final char readChar() throws IOException;
```

```
    public final double readDouble() throws IOException;
    public final float readFloat() throws IOException;
    public final void readFully(byte b[]) throws IOException;
    public final void readFully(byte b[], int off, int len) throws IOException;
    public final int readInt() throws IOException;
    public final String readLine() throws IOException;
    public final long readLong() throws IOException;
    public final short readShort() throws IOException;
    public final int readUnsignedByte() throws IOException;
    public final int readUnsignedShort() throws IOException;
    public final String readUTF() throws IOException;
    public native void seek(long pos) throws IOException;
    public int skipBytes(int n) throws IOException;
    public void write(byte b[]) throws IOException;
    public void write(byte b[], int off, int len) throws IOException;
    public native void write(int b) throws IOException;
    public final void writeBoolean(boolean v) throws IOException;
    public final void writeByte(int v) throws IOException;
    public final void writeBytes(String s) throws IOException;
    public final void writeChar(int v) throws IOException;
    public final void writeChars(String s) throws IOException;
    public final void writeDouble(double v) throws IOException;
    public final void writeFloat(float v) throws IOException;
    public final void writeInt(int v) throws IOException;
    public final void writeLong(long v) throws IOException;
    public final void writeShort(int v) throws IOException;
    public final void writeUTF(String str) throws IOException;
}
```

In terms of organization, the class can be viewed simply as implementing the two interfaces `DataInput` and `DataOutput`. Class `RandomAccessFile` does not add much functionality beyond the methods defined in these interfaces. Here is the definition for interface `DataOutput`:

```
public interface DataOutput extends Object {
    public abstract void write(byte b[]) throws IOException;
    public abstract void write(byte b[], int off, int len) throws IOException;
    public abstract void write(int b) throws IOException;
    public abstract void writeBoolean(boolean v) throws IOException;
```

```
    public abstract void writeByte(int v) throws IOException;
    public abstract void writeBytes(String s) throws IOException;
    public abstract void writeChar(int v) throws IOException;
    public abstract void writeChars(String s) throws IOException;
    public abstract void writeDouble(double v) throws IOException;
    public abstract void writeFloat(float v) throws IOException;
    public abstract void writeInt(int v) throws IOException;
    public abstract void writeLong(long v) throws IOException;
    public abstract void writeShort(int v) throws IOException;
    public abstract void writeUTF(String str) throws IOException;
}
```

The DataOutput interface specifies a list of output (writing) methods that allow you to write any kind of simple Java type. It also requires all implementing classes to be able to write bytes or blocks of bytes. Outputting objects (apart from strings) is not supported. The exact bitstream produced by these methods should not concern you because a symmetrical interface (DataInput) specifies the equivalent reading methods that allow you to read back any data written out.

Here is the definition for the companion DataInput interface:

```
public interface DataInput extends Object {
    public abstract boolean readBoolean() throws IOException;
    public abstract byte readByte() throws IOException;
    public abstract char readChar() throws IOException;
    public abstract double readDouble() throws IOException;
    public abstract float readFloat() throws IOException;
    public abstract void readFully(byte b[]) throws IOException;
    public abstract void readFully(byte b[], int off, int len) throws IOException;
    public abstract int readInt() throws IOException;
    public abstract String readLine() throws IOException;
    public abstract long readLong() throws IOException;
    public abstract short readShort() throws IOException;
    public abstract int readUnsignedByte() throws IOException;
    public abstract int readUnsignedShort() throws IOException;
    public abstract String readUTF() throws IOException;
    public abstract int skipBytes(int n) throws IOException;
}
```

Some of the asymmetrical differences are the `skipBytes()` method, the unsigned number reading methods, and the `readLine()` method instead of the `writeByte()`/`Chars()` methods. Apart from those superficial differences, the two interfaces really are each other's opposites. Class `RandomAccessFile` then, if you look back at its definition, is mainly the implementation of these two interfaces. The following are the main additional methods in `RandomAccessFile`:

```
void seek(long pos) throws IOException
long getFilePointer() throws IOException
long length() throws IOException
void close() throws IOException
```

There is no `open()` method, because constructing a `Random-AccessFile` object opens the file for you. The `seek()` method is the method that reflects the class's random-access reading and writing capability. Using `seek()`, you can position the file pointer to any position within the file to read or write in any place. You are not limited to sequential reads or writes (although that is what the reading and writing methods default to). Method `getFilePointer()` lets you find out where the next read or write will occur. For a newly opened file, it is always position 0; in other words, the beginning of the file.

By now, you have noticed the universal exception type used by class `RandomAccessFile` (and the `DataInput` and `DataOutput` interfaces), which signals a failure within any of its methods: exception `IOException`. The explicit `throws` clause at the end of every method's signature means you are required to either:

- Add explicit error-handling code to your methods that use `RandomAccessFiles` by enclosing any uses with a `try-catch` pair.

- Let the exception bubble up to your method's caller by declaring your methods to throw `IOException` in turn.

As an example of using this class, including the explicit handling of possible exceptions, the following program uses two RandomAccess-File objects to compare two files:

```java
import java.io.RandomAccessFile;

class Diff {

//----------------------------------------------------------------------
// program main()
//
// check command-line argument (filename)
// open & load files
// process files
// close files
//----------------------------------------------------------------------

public static void main (String args[]) {

RandomAccessFile     fh1 = null;
RandomAccessFile     fh2 = null;

int     tail;            // difference in length
int     bufsize;         // size of smallest file
long    filesize1 = -1;
long    filesize2 = -1;
byte[]  buffer1;         // the two file caches
byte[]  buffer2;

        // check what you get as command-line arguments


    if (args.length == 0 || args[0].equals("?") ) {
        System.out.println("File Diff v1.0 (c) 04/96 L. Vanhelsuwe");
        System.out.println("————");
        System.out.println("USAGE: java Diff <file1> <file2> | ?");
        System.out.println();

        System.exit(0);
    }
```

```
       // open file ONE for reading

   try {
      fh1 = new RandomAccessFile(args[0], "r");
      filesize1 = fh1.length();
   } catch (Exception ioErr) {
      System.out.println("Could not find " + args[0]);
      System.out.println( ioErr );
      System.exit(100);
   }
       // open file TWO for reading

   try {
      fh2 = new RandomAccessFile(args[1], "r");
      filesize2 = fh2.length();
   } catch (Exception ioErr) {
      System.out.println("Could not find " + args[1]);
      System.out.println( ioErr);
      System.exit(100);
   }

   tail = (int) (filesize2 - filesize1);

   if (tail != 0) {
      System.out.println("Files differ in size !");
      System.out.println("'" + args[0] + "' is " + filesize1 + " bytes");
      System.out.println("'" + args[1] + "' is " + filesize2 + " bytes");
   }

       // allocate two buffers large enough to hold entire files

   bufsize = (int) Math.min(filesize1, filesize2);
   buffer1 = new byte [ bufsize ];
   buffer2 = new byte [ bufsize ];

   try {
      fh1.readFully(buffer1,0,bufsize);
      fh2.readFully(buffer2,0,bufsize);

         // now the HEART of the program...

      for (int i = 0; i < bufsize; i++) {
```

```
        if (buffer1[i] != buffer2[i]) {
            System.out.println ("Files differ at offset " + i);
            break;
        }
      }
    } catch (Exception ioErr) {
        System.out.println("ERROR: An exception occurred while processing the
                            files");
        System.out.println( ioErr.toString() );
    }

    finally {
        try {
            fh1.close();
            fh2.close();
        } catch (Exception ignored) {}
    }
}}
```

The program uses a performance-enhancing trick that is often useful when processing files. It buffers the entire files in memory by reading them, in one swoop, using `readFully()`. This technique can be orders of magnitude quicker than reading a file bit by bit in a loop. Once the two files are cached in memory, they can be compared very quickly using simple array accesses (the nearest Java gets to the even more efficient pointer addressing of C and C++).

Note how the I/O method invocations needed to be surrounded by `try-catch` statements. This is because all `RandomAccessFile` methods can potentially throw an `IOException`. Because Java (quite rightly) insists that programs catch potential exceptional circumstances or events, you must explicitly add error-handling code for those occasions. The alternative would be to declare the `main()` method as being able to throw an `IOException` itself. While this strategy would have made the example easier to read, it would not be good programming practice. The `main()` method is the topmost method, and any exceptions it throws will be thrown straight into the user's face. This is not acceptable, so you should opt to catch the errors explicitly and translate them into more user-friendly error messages (instead of erroneous behavior!).

Because exceptions can seriously disturb an algorithm's programmed flow of control (exceptions are essentially `goto` statements), you need to ensure that both files are closed under all circumstances. You do this in the `finally` statement at the end of the `main()` method. Regardless of whether exceptions occurred or not, the code within the `finally` statement will always be executed, so that statement is the perfect place to put your file `close()` calls.

Java's I/O Stream-Manipulation Methods

The invention of streams is surprisingly recent, dating back to 1984 when Dennis Ritchie (who codesigned the C language with Brian Kernighan) implemented the first stream I/O system for AT&T's Unix operating system. Software streams are linear flows of data, and, as with real rivers of water, users can come up to a stream and sequentially fish out (in other words, read) items floating toward them, or they can throw items into the stream (that is, write) in the secure knowledge that the items will be carried to a known destination at the end of a stream.

Every stream has either a data source (like a spring), in the case of input streams, or a destination (called a *sink*, like a river's delta), in the case of output streams. Both input and output streams, therefore, have the need to be connected to "something" before they will do any useful work. Input streams should be connected to some device producing data, and output streams should be connected to some device that can accept data (see Chapter 9).

The package `java.io` consists mostly of stream, reader, and writer I/O classes. Stream input and output classes manipulate bytes; readers and writers manipulate characters (recall that in Java, unlike C, a character is two bytes). The package defines four root classes from which most of the package's stream subclasses are derived. Not surprisingly, they are called `InputStream`, `OutputStream`, `Reader` and

`Writer`. Study these abstract classes before tackling any of the concrete stream classes; all stream classes rely on the fundamental functionality of the superclasses.

Input Streams and Readers

All input streams can read bytes of data from some kind of data source. Their core functionality is reading data in the form of bytes (and only bytes). This reading can be done on a byte-by-byte basis, or it can be done by blocks of arbitrary length. All other functionality encapsulated in `InputStream` is peripheral to this elementary reading functionality. Here is the full definition of class `InputStream`:

```
public abstract class InputStream extends Object {
    public InputStream();
    public abstract int read() throws IOException;
    public int read(byte b[]) throws IOException;
    public int read(byte b[], int off, int len) throws IOException;
    public long skip(long n) throws IOException;
    public int available() throws IOException;
    public void close() throws IOException;
    public synchronized void mark(int readlimit);
    public synchronized void reset() throws IOException;
    public boolean markSupported();
}
```

The three mark-related methods—`mark()`, `reset()`, and `mark-Supported()`—deal with an optional input stream support for undoing `read()` methods. All input streams should implement `markSupported()` but are free to return either `true` or `false`. Most return `false`, meaning that `mark()` and `reset()` don't do anything (or throw exceptions). Abstract class `InputStream` itself implements `markSupported()` to return `false`, so all classes that inherit from `InputStream` without overriding this method do not support marks.

When the mark feature is supported, the system works as follows: You can mark any position (in an input stream) to come back to later if you want to undo the reading of data that has been read since the mark was placed. The `readlimit` argument to the `mark()` method determines how far you can read ahead while still legally being able to `reset()` the reading position to the marked position. The `readlimit` is expressed in bytes. It is used to internally allocate a buffer for all the data that potentially needs to be rewound. If you read past the `readlimit` and still do a `reset()`, the results are undefined.

A whole collection of concrete classes descends from class `InputStream`:

- `FileInputStream`

- `ByteArrayInputStream`

- `StringBufferInputStream`

- `SequenceInputStream`

- `PipedInputStream`

- `ObjectInputStream`

- `FilterInputStream`

  - `BufferedInputStream`

  - `DataInputStream`

  - `LineNumberInputStream`

  - `PushbackInputStream`

All of these classes have one thing in common (apart from being subclasses of `InputStream`): All their constructors let you specify a data source in one way or another. In the case of the `FileInput-Stream`, `ByteArrayInputStream`, `StringBufferInputStream`, `SequenceInputStream`, `ObjectInputStream`, and `PipedInput-Stream` classes, this data source is the attribute that differentiates that class from the others in that list. A `FileInputStream`, for example, is just that because the data stream that flows from it is sourced from a file that is part of your machine's filing system. In the same way, a `PipedInputStream` is just that because the stream that flows from it is sourced from a pipe (a *pipe* is a mechanism that allows two different processes to communicate). And so on...

All the `FilterInputStream` descendants have a very different purpose. Their constructors also allow you to specify a data source, but this is in the form of another input stream as the source for the stream. However, if that was all `FilterInputStreams` could do, there would be little point in them; they would simply pass on the data unmodified. But the purpose of `FilterInputStreams` is not to connect to any specific data source (like the previous classes) but to enhance streams. Streams can be enhanced either by altering the stream's data itself (for example, by compressing it) or by adding handy features to the minimal functionality enshrined in class `InputStream`.

The abstract `Reader` class is very similar to `InputStream`. Here is its definition:

```
public abstract class Reader extends Object  {
    abstract public void close() throws IOException;
    public abstract int read(char cbuf[], int off, int len) throws IOException;
    public void mark(int readAheadLimit) throws IOException;
    public boolean markSupported();
    public int read() throws IOException;
    public int read(char cbuf[]) throws IOException;
    public boolean ready() throws IOException;
    public void reset() throws IOException;
    public long skip(long n) throws IOException;
}
```

The difference between readers and input streams is that readers manage characters while input streams manage bytes. `Reader` has the following subclasses:

- `FileReader`
- `CharArrayReader`
- `StringReader`
- `PipedReader`

- `InputStreamReader`
- `FilterReader`
  - `BufferedReader`
  - `LineNumberReader`
  - `PushbackReader`

Readers, like input streams, have various possible data sources, such as files and strings. The filter subclasses take other readers as their data sources and modify the source's characters. Most (but not all) of the input stream classes have corresponding reader classes.

FileInputStream and FileReader

Class `FileInputStream` is an input stream whose data is sourced from an everyday file. As such, you could consider it as (nearly) half of class `RandomAccessFile`, which allows you to read and write files. You could use two `FileInputStream` objects to implement the featured file difference program with equal ease. The constructors for class `FileInputStream` are what the class really adds to the abstract class `InputStream`:

```
public FileInputStream(String name) throws FileNotFoundException

public FileInputStream(File file) throws FileNotFoundException

public FileInputStream(FileDescriptor fd) throws FileNotFoundException
```

These constructors create a new `FileInputStream` object and, at the same time, open the file, ready for reading. The first constructor takes a filename as a `String`, but you should avoid doing this if the filename has any platform-dependent characters in it. For example, a filename of abc\def would work fine on a Windows platform but would fail on a Unix machine.

The second constructor is the one more commonly employed. It takes a platform-independent `File` object describing which file needs to be accessed.

The constructors for `FileReader` are identical to those for `FileInputStream`:

```
public FileReader(String name) throws FileNotFoundException
public FileReader(File file) throws FileNotFoundException
public FileReader(FileDescriptor fd) throws FileNotFoundException
```

File input streams should be used only for reading byte-oriented data. For text files, file readers are preferred, because reader classes support full 16-bit characters.

Here is a program that uses the `FileReader` class to read a text file and calculate its word frequencies:

```
import java.io.*         ;
import java.util.Hashtable  ;
import java.util.Enumeration;

class WC {

public static void main(String args[]) throws IOException {

WordFrequencyCounter wfr;
FileReader           longText;
StreamTokenizer      wordStream;
String               word;
int                  tok;

    if (args.length != 1) {
        System.out.println( "Usage: java WC <textfile>" );
        System.exit(10);
    }

    wfr        = new WordFrequencyCounter();
    longText   = new FileReader( args[0] );
    wordStream = new StreamTokenizer( longText );

        // treat any punctuation as word delimiters

    wordStream.whitespaceChars('!','@');
```

```
      while( (tok = wordStream.nextToken()) != StreamTokenizer.TT_EOF ) {
         if (tok == StreamTokenizer.TT_WORD ) {
            word = wordStream.sval;
            wfr.count( word );
         }
      }

      Enumeration e = wfr.keys();
      while ( e.hasMoreElements() ) {
         word = (String) e.nextElement();
         System.out.println( wfr.frequency(word) + " " + word );
      }
}}
//———————————————————————————————————————————————————————————
class WordFrequencyCounter extends Hashtable {

// no constructor needed; this class is just a fancy Hashtable


//———————————————————————————————————————————————————————————
// first see if this word has already been encountered;
// if not, then create a fresh counter for it;
// otherwise, increment its counter
//———————————————————————————————————————————————————————————


public synchronized int count (String word) {

Integer counter;

   counter = (Integer) get(word);
   if (counter == null) {
      counter = new Integer(1);
   } else {
      counter = new Integer( counter.intValue() + 1);
   }
   put(word, counter);
   return counter.intValue();
}


//———————————————————————————————————————————————————————————
// find out how many times this word has been encountered
//———————————————————————————————————————————————————————————


public synchronized int frequency (String word) {
```

```
Integer counter;

    counter = (Integer) get(word);
    if (counter == null) {
        return 0;
    } else {
        return counter.intValue();
    }
}} // End of class WordFrequencyCounter
```

The program consists of two classes: the main driver class WC (which stands for Word Counter, in case you were wondering) and a thoroughly reusable WordFrequencyCounter class. The main class (WC) opens the file specified as a command-line argument by creating a FileReader object. It then passes that object straight to another java.io class: StreamTokenizer.

Class StreamTokenizer takes an input stream as argument to its constructor and then allows you to have the stream tokenized. In this case, *tokenized* simply means chopped up into its constituent words. The StreamTokenizer method nextToken() divides the file stream up into words and makes the stream of words available via the StreamTokenizer instance variable sval (String value). The StreamTokenizer class is discussed in more detail later in the chapter.

The individual words thus extracted from the stream are then passed on to the WordFrequencyCounter object, whose duty it is to keep track of which words have already been encountered and, if so, how many times. It keeps track by relying heavily on the functionality provided by class Hashtable, part of package java.util.

A Java Hashtable implements a dictionary data structure. Dictionaries consist of paired entries: the first half called the *key*, and the second half called the *value*. The program uses a dictionary to track the number of occurrences of each word, because dictionary keys cannot occur more than once. Therefore, the word itself is the key to the dictionary entry, with the count being the value of the entry. Although the word count need only be a humble integer, a Java Hashtable requires objects for both keys and values. Primitive datatypes (like `boolean`, `char`, and `int`) are not supported. That's the reason to use a heavyweight `Integer` object instead, to hold the counter. The main `Hashtable` methods are put(`key, value`) and get(`key`). Because the `WordFrequencyCounter` class extends `Hashtable`, it is able to use these methods unqualified, in other words acting on itself (the `this` object reference is implied).

There's one more interesting aspect to this program: To actually list every encountered word, along with its associated frequency, the program uses the enumerating capability of all `Hashtables`. The last four lines of the `main()` method of class `WC` reflect the standard Java idiom for enumerating or listing every element of some collection. The code relies on the `Enumeration` interface, which has this definition:

```
public interface Enumeration extends Object {
    public abstract boolean hasMoreElements();
    public abstract Object nextElement() throws NoSuchElementException;
}
```

Any object of type `Enumeration` will obey the two methods of the definition: `hasMoreElements()` and `nextElement()`. Using these two methods, it then becomes a simple matter to construct a generic list-processing loop of this form:

```
Enumeration e = <any Enumeration object>;
while ( e.hasMoreElements() ) {
    <anObject> = (<cast>) e.nextElement();
    <process anObject>
}
```

And if you look back at the `main()` method, that is exactly what `main()` does to list the text file's words and their frequencies.

ByteArrayInputStream and StringBufferInputStream

The `ByteArrayInputStream` and `StringBufferInputStream` classes are virtually identical. They both create input streams from strings of bytes. `ByteArrayInputStream` does this literally, from an array of bytes. `StringBufferInputStream` uses a `String` (and not a `StringBuffer`) as its array of bytes.

Because Java `String`s are essentially arrays of Java `char`s (in other words, 16-bit wide Unicode characters), you might wonder how the resulting byte (input) stream is structured: low byte first or high byte first? Well, neither. `StringBufferInputStream` discards the high byte of the Unicode characters. Although this is fine for Java characters in the range 0 to 255, all other characters that make use of Unicode's vastly expanded encoding space will lose information or be corrupted in the string-to-stream transformation.

The following are the main constructors for the two classes:

```
public ByteArrayInputStream( byte buf[] )
public StringBufferInputStream( String s )
```

There is one major but subtle difference between the two classes. Both classes do not copy their respective input data into internal buffers. Therefore, in the case of `ByteArrayInputStream`, the source array might be modified at any time while the stream is being used. This type of conflict can be the source of bugs that are very hard to find. This problem cannot occur for `StringBufferInputStreams`, because the source `String` can never be modified "under the stream's nose." For this reason alone, it is safer to always convert a byte array that will be used as a stream into a string by using the `String` constructor `String(byte[] array, int hibyte)`.

CharArrayReader and StringReader

The `CharArrayReader` and `StringReader` classes are the character-oriented counterparts of byte array input streams and string buffer input streams. The main constructors for these classes are:

```
public CharArrayReader(char chars[])
public StringReader(String s)
```

As with the corresponding streams, there is a possible data-integrity problem. If a `char` array reader's array is modified, the reader's behavior could be unpredictable. This is not an issue with a string reader, because the data source is an unchangeable string.

SequenceInputStream

Class `SequenceInputStream` allows you to seamlessly glue together two or more input streams to create one long, concatenated stream. (There is no corresponding reader class.) Whenever you read from such a "super" stream and an EOF (end of file) is encountered by one of the building block streams, class `SequenceInputStream` proceeds to the next stream in the list (without letting the EOF reach you). Only when the last input stream is exhausted do you get an EOF (a -1 returned by `read()`). The constructors give you two ways of specifying the sequence of streams:

```
public SequenceInputStream(InputStream s1, InputStream s2)
public SequenceInputStream(Enumeration e)
```

The first form is convenient when you only need to glue two input streams together. The second form is more general in its ability to take an open-ended list of input streams. The required argument type is rather surprising, though. You would expect a type-safe array of `InputStream` (for example, an `InputStream[]` list) to be the ideal way to specify an ordered list of `InputStreams`. Instead, a much fuzzier `Enumeration` object is expected. As explained earlier, any `Enumeration` object must implement the `hasMoreElements()` and `nextElement()` methods. You might think this means you need to create a brand-new class that implements interface `Enumeration` simply to specify a list of input streams to this constructor, but there's an easier work-around: Declare a simple `Vector` in which you `addElement()` the sequence of `InputStreams`, and then use the `Vector` method `elements()` to get an `Enumeration` object that will do the trick.

PipedInputStream and PipedReader

Pipes are another Unix invention. In fact, the concept is very close to the stream concept, except that the application of pipes is less generic. Pipes are (typically) used when two different processes (or tasks or threads) need to communicate large(ish) amounts of data in a synchronized fashion.

Remember from Chapter 8 that one of the most difficult aspects of using multiple threads is their synchronization. Few multithreaded systems can avoid the need, at one time or other, to have some threads rendezvous for whatever purpose. If that purpose is the exchange of data, pipes can be used to cleanly solve the problem. A less technical example is the use of the vertical-bar character | (pipe) to chain together programs at the Unix or DOS command prompts. For example:

```
C:\> DIR | SORT | MORE
```

creates two pipes, the first connecting the output of the DIR command to the input of the SORT command. The second pipe would similarly connect the output of SORT to the input of MORE. The result would be a directory listing that is sorted by the MORE utility before being displayed page by page.

Class `PipedInputStream` requires you to connect it with another pipe, an instance of `PipedOutputStream`. The two classes can only be used with each other and are useless without one another. Their respective constructors are as follows:

```
public PipedInputStream(PipedOutputStream src) throws IOException
public PipedOutputStream(PipedInputStream snk) throws IOException
```

The reader/writer constructors are:

```
public PipedReader(PipedWriter src) throws IOException
public PipedWriter(PipedReader snk) throws IOException
```

Perfect symmetry! (Don't you just love it when software is this beautiful?) If you analyze these constructors long enough, you will notice that something is in fact missing: How do you create a connection between two pipes if you need to pass the (already constructed) instance of the other type as an argument to the constructor? It's a Catch-22 situation that you need to bypass using one of the other types of constructors:

```
public PipedInputStream()
public PipedReader
public PipedOutputStream()
public PipedWriter
```

These four constructors allow you to create a pipe object that is not connected yet. To complete the actual connection, you call the respective `connect()` method.

ObjectInputStream

Object input and output streams support object *serialization*. With serialization, what is read or written is not a byte or an array of bytes, but an object and everything it refers to. This is certainly more complicated than writing any other kind of data. Many issues are involved, including security, data privacy, and class version management.

With serialization, an object can be stored outside the Java VM (Virtual Machine) that created it, and restored at a later time. For example, a painting program might represent its state as an object of a class (probably a quite complicated class) called `Picture`. When the user wants to save the painting, the program can open a file output stream and pass that stream to the constructor of an object input stream. Then, with a single method, the program can call the entire `Picture`, which can be written to the object output stream, through the file output stream, and onto the disk. Later, perhaps in a different invocation of the painting program, an object input stream and a file input stream can be used to restore the `Picture` object so that the user can continue working.

Serialization also plays an essential role in Remote Method Invocation (RMI), whereby a Java program can make a method call on an object running on a different machine. RMI must support passing method parameters to the remote object and returning return values to the caller. Parameters and return values might be objects; if this is the case, the RMI infrastructure uses object input streams and object output streams to serialize the data. Chapter 22 discusses RMI and serialization in more detail.

InputStreamReader

The input stream reader was designed for converting byte-oriented situations to character-oriented situations. An input stream reader reads bytes from an input stream and converts them to characters, according to a mapping algorithm. The default mapping recognizes bytes as common ASCII characters and converts them to Java's Unicode characters.

The constructor for the `InputStreamReader` class takes an input stream as its data source:

```
public InputStreamReader(InputStream src)
```

FilterInputStream and FilterReader

Classes `FilterInputStream` and `FilterReader` are the superclasses for the `java.io` classes `BufferedInputStream`, `BufferedReader`, `DataInputStream`, `LineNumberInputStream`, `LineNumberReader`, `PushbackInputStream`, and `PushbackReader`. `FilterInputStream` is pseudo-abstract, and `FilterReader` is genuinely abstract. The important point is that they are both for subclassing, not for instantiating.

The `FilterInputStream` class looks like this:

```
public class FilterInputStream extends InputStream {

    protected InputStream in;
    public int read() throws IOException;
    public int read(byte b[]) throws IOException;
    public int read(byte b[], int off, int len) throws IOException;
```

```
    public long skip(long n) throws IOException;
    public int available() throws IOException;
    public void close() throws IOException;
    public synchronized void mark(int readlimit);
    public synchronized void reset() throws IOException;
    public boolean markSupported();
}
```

Not surprisingly, class `FilterReader` is similar:

```
public abstract Class FilterReader extends Reader
{
    protected Reader in;

    public void close() throws IOException;
    public void mark(int readAheadLimit) throws IOException;
    public boolean markSupported();
    public int read() throws IOException;
    public int read(char cbuf[], int off, int len) throws IOException;
    public boolean ready() throws IOException;
    public void reset() throws IOException;
    public long skip(long n) throws IOException;
}
```

BufferedInputStream and BufferedReader

Class `BufferedInputStream` enhances bare-bones `InputStream` by adding a buffer of bytes to `InputStream`, which usually improves reading performance significantly. `BufferedReader` adds a buffer of characters to `Reader`. To demonstrate the speed-up, here's a program that uses a vanilla `FileReader` to read in a whole file, byte by byte:

```
import java.io.*;

class Unbuffered {

public static void main (String args[]) {
Reader reader;
int ch;
```

```
System.out.println("Start !");

try {
   reader = new FileReader( args[0] );
   while ( (ch=reader.read()) != -1) {
      // read entire file
   }
} catch (Exception ioErr) {
   System.out.println( ioErr.toString() );
   System.exit(100);
}

System.out.println("Stop !");
}}
```

When you run this program on a reasonably large file (for example, Windows 95's COMMAND.COM, which is 92,870 bytes), it takes 16 seconds to simply read in every byte. Now if you change the Input-Stream assignment line into the following two lines:

```
FileReader fr = new FileReader( args[0] );
reader = new BufferedReader( fr );
```

the time has been reduced to less than 3 seconds! A five-fold improvement. Clearly, taking the trouble to "wrap" nonbuffered input streams up in an instance of a BufferedReader pays off handsomely. The exact performance gain is determined by the size of the buffer that is used by the BufferedReader object. While the example uses the default constructor (resulting in a default, but undefined, buffer size being used), you can explicitly set the buffer size, at constructor time, by using constructors with the following, predictable signatures:

```
public BufferedInputStream(InputStream in, int size)
public BufferedReader(Reader in, int size)
```

Classes BufferedInputStream and BufferedReader are among the few standard java.io classes that implement the mark and reset mechanism.

DataInputStream

Remember the DataInput interface discussed earlier in the chapter as part of class RandomAccessFile? Well, here is the only other class that implements this interface: class DataInputStream. This RandomAccessFile/DataInputStream kinship also exists in the output branch of the java.io classes: Class DataOutputStream implements interface DataOutput, which was also implemented by RandomAccessFile. Therefore, there is a data-format compatibility between data written by RandomAccessFile and data read back in by DataInputStream, or, conversely, data written by DataOutputStream can be read back via a RandomAccessFile. In practice though, this cross-communication does not occur often, because data will be written and read back using the naturally corresponding class, most often simply DataOutputStream and DataInputStream.

Here is the definition of class DataInputStream:

```
public class DataInputStream extends FilterInputStream implements DataInput {
    public DataInputStream(InputStream in);
    public final static String readUTF(DataInput in) throws IOException;
    public final int read(byte b[]) throws IOException;
    public final int read(byte b[], int off, int len) throws IOException;
    public final boolean readBoolean() throws IOException;
    public final byte readByte() throws IOException;
    public final char readChar() throws IOException;
    public final double readDouble() throws IOException;
    public final float readFloat() throws IOException;
    public final void readFully(byte b[]) throws IOException;
    public final void readFully(byte b[], int off, int len) throws IOException;
    public final int readInt() throws IOException;
    public final String readLine() throws IOException;
    public final long readLong() throws IOException;
    public final short readShort() throws IOException;
    public final int readUnsignedByte() throws IOException;
    public final int readUnsignedShort() throws IOException;
    public final String readUTF() throws IOException;
    public final int skipBytes(int n) throws IOException;
}
```

The `DataInput` interface implicitly specifies that implementing classes should handle an EOF differently than by simply returning -1 (EOF is used to denote end of stream, not just files). Instead, methods should throw an `EOFException` object (class `EOFException` is a subclass of `IOException`; this is why the definition does not talk about `EOFException`). This means that a different coding template can be used to read streams via a `DataInputStream`. You can simply implement an endless loop that does not check for EOF, and rely on exception-catching code to correctly handle the EOF condition. The following program demonstrates this:

```java
import java.io.*;

class EOF {

public static void main(String[] args) {

DataInputStream is;
byte ch;

    try {

        is = new DataInputStream(new FileInputStream("EOF.java"));

        while (true) {  // no need to check for EOF: exception deals with it

            ch = is.readByte();
            System.out.print( (char) ch );
            System.out.flush();
        }

    } catch (EOFException eof) {
        System.out.println(" >> Normal program termination.");
    } catch (FileNotFoundException noFile) {
        System.out.println("File not found! " + noFile);
    } catch (IOException io) {
        System.out.println("I/O error occurred: " + io);
    } catch (Throwable anything) {
        System.out.println("Abnormal exception caught !: " + anything);
    }
}} // End of class EOF
```

LineNumberReader

Class LineNumberReader adds line-number tracking for text-input streams. The following two methods are provided to manage the line-number tracking feature:

```
public void setLineNumber(int lineNumber)
public int getLineNumber()
```

The following program uses the class to print any text file with line numbers starting each line:

```java
import java.io.*;

class Lineno {

public static void main (String args[]) {

FileReader          fileReader = null;
BufferedReader      bufferedReader = null;
LineNumberReader    lineNumberReader = null;
String              line;

  try {
     fileReader = new FileReader( args[0] );
     bufferedReader = new BufferedReader( fileReader );
     lineNumberReader = new LineNumberReader( bufferedReader );

     while ( (line = lineNumberReader.readLine()) != null) {
        int lineNo = lineNumberReader.getLineNumber();
        System.out.println(lineNo + " " + line);
     }
  } catch (Exception ioErr) {
     System.out.println( ioErr.toString() );
     System.exit(100);
  } }}
```

The program uses a three-stage input pipeline:

```
agrs[0] file -> fileReader -> bufferedReader -> lineNumberReader
```

The data read from lineNumberReader travels the length of the stream, originating in the file specified in the command line and passing through fileReader and bufferedReader. The BufferedReader was used to turbo-charge the whole program, and the LineNumber-Reader was used to provide the line numbers themselves.

Note that the order of the different stream types can be important. In this example, it wouldn't make any sense to, say, put the buffered reader object last in the chain. Buffered input streams and readers always need to be the second link in the chain so that all downstream stages can benefit from the buffering (equivalent BufferedOutput-Stream and BufferedWriter objects always need to be last-but-one in any output chain).

NOTE In this case, you could have easily tracked the line number by trivially using an integer variable that is incremented for every loop iteration, but it would be reinventing the wheel, which is not what object-oriented programming is about. The Java API classes represent software reuse handed to us on a plate. If you want software reusability to mean something within your software-development cycle, you should make a valiant effort to become familiar with the valuable functionality provided by the different Java packages. This way, you can cut your program-development time by simply relying on prewritten (and debugged!) classes.

PushbackInputStream and PushbackReader

Classes PushBackInputStream and PushbackReader add a pushback (undo) capability to an input stream or reader. In both classes, the following methods deal with the new feature:

```
public void unread(int ch) throws IOException
public void unread(char ch[]) throws IOException
public void unread(char ch[], int offset, int len) throws IOException
```

Note that these methods allow you to do slightly more than simply undo the last read: They allow you to cheat and push back different characters than the ones originally read.

Tokenizing Input Streams

There's one `java.io` input class that does not descend from `InputStream` but really ought to: class `StreamTokenizer`. You already briefly encountered the class in the word-frequency program presented in the discussion of `FileInputStream`.

Tokenizing some input means reducing it to a simpler stream of tokens. These tokens represent recurring chunks of data in the stream. Any Java compiler, for example, would check for grammatical correctness of your programs by checking the sequence of tokens representing reserved word strings like `class`, `import`, `public`, `void`, and so on. By not requiring you to deal with the exact character sequences themselves, tokenizing as a technique has two main advantages:

- It reduces code complexity.

- It allows for flexible, quick changes in input syntax.

If, for instance, the Java designers had at some stage wanted to rename the reserved word `extends` to `subclasses`, they could have done so easily without it impacting the compiler in any way. The tokenizing stage of the compiler would still deliver the same TOKEN_ EXTENDS token to the grammar-checking stage, even though Java source codes would now contain the word `subclasses` everywhere.

StreamTokenizer

Class `StreamTokenizer` can be used to turn any input stream into a stream of tokens. The programming model for the class is that a stream can contain three types of entities:

- Words (that is, multicharacter tokens)

- Single-character tokens

- Whitespace (including C/C++/Java-style comments)

Before you start processing a stream into tokens, you must define which ASCII characters should be treated as one of the three possible input types, called *defining the syntax table* for the stream. Once the syntax table is defined, you can proceed by extracting actual tokens. Look at how it is done in practice by first checking out the structure and services of class `StreamTokenizer`:

```
public class StreamTokenizer extends Object {
public static final int TT_EOF = -1;
public static final int TT_EOL = '\n';
public static final int TT_NUMBER = -2;
public static final int TT_WORD = -3;
public double nval;
public String sval;
public int ttype;

public StreamTokenizer(InputStream is);
public StreamTokenizer(Reader r);


    public void resetSyntax();
    public void wordChars(int low, int hi);
    public void whitespaceChars(int low, int hi);
    public void ordinaryChars(int low, int hi);
    public void ordinaryChar(int ch);
    public void commentChar(int ch);
    public void quoteChar(int ch);
    public void parseNumbers();
    public void eolIsSignificant(boolean flag);
    public void slashStarComments(boolean flag);
    public void slashSlashComments(boolean flag);

    public void lowerCaseMode(boolean flag);
    public int nextToken() throws IOException;
    public void pushBack();
    public int lineno();
    public String toString();}
```

To begin with, this class has some public instance variables: `ttype`, `sval`, and `nval`. These stand for token type, string value, and number value, and, contrary to object-oriented rules, the class expects clients to actually access these fields. This you need to do after calling the core method for class `StreamTokenizer`: `nextToken()`. This method is the token-producing conveyor belt. Its return value tells you what type of token it produced: It can either be a multicharacter `TT_WORD` token or a single-character token, in which case the return value holds the ASCII code for that character. If the stream is exhausted, `nextToken()` returns `TT_EOF`. If you have enabled end-of-line checking by invoking `eolIsSignificant(true)`, `TT_EOL` will be returned each time the end of a line is reached. If you have enabled number parsing by invoking `parseNumbers()`, `TT_NUMBER` will be returned each time numbers are encountered in the stream (possibly in scientific notation).

When `nextToken()` returns either a `TT_WORD` or `TT_NUMBER` token-type return value, you need to dig the actual string or numeric values out of the `sval` and `nval` instance variables, respectively. (This is very un-object-oriented; simple access methods could have been provided—like `getWord()` and `getNumber()`—to accomplish those same tasks.)

Before starting to call `nextToken()`, you should set up the syntax table for the input stream. This setup is done via a number of methods that assign different types of significance to different input characters. Method `whitespaceChars()` lets you define a character range with no significance whatsoever: `Whitespace` can be skipped altogether by the stream tokenizer. Method `wordChars()` lets you define another range of characters that should be treated as building-block characters for "words." In the Java compiler example, all characters that can legally be part of identifiers (like variable names or method names) should be defined as word characters. This definition lets the tokenizer treat identifiers, for example, as the atomic wholes they actually are.

An Example: Tokenizing HTML

The following sample program uses class `StreamTokenizer` to tokenize another structured language that is very relevant to the Java developer: HTML. The program consists of a new subclass of `StreamTokenizer` called `HTMLTokenizer` (what else?), which can identify a common subset of HTML 2 tags. The driver program (HTMLtext) uses the new class to extract all text from a Web page. Here is the listing for the HTMLtext program:

```java
import java.io.*;

class HTMLtext {

public static void main(String args[]) throws IOException {
FileReader       htmlInput;
HTMLTokenizer    htmlTokens;
int tagType;

   if (args.length != 1) {
      System.out.println("Usage: HTMLtext <file.html>");
      System.exit(10);
   }

   htmlInput = new FileReader( args[0] );
   htmlTokens= new HTMLTokenizer( htmlInput );

   while( (tagType = htmlTokens.nextHTML()) != HTMLTokenizer.HTML_EOF ) {

      if (tagType == HTMLTokenizer.HTML_TEXT) {
         System.out.println("TEXT: " + htmlTokens.sval);
      } else
      if (tagType == HTMLTokenizer.HTML_UNKNOWN) {
         System.out.println("UNKNOWN TAG: '" + htmlTokens.sval +"'");
      } else
      if (tagType == HTMLTokenizer.TAG_PRE) {
         if (htmlTokens.nextHTML() == HTMLTokenizer.HTML_TEXT) {
            System.out.println(htmlTokens.sval);
            htmlTokens.nextHTML();  // swallow </PRE>
         }
      }
   }
}}
```

```
//————————————————————————————————————————————————————————————
// Class HTMLTokenizer is a form of StreamTokenizer that knows about
// HTML tags (but not HTML structure!).
//————————————————————————————————————————————————————————————
class HTMLTokenizer extends StreamTokenizer {

static int HTML_TEXT        = -1;
static int HTML_UNKNOWN     = -2;
static int HTML_EOF         = -3;


// The following class constants are used to identify HTML tags.
// Note that each tag type has an odd- and even-numbered ID, depending on
// whether the tag is a start or end tag.
// These constants are returned by nextHTML().

static int TAG_HTML         = 0    , TAG_html         = 1;
static int TAG_HEAD         = 2    , TAG_head         = 3;
static int TAG_BODY         = 4    , TAG_body         = 5;
static int TAG_H1           = 6    , TAG_h1           = 7;
static int TAG_H2           = 8    , TAG_h2           = 9;
static int TAG_H3           = 10   , TAG_h3           = 11;
static int TAG_H4           = 12   , TAG_h4           = 13;
static int TAG_H5           = 14   , TAG_h5           = 15;
static int TAG_H6           = 16   , TAG_h6           = 17;
static int TAG_H7           = 18   , TAG_h7           = 19;
static int TAG_CENTER       = 20   , TAG_center       = 21;
static int TAG_PRE          = 22   , TAG_pre          = 23;
static int TAG_TITLE        = 24   , TAG_title        = 25;
static int TAG_HORIZONTAL   = 26;
static int TAG_DT           = 28   , TAG_dt           = 29;
static int TAG_DD           = 30   , TAG_dd           = 31;
static int TAG_DL           = 32   , TAG_dl           = 33;
static int TAG_IMAGE        = 34   , TAG_image        = 35;
static int TAG_BOLD         = 36   , TAG_bold         = 37;
static int TAG_APPLET       = 38   , TAG_applet       = 39;
static int TAG_PARAM        = 40   , TAG_param        = 41;
static int TAG_PARAGRAPH    = 42;
static int TAG_ADDRESS      = 44   , TAG_address      = 45;
static int TAG_STRONG       = 46   , TAG_strong       = 47;
static int TAG_LINK         = 48   , TAG_link         = 49;
static int TAG_ORDERED_LIST = 50   , TAG_ordered_list = 51;
static int TAG_LIST         = 52   , TAG_list         = 53;
```

```
static int TAG_LIST_ITEM    = 54   , TAG_list_item  = 55;
static int TAG_CODE         = 56   , TAG_code       = 57;
static int TAG_EMPHASIZE    = 58   , TAG_emphasize  = 59;

// When extending this list, make sure that substring collisions do not
// introduce bugs. For example: tag "A" has to come after "ADDRESS";
// otherwise all "ADDRESS" tags will be seen as "A" tags.

String[] tags = {"HTML", "HEAD", "BODY"
                ,"H1", "H2", "H3", "H4", "H5", "H6", "H7"
                ,"CENTER", "PRE", "TITLE", "HR"
                ,"DT", "DD", "DL", "IMG", "B"
                ,"APPLET", "PARAM"
                ,"P", "ADDRESS", "STRONG"
                ,"A", "OL", "UL", "LI", "CODE", "EM"
                };

boolean outsideTag = true;

//————————————————————————————————————————————————————————————————————
// The HTMLTokenizer relies on a two-state state machine: the stream
// can be "inside" a tag (between < and >) or "outside" a tag
// (between > and <).
//————————————————————————————————————————————————————————————————————
public HTMLTokenizer (Reader reader) {
    super(reader);

    resetSyntax();              // start with a blank character type table
    wordChars(0, 255);          // you want to stumble over < and > only,
    ordinaryChars('<','<');     // all the rest is considered "words"
    ordinaryChars('>','>');

    outsideTag = true;          // you start being outside any HTML tags
}
//————————————————————————————————————————————————————————————————————
// grab next HTML tag, text, or EOF
//————————————————————————————————————————————————————————————————————
public int nextHTML() throws IOException {
int tok;

    switch ( tok = nextToken() ) {
        case StreamTokenizer.TT_EOF :    return HTML_EOF;
```

```
        case '<'                        :    outsideTag = false; // we're inside
                                             return nextHTML();   // decode type

        case '>'                        :    outsideTag = true;
                                             return nextHTML();

        case StreamTokenizer.TT_WORD:
            if ( ! outsideTag ) {
                return tagType();      // decode tag type
            } else {
                if ( onlyWhiteSpace(sval) ) {
                    return nextHTML();
                } else {
                    return HTML_TEXT;
                }
            }
        default:        System.out.println("ERROR: unknown TT " + tok);
    }
    return HTML_UNKNOWN;
}
//————————————————————————————————————————————————————————————————————
// Inter-tag words that consist only of whitespace are swallowed
// (skipped); this method tests whether a string can be considered
// whitespace.or not.
//————————————————————————————————————————————————————————————————————
protected boolean onlyWhiteSpace( String s ) {

char ch;

    for(int i=0; i < s.length(); i++) {
        ch = s.charAt(i);
        if ( ! (ch==' ' || ch=='\t' || ch=='\n' || ch=='\r') ) {
            return false;
        }
    }
    return true;
}
//————————————————————————————————————————————————————————————————————
// You've just hit a '<' tag start character; now identify the type of tag
// you're dealing with.
//————————————————————————————————————————————————————————————————————
protected int tagType () {
```

```
boolean endTag = false;
String input;
int start = 0;
int tagID;

    input = sval.substring(1);      // skip leading space (bug in StreamTok)

    if (input.charAt(0) == '/') {   // is this an end tag (like </HTML>) ?
       start++;                     // skip slash
       endTag = true;
    }
       // go through the list of known tags, try to match one
    for (int tag=0; tag < tags.length; tag++) {
       if (input.regionMatches(true, start, tags[tag], 0, tags[tag].length()
)) {
          tagID = tag*2 + (endTag ? 1 : 0);
          return tagID;
       }
    }
    return HTML_UNKNOWN;

}} // End of class HTMLTokenizer
```

Because the HTMLTokenizer class extends StreamTokenizer, it is no surprise that the example followed the StreamTokenizer's programming model, even if it is less than perfect. The new class needs no syntax table initialization, though, nor does it provide any methods in this respect. Its key method is nextHTML(), which is modeled after nextToken(). Method nextHTML() returns token IDs of the form TAG_*XXX* where *XXX* is some HTML tag type. To help remember all the different HTML token constants, the convention of using a lowercased equivalent, TAG_*xxx*, is used to denote end tags. For example, if <HEAD> is a start tag, then </HEAD> is its corresponding end tag. Their respective token constants are TAG_HEAD and TAG_head.

The parsing approach embodied by HTMLTokenizer is to treat the opening and closing angle brackets (< and >) as the only special characters in the HTML input stream. All other characters are regarded as "word" characters, even whitespace. This unconventional syntax table approach greatly simplifies the remaining logic of the class and is

implemented in the constructor for HTMLTokenizer. The nextHTML()
method can rely on always either being inside or outside a tag. If it
switches from out to in, it is a simple matter of identifying the tag
while noting whether this is a start or an end tag (end tags have a
slash character before the tag label).

Because inter-tag whitespace should not be taken into account
when parsing HTML files, it is filtered out manually (Stream-
Tokenizer's whitespace-filtering capability is not relied on). All
other inter-tag data is the raw text for the Web page, stripped of any
HTML markups.

> **TIP**
>
> **Because this sample program does not implement support for
> HTML 3 tags, you may wish to enhance the program yourself. The
> program is very easily enhanced by adding new tag strings to the
> tags array and adding the corresponding** TAG_xxx **ID constant for
> the new tag.**

Output Streams and Writers

The second main hierarchy branch in package java.io consists of
all stream and writer classes concerned with output. The roots for
this branch are the classes OutputStream and Writer. Here is the
full definition of class OutputStream:

```
public abstract class OutputStream extends Object {
    public OutputStream();
    public abstract void write(int b) throws IOException;
    public void write(byte b[]) throws IOException;
    public void write(byte b[], int off, int len) throws IOException;
    public void flush() throws IOException;
    public void close() throws IOException;
}
```

The definition for Writer is nearly identical:

```
public abstract class Writer extends Object {
    public Writer();
```

```
    public Writer(Object lock);
    public abstract void write(int b) throws IOException;
    public void write(byte b[]) throws IOException;
    public void write(byte b[], int off, int len) throws IOException;
    public void flush() throws IOException;
    public void close() throws IOException;
}
```

The second form of the constructor takes an object as an argument. When this form is used, the writer will synchronize its writing, flushing, and closing operations on the object's lock; this prevents competing threads from corrupting the writer's data. (See Chapter 8 for information about locks and synchronization.)

Output streams and writers are even simpler than input streams and readers in that they do not support the mark/reset mechanism (it simply does not make sense for output). The core functionality is to be able to write bytes or characters one at a time or in blocks. The destination for this written data can be anything, in theory; in practice, the concrete destinations of files, byte arrays, and network connections are supported (the latter via java.net classes, discussed in Chapter 16). Because there is very little difference between output and input (apart from the direction of information flow), what follows is a condensed overview of the output stream and writer classes.

ByteArrayOutputStream and CharArrayWriter

The ByteArrayOutputStream and CharArrayWriter classes are the exact opposites of ByteArrayInputStream and CharArray-Reader. The classes provide for some extra methods above the minimal write() methods defined by OutputStream and Writer. Here is the full definition of ByteArrayOutputStream:

```
public class ByteArrayOutputStream extends OutputStream {
    protected byte buf[];
    protected int count;

    public ByteArrayOutputStream();
```

```
    public ByteArrayOutputStream(int size);
    public synchronized void reset();
    public int size();
    public synchronized byte toByteArray()[];
    public String toString();
    public String toString(int hibyte);
    public String toString(String enc) throws UnsupportedEncodingException;
    public synchronized void write(byte b[], int off, int len);
    public synchronized void write(int b);
    public synchronized void writeTo(OutputStream out) throws IOException;
}
```

The definition of CharArrayWriter is almost identical:

```
public Class CharArrayWriter extends Writer {
    public CharArrayWriter();
    public CharArrayWriter(int initialSize);
    public void close();
    public void flush();
    public void reset();
    public int size();
    public char toCharArray()[];
    public String toString();
    public void write(char c[], int off, int len);
    public void write(int c);
    public void write(String str, int off, int len);
    public void writeTo(Writer out) throws IOException;
}
```

After these classes have been written to, the data may be retrieved by calling toByteArray() (for a ByteArrayOutputStream) or toCharArray() (for a CharArrayWriter).

WARNING Byte array output streams and character array writers write to memory. They should be used only when the amount of data to be written can safely be accommodated in memory. Writing a few bytes or a few thousand bytes is reasonable; writing a few megabytes will cause problems!

FilterOutputStream and FilterWriter

The `FilterOutputStream` and `FilterWriter` classes are the superclasses of the higher-level filtering output streams and writers. Like their input counterparts, they are supposed to be subclassed, not directly instantiated. The following is the definition of `Filter-OutputStream`:

```
public class FilterOutputStream extends OutputStream
{
    public FilterOutputStream(OutputStream out);
    public void close() throws IOException;
    public void flush() throws IOException;
    public void write(byte b[]) throws IOException;
    public void write(byte b[], int off, int len) throws IOException;
    public void write(int b) throws IOException;
}
```

And here is the definition of `FilterWriter`:

```
public abstract class FilterWriter extends Writer
{
    public void close() throws IOException;
    public void flush() throws IOException;
    public void write(char cbuf[], int off, int len) throws IOException;
    public void write(int c) throws IOException;
    public void write(String str, int off, int len) throws IOException;
}
```

BufferedOutputStream and BufferedWriter

Buffering output can enhance writing performance in exactly the same way as buffering input enhances reading performance. The `BufferedOutputStream` and `BufferedWriter` classes are the same as `BufferedInputStream` and `BufferedReader`, except they work with output. The following program highlights the difference a write buffer makes by writing a file without buffering and then writing a file with buffering:

```
import java.io.*;
import java.util.*;

class BufferDiff {
```

```
public static void main (String args[]) throws IOException {

FileOutputStream        unbufStream;
BufferedOutputStream    bufStream;

    unbufStream = /* a raw file stream */  new FileOutputStream("test.one");
    bufStream   = new BufferedOutputStream(new FileOutputStream("test.two"));

    System.out.println("Write file unbuffered: " + time( unbufStream ) + "ms");
    System.out.println("Write file   buffered: " + time( bufStream   ) + "ms");
}

static int time (OutputStream os) throws IOException {

Date then = new Date();

    for (int i=0; i<50000; i++) {
       os.write(1);
    }
    os.close();
    return (int)  ((new Date()).getTime() - then.getTime());
}
}
```

When run, the program produced the following statistics on my machine:

```
Write file unbuffered: 8190ms
Write file   buffered: 1370ms
```

As you can see, the simple wrapping of a `BufferedOutputStream` object around the final destination stream (that is, the last stage in a chain of output streams) substantially improves write performance.

DataOutputStream

Class `DataOutputStream` implements the `DataOutput` interface, which was described earlier in the chapter in the discussion of class `RandomAccessFile`. Basically, interface `DataOutput` specifies methods for saving (writing) every type of Java primitive type plus `Strings`. Although the exact representation of the types output this way is irrelevant, the reality is that `DataOutputStream` generates a binary stream; that is, output not interpretable by people.

When you need to keep external databases whose sizes are an issue, binary is usually the most efficient representation. Say your application manipulates large 3-D models. The definition for those models consists of large amounts of (x,y,z) triplets of `doubles`, plus extra data of various data types. Such models would probably best be saved in binary to conserve storage resources.

> **NOTE**   There is no writer equivalent to `DataOutputStream`. **This makes sense, because writers deal with characters, not with binary representations of other data types.**

For smaller entities, say configuration files, binary is not your best choice. Representing data in readable ASCII format is much more attractive. Another output stream class, class `PrintStream` (discussed shortly), can be used instead to create a readable stream of data, but `PrintStream` is not as useful as it seems because of a major flaw in the `java.io` hierarchy: There is no corresponding input class to read the data back in. If you need to design a file format for a configuration file, a completely different class might be the best solution: class `Properties` from package `java.util` (also discussed in a bit).

ObjectOutputStream

As explained in the discussion of `ObjectInputStream`, object input and output streams read and write entire objects. More precisely, they write the state of object's instance variables. This is a more complicated operation than you might guess. Some instance variables are themselves references to other objects, and they also must be written to an object output stream or read from an object input stream.

The Endian Wars Are Over

Whenever binary files containing numbers are moved from one architecture to another, the issue of "endianness" crops up. Different CPUs order the bytes in a multibyte number (say a four-byte `int`) according to little-endian (least significant byte at lowest address) or big-endian (most significant byte at lowest address) schemes.

When a number is written to a file by a little-endian processor, and then subsequently read back by a big-endian processor (or vice versa), the number will have been corrupted (unless it is 0 or −1). Java's `Data-OutputStream` and `DataInputStream` classes protect you from this pitfall because, although Java data files are exchanged between very different physical machines, the exchange actually takes place between two (identical) Java VMs (which, by the way, both use the big-endian scheme).

The process of writing out an object's state is called *serialization*. Reading in an object's state is called *deserialization*. Serialization and deserialization are useful in their own right; they are also essential for RMI, which allows method calls to be made on objects running on external machines. For more information about serialization, deserialization, and RMI, see Chapter 22.

Properties

Although the `Properties` class is not part of the `java.io` package (it is part of `java.util`), it is so closely related to I/O issues that it is discussed here. This class has the following definition:

```
public class Properties extends Hashtable {
    public Properties();
    public Properties(Properties defaults);
    public String getProperty(String key);
    public String getProperty(String key, String defaultValue);
    public void list(PrintStream out);
```

```
    public void list(PrintWriter out);
    public synchronized void load(InputStream in) throws IOException;
    public Enumeration propertyNames();
    public synchronized void save(OutputStream out, String header);
}
```

Class `Properties` is basically a `Hashtable` with `load()` and `save()` methods added. These take input and output streams, respectively, as arguments, so you can send or receive your `Properties` objects to or from more than just an external file. You can think of a configuration file as a kind of dictionary, pairing configuration variables with their values.

The following program demonstrates how a set of configuration variables can be saved as a `Properties` configuration file.

```
import java.io.*;
import java.util.*;

class Config {

public static void main (String args[]) {

Properties      config;
FileOutputStream fos;

// some dummy configuration variables to be saved in a config file

Double proficiencyScore = new Double(Math.PI);
Boolean hasCDROM = Boolean.FALSE;
String userName = "Peewee";

   try {
      fos = new FileOutputStream("myprogram.cfg");

      config = new Properties();

      config.put("proficiency", proficiencyScore.toString() );
      config.put("hasCDROM"   , hasCDROM.toString() );
      config.put("name"       , userName.toString() );
```

```
        config.save( fos, "My Program's very own config file" );
   } catch (Exception io) {
      System.out.println("Failed to save configuration file... what now ?");
      System.out.println(io);
   }
}}
```

The imaginary configuration variables `proficiencyScore`, `hasCDROM`, and `userName` are saved in an ASCII file of the following format:

```
#My Program's very own config file
#Thu Jun 27 20:30:38  1997
hasCDROM=false
proficiency=3.141592653589793
name=Peewee
```

As you can see, the `Properties` class `timestamps` and `datestamps` these files internally and adds the `String` you passed to the `save()` method to the top of the file (as a comment). This allows you to store copyright or other information in the file.

Note that all configuration variables saved via a `Properties` object must be objects (primitive types are not supported) and also must be converted to `Strings` before being put into the `Properties` dictionary using the `put()` `Hashtable` method. To read back the configuration file and initialize your variables from it, you need to `load()` the `Properties` object back (via an input stream) and then extract and convert the variables stored as `Strings`. Here is the other half of the sample program:

```
import java.io.*;
import java.util.*;

class LoadConfig {

public static void main (String args[]) {

Properties      config;
FileInputStream  fis;
```

```
Double proficiencyScore;
Boolean hasCDROM;
String userName;

    try {
        fis = new FileInputStream("myprogram.cfg");

        config = new Properties();
        config.load( fis );

        proficiencyScore = Double.valueOf(config.getProperty("proficiency"));
        hasCDROM         = Boolean.valueOf(config.getProperty("hasCDROM"));
        userName         = config.getProperty("name");


        System.out.println("proficiency = " + proficiencyScore );
        System.out.println("hasCDROM    = " + hasCDROM );
        System.out.println("name        = " + userName );

    } catch (Exception io) {
        System.out.println("Failed to load configuration file... what now ?");
        System.out.println(io);
    }
}}
```

PrintStream and PrintWriter

Class PrintStream resembles class DataOutputStream, because
the methods it defines mirror the type of write() methods provided
by DataOutputStream. The difference is that they come in two
flavors: print(..) and println(..). Here is the definition of
class PrintStream:

```
public class PrintStream extends FilterOutputStream {
    public PrintStream(OutputStream out, boolean autoFlush);
    public PrintStream (OutputStream out);
    public boolean checkError();
    public void close();
    public void flush();
    public void print(char c);
    public void print(char s[]);
```

```
        public void print(double d);
        public void print(float f);
        public void print(int i);
        public void print(long l);
        public void print(Object obj);
        public void print(String s);
        public void println(boolean x);
        public void println(char x);
        public void println(char x[]);
        public void println(double x);
        public void println(float x);
        public void println(int x);
        public void println(long x);
        public void println(Object x);
        public void println(String x);
        public void write(int b);
        public void print(boolean b);
        public void println();
        public void write(byte buf[], int off, int len);
}
```

The PrintWriter class is similar. Here is its definition:

```
public class PrintWriter extends Writer
{
    public PrintWriter(Writer out, boolean autoFlush);
    public PrintWriter(OutputStream out);
    public PrintWriter(OutputStream out, boolean autoFlush);
    public PrintWriter (Writer out);
    public boolean checkError();
    public void close();
    public void flush();
    public void print(char c);
    public void print(char s[]);
    public void print(double d);
    public void print(float f);
    public void print(int i);
    public void print(long l);
    public void print(Object obj);
    public void print(String s);
    public void println(boolean x);
    public void println(char x);
    public void println(char x[]);
```

```
    public void println(double x);
    public void println(float x);
    public void println(int x);
    public void println(long x);
    public void println(Object x);
    public void println(String x);
    public void write(int c);
    public void print(boolean b);
    public void println();
    public void write(char buf[], int off, int len);
    public void write(char buf[]);
    public void write(String s, int off, int len);
    public void write(String s);
}
```

The PrintStream class has not formally been deprecated in JDK 1.1, but use of PrintWriters is strongly encouraged.

There is a difference between these print() methods and the write() methods of DataOutputStream. PrintStream and PrintWriter convert all of their arguments to character representations. PrintStream converts to 8-bit ASCII representations; PrintWriter converts to 16-bit bytecode representations.

You have actually been using a PrintStream object ever since your first encounter with Java:

```
System.out.println("Hello World!");
```

Object out is a static PrintStream variable in class System. Various instances of the overloaded print() and println() methods have been used in most of the programs. The difference between the two is that print() does not force the immediate writing of the data (called *flushing*). It can remain buffered in the stream until a newline character is written or until an explicit flush() is done on the PrintStream.

Classes PrintStream and PrintWriter allow you to pass any object as argument. The mechanism used to convert any object into a string representation is to call the object's toString() method. If you create a new class that doesn't override toString() of class Object, you will inherit its default implementation, which is to output the class name along with the object's hashcode, produced by the hashCode() Object method. The following program demonstrates a println() on an instance of a brand new class:

```
class Print {

public static void main (String args[]) {
BrandNew anObject = new BrandNew();

    System.out.println( anObject );
}}

class BrandNew {

}
```

The new class BrandNew (which is empty and doesn't even have a custom constructor) is no problem for the println (Object obj) method because it can still invoke the parent Object toString() method, which, in this case, produces the following output for object anObject:

```
BrandNew@1ec614
```

The consistent overloading of both print() and println() methods means that you can literally throw any (single) argument at these methods, without needing to cast, and they will perform what you intuitively would expect them to: convert the argument to a string representation and write this string to the output stream.

Summary

Computers need to interact with the outside world in order to be useful. They need to input external information, process it, and output results. Almost every computer language includes a generic I/O support layer that shields applications, written in those languages, from the more turbulent world of rapidly changing and very different I/O devices "out there." Java's answer to (or rather, its arsenal to cope with) the I/O issue is the `java.io` package, which provides device- and platform-independent classes for file and stream manipulation.

The way that Java supports streams is especially powerful and flexible. The stream classes support an unlimited chaining mechanism that allows you to mix and match stream classes to achieve any desired I/O functionality. Creating your own enhanced stream classes, to be inserted anywhere along an input or output chain, is straightforward. The type of power and flexibility that the `java.io` hierarchy puts in developers' hands is possible only because of the application of pure object-oriented techniques, and, it has to be said, clever design.

CHAPTER
SIXTEEN

16

Network Programming

- The TCP/IP protocol suite

- Internet addressing methods

- Low-level communication using UDP

- Connecting to servers using TCP

- Java's Web support classes

- Server system design

- The Factory design pattern

When Java was developed, GUIs had already become common-place, so Java is accompanied by its AWT. But Java is also a child of the Internet era, and so it comes with an entire package of classes devoted to Internet and Web support.

Java is the first mainstream programming language to provide built-in support for high-level Internet programming. Using other languages, the only way to write applications for the Internet is to descend into the technical depths of operating system-dependent networking APIs. With Java, writing a program that accesses a computer on the other side of the planet is easier than ever, and there is no need to grind through your machine's reference volumes for operating system networking support.

This chapter provides a brief review of the main networking protocols, and then describes the classes in the `java.net` package. The examples presented here demonstrate how to connect to remote servers and fetch resources, as well as how to design a simple server system. You'll also learn about the Factory design pattern and the factory interfaces in `java.net`.

Java's Networking Protocols: TCP/IP

Java's view of networking means TCP/IP, and only TCP/IP. Novell, IBM, and DEC proprietary networking protocols do not make the grade—and quite rightly so, since TCP/IP is the only true "open" networking standard that links together the four corners of our globe, via the Internet.

TCP/IP stands for Transmission Control Protocol/Internet Protocol, the two data communication protocols on which the Internet relies for all its functionality. In practice, however, TCP/IP stands for a whole collection of related protocols (a *suite*, in communications jargon) all based around TCP and IP. SMTP (Simple Mail Transfer Protocol) and NNTP (Network News Transfer Protocol) are examples of some older (but still ubiquitous) protocols that are considered part of the TCP/IP suite. The new kid on the block, HTTP (Hypertext Transfer Protocol), has become so much a part of the Internet (and therefore TCP/IP) that many people confuse the Web with the Internet.

IP: The Heart of Internet Data Communications

Whatever application protocol is used to implement some Internet service, IP lies at the heart of all Internet data communications. IP is a datagram protocol, which means that transmitted packets of information (*packets*, for short) are not guaranteed to be delivered. IP packets also do not form part of a stream of related packets; IP is a *connectionless* protocol. Each IP packet travels on its own, like an individual letter in a postal network (or a guru looking for enlightenment). Figure 16.1 shows the structure of an IP packet.

FIGURE 16.1

The IP datagram packet format

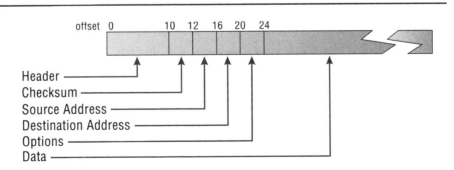

The various fields at the beginning of the *frame* (another word for packet) are collectively known as the *frame header*. The IP packet header determines the IP protocol's functionality and its limitations. Foremost in this respect is the addressing structure employed to encode the source (sender) and destination addresses. There have been 32 bits allocated for each of these address fields, which means the Internet can have a maximum of 2^32 (4,294,967,296) different machines connected to its global network.

> **NOTE** The maximum number of machines may sound sufficient, but this address space is already close to being exhausted. The Internet Architecture Board (IAB) is working hard to introduce a less restrictive upgrade to IP, called IP Next Generation (IPng).

Instead of writing down 32-digit long bitstrings, like 11001110110000110001011111010000, Internet addresses are almost always expressed in their human-readable, textual form (for example, www.sybex.com). On the rarer occasions when the address needs to be expressed numerically, these 32-bit IP addresses are written as four decimal bytes (for example, 192.31.32.255). The remainder of the header portion of the packet encodes a collection of fields, including the total packet length in bytes. Sixteen bits are allocated for this field, so an IP packet can be a maximum of 64KB long.

TCP: For Guaranteed Delivery

Since IP packets are never guaranteed to arrive at their destination, a higher-level protocol, TCP, is used to provide a basic service that does guarantee delivery. TCP manages this by using IP as a building block. The structure of a TCP packet is shown in Figure 16.2.

FIGURE 16.2

TCP packet format

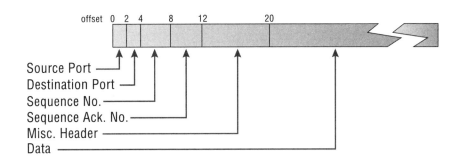

Source Port
Destination Port
Sequence No.
Sequence Ack. No.
Misc. Header
Data

Whereas IP is a datagram service, TCP presents a *connection-oriented* data stream service (like the telephone network). Before sending data via TCP, a computer needs to connect with the computer at the other end; only then can data be exchanged. Another difference is that the TCP protocol allows you to send or receive arbitrary amounts of data as one big stream of byte data. IP is theoretically limited to sending a 65,536-byte packet, which would be insufficient for sending many files or even many large GIF images embedded in Web pages. TCP solves this problem by breaking up the user's data stream into separate IP packets, numbering them, and then reassembling them on arrival. This is the function of the sequence number and sequence acknowledge number fields.

The most important TCP header fields, from a user's standpoint, are the source and destination port fields. While IP allows you to send an IP packet to an individual machine on the network, TCP forces you to refine this addressing by adding some destination port address. Every machine that talks TCP/IP has 65,536 different TCP ports (or *sockets*) it can talk through, as shown in Figure 16.3.

A large collection of standard port numbers has been defined. Table 16.1 shows some port addresses for familiar Internet services; for example, port 21 is universally used for file transfers using the FTP (File Transfer Protocol), and port 80 is used for all communications with World Wide Web HTML servers. In later examples, you will talk to port 25 on your Internet provider's machine to send e-mail, and to port 80 of any Web server in the world to request a Web page to be transmitted to you.

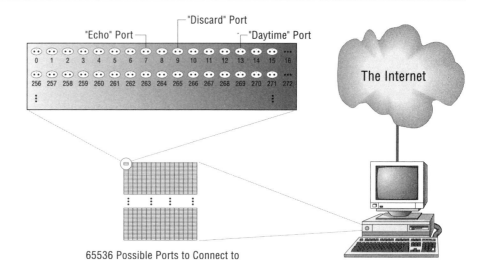

FIGURE 16.3

TCP ports and well-known port numbers

> **TIP**
>
> You might be able to find out more about standard port numbers if you have access to the TCP/IP configuration files on your machine. The file that lists many port numbers is called services. On Windows 95 machines, the file is called C:\WINDOWS\SERVICES. On Unix systems, the file is located in the /etc directory. If you can access it, be sure not to modify it in any way; if you do, you risk losing part or all of your Internet connectivity.

TABLE 16.1   Standard TCP Port Numbers

Port Name	Port Number	Service Description
echo	7	Echoes whatever you send to it
discard	9	Discards whatever you send to it
daytime	13	Produces the destination machine's local time
qotd	17	Produces the "quote of the day" for that machine

TABLE 16.1   Standard TCP Port Numbers (*Continued*)

Port Name	Port Number	Service Description
chargen	19	Produces a test stream of characters (character generator)
ftp	21	FTP port
telnet	23	Telnet protocol port
smtp	25	SMTP port
finger	79	Finger protocol port
http	80	Web server port
pop3	110	POP version 3 port
nntp	119	NNTP port

The majority of application-level TCP/IP protocols (like SMTP for e-mail transfer) rely on TCP, not IP, to achieve their functionality. This is because they invariably need guaranteed or error-free transmission of unlimited amounts of data.

There is one more low-level TCP/IP protocol that builds on IP to achieve its functionality: UDP (User Datagram Protocol). UDP is a datagram protocol with the same 64KB packet-size limit of IP, but it also allows port addresses to be specified. In fact, every machine has two sets of 65,536 ports to communicate through: one for TCP and one for UDP.

Now that you have reviewed some TCP/IP basics, you are ready to explore the core `java.net` package classes.

Internet Addressing

One of the `java.net` classes allows you to manipulate a 32-bit IP address (that is, an Internet host address) in a more high-level fashion than by just using a single 32-bit integer. Class `InetAddress` essentially lets you convert a textual Internet address of the form *host.subdomain.domain* into an object representing that address.

Here is the definition for class InetAddress:

```
public final class InetAddress extends Object
implements java.io.Serializable {
    public static InetAddress[] getAllByName(String host)
        throws UnknownHostException;
    public static InetAddress getByName(String host)
        throws UnknownHostException;
    public static InetAddress getLocalHost()
        throws UnknownHostException;
    public boolean equals(Object obj);
    public byte[] getAddress();
    public String getHostAddress();
    public String getHostName();
    public int hashCode();
    public boolean isMulticastAddress();
    public String toString();
}
```

The class deviates from the object-oriented norm by not providing a constructor and relying instead on static class methods, getByName() and getAllByName(), to create instances of InetAddresses. These methods take as their argument the textual address of any host on the Internet, in the form of a String. You can also turn the Internet address of your own machine (localhost) into an InetAddress by calling InetAddress.getLocalHost().

To experiment with the InetAddress methods, and most other java.net methods and classes, you need to have your machine online; that is, you need to be connected to a live TCP/IP network, if not the Internet itself. One of the reasons for this is that the java.net classes need to be able to do full domain name lookups via the Domain Name System (DNS). You already learned that Internet addresses are encoded as 32-bit integers within the IP packets exchanged on the Internet. Mnemonic addresses like www.microsoft.com or www.mit .edu are used only for your benefit, and they must be translated to 32-bit addresses for any real Internet communication to be initiated based on those addresses.

The Domain Name System

How does the translation from textual address to numeric address take place? Does your machine contain a huge file listing every Internet machine in the world, along with its numeric address? Not nowadays. This was the situation during the earlier years of the Internet when there were a couple of hundred machines worldwide. With the exponential growth in hosts connecting to the Internet, this approach became unsustainable (it did not scale well).

Today, every machine configured to talk TCP/IP needs to know at least one numeric address of another, very special, machine it can talk to directly, without needing to translate any textual address to the real 32-bit address—the address of a DNS server. This DNS server is responsible for translating the cozy textual Internet addresses into hard (but efficient) numeric Internet addresses.

The Internet's DNS system is like a global (distributed) telephone book for all of the Internet's host machines; given a mnemonic address, the DNS system will return the IP address (the telephone number) of a host.

Looking Up a Textual Address

Method `getByName()` in class `InetAddress` is the transparent interface to the DNS service. When you invoke `getByName()`, the DNS server will be contacted "directly" (using its numeric address) and asked to look up and return the numeric address for the textual address you passed to `getByName()`. If your machine is not online, this lookup mechanism will fail, and an `UnknownHostException` will be thrown (which is why you generally need to be online when working with `java.net` classes), unless you are looking up your own machine's IP address, passing your machine's name as a string.

The following program demonstrates the address lookup possibilities of class InetAddress.

```
import java.net.*;

class DNSLookup {

public static void main (String[] args) throws UnknownHostException {
InetAddress someHost;
byte[] bytes;
int[] fourBytes = new int[4];

   if (args.length == 0) {
      someHost = InetAddress.getLocalHost();
   } else {
      someHost = InetAddress.getByName( args[0] );
   }

   System.out.print( "Host '"+ someHost.getHostName() +"' has address: ");

   bytes = someHost.getAddress();
   for(int i=0; i<4; i++) {
      fourBytes[i] = bytes[i] & 255;
   }

   System.out.println( fourBytes[0] +"."+
                   fourBytes[1] +"."+
                      fourBytes[2] +"."+
                         fourBytes[3] );
}
}
```

The program takes a host name string as a command-line argument. If no host name is specified, the lookup will be performed for your own machine's address. Here is an example of the output when no command-line arguments are entered:

```
Host 'telework.demon.co.uk' has address: 194.222.15.21
```

Getting a Numeric Address

To get the numeric address, use getAddress(), which returns an array of four bytes. To print these bytes, interpreted as unsigned values, you cannot just cast to an int datatype; negative byte values will be sign-extended to equally negative int values. The bytes need to be copied into an array of integers while ANDing with 255 to undo the sign-extending.

Note that class InetAddress overrides toString() (like all good classes), which, in this context, outputs a String containing much the same information as we constructed manually. For example, using this code:

```
System.out.println(InetAddress.getLocalHost())
```

produces this:

```
telework.demon.co.uk/194.222.15.21
```

Communicating with Remote Systems

Now that you know how to specify an Internet destination using instances of class InetAddress, how do you actually communicate with a remote system? Package java.net provides several ways.

Low-Level Communication Using UDP

The most basic method of communicating with a remote system is to use UDP datagrams. A UDP datagram is embodied in an instance of class DatagramPacket:

```
public final class DatagramPacket extends Object {
    public DatagramPacket(byte ibuf[], int ilength);
    public DatagramPacket(byte ibuf[], int ilength, InetAddress iaddr,
        int iport);
```

```
     public InetAddress getAddress();
     public byte[] getData();
     public int getLength();
     public int getPort();
}
```

Class `DatagramPacket` provides two constructors: one to receive datagrams and another to transmit datagrams. With both constructors, you need to specify a byte buffer and its length (the `ibuf` array can be bigger than `ilength`, but not smaller). The second constructor additionally needs the destination machine and port number for the datagram (in this constructor's case, the byte buffer contains the message).

As you can see, the class does not actually give you the means for sending or receiving any datagrams. This functionality is the responsibility of a companion class, class `DatagramSocket`:

```
public final class DatagramSocket extends Object {
   public DatagramSocket() throws SocketException;
   public DatagramSocket(int port) throws SocketException;
   public DatagramSocket(int port, InetAddress laddr)
      throws SocketException;
   public void close();
   public InetAddress getLocalAddress();
   public int getLocalPort();
   public synchronized int getSoTimeout() throws SocketException;
   public synchronized void receive(DatagramPacket p) throws IOException;
   public void send(DatagramPacket p) throws IOException;
   public synchronized void setSoTimeout(int timeout)
      throws SocketException;
}
```

The methods of interest here are the `send()` and `receive()` methods. The `send()` method simply takes a `DatagramPacket` instance and sends the datagram's data to the previously defined host and port address. The `receive()` method also takes a `DatagramPacket` instance, but this time as a recipient for a datagram to be received. You can extract the data from a received datagram using the `getData()` method in class `DatagramPacket`. To demonstrate the use of both classes in their transmit and receive capacities, here is a short example that addresses Sybex's Web server and asks it what the local time is (at Sybex headquarters, this is Pacific Standard Time).

```
import java.net.*;

class GetDate {

final static int PORT_DAYTIME = 13;  // well-known daytime port

public static void main(String[] args) throws Exception {
DatagramSocket  dgSocket;
DatagramPacket  datagram;
InetAddress     destination;
byte[]  msg = new byte[256];

    dgSocket    = new DatagramSocket();
    destination = InetAddress.getByName("www.sybex.com");

    datagram    = new DatagramPacket(msg, msg.length, destination,
                                PORT_DAYTIME);
    dgSocket.send(datagram);

    datagram    = new DatagramPacket(msg, msg.length);
    dgSocket.receive(datagram);

    String received = new String(datagram.getData());
    System.out.println("The time in sunny California is now: " + received);

    dgSocket.close();

}} // end of class GetDate
```

The program first creates a datagram socket that it will use to both transmit and receive. It then proceeds by creating an instance of a transmit datagram packet, to be sent to the daytime port service on Sybex's server. The server's mechanical response is always to return a time-stamped datagram (in ASCII). This datagram must be caught in a brand new `DatagramPacket` instance. (The program does not reuse the transmit packet for receive purposes; the only reuse that occurs is the reuse of the variable name datagram.) Once the response datagram is received, the time is extracted from the datagram as an ASCII byte array and converted to a `String` that is printed to the console.

The simplicity of this example hides a serious problem: Neither the sent or the received datagrams are ever guaranteed to arrive at their destinations. This means that the server might never receive your initial datagram. And if it does, its response might never reach your machine. UDP is useful mainly whenever low-value information needs to be broadcast or when information needs to be transmitted on a frequent basis, so that losing a communication now and then does not affect the service. For most communications, however, you need guaranteed delivery of your data—and that is TCP's domain.

Connecting to Servers Using TCP

The programming model for TCP communication is similar to that of UDP, except that it does not rely on a class to encapsulate TCP packets. This is to be expected, because TCP is a stream protocol: It allows you to send arbitrary amounts of data. The core class is simply called `Socket`:

```
public class Socket extends Object {
    public Socket(String host, int port) throws UnknownHostException, IOException;
    public Socket(InetAddress address, int port) throws IOException;
    public Socket(String host, int port, InetAddress localAddr, int
        localPort) throws IOException;
    public Socket(InetAddress address, int port, InetAddress localAddr,
        int localPort) throws IOException;
    public Socket(String host, int port, boolean stream) throws IOException;
    public Socket(InetAddress host, int port, boolean stream)
        throws IOException;
    public static synchronized void setSocketImplFactory(SocketImplFactory fac)
        throws IOException;
    public synchronized void close() throws IOException;
    public InetAddress getInetAddress();
    public InputStream getInputStream() throws IOException;
    public InetAddress getLocalAddress();
    public int getLocalPort();
    public OutputStream getOutputStream() throws IOException;
    public int getPort();
    public int getSoLinger() throws SocketException;
```

```
public synchronized int getSoTimeout() throws SocketException;
public boolean getTcpNoDelay() throws SocketException;
public void setSoLinger(boolean on, int val) throws SocketException;
public synchronized void setSoTimeout(int timeout)
    throws SocketException;
public void setTcpNoDelay(boolean on) throws SocketException;
public String toString();
}
```

To use the class, you need to understand the `Socket` constructors and the two stream access methods. The constructors need to have an instance of an `InetAddress` object or a `String` to specify the destination machine you want to connect to. If this were an IP support class, this would be all that is required. But since this is a TCP support class, the constructors also need a port address for the remote machine. Using this class puts you in the role of a client (within the client/server application model), so you cannot just specify any old number for this port address; you must stick to one of the well-known port numbers (see Table 16.1, earlier in the chapter).

All TCP connections actually involve two ports: the port on the remote machine and a port on the local machine, through which the client communicates. You do not need to specify the local port number, because the TCP/IP software allocates these ephemeral ports dynamically. They are called *ephemeral* ports because, unlike server ports, they exist only for the duration of a volatile client/server transaction. Server ports remain in use as long as the server software (also called a *daemon*) is up (that is, running).

NOTE On Unix, the server programs that manage the different ports are all implemented as background daemon tasks. That is why their names all end with *d*, as in smtpd for the SMTP service, ftpd for the FTP service, telnetd for the Telnet service, and so on.

Now you will work through some examples that rely on the `Socket` class to reach out into that cyberspace called the Internet.

Connecting to an SMTP Mail Server

If you want to deliver e-mail to a machine, you need to knock on that machine's port number 25. Once invited in, you also need to talk to the entity behind that port using a very strict, but simple, data communications protocol called SMTP. The way that this protocol works can be summarized in the following steps:

1. The SMTP server sends an initial identification string.

2. You reply by telling it which machine you are sending from.

3. If okay, the server replies with an acknowledge.

4. You reply by giving it the "From:" e-mail address (the sender's address).

5. If okay, the server replies with an acknowledge.

6. You reply by giving it the "To:" e-mail address (the address of the person you want the message to travel to).

7. If okay, the server replies with an acknowledge.

8. You send the entire e-mail message, line by line, and end the message with a single line containing a full stop ('.').

9. The server again acknowledges receipt of the message.

10. You sign off by sending QUIT.

The entire exchange is done in readable ASCII—no binary flags or cryptic fields are used within this protocol. If you delve into the fascinating world of Internet protocols, you will see that this is in fact very common among Internet protocols. (Data communications protocols outside the Unix-derived sphere of the Internet usually rely on complex packet structures encoded in binary.) Few of the Internet's application protocols employ the much more complex (but more efficient) binary representation for their protocol data units (PDUs; these are the packet types used to manage a communications protocol between two peers).

TIP You can obtain the full specifications for every Internet protocol (IP, UDP,4 TCP, SMTP, FTP, HTTP, and so on) by retrieving the standards documents themselves. These are called Request For Comments (RFCs). For example, RFCs 821 and 822 contain all the information about SMTP. RFCs are available by anonymous FTP from various sites, including mit.edu. An even more convenient way is to send an e-mail message to rfc-info@isi.edu, with a body containing two lines, such as:

> Retrieve: RFC
> Doc-ID: RFC0821

The server will send you the document (ASCII of course) by e-mail within the next 24 hours. What a service!

An Example: Sending an E-Mail Message

The sample program presented here demonstrates how easy it is to talk TCP with any (willing) port on a remote machine. It actually allows you to send an e-mail message from the command line by specifying the filename of the message to send, the "From" and "To" e-mail addresses, and the address of a mail host that will accept (and possibly forward) the mail message. You should use your usual mail drop-off point.

```
import java.io.*;
import java.net.*;

class SMTPDemo {

public static void main(String[] args)
   throws IOException, UnknownHostException {
String msgFile;
String from, to, mailHost;
```

```java
    if (args.length != 4) {
       System.out.println("Usage: java SMTPDemo msgFile from to mailHost");
       System.exit(10);
    }

    msgFile   = args[0];
    from      = args[1];
    to        = args[2];
    mailHost  = args[3];

    checkEmailAddress(from);
    checkEmailAddress(to);

    SMTP mail = new SMTP(mailHost);
    if (mail != null) {
       if (mail.send(new FileReader(msgFile), from, to) ) {
          System.out.println("Mail sent.");
       } else {
          System.out.println("Connect to SMTP server failed!");
       }
    }
    System.out.println("Done.");
}

static void checkEmailAddress(String address) {
    if (address.indexOf('@') == -1) {
       System.out.println("Invalid e-mail address '" + address + "'");
       System.exit(10);
    }
}
}


//————————————————————————————————————————————

//————————————————————————————————————————————
class SMTP {

public final static int SMTP_PORT = 25;

InetAddress mailHost;
InetAddress ourselves;
BufferedReader in;
```

```
PrintWriter out;

public SMTP (String host) throws UnknownHostException {

    mailHost = InetAddress.getByName(host);
    ourselves= InetAddress.getLocalHost();

    System.out.println("mailhost = " + mailHost);
    System.out.println("localhost= " + ourselves);
    System.out.println("SMTP constructor done\n");
}

public boolean send (FileReader msgg, String from, String to) throws
IOException {
Socket smtpPipe;
InputStream inn;
OutputStream outt;
BufferedReader msg;

    msg = new BufferedReader(msgg);

    smtpPipe = new Socket(mailHost, SMTP_PORT);
    if (smtpPipe == null) {
        return false;
    }

    // get raw streams
    inn  = smtpPipe.getInputStream();
    outt = smtpPipe.getOutputStream();

    // turn into usable ones
    in  = new BufferedReader(new InputStreamReader(inn));
    out = new PrintWriter(new OutputStreamWriter(outt));

    if (inn==null || outt==null) {
        System.out.println("Failed to open streams to socket.");
        return false;
    }

    String initialID = in.readLine();
    System.out.println(initialID);
```

```
System.out.println("HELO " + ourselves);
      out.println("HELO " + ourselves);
out.flush();

String welcome = in.readLine(); System.out.println(welcome);

System.out.println("MAIL From:<" + from + ">");
      out.println("MAIL From:<" + from + ">");
out.flush();

String senderOK = in.readLine(); System.out.println(senderOK);

System.out.println("RCPT TO:<" + to + ">");
      out.println("RCPT TO:<" + to + ">");
out.flush();

String recipientOK = in.readLine(); System.out.println(recipientOK);

System.out.println("DATA");
      out.println("DATA");
out.flush();

String line;
while( (line = msg.readLine()) != null) {
   out.println(line);
   out.flush();
}
System.out.println(".");
      out.println(".");

String acceptedOK = in.readLine(); System.out.println(acceptedOK);

System.out.println("QUIT");
      out.println("QUIT");
out.flush();

return true;
   }
}
```

The SMTP demonstration program defines a new class called SMTP that provides a single method, send(). This method allows clients to send some e-mail message to an e-mail recipient. Note that this implementation of `send()` simply swallows the responses from the server without checking for errors. This is not robust enough to be used in the real world (see RFC 821 for the error codes to check for in a secure implementation of `send()`). However, the main program does do a simple check on the e-mail addresses to see if they at least contain the @ character, something all fully qualified addresses require.

Looking at the program's source code, you might wonder where all the low-level, technical data communications code is hiding. The bulk of the program simply uses stream input and output methods. That is exactly where the protocol logic is hiding: class `Socket` lets clients communicate via everyday input and output streams that happen to connect all the way to the machine and its socket at the other end. These streams are obtained via the `getInputStream()` and `getOutputStream()` methods. It is therefore possible (and desirable, as was done in the `send()` method) to upgrade the raw `InputStream` and `OutputStream` streams by encapsulating them in more high-level streams like a `BufferedReader` to read and a `PrintWriter` to write. (See Chapter 15 for a details about the I/O stream classes.) Using these two stream enhancers, you can treat both incoming and outgoing data as lines of ASCII text, which, in the case of the SMTP, is most appropriate.

Connecting to an HTTP Web Server

Another protocol that operates in this transparent, ASCII line-based format is HTTP, on which the Web relies. The HTTP protocol is based on an exchange of multiline request and response headers. As is always the case in a client/server situation, it is the client (that is, the browser) that initiates the communication by sending the server a request header. The server then replies to this request by sending a response header, which usually includes any requested resources (Web page, image file, audio clip, and so on) as appended data.

The most common type of request header formats is appropriately called a "GET" request. The format of the GET header is as follows:

```
"GET" <URL> "HTTP/1.0"
```

This client request header has three components:

- The request method (GET)

- The resource URL

- The version of the HTTP protocol used for the exchange (HTTP/1.0)

If the request can be satisfied by the server, it replies with a response header. Here is an example of a server's response header:

```
HTTP/1.0 200 OK
Server:Apache/1.0.2
Content-type: text/html
Last-Modified: Mon, 04 Sep 1995 12:34:51 PST

<HTML><HEAD>..
..
..
```

The following are the important aspects to note about the HTTP response header:

- It starts with a status reply (the 200 OK).

- It contains the type of resource returned (in the Content-type field).

- It contains an empty line that separates the header from the actual data.

In the response header example, you can see the beginning of a requested HTML file stream in (right after the blank line). Other non-ASCII resources would similarly start just past the empty line. In the case of an audio clip, for example, this data might be encoded in non-readable binary.

An Example: Downloading a Web Page

The following program allows you to grab any Web page off the Internet from the command line. Here is the program's source code:

```
import java.io.*;
import java.net.*;

class GetWebPage {

public static void main(String[] args)
   throws IOException, UnknownHostException {
String resource, host, file;
int slashPos;

   if (args.length != 1) {
      System.out.println("Usage: java GetWebPage <URL>");
      System.exit(10);
   }

   if ( ! args[0].startsWith("http://")) {
      System.out.println("Please specify a legal http URL.");
      System.exit(10);
   }

   resource = args[0].substring(7);    // skip HTTP://

   slashPos = resource.indexOf('/');   // find host/file separator
   if (slashPos < 0) {
      resource = resource + "/index.html";
      slashPos = resource.indexOf('/');
   }
   file = resource.substring(slashPos); // isolate host and file parts
   host = resource.substring(0,slashPos);

   System.out.println("Host to contact: '" + host +"'");
   System.out.println("File to fetch   : '" + file +"'");

   HTTP webConnection = new HTTP(host);
   if (webConnection != null) {
      BufferedReader in = webConnection.get(file);
      String line;
```

```
        while( (line = in.readLine()) != null) {  // read until EOF
          System.out.println( line );
        }
    }
    System.out.println("\nDone.");
}}


//—————————————————————————————————————————————————————
//—————————————————————————————————————————————————————
class HTTP {

public final static int HTTP_PORT = 80;

InetAddress WWWhost;
DataInputStream in;
PrintStream out;

public HTTP (String host) throws UnknownHostException {

   WWWhost = InetAddress.getByName(host);

   System.out.println("WWW host = " + WWWhost);
}

public BufferedReader get (String file) throws IOException {
Socket httpPipe;
InputStream inn;
OutputStream outt;
BufferedReader ir;
PrintWriter out;

   httpPipe = new Socket(WWWhost, HTTP_PORT);
   if (httpPipe == null) {
      return null;
   }

   // get raw streams
   inn  = httpPipe.getInputStream();
   outt = httpPipe.getOutputStream();


   // turn into useful ones
```

```
ir  = new BufferedReader(new InputStreamReader((inn)));
out = new PrintWriter(new OutputStreamWriter(outt));

if (inn==null || outt==null || ir==null || out==null) {
   System.out.println("Failed to open streams to socket.");
   return null;
}

   // send GET request
System.out.println("GET " + file + " HTTP/1.0\n");
out.println("GET " + file + " HTTP/1.0\n");
out.flush();

   // read response until blank separator line
String response;
while ( (response = ir.readLine()).length() >0) {
   System.out.println(response);
}

return ir;  // return BufferedReader to let client read resource
}}
```

As with the SMTP demonstration program, a separate class, HTTP in this example, is created to encapsulate the details about the protocol. Instead of a send() method, a get() method is implemented. This get() method creates a new Socket in the same way the SMTP class did. It then proceeds to get the input and output streams associated with the socket, so it can send and receive data over the HTTP link. The heart of the get() method is the sending of the GET HTTP header followed by the "parsing" of the response header returned by the Web server.

The minimalistic implementation given here restricts itself to simply reading and echoing the response header lines until the separator line is encountered. From that point on, all remaining data is part of the resource requested by the main program, so the input stream itself is returned to the caller, who can then proceed with reading the resource stream (oblivious of the fact that an ASCII header preceded it).

Here is a transcript of a sample session with the GetWebPage program:

```
C:\>java GetWebPage http://www.ping.be/~ping3100/index.html
Host to contact: 'www.ping.be'
File to fetch  : '/~ping3100/index.html'
WWW host = www.ping.be/193.74.114.17
GET /~ping3100/index.html HTTP/1.0

HTTP/1.0 200 OK
Server: Netscape-Communications/1.1
Date: Sunday, 06-Jul-97 18:55:39 GMT
Content-type: text/html

<HTML>
<HEAD>
<TITLE>
Home Page for Laurence Vanhelsuwe
</TITLE>
</HEAD>
─────── Bulk of HTML file cut ───────
</HTML>

Done.
```

If you specified a nonexistent file on a Web server you would get the familiar browser error "404: Not Found." Here is what the GetWebPage program prints when we ask it to get a nonexistent file:

```
HTTP/1.0 404 Not Found
Server: Netscape-Communications/1.1
Date: Sunday, 06-Jul-97 18:55:39 GMT
Content-type: text/html

<HEAD><TITLE>File Not Found</TITLE>
</HEAD>
<BODY> Error 404: Not Found <P> The file or resource you
       requested could not be found anywhere on this server.
</BODY>
```

Fetching Other Web Resources

Note that the content type field returned by all Web servers uses a standard format called the MIME (Multipurpose Internet Mail Extensions) type. Table 16.2 shows some common MIME types and their meanings.

TABLE 16.2   Standard MIME Types

MIME Type	Origin
application/octet-stream	Generic binary byte stream emanating from unspecified application
application/postscript	PostScript language file
application/rtf	Rich Text Format word-processor file
application/x-tex	TeX Typesetter file
audio/basic	.snd or .au sound clip file
audio/x-aiff	Audio IFF file
audio/x-wav	.wav file
image/gif	.gif image file
image/jpeg	.jpg image file
image/tiff	.tif image file
image/x-xbitmap	.xbm image file
text/html	.html or .htm file
text/plain	.txt, .c, .cpp, .h, .pl, .java files
video/mpeg	.mpg file
video/quicktime	.mov or .qt Apple QuickTime file
video/x-sgi-movie	.movie Silicon Graphics file

To fetch other Web resources like images or audio files, you could use the same technique as demonstrated in the GetWebPage program, except that you would need to have different methods or classes to deal with the different types of content returned by the server.

Before you start investing mammoth amounts of effort to deal with each of these content types, you should know that Java already has a general solution in store:

```java
import java.net.*;
import java.io.*;

class GetContent {

public static void main (String[] args)
                    throws MalformedURLException, IOException {
Object obj;

   obj = (new
URL("http://www.ping.be/~ping3100/gif/ball.gif")).getContent();
   System.out.println( obj.getClass().getName() );
}
}
```

This two-line program (if you ignore the necessary skeleton code) essentially does the same as the 90-odd line GetWebPage program! The only difference is that the GetContent program retrieves an image file from a Web server instead of an HTML file. No more sockets, no more input or output streams, and no more protocol-specific concerns. But how does it work? And does it work for all the MIME types listed in Table 16.2? The answer to these questions lies in a new class introduced in the program: class URL. This class is discussed next.

Performing Operations on URLs

Class URL defines a Web URL (Uniform Resource Locator) plus some operations you can perform on URLs. In its most primitive capacity, this class is similar to InetAddress in that it just lets you create an object that addresses, or points to, something. In the case of class InetAddress, its instances point to Internet hosts; in the case of class URL instances, these objects point to Web resources (Web pages, text files, image files, sound clips, and so on). Here is the definition of class URL:

```
public class URL extends Object implements java.io.Serializable {
    public URL(String protocol, String host, int port, String file)
        throws MalformedURLException;
    public URL(String protocol, String host, String file)
        throws MalformedURLException;
    public URL(String spec) throws MalformedURLException;
    public URL(URL context, String spec) throws MalformedURLException;
    public static synchronized void
        setURLStreamHandlerFactory(URLStreamHandlerFactory fac);
    public boolean equals(Object obj);
    public final Object getContent() throws java.io.IOException;
    public String getFile();
    public String getHost();
    public int getPort();
    public String getProtocol();
    public String getRef();
    public int hashCode();
    public URLConnection openConnection() throws java.io.IOException;
    public final InputStream openStream() throws java.io.IOException;
    public boolean sameFile(URL other);
    public String toExternalForm();
    public String toString();
}
```

The arguments for the simplest constructor reflect the basic structure of all well-formed URL addresses:

```
<protocol> <host address> [<:port number>] <resource spec>
```

The fields hold the following information:

- The protocol field can be `http:`, `ftp:`, `gopher:`, `news:`, `telnet:`, or `mailto:`.

- The host address is any legal host address, such as www .apple.com.

- The port number field is optional and denotes the port number to connect to, if the default port for this protocol is to be overridden.

- The resource specification field is usually the full path of a file on the remote machine's file system, although this can be anything the protocol requires—for example, the name of a newsgroup for the `news:` protocol.

Here are some legal URL examples:

http://www.who.org:8080/index.htm

http://java.sun.com/Developers/welcome.html#footer

ftp://ftp.uni-paderborn.de/pub/Aminet/README

news:comp.sys.amiga.*

gopher:gopher.ucdavis.edu

mailto:president@whitehouse.gov

Note the first URL, which overrides the standard Web server port (80) to a less common port 8080. Note also the second URL, which specifies a reference (that is, a location) within the welcome.html document by appending a #, followed by the name of the reference in the document.

The first URL object constructor mirrors these URL components in its list of arguments. The second constructor is very similar, except that it omits the need to specify a port number explicitly; it uses the default for the given protocol (port 21 for FTP, port 80 for HTTP, and so on). The GetContent program in the previous section uses the third constructor (the most compact) to create a class URL instance. It just takes a URL string as you would type it into any Web browser's URL text-entry field.

Controlling the HTTP Link

Once you have constructed a class URL instance, you can extract any of the URL component fields using the getPort(), getProtocol(), getHost(), getFile(), and getRef() methods. The core URL method, however, is getContent(), which is used in the demonstration program. You do not need to explicitly specify the type of resource addressed; the program will fetch the resource and return it in an appropriate form. For example, an Image object would be returned for a GIF or JPEG image resource. What class URL hides is that it relies heavily on a closely related class, class URLConnection, to do all its dirty work:

```
public abstract class URLConnection extends Object {
    public static FileNameMap fileNameMap;
    public static boolean getDefaultAllowUserInteraction();
    public static String getDefaultRequestProperty(String key);
    public static String guessContentTypeFromStream(InputStream is)
        throws IOException;
    public static synchronized void
        setContentHandlerFactory(ContentHandlerFactory fac);
    public static void setDefaultAllowUserInteraction(boolean
        defaultallowuserinteraction);
    public static void setDefaultRequestProperty(String key, String value);
    public abstract void connect() throws IOException;
    public boolean getAllowUserInteraction();
    public Object getContent() throws IOException;
    public String getContentEncoding();
    public int getContentLength();
    public String getContentType();
    public long getDate();
    public boolean getDefaultUseCaches();
    public boolean getDoInput();
    public boolean getDoOutput();
    public long getExpiration();
    public String getHeaderField(int n);
    public String getHeaderField(String name);
    public long getHeaderFieldDate(String name, long Default);
    public int getHeaderFieldInt(String name, int Default);
    public String getHeaderFieldKey(int n);
```

```
public long getIfModifiedSince();
public InputStream getInputStream() throws IOException;
public long getLastModified();
public OutputStream getOutputStream() throws IOException;
public String getRequestProperty(String key);
public URL getURL();
public boolean getUseCaches();
public void setAllowUserInteraction(boolean allowuserinteraction);
public void setDefaultUseCaches(boolean defaultusecaches);
public void setDoInput(boolean doinput);
public void setDoOutput(boolean dooutput);
public void setIfModifiedSince(long ifmodifiedsince);
public void setRequestProperty(String key, String value);
public void setUseCaches(boolean usecaches);
public String toString();
}
```

As the size of class URLConnection suggests, it gives you much more control over the HTTP link created when activating (opening) a URL connection. For example, the following methods are all convenience methods that let you query the values of the HTTP response header fields the Web server sends back:

String getContentType()   Returns the MIME type of this resource.

int getContentLength()   Returns the size in bytes of this resource.

String getContentEncoding()   Returns the encoding used to transmit the resource.

long getDate()   Gets the date and time stamp for this response header.

long getExpiration()   Gets the date and time when this resource becomes stale (and should be reloaded to get an up-to-date version).

long getLastModified()   Gets the date and time stamp for the moment the resource was last altered.

Only the content type field is mandatory, so all other methods can return nulls (for `String` return types) or 0 (for numeric return types), if the server does not volunteer the information.

> **NOTE**
>
> Content type and content encoding are two different things. Content encoding tells you in which encoding scheme the resource is returned. Common encodings are straight 8-bit binary, UUencoded, and base64 encodings. The last two are used when the entire HTTP response needs to be "seven-bit clean"—that is, the most significant bit of every byte needs to be zero.

Two `URLConnection` methods are similar to the two key `Socket` methods you saw earlier: `getInputStream()` and `getOutput-Stream()`. These methods are also important within the context of class `URLConnection`. Class `URL` also makes available a `getInput-Stream()` method (but no corresponding output stream method), by calling the underlying `URLConnection` class' `getInputStream()`.

Several methods within class `URLConnection` deal with resource-caching issues. It is common for Web browsers to cache in-line images, and even entire source Web pages, for future, accelerated loading and display. The downside of this caching is that the original Web pages and/or pictures may undergo important changes that would pass you by if the browser's caching kept all cached resources indefinitely.

The following methods deal with this resource caching:

`void setDefaultUseCaches(boolean defaultusecaches)` Sets the default caching behavior (on or off) for future instances of the class.

`boolean getDefaultUseCaches()`   Queries whether or not future instances will use caching.

`void setUseCaches(boolean usecaches)`   Allows you to change the caching behavior of a `URLConnection` object on the fly.

boolean getUseCaches() Queries whether or not a URL-Connection object caches resources.

Finally, two utility functions are provided to guess the content:

protected static String guessContentType From-Name(String fname) Guesses the content of a file, judging by its name alone.

protected static String guessContentType From-Stream(InputStream is) Guesses the content of a stream by peeking at its actual content, relying on mark()/reset() to avoid consuming any data.

Unfortunately, these methods are declared protected, which means you need to subclass URLConnection before you can use them.

Writing Server Systems

So far, this chapter has focused on the client aspect of client/server computing, since the majority of Java developers will view the world from that perspective. If you are part of that minority that needs to write server (not client) software, this section is for you. The java.net package contains all you need to write any server system, using class ServerSocket:

```
public class ServerSocket extends Object {
public ServerSocket(int port) throws IOException;
public ServerSocket(int port, int backlog) throws IOException;
public ServerSocket(int port, int backlog, InetAddress bindAddr)
   throws IOException;
public static synchronized void setSocketFactory(SocketImplFactory fac)
   throws IOException;
public Socket accept() throws IOException;
public void close() throws IOException;
public InetAddress getInetAddress();
public int getLocalPort();
public synchronized int getSoTimeout() throws IOException;
```

```
    public synchronized void setSoTimeout(int timeout) throws
        SocketException;
    public String toString();
}
```

The first constructor is all you need to get going; it creates a new listening socket on your machine that can accept incoming connections from clients across the network.

The port number argument specifies on which server port your server will be available to the world. If you want to write a standard server, such as an SMTP or FTP server, you need to use its respective well-known port addresses. On the other hand, if you want to create a brand new Internet service, you will need to use a port number that no one else is using. Since the full port number range is 0–65,535, there are plenty of choices, provided that you stay clear of certain ranges:

- The range 0–1023 is reserved for "standard" Internet protocols. These ranges are controlled by the IANA (Internet Assigned Numbers Authority).

- The region from 1024 onward is used for client ephemeral ports.

- Some systems use the range starting at 32768 for ephemeral ports too, so it is best to avoid these numbers as well.

For testing purposes, port number 8001 is quite commonly used, although anything within the 8–16K or 48–64K ranges is fine.

Once a new ServerSocket object is created, it does not listen yet on its port for client requests to arrive. This only starts when you call the accept() method on the ServerSocket object. The accept() method will not return until a client connects to the server. If you like, you can call the setSoTimeout() method to assign a timeout to the server socket (this must be done before the accept() call). If no client connects to the server before the timeout expires, a java.io.InterruptedIOException will be thrown.

As you can see from the list of methods class ServerSocket provides, there are no reading or writing methods, nor does

ServerSocket let you have the input and output streams to the socket. This is because a ServerSocket is not used for the actual communication: A ServerSocket produces a new Socket instance for the server software to talk to the connecting client. This Socket instance is created (and returned) when a connection is accepted by the accept() method. This means the server programming model is almost identical to that of the client programming model; you just use the input and output streams connected to a socket to implement the required protocol.

A Simple Server Program

The example presented here is a simplistic server that actually behaves like a real server. When a client connects to its port, it sends an initial welcome identification string, then waits for a client command (the server protocol is modeled on the SMTP). The only commands the program implements are "HELP" and "QUIT"—not very functional, but these two commands should be implemented by all line-based protocols (and SMTP, NNTP, and FTP support HELP and QUIT). Here is the server:

```
import java.util.*;
import java.io.*;
import java.net.*;

public class ServerTest {

final static int SERVER_PORT = 8001;  // our server's own port

public static void main(String[] args) {
Server server;
String clientRequest;
BufferedReader reader;
PrintWriter writer;

    server = new Server(SERVER_PORT);
    reader = new BufferedReader(new InputStreamReader(server.in));
    writer = new PrintWriter(new OutputStreamWriter(server.out));
```

```
           // send initial string to client.
       writer.println("Java Test server v0.02, " + new Date() );
       writer.flush();

       while ( true ) {
          try {
                // what does client have to say to us ?
             clientRequest = reader.readLine();
             System.out.println("Client says: " + clientRequest);
             if (clientRequest.startsWith("HELP")) {
                writer.println("Vocabulary: HELP QUIT");
                writer.flush();
             } else

             if (clientRequest.startsWith("QUIT")) {
                System.exit(0);
             } else {
                writer.println("ERR: Command '" + clientRequest +"' not understood.");
                writer.flush();
             }

          } catch (IOException e) {
             System.out.println("IOEx in server " + e);
          }
       }
   }
}}
//————————————————————————————————————————————————————————————
class Server {

private ServerSocket server;
private Socket socket;

public InputStream in;
public OutputStream  out;

public Server(int port) {

   try {
      server = new ServerSocket(port);
      System.out.println("ServerSocket before accept: " + server);
      System.out.println("Java Test server v0.02, on-line!" );
```

```
    // wait for a client to connect to our port
  socket = server.accept();
  System.out.println("ServerSocket after  accept: " + server);

  in  = socket.getInputStream();
  out = socket.getOutputStream();

} catch (IOException e) {
  System.out.println("Server constructor IOEx: " + e);
}
}
}
```

When you run this program, your console should print:

```
C:\LANG\JAVA\SRC\NET> java ServerTest
ServerSocket before accept: ServerSocket[addr=0.0.0.0,port=0,localport=8001]
Java Test server v0.02, on-line!
```

The Client for the Sample Server

The sample server seems to work; however, you do not have any client that knows about the protocol just invented, and the server expects clients to talk only to this protocol. You can quickly solve this problem by writing a client program customized to talk to your new server. The fact that both the client and the server will be tested on the same machine does not matter; the client program will simply connect to machine "localhost" at port 8001 (your server's port). Here is the client:

```
import java.io.*;
import java.net.*;

public class ClientTest {

public static void main(String[] args) {
String welcome, response;
Client client;
BufferedReader reader;
PrintWriter writer;
```

```
   client = new Client("localhost", 8001);

   try {
      reader = new BufferedReader(new InputStreamReader(client.in));
      writer = new PrintWriter(new OutputStreamWriter(client.out));

      welcome = reader.readLine();
      System.out.println("Server says: '"+ welcome +"'");

      System.out.println("HELLO");
      writer.println("HELLO");
      writer.flush();
      response =  reader.readLine();
      System.out.println("Server responds: '"+ response +"'");

      System.out.println("HELP");
      writer.println("HELP");
      writer.flush();
      response = reader.readLine();
      System.out.println("Server responds: '"+ response +"'");

      System.out.println("QUIT");
      writer.println("QUIT");writer.flush();
   }
   catch (IOException e) {
      System.out.println("IOException in client.in.readln()");
      System.out.println(e);
   }
   try {Thread.sleep(2000);} catch (Exception ignored) {}
}}
//─────────────────────────────────────────────────────────────
class Client {

   // make input and output streams available to user classes
public InputStream in;
public OutputStream out;

   // the socket itself remains ours though...
private Socket client;

public Client(String host, int port) {
```

```
try {
    client = new Socket(host, port);
    System.out.println("Client socket: " + client);

    out= client.getOutputStream();
    in = client.getInputStream();
}
catch (IOException e) {
    System.out.println("IOExc : " + e);
}
}}
```

If you run this client program in a new console window, while the server is still online and waiting for client connections, you should see the client go through its paces as follows:

```
C:\LANG\JAVA\SRC\NET> java ClientTest
Client socket:
Socket[addr=localhost/127.0.0.1,port=8001,localport=1034]
Server says: 'Java Test server v0.01, Mon Jul 08 10:12:37  1996'
HELLO
Server responds: 'ERR: Command 'HELLO' not understood.'
HELP
Server responds: 'Vocabulary: HELP QUIT'
QUIT

C:\LANG\JAVA\SRC\NET>
```

While the client printed these lines, your server printed the following lines, reflecting its perspective on the exchanges:

```
ServerSocket after accept:
ServerSocket[addr=0.0.0.0,port=0,localport=8001]
Client says: HELLO
Client says: HELP
Client says: QUIT

C:\LANG\JAVA\SRC\NET>
```

As you can see, both parties communicate together without a hitch. Of course, this is because the protocol used here is trivial—it is stateless to start with, which always keeps things very simple indeed—and no real network was involved. Although real TCP packets were created, they didn't travel far; they just looped back internally within the TCP/IP stack.

Real protocols usually rely heavily on a number of states the protocol can find itself in—for example, idle, connecting, connected, resyncing, disconnecting. These different states require you to implement state machines to manage the protocol. State machines that have more than just a few states and accept more than just a few possible events quickly become very complex, necessitating formal mathematical methods to prove their correctness.

Unfortunately, protocol state machines usually are nontrivial because real networks can be the cause of many different types of events and situations. Packets can become corrupted due to line noise; packets can fail to arrive altogether if networking equipment suddenly fails. Packets can even be delayed for so long that the receiver thinks the packet got lost and then suddenly—"pop!"—the original packet arrives, throwing the receiver out of synchronization with the sender. All these factors need to be taken into account when designing a protocol, unless you build your application protocol on a protocol that already takes care of these issues, and that is exactly the function of TCP, on which most (but not all) Internet protocols are based.

TIP

Developing and debugging client/server protocols are much easier if you use a line-based ASCII protocol and use Telnet to exercise the server. You can even test the ServerTest program by using Telnet to connect to it instead of using the ClientTest program. Try it yourself with "telnet localhost 8001" after starting up the server again. You will also discover that writing your own Telnet utility (in Java) is very easy indeed.

Factories and the Factory Design Pattern

While browsing the classes in `java.net`, you might have noticed the term *factory* here and there. Package `java.net` contains three interfaces that all contain the word *factory* in their names. In order to understand how these interfaces work, you need to know what factory classes are in the context of object-oriented software.

Solving Problems with Factory Classes

You know what factories are in real life—organizations that produce a variety of related products. In object-oriented software, the factory metaphor applies to classes that can construct objects with diverging (but related) characteristics without invoking the constructors for the objects' concrete classes. The Factory design pattern can be used whenever a class needs to instantiate objects from classes it doesn't yet know about.

As an example, consider how a Web browser might need the factory design pattern to solve a problem. Most Web resources are transferred by browsers using the HTTP protocol, but you might have noticed that this is not always the case. At some point, your browser's address input field might start with the characters *ftp://* instead of *http://*. What's going on? Your browser was instructed to fetch a resource using a different protocol than the usual HTTP. It switched to FTP to fetch a file or a directory, but without informing you of the quite dramatic change in internal operation. If a resource's URL specified a protocol other than one of those that currently supported (HTTP, FTP, NNTP, and so on), your browser would have a problem: It would not know how to handle this foreign protocol.

An analogous obstacle can occur within Web pages themselves. Most browsers can deal with in-line images in GIF or JPEG format, but not some future popular image format. In the cases of new protocols and new image file formats, the browser software is stuck because of its lack of dynamic extensibility (addressed by Plug-Ins in Netscape's browser, as described in Chapter 1). If it could only load or call on classes that can deal with new protocols or new image or file formats, there would be no problem. And that is exactly what Sun's HotJava browser (which is written in Java, of course) can do, by relying on the Factory design pattern to get around these problems transparently. Factory classes can construct new protocol or content handlers to allow a browser to support an emerging standard without changing the browser itself.

Factory classes obviously cannot suddenly manufacture new objects on the fly to deal with these new developments. (For this to be possible, a lot more effort on the part of our artificial intelligence colleagues would be needed.) The way the factory classes are able to produce the goods is by loading new protocol or file format handler classes off the Internet. They do this the first time the new protocol or format is encountered; subsequently, they just load the classes off the client's local disk, as with all other classes. The Factory design pattern essentially decouples systems from each other, thereby adding a new level of flexibility.

Java's Factory Interfaces

Now that you have some insight into the Factory design pattern, you can examine the three `java.net` factory interfaces:

`ContentHandlerFactory` Builds `ContentHandler` objects.

`URLStreamHandlerFactory` Builds `URLStreamHandler` objects.

`SocketImplFactory` Builds `SocketImpl` objects.

Note that these are all interfaces rather than classes. None of the existing `java.net` classes implement any of these interfaces, but several `java.net` classes rely on external classes to be of one or other above factory type. (These classes are external and unknown, by definition, because that is the mechanism that allows future browser extensions without needing to alter the browser any further.) Class URL, for example, requires a `URLStreamHandlerFactory` (-typed) object for its `setURLStreamHandlerFactory()` method. Similarly, class 6URLConnection requires a `ContentHandler-Factory` object for its `setContentHandlerFactory()` method. `Socket` and `ServerSocket` work similarly with interface `Socket-ImplFactory`. These lean heavily on their respective factories to off-load nitty-gritty functionality to objects created by those factories.

As an example, consider what goes on behind the scenes when you invoke `getContent()` on a plain URL instance (as in the example for the URL class, presented earlier in the chapter). First, a connection is created to the resource, giving you a `URLConnection` object. Then, `getContent()` is called on the new `URLConnection` object instead (`getContent()` is also a method for class `URLConnection`). The `URLConnection` object has associated with it a `ContentHandler-Factory` object that can produce appropriate content handlers via its sole `createContentHandler()` method. The argument that this factory method takes is a `String` specifying a MIME type. Now the HTTP protocol dictates that Web servers always respond to GET HTTP requests using an HTTP response header that specifies the type of data it replies, as in the following header for a GIF picture:

```
Server:Apache/1.0.2
Content-type: image/gif
Content-length: 23746
Last-Modified: Fri, 21 Sep 1997 12:34:51 PST
```

Without "touching" the resource itself (say, to read the first ten bytes to figure out what type of resource it is), the `URLConnection` object can already determine the exact MIME type for the resource. And given the MIME type, the factory can then produce a subclass of `ContentHandler` that can deal with this type of content.

If you look at the simple definition of the `ContentHandler` super-class, you will see a very relevant method waiting in hiding:

```
public abstract class ContentHandler {
() public abstract Object getContent(URLConnection urlc) throwsIOException;
}
```

Yet another `getContent()`! This is the one (or, rather, the one implemented by the subclass produced by the factory method) that does the real content fetching and produces an object of the appropriate type for the resource. For example, if a GIF image was fetched, the `getContent()` method would return an `Image`, and not a (useless) simple `Object`, as hinted at by the method signature for `get-Content()`. Figure 16.4 illustrates how class URL relies on a factory to discover the resouce content.

FIGURE 16.4

How the URL class uses
a factory class

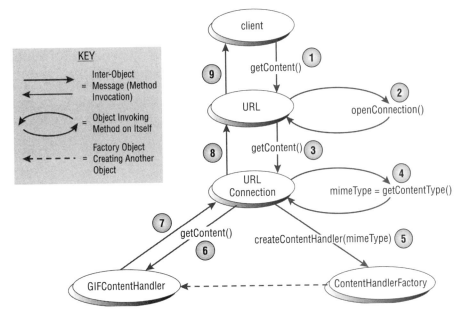

Here is a summary of the steps described here and depicted in the figure:

1. A client class wants to get the content for a resource defined by a URL.

2. The URL opens an HTTP connection to the Web server, creating a URLConnection object.

3. The URL object calls getContent() on the URLConnection object.

4. The URLConnection determines which type of resource this is from the HTTP response header (the Content-type field).

5. The URLConnection calls its ContentHandlerFactory to provide it with an appropriate ContentHandler subclass.

6. Upon instantiation of this content handler, the URLConnection calls it to deal with the specific resource (a GIF image in this example).

7. The prefabricated content handler returns the resource in a form best suited to it (Image for GIF images, String for text files, and so on).

8. The URLConnection passes the resource object back to the URL.

9. The URL passes the resource object back to the client (who now is very happy).

> **NOTE**
>
> There are actually more steps involved than those shown in Figure 16.4. The extra steps are an attempt to reduce the poor performance resulting from needing to create a new ContentHandler object for every client getContent() invocation. What class URLConnection adds to the picture is a caching step (involving a Hashtable, between steps 4 and 5), which often means that a suitable ContentHandler is already available without needing to be fabricated by the factory (at, more or less, great expense).

Summary

Java supports network programming through various classes dealing with the TCP/IP suite of data communication protocols. The core `java.net` class is class `Socket` that, together with class `InetAddress` to address hosts, allows you to write client software that connects itself to any server on the Internet. These connections are brought about via specific ports—called well-known ports on the server side, and ephemeral ports on the client side.

You also learned how most of the Internet's application-level protocols (SMTP, FTP, HTTP, NNTP, and so on) are ASCII, line-based protocols. This greatly facilitates development, debugging, and day-to-day protocol problem-solving, because the communication link can be intercepted and deciphered easily by any person familiar with the protocol. For example, the HTTP was shown to use a simple system of request and response headers that can be generated and viewed using a simple, standard tool like Telnet.

Finally, you learned about the nontrivial workings of the factory classes and their relationship to Java's key, dynamic extensibility in the field of yet-to-be-developed protocols and future Web resource types.

PART III

Advanced Topics

CHAPTER
SEVENTEEN

17

The Java Virtual Machine

- How the Java Virtual Machine works

- The architecture of the Java Virtual Machine

- Security and the Java Virtual Machine

- Just-In-Time (JIT) compilers for improving Java Virtual Machine performance

- Licensing and the Java Virtual Machine

In Chapter 1, you were briefly introduced to the Java Virtual Machine (VM) as part of the explanation of how Java works, and it has been mentioned in other chapters. This chapter focuses on the Java VM from a Java program developer's perspective. This knowledge is important to developers because the Java platform differs from traditional systems and follows the new paradigm "network is the computer." The Java platform extends the object-oriented systems to networked computers for encapsulated programs and data. The Java VM is central to the Java platform. Many of the attributes that make Java a universal development platform stem from the Java VM concept and implementation.

What Is a Java Virtual Machine?

At the most elementary level, the Java VM is a software CPU with the Java bytecode as the instruction set. Figure 17.1 shows a Java system flow diagram, including the Java VM. This figure illustrates the path of the bytecodes from the beginning. A developer writes a Java program and stores the program in a .java file. The Java compiler converts this Java program in the .java file into a .class file consisting of bytecodes. The bytecodes are the instruction set (like the machine code for a CPU) for the Java VM. The bytecodes are of the form:

<opcode> <... Parameters>

The instruction code, or opcode, is one byte long (hence, the name bytecodes) and can have many parameters. Currently, there about 220 bytecode instructions defined in the Java VM specification.

FIGURE 17.1

The Java system flow diagram

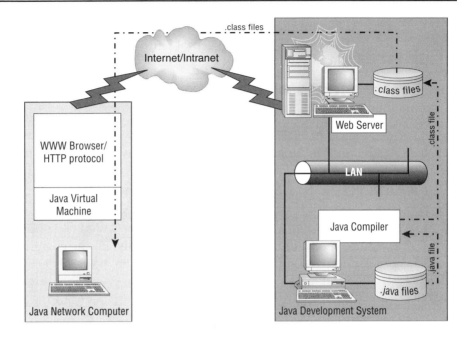

Like normal program loaders, the Java VM starts the execution of a program by loading the .class files from either the network or local storage. Since Java does not trust anything that comes across the network, the Java VM verifies only the bytecodes of .class files that are passed across a network. If the .class file does not pass the verification, the execution stops there with an error message. If the program successfully passes the verification phase, the Java VM runtime interpreter reads the bytecodes, translates them to the specific operating system/hardware instructions, and executes them in the target CPU.

To run the Java bytecodes, a hardware manufacturer or operating system vendor implements the Java VM on its hardware/operating system combination. The Java VM program modules are usually written in C, C++, or in assembly for an operating system/CPU. The Java VM uses the host operating system facilities for memory functions, file system, display, mouse, keyboard, network, other device drivers, processing of threads, and so on. Most of the current Java

VMs available now interpret the Java bytecodes versus the normal compilation process of C/C++ programs. As you can see in Figure 17.1, a Java VM executable unit is the .class file.

Benefits of Class Files

On a conceptual level, each .class file corresponds to one object. Unlike traditional applications, in the Java VM architecture there is no monolithic executable file that is loaded with all of the program code. One .class file could refer to many other .class files. (In the Java language, this is done using the `import`, `implements`, or `extends` clauses.) The Java VM loads the .class files (called classes) from the network or local file system as they are needed by the currently running class. Extending this concept further, the different classes/objects can be developed by different developers and exist in separate servers, and the Java VM will dynamically load and bind the class files as required.

NOTE Currently, the security scheme implemented by Netscape Navigator allows applets to load classes only from the servers from which the applets themselves are loaded. Netscape Navigator 3.0 and Microsoft Explorer 3.0 both maintain security using signed applets and certificates. The browsers maintain a list of the trusted applet and application suppliers, and warn the operator if an untrusted applet has been detected in the download process. The security systems used by these browsers is not the same as Java's built-in security and predates the release of Java 1.1.

This dynamic loading and binding architecture enables you to update the .class files on the servers, providing clients with the latest version of the software. These updates can be bug fixes or new versions of software with additional features. It is precisely the zero-administration client, versionless software and Just-In-Time (JIT) software delivery architecture that make the Java platform so successful. The JIT compiler concept, which is now being offered as a product by many vendors, is an important development for Java VM performance enhancement. The JIT compiler is discussed later in this chapter.

Additionally, with the Java VM architecture, the .class files are cross-platform and architecture-neutral. The same .class files can be run on any computer that has a Java VM implementation. This is the "compile once, run anywhere" paradigm, revered by software professionals all over the world, and one more compelling reason for the popularity of the Java platform.

The platform-neutral, portable .class file architecture means that the Java VM's universe starts with a .class file. It knows how a .class file should look and what it can contain, but it is not concerned with which language the source was in.

NOTE   In the future, the Java VM will need to perform verification of signed classes, and as a result, the origin of the .class file will be relevant to the Java VM.

As it currently stands, any compiler can output the Java bytecodes in a .class file, and the Java VM will run the program as long as it conforms to the Java VM specification. If the output was not in the appropriate format, the Java VM would be unable to load, verify, and execute the classes.

Because the compiler does not matter to the Java VM, you can actually write for the Java VM without knowing the Java language. Extending this idea a bit further (and people are doing just that), you could write programs in a language like Ada, Visual Basic, or C, and if a compiler can generate Java bytecodes from those source files, it is effectively writing applications that will run on any Java VM. By the same token, if manufacturers want to bring new, intelligent appliances to the market, they can take advantage of the existing talent by incorporating the Java VM into the appliances with software like JavaOS or on a chip like the picoJava. See Chapter 23 for more information about JavaOS and picoJava chips.

Java VM Performance

One important issue on everybody's mind is performance. Because of the additional Java VM layer over the host operating system (compared to traditional compiled languages like C and C++), the current Java VMs are considered to be 10 to 20 times slower than native compiled code. The current version of the Java VM (1.1) has been benchmarked at roughly twice the performance of the previous version (1.0.2). There will undoubtedly be faster Java VM implementations coming along very soon (probably by the time you finish this chapter!), but for now, performance is still a legitimate concern for developers. The following sections explain some of the reasons that the Java VM is relatively slower than traditional executables. But keep in mind that there is a lot of work being done to address the issues raised here, some of which will be touched upon shortly.

The Verification Process

The verification process takes time. As a class is read in, it is verified during runtime, whereas traditional compilers perform verification processes during the compilation of the program. Also, as part of the class is executed, the Java bytecodes are converted to native machine instructions. If the same section is executed multiple times, it is converted to native instructions multiple times. It does not cache previously converted bytecodes. Additionally, as each instruction is executed, there are multiple safety checks being performed. For instance, when accessing an array element, the Java VM ensures that you are not reading past the end of it.

Instruction Size

Java instructions are all byte-sized codes. Since most operations require objects that are larger than a byte (an integer is 32 bits), multiple bytecodes would need to be read to get the various operators and their parameters.

Java as a Stack Machine

Java is implemented as a stack machine, which means that the instructions take the parameters from the operand stack and return the results to the stack. This is due to the fact that the Java VM does not assume any particular CPU architecture, including the word size and register combinations. Many of the intended applications might run on systems with only a few registers, or none at all.

Normally, compiled programs use very fast register operations, and the parameters needed for an operation are available in the CPU registers most, if not all, of the time. Because registers are in the CPU while a stack is in the main memory, register operations are many times faster than stack operations. Also, traditional compilers perform many types of code optimization during compilation, including operation optimization where the results of operations are kept in registers and subsequent operations access the results of previous operations from the registers.

NOTE The Java VM implementor has the freedom and latitude to optimize the system for the target hardware and operating system. The implementation can be fine-tuned to exploit the target system's strengths and compensate for the target system's weaknesses or limited resources. For example, the stack machine can be implemented with the stack-caching technique (which emulates a stack with CPU registers) for a CPU that has registers like the Pentium or the UltraSparc chip.

Garbage Collection by the System

The system performs automatic garbage collection for you, which inevitably impacts performance since everything must stop when the garbage collector runs. Automatic garbage collection is covered in more detail later in the chapter.

The Java VM Architecture

The Java VM specification describes all of the required elements needed for a Java VM architecture using the following elements:

- Datatypes
- Instruction set
- Class file format
- Registers
- Method area
- Operand stack
- Garbage-collected heap

Figure 17.2 shows the major modules of a Java VM and how they fit in with the host operating system and hardware.

FIGURE 17.2

Main elements of the Java VM

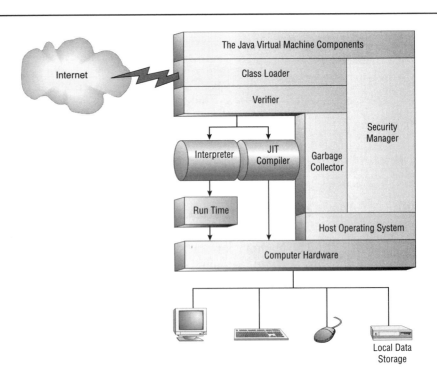

TIP

Sun is the keeper of the Java VM specification. The complete specification can be found in a book called *The Java Virtual Machine Specification*, published by Addison Wesley. As the Java VM matures, Sun promises any changes will not break past implementations. To ensure compliance with the specification, Sun maintains a compatibility suite. If a vendor implements its own Java VM and it passes the compatibility suite, it gets Sun's blessing, is deemed compatible, and boasts that it is "Java Compatible." (The licensing details are discussed later in the chapter.) If you have any additional comments or concerns regarding the Java VM, you can send them to jvm@javasoft.com.

Datatypes Supported by the Java VM

Table 17.1 lists the datatypes supported by the Java VM. Integers are implemented as 32-bit sized and floating points in the IEEE 754 format. The sizes of all datatypes are the same across all operating systems and hardware. The implementor does not have the latitude to change the datatypes. Arrays of all the datatypes, including objects, are possible. In fact, the arrays themselves are implemented as objects.

TABLE 17.1   Java VM Datatypes

Type	Size	Description
byte	1 byte	Signed 2's complement integer
short	2 bytes	Signed 2's complement integer
int	4 bytes	Signed 2's complement integer
long	8 bytes	Signed 2's complement integer
float	4 bytes	IEEE 754 single-precision float
double	8 bytes	IEEE 754 double-precision float
char	2 bytes	Unsigned Unicode character
object	4 bytes	Reference to a Java object; called a handle
returnAddress	4 bytes	Used with jsr/ret/jsr_w/ret_w (jump subroutine and return from subroutine) instructions

The Java VM Instruction Set

The Java VM has roughly 220 instructions. These instructions are normal machine code types of instructions for loading variables, branching, arithmetic operations, stack manipulation, and so on. Each instruction consists of an instruction code called the *opcode*, which is 8 bits, and a variable set of operands, which are operated out of the stack. This means that the operations pull their operands from the operand stack and push the results back into the stack.

Even though Java VM assumes a 32-bit platform, the implementor has the choice to optimize for a larger word size machine/operating system, like a 64-bit Windows NT system. All operands are stored as one byte long in the class file, so to make a 16- or 32-bit operand, multiple operands are combined in big-endian (memory), or network, order.

> **NOTE**
> Big-endian ordering is also called network ordering. In big-endian ordering, high bytes of a word are stored first in memory; for example, 0x1234 will be stored in memory as 0x12 0x34 (the big end comes first). RISC and Motorola processors use big-endian byte ordering. The Intel 80x86 processors use the little-endian byte ordering. In the little-endian ordering, the word will be stored as 0x34 0x12 in memory (the little end comes first).

As an opcode example, take a look at the most fundamental operation that computers are good at: addition. The addition of two numbers is achieved in the Java VM by the opcodes `iadd (96)` for the integer type, `ladd (97)` for adding two long integers, `fadd (98)` for adding two numbers of float type, and `dadd (99)` for adding two numbers of double type.

> **NOTE**
> In the example `iadd (96)`, `iadd` is the mnemonic used for the description in the Java VM specification and `96` is the actual opcode stored in the .class file representing the `iadd` operation.

Figure 17.3 shows a schematic diagram of the `iadd` operation. You can see that the operand stack contains the first and second (32-bit) numbers to be added. The Java VM will add the two numbers at the top of the stack. At the end of the operation, the result will be pushed onto the stack. Opcodes `96` through `131` perform the addition (`.add`), subtraction (`.sub`), multiplication (`.mul`), division (`.div`), modulo (`.mod`), negation (`.neg`), and other operations in a similar manner.

FIGURE 17.3

How the Java VM's iadd operation works

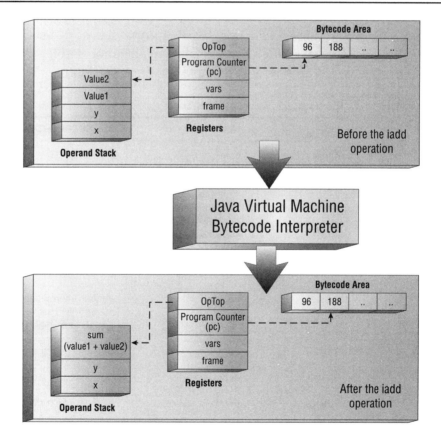

Another example is the opcodes for array manipulation. To create an array, the new array (`188`) opcode is used. This opcode requires the array type as a parameter and the array size in the operand stack. The Java VM then allocates enough space for the array, initializes all elements to zero, and returns the reference handle at the top of the stack.

Class File Format

As explained earlier, the Java compiler converts the Java source code into the .class file. Each source file will have one corresponding .class file. This file is a stream of bytes, and each byte is 8 bits long. Bigger entities of 16 or 32 bits are constructed by reading in 2 or 4 bytes in the big-endian, or network, format. Table 17.2 lists the major elements in a .class file. (For a detailed explanation and the underlying data structures, refer to the Java VM specification.)

TABLE 17.2 Class File Format

Size	Name	Default/Value/Description
4 bytes	magic	OxCAFEBABE
2 bytes	minor_version	Minor version of the Java compiler
2 bytes	major_version	Major version of the Java compiler
2 bytes	constant_pool_count	Number of constant pool info variables in following field
variable	Constant pool info	Constant pool information (constant_pool_count-1)
2 bytes	access_flags	Various information flag bits. For example, 0x0100 means it is a native method or 0x0010 means it is a final class, method, variable
2 bytes	this_class	Constant pool index to this class
2 bytes	super_class	Constant pool index to the superclass if one exists
2 bytes	interface_count	Number of interface variables in following field
2 × interface_count	interfaces	Index to constant pool for each interface
2 bytes	fields_count	Number of fields variables in following field

TABLE 17.2   Class File Format (Continued)

Size	Name	Default/Value/Description
variable	fields	Information on all fields, including index to constant pool
2 bytes	method_count	Number of methods
variable	methods	Information on each method
2 bytes	attributes_count	Number of additional attributes about this class
variable	attributes	Extra attributes about this class

NOTE The current Java VM specification supports only the source file attribute. The attributes_count field will contain the number 1. The attributes data structure contains a two-byte constant pool index, which is "SourceFile," and a four-byte attribute length, which is 2. The "SourceFile" constant pool index points to the constant, where the name of the source file, from which this class file was compiled, is kept.

Registers

The Java VM requires four 32-bit registers:

pc   Program counter register, which contains the address of the next bytecode instruction.

frame   Pointer to the method area of the method that is being executed.

vars   Local variables pointer.

optop   Top of the operand stack pointer.

Method Area

The Java VM specification gives each method invocation its own space for local variables, symbol tables, and so on.

The detailed information about each method is found in the .class file on the methods structure (with the name CODE). This information includes the maximum stack size, local variable size, the byte-code length, the actual bytecodes, and exception details. Also, this area has the `LineNumberTable` and `LocalVariable` table for debugging. The Java VM creates an area to store the transient data and execute the method.

Operand Stack

As you have seen, the instructions need an operand stack to pop parameters and push the operation results. The operand stack is 32 bits wide.

The instructions can perform only the specified operations on the stack. For example, the `iadd` instruction can pop two 32-bit numbers from the stack and should push a 32-bit number back after the operation. It cannot join two 32-bit numbers and form a 64-bit number or push two numbers into the stack. The bytecode verifier will catch such misbehaved operations and will raise an error.

Garbage-Collected Heap

The garbarge-collected heap is where the objects are created during the program execution. Each object in a Java program has a 32-bit pointer to the heap. This limits the maximum heap size to 4GB of memory.

As explained earlier, arrays are also implemented as objects, and the space for arrays is allocated in this heap. This heap is garbage-collected automatically by the Java VM.

Java VM Automatic Garbage Collection

The Java VM automatically performs garbage collection to free resources. The Java VM specification does not specify any garbage-collection schemes or algorithms. Instead, it relies on the implementor to research and develop an efficient and appropriate garbage-collection algorithm.

Because the Java language has no constructs for freeing memory, deleting objects, and performing other similar tasks, it is the responsibility of the garbage collector to reclaim discarded memory.

The Java VM specification does not guarantee any timing on the garbage collection, so a Java programmer cannot assume that unused memory will be available immediately after an object ceases to exist in the program. The implication is that you should be careful when developing memory-hungry programs that declare and use objects with large data structures. Even though memory used by a huge data structure will be reclaimed when the structure is discarded, you should not declare another huge structure immediately, especially when there is not enough memory space for both structures (and you need huge arrays for multimedia types of data). Similarly, when you pack linked lists and other structures, you should not assume that the memory freed by the packing routines will be available immediately.

NOTE Runtime automatic garbage collection is not a new concept. During the creation and runtime redimensioning of arrays, the Microsoft Visual Basic memory management is one very efficient runtime implementation of garbage collection. The Microsoft implementation of garbage collection in Basic runtime was a point of discussion for many years by programmers, particularly among beta testers. Usually, a bug in the memory management and garbage collection would manifest itself as the dreaded general protection faults (GPFs) in the Windows environment. The memory allocation and deallocation techniques have matured over the years through many versions of the product.

Java VM Security

The compiled Java bytecode does not contain any absolute memory references or addresses. Gone are the days of Poke and Peek, or defining arrays at absolute memory references like 0xB8000 (which is the memory reference for the display buffer in IBM PC-compatible display cards). The Java VM handles the memory allocation and referencing.

As mentioned earlier, you can create bytecodes directly, without a compiler, or you can write a compiler to generate bytecodes that could possibly snoop around the system, causing security risks. This is guarded by the bytecode verifier. Before the code is run for the first time, the bytecode verifier checks the bytecodes fully for things like mismatched parameters, bypassing access restrictions, and so on.

To prevent valid bytecode programs from causing damage, such as deleting all files, corrupting hard disks, or sending local information across the network without permission from the user, the Java VM can have user-configurable access restrictions, such as deny local write, deny network access to other sites, and a host of others.

Most of the security measures rely upon a virus-free Java VM. Obviously the security measures cannot prevent a faulty or Trojan horse–type Java VM from causing damage. If you download a Java VM that has viruses built into it, there is no safeguard. So, if you glean only one thing from this section, let it be that the Java VM should be acquired very carefully. Be extremely careful when you are downloading a Java VM environment. Established vendors like Sun, Symantec, and Microsoft check their Java VMs thoroughly, and these are usually safe to download and operate. (There are known instances of major software companies having released viruses on their commercial releases.) The Java VM is similar to an operating system and should be given the same considerations. Obtaining a secure Java VM from an established vendor is the first line of defense against virus-ridden Java programs.

We are entering an era of encrypted, authenticated, and secure Java VMs and Java applets. All companies, including Microsoft and Sun, are working on public-key/certificate-encrypted delivery systems and signed classes. With signed applets, another level of trust is added.

Among the many levels of security, the two major mechanisms are the `SecurityManager` and the Java class file verifier. These are discussed in the next sections.

Java's SecurityManager

The `SecurityManager` acts as the enforcer of security. It is an extensible class, thus providing application or system-specific added security implementations. It implements the security envelope and policies configured in the Java VM/browser setup. The `SecurityManager` establishes a namespace for the Java program that can restrict access to network, local file system, and other parts of the program.

NOTE A namespace is the boundary for a program established by the operating system or, here, by the Java VM. A program cannot access resources beyond its own namespace.

Applet Security

The `SecurityManager` policies are configurable for an applet loaded through a Web browser. In the most common security scheme (used by Netscape Navigator), an applet downloaded from the network can load class files only from the same source as the code requesting the class. These are called *untrusted applets.* If untrusted applets try to access local storage or to communicate with some other server in the Internet, the `SecurityManager` will generate a security exception. An applet loaded from the local hard disk can be allowed full access to all resources, at which point the `SecurityManager` will allow the applets loaded locally to access local resources and connect to remote servers.

The use of digitally signed applets, called *signed classes*, is an important development in the area of security. In this security system, the user can configure a table of trusted entities. The table contains certificates, digital signatures, and other related material for identifying the entity, and all entities sign the Java applets/classes that they develop. The `SecurityManager` can allow more privileges to classes developed by trusted entities. If it is verified that the applet is signed by Microsoft, it can be given wider namespace than an untrusted applet downloaded from http://www.virus.com. The signed class architecture can be applied to applets as well as Java applications, which ensures that security policies will be uniform across Web browsers and applications.

Application Security

In the case of Java applications, there are no default security restrictions—all local and remote resource accesses are open to Java applications. However, security may be implemented with the extensible `Security` class. It is therefore the responsibility of the application programmer to implement the `SecurityManager` methods required by an application.

The Java Verifier

The Java verifier runs on a .class file and performs the security function to make sure that the Java bytecodes comply with the Java VM specification. The bytecode verifier is one of the many levels of security assurance by the Java platform to check that viruses and other malicious programs will not wreak havoc on the local system.

The verifier looks for syntax and semantic correctness of the class files, performs version and API conformance checking, and so on. Obviously, this is done before executing the Java program. Among other things, the verifier protects against compiler bugs and the intentional addition of malicious bytecodes. Overflow and underflow of values during arithmetic operations are identified during the verifier check run. Also, many other runtime checks are done by the verifier, thus making the Java Interpreter run faster.

> **NOTE** As mentioned earlier, you really do not need the Java language for the Java VM—a C++ or a BASIC compiler can generate Java bytecodes; however, it is the function of the verifier to make sure the generated bytecodes are executable safely and securely.

The verifier is implemented as a four-pass operation:

Pass 1, class file verification   This pass verifies the class file structure. The first four bytes should be 0xCAFEBABE. It also checks that the file does not contain any extra bytes at the end, and runs the class file structure verification.

Pass 2, type system verification   This pass, as the name indicates, does system-level verifications, such as valid subclassing, valid constant, and pool pointers.

Pass 3, bytecode verification   This pass does an exhaustive analysis of the actual bytecodes for each method, including operand stack analysis, method argument validation, and variable initialization.

Pass 4, runtime type and access checking   The final pass is where many runtime checks and associations are done. By the time this pass is invoked, the system knows the methods, parameters, and return values. During this pass, it checks their validity and does runtime optimization, such as replacing indirect references with direct references. Also, in this pass, the access levels for the variables and methods are verified. For example, it verifies that the bytecodes were not tweaked to provide access to private/protected variables/methods, and so on. This pass can be optimized by the Java VM implementor.

The verifier is the target of many virus attacks, so this process should be very thorough and fully tested. If a bug or a malicious operation passes the verifier, it could damage the system by deleting files or compromising the security.

Just-In-Time (JIT) Compilers

It is no secret that the Java VM is slower in performance than traditional compiled languages. The JIT compiler is a technique currently available and being developed by Symantec, Borland, Sun, and Microsoft, among others, that greatly improves performance. The JIT compiler translates the bytecode to native machine code just before execution, so you get a bytecode compiler instead of an interpreter. It provides portability without sacrificing speed.

For example, Symantec Café has a JIT for the Apple Macintosh and 68K platform. Symantec claims that its JIT provides significant performance improvements when running Java-powered applets on the Macintosh. Applets run up to three times faster when compared to Sun's current Java VM for the Macintosh. Symantec's JIT compiler for Windows is also many times faster than Sun's current Java VM.

The Microsoft JIT compiler, which comes with Microsoft's Visual J++ Java development system, reads and compiles the bytecodes to machine code and then keeps a pointer to the compiled code with the bytecode in the method area. This means that when the bytecode is to be executed again (which happens most of the time; programs consist of do and for loops), it need not go through the JIT. It is rumored that Microsoft might even develop an executable generator for Java programs on Microsoft platforms.

Borland's JIT Java AppAccelerator is an integral part of Navigator 3.0. The AppAccelerator makes Java applications run five to fifteen times faster than the native interpreted code. With the Netscape

Communicator line of Internet and networking tools, the Symantec JIT compiler has been adopted, and it appears in Navigator 4.0 and later.

For Unix and Solaris, Sun has developed its own JIT compiler to increase the execution speed of Java on those platforms.

Most probably, a JIT compiler will become an integral part of the Java VM in the future, thus alleviating any performance concerns. This part of the VM would be supplied by the vendor of the VM or browser, because the JIT compiler will produce machine code specific to that platform. JavaSoft is committed to platform-independent bytecode and the flexibility it provides.

Java Licensing

Every day, there is more news about companies licensing Java. Almost all of the major companies, including Apple, IBM, Microsoft, Novell, and Hewlett-Packard have licensed Java. What are they getting for their license? More important, as a developer, what is its significance?

The standard JavaSoft license covers the Java class libraries and the Java VM. Each vendor will then become the custodian of Java on its platform, optimizing the engine for system performance and ensuring that Java applets, which are intended to be platform independent, run just as well on their systems as they do on others. The contracts also require licensees to add all future Java APIs into their implementations.

Microsoft's Java VM implementation is as a 32-bit operating system DLL (dynamic-link library) on NT and Windows 95. This is called the Windows Virtual Machine for Java. As a DLL, it acts as an operating system extension, so Java is available from all Windows applications. Microsoft has licensed the Windows Virtual Machine for Java back to Sun as a reference implementation for the Windows platform.

Apple is getting its Java VM from a third-party vendor and may possibly build one later. Apple's Newton and Pippin are covered under the Java license. Novell has licensed to embed the Java VM into the Novell NetWare, which will add Java capabilities to NetWare servers and clients, while providing capabilities for the distributed network services to create distributed applications for the Smart Global Network.

IBM is the first to include the Java VM in its latest desktop operating system, code named Merlin and released as OS/2 Warp version 4.0. This operating system is Java-enabled right out of the box; applets or applications loaded over the network can be run without the aid of a browser or Java runtime. This may be the shape of desktop operating systems to come.

There are two types of licensable logos from Sun related to Java (although one can assume that there will be more coming later):

- The "Java Powered" Logo (no license fees) for applets and programs, which are developed using the Java language and unmodified Java binaries

- The "Java Compatible" Logo for OEMs who integrate the Java VM

A clean room Java VM implementation would successfully complete the Java Test Suites and should maintain applet API compatibility on all platforms. There is no logo for this compliance.

NOTE A clean room implementation is a Java VM designed and programmed from scratch. "Clean room" implies that the design and implementation are done without copying or reverse-engineering any of JavaSoft's Java VM.

Summary

You can see how the Java VM concept and the design of its elements, like the verifier and `SecurityManager`, have aided the advancement of the current Internet/Intranet frenzy. The Java VM has truly marshaled us into the next era of computing. As the technology matures, there will be more efficient implementations to better address the performance and security issues.

CHAPTER

EIGHTEEN

Java Database Connectivity (JDBC)

- Two- and three-tier database design

- The JDBC API

- A sample Java database application

- Types of JDBC drivers

- RMI and CORBA as alternative connectivity strategies

In the information age, the database is a tool used to collect and manipulate data. The database forms the foundation of the infrastructure of many companies. While the database system is well-suited to the storage and retrieval of data, human beings need some sort of front-end application in order to see and use the data stored.

The problem is complicated by the heterogeneous nature of the computers in most companies. The art and marketing departments have Macintosh systems, the engineers have high-end Unix workstations, and the sales people are using PCs. In order to expose the data in the database, developers must consider all of the various permutations of systems on which they wish to deploy.

This chapter will look at Java as the way to solve the Tower of Babel of database front ends, by providing a single and consistent application programming interface: the Java Database Connectivity (JDBC) API.

Java as a Database Front End

Java offers several benefits to the developer creating a front-end application for a database server. Java is a "write once, run anywhere" language. This means that Java programs may be deployed without change on any of the computer architectures and operating systems that run the Java VM. For large corporations, just having a common development platform is a big savings: No longer are programmers required to write to the many platforms a large corporation may have. Java is also attractive to third-party developers—a single Java program can answer the needs of a large corporate customer.

In addition, there is a cost associated with the deployment and maintenance of the hardware and software of any system (client) the corporation owns. Systems such as Windows PCs, Macintoshes, and Unix desktop-centric clients (*fat clients*) can cost corporations between $10,000 and $15,000 per installation seat. Java technology now makes it possible for any company to use a smaller system footprint. These systems are based on a Java chip set and can run any and all Java programs from a built-in Java operating system.

Java-based clients (*thin clients*) that operate with a minimum of hard resources and yet run the complete Java environment are expected to cost less than $2,500 per seat. According to various studies, the savings for a corporation moving 10,000 fat client systems to thin clients could be as much as $100 million annually.

It follows, then, that the incentive to create Java-based applications and applets for corporate systems is high. Corporations are extremely interested in shifting their applications from architecture- and operating-system-specific models to network-centric models. Java represents a long-term strategy in saving resource costs.

For the developer, Java represents a huge market opportunity. There are very few medium-to-large organizations that do not use databases for some portion of their business operation; most use databases for *every* aspect of their business, from human resources to front-line customer sales.

Database Designs for Client/Server Systems

The evolution of relational data storage began in 1970 with the work of Dr. E. F. Codd, who proposed a set of 12 rules for identifying relationships between pieces of data. Codd's rules for relational modeling of data formed the basis for the development of systems to manage data. Today, Relational Database Management Systems (RDBMS) are the result of Codd's vision.

Data in an RDBMS is stored as rows of distinct information in tables. A structured language is used to query (retrieve), store, and change the data. The Structured Query Language (SQL) is an ANSI standard, and all major commercial RDBMS vendors provide mechanisms for issuing SQL commands.

The early development of RDBMS applications was based on an integrated model of user interface code, application code, and database libraries. This single binary model ran only on a local machine, typically a mainframe. The applications were simple but inefficient, and did not work over local-area networks. The model did not scale, and the application and user interface code were tightly coupled to the database libraries. Furthermore, the monolithic approach did not allow multiple instances of the application to communicate with *each other*, so there was often contention between instances of the application. Figure 18.1 illustrates the monolithic, single-tier database design.

FIGURE 18.1

The monolithic, single-tier database design

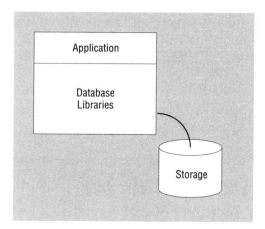

The terms RDBMS and DBMS (Database Management System) are often used interchangeably, because almost all major commercial databases are relational and support some form of SQL to allow the user to query the relations between data tables.

Two-Tier Database Design

Two-tier models appeared with the advent of server technology. Communication protocol development and extensive use of local- and wide-area networks allowed the database developer to create an application front end that accessed data through a connection (*socket*) to the back-end server. Figure 18.2 illustrates a two-tier database design, where the client software is connected to the database through a socket connection.

FIGURE 18.2

The two-tier database design

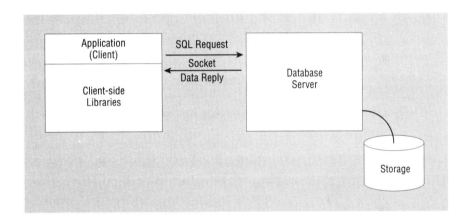

Client programs (supplying a user interface) send SQL requests to the database server. The server returns the appropriate results, and the client is responsible for formatting the data. Clients still use a vendor-provided library of functions that manage the communication between client and server. Most of these libraries are written in the C language.

Commercial database vendors realized the potential for adding intelligence to the database server. They created proprietary techniques that allowed the database designer to develop macro programs for simple data manipulation. These macros, called *stored procedures*, can cause problems relating to version control and maintenance. Because a stored procedure is an executable program residing on the database, it is possible for the stored procedure to attempt to access named columns of a database table when the table has been changed. For example, if the name of the `id` column is changed to `cust_id`, the meaning of the original stored procedure is lost. The use of *triggers*, which are stored procedures executed automatically in response to some action with a particular table or tables, can compound these difficulties when the data returned from a query is not expected. Again, this can be the result of the trigger reading a table column that has been altered.

Despite the success of client/server architectures, two-tier database models suffer a number of limitations:

- They are limited by the vendor-provided library. Switching from one database vendor to another requires rewriting a significant amount of code for the client application.

- Version control is an issue. When the vendor updates the client-side libraries, the applications that use the database must be recompiled and redistributed.

- Vendor libraries deal with low-level data manipulation. Typically, the base library deals with only fetches and updates on single rows or columns of data. This can be enhanced on the server side by creating a stored procedure, but this increases the complexity of the system.

- All of the intelligence associated with using and manipulating the data is implemented in the client application, creating large client-side runtimes. This drives up the cost of each client seat.

Three-Tier Database Design

Today, there is a great deal of interest in multitier design. The design is not limited to three tiers, but conceptually this is the next step. In a multitier design, the client communicates with an intermediate server that provides a layer of abstraction from the RDBMS. Figure 18.3 illustrates a three-tier database design.

FIGURE 18.3

A three-tier database
design

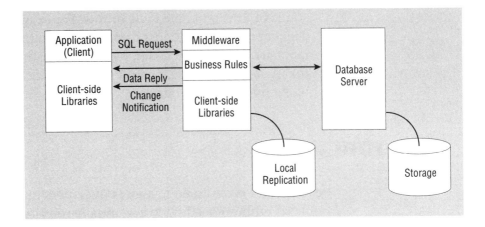

The intermediate layer is designed to handle multiple client
requests and manage the connection to one or more database servers.
The intermediate-tier design provides several advantages over the
two-tier design. The middle tier has the following benefits:

- It is multithreaded to manage multiple client connections
  simultaneously.

- This tier can accept connections from clients on a variety of
  vendor-neutral protocols (from HTTP to TCP/IP), then marshal
  the requests to the appropriate vendor-specific database servers
  and return the replies to the appropriate clients.

- The designer can program the middle tier with a set of "business
  rules" that manage the manipulation of the data. Business rules
  may include anything from restricting access to certain portions
  of data to making sure that data is properly formatted before
  being inserted or updated. Furthermore, because the client
  application is isolated from the database system, a company can
  switch database systems without needing to rework the business rules.

- By centralizing process-intensive tasks and abstracting data representation to a higher level, the use of an intermediate tier prevents the client from becoming too heavy.

- The middle tier can asynchronously provide the client with a status of a current data table or row. For example, suppose that a client application had just completed a query of a particular table. If a subsequent action by another distinct client *changed* that data, the first client could receive notification from an intelligent middle-tier program.

The JDBC API

The JDBC API is designed to allow developers to create database front ends without needing to continually rewrite their code. Despite standards set by the ANSI committee, each database system vendor has a unique way of connecting and, in some cases, communicating with its system.

The ability to create robust, platform-independent applications and Web-based applets prompted developers to consider using Java to develop front-end connectivity solutions. At the outset, third-party software developers met the need by providing proprietary solutions, by using native methods to integrate client-side libraries, or by creating a third tier and a new protocol.

JavaSoft worked in conjunction with database and database-tool vendors to create a DBMS-independent mechanism that would allow developers to write their client-side applications without concern for the particular database being used. The result is the JDBC API.

How JDBC Works

JDBC provides application developers with a *single* API that is uniform and database independent. The API provides a standard to write to, and a standard that takes all of the various application designs into account. The solution is a set of Java interfaces that are implemented by a driver. The driver translates the standard JDBC calls into the specific calls required by the database it supports. The application can be written once and moved to the various drivers. The application remains the same; the drivers change. Drivers may be used to develop the middle tier of a multitier database design, also known as *middleware*. Both of these designs are illustrated in Figure 18.4.

FIGURE 18.4

JDBC database designs

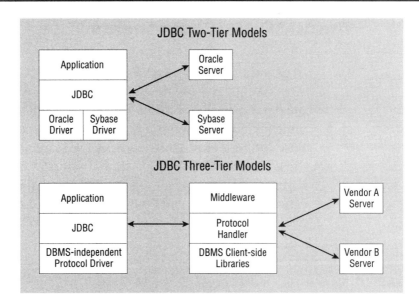

In addition to providing developers with a uniform and DBMS-independent framework, JDBC also provides a means of allowing developers to retain the specific functionality that their database vendor offers. JDBC drivers must support ANSI SQL-2 Entry Level, but JDBC allows developers to pass query strings directly to the connected driver. These strings may or may not be ANSI SQL, or SQL at all. The use of these strings is up to the underlying driver. (Of course, use of this feature limits the freedom of the application developer to change database back ends.)

JDBC is *not* a derivative of Microsoft's Open Database Connectivity (ODBC) specification. JDBC is written entirely in Java; ODBC is a C interface. However, both JDBC and ODBC are based on the X/Open

SQL Command Level Interface (CLI). Having the same conceptual base allows work on the API to proceed quickly and makes acceptance of the API easier. JavaSoft provides a JDBC-ODBC bridge that translates JDBC to ODBC. This implementation, done with native methods, is very small and efficient. The JDBC-ODBC bridge is discussed in more detail later in the chapter.

The JDBC API Components

In general, there are two levels of interface in the JDBC API: the Application layer, where the developer uses the API to make calls to the database via SQL and retrieve the results, and the Driver layer, which handles all communication with a specific driver implementation. Although the driver vendors are responsible for implementing the Driver layer, it is important to understand how this layer works, if only to realize that some of the objects that are used at the Application layer are created by the driver. Figure 18.5 illustrates the connection between the Driver and Application layers.

FIGURE 18.5

JDBC API components

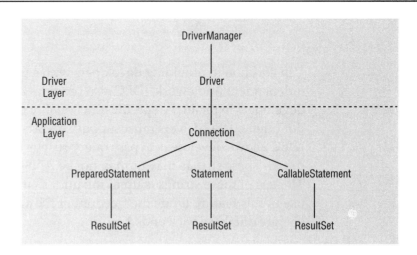

Fortunately, the application developer needs to use only the standard API interfaces in order to guarantee JDBC compliance. The driver developer is responsible for developing code that interfaces to the database and supports the JDBC Application level calls.

There are four main interfaces that every Driver layer must implement, and one class that bridges the Application and Driver layers. The four interfaces are the `Driver, Connection, Statement`, and `ResultSet`. The `Driver` interface implementation is where the connection to the database is made. In most applications, the `Driver` is accessed through the `DriverManager` class, providing one more layer of abstraction for the developer.

The `Connection, Statement`, and `ResultSet` interfaces are implemented by the driver vendor. These interfaces represent the methods that the application developer will treat as real object classes and allow the developer to create statements and retrieve results. The distinction made here between Driver and Application layers is artificial, but it allows the developer to create database applications without needing to think about where the objects are coming from or worry about what specific driver the application will use.

The Driver Layer

There is a one-to-one correspondence between the database and the JDBC driver. This approach is common in multitier designs. The `Driver` class is an interface implemented by the driver vendor. The other important class is the `DriverManager` class, which sits between the Driver and Application layers. The `DriverManager` is responsible for loading and unloading drivers and making connections through drivers. The `DriverManager` also provides features for logging and database login timeouts.

> **NOTE** As shown earlier in Figure 18.4, the driver does not need to connect directly to a database and can support a new protocol for a multitier database design.

The Driver Interface   Every JDBC application or applet must have at least one JDBC driver, and each driver is specific to the type of DBMS used. A driver does not, however, need to be directly associated with a database. The `Driver` interface allows the `Driver-Manager` and JDBC Application layer to exist independently of the particular database used. A JDBC driver is an implementation of the `Driver` interface class.

Drivers use a string to locate and access databases. The syntax of this string is very similar to a URL string. The purpose of a JDBC URL string is to separate the application developer from the driver developer. JavaSoft defines the following goals for driver URLs:

- The name of the driver-access URL should define the type of database being used.

- The user (application developer) should be free from any of the administration of creating the database connection; therefore, any database connection information (host, port, database name, user access, and passwords) should be encoded in the URL.

- A network naming system may be used in order to prevent the user from needing to specifically encode the exact host name and port number of the database.

The URL syntax used by the World Wide Web supports a standard syntax that satisfies these goals. JDBC URLs have the following syntax and structure:

```
jdbc:<subprotocol>:<subname>
```

where `<subprotocol>` defines the type of driver, and `<subname>` provides the network encoded name—for example:

```
jdbc:oracle:products
```

Here, the database driver is an Oracle driver and the subname is a local database called `products`. This driver is designed to know how to use the subname when making the connection to the Oracle database.

A network naming service may also be specified as the subprotocol, rather than using a specific database driver name. In this case, the subprotocol would define the naming service:

```
jdbc: localnaming:human-resources
```

Here, the subprotocol defines a local service that can resolve the subname human-resources to a database server. This approach can be useful when the application developer wants to isolate the user from the actual location, name, database username, and database password. This URL specifies that a driver named localnaming be specified; this could be a Java program that contains a simple flat-file lookup, translates human-resources into hrdatabase1.eng:888/personnel, and knows to use the username user and password "matilda." The details of the connection are kept hidden from the user.

Typically, the application developer will know specifically where the database is located and may not wish to use network indirection to locate the database. In this case, the URL may be expanded to include the location of the host and specific port and database information:

```
jdbc:msql://dbserver.eng:1112/bugreports
```

Here, an msql database driver type is to locate a server named dbserver in the eng domain and attempt to connect to a database server on port 1112 that contains a bugreports database, using the default username and password to connect.

> **NOTE** Subprotocol names will eventually overlap, and there will need to be a registry of reserved names. For more information about registering a JDBC subprotocol name, consult the JDBC Specification.

The `Driver` interface is implemented by the driver vendor by creating methods for each of the following interface methods.

Signature: `interface java.sql.Driver`

`public abstract Connection connect (String url, Properties info) throws SQLException` The driver implementation of this method should check the subprotocol name of the URL string passed for a match with this driver. If there is a match, the driver should then attempt to make a connection to the database using the information passed in the remainder of the URL. A successful database connection will return an instance of the driver's implementation of a `Connection` interface (object). The `SQLException` should be thrown only if the driver recognizes the URL subprotocol but cannot make the database connection. A null is returned if the URL does not match a URL the driver expected. The username and password are included in a container class called `Properties`.

`public abstract boolean acceptsURL (String url) throws SQLException` It is also possible to explicitly "ask" the driver if the URL is valid, but note that the implementation of this method (typically) checks only the subprotocol specified in the URL, not whether the connection can be made.

The `Driver connect()` method is the most important method, and it is called by the `DriverManager` to obtain a `Connection` object. As shown earlier in Figure 18.5, the `Connection` object is the starting point of the JDBC Application layer. The `Connection` object is used to create `Statement` objects that perform queries.

The `Driver connect()` method typically performs the following steps:

- Checks to see if the given URL string is valid.
- Opens a TCP connection to the host and port number specified.
- Attempts to access the named database table (if any).
- Returns an instance of a `Connection` object.

> **NOTE**
>
> `Connection` is a Java interface, so the object returned is actually a reference to an instance of the driver's implementation of the `Connection` interface.

The DriverManager Class   The `DriverManager` class is actually a utility class used to manage JDBC drivers. The class provides methods to obtain a connection through a driver, register and deregister drivers, set up logging, and set login timeouts for database access. All of the methods in the `DriverManager` class listed below are static and may be referenced through the following class name:

```
public class java.sql.DriverManager
  public static synchronized Connection getConnection
  (String url, Properties info) throws SQLException
```
This method (and the other `getConnection()` methods) attempts to return a reference to an object implemented from the `Connection` interface. The method sweeps through a vector of stored `Driver` classes, passing the URL string and `Properties` object `info` to each in turn. The first `Driver` class that returns a `Connection` is used. `info` is a reference to a `Properties` container object of tag/value pairs, typically username/password. This method allows several attempts to make an authorized connection for each driver in the vector.

```
  public static synchronized Connection getConnection
  (String url) throws SQLException
```
This method calls `getConnection (url, info)` with an empty `Properties` object (`info`).

```
  public static synchronized Connection getConnection
  (String url, String user, String password) throws
  SQLException
```
This method creates a `Properties` object (`info`), stores the user and password strings into it, and then calls `getConnection (url, info)`.

public static synchronized void registerDriver(java
.sql.Driver driver) throws SQLException This method
stores the instance of the Driver interface implementation into a
vector of drivers, along with an instance of securityContext,
which identifies where the driver came from.

public static void setLogStream(java.io.PrintStream
out) This method sets a private, static java.io.PrintStream
reference to the PrintStream object passed to the method.

TIP

The driver implementation can make use of two static object references that are stored through set*Type* methods and accessed
by the driver through get*Type* methods: an integer that specifies
a login timeout and a PrintStream object used to log driver
information.

Drivers are registered with the DriverManager class, either at
initialization of the DriverManager class or when an instance of the
driver is created.

When the DriverManager class is loaded, a section of static code
(in the class) is run, and the class names of drivers listed in a Java
property named jdbc.drivers are loaded. This property can be
used to define a list of colon-separated driver class names, such as:

```
jdbc.drivers=imaginary.sql.Driver:oracle.sql.Driver:weblogic
.sql.Driver
```

Each driver name is a class filename (including the package declaration) that the DriverManager will attempt to load through the current CLASSPATH. The DriverManager uses the following call to
locate, load, and link the named class:

```
Class.forName(driver);
```

If the jdbc.drivers property is empty (unspecified), the application programmer must create an instance of a driver class.

In both cases, the `Driver` class implementation must explicitly register itself with the `DriverManager` by calling:

```
DriverManager.registerDriver (this);
```

Here is a segment of code from the imaginary `Driver` (for the Mini-SQL database). The `Driver` registers itself whenever an instance of the imaginary driver is created:

```
...
public class iMsqlDriver implements java.sql.Driver {
 static {
  try {
   new iMsqlDriver();
  }
  catch( SQLException e ) {
   e.printStackTrace();
  }
 }
 /**
  * Constructs a new driver and registers it with
  * java.sql.DriverManager.registerDriver() as specified
  * by the JDBC draft protocol.
  */
 public iMsqlDriver() throws SQLException {
  java.sql.DriverManager.registerDriver(this);
 }
...
```

The primary use of the `DriverManager` is to get a `Connection` object reference through the `getConnection` method:

```
Connection conn = null;
conn = DriverManager.getConnection ("jdbc:sybase://dbserver:
➥8080/billing", dbuser, dbpasswd);
```

This method goes through the list of registered drivers and passes the URL string and parameters to each driver in turn through the driver's `connect()` method. If the driver supports the subprotocol and subname information, a `Connection` object reference is returned.

The `DriverManager` class is not required to create JDBC applications; it is possible to get a `Connection` object directly from the `Driver`:

```
Connection conn = null;
conn = new Driver().connect("jdbc:sybase://dbserver:8080/billing",
➥props);
```

This means of obtaining a connection is not as clean and leaves the application developer dependent on the `Driver` implementation class to provide security checks.

The Application Layer

The Application layer encompasses three interfaces that are implemented at the Driver layer but are used by the application developer. In Java, the interface provides a means of using a general name to indicate a specific object. The general name defines methods that *must* be implemented by the specific object classes. For the application developer, this means that the specific `Driver` class implementation is irrelevant. Just coding to the standard JDBC APIs will be sufficient (assuming that the driver is JDBC compliant—that the database is at least ANSI SQL-2 Entry Level).

The three main interfaces are `Connection`, `Statement`, and `ResultSet`. A `Connection` object is obtained from the driver implementation through the `DriverManager.getConnection()` method call. Once a `Connection` object is returned, the application developer may create a `Statement` object to issue against the database. The result of a `Statement` is a `ResultSet` object, which contains the results of the particular statement (if any).

Connection Basics   The `Connection` interface represents a session with the database connection provided by the `Driver`. Typical database connections include the ability to control changes made to the actual data stored through transactions. On creation, JDBC `Connections` are in an *auto-commit* mode—there is no rollback possible. Therefore, after getting a `Connection` object from the driver, the developer should consider setting auto-commit to `false` with the `setAutoCommit(boolean b)` method. When auto-commit is disabled, the `Connection` will support both `Connection.commit()` and `Connection.rollback()` method calls. The level of support for transaction isolation depends on the underlying support for transactions in the database.

> **NOTE** A *transaction* is a set of operations that are completed in order. A *commit* action makes the operations store (or change) data in the database. A *rollback* action undoes the previous transaction before it has been committed.

A portion of the `Connection` interface definition follows:

Signature: `public interface Connection`

`Statement createStatement () throws SQLException` The `Connection` object implementation will return an instance of an implementation of a `Statement` object. The `Statement` object is then used to issue queries.

`PreparedStatement prepareStatement (String sql) throws SQLException` The `Connection` object implementation will return an instance of a `PreparedStatement` object that is configured with the `sql` string passed. The driver may then send the statement to the database, if the database (driver) handles precompiled statements. Otherwise, the driver may wait until the `PreparedStatement` is executed by an execute method. An exception may be thrown if the driver and database do not implement precompiled statements.

`CallableStatement prepareCall (String sql) throws SQLException` The `Connection` object implementation will return an instance of a `CallableStatement`. A `CallableStatement` is optimized for handling stored procedures. The driver implementation may send the `sql` string immediately when prepareCall() is complete or may wait until an execute method occurs.

void setAutoCommit (boolean autoCommit) throws SQLException   Sets a flag in the driver implementation that enables commit/rollback (false) or makes all transactions commit immediately (true).

void commit () throws SQLException   Makes all changes made since the beginning of the current transaction (either the opening of the Connection or since the last commit() or rollback()).

void rollback() throws SQLException   Drops all changes made since the beginning of the current transaction.

The primary use of the Connection interface is to create a statement:

```
Connection msqlConn = null;
Statement stmt = null;

msqlConn = DriverManager.getConnection (url);
stmt = msqlConn.createStatement ();
```

This statement may be used to send SQL statements that return a single result set in a ResultSet object reference. Statements that need to be called a number of times with slight variations may be executed more efficiently using a PreparedStatement. The Connection interface is also used to create a CallableStatement whose purpose is to execute stored procedures.

Most of the time, the developer knows the database schema beforehand and creates the application based on the schema. However, JDBC provides an interface that may be used to dynamically determine the schema of a database. The Connection interface getMetaData method will return a DatabaseMetaData object. The instance of the class that implements the interface provides information about the database as a whole, including access information about tables and procedures, column names, datatypes, and so on. The implementation details of `DatabaseMetaData` depend on the database vendor's ability to return this type of information.

Statement Basics   A *statement* is the vehicle for sending SQL queries to the database and retrieving a set of results. Statements can be SQL updates, insertions, deletions, or queries (via Select). The `Statement` interface provides a number of methods designed to make the job of writing queries to the database easier.

Signature: `public interface Statement`

`ResultSet executeQuery(String sql) throws SQL-Exception`   Executes a single SQL query and returns the results in an object of type `ResultSet`.

`int executeUpdate(String sql) throws SQLException` Executes a single SQL query that returns a count of rows affected rather than a set of results.

`boolean execute(String sql) throws SQLException` A general SQL statement that may return multiple result sets and/or update counts. This method is used to execute stored procedures that return Out and Inout parameters. The `getResultSet()`, `getUpdateCount()`, and `getMoreResults()` methods are used to retrieve the data returned.

> **NOTE**   *In parameters* are parameters that are passed into an operation. *Out parameters* are parameters passed by reference; they are expected to return a result of the reference type. *Inout parameters* are Out parameters that contain an initial value that may change as a result of the operation. JDBC supports all three parameter types.

`ResultSet getResultSet () throws SQLException` Returns the current data as the result of a statement execution as a

ResultSet object. Note that if there are no results to be read or if the result is an update count, this method returns a null. Also note that once read, the results are cleared.

int getUpdateCount() throws SQLException   Returns the status of an Update, Insert, or Delete query or a stored procedure that returns a row status. A -1 is returned if there is either no update count or if the data returned is a result set. Once read, the update count is cleared.

boolean getMoreResults() throws SQLException Moves to the next result in a set of multiple results/update counts. This method returns true if the next result is a ResultSet object. This method will also close any previous ResultSet read.

Statements may or may not return a ResultSet object, depending on the Statement method used. The executeUpdate() method, for example, is used to execute SQL statements that do not expect a result (except a row-count status):

```
int rowCount;
rowCount = stmt.executeUpdate ("DELETE FROM Customer WHERE
➥CustomerID = 'McG10233'");
```

SQL statements that return a single set of results can use the executeQuery() method. This method returns a single Result-Set object. The object represents the row information returned as a result of the query:

```
ResultSet results;
results = stmt.executeQuery ("SELECT * FROM Stock");
```

SQL statements that execute stored procedures (or trigger a stored procedure) may return more than one set of results. The execute() method is a general-purpose method that can return either a single result set or multiple result sets. The method returns a boolean flag that is used to determine whether there are more result sets. Because a result set could contain either data or the count of an operation that returns a row count, the `getResultSet()`, `getMoreResults()`, and `getUpdateCount()` methods are used. For example:

```
// Assume SQLString returns multiple result sets
// true if a ResultSet is returned
if (stmt.execute (SQLstring)) {
   results = stmt.getResultSet();
// false, an UpdateCount was returned
} else {
   count = stmt.getUpdateCount();
}

// Process the first results here ....

// Now loop until there are no more results or update counts
do {
   // Is the next result a ResultSet?
   if (stmt.getMoreResults()) {
      results = stmt.getResultSet();
   else {
      count = stmt.getUpdateCount();
   }

   // Process next results here ....

} while ((results != null) && (count != -1));
```

The `PreparedStatement` interface extends the `Statement` interface. When there is a SQL statement that requires repetition with minor variations, the `PreparedStatement` provides an efficient mechanism for passing a precompiled SQL statement that uses parameters.

```
public interface PreparedStatement extends Statement
```

`PreparedStatement` parameters are used to pass data into a SQL statement, so they are considered In parameters and are filled in by using set*Type* methods.

```
// Assume priceList is an array of prices that needs to
// be reduced for a 10% off sale, and reducedItems
// is an array of item IDs
int reduction = 10;
```

```
PreparedStatement ps = msqlConn.prepareStatment ("UPDATE Catalog
➡SET Price = ? WHERE ItemID = ?");
// Do the updates in a loop
for (int i = 0; i < reducedItems.length(); i++) {
   // Note that the setType methods set the value of the
   // parameters noted in the SQL statement with question
   // marks (?). They are indexed, starting from 1 to n.
   ps.setFloat (1, (priceList[i]*((float)(100-reduction)/100)));
   ps.setString (2, reducedItems[i]);
   if (ps.executeUpdate() == 0) {
      throw new SQLException ("No Item ID: " +
         reducedItems[i]);
   }
}
```

Parameters hold their current values until either a new set*Type*
method is called or the method clearParameters() is called for
the PreparedStatement object. In addition to the execute methods inherited from Statement, PrepareStatement declares the
set*Type* methods listed in Table 18.1. Each method takes two arguments: a parameter index and the primitive or class type.

NOTE The set*Type* methods fill the value of parameters (marked by question marks) in a PreparedStatement. These parameters are indexed from 1 to *n*.

The CallableStatement interface is used to execute SQL stored
procedures. CallableStatement inherits from the Prepared-
Statement interface, so all of the execute and set*Type* methods
are available. The syntax of stored procedures varies among database
vendors, so JDBC defines a standard way for all RDBMSs to call
stored procedures.

```
public interface CallableStatement extends PreparedStatement
```

TABLE 18.1   set*Type* Methods

Method Signature	Java Type	SQL Type to the Database
`void setByte (int index, byte b)`	`byte`	TINYINT
`void setShort (int index, short x)`	`short`	SMALLINT
`void setInt (int index, int i)`	`int`	INTEGER
`void setLong (int index, long 1)`	`long`	BIGINT
`void setFloat (int index, float f)`	`float`	FLOAT
`void setDouble (int index, double d)`	`double`	DOUBLE
`void setBigDecimal (int index, BigDecimal x)`	`java.lang.BigDecimal`	NUMERIC
`void setString (int index, String s)`	`java.lang.String`	VARCHAR
`void setAsciiStream (int index, InputStream x, int length)`	`java.io.InputStream`	LONGVARCHAR
`void setUnicodeStream (int index, InputStream x, int length)`	`java.io.InputStream`	LONGVARCHAR
`void setBytes (int index, byte x[])`	byte array	VARBINARY
`void setBinaryStream (int index, InputStream x, int length)`	`java.io.InputStream`	LONGVARBINARY
`void setDate (int index, Date d)`	`java.sql.Date`	DATE
`void setTime (int index, Time t)`	`java.sql.Time`	TIME
`void setTimestamp (int index, Timestamp ts)`	`java.sql.Timestamp`	TIMESTAMP
`void setNull (int index, int sqlType)`	—	`java.sql.Types` has constants for each of the SQL types
`void setBoolean (int index, boolean b)`	`boolean`	BIT

The JDBC uses an escape syntax that allows parameters to be passed as In parameters and Out parameters. The syntax also allows a result to be returned; if this syntax is used, the parameter must be registered as an Out parameter.

Here is an example of a `CallableStatement` returning an Out parameter:

```
CallableStatement cs = conn.prepareCall ("{call getQuote
➥(?, ?)}");
cs.setString (1, stockName);
// java.sql.Types defines SQL datatypes that are returned
// as Out parameters
cs.registerOutParameter (2, Types.FLOAT);
stmt.executeUpdate();
float quote = stmt.getFloat (2);
```

`CallableStatement` defines a set of get *Type* methods that convert the SQL types returned from the database to Java types. These methods match the set *Type* methods declared by `Prepared-Statement`, as shown in Table 18.2.

NOTE   The get *Type* methods access data in each column as the result a query. Each column can be accessed by either its position in the row, numbered from 1 to *n* columns, or by its name, such as `custID`.

TABLE 18.2   get*Type* Methods

Method Signature	Java Type	SQL Type from the Database
`boolean getBoolean (int index)`	`boolean`	BIT
`byte getByte (int index)`	`byte`	TINYINT
`short getShort (int index)`	`short`	SMALLINT
`int getInt (int index)`	`int`	INTEGER
`long getLong (int index)`	`long`	BIGINT
`float getFloat (int index)`	`float`	FLOAT
`double getDouble (int index)`	`double`	DOUBLE

TABLE 18.2   get*Type* Methods (Continued)

Method Signature	Java Type	SQL Type from the Database
BigDecimal getBigDecimal (int index, int scale)	java.lang.BigDecimal	NUMERIC
String getString (int index)	string	CHAR, VARCHAR or LONGVARCHAR
byte[] getBytes (int index)	byte array	BINARY or VARBINARY
Date getDate (int index)	java.sql.Date	DATE
Time getTime (int index)	java.sql.Time	TIME
Timestamp getTimestamp (int index)	java.sql.Timestamp	TIMESTAMP

NOTE   It is the responsibility of the JDBC driver to convert the data passed from the database as SQL datatypes into Java values.

ResultSet Basics   The `ResultSet` interface defines methods for accessing tables of data generated as the result of executing a `Statement`. `ResultSet` column values may be accessed in any order; they are indexed and may be selected by either the name or the number (numbered from 1 to *n*) of the column. `ResultSet` maintains the position of the current row, starting with the first row of data returned. The `next()` method moves to the next row of data.

A partial look at the `ResultSet` interface follows:

Signature: `public interface ResultSet`
    `boolean next () throws SQLException`   Positions the `ResultSet` to the next row; `ResultSet` row position is initially the first row of the result set.

`ResultSetMetaData getMetaData throws SQLException` Returns an object that contains a description of the current result set: the number of columns, the type of each column, and properties of the results.

void close () throws SQLException Normally, a `ResultSet` is closed when another `Statement` is executed, but it may be desirable to release the resources earlier.

As with `CallableStatement`, the resulting data can be read through get *Type* methods. For example:

```
// Pass a query to the statement object
ResultSet rs = stmt.executeQuery
            ("SELECT * FROM Stock WHERE quantity = 0");

// Get the results as their Java types
// Note that columns are indexed by an integer starting
// with 1, or by the name of column, as in "ItemID"
System.out.println ("Stock replenishment list");
while (rs.next()) {

   System.out.println ("Item ID: " + rs.getString("ItemID"));
   System.out.println ("Next ship date: " + rs.getDate(2));
   System.out.println ("");
}
```

ResultSetMetaData Besides being able to read data from a `ResultSet` object, JDBC provides an interface to allow the developer to determine what type of data was returned. The `ResultSetMetaData` interface is similar to the `DatabaseMetaData` interface in concept, but it is specific to the current `ResultSet`. As with `DatabaseMetaData`, it is unlikely that many developers will use this interface, because most applications are written with an understanding of the database schema and column names and values. However, `ResultSetMetaData` is useful in dynamically determining the `MetaData` of a `ResultSet` returned from a stored procedure.

Sending and Receiving Large Data Chunks SQL `LONGVARBINARY` and `LONGVARCHAR` datatypes can be of arbitrary size. The `getBytes ()` and `getString ()` methods can read these types up to the limits imposed by the driver. The limits can be read through the `Statement.getMaxFieldSize()` method. For larger blocks of data, the JDBC allows developers to use `java.io.Input-Stream` parameters to return the data in chunks.

NOTE   Streams must be read immediately following the query execution; they are automatically closed at the next retrieval of a `ResultSet`.

Sending large blocks of data is also possible using `java.io.Output-Stream` as parameters. When a statement is executed, the JDBC driver makes repeated calls to read and transmit the data in the streams.

Database Applications versus Applets

As you know, there are two types of programs in the Java world: applications and applets. Each program type provides benefits, and the use of each is generally determined by the way in which the developer wishes the user to access the program. The following sections discuss the use of applications versus applets for database systems.

Java Database Applications

Applications are Java programs that are developed as stand-alone executables. The user is expected to have access to the program executable (class file) and the Java interpreter locally. For an Intranet-based database front end, this strategy offers the benefits of faster startup (class files are local) and local disk utilization.

In addition, Java applications are trusted and are allowed greater flexibility with socket connections. This makes it possible for the client program to access multiple database systems on remote servers.

Java applications are becoming more prevalent as tools become available for GUI development and speed improvements are made possible through Just-In-Time (JIT) compilers/interpreters. Applications can also reduce or eliminate issues with browser security models and the differences in the browser's implementation of Java widgets.

Java Database Applets

Applets are mini Java programs that require a Java-enabled browser to run. The browser provides an environment for the applet to run in, including drawing and viewing resources directly on the browser page. When a user moves or "surfs" to a browser page that contains an applet, the applet is automatically executed.

The process involves downloading the necessary Java applet code, including JDBC drivers and Application layer software; automatically checking security restrictions on the code; and running the applet if the restrictions do not prevent this.

Applets provide several key benefits over applications:

Version control　It is possible to modify an applet almost on the fly by replacing the class file in the HTML page references.

Easier execution model　It takes very little effort to learn to use even the most sophisticated browsers and to execute a front-end client; the user simply navigates to the page where the application is located.

Online help　Creating the running program on a browser HTML page makes it extremely easy to embed help links that can be developed separately from the running program.

A typical use of applets might be for training within a large organization, where the data being delivered is not critical and access can be limited to a two-tier model (three-tier models are possible but involve more complex layering schemes). Another use may be the simple presentation of data to the Internet community—again, where the quantity of data is not great and security of the data message is not paramount.

Applets, however, are severely constrained by the browser environment. Applets are not allowed to do the following:

- Access any local files. This limits the use of local caching and table manipulation and storage to in-memory during the life of the applet.

- Connect to arbitrary hosts. Socket connections are allowed only between the applet and the host for which the applet originated.

- Load or run drivers that contain native methods (C language calls).

Additionally, there is a considerable performance hit involved in loading applet code across an Internet (wide-area) network connection.

Some of these constraints may be lifted or reduced with the introduction of trusted applets (which are now being considered in the development of the Java security model) and browsers that accept them. Trusted applets may be code-signed with a cryptographic key or may be stored in a trusted location. If the browser environment believes that the applet's source is trusted, for security purposes, it may be treated like an application (although there may still be limits regarding the location of databases on an internet).

The other alternative that is more tangible and available today is the use of a three-tier model. In this approach, the applet is loaded from a middleware tier that provides both the HTML page and HTTP server, and a multithreaded application (Java, C, or C++) that supports socket connections for multiple clients and, in turn, contacts remote database systems. Calls to the third tier can be managed by developing a custom (proprietary) protocol, by using Remote Method Invocation (RMI), or by using an Object Request Broker (ORB). See the "Alternative Connectivity Strategies" section later in this chapter for more information.

Security Considerations

The JDBC API follows the standard Java security model. In short, applications are considered trusted code, and applets are considered untrusted. In general, the job of writing a secure JDBC driver is left to the driver vendor.

The Java VM employs its own, well-documented security checks for untrusted applets, including the aforementioned restrictions. However, if a JDBC driver vendor wants to extend the model by adding features to its driver—for example, allowing multiple applets to use the same TCP socket connection to talk to a database—it becomes the responsibility of the vendor to check that each applet is allowed to use the connection.

In addition to maintaining the integrity of the Java security model, both the JDBC driver vendor and JDBC application developer need to keep in mind that the JDBC API defines a means of executing database calls and does not define a network security model. The data sent over the network to the database and the resulting table information (for example, to request customer credit card information) are exposed and can be read by any terminal that is capable of snooping the network.

A JDBC Database Example

The following is an example that uses the concepts presented in this chapter; it is artificial and intended only to illustrate the use of `Statement`, `PreparedStatement`, and `CallableStatement`.

The simple database contains a table called Customer, which has the schema shown in Table 18.3.

TABLE 18.3   Customer Data Table

Column Name	Datatype
CustomerID	VARCHAR
LastName	VARCHAR
FirstName	VARCHAR
Phonenumber	VARCHAR
StreetAddress	VARCHAR
Zipcode	VARCHAR

Table 18.3 is part of a larger database that stores information related to a large catalog ordering system. Here is the definition of a simple `Customer` object with two primary methods: `insertNew-Customer()` and `getCustomer()`:

```
public class Customer
```

`public Customer (Connection conn)`   The constructor for the class. The `Customer` constructor receives a `Connection` object, which it uses to create `Statement` references. In addition, the constructor creates a `PreparedStatement` and three `CallableStatements`.

`public String insertNewCustomer (String lname, String fname, String pnum, String addr, String zip) throws insertFailedException, SQLException` Creates a new customer record, including a new ID. The ID is created through a stored procedure that reads the current list of customer IDs and creates a new reference. The method returns the new ID created or throws an exception if the insertion failed.

`public CustomerInfo getCustomer (String custID) throws selectException, SQLException`   Returns an object that contains the data in the Customer table. An exception is thrown if the customer ID passed does not exist or is not properly formatted, or if the SQL statement fails.

`public static synchronized boolean validateZip (String zip) throws SQLException` A utility method to validate the zip code. A `true` value is returned if the zip code exists in the ZipCode table in the database.

`public static synchronized boolean validateID (String id) throws SQLException` A utility method to validate a customer ID. If the ID exists, the method returns `true`.

The source code is as follows:

Customer.java

```
// Customer record class
// This class is used to store and access
// customer data from the database
import java.sql.*;

public class Customer {

    private Connection conn;
    private PreparedStatement insertNewCustomer;
    private CallableStatement getNewID;
    public static CallableStatement checkZip;
    public static CallableStatement checkID;

    // Customer constructor: store a local copy of the
    // Connection object
    // Create statements for use later
    public Customer (Connection c) {
        conn = c;

        try {
            insertNewCustomer = conn.prepareStatement
            ("INSERT INTO Customers VALUES (?, ?, ?, ?, ?, ?)");

            getNewID = conn.prepareCall
                ("{call getNewID (?)}");
```

```
        checkID = conn.prepareCall
              ("{call checkID (?,?)}");

        checkZip = conn.prepareCall
              ("{call checkZip (?, ?)}");
    } catch (SQLException e) {
    System.out.println
    ("Unable to create prepared and callable statements");
    }
}

// Method for creating a new customer record
// The customerID is generated by a stored procedure
// call on the database
public String insertNewCustomer (String lname, String fname,
String pnum, String addr, String zip)
throws insertFailedException, SQLException {

    String newID;

    // Get a new customer ID through the
    // stored procedure
    if ((newID = getNewID ()) == null) {
       throw new insertFailedException
             ("could not get new ID");
    }

    // Insert the new customer ID
    insertNewCustomer.setString (1, newID);
    insertNewCustomer.setString (2, lname);
    insertNewCustomer.setString (3, fname);
    insertNewCustomer.setString (4, pnum);
    insertNewCustomer.setString (5, addr);
    insertNewCustomer.setString (6, zip);

    // Execute the statement
    if (insertNewCustomer.executeUpdate() != 1) {
       throw new insertFailedException
             ("could not execute insert");
    }
    return (newID);
}
```

```
// Get a single customer record with this ID
// Note: this method maps the returned data onto a
// CustomerInfo container object
public CustomerInfo getCustomer (String custID)
throws selectException, SQLException {

   // Check the ID first
   if (!validateID (custID)) {
      throw new selectException
         ("no customer with ID: " + custID);
   }

   // Create the select statement
   Statement stmt = conn.createStatement();

   // Get the results
   ResultSet rs = stmt.executeQuery
   ("SELECT FROM Customer WHERE CustID = " + custID);

   // Create a CustomerInfo container object
   CustomerInfo info = new CustomerInfo ();

   // Populate the CustomerInfo object
   // Columns are indexed starting with 1
   info.CustomerID = rs.getString (1);
   info.LastName = rs.getString (2);
   info.FirstName = rs.getString (3);
   info.PhoneNumber = rs.getString (4);
   info.StreetAddress = rs.getString (5);
   info.Zip = rs.getString (6);

   return (info);
}

// Method for validation of a customer's zip code
// This method is public so that it can be called from
// a user interface
public static synchronized boolean validateZip (String zip)
throws SQLException {

   // Make call to stored procedure to validate zip code
   checkZip.setString (1, zip);
   checkZip.registerOutParameter (2, Types.BIT);
```

```
        checkZip.executeUpdate();
        return (checkZip.getBoolean(2));


    }


    // Method for validating a customer ID
    // This method is public so that it can be called from
    // a user interface
    public static synchronized boolean validateID (String id)
    throws SQLException {

        // Make call to stored procedure to validate
        // customer id
        checkID.setString (1, id);
        checkID.registerOutParameter (2, Types.BIT);
        checkID.executeUpdate();
        return (checkID.getBoolean(2));
    }


    // Method for retrieving a new customer ID from the database
    private String getNewID () throws SQLException {

        // Make call to stored procedure to get
        // customer ID from DB
        getNewID.registerOutParameter (1, Types.VARCHAR);
        getNewID.executeUpdate();
        return (getNewID.getString (1));
    }
}


// Exceptions

// insertFailedException is a general exception for
// SQL insert problems
class insertFailedException extends SQLException {

    public insertFailedException (String reason) {
        super (reason);
    }

    public insertFailedException () {
        super ();
    }
}
```

```
// selectException is a general exception for
// SQL select problems
class selectException extends SQLException {

    public selectException (String reason) {
        super (reason);
    }

    public selectException () {
        super ();
    }
}
```

> **TIP**
>
> The `CustomerInfo` class is a simple container object. Container classes make it easier to pass a complete customer record to and from any method that manipulates the Customer table in the database. Data can be stored in the container class and passed as a single object reference, rather than having to pass each element as a single reference.

CustomerInfo.java

```
// A container object for the Customer table
public class CustomerInfo {

    String CustomerID;
    String LastName;
    String FirstName;
    String PhoneNumber;
    String StreetAddress;
    String Zip;

}
```

Finally, to test the simple `Customer` class, here is a simple Java application that illustrates loading a Sybase driver, then making a connection and passing the `Connection` object returned to a new instance of a `Customer` object.

Example.java

```
// A simple Java application that illustrates
// the use of DriverManager, Driver, Connection,
// Statement, and ResultSet

import java.sql.*;
import sybase.sql.*;

public class Example {

    Connection sybaseConn;

    // main
    public static void main (String arg[]) {

        // Look for the url, username, and password
        if (arg.length < 3) {
            System.out.println ("Example use:");
            System.out.println
            ("java Example <url> <username> <password>");
            System.exit (1);
        }

        // Create an instance of the class
        Example ex = new Example ();

        // Initialize the connection
        ex.initdb (arg[0], arg[1], arg[2]);

        // Test the connection—write a customer and
        // then read it back
        ex.testdb ();
    }

    // method to initialize the database connection
    // The Connection object reference is kept globally
    public void initdb (String url, String user, String passwd) {
        // Try to open the database and get the connection
        try {

            // Note that this example assumes that
            // Java property "jdbc.drivers"
```

```
            // is loading the appropriate driver(s) for
            // the url passed in the getConnection call.
            // It is possible to explicitly create an
            // instance of a driver as well, for example:
            // new sybase.sql.driver ();

            // Create a connection
            sybaseConn = DriverManager.getConnection
                    (url, user, passwd);

        } catch (SQLException e) {
            System.out.println
                ("Database connection failed:");
            System.out.println (e.getMessage());
            System.exit (1);
        }
    }

    // Simple method to test the Customer class methods
    public void testdb () {
        String custID = null;

        // Create the instance of the Customer class
        Customer cust = new Customer (sybaseConn);

        try {
            // Now insert a new Customer
            custID = cust.insertNewCustomer
            ("Jones", "Bill", "555-1234", "5 Main Street",
             "01234");

        } catch (SQLException e) {

            System.out.println ("Insert failed:");
            System.out.println (e.getMessage());
            System.exit (1);
        }

        try {
            // Read it back from the database
            CustomerInfo info = cust.getCustomer (custID);

        } catch (SQLException e) {
```

```
        System.out.println ("Read failed:");
        System.out.println (e.getMessage());
        System.exit (1);
    }
  }
}
```

This example illustrates the use of the `CallableStatements` to issue stored procedure calls that validate the zip code and validate the customer ID, and the `PreparedStatement` to issue an Insert SQL statement with parameters that will change with each insert. It also illustrates code that will run with any JDBC driver that will support the stored procedures used in the `Customer` class. The driver class names are loaded from the `jdbc.drivers` property, so code recompilation is not required.

JDBC Drivers

One of the real attractions of the JDBC API is the ability to develop applications knowing that all of the major database vendors are working in parallel to create drivers. A number of drivers are available from database vendors and third-party developers. In most cases, it is wise to shop around for the best features, cost, and support.

Drivers come in a variety of flavors according to their construction and the type of database they are intended to support. JavaSoft categorizes database drivers in four ways, described in the following sections.

TIP JDBC drivers are being released from so many vendors and at such a rapid rate that a definitive list is just not practical and would be obsolete by the time it was printed. For information on current driver vendors, their product names, and what databases they support, a good source is http://splash.javasoft.com/jdbc/jdbc.drivers.html.

The JDBC-ODBC Bridge Driver

The JDBC-ODBC bridge is a JDBC driver that provides translation of JDBC calls to ODBC operations. There are a number of DBMSs that support ODBC.

The JDBC-ODBC bridge driver, shown in Figure 18.6, is implemented with ODBC binary code and, in some cases, a client library as well. The bridge driver is made up of three parts:

- A set of C libraries that connect the JDBC to the ODBC driver manager

- The ODBC driver manager

- The ODBC driver

FIGURE 18.6

JDBC-ODBC bridge
driver

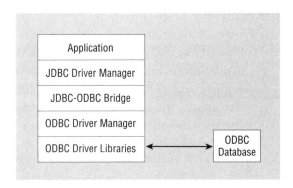

As mentioned earlier, both JDBC and ODBC are based on the X/Open CLI, so the translation between JDBC and ODBC is relatively straightforward. ODBC is a client-side set of libraries and a driver that is specific to the client's operating system and, in some cases, specific to the machine architecture.

From the developer's perspective, using a JDBC-ODBC bridge driver is an easy choice—applications will still speak directly to the JDBC interface classes, so it is exactly the same as using any other JDBC driver. However, the implementation of a JDBC-ODBC bridge requires that the developer be aware of what is required to run the application. Because ODBC calls are made using binary C calls, the client must have a local copy of the ODBC driver, the ODBC driver manager, and the client-side libraries.

For these reasons, JavaSoft recommends that the JDBC-ODBC bridge not be used for Web-based database access. For Intranet access, the developer must distribute the Java program to the client machines as either a Java application or Java applet (which would run as a trusted source from the local client file system).

The Native Library-to-Java Driver

The native library-to-Java implementation is illustrated in Figure 18.7. This driver uses native C language library calls to translate JDBC to the native client library. These drivers use C language libraries that provide vendor-specific functionality and tie these libraries (through native method calls) to the JDBC. These drivers were the first available for Oracle, Sybase, Informix, DB2, and other client-library-based RDBMSs.

FIGURE 18.7

Native library-to-Java driver

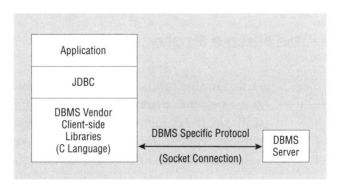

The Network Protocol Driver

With a network protocol Java driver, JDBC calls are translated by this driver into a DBMS-independent protocol and sent to a middle-tier server over a socket. The middle-tier code contacts a variety of databases on behalf of the client. This approach, which is illustrated in Figure 18.8, is becoming the most popular and is by far the most flexible. This approach also deals specifically with issues relating to network security, including passing data through firewalls.

FIGURE 18.8

DBMS-independent network protocol driver

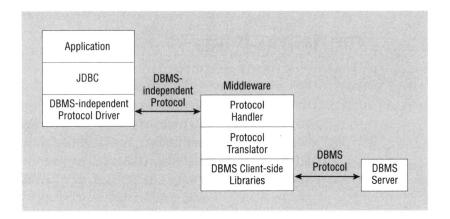

The Native Protocol Driver

With a native protocol Java driver, JDBC calls are converted directly to the network protocol used by the DBMS server. In this driver scenario, the database vendor supports a network socket, and the JDBC driver communicates over a socket connection directly to the database server. The client-side code can be written in Java. This solution has the benefit of being one of the easiest to implement and is very practical for Intranet use. However, because the network protocol is defined by the vendor and is typically proprietary, the driver usually is available only from the database vendor. Figure 18.9 illustrates how a native protocol driver works.

FIGURE 18.9

Native protocol driver

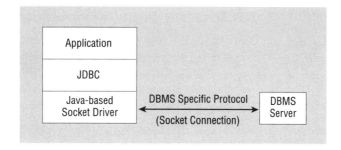

Alternative Connectivity Strategies

JDBC represents a very easy way to save time and future investment when developing database applications. The API guarantees that a client program written to the JDBC standard will work with any JDBC-compliant driver and database combination. Two alternative technologies that provide a flexible way to preserve a development investment are Remote Method Invocation (RMI) and the Common Object Request Broker Architecture (CORBA). Both RMI and CORBA can also be used to connect client applications to databases, although there are some caveats to consider. Other connectivity alternatives are the use of object databases and Web-based database systems.

Using RMI

RMI is analogous to Remote Procedure Calls (RPC), but while RPC was not designed for distributed object systems, this is RMI's strength. RMI is designed to allow client applications to execute the methods of objects that exist on a remote server, and execute these methods in such a way that it *appears* that the objects are local.

For database connectivity, this means that the developer can create an application that accesses database objects directly, even though these objects are actually implemented on the database server host. Because RMI provides mechanisms for allowing objects to be passed as serialized streams, it also supports protocols for passing these streams through firewalls.

Because RMI is a Java-to-Java solution, it is also possible to combine the best of JDBC and RMI for a multitier solution. For example, if the JDBC driver is written using RMI, it becomes possible to write to a standard database interface definition and also use object persistence and remote method calls via RMI, thereby extending the JDBC model.

> **TIP** For more information about RMI, see Chapter 22. You can also take a look at the Web page http://chatsubo.javasoft.com/current/rmi/.

Using CORBA

For the database application developer, CORBA provides the ultimate flexibility in a heterogeneous development environment. The server could be developed in C or C++, and the client could be a Java applet. Currently, JavaSoft is in the process of providing a Java Interface Definition Language (IDL) compiler that takes a CORBA 2.0 IDL file and creates the necessary stub files for a client implementation.

CORBA is a standard (at version 2.0 as of this writing) that defines a definition language that is vendor- and language-neutral. The IDL is used to create a contract between a client and server implementation. IDL is not an implementation language itself; it merely describes object services and operations that may be performed on an implementation of the those services.

> **TIP**
>
> CORBA is the result of years of work by the Object Management Group (OMG). The OMG is a consortium of more than 500 companies that have compiled a specification for a communications infrastructure that allows different computer languages on different computer architectures to access a distributed collection of objects. For a closer look at CORBA and a wealth of information on the OMG consortium, see the group's Web page: http://www.omg.org/.

At the core of CORBA is the Object Request Broker (ORB). The ORB is the principal component for the transmission of information (requests for operations and their results) between the client and server of a CORBA application. The ORB manages marshaling requests, establishes a connection to the server, sends the data, and executes the requests on the server side. The same process occurs when the server returns the results of the operation.

The CORBA 2.0 specification also defines an Internet interoperability protocol (IIOP) for the connection between the client and server through the ORB. This allows developers to choose a client IDL compiler and server IDL compiler from two different vendors.

Besides JavaSoft, there are several vendors that provide CORBA 2.0 compliance, including IIOP and Java IDL compilers.

Connectivity to Object Databases

Besides RMI and CORBA, another alternative is to use an object database, specifically one that supports Java's object model. There are several object database products for Java, but currently there are no existing standards. Fortunately, there is an object database standards committee, the Object Database Management Group (ODMG), working on a standard API for Java object databases. The ODMG 2.0 release is expected to be published sometime in 1997.

> **TIP**
>
> For more information about the ODMG's work on a standard Java object database, see the group's Web page: http://www.odmg .org/java.html.

Connectivity with Web-Based Database Systems

While not specifically JDBC, and not always related to Java, there is another alternative to accessing databases from Web pages. It is possible to use HTML pages to send information to CGI (Common Gateway Interface) scripts. The CGI scripts, in turn, connect to the database and return results to the HTML page. Vendors in the Web-based database market have a variety of strategies for improving the performance of CGI with multithreaded applications written in C or C++ that handle the database connection and queries.

JavaSoft is also working to provide a technology that exceeds the performance of CGI. The Java Web Server API presents a collection of classes that allow applets to execute small *servlets* (also written in Java) on a server to perform a task. The servlet can be instructed to open a database connection, retrieve a result, and return the data to the applet.

> **TIP**
>
> For more information about servlet technology, see Chapter 21. You can also see the Web page http://www.javasoft.com/products/ java-server/. Other Web pages of interest are http://www.stars .com/Vlib/Providers/Database.html, which lists Web-based database connectivity products, and http://www. odi.com, which is ObjectStores page.

Summary

The interest in Java has created a number of new strategies for moving data between the database system and the front-end user. In this chapter, the JDBC API was presented as the primary technique for connecting Java applications to database systems. The JDBC solves the problem of connecting a single application to a multitude of database systems by isolating the interface that the developer uses and the driver that is used to connect to the database.

In addition, the chapter looked briefly at alternative connectivity strategies, including Remote Method Invocation (RMI) and the Common Object Request Broker Architecture (CORBA).

The Java Electronic Commerce Framework (JECF)

- JECF's Merchant Applet layer

- JECF's Wallet layer

- JECF's Cassette layer

The Java Electronic Commerce Framework (JECF) provides support for applet-based shopping and other financial transactions. Pre-Java shopping sites on the World Wide Web have tended to standardize on the metaphor of a shopping cart. Users click on items they wish to purchase to add the items to a virtual shopping cart. At the end of the shopping session, the user specifies a payment instrument (typically a credit card), clicks on a Pay button, and hopes that the goods arrive a few days later.

The JECF standardizes computer-aided shopping (CASH) and provides a rich infrastructure for making the shopping experience seamless, intuitive, and secure. The JECF also provides functionality for applets to charge for their use and for banks and other financial institutions to offer Web-based services.

The JECF architecture is based on a three-layer structure: the Merchant Applet layer, Wallet layer, and Cassette layer. This chapter briefly examines each of these layers.

The Merchant Applet Layer

The JECF's Merchant package (`java.commerce.merchant`) is simply a set of subclasses of `java.applet.Applet`. Merchants (that is, providers of Web-based shopping services) may use these applets for easy and standard support of the common shopping functions.

The applet subclasses in this layer fall into four families:

- Shopping Cart

- Identity
- Tally
- Payment Instrument Selection

These applet subclasses are discussed in the following sections.

The Shopping Cart Applet

Shopping Cart applets implement the metaphor of adding desired merchandise to a virtual shopping cart. This is the first phase of the user's experience. Sophisticated online shopping sites may offer dozens or even hundreds of Web pages of merchandise description. As the user browses these pages, he or she can click on any desired products, thus adding them to the user's shopping cart.

Eventually, the product-selection phase of the shopping trip is over, and the user clicks on a Pay button. When this happens, the applet code must verify the user's identity and access a private database containing transaction information specific to the user. This functionality is supported by the Wallet and Cassette layers, which are described in the next two sections.

The Identity, Tally, and Payment Instrument Selection Applets

After verifying identity and opening the database, the Shopping Cart applet typically will display a single Web page containing three applets:

Identity applet   Verifies the identity of the seller. The Identity applet establishes that the seller is the entity it claims to be in the applet. This makes it difficult for counterfeit sites to pretend to be reputable merchants.

Tally applet   Describes the merchandise in the user's virtual shopping cart, along with quantity and price. It is common at this point to offer the user the opportunity to modify the desired quantity of any item. The Tally applet also displays the total price of the user's purchases.

There is a clear advantage to having an applet handle the tallying chore, as opposed to using CGI (Common Gateway Interface) scripts. With a CGI solution, any change to the shopping cart (for example, deciding after all not to buy a certain product) must fire off a script. This script consumes CPU cycles on the server and results in loading a new page into the browser. With a JECF applet, minor adjustments are all handled locally without the server's involvement.

Payment Instrument Selection applet   Allows the user to select the method of payment. The shopper's private database contains information from which the JECF is able to build a "wallet" that contains, among other things, representations of the various electronic payment instruments that have been issued to the shopper. Because this applet has access to the contents of the shopper's wallet, it can format a personalized screen so that the shopper can select from among those instruments that have actually been issued to that user. A user who does not have a VISA card, for example, need not be shown an option to charge the purchases to a VISA card. A user with four VISA cards may choose which of these credit cards to use.

Somewhere in these three applets (most likely in Payment Instrument Selection), there is an ultimate OK or Apply button. Clicking on this button brings up one final screen. Unlike the previous applets, which are customized by the merchant and provided on the merchant's Web pages, this final screen is brought up by the JECF. This screen is called the *final confirmation window*. If the user confirms one last time that the purchase is desired, the JECF code initiates the sequence of electronic financial transactions that will cause the payment instrument to be debited and will notify the merchant that the purchase has taken place. The vital payment instrument information (VISA card number and expiration date, for example) is not visible to the merchant.

The final step in the process is for the JECF to display a verification page to the user. This page documents the shopping transaction that just took place. This information is also stored in the shopper's private database, in an entity called the user's *transaction register*. The JECF provides support for service software that can analyze the transaction register.

The Wallet Layer

As described in the previous section, the JECF extends the shopping-cart metaphor to include the act of opening a wallet, looking inside, and selecting an instrument of payment. Two very important characteristics of real-world wallets are that they are personal and they are private. A JECF wallet is built on a user's individual database. The information within the wallet—and most especially the information that grants permission to spend the user's money—is guarded by security mechanisms that are new in revision 1.1 of the JDK. The JECF security apparatus relies heavily on the digital signature mechanism.

> **NOTE** Digital signatures are part of the Java 1.1 Security API. Signatures are based on a public key/private key encryption scheme. With such a scheme, entities (people and organizations) have public and private keys. These keys are large numbers that are mathematically related according to a complicated algorithm. The private key is known only to the entity; the public key is published. The public key is used to verify that a digital signature has been generated by the owner of the private key. The advantage of this scheme is that it is impossible (or nearly impossible) to deduce the private key from the public key.

A wallet is a collection of cassettes, or instruments, which are signed collections of Java class packages. Cassettes are described in the next section.

The Cassette Layer

The JECF uses the cassette mechanism to represent payment instruments and financial service applications. Payment instruments include the following:

- Credit cards

- Debit cards

- Pre-authorized payments

- Electronic checks

- Frequent flier miles

- Coupons

Service applications include the following:

- Accounting

- Budgeting and household management

- Tax analysis

- Banking

- Stock and bond brokerage

A *cassette* is a collection of Java packages. These packages are combined into a compressed Java Archive file (JAR file) and signed by a trusted authority. This trusted authority might be the issuer of the credit card represented by the cassette. The JECF uses the identity of the authority to grant access permissions to the user's private database.

Cassette Identity

As a security safeguard, every JECF cassette must have an *identity*. An identity is a subclass of the new `CassetteIdentifier` class (in package `java.commerce.cassette`). The organization that signs the cassette puts identical `CassetteIdentifier` classes in each package in the cassette. The cassette specification requires every package to have an identity, and the Java language specifies that every class name within a package must be unique. Thus, it is impossible for an attacker to insinuate a counterfeit identity into a cassette's package.

The `CassetteIdentifier` class (and therefore its subclasses) provides methods that describe the signer. The following are some of the methods of the `CassetteIdentifier` class:

`String getName()`   Returns the identity's common name.

`String getVersion()`   Returns the version of the identity.

Along with an identity, the JECF uses the digital-signature method for authentication.

Roles and Access Control

The JECF uses a design model of *roles*, *ultimate objects*, and *permit objects* to enforce access control. The `Ticket.stamp()` method tells whether an object plays a particular role. Tickets are discussed in the next section.

To understand the role mechanism and the JECF access control model, consider two cassettes. One implements a credit card payment instrument, and it will need to both read and write the user's private database. The other cassette implements a budget-analysis service. It will certainly need to read the database, but there is no reason for it to write the database. Clearly, the first cassette should have read/write permission on the database; the second should have read-only permission. In the vocabulary of roles, the credit card payment instrument cassette plays a *modifier* role with respect to the database, and the budget-analysis service cassette plays a *reader* role with respect to the database.

The JECF uses a design pattern called Capability to provide a flexible permission scheme that is extremely robust. To extend the example of the two cassettes accessing the user's database, suppose that access to the database is provided by an object called `userDB`. In the Capability design pattern, `userDB` is known as the *ultimate object*. An additional layer is created between the cassettes and the database, but it is `userDB` that the cassettes ultimately wish to access.

The extra layer is called the *permit* layer. Cassettes never make direct method calls to the `userDB` object. Instead, they obtain an object from the permit layer and make calls to that permit object; it is the permit object that makes calls to the `userDB` object. Each permit type corresponds to a role. In our example there are two roles: *database modifier* and *database reader*.

Permits are interfaces, not classes. This allows the JECF to take advantage of the fact that interfaces may have multiple inheritance.

> **NOTE** It is illegal in Java to define a class that extends two or more superclasses. It is perfectly legal, however, to do this with interfaces. Thus there is nothing wrong with the following declaration:
>
> ```
> interface A extends B, C, D, E, F { … }.
> ```

The example needs to have one permit type that supports database reading and writing, and another that supports only reading. The JECF style would be to create three interfaces: one to support reading, one to support writing, and one to support both. The last interface would simply inherit from the first two. The code below shows how this would be done, assuming the existence of a class called `Data` that represents information to be read or written.

```
interface DBReadPermit
{
    Data read();
}

interface DBWritePermit
{
    void write(Data d);
}

interface DBReadWritePermit extends DBReadPermit, DBWritePermit
{
    // Nothing in here; all methods are inherited.
}
```

Consider the budget-analysis cassette. It never receives a handle to the `userDB` object, which is the ultimate object. Because its role is database reader, it can only receive a handle to some object that implements the `DBReadPermit` interface. This permit object forbids writing to the database because it has no methods that write. This is the essence of the Capability design pattern.

The next section examines the mechanism for providing appropriate permits.

Tickets, Gates, and Permits

Access permission for a particular JECF resource is based on the identity of the client code (the client being the software entity that wishes to access the resource) and the role played by that client. In the example, one client is the credit card payment instrument. The resource is the database, and the role is database modifier. The JECF uses a ticket/gate architecture to ensure that clients receive access permits that correspond to their roles.

A *ticket* is an object that describes an identity and a role. Anyone can create a *role*, which is essentially a public-private key pair. The role's public key could be embedded in the financial institution's cassette. Clients could then use these tickets to prove their identity and role. In particular, tickets are used as inputs to *gate* methods, which return permits. In the example, there would be three gate methods:

```
DBReadPermit dataBase_ReadPermit(Ticket t, // other params)
DBWritePermit dataBase_WritePermit(Ticket t, // others)
DBReadWritePermit dataBase_ReadWritePermit(Ticket t, // others)
```

The form of each of these would be similar to the first:

```
DBReadPermit dataBase_ReadPermit (Ticket t) Throw SecurityException {
    if (t.stamp (ReadDBRole))
        return new DBReadPermit();
        else
            throw new SecurityException();
```

> **TIP**
>
> The JECF uses very specific naming conventions for permits, tickets, and gate methods. Sun has posted a document called "Writing Code for the JECF" that details these conventions. The document is available from the JECF home page, which is http://www.javasoft.com/products/commerce/.

The gate methods inspect the tickets to determine whether the client may access the requested resource. (The resource is specified in the other input parameters to the gate methods, designated by `// other params` in the list above.) If the resource request is legitimate, the gate method returns a permit object to the client; otherwise, a `SecurityException` is thrown. This permit object provides methods that support the operations permitted to the client; operations forbidden to the client are not supported by the permit object.

Summary

The JECF provides support for applet-based shopping and other financial transactions. The three layers in the JECF architecture are the Merchant Applet layer, Wallet layer, and Cassette layer.

The JECF is both secure and extensible. New payment instruments and new online financial services will likely be invented as electronic shopping and other forms of Internet commerce become an accepted part of everyday life. These instruments and services can be implemented as JECF cassettes and will be able to take advantage of the Java security apparatus.

CHAPTER
TWENTY

20

Java Beans

- The Java Bean component model

- The Java "Bean"

- Bean introspection and customization

- Bean applications and the Beans Development Kit (BDK)

- Beans and other developing technologies

One of the real goals of software development is to recoup the investment in code by making it possible for the code to be reused in other development efforts, either in the same company or in other companies. In recent years, programmers have expended great energy on creating reusable software. The early efforts spent on OOP (object-oriented programming) are now coming full circle with the development of a programming language like Java, where the software will run on a variety of platforms without any additional work.

However, Java does not automatically allow software to be reusable. Java code may be well written, and thus allow another developer to make changes to the code easily, but the goal of reusable software is to allow developers to use the code *without* needing to recompile the code. Furthermore, true reuse implies that developers can integrate code pieces into their designs without needing to recompile *their* code either.

These are the goals of the Java Beans API, which is the focus of this chapter. The Java Beans API is not yet a formal part of the language, but enough of the design is available to make it possible for developers to get started with this very exciting and powerful technology.

The Java Beans Component Model

Java Beans are based on a software component model for Java. The model is specifically designed to allow third-party vendors to create and sell Java components that are integrated into other software products by other developers.

An application developer will purchase off-the-shelf components from a vendor, drag-and-drop them onto a developer tool container, make any necessary modifications to each component, test them, and revise them as necessary without needing to write and compile code. Within the Java model, components may be modified or combined with other components to create new components or complete applications.

At runtime, the end user may also modify components through properties that the component designer (or application developer) built in. These may be simple properties, like color or shape, or more sophisticated properties that affect the overall behavior of the component.

The component model specified by the Java Beans 1.00-A Specification defines five major services:

Introspection　A mechanism that allows components to publish the operations and properties they support and a mechanism to support the discovery of such mechanisms in other components.

Communication　An event-handling mechanism for creating or "raising" an event to be received as a message by other components.

Persistence　A means of storing the state of a component.

Properties　A mechanism for control over the layout of a component. This includes the physical space that a component takes and the relationship of the component to other components when they are placed together on a container.

Customization　A mechanism for allowing developers control over changes that each component requires. Components should provide visibility for properties and operations (behavior) to a builder application. The application can then provide a developer with a means for modifying the component pieces in order to construct the appropriate application.

The component model allows software to be designed for modification. Each piece of software contains a set of properties, operations, and event handlers. Combining several components can create the specific runtime behavior a designer or developer wants. Components are held together in a container or toolkit, which provides the context for the application.

The Java Bean

A Java "Bean" is a single reusable software component. Beans are manipulated in a builder's tool (container) to provide specific operational behavior. Beans are building blocks for creating applications. The most common Bean will most likely be a small-to-medium control program, but it is also possible to create a Bean that encompasses a complete application and to embed that Bean into a compound document. For example, Figure 20.1 illustrates a container panel that holds three components.

FIGURE 20.1

A set of Bean components on a container

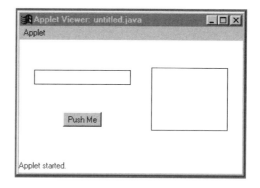

In general, Beans can be represented by simple GUIs; they can be button components, sliders, menu lists, and so on. These simple components provide a straightforward means of letting the user know what a Bean does. However, it is possible to create "invisible" Beans that are used to receive events and work behind the scenes. In any case, it is easiest to think of Beans as component building blocks designed to receive an event and process it so that some operation is carried out.

TIP The slides from the first Java Beans conference at Long Beach are available from http://splash.javasoft.com/beans/LongBeach/.

A Bean is neither a class library nor an API like JDBC. JDBC provides a means of querying databases; the Bean connects the user to the JDBC queries (see Chapter 18 for information about JDBC). For example, a Bean may be used to provide a simple Select button in an application's user interface. This may, in turn, be a Bean that composes the appropriate database select statement and issues the request. Visually, the Bean used in this case would resemble a Java button, similar to the Bean shown here which looks like a Select button.

Bean Architecture

Beans are composed of three parts: properties, methods, and events. These parts are illustrated in Figure 20.2.

FIGURE 20.2

Bean architecture

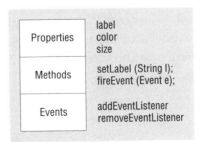

Properties	label color size
Methods	setLabel (String l); fireEvent (Event e);
Events	addEventListener removeEventListener

Bean properties describe the state attributes of the Bean, including its physical representation. Bean properties are the primary mechanisms of change within a Bean, and they are set or retrieved through methods. In addition, methods are used to fire and receive events, the mechanism by which Beans communicate. Multiple Beans, connected by event methods, make up a complete system or application, as shown earlier in Figure 20.1.

Bean Event Model

Bean events are the mechanism for notification between Beans, and between Beans and containers. A Bean uses an event to notify another Bean to take an action or to inform the Bean that a state change has occurred. An event is registered or published by the source and propagated (through a method call) to one or more target listeners.

Bean events are passed as an object, an instance of a class that extends from `java.util.EventObject`. The event can be created directly from this class, as in the following example:

```
public class MyEvent extends java.util.EventObject {
   public MyEvent (Object source) {
      super (source);
   }
}
```

The Java Beans model closely follows the JDK 1.1 AWT event model. This is helpful because many Bean components are visual GUI elements that are part of the AWT hierarchy. At the lowest level, events are sent as the result of some change, input, or other occurrence on the visual component. The AWT defines the low-level hierarchy as follows:

```
java.util.EventObject
   java.awt.AWTEvent
      java.awt.event.ComponentEvent
      java.awt.event.ContainerEvent
```

```
java.awt.event.FocusEvent
java.awt.event.InputEvent
java.awt.event.KeyEvent
java.awt.event.MouseEvent
java.awt.event.WindowEvent
```

The AWT event hierarchy also defines a set of events that are used to provide events that occur at the higher level of the user interface. These higher-level events apply to multiple component types, as in the following:

```
java.util.EventObject
    java.awt.AWTEvent
        java.awt.event.ActionEvent
        java.awt.event.AdjustmentEvent
        java.awt.event.ItemEvent
        java.awt.event.TextEvent
```

Beans send events as the single parameter to an event method of the target Bean. However, events encapsulate elements that may be used by the recipient of the event—for example:

```
public void fireAction (String command) {
    if (listener != null) {
        ActionEvent actionEvt =
            new ActionEvent(this, 0, command);
        listener.actionPerformed(actionEvt);
    }
}
```

Here, an event object with a `String command` is sent to the `listener` object, and the event method to be triggered is the `actionPerformed()` event.

Event Sources and Targets

The event model in Java Beans is defined by event sources and event targets. The event source identifies itself as the initiator of an event by registering one or more event targets. Both the event source and the event target establish a set of methods that the event source will use to call event listeners.

An event source attempts to send a desired event to an arbitrary collection of event targets. This mode is the default behavior of the event source and is called *multicast*. The event source keeps track of the event listeners for each kind of event it fires and notifies each target when an event is fired.

A multicast event allows a source object to notify several event listeners all at once, which is accomplished by keeping the state of every event listener registered in a `Vector` class:

```
private Vector listenerList = new Vector ();

public synchronized void addActionListener (ActionListener 1) {
    listenerList.addElement (1);
}

public synchronized void removeActionListener (ActionListener 1) {
    listenerList.removeElement (1);
}
```

NOTE The `add/remove ActionListener` pair is typically synchronized to avoid multithread race conditions. (Race conditions occur when multiple processes try to do something with shared data and the outcome depends on the order of operations.)

Event sources may also be *unicast* sources, where the event source is required to keep track of a single target listener for each type of event it fires. A unicast event is sent to the specific single target listener.

The unicast event allows only one listener to be registered; otherwise, an exception, `java.util.TooManyListenersException`, is thrown. The unicast event listener stores just one instance of a listener:

```
private ActionListener 1;

public synchronized void addActionListener (ActionListener 1)
    throws java.util.TooManyListenersException {
    if (1 == null) {
```

```
      this.1 = 1;
   } else {
      throw new java.util.TooManyListenersException ();
   }
}

public synchronized void removeActionListener (ActionListener 1)
{
   1 = null;
}
```

The event target is an instance of a class that implements some (or all) of the `EventListener` interface—specifically, the event methods that class is interested in.

Each event type is tied to a single method, and event methods are typically grouped by their application—for example:

```
import java.awt.event.*;
public class MyActionEventListener implements ActionListener {

   // Provide an event method for the actionPerformed event
   public void actionPerformed (ActionEvent e) {

      // Pull the command out of the event
      String command = e.getActionCommand ();

      if (command.equals ("add")) {
         ...
      }
   }
}
```

The following is an example of the use of a multicast event source and event listener. This example illustrates how an event listener is registered with an event source and how the event source sends an event to each of the listeners registered.

```
import java.util.Vector;
import java.awt.event.*;
public class MyApp {
```

```
private Vector listenerList = new Vector ();
private MyActionEventListener myListener;

   public MyApp () {
      myListener = new MyActionEventListener ();
      addActionListener (myListener);
}

public synchronized void addActionListener(ActionListener l)
   {
      listenerList.addElement (l);
}

public synchronized void removeActionListener
   (ActionListener l) {
      listenerList.removeElement (l);
}

public void fireAction (String command) {
   Vector targets;
   synchronized (this) {
      targets = (Vector) listenerList.clone();
   }
   ActionEvent actionEvt =
            new ActionEvent(this, 0, command);
      for (int i = 0; i < targets.size(); i++) {
         ActionListener target =
                  (ActionListener)targets.elementAt(i);
         target.actionPerformed(actionEvt);
      }
   }
   ...
}
```

In some cases, the event target cannot implement the interface directly, and an instance of an event-adapter class may be used to interpose between the source and one or more listeners.

The event adapter implements one or more listener interfaces and allows a developer to use a single event to be sent to two different adapter classes that interpose between the source and listener. Besides allowing a developer to use a single event with multiple event sources to a single listener, adapters are useful for filtering events and implementing advanced features like event queues.

Bean Properties

The *properties* of a Bean describe attributes associated with the Bean, such as color, size, or the string to be used as a label. Properties may be used in a number of ways, depending on the environment in which the Bean is accessed. Properties can be changed at runtime through their `get`/`set` methods, through a scripting environment, or in a property sheet that is part of a Bean builder/customization tool.

A property can be changed by the end user through a pair of `get`/`set` methods that is specific to the property. For example, there may be a color property for the Bean, and the end user can change the color of the Bean through a properties dialog box provided with the Bean. The Bean provides two methods to allow the private color property to be changed:

```
public Color getFillColor (); // This Bean's object fill color
public void setFillColor (Color c);
```

Properties may be indexed to support a range of values, where the indexes are specified by `int` values. Indexed properties have four access signatures, where the arrays of values may be accessed by either a single element or by the entire array:

```
void setLabel (int index, String label);
String getLabel (int index);
void setLabel (String [] labels);
String [] getLabel ();
```

The indexed methods should check array bounds and throw `java` `.lang.ArrayIndexOutOfBoundsException` if the index is outside those bounds.

Other property types include bound properties and constrained properties. A bound property sends a notification of a change in property to other Beans and/or the container when a property change occurs. A bound property raises an event when a change is made.

A bound property sends a notification that a change has been made. The notification process occurs by *binding* the property type to a PropertyChangeListener event listener. A Bean that wishes to notify itself, some other Bean, or the Bean container tool will include a pair of multicast event listener registration methods:

```
public void addPropertyChangeListener (PropertyChangeListener l);
public void removePropertyChangeListener (PropertyChangeListener l);
```

The Java Beans API provides a class that supports bound properties. This class may be used to display a property sheet editor for a particular property. For example:

```
private PropertyChangeSupport changes =
    new PropertyChangeSupport(this);

public void setFillColor (Color newColor) {
   Color oldColor = currColor;
   currColor = newColor;
   changes.firePropertyChange ("color", oldColor, newColor);
   ...
}
```

The firePropertyChange() method will call the property-Change() method on the object that implements the Property-ChangeListener interface. Typically, this object would be part of a builder tool and would call an appropriate property sheet method to open a property editor.

Constrained properties are validated internally and rejected if they are inappropriate. The user or developer is notified of a rejected property through an exception—for example:

```
public Dimension getSize () {
   return currSize;
}
public void setSize (Dimension d)
```

```
    throws SizeChangeRejectedException (){
    // Check the size and throw an exception
    // if it exceeds some preset value
    ...
}
```

Constrained properties use the `VetoableChangeListener` interface to validate changes. These are implemented in the Bean by including a pair of `add`/`remove` methods:

```
public void addVetoableChangeListener (VetoableChangeListener v);
public void removeVetoableChangeListener (VetoableChangeListener v);
```

Of course, the Bean property method should fire an event before the property is changed—for example:

```
private VetoableChangeSupport vetos =
    new VetoableChangeSupport(this);

public void setSize (Dimension newSize)
    throws PropertyVetoException {
  Dimension oldSize = currSize;
  vetos.fireVetoableChange ("size", oldSize, newSize);
  // No one vetoed, make the change
  currSize = newSize;
  changes.firePropertyChange ("size", oldSize, newSize);
  ...
}
```

Bean Methods

Bean methods are the operations that are called from other components (that have an instance of the Bean), the container, or from a scripting environment. Bean methods may be exported by making them public; this makes it possible to view the methods with a builder tool using Java introspection (more on this later).

Methods are used to set and get properties and fire and catch events. Bean methods may be either public or private. Methods that are private may not be seen or modified by builder tools.

Bean Storage

Beans are stored in a JAR (Java Archive) format. Essentially, JAR files are Zip-formatted archive files with an optional component called a manifest file that can contain additional information about the contents of the JAR file.

Applications that use Beans are not required by the Java Beans Specification to use JAR files or even to store beans as JAR files; however, the specification does propose that Beans should be shipped as JAR files initially.

NOTE   For more information about Bean storage, see Chapter 11, "Packaging," of the Java Beans Specification, version 1.00-A, and the JAR HTML file in the Beans Development Kit, under <installation directory>/beans/doc/jar.html.

Inspecting and Customizing Beans

Beans will be received as pieces of software from vendors or developed internally within companies. A Bean is likely to be developed as a generic component; that is, designed to be customized by the developer at application creation. This happens through two Java technologies that are maturing with the Java Beans API:

- The Java Reflection API, a set of classes that is used to look into a class file and discover the properties (variables) and methods of the class.

- The Java Serialization API, which is used to create a permanent storage of a class, including its current state.

These two technologies are used to allow Beans to be investigated and discovered by a builder tool, then modified and stored for a particular application use.

The Bean Introspection Process

The Java Bean introspection process exposes the properties, methods, and events of a Bean. The introspection process is actually quite rote. Bean classes are assumed to have properties if there are methods that either set or get a property type:

```
public <PropertyType> get<PropertyName> ();
public void set<PropertyName> (<PropertyType> p>);
```

If only one of the get/set methods is discovered, then Property-Name is determined to be read-only or write-only.

Properties that are boolean—that is, return a boolean type—may also have a boolean method:

```
public boolean is<PropertyName> ();
```

Indexed properties are also discovered when the method signatures include them:

```
public <PropertyElement> get<PropertyName> (int a);
public void set<PropertyName> (int a, <PropertyElement> b);
```

These are replaced by the four access signatures described earlier.

Events are discovered by a pair of add/remove event methods. These are assumed to begin with add and remove and take an <EventListenerType> argument that extends the java.util .EventListener interface, where the type name ends with Listener. For example:

```
public void add<EventListenerType> (<EventListenerType> a);
public void remove<EventListenerType> (<EventListenerType> a);
```

Methods are discovered if the method access is public. This includes all of the property and event methods.

The BeanInfo Interface

The Java Bean API also provides an explicit interface to allow Bean designers to expose the properties, events, methods, and any global information about a Bean. A Bean vendor provides a `BeanInfo` interface by supplying a class that extends the `BeanInfo` interface and appends `BeanInfo` to the class name:

```
public class myBeanBeanInfo implements java.util.BeanInfo {…
```

The `BeanInfo` interface provides a series of methods to access Bean information, but a Bean developer can also include private description files that the `BeanInfo` class uses to define Bean information. By default, a `BeanInfo` object is created when introspection is run on the Bean.

The process follows these steps to discover the inner workings of a Bean:

- Walk the class and superclass chain of each target class.

- Look for a `BeanInfo` class name (the class name with `BeanInfo` appended to the end of the name).

- Use low-level reflection to study the class and create a `BeanInfo` object with the results.

Bean Persistence

Java Beans are components that rely on state. When a Bean receives a state change, the Bean designer may desire to store, or *persist*, the changed state. State changes may occur as the result of some action, either during runtime or development.

Beans may be stored in one of two ways: automatically through the Java Object Serialization mechanism, or through a future externalization stream mechanism that will allow the Bean object complete control over the writing of its state, including the ability to mimic arbitrary existing data formats.

Normally, a Bean will store the parts of its internal state that would be used to define the Bean on re-creation. Typically, these are the Bean's look and feel and the Bean's behavior. A Bean that references other Beans may wish to store these references, but this activity is inherently dangerous because it assumes the *referenced* Beans are also saved. Instead, references to other Beans should be rebuilt during the re-creation process. In this way, Beans may mark references as "transient" to specify that the reference is volatile and will be rebuilt as necessary.

The Beans Development Kit (BDK)

The BDK is a pure Java application that allows Java developers to create reusable components that use the Bean event model. The BDK is dependent only on the current release of the JDK 1.1, and it is available for both Solaris Unix and Win32 platforms. The BDK is not intended as a commercial product; instead, the BDK provides a first look at Beans: how they are constructed and how they are applied through a simple and easy-to-use builder application.

TIP In December 1996, JavaSoft announced the JDK version 1.1 Beta release, followed four days later by a minor update of the JDK to 1.1 Beta 2. At the same time, JavaSoft announced a Beta version (followed by a Beta 2 version) of the BDK. The final (first customer ship) BDK is planned for the first quarter of 1997. The BDK is available from http://splash.javasoft.com/beans/; the current JDK release is available from http://www.javasoft.com/products/JDK/1.1/.

Installing the BDK

The Beta BDK is a complete system and contains source code for all of the applications, examples, and documentation. The BDK also contains a sample Bean builder and customizer application called BeanBox.

The Beta BDK is downloaded as either a Bourne shell executable (bdk_beta3.sh) for Solaris Unix or as a Win32 exe file (bdk_beta3.exe) for Windows 95 and NT systems. For Solaris Unix, the BDK is unpacked by running the shell executable:

% sh bdk_beta3.sh

For Win32 systems the BDK is installed by copying the bdk_beta3 .exe file into a folder and double-clicking on it. This will unpack the distribution and create a setup batch script. To continue the installation, double-click on this script.

Both installations ask the user to agree to the terms of the distribution license agreement and then create a beans directory that contains the following subdirectories:

apis   Contains the source code for the Bean API.

beanbox   Contains the sample Bean builder tool, BeanBox.

classes   Holds the compiled Bean class files.

demo   Stores the sample Beans in the BeanBox.

doc   Contains HTML files that describe the Bean API, the Bean-Box, and examples.

jars   Holds the JAR files of the sample Beans that the BeanBox application will read and load.

To use the Beta BDK, the JDK 1.1 Beta 3 must also be loaded, and the CLASSPATH environment variable should include: <installation directory>/beans/classes.

Using the BDK BeanBox

The BDK BeanBox application (located in the beanbox directory under the beans installation directory) is a simple test container that allows you to work with Bean components as follows:

- Drop Beans onto a composition window.

- Resize and move Beans.

- Alter Beans with property sheets.

- Customize Beans with a customizer application.

- Connect Beans together.

- Save Beans through serialization.

- Restore Beans.

You can also add new Beans to the BeanBox and then use existing components to create simple applications.

Figure 20.3 shows the BeanBox composition window (center), Tool-Box palette (left), and PropertySheet window (right). The ToolBox palette displays the Beans that are available to be dropped onto the composition window. When a Bean is selected, the PropertySheet window displays the properties of the Bean that are available for editing.

To place a Bean in the composition window, select the Bean from the Bean's icon or name on the ToolBox palette, then click the mouse where the center of the Bean should go. The Bean is then drawn onto the composition window with a black-and-white-hashed boundary, as shown in Figure 20.4.

The File menu in the BeanBox composition window allows the current composition to be saved, cleared, or exited. The Load option on the File menu is used to restore the state of a saved composition.

FIGURE 20.3

The BeanBox application

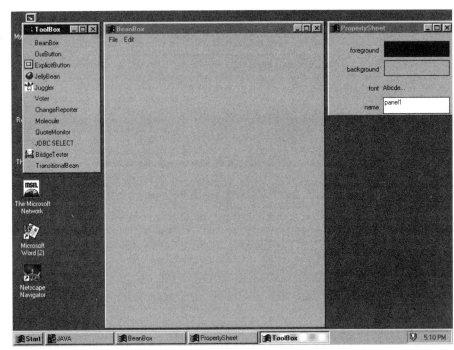

FIGURE 20.4

A Bean in the BeanBox window

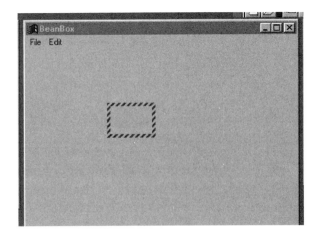

The Edit menu is used to change the currently selected Bean (or the composition window if no Bean is selected). The Edit menu includes Cut, Copy, and Paste options for selected Beans. Depending on the Bean selected, the Edit menu will also list the Events option, which allows you to "connect" Beans together.

The Sample Beans

The BeanBox comes with a set of 12 sample Beans. Each of these has a different function and provides an example of various aspects of the Java Beans API. The Beans provided with the BeanBox are listed in the ToolBox palette and described in Table 20.1.

TABLE 20.1   Sample Beans in the BeanBox

Bean	Description
BeanBox	This composition window itself is a Bean, and a BeanBox can be nested inside another.
OurButton	A subclass of a `java.awt.Canvas`. This Bean is the simplest button GUI component. When clicked, it will send a standard AWT `actionPerformed` method. OurButton exposes four properties: (`label`, `fontSize`, `largeFont`, and `debug`) in addition to the standard `java.awt.Component` properties. These properties illustrate the use of getter/setter methods for `String`, `int`, `Font` class, and boolean parameter types.
ExplicitButton	A simple subclass of the OurButton Bean, which illustrates the effect that a `BeanInfo` class can have. The `ExplicitButtonBeanInfo` class includes a `PropertyDescriptor` method that defines default values for the `label`, `fontSize`, `largeFont`, and `debug` parameters. The `ExplicitButtonBeanInfo` class also illustrates how to define icons that will appear to the left of the Bean name in the ToolBox palette and makes use of a simple `customizer` class, the `OurButtonCustomizer` class. This `customizer` appears in the Edit menu when this Bean is selected and allows the developer to edit the button label.
JellyBean	A simple visual component that draws a colored oval "jelly bean." This Bean illustrates the use of bound and constrained properties. The `color` property is a bound component and notifies the JellyBean when a change is made to the component. The `priceInCents` property is an example of a constrained property.
Juggler	Represents a threaded animation component that may be started and stopped by connecting a button-push event from an ExplicitButton or OurButton to the `start` and `stop` event methods supported by the Juggler Bean.

TABLE 20.1   Sample Beans in the BeanBox (Continued)

Bean	Description
Voter	Designed to handle a `vetoableChange` event. By default, the Bean will reject all change requests (it is initially set to NO), but change requests will be accepted if the `vetoAll` property is set to `false`.
ChangeReporter	A `TextField` component that can be used to display `PropertyChange` events.
Molecule	Similar to Juggler in concept. The Bean displays a 3-D representation of a molecule and accepts mouse input to rotate the molecule. It is also possible to rotate the molecule by attaching buttons to the `rotateX()` and `rotateY()` methods.
QuoteMonitor	Uses Remote Method Invocation (RMI) to contact a remote (or local) quote server and request a real or imaginary stock quote value. The RMI server is started by changing directories to the `demo` directory and executing `gnumake -f quote.gmk run &` on Solaris Unix or `start nmake -f quote.mk run` from a DOS prompt on a Win32 system.
JDBC Select	Uses the JDBC API to connect to a database at a specified URL and issue a select statement. It is complex and requires its own `customizer` to configure the JDBC URL string, database username, and password.
BridgeTester	Provides a set of property types and events that may be used to test other Bean components.
TransitionalBean	Uses the JDK 1.0.2 event model and will work with both JDK 1.1 and JDK 1.0.2.

Connecting Beans

You can connect Beans visually in the BeanBox tool. Figure 20.5 shows the Juggler Bean with two ExplicitButton Beans. The next step in making a simple animation application is to connect one of the buttons to the `start()` event method on the Juggler Bean and connect the other to a `stop()` event method.

After selecting one of the ExplicitButton Beans, you would choose Events from the Edit menu, then button push, then actionPerformed. This procedure is shown in Figure 20.6.

FIGURE 20.5

The Juggler application

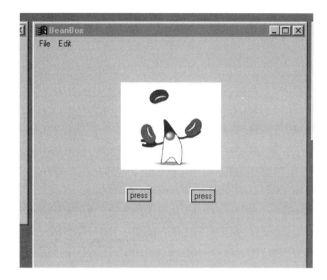

FIGURE 20.6

Selecting the action-
Performed event

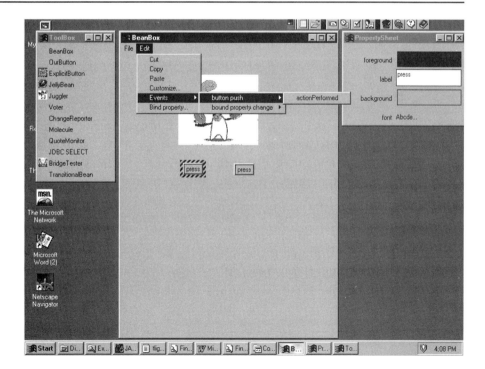

After this event is selected, the BeanBox will draw a rubber-banding line from the ExplicitButton Bean. This line illustrates the event source. The event target (listener) is selected by clicking on the Bean that the event source should go to. In this case, the Juggler Bean will receive an `actionPerformed` event. The Juggler Bean supports two methods that can receive an `actionPerformed` event: `start()` and `stop()`. These appear in an EventTargetDialog pop-up window, as shown in Figure 20.7.

FIGURE 20.7

The EventTargetDialog pop-up window for Juggler

Selecting the `start()` method will connect the ExplicitButton's `actionPerformed` event to the `start()` method of the Juggler Bean. The two Beans are now connected. Clicking on the ExplicitButton with the mouse will send the event to the Juggler Bean, and the Bean will begin the animation. To connect the other ExplicitButton to the Juggler `stop()` method, the steps above are repeated, and the `stop()` method is selected. The application is now completely functional after just a few mouse clicks. To complete the application, the two ExplicitButtons are labeled Start and Stop to indicate what actions they will have on the Juggler Bean.

Saving and Restoring Bean Applications

You can save Bean applications created in the BeanBox in their current state (including running or stopped, as in the case of the Juggler application) by selecting the Save option from the File menu. This opens a dialog box in which you can specify the name of the file that the current set of Beans in the composition window is saved to. To restore the application, use the File menu's Load option.

The current BeanBox composition window is in a beta state and not intended for commercial use. There are two important things to note:

- The Clear and Load options on the File menu will clear the current set of Beans in the composition window without any warning, even if they are not already saved.

- The Save option on the File menu will not ask if you want to overwrite any current Bean application.

Creating a New Bean

The BDK also provides a means for adding new Beans to the BeanBox and testing them. The example presented here illustrates the process.

In the example, the new Bean will emulate the operation of a traffic signal light. The traffic signal is a rectangular component with three colored circles: red, yellow, and green. These are meant to emulate the functions of a real-life traffic signal: stop, slow, and go.

The traffic component will respond to a signal from a Walk button to cycle between its current state (either red or green; yellow is a transient state) to allow someone to cross the street. For simplicity, the component will be represented by a two-dimensional rectangle, as shown here.

This component is a visual component, so it will need to subclass from an AWT component. In addition to responding to a signal from the Walk button, the component should signal or support a second traffic light slave that would appear at a four-way intersection.

The TrafficLight Bean

The BDK provides a directory where it stores the example source code and a set of make files that are used to create the JAR files that the BeanBox requires. This directory is just below the installation directory of the BDK, in a directory named demo.

This directory contains the GNU and nmake files for Solaris and Win32 systems. There is also a directory sun/demo, where the source files for the sample Beans are stored. For simplicity, the directory containing TrafficLight, called tlight, is created in this location. Using this directory path and structure makes it possible to copy one of the existing make files in the BDK demo directory.

The TrafficLight Bean subclasses a `java.awt.Canvas` component. TrafficLight exposes two properties: `defaultLight`, which is a `String` representing the starting color of the light in its resting state, and a `boolean debug` property, which may be turned on or off through a property sheet in order to see the result of events as they are passed to and from the TrafficLight component.

Here is the source code, which is for the TrafficLight component:

TrafficLight.java

```
package sun.demo.tlight;

import java.awt.*;
import java.awt.event.*;
import java.awt.image.*;
import java.beans.*;

// A Simple bean that represents a traffic light component
```

```
public class TrafficLight extends Canvas implements Runnable {

   private ActionListener l = null;

   private Thread me = null;

   private String defaultLight = "RED";
   private String currLight = defaultLight;

   private boolean debug = false;

   // Set the size of the Bean display
   public TrafficLight () {
      setSize (100, 200);
   }

   // Turn debugging on/off
   public void setDebugging (boolean state) {
      debug = state;
   }

   public boolean getDebugging () {
      return debug;
   }

   // Methods for get/set of the default light state
   public synchronized String getDefaultLightState () {
      return defaultLight;
   }

   public void setDefaultLightState (String state) {
      defaultLight = state;
      currLight = state;
      repaint();
   }

   // Display the current traffic light state
   public void paint (Graphics g) {

      // Put a black border around it
      g.setColor (Color.black);
      g.drawRect (1, 1, 98, 198);
```

```
// Paint the outline of the traffic light
g.setColor (Color.white);
g.fillRect (2, 2, 96, 196);

// Paint the outline of the lights
g.setColor (Color.black);
g.drawOval (30, 30, 40, 40);
g.drawOval (30, 80, 40, 40);
g.drawOval (30, 130, 40, 40);

// Debug
if (debug) {
   System.out.println
      ("Current light state is: " + currLight);
}

// Which light is on?
if (currLight.equals("RED")) {
   g.setColor (Color.red);
   g.fillOval (30, 30, 40, 40);
} else {
   if (currLight.equals("YELLOW")) {
      g.setColor (Color.yellow);
      g.fillOval (30, 80, 40, 40);
   } else   {
      if (currLight.equals("GREEN")) {
         g.setColor (Color.green);
         g.fillOval (30, 130, 40, 40);
      }
   }
}

}

// Send a message to the light to start a cycle
public void start (ActionEvent x) {
   // Debug
   if (debug) {
      System.out.println ("Got a start Event!");
   }
   startCycle ();
}
```

```
// Start a light cycle
private synchronized void startCycle () {
   // Don't bother unless there is no cycle running already
   if (me == null) {
      me = new Thread (this);
      me.start ();
   }
}

// The run method
public void run () {
   // Debug
   if (debug) {
      System.out.println ("Started cycle");
   }

   while (me != null) {
      try {
         me.sleep (3000);
      } catch (InterruptedException e) {
      }

      // Get the current light state
      if (currLight.equals ("RED")) {
         // Cycle to green
         currLight = "GREEN";
         fireAction(currLight);
      } else {
         if (currLight.equals("GREEN")) {
            // Cycle through yellow to red
            currLight = "YELLOW";
         } else {
            // Otherwise, we are at YELLOW,
            // so cycle to RED
            currLight = "RED";
            fireAction(currLight);
         }
      }
      repaint ();
      // Break the cycle when the default state is reached
      if (currLight == defaultLight) {
```

```
                    me = null;
                }
            }

        }

        // Get an event that indicates a light
        // Change from another light
        // In which case, we will act as slave
        public void lightChange (ActionEvent x) {
            // Check the state of this event
            String command = x.getActionCommand();
            // Debug
            if (debug) {
                System.out.println
                    ("Received event from traffic light: "
                    + defaultLight + " command: go to " + command);
            }

            // If the other light went red, then check our default
            if (command.equals ("RED")) {
                if (currLight.equals ("GREEN")) {
                    // ok, do nothing
                } else {
                    // Cycle
                    currLight = "GREEN";
                    repaint ();
                }
            } else {
                if (command.equals ("GREEN")) {
                    if (currLight.equals ("RED")) {
                        // ok, do nothing
                    } else {
                        // Cycle
                        currLight = "YELLOW";
                        repaint ();
                        try {
                            Thread.sleep (3000);
                        } catch (InterruptedException e) {}
                        currLight = "RED";
                        repaint ();
```

```
            }
         }
      }
   }

   // The fireAction method sends an event to the
   // slave TrafficLight to tell it we are changing
   // state
   public void fireAction (String s) {
      // Debug
      if (debug) {
         System.out.println ("Firing action event");
      }

      if (1 != null) {
         ActionEvent actionEvt = new ActionEvent(this, 0, s);
         1.actionPerformed(actionEvt);
      }
   }

   // List ourselves as the source of an event
   // Just use Action for now...
   public void addActionListener (ActionListener 1)
      throws java.util.TooManyListenersException
   {
      // Debug
      if (debug) {
         System.out.println ("Registering a listener");
      }

      // Is there an event listener already?
      if (this.1 != null) {
         throw new java.util.TooManyListenersException ();
      }
      this.1 = 1;
   }

   public void removeActionListener (ActionListener 1) {
      1 = null;
   }
}
```

The TrafficLight component uses a pair of `set`/`get` methods to expose the `Debugging` and `DefaultLightState` properties. The `paint()` method for the component paints a white rectangle and three empty circles to indicate the red, yellow, and green lights for the TrafficLight Bean.

Public methods that take an `ActionEvent` argument may be connected to an `actionPerformed` event (like the Juggler Bean example discussed in the previous section). The TrafficLight Bean supports two such methods: a `start()` method that calls a private `startCycle()` method that, in turn, creates a thread and begins the cycle of changing the TrafficLight from its current state to its opposite state and back again. This method is intended to support the Walk button.

The `lightChange()` method is used to support a second traffic light slave. This method is used to connect two TrafficLight Beans. When one light is cycling, the other is notified through an event that the light should change. For example, if the first traffic light changes from green to red, then the second light (on the other intersection) will change from red to green.

The `fireAction()` method is used to notify another TrafficLight Bean that is registered as an `ActionListener`. Note that the TrafficLight Bean is an example of a unicast event source and therefore does not support more than a four-way intersection. The source code for the TrafficLight Bean is included on the CD-ROM accompanying this book.

Compiling the TrafficLight Bean   The BDK provides a set of make files that make it easier to compile Bean components and place them in the appropriate classes directory, as well as putting them into JAR files that the BeanBox can read.

The following listing is an example of a GNU make file copied and modified from one of the existing make files in the demo directory below the installation directory of the BDK.

tlight.gmk

```
CLASSFILES= \
    sun/demo/tlight/TrafficLight.class
#   sun/demo/tlight/TrafficLightBeanInfo.class

#GIFFILES= \
#   sun/demo/tlight/TrafficLightIcon.gif

JARFILE= ../jars/tlight.jar

all: $(JARFILE)

# Create a JAR file with a suitable manifest.

$(JARFILE): $(CLASSFILES) $(GIFFILES)
    echo "Manifest-Version: 1.0" > manifest.tmp
    echo "" >> manifest.tmp
    echo "Name: sun/demo/tlight/TrafficLight.class" >> manifest.tmp
    echo "Java-Bean: True" >> manifest.tmp
    jar cfm $(JARFILE) manifest.tmp sun/demo/tlight/*.class $(GIFFILES)
    ➡@/bin/rm manifest.tmp

%.class: %.java
    export CLASSPATH; CLASSPATH=../classes:.; \
    javac $<

clean:
    /bin/rm -f sun/demo/tlight/*.class
    /bin/rm -f $(JARFILE)
```

NOTE For a Win32 system, the make file for TrafficLight should be a copy of one of the .mk files, and the nmake utility is used to compile the make file.

To compile and create a JAR file (under Solaris Unix) the make file is compiled with gnumake, a GNU make utility:

```
% cd Beans/demo
% gnumake tlight.gmk
```

Once compiled correctly, the make file will create a manifest file for the TrafficLight.class file and create an appropriate JAR file. The new JAR file is then copied into the jars directory, where the BeanBox can read it.

Inserting the New Bean into the BeanBox

When the BeanBox is started through its make file, the BeanBox application will load the JAR files that are located in the jars directory. To add the tlight JAR file created by the make file above, the BeanBox application is started through the make file:

```
%cd beans/beanbox
%gnumake run
```

> **NOTE** For a Win32 system, the BeanBox will reload the JAR files with the command **nmake run**.

This forces the BeanBox to reload the JAR files in the jars directory and re-create the ToolBox palette with the TrafficLight component, as shown in Figure 20.8.

FIGURE 20.8

The ToolBox with the TrafficLight Bean

Testing the New Bean

To test the TrafficLight Bean, two instances of the new Bean and one instance of an ExplicitButton (for the Walk signal) are placed in the composition window, as shown in Figure 20.9.

FIGURE 20.9

Two instances of the TrafficLight Bean and an ExplicitButton in the composition window

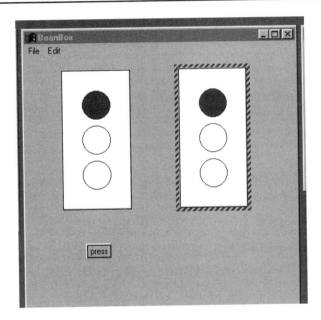

Using the Edit menu's Event item, the ExplicitButton `action-Performed` event is connected to the `start()` event method of the first TrafficLight Bean. When the button is clicked with the mouse, the TrafficLight Bean will cycle to green, yellow, and then back to red, with a brief (three-second) delay between light changes.

Both TrafficLight Beans are in a RED state by default, so the second Bean's `defaultLightState` is changed to GREEN by entering the string **GREEN** in the PropertySheet window for the second Bean.

Next, the first traffic light is connected to the second traffic light through an `actionPerformed` method to the second traffic light's lightChange() method. This is done by repeating the steps for connecting the ExplicitButton. As a final step, the label of the Explicit-Button is changed from Press to Walk, as shown in Figure 20.10.

FIGURE 20.10

The completed traffic light application

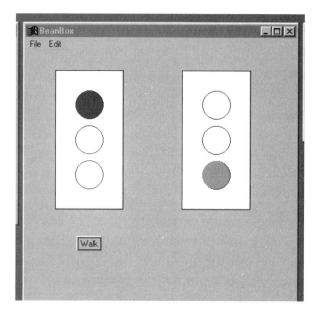

When the Walk button is clicked with the mouse, the first traffic light sends a signal to the second light to change and then begins its own change cycle. The second light changes from green to yellow, and then red, as the first traffic light changes from red to green, then to yellow, and finally to red.

Integrating Beans in Other Technologies

Besides being reusable software components, Beans also will allow developers to integrate their code with other technologies, including access to Microsoft's ActiveX API, AppleSoft's OpenDoc technology, and Netscape's JavaScript and LiveConnect technologies.

Java Beans will allow developers to create controls for ActiveX through COM events. The result is that the Bean will run in the ActiveX environment without any knowledge of the underlying environment and without needing to create any C++ code or tie the Bean development into any Microsoft tools.

Beans under OpenDoc will run as OpenDoc parts, and it will be possible to create a Bean that acts as an OpenDoc container. Beans under Netscape will be able to fire events to JavaScript, and JavaScript will be able to make property changes on Beans. These technologies are currently under development by their respective companies.

In addition to integration with other technologies, the Java Bean specification has several authors and partners from other industries, including Borland (J Builder), IBM (Visual Age for Java), Penumbra Software (Mojo), SunSoft (Java Workshop and Java Studio), Symantec (Visual Café), and others. These partners are creating builder tools that facilitate Bean development and deployment.

Summary

The Java development environment continues to add more functionality and features. The Java language has gone from being an interesting departure from C++ to a serious multiplatform development language. The Java Beans specification and the BDK will move Java into a next-generation tool, allowing developers to concentrate on writing code that is cross-platform and truly reusable.

Java Servlets

- Advantages of servlets

- Servlet classes and methods

- Java Web Server configuration for servlets

- Server-side includes

- Communication between servlets

The Java Web Server, formerly known as Jeeves, is JavaSoft's own Web server. The Java Web Server is just a part of a larger framework, intended to provide you not just with a Web server, but also with tools to build customized network servers for any Internet or Intranet client-server system. The most interesting part of the Java Web Server distribution, from a programmer's point of view, is the Servlet API. Servlets are to a Web server what applets are to the browser.

This chapter discusses the Servlet API and the origin of the servlet as an improved form of CGI (Common Gateway Interface). The examples demonstrate the use of servlets in HTTP environments, and the key Servlet API mechanisms are introduced.

Although, as programmers, you will be mainly concerned with the techniques for coding servlets, the chapter also covers some of the basic elements of the Java Web Server configuration. This knowledge will allow you to set up the server for servlet support and install and try out the examples.

In addition to the fundamental facilities of servlets and the supporting Web server configuration, this chapter also discusses the server-side include (SSI) mechanism as it applies to servlets, as well as a number of techniques for arranging communication between servlets.

CGI Limitations

When HTML and the World Wide Web were first invented, the content of each displayed page was essentially static. Each URL referred directly to either a fixed page or a fixed element of a page. To allow for the possibility of more interaction, and hence for pages that are tailored to an individual request, the CGI mechanism was introduced.

CGI allows a URL to contain a basic reference, which is not to a page of HTML, but to a program. In addition to that basic reference, parameters to control the execution can also be passed from the browser into the CGI program.

Although CGI is quite simple to use, both from the user's and the server administrator's point of view, it has a number of weaknesses:

Low performance Most CGI programs are written using interpreted languages such as Unix shell scripts and PERL. This is not a requirement of the CGI specification, but appears to be the popular option. Using compiled languages improves speed but tends to raise platform-dependency issues.

Startup time CGI programs run as separate processes, which generally involves significant startup time. This overhead occurs each time the program is invoked. The startup time is compounded if you are using an interpreter.

Poor inter-CGI communication Because each invocation of a CGI program starts a separate process, communicating between invocations must usually be done via files, and hence can be quite slow. Communicating between different CGI programs on the same server is similarly cumbersome.

Security Some variations of CGI have suffered from significant security weaknesses. Even when more recent standards and relatively safe languages like PERL are used, the system does not have a basic security framework, but relies instead on a collection of ad hoc rules.

A number of enhancements have been made to CGI to address these limitations. FastCGI avoids the process-startup overhead by using persistent processes, but using FastCGI interprocess communication is still slow. Some C language APIs allow for programs to run inside the server, but these APIs are platform dependent and difficult to secure; they also tend to be rather complex.

Another choice that you now have is to use a servlet. Servlets can do the things that CGI is used for, and they have many advantages over CGI scripts.

Introducing Servlets and the Java Web Server

Since the arrival of Java, applets have provided a mechanism for Web pages to have not just tailored information, but actually interactive and dynamic content. As you've learned, with an applet, the process is run on the browser's own machine. In general, this configuration is an advantage because it improves response time and reduces network bandwidth requirements. But this configuration might present problems if your program has either of these requirements:

Privileged access to server facilities   An applet generally does not have any special access to services and information on a server. Even the server that supplied the applet cannot, in the absence of something like a digital signature, distinguish between a request from an applet that it might want to trust and any other request. Hence, an applet cannot be granted the right to read, say, a database on the server unless full access to that database is given to any HTTP request.

Protection of proprietary algorithms   In a number of ways, Java's bytecode is easier to reverse-engineer than other machine languages. This is partly because it is difficult to generate obfuscated bytecodes—the demands of the bytecode verifier will reject as illegal many forms of code that are not straightforward. Because of this fact, a proprietary algorithm of significant value should generally not be entrusted to an applet.

If either of these considerations applies, a servlet might be the better choice. With a servlet approach, the server can grant full access to local facilities, such as databases, and trust that the servlet itself will control the amount and precise nature of access that is effectively afforded to external users. So, for example, the rate at which requests can be made could be limited, and the origin of requests can be monitored and verified. If a proprietary algorithm is built into a servlet, the code never passes beyond the boundaries of the server; only the results that it produces do. If the code is not passed to the client, it cannot be saved and disassembled.

A servlet and applet can be used as a pair to gain both the benefits of servlets and of the interactive nature of applets. This paired approach can also be used to provide optimization of the data stream, possibly involving actual compression, and, if desired, encryption. The data streams can be optimized in many cases simply by appropriate use of the binary methods of the `DataInputStream` and `DataOutputStream` classes in the `java.io` package, or by using object serialization, which is covered in Chapter 22. Encryption is typically handled by classes such as `SSLSocket`, which implements a Secure Sockets Layer for use in a Java program.

To accompany the introduction of the new servlet standard, a new Web server has been produced. The Java Web Server is JavaSoft's Web server, written in Java, which supports the use of servlets. It is not part of the JDK distribution, but you can download it from the JavaSoft site: http://jeeves.javasoft.com. Because Java Web Server is written in Java, it can be used on any Java-capable platform. It also provides the security reassurances of Java in a networked environment. Other servers are already starting to announce support for this mechanism. For example, support for Netscape Enterprise and FastTrack 2.x is provided, with Microsoft IIS 2.x/3.x and Apache expected in the next release.

> **NOTE**
>
> Running servlets requires a degree of administrative effort. Early versions of the Java Web Server had very few administrative support tools, requiring that all configuration be done with a text editor. More recently, interactive GUI-based administration tools have been added. Other Web servers have their own configuration mechanisms, which are likely to be similar to the ones in JavaSoft's Web server. Configuration for the Java Web Server is discussed in this chapter. If you will be using another type of Web server with your Java servlets, see the documentation for your system for configuration information.

The Java Servlet Development Kit

Before creating any servlets, you need to install JavaSoft's Java Servlet Development Kit (JSDK). The kit includes the `java.servlet` and `sun.servlet` packages, sample servlets, and, for Windows 95 and NT, ServletRunner, which is an appletviewer-like tool to test servlets.

> **TIP**
>
> For more information about the Windows-specific ServletRunner, refer to the online documentation provided with the JSDK.

In order for your servlets to find the servlet packages, you need to add their location to your `CLASSPATH` environment variable. For example, on a Windows 95 or NT system, with the JSDK installed in the default location, the following will do the trick:

```
set CLASSPATH=%CLASSPATH%;C:\Program Files\JSDK\lib\classes.zip
```

The Servlet API

At a superficial level, a servlet is much like an applet. It does not run as an application or start at a static `main()` method; rather, it is loaded, and an instance is created. When the instance exists, it is given an environment from which it can determine details, such as the parameters with which it has been invoked.

In an `Applet` class, the behavior is largely determined by a few methods, which are called by the browser. These methods are `init()`, `start()`, `stop()`, `destroy()`, and `paint()`. In a `Servlet` class, the same basic concept is used, but the particular methods of interest are slightly different.

When a `Servlet` instance is created, its `init()` method is called. This closely parallels the life cycle of an applet and is intended to allow the servlet to initialize itself.

TIP

The general rule with the `Applet` class is that `init()` should be called only once, just after construction. A number of browsers have slightly different behaviors in this respect, so that in some environments `init()` might be called several times for less-than-obvious reasons. This situation is best handled by writing `init()` in such a way that it is only necessary to run it once, and if it is called again, it simply reinitializes the applet. This condition is easy to achieve with careful use of the constructor. It seems a sensible precaution to treat `init()` in a `Servlet` class in the same way.

A servlet does not need to become active or inactive in the way that an applet does when it moves in and out of the current page. Also, a servlet does not have a GUI of its own. The `Servlet` class, therefore, does not define the `start()`, `stop()`, or `paint()` methods. The main behavior of the servlet is required in response to a new connection at the server, and that connection results in a call to the `service()` method of the servlet.

The `service()` method takes two parameters. These are defined by interface types called `ServletRequest` and `ServletResponse`. These interface types provide accessor methods that allow the servlet to examine its environment, determine how it has been executed, and then decide what request it has received and what to do to provide a proper response. In particular, the input and output streams that are connected to the browser client are accessible through these parameters.

NOTE   The `Servlet` class is declared as abstract because the `service()` method is actually undefined. Hence, to implement a servlet, it is essential to override this method. The nature of the servlet is such that it could not actually perform useful work otherwise.

The basic `Servlet` class is not protocol-specific. However, because a large proportion of servlets are likely to use HTTP as the basis of their communication, a subclass of the `Servlet` class, the `HttpServlet` class, is provided to give additional support methods that are useful when handling this protocol. Most of the examples in this chapter use the `HttpServlet` class.

Two additional support interfaces are defined for use with the `HttpServlet` class: the `HttpServletRequest` interface and the `HttpServletResponse` interface. These interfaces extend the `ServletRequest` and `ServletResponse` interfaces, and provide definitions of additional accessor methods for handling HTTP-specific aspects of a servlet's environment, such as the header information that forms the initial part of an HTTP transaction.

The information that may be read from an `HttpServletRequest` includes the details of the request, such as the path and query string, along with authorization type and header fields. The `HttpServlet-Response` class supports sending of HTTP-specific errors and also of redirects.

A Simple Servlet Example

The following example demonstrates the working environment of an `HttpServlet` object, reporting the values of significant parameters as supplied by the call it receives.

```java
import java.io.*;
import java.util.*;
import java.servlet.*;
import java.servlet.http.*;
public class HelloServlet extends HttpServlet {
   public void init() {
      System.out.println("HelloServlet got an init()!");
      File f = new File("");
      f = new File(f.getAbsolutePath());
      System.out.println("HelloServlet current directory is " + f);
   }
   public void service(HttpServletRequest req,
                       HttpServletResponse resp) {
      try {
         ServletOutputStream out = resp.getOutputStream();
         resp.setContentType("text/html");
         resp.setStatus(HttpServletResponse.SC_OK);
         out.println ("<html>");
         out.println ("<head><title>Hello World</title></head>");
         out.println ("<body>");
         out.println ("<H1>Hello World!</H1>");
         out.println ("<H2>This servlet was invoked with:</H2>");
         out.println ("<dl>");
         Enumeration e = req.getHeaderNames();
         while (e.hasMoreElements()) {
            String name = (String)e.nextElement();
            out.println ("<dt>" + name + "</dt><dd>" +
               req.getHeader(name) + "</dd>");
         }
         out.println ("<dt>Request method:</dt><dd>" +
            req.getMethod() + "</dd>");
         out.println ("<dt>Translated Request path info:</dt><dd>" +
            req.getPathTranslated() + "</dd>");
         out.println ("<dt>Request query string:</dt><dd>" +
            req.getQueryString() + "</dd>");
```

```
        out.println ("</dl>");
        out.println ("</body></head></html>");
    } catch (IOException e) {
        // Ignore it. Let the client worry...
    }
  }
}
```

Running the Servlet

To run any servlets, you need a Web server that supports them. This chapter describes the use of JavaSoft's Java Web Server, but any other servlet-enabled server will work. To run a servlet, follow this sequence of actions:

1. Start your Web server, if it is not already running.

2. Configure the server to install the servlet (the servlet must be installed in the Web server).

3. Start your Web browser.

4. Direct the browser to the particular URL that refers to the new servlet.

NOTE Some servers might require that you restart them after installing a new servlet, but this is not the case with JavaSoft's server when using the Web-based interactive administration tools. If you have a server that requires restarting after a servlet is installed, you should perform step 2 before step 1 in the above list.

You will find the source code and bytecode files for this servlet on the CD-ROM. If you are using JavaSoft's server and are unfamiliar with its configuration for running servlets, see the "Servlet Configuration," section later in this chapter. Install the servlet into the Web server and direct your browser to this URL:

```
http://localhost:8080/servlet/HelloServlet?Hello+World
```

Notice that this assumes that you have configured your server to use port 8080. This is the default for the early releases of JavaSoft's server, and it is a sensible choice in any case because it allows the server to run on Unix systems without requiring root privilege.

When the browser has loaded, the page should show a heading and several entries in a list. Figure 21.1 shows an example of the kind of output you can expect to see.

FIGURE 21.1

Typical output from HelloServlet

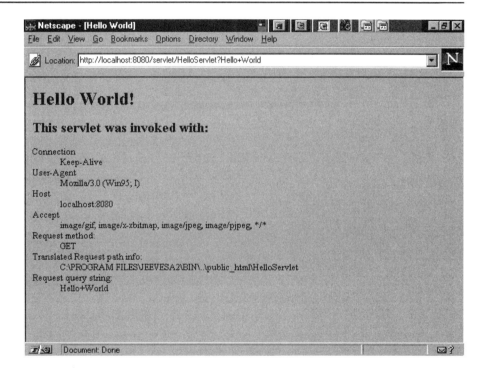

Changing the Query String   You can experiment with modifications to the URL. The first part, which describes the protocol, host, port, and path, cannot be changed. The parts after the query character (?) form the *query string*.

The query string is qualifying information that may be changed within certain restrictions. You should not put spaces or nonalphanumeric characters in this string, except for the plus symbol (+), which signifies a space. If you need to represent any other characters, you should find the appropriate ASCII code for the character, in hexadecimal, and use that with a percent symbol (%) as a prefix. For example, the percent symbol itself is represented as %25.

When you change the query string, observe that all the output, except for the last line, remains the same. If you omit the query string entirely and simply use the following:

```
URL http://localhost:8080/servlet/HelloServlet
```

the output reports the request query string as null, which results from attempting to convert a null reference to a String object in the servlet itself.

HelloServlet's Classes and Methods

The HelloServlet example simply extracts some of the available environment information from the HttpServletRequest and HttpServletResponse objects that are provided to it as the arguments to its service() method. HTML-formatted output is then returned to the caller via the output stream supplied by the server.

The HelloServlet class is a subclass of the HttpServlet class, rather than a direct subclass of the GenericServlet class, because a number of useful utility methods and definitions are provided by the HttpServlet class, and most servlets will use HTTP as their protocol. If you wish to write a servlet that uses some other—perhaps entirely proprietary—protocol, you should extend the GenericServlet class.

NOTE The Java Web Server is part of the much larger Server Toolkit. This kit allows you to build your own network server for arbitrary protocols, including ordinary client/server systems; it is not limited to HTTP and Web-related services. However, HTTP servlets provide good examples of the essence of any servlet and are the focus of this chapter. If you will be writing servlets for radically different services, see Chapter 16, which covers network programming. It describes other useful aspects of writing client/server systems with Java.

The GenericServlet class, or more precisely the Servlet interface, defines a method called service(), which takes two arguments that are objects that implement the ServletRequest and ServletResponse interfaces, respectively. The HttpServlet class defines a new method called service() that takes different argument types. These two arguments are objects that implement the HttpServletRequest and HttpServletResponse interfaces, respectively. The new service() method therefore overloads the method name, rather than overriding it. Because the Web server thinks of the servlet simply as an object that implements the Servlet interface, and the Web server knows nothing about the HttpServlet class, it will call only the first service() method. In the HttpServlet class, this original service() servlet method is written to pass the call to the new service() method instead.

Inside a servlet, two streams are available for communication with the remote client. This example produces only a page of HTML; it does not read input from the client. Therefore, it requires only the output stream. In either a ServletResponse object or—as is the case with an HttpServlet class like the HelloServlet example—an HttpServletResponse object, you can extract the output stream using the getOutputStream() method. If you are implementing bidirectional communication, such as is required for the POST protocol, you will also need to use the getInputStream() method on the ServletRequest object.

The output from the servlet has two broad parts, which can be thought of as the status part and the content part. In the status part, this example specifies that the content type of its reply is text/html and the status is OK. Both of these operations use methods of the HttpServletResponse object. The first, setContentType(), takes an argument of the String class, which is used to specify the MIME-type string of the response that is to be sent. The status is specified using the setStatus() method, although for a reply of OK, this method is actually redundant.

> **NOTE**
>
> The `setContentType()` method is actually a member of the parent class `ServletResponse`, and is therefore available for use in servlets using protocols other than HTTP. The `setStatus()` method, however, is defined in the `HttpServletResponse` class and not in its parent class.

After setting up the status parts of the reply, `HelloServlet` then generates the HTML text, which is presented to the user in the client browser window. The output stream obtained from the `HttpServletResponse` object is an instance of the `java.servlet.ServletOutputStream` class, which defines `println()` methods with a variety of overloads supporting different argument types. For this reason, it is not necessary to create an intervening `DataOutputStream`, `PrintStream`, or `PrintWriter` object, although this would be typical practice in similar situations where a stream has been obtained from an underlying service.

There is a minor irritation with the `ServletOutputStream` class, which is that it declares the `println()` method as throwing an `IOException` if trouble occurs with the connection. The `println()` method of the more familiar `PrintStream` class hides this exception from the caller. Because of this exception, the bulk of the body of this `service()` method is wrapped in a `try` block. If the exception occurs in this example, it is simply ignored. In a servlet intended for production use rather than a simple example, the error would probably be logged. Later sections of this chapter examine the log mechanisms available to servlets.

Once the output stream has been obtained, the servlet must construct the page to provide to the client browser. Normally, this will involve some form of calculated or conditional response; otherwise, the page should be defined by a simple HTML text file. The `HelloServlet` object will return an HTML page, which is a typical action, especially for servlets that are constructed based on the `HttpServlet` class. The HTML page is generated through a series of `println` statements.

> **NOTE** An earlier version of the development kit included a package of HTML-generation support classes, but that was removed from the current beta release. If they return in the final release, they will make your life easier.

After the initial page headings, a definition list is created. A *definition list* in HTML takes a series of entries, which are headings and body text pairs. The corresponding HTML tags used to define entries in such a list are <DT> and <DD>. The result has the general form of the latter part of this servlet's output, as shown earlier.

Construction of the list does not require any arguments, because the HTML definition list does not have a title of its own, only separate elements. After it has been constructed, the individual elements are added by lines like this one:

```
out.println ("<dt>Request method:</dt><dd>" +
    req.getMethod() + "</dd>");
```

Notice that two arguments are supplied. The first is the title part of the list element, and the second is the text that follows.

The information provided in this particular list is obtained from the request information carried by the first argument of the `service()` method. This argument is an instance of the `HttpServletRequest` class. In the `HelloServlet` example, several pieces of information are extracted and placed into the list; the first few pieces of information that are added are the header values.

An HTTP request has a number of attendant headers that define general aspects of the connection. The precise set of headers will depend on the browser being used to issue the request. You can see from the sample output of this servlet that information describing the actual browser forms one of the header fields. To obtain the headers, a servlet can use one of a number of `getHeader()` methods. This example, because it is simply going to output all the headers, uses the variation that fetches the enumeration of header names and loops until no more are found.

Normally, a particular header—such as the Accept list, which describes the preferred response types—would be required, and for this purpose another overloaded getHeader() method is provided. This method accepts a String object as an argument and attempts to find the particular header specified by name in that argument. If any of these getHeader() methods cannot find the requested header, they simply return null.

In addition to accessing the headers, several other data items are available to the servlet. The HelloServlet example demonstrates three of them, which are obtained using the getMethod(), getPathTranslated(), and getQueryString() methods.

The getMethod() method returns the request type. This type is almost always one of the three strings GET, POST, or HEAD, although some other strings are permitted by the definition of HTTP. These strings name the type of request that the Web server received. The method used for general requests from a browser is GET. This type of request carries all the information from the browser to the server as part of the URL string. Requests from HTML forms commonly use the POST method, which sends the bulk of its data to the server as a stream rather than as part of the URL. In a servlet, this data stream is the input stream obtained from the ServletRequest object using the getInputStream() method. In the standard JDK HTTP protocol handler, opening the output stream from the client applet automatically makes the request into a POST type. The HEAD method constitutes a request for header information only, and it is typically used to determine if a cache entry can be reused or if it should be replaced with newer information.

The path information, returned from the getPathTranslated() method, describes the path on the server machine from which the servlet was loaded. Hence, for this example, the path information returned, which is specific to the particular installation of the server, is C:\JEEVES\BIN\..\public_html\HelloServlet. This information might be very useful if a servlet needs to read from support files.

> **NOTE** Also related to paths is the `getPathInfo()` method, which returns the path part of the original URL. In the conditions of this example, the `getPathInfo()` method returns `/HelloServlet`, treating the `servlet` part of the original URL as a server directive, not as part of the path itself. This treatment is entirely consistent because it is not actually a directory name (for instance, in the Java Web Server, servlets are typically placed in a directory called servlets, and a translation takes place to convert the /servlet part of the URL). In general, the `getPathInfo()` method is less useful because it does not relate directly to the local file system.

In many conventional requests to CGI services, the URL carries additional argument information that qualifies the particular request. The sample output shown earlier resulted from the full URL:

```
http://localhost:8080/servlet/HelloServlet?Hello+World
```

and, in this case, the query string was reported as `Hello+World`.

The `getQueryString()` method returns the full text of the query string from the invoking URL. Notice that the returned value is still in the URL-encoded format and might need to be converted before it is used.

> **NOTE** At the time of writing, no standard method existed to facilitate decoding a URL-encoded string, which is surprising because the `URLEncoder` class exists to encode the string in the first place. It is also unfortunate because, although the decoding is a simple operation, it is still one more step you need to take.

Finally, after the definition list has been constructed, the closing HTML statements are added.

Other Important Servlet Methods

The preceding section described the basic use of the `HttpServlet` class and a number of supporting classes. A considerable number of additional methods are provided in the various classes that support servlets.

General Servlet Methods

When the server needs a servlet for the first time, it starts by loading the class, then creating an instance of it. The next step is to call the `init()` method, which can be used for general initialization of the servlet. You should ensure that only initialization is performed in the `init()` method, because it might be called to reset the servlet after it has been used, as explained earlier in this chapter.

Web servers generally keep records about the accesses they receive, and servlets have the opportunity to do so, too. The `log()` method of the `ServletContext` interface takes a `String` argument with which it builds an entry that is written to the server's log file. Logs are generally written into a directory called logs under the server's home directory.

Information about the Request

Five more methods supply additional details about the request itself: `getContentLength()`, `getContentType()`, `getProtocol()`, and the pair `getParameter()` and `getParameterNames()`. These are all member methods of the `ServletRequest` object.

The `getContentLength()` method returns the number of bytes of input that are to be supplied, or `-1` in the event that this number is unknown. It is not good practice to allow a servlet to depend functionally on the content length that is reported, because the responsibility for providing this information rests with the client browser, and therefore the accuracy of the content length information is beyond your control. In general, input on an HTTP connection to a servlet will occur with a `POST` type request, so this value can be ignored for `GET` requests.

The `getContentType()` method returns a string that contains the MIME content type for the data that is to be sent to the servlet from the client browser. If no type has been specified by the client, or the connection is not issuing any data for use by the server, this method returns null. Some browsers specify content types of `text/plain` to indicate that the data is of no special type, some use `content/unknown`, and some use `application/octet-stream`. In general, it is likely that most servlets will expect a fairly specific type of data and may be written to handle just that. It also is likely that one particularly common input type will be argument values from a `POST` request. Form results in a `POST` request are normally reported using the MIME-type `application/x-www-form-urlencoded`.

The protocol used, which will typically be some version of HTTP, is reported by the `getProtocol()` method. This method returns a string of the form `<Protocol>/<major_version>.<minor_version>`. `HTTP/1.0` is a typical return value from a Web browser client, although older browsers still exist that use `HTTP/0.9`. If the browser does not explicitly state the protocol type that it is using, the default (`HTTP/0.9`) is assumed and reported by the `getProtocol()` method.

CGI requests commonly include parameter information encoded onto the end of the URL itself in the form of *name=value* assignments. Multiple parameters should be separated using the ampersand character (`&`). Note that neither the equals symbol nor the ampersand should be converted to the external form using the percent (%) representation discussed earlier, or they will lose their special meaning as separators and simply become part of the query string. Such information can be accessed by a servlet by using the `getParameterNames()` and `getParameter()` methods. If a particular named parameter is expected, it is sufficient to use the `getParameter()` method, which takes a string argument specifying the name of the parameter to match and returns a string that represents the associated value. For example, given a URL like this:

`http://localhost:8080/servlets/getparameter?quantity=maximum`

the method call `getParameter("quantity")` would return the `String` value `maximum`. As with applets, all parameters are returned as `String` objects. If your servlet expects, say, an `int`, you must convert it.

In some servlets, it might be inconvenient or impossible to predict the parameter names that are acceptable in advance of the call. In these circumstances, the `getParameterNames()` method is useful. This method returns an enumeration of the strings representing the names, but not the values, of the parameters that have been passed. For each of these names, the associated value can be obtained by calling the `getParameter()` method.

Information about the Client

The request also carries information about the host of the client browser. The `getRemoteAddr()` method returns the IP address of the remote host, and the `getRemoteHost()` method returns its name.

> **WARNING** You should not attribute trust to any remote machine based solely on its name as extracted from either the `getRemoteAddr()` or `getRemoteHost()` method. Such a name will have been obtained from a reverse DNS lookup—a translation of the address into a name—and this process can be subverted by untrusted outsiders. If you need to allocate trust to particular hosts, either look up the name you trust and verify that the remote address you have matches one of those returned, or simply use addresses directly. Forward DNS lookups—that is, name-to-address translation—and actual IP addresses are much more difficult to subvert, especially when the machines are in the same network.

Length of Reply

In addition to the `getOutputStream()` and `setContentType()` methods, the `ServletResponse` object also provides a method for specifying the length of content that is to be returned.

The `setContentLength()` method takes an integer argument that specifies the number of bytes of data that will be returned. Nothing in this method constrains the actual amount of data sent, so be careful to ensure that the value specified is correct. It is not necessary to use this method to set any value if it is difficult or inconvenient to calculate the correct value. However, if you choose not to use the `setContent-Length()` method, the client browser will not be able to display a progress monitor.

TIP Determining the size of a dynamically constructed page is easiest if the whole page is constructed in a buffer and then transmitted as a whole when complete. This strategy allows the size to be taken from the buffer size.

Accessing HTTP Header Information

A variety of headers are meaningful in the HTTP environment, and these can be accessed using methods in the `HttpServletRequest` and `HttpServletResponse` classes. Header values can be read using methods in the `HttpServletRequest` class. The `Hello-Servlet` example uses the `getHeaderNames()` method; this accesses the headers by their order. Another `getHeader()` method takes a `String` object as an argument and allows searching for specific headers.

Both the `getHeader()` method and `getHeaderNames()` return strings, or an enumeration of strings. Convenience methods are provided to interpret these strings into either integer or date format.

When generating a reply, the headers may be set using a similar set of methods. In this case, the methods are members of the `HttpServlet-Response` object. The basic `setHeader()` method takes two strings as arguments: the first names the header field, and the second specifies the value to be associated with the header. The `setIntHeader()` and `setDateHeader()` methods are convenience methods that take an `int` and a `long` representing a date, respectively.

Servlet Initialization Parameters

When a servlet is first loaded into a server, it can be configured via initialization parameters. These parameters are set by the administrator and are used for localization and installation of the servlet rather than configuration of a particular request. The initialization parameters are named, and the values associated with them can be read into the servlet from the `ServletContext` object—which is an interface to the server itself—by the method `getInitParameter()`. This method takes a string argument that should match the string name of the parameter in question. To obtain a list of all the parameters that have been configured, use the `getInitParameterNames()` method.

Servlet Configuration

In JavaSoft's Java Web Server, a servlet cannot be loaded or executed without prior configuration from the administrator. This is an important security feature. This section briefly outlines how to configure the Java Web Server to enable a servlet.

The Java Web Server is supplied with a collection of servlets and an applet to support configuration from the browser interface. Two particular views within the administration applet are of interest for servlet configuration: the log-in view and the servlet-loading view. The main entry to the administration system is via the URL http://localhost :9090applet.html and is accessed via a Java-enabled browser (port 9090 is the administration port).

In the log-in view, two text fields and a Log in button are presented, as shown in Figure 21.2. The text fields prompt for a username and a password. By default, the administration login uses the username and password `admin`. Entering these into the text fields and selecting the Log in button changes the view to a supervisory control-panel view. This view has a list of the available services. Selecting the Web Page Service choice and clicking on the Manage button displays the administration functions. Selecting the Servlets button changes the view again. Figure 21.3 shows this form.

FIGURE 21.2

Logging in to the Java Web Server

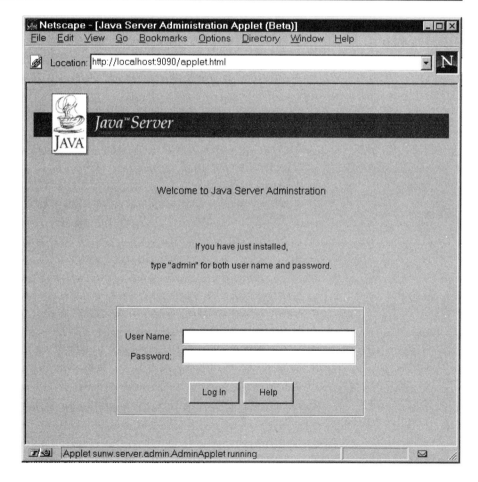

FIGURE 21.3

The servlet form in the
Java Web Server

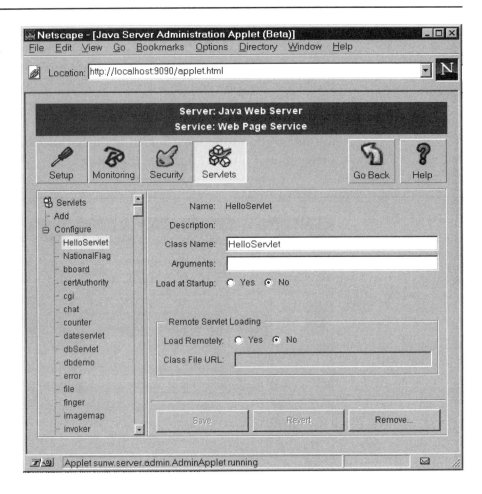

In the servlet-loading view, a list of currently known servlets is
shown along with Add and Configure options. With the Add option,
two text fields are provided for servlet name and class name. After
you add a servlet, you can configure it to have arguments and possibly
remote loading. The name of a servlet can be a descriptive name and
is not restricted to being the same as the class name. The class name
entered should be the fully qualified class name, and the path should
describe the base of any package hierarchy that should be searched.
For HelloServlet, just place **HelloServlet** in both fields, since the servlet
is in the default package.

In configure mode, a pair of radio buttons allow you to indicate whether the servlet should be loaded automatically when the server starts. If this option is not selected, the servlet will be loaded in response to the first client request for its service. Once loaded, a servlet will remain resident in the server until it is shut down. Therefore, most servlets should be loaded at startup unless there is a real possibility that the servlet will not be invoked at all during a server session.

The administration servlets actually act on underlying configuration files, which are maintained in the form of properties in a file called servlets.properties in the server installation's admin\properties\process\javawebserver\adminservice directory. A servlet is defined primarily by an entry of the form `servletname.code=classname`. For example, if a servlet referred to as `Useful` is defined in a class called `Use1`, the entry in the servlets.properties file would be `Useful.code=Use1`. Such an entry represents, in a single record, both the servlet name and the class that is to be loaded.

The code base for a servlet defaults to the `servlets` directory of the server installation but may be overridden by an entry of the form `servletname.codebase=URL`.

Arguments to the servlet are specified in the servlets.properties files by an entry of the form `servletname.initArgs=comma_separated_list`. For example, if two arguments called `one` and `two` are to be specified for a servlet called `Test`, and the arguments are to have the values `yes` and `maybe`, respectively, the servlet.properties file would contain the entry `Test.initArgs=one=yes,two=maybe`.

A Fuller Example of a Servlet

Now you are ready for a fuller servlet example. The following servlet combines a number of techniques to return an image representing the national flag of the country in which the host is apparently located. Of course, this idea is not entirely reliable, because many multinational and US-based companies use the .com top-level domain for all their offices, regardless of geographical location. Hence, a connection from a Sun Microsystems office in the United Kingdom would appear as being from sun.com and be treated as if it were of US origin. However, despite this limitation, the example demonstrates a number of interesting and useful techniques.

```java
import java.io.*;
import java.util.*;
import java.servlet.*;
import java.servlet.http.*;

public class NationalFlag extends HttpServlet {
    File flagDir;
    Hashtable flags = new Hashtable();

    private static final int SUFFIX      = 0;
    private static final int FILENAME    = 1;
    private static final int CONTENTTYPE = 2;

    private String defflagname[] = {
       "us",    "usa-flag.jpg", "image/jpeg"
    };

    private String flagnames[][] = {
       {"nl",    "nl-flag.jpg",    "image/jpeg"},
       {"fr",    "fr-flag.jpg",    "image/jpeg"},
       {"uk",    "uk-flag.jpg",    "image/jpeg"}
};

    public void init() throws ServletException {
       String fileDir = getInitParameter("flagDirectory");
       if (fileDir == null) {
          fileDir = "servlets" + File.separator;
       }
       flagDir = new File(fileDir);
       if (!(flagDir.exists() && flagDir.isDirectory())) {
          log("Invalid flagDirectory value specified");
          throw new ServletException("Can't find flag Directory");
       }
```

```
   else {
      File f = new File(flagDir, defflagname[FILENAME]);
      if (!(f.exists() && f.canRead())) {
         log("can't find default flag ");
         throw new ServletException("Can't find default flag");
      }
   }
}
   for (int i = 0; i < flagnames.length; i++) {
      flags.put(flagnames[i][0], flagnames[i]);
   }
}

public void service(HttpServletRequest req,
                                  HttpServletResponse resp)
   throws IOException {
   String country = null;
   if (req.getParameter("country") != null) {
      country = req.getParameter("country");
   }
   else {
      country = req.getRemoteHost();
      int i = country.lastIndexOf('.');
      if (i != -1) {
         country = country.substring(i + 1);
      }
   }

   String [] flagdef = (String [])(flags.get(country));
   if (flagdef == null) {
      flagdef = defflagname;
   }

   try {
      resp.setContentType(flagdef[2]);
      File f = new File(flagDir + flagdef[1]);

      int size = (int)f.length();
      resp.setContentLength(size);

      byte [] buffer = new byte[size];
      FileInputStream in = new FileInputStream(f);
      in.read(buffer);
```

```
        resp.getOutputStream().write(buffer);
      }
      catch (IOException e) {
        log("Trouble: " + e);
        throw e;
      }
      finally {
        resp.getOutputStream().close();
      }
    }
  }
```

Running the Servlet

To run this example, you need a running Web server that supports the servlet mechanism. Copy the class file from the CD-ROM into the appropriate directory in your server hierarchy.

This example requires the flag image files, too. Copy all the .jpg files from the CD-ROM into the servlet directory of your server.

In operation, this servlet must be able to locate the flag files. Although it uses the initialization parameter flagDirectory to allow these to be placed anywhere convenient, the servlet calculates a default directory if this parameter is not set. Provided your servlet directory is called servlets and is a subdirectory beneath the server's default directory, you will not need to set this parameter. (Note that this default directory might change between releases.)

Once the files are in the correct places, configure the server to load this servlet and then load the servlet from a browser. Typically, this would mean loading the URL:

```
http://localhost:8080/servlet/NationalFlag
```

If you have completed the installation according to the needs of your server, you should expect to see a flag. It will probably be the Stars and Stripes, as the local connection suggested here will probably not advertise your full domain name, even if you are in a non-US domain. However, you might see a representation of another national flag.

Because it is difficult in most cases to test this servlet from different geographical locations—or even to simulate the effect by modifying naming tables—and because the genuine local host name will be hidden in many installations, this example checks for a parameter that overrides the host name in controlling the choice of flag to return. The parameter is called country, and it may be set to any of the values usa, uk, nl, or fr. These are the only countries that are supported by the image files on the CD-ROM. Test other countries by directing your browser to a URL of this form:

```
http://localhost:8080/servlet/NationalFlag?country=uk
```

You should find that the flag displayed changes to one appropriate to the country parameter value. In this particular case, you should see the Union Jack.

In normal use, this servlet would be embedded in a page using the IMG tag. A sample Web page is located on the CD-ROM in the file NatFlag.html.

Copy this file into a suitable subdirectory in a public directory of your server and direct your browser to that URL. Provided you installed the NationalFlag servlet so that it is at the URL used above, you will see the Stars and Stripes embedded in a normal HTML page. If your servlet installation is different, you will need to edit the NatFlag.html file to reflect the particulars of your installation.

The NationalFlag Servlet's Classes and Methods

The first part of the NationalFlag servlet is its init() method. This method determines the directory from which image files are to be loaded and verifies that the default flag can be found in that directory. The init() method completes by building a hashtable containing the other flags that are available.

Each time the servlet is invoked, it tests to see whether the country parameter has been supplied; if it has, this value is used to determine which flag to return. If not, the host name of the client is used instead. Once the flag has been chosen, it is loaded into a buffer. The content type and length are set appropriately, and then the image data is sent to the client.

The servlet comprises two parts: the `init()` method and the `service()` method itself. The `init()` method performs the one-time initialization. First, it checks whether an initialization parameter called `flagDirectory` has been set. This parameter may be used to specify the directory in which the supporting flag image files are located. If no value is found for the `flagDirectory` variable, a default is assumed, which is the subdirectory servlets beneath the servlet's default directory. For the Java Web Server, the current working directory of a running servlet is the base directory of the server, and hence is the parent directory of the servlets directory.

Once a directory has been chosen as a string, a `File` object is constructed to represent it. Using that object, the `init()` method checks whether the file it describes is an existing directory. If it isn't, a log entry is made indicating the nature of the problem, and a servlet exception is thrown.

Provided the directory chosen exists, the `init()` method proceeds by checking whether it contains a readable file for use as the default flag. The name for this file is taken from the `defflagname` array of strings. As before, if this is found not to be the case, a log entry is made, and a servlet exception is thrown to indicate the problem.

If the `init()` method has found the default flag file, a `Hashtable` object is filled with descriptions of each known country, the associated flag filename, and the content type that describes the file. In this example, the `Hashtable` is filled from a predefined array, but in a production implementation, it could be filled using either properties or some other external file. Such an approach would allow greater flexibility and, hence, permit the addition of new flags without requiring recompilation.

NOTE

The definitions of the `init()` method in the `Servlet` interface, the `GenericServlet` class, and the `HttpServlet` class allow the method to throw a `ServletException` object if required. This allowance is important because it provides a means for the servlet to indicate to the server that the initialization has failed. If no exception is thrown, the `init()` method would be incorrectly deemed to have completed successfully, and the servlet would be called whenever a request was received. This would then need to be rejected each time by the `service()` method.

The `service()` method must determine which flag image should be returned. If a `country` parameter is set for the request, the value of that parameter is used to determine the flag. However, if no `country` parameter is defined, the host name of the client is looked up, and the last part, following the last occurrence of a period, is used. The intention is that if a connection is received from a machine with, for example, the host name `jaques.delores.fr`, the `fr` part is extracted and taken to represent the connection's country of origin.

Once a country value has been determined, either from the end of the host name or from a parameter, it is used as the key to look up the corresponding flag in the hashtable of known flags. If no match is found in that table, the default flag is used. Note that in the NationalFlag example, the default flag is not actually entered in the `Hashtable` itself, which means that the handling of US connections is indistinguishable from the handling of undetermined connections. If you change this behavior under default conditions to return a special image indicating an unrecognized connection, all the various US suffixes (.com, .edu, and so forth) should be added to the `Hashtable`.

Each entry in the hashtable is an array of three strings. These describe the country identifier, the name of the flag file, and the MIME content type of the file. The country identifier is used as the key for the hashtable because this is the value that must be looked up to determine which flag is required. When a country has been identified, the MIME content type of the response is specified using the third of these strings from the hashtable entry. A `File` object is also created using the directory that was determined by the `init()` method and the individual filename from the second element of the hashtable entry. This `File` object is used to determine the actual size in bytes of the flag file, and this value is used to set the content length of the response. The length allows the client browser to indicate correctly the progress of the download.

A buffer is allocated using the indicated file size, and the whole file is read in via a `FileInputStream` object. Once this buffer has been filled, it is written to the output stream of the `HttpServletResponse` object, and thereby to the client.

During the execution of the `service()` method, a number of different methods are called that might cause an `IOException` object to be thrown. Any of these would be very difficult to recover from effectively, so in this servlet any such problem simply causes a log entry and is passed back to the server.

Regardless of any exceptions that might occur, the output channel is closed before the servlet returns. Any exception that occurs during this closure is simply passed to the server and otherwise ignored.

Server-Side Includes

The Java Web Server has the ability to perform a *server-side include* (SSI) using a servlet. With server-side inclusion, the server converts a placeholder in an HTML document into alternative dynamically calculated text each time the document is served to a client.

A server-side include is requested in two ways:

- The document carries the extension .shtml rather than the normal .html.

- The point at which the inclusion should be made is marked with a special tag.

Most servers, other than the Java Web Server, have adopted an HTML comment format to indicate the point of inclusion. In Java-Soft's server, the servlet tag is used. The format of the servlet tag is similar to the applet tag, and in its minimum form looks like this:

```
<servlet name=ServletName>
</servlet>
```

The servlet itself does not have a user interface at the client; there-fore, a servlet tag, unlike an applet tag, does not require, and in fact cannot have, a width or height parameter. Furthermore, because the servlet is conventionally referenced by a name other than its class name, it is not necessary to specify a class name in this tag. If both a name and the class name are specified in the servlet tag, and the named servlet is already loaded in the server, that servlet will be invoked by its name. But if the servlet tag in an .shtml file has only the servlet name part, without a class name specified, the server checks all loaded servlets for the name given. If the servlet is not found preloaded, the tag is simply ignored.

However, with an appropriate servlet tag, it is not always neces-sary for a servlet to be preloaded. If the class name and servlet name are specified in the servlet tag, and the servlet is not found by name, it will be loaded using the specified class name and registered in the server for future use by the name given. If a class name part, but no servlet name part, is specified in the tag, the servlet will be reloaded every time the include is requested, which should be avoided.

The full format for specifying a server-side included servlet is:

```
<servlet name=ServletName code=ServletCode
    initParam1=initArg1 initParam2=initArg2 ...>
    <param name=param1 value=val1>
</servlet>
```

Notice that named parameters can be specified, using a format that exactly mimics the one used for applet parameters. Also, initializa-tion parameters can be specified as part of the main part of the servlet tag.

Inter-Servlet Communication

One of the difficulties with standard CGI is that of communication. With traditional CGI mechanisms, communication between different CGI scripts tends to be rather slow because it involves either reading and writing files, or perhaps using pipes to communicate between different processes.

Servlets are persistent in that once the server starts one, the servlet remains in existence to service all future requests, and, also, servlets all exist in the same Virtual Machine (VM) and hence in the same process space. These two considerations make it possible for different servlets to communicate conveniently and efficiently.

To effect communication between two servlets, the servlets must be able to obtain references to each other and must be designed to communicate. This section discusses these two aspects. Of course, the servlets must also have something useful to say to each other.

Finding a Servlet

When a servlet runs, it does so inside a Web server. The server provides a number of facilities to the servlets it runs, including the ability to locate other servlets on the same server. The Web server, from the API point of view, is encapsulated in the `ServletContext` interface, similar in principle to `AppletContext`. The servlet itself can obtain a reference to the Web server by issuing a call to the `getServletContext()` method. Note that this method is not defined in the `Servlet` interface, but in the `GenericServlet` class.

Once the servlet context has been obtained, two methods are available for locating servlets:

`getServlets()`   Returns an enumeration of all the servlets in the server. Inside a servlet, this method cannot return an empty enumeration, because the servlet itself must be included in the list.

`getServlet()` Takes a string argument and returns a reference to the servlet named by that string. This method will return null if the server does not know about the servlet that was requested.

Both the `getServlets()` and `getServlet()` methods will return only those servlets that are currently loaded. Neither will cause the server to load any servlet, even if its name is known. For this reason, it is usually required that if servlets are to communicate, they be marked as loaded at startup in the administration system.

Communicating between Servlets

You can implement communication between servlets in several different ways. These are methods that allow programs of various types to communicate, and are not specific to servlets.

Calling Each Other's Methods

If the two servlets are written at the same time and are able to know each other's public API when they are compiled, they can call each other's methods. This situation would allow, for example, each servlet to implement a `getInfo()` and `setState()` method—the actual names are unimportant—so that each can call the appropriate method to control the other.

Using Stream Classes

It might be appropriate to use the `PipedInputStream` and `Piped-OutputStream` classes. These classes are discussed in Chapter 15 as one of the ways that different threads can communicate, and their use is equally appropriate for servlets. To set up such a communication, each servlet must be able to obtain a handle on the streams of the other. One possible approach is described by the following code fragments:

```
public class TalkerServlet extends GenericServlet {
   public final PipedOutputStream myOutput = new PipedOutputStream();
```

```
// body of class...
}

public class ListenerServlet extends GenericServlet {
    private PipedInputStream myInput = null;
    public void service(ServletRequest req,
                        ServletResponse resp)
        throws ServletException {
        if (myInput == null) {
            ServletContext context = getServletContext();
            Servlet theTalker = context.getServlet("TalkerServlet");
            if ((theTalker == null) ||
                !(theTalker instanceof TalkerServlet)) {
                throw new ServletException("Cannot find Talker");
            }
            TalkerServlet ts = (TalkerServlet)theTalker;
            try {
                    myInput = new PipedInputStream(ts.myOutput);
            }
            catch (IOException io) {
                    myInput = null; // ?
            }
        }
        // main body of service()
    }
}
```

In this scheme, one end of the input/output stream pair must be created first; in this case, the output has been chosen, and it is created at the moment the `TalkerServlet` object is instantiated. Some time later, the other end of the stream can be created. In this example, the other end of the stream is not created in an `init()` method because there would be a risk of the servlets being created in the wrong order. To avoid this problem, the other end of the stream is created during the first call to the `service()` method of the `ListenerServlet` object. Provided that both the talker and the listener are loaded at server startup, this approach will work safely.

This approach is equally applicable for bidirectional communication. Although this sample code shows only one stream being set up, it would be simple to add an instance of the `PipedInputStream` class to the `TalkerServlet` class and attach that to an output stream in the listener in the same way.

Using Static Variables

It is possible to use static variables as the basis for communication between classes. For example, using input and output streams, the mechanism shown in the previous section could be modified to use a static variable to provide access to the output stream. In this way, it would not be necessary to use the `ServletContext` object to obtain a handle on the other `Servlet` object. Consider the following code fragments:

```
public class TalkerServlet extends GenericServlet {
   public static final PipedOutputStream myOutput;

   static {
      try {
         myOutput = new PipedOutputStream();
      }
      catch (IOException e) {
      }
   // body of class...
}

public class ListenerServlet extends GenericServlet {
   private PipedInputStream myInput;
public ListenerServlet() throws IOException {
      myInput = new PipedInputStream(
TalkerServlet.myOutput);
   }
   // main body of class
}
```

Usually, the fact that the value of a static variable is shared between all instances makes this type of variable subject to misuse and misunderstanding in a fashion similar to global variables in non–object-oriented languages. However, in this case, because only one instance of a servlet is ever created in a Web browser environment, these particular difficulties do not arise.

By using the static variable, observe that the `TalkerServlet` class can create and advertise its `PipedOutputStream` object at the moment the class is loaded, which ensures that the `ListenerServlet` object can refer to that output stream immediately. The approach also avoids the earlier requirement of ensuring that the servlets be loaded by the server at startup, because the VM itself will resolve any dependencies between the classes, as the language clearly defines the proper behavior. So if the `ListenerServlet` class refers to the `TalkerServlet` class in this way, the system, rather than the browser, ensures that the `TalkerServlet` class will be loaded if it is not already loaded.

Using Once Objects

A variation on the static variable idea is the concept of a *once* object. The once object is effectively an object that is created and advertised as a static variable but that has some protection against corruption from outside the class. You can set up a once object by adhering to the following guidelines:

- Declare at least one constructor and mark all constructors for the class as private.

- Declare a private static variable of the same type as the class itself.

- Declare a nonprivate synchronized static method, which returns an instance of the class.

- In the static method, if the private variable described above is non-null, simply return it. However if the variable is null, create an instance of the class (remember, the private constructors are accessible to this method) and put the reference to the new object into the variable. Now return the value of that variable.

A code fragment following these guidelines looks like this:

```
public class Once {
  private static Once myself;
  private Once() {
```

```
        // set me up
    }
    public static synchronized Once newOnce() {
        if (myself == null) {
            myself = new Once();
        }
        return myself;
    }
}
```

Now if two servlets need to communicate, they can both have instances variables that are of this Once class. The variables themselves do not need to be static, and can be private, but they will necessarily both refer to the same object. The classes would look like this:

```
public class XXXXServlet extends HttpServlet {
    private Once myOnce = Once.newOnce();
    // rest of class
}
```

This approach is effectively just syntactic sugar on the basic idea of a static variable in the classes, but has the—potentially great—advantage of loosening the coupling between the talker and listener classes. When you use static variables directly, one of these classes must know about, and use explicitly, the other class and the variable name within it. Such coupling reduces maintainability of the classes. With the once object approach, this coupling is significantly reduced. The talker class could change its name and function entirely, the variable in which it stores its reference to the shared object could be changed or even deleted entirely, and the listener class would be unaffected.

> **TIP**
>
> The applicability of the once object approach is not restricted to servlets. It is a powerful design pattern in general object-oriented programming, also known as Singleton. Its value derives from its ability to loosen the coupling between components as just described.

Summary

This chapter started by explaining the limitations of using CGI, an earlier mechanism for dynamically calculated content. Then it described the relative advantages of using servlets and a Java-capable Web server for providing these services.

You have learned how to use the Servlet API classes and methods for creating servlets, including the `service()` method and the `HttpServletRequest` and `HttpServletResponse` classes.

Next, you learned how to configure the Java Web Server, JavaSoft's Web server, to support your servlets. Other Java-based Web servers are available, and it is likely that they will need similar configuration to support servlets.

Finally, a number of possible mechanisms for implementing communication between servlets were described. These mechanisms are appropriate for a variety of purposes and can actually be used for communication between all sorts of classes, not just servlets.

If you expect to be writing extensive network-based services, the Java Web Server and the Servlet API are likely to reward your study. In addition, if those services will connect to corporate databases, you should ensure that you are familiar with the general techniques of one of the database interface mechanisms, such as JDBC (Java Database Connectivity), which is used for relational database interfacing. For more information about JDBC, see Chapter 18.

Serialization and Remote Method Invocation

- Serialization for recording objects

- Deserialization for restoring objects

- The RMI (Remote Method Invocation) feature

- Steps for RMI application development

The JDK 1.1 release includes support for object persistence through serialization and deserialization. It also includes a Remote Method Invocation (RMI) feature for making method calls on remote objects. This chapter explains these two concepts, discusses Java's support for them, and shows how they are related.

Object Persistence and Serialization

A Java object ordinarily lasts no longer than the program that created it. An object may cease to exist during runtime if it is reaped by the garbage collector. If it avoids that fate, it still goes away when the user terminates the browser (for an applet) or the object's runtime environment (for an application).

In this context, *persistence* is the ability of an object to *record* its state so it can be reproduced in the future, perhaps in another environment. For example, a persistent object might store its state in a file. The file can be used to *restore* the object in a different runtime environment. It is not really the object itself that persists, but rather the information necessary to construct a replica of the object.

An object records itself by writing out the values that describe its state. This process is known as *serialization* because the object is represented by an ordered series of bytes. Java provides classes that write objects to streams and restore objects from streams.

The main task of serialization is to write the values of an object's instance variables. If a variable is a reference to another object, the referenced object must also be serialized. This process is recursive; serialization may involve serializing a complex tree structure that consists of the original object, the object's objects, the object's object's objects, and so on. An object's ownership hierarchy is known as its *graph*.

Criteria for Serialization

Not all classes are capable of being serialized. Only objects that implement the `Serializable` or `Externalizable` interfaces may successfully be serialized. Both interfaces are in the `java.io` package. A serializable object can be serialized by an external object, which in practice is a type of output stream; an externalizable object must be capable of writing its own state, rather than letting the work be done by another object.

You can serialize any class as long as the class meets the following criteria:

- The class, or one of its superclasses, must implement the `java.io.Serializable` interface.

- The class must participate with the `writeObject()` method to control data that is being saved and append new data to existing saved data.

- The class must participate with the `readObject()` method to read the data that was written by the corresponding `writeObject()` method.

If a serializable class has variables that should not be serialized, those variables must be marked with the `transient` keyword; the serialization process will ignore them. In general, references to AWT classes that rely on system peers should be marked as transient.

The Serializable Interface

The `Serializable` interface does not have any methods. When a class declares that it implements `Serializable`, it is declaring that it participates in the serializable protocol. When an object is serializable, and the object's state is written to a stream, the stream must contain enough information to restore the object. This must hold true even if the class being restored has been updated to a more recent (but compatible) version.

The Externalizable Interface

The Externalizable interface identifies objects that can be saved to a stream but that are responsible for their own states. When an externalizable object is written to a stream, the stream is only responsible for storing the name of the object's class; the object must write its own data. The Externalizable interface is defined as:

```
public interface Externalizable extends Serializable {

    public void writeExternal (ObjectOutput out)
        throws IOException;

    public void readExternal (ObjectInput in)
        throws IOException, ClassNotFoundException;
}
```

An externalizable class must adhere to this interface by providing a writeExternal() method for storing its state during serialization and a readExternal() method for restoring state during deserialization.

Creating Output Streams for Serialization

Objects that can serialize other objects implement the ObjectOutput interface from the java.io package. This interface is intended to be implemented by output stream classes. The interface's definition is:

```
public interface ObjectOutput extends DataOutput {
    public void writeObject(Object obj)
        throws IOException;
    public void write (int b) throws IOException;
    public void write(byte b[]) throws IOException;
    public void write(byte b[], int off, int len)
        throws IOException;
    public void flush() throws IOException;
    public void close() throws IOException;
}
```

The essential method of the interface is `writeObject(Object obj)`, which writes `obj` to a stream. Static and transient data of `obj` is ignored; all other variables, including private ones, are written.

Exceptions can occur while accessing the object or its fields or when attempting to write to the storage stream. If these occur, the stream that the interface is built on will be left in an unknown and unusable state. If this happens, the external representation of the object is corrupt.

The `ObjectOutput` interface extends the `DataOutput` interface. `DataOutput` methods support writing of primitive datatypes. For example, the `writeDouble()` method writes data of type `double`, and `writeBoolean()` writes data of type `boolean`. These primitive-type writing methods are used for writing an object's primitive instance variables.

The primary class that implements the `ObjectOutput` interface is `ObjectOutputStream`. This class is similar to other output stream classes, which are discussed in Chapter 15. Note that objects are represented as streams of bytes, rather than characters, so they are represented by streams rather than character-oriented writers.

When an object is to be serialized to a file, the first step is to create an output stream that talks to the file:

```
FileOutputStream fos = new FileOutputStream("obj.file");
```

The next step is to create an object output stream and chain it to the file output stream:

```
ObjectOutput objout = new ObjectOutputStream(fos);
```

The object output stream automatically writes a header into the stream; the header contains a magic number and a version. This data is written automatically with the `writeStreamHeader()` method when the object output stream is created. As explained later in this chapter, an object input stream reads this header and verifies the object before returning its state.

After writing the header, the object output stream can write the bit representation of an object to the output stream using the `write-Object()` method. For example, the following code constructs an instance of the `Point` class and serializes it:

```
objout.writeObject(new Point(15, 20));
objout.flush();
```

This example shows that serializing an object to a stream is not very different from writing primitive data to a stream. The next section investigates restoring serialized objects from input streams. The example writes objects to a file, but the output stream can just as easily be chained to a network connection stream.

Using Object Input Streams for Deserialization

The `ObjectInputStream` class deserializes a serialized stream. It is responsible for maintaining the state of the stream and all of the objects that have been serialized to the stream. By using the methods of this class, a program can restore a serialized object from the stream, as well as the entire tree of objects referred to by the primary object. Primitive data types may also be read from an object input stream.

There is only one class constructor in the `ObjectInputStream` class:

```
public ObjectInputStream(InputStream in) throws IOException,
    StreamCorruptedException
```

The constructor calls the class's `readStreamHeader()` method to verify the header and the version that were written into the stream by the corresponding object output stream. If a problem is detected with the header or the version, a `StreamCorruptedException` is thrown.

The primary method of the `ObjectInputStream` class is `read-Object()`, which deserializes an object from the data source stream. The deserialized object is returned as an `Object`; the caller is responsible for casting it to the correct type.

During deserialization, the system maintains a list of objects that have been restored from the stream. This list is called the *known objects table*.

If the data being maintained is of a primitive type, it is simply treated as a sequence of bytes and restored from the input stream. If the data being restored is a string, it is read using the string's UTF (Unicode Transfer Format) encoding; the string will be added to the known objects table. If the object being restored is an array, the type and length of the array are determined. Next, memory for the array is allocated, and each of the elements contained in the array is read using the appropriate reading method. Once the array is reconstructed, it is added to the known objects table; if it is an array of objects (as opposed to primitives), then each object is deserialized and added to the known objects table. When an ordinary object (that is, not a string or an array) is restored, it is added to the known objects table; then the objects to which the original object refers are restored recursively and added to the known objects table.

Once an object has been retrieved from a stream, it must be validated so it can become a full-fledged object and be used by the program that deserialized it. The `validateObject()` method is called when a complete graph of objects has been retrieved from a stream. If the primary object cannot be made valid, the validation process will stop, and an exception will be thrown.

Security Considerations for Serialized Objects

Serialization can involve storing an object's data on a disk file or transmitting the data across a network. In both cases, there is a potential security problem because the data is located outside the Java runtime environment, beyond the reach of Java's security mechanisms.

The `writeExternal()` method is public, so any object can make an externalizable or serializable object write itself to a stream. Caution should be exercised when deciding whether or not `writeExternal()`

should serialize sensitive private data. When an object is restored via an ordinary `readExternal()` call, its sensitive values are restored back into private variables and no harm is done. However, while the serialized data is outside the system, an attacker could access the data, decode its format, and obtain the sensitive values. A similar form of attack would involve modifying data values so, for example, a password is replaced or a bank balance is incremented. A less precise attack would simply corrupt the serialized data.

When an object is serialized, all the reachable objects of its ownership graph are potentially exposed. For example, a serialized object might have a reference to a reference to a reference to an instance of the `FileDescriptor` class. An attacker could reserialize the file descriptor and gain access to the file system of the machine where the serialized object originated.

The best protection for an object that has fields that should not be stored is to label those fields with the `transient` keyword. Transient fields, like static fields, are not serialized and are therefore not exposed.

If a class cannot be serialized in a manner that upholds the integrity of the system containing it, that class should not implement the `Serializable` interface. Moreover, it should not be referred to by any class that will be serialized.

Externalizable objects (that is, ones that take care of writing their own data) often use the technique of including invariant data among their instance variables. These invariants serve no useful purpose during normal operation of the class. They are inspected after deserialization; an unexpected value indicates that the external serialized representation has been corrupted.

Serialization Exceptions

There are seven types of exceptions that can be thrown during serialization or deserialization of an object. All seven types are extensions of

`ObjectStreamException`, which is an extension of `IOException`. The exceptions are described below.

`InvalidClassException`   Typically thrown when the class type cannot be determined by the reserializing stream or when the class that is being returned cannot be represented on the system retrieving the object. The exception is also thrown if the deserialized class is not declared public, or if it does not have a public default (no-argument) constructor.

`NotSerializableException`   Typically thrown by externalizable objects (which are responsible for their own reserialization) on detection of a corrupted input stream. The corruption is generally indicated by an unexpected invariant value.

`StreamCorruptedException`   Thrown when a stored object's header or control data is invalid.

`NotActiveException`   Thrown if the `registerValidation()` method is not called during a call to `readObject()`.

`InvalidObjectException`   Thrown when a restored object cannot be made valid after deserialization.

`OptionalDataException`   Thrown when a stream is supposed to contain an object in it, but it actually contains only primitive data.

`WriteAbortedException`   Thrown during reserialization (reading), when an input stream detects that its data is incomplete because of abnormal termination of the writing process.

Writing and Reading an Object Stream

Writing an object to a stream is a simple process, similar to the process of writing any other kind of high-level structure. This process is explained in detail in Chapter 15. You must create a low-level output stream to provide access to the external medium (generally a file or network). Next, a high-level stream is chained to the low-level stream; for serialization, the high-level stream is an object output stream.

The following code fragment constructs an instance of `Point` and writes it to a file called `point.ser` on the local file system:

```
Point p = new Point(13, 10);
FileOutputStream f = new FileOutputStream("Point.ser");
ObjectOutputStream s = new ObjectOutputStream (f);
try
{
    s.writeObject (p);
    s.flush ();
} catch (IOException e) { }
```

Restoring the object involves opening a file input stream on the file and chaining an object input stream to the file input stream. The `Point` object is read by calling `readObject()` from the object input stream; the return value is of type `Object` and must be cast by the caller. The following code fragment shows how all this is accomplished:

```
Point p = null;
FileInputStream f = new FileInputStream("Point.ser");
ObjectInputStream s = new ObjectInputStream (f);
try
{
    p = (Point)s.readObject ();
}
catch (IOException e) {}
```

The next section develops a simple sample program that saves and restores an object.

A Serialization Example

The example presented here is a simple painting program that can store its display list to a file. (A *display list* is a data structure that contains an abstract description of what should appear on the screen.) The program allows the user to draw rectangles with the mouse;

pressing down on the mouse button defines one corner of a rectangle and releasing the button defines the opposite corner. The display list is a vector that contains two instances of the `Point` class for each rectangle. One point represents the mouse-down corner of the rectangle.

The PersisTest application is a subclass of `Frame`. A panel across the top of the frame contains four control buttons. The frame's `paint()` method clears the screen to white and then traverses the display list vector, drawing one black rectangle for each pair of points in the vector.

The four control buttons support clearing, saving, restoring, and quitting. The handler for the Save button uses the writing technique discussed in the previous section to store the display list vector in a file. The filename must be specified in the command-line argument. The handler for the Restore button deserializes a vector, replacing the old display list with the new vector.

To test the application, invoke it with a filename as a command-line argument:

java PersisTest *filename*

Then use the mouse to draw some rectangles. Next, click on the Save button to write the display list to the file. Clear the screen or draw more rectangles. Finally, click on the Restore button. The display will change back to the state it was in when the Save button was clicked. You can even terminate the application and restart it; it will still restore correctly from the external file.

This example could achieve the same result by opening a data output stream instead of an object output stream and writing four `int` values for each rectangle. The benefit to using serialization lies in the dramatic improvement in program maintainability. If you were to store and restore the display list by using data input and output streams, any change in the format of the display list would force a change in both the writing and the reading code. With serialization, the display list data format is irrelevant.

The following is the source code listing for the PersisTest program.

```java
import java.awt.*;
import java.awt.event.*;
import java.io.*;
import java.rmi.*;
import java.util.Vector;


public class PersisTest extends Frame
implements MouseListener, ActionListener
{
    Vector      displayList;
    String      pathname;
    Button      clearBtn, saveBtn, restoreBtn, quitBtn;


    public static void main(String args[])
    {
        if (args.length == 0)
        {
            System.out.println("Usage: java PersisTest filename");
            System.exit(0);
        }

        PersisTest that = new PersisTest(args[0]);
        that.show();
    }


    public PersisTest(String pathname)
    {
        this.pathname = pathname;
        displayList = new Vector();

        // Handle our own mouse clicks.
        addMouseListener(this);

        // Build the GUI. Make this object a listener for all actions.
        setLayout(new BorderLayout());
        Panel pan = new Panel();
```

```
      clearBtn = new Button("Clear");
      clearBtn.addActionListener(this);
      pan.add(clearBtn);
      saveBtn = new Button("Save");
      saveBtn.addActionListener(this);
      pan.add(saveBtn);
      restoreBtn = new Button("Restore");
      restoreBtn.addActionListener(this);
      pan.add(restoreBtn);
      quitBtn = new Button("Quit");
      quitBtn.addActionListener(this);
      pan.add(quitBtn);
      add("North", pan);

      resize(350, 200);
   }


public void paint(Graphics g)
{
   // Clear to white.
   g.setColor(Color.white);
   g.fillRect(0, 0, getSize().width, getSize().height);

   // Traverse display list, drawing 1 rect for each 2 points
   // in the vector.
   g.setColor(Color.black);
   int i = 0;
   while (i < displayList.size())
   {
      Point p0 = (Point)(displayList.elementAt(i++));
      Point p1 = (Point)(displayList.elementAt(i++));
      int x = Math.min(p0.x, p1.x);
      int y = Math.min(p0.y, p1.y);
      int w = Math.abs(p0.x - p1.x);
      int h = Math.abs(p0.y - p1.y);
      g.drawRect(x, y, w, h);
   }
}
```

```java
public void mousePressed(MouseEvent e)
{
   // Store x and y in display list vector.
   Point p = new Point(e.getX(), e.getY());
   displayList.addElement(p);
}


public void mouseReleased(MouseEvent e)
{
   // Store x and y in display list vector, and request repaint.
   Point p = new Point(e.getX(), e.getY());
   displayList.addElement(p);
   repaint();
}


// Unused methods of MouseListener interface.
public void mouseClicked(MouseEvent e) { }
public void mouseEntered(MouseEvent e) { }
public void mouseExited(MouseEvent e)  { }


public void actionPerformed(ActionEvent e)
{
   if (e.getSource() == clearBtn)
   {
      // Repaint with an empty display list.
      displayList = new Vector();
      repaint();
   }
   else if (e.getSource() == saveBtn)
   {
      // Write display list vector to an object output stream.
      try
      {
         FileOutputStream fos = new FileOutputStream(pathname);
         ObjectOutputStream oos = new ObjectOutputStream(fos);
         oos.writeObject(displayList);
         oos.flush();
         oos.close();
         fos.close();
      }
```

```
        catch (Exception ex)
        {
            System.out.println("Trouble writing display list vector");
        }
    }
    else if (e.getSource() == restoreBtn)
    {
        // Read a new display list vector from an object input stream.
        try
        {
            FileInputStream fis = new FileInputStream(pathname);
            ObjectInputStream ois = new ObjectInputStream(fis);
            displayList = (Vector)(ois.readObject());
            ois.close();
            fis.close();
            repaint();
        }
        catch (Exception ex)
        {
            System.out.println("Trouble reading display list vector");
        }
    }
    else if (e.getSource() == quitBtn)
    {
        hide();
        dispose();
        System.exit(0);
    }
    }
}
```

RMI for Distributed Computing

Java's RMI (Remote Method Invocation) feature enables a program running on a client computer to make method calls on an object located on a remote server machine. The RMI feature gives Java programmers the ability to distribute computing across a networked environment. Object-oriented design requires that every task be executed by the object most appropriate to that task. RMI takes this concept one step further by allowing a task to be performed on the *machine* most appropriate to the task.

RMI defines a set of remote interfaces that can be used to create remote objects. A client can invoke the methods of a remote object with the same syntax that it uses to invoke methods on a local object. The RMI API provides classes and methods that handle all of the underlying communication and parameter referencing requirements of accessing remote methods. RMI also handles the serialization of objects that are passed as arguments to methods of remote objects.

The `java.rmi` and `java.rmi.server` packages contain the interfaces and classes that define the functionality of the Java RMI system. These packages and interfaces provide the building blocks for creating server-side objects and client-side object stubs. A *stub* is a local representation of a remote object. The client makes calls to the stub, which automatically communicates with the server.

Object Persistence and RMI

When a Java program makes a remote method invocation, method parameters must be transmitted to the server, and a return value must be sent back to the client. Primitive values can simply be sent byte by byte. However, passing objects, either as parameters or return values, presents a problem.

Object persistence is a useful feature in its own right. It is also indispensable for remote invocation. The server-side object needs access to a parameter object's entire graph of referenced objects. The remote method might construct and return a complicated object that owns references to other objects. If this occurs, the entire graph must be returned.

For the RMI feature to support passing and returning objects as well as primitives, there must be a full-featured object-serialization system, which is why serialization and persistence are generally discussed together. Any object passed to or returned from a remote method must implement either the `Serializable` or the `Externalizable` interface.

> **NOTE**
>
> RMI is similar to the Remote Procedure Call (RPC) feature introduced by Sun in 1985. RPC also requires a way to serialize parameter and return value data, although the situation is simpler because of the absence of objects. Sun developed a system called External Data Representation (XDR) to support data serialization. One significant difference between RPC and RMI is that RPC uses the fast but less-than-reliable UDP protocol; RMI uses the slower but more reliable TCP/IP protocol.

The RMI Architecture

The RMI architecture consists of three layers: the Stubs/Skeleton, Remote Reference, and Transport layers. The relationships among these layers are shown in Figure 22.1.

FIGURE 22.1

The RMI architecture

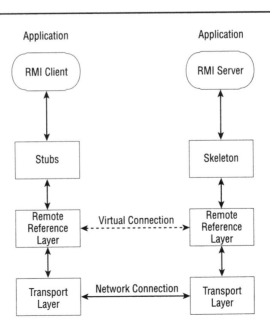

When a client invokes a remote method, the request starts at the top with the stub on the client side. The client references the stub as a proxy for the object on the remote machine; all the underlying functionality shown in Figure 22.1 is invisible to the client. The stub code is generated with the rmic compiler and uses the Remote Reference layer (RRL) to pass method invocation requests to the server object.

Stubs for RMI

The *stub* is the client-side proxy representing the remote object. Stubs define all of the interfaces that the remote object implementation supports. A program running on the client machine references the stub in the same way that it references any other local object. It looks like a local object on the client side; it also maintains a connection to the server-side object.

The RRL on the client side returns a *marshal stream* to the stub. The marshal stream is used by the RRL to communicate to the RRL on the server side. The stub serializes parameter data, passing the serialized data into the marshal stream. After the remote method has been executed, the RRL passes any serialized return values back to the stub, which is responsible for deserializing.

The Skeleton for RMI

The *skeleton* is the server-side construct that interfaces with the server-side RRL. The skeleton receives method invocation requests from the client-side RRL. The server-side RRL must unmarshal any arguments that are sent to a remote method. The skeleton then makes a call to the actual object implementation on the server side. The skeleton is also responsible for receiving any return values from the remote object and marshaling them onto the marshal stream.

The RRL for RMI

The *RRL* is responsible for maintaining an independent reference protocol that is not specific to any stub or skeleton model. This flexibility allows you to change the RRL (if desired) without affecting the other two layers. The RRL deals with the lower-level transport interface and is responsible for providing a stream to the Stub/Skeleton layer.

The RRL uses a server-side and a client-side component to communicate via the Transport layer. The client-side component contains information specific to the remote server. This information is passed to the server-side component and therefore is dependent only on the server-side RRL. The RRL on the server side is responsible for the reference semantics and deals with those semantics before delivering the remote method invocation to the skeleton. The communication between client- and server-side components is handled by the Transport layer.

The Transport Layer for RMI

The *Transport layer* is responsible for creating and maintaining connections between the client and server. The Transport layer consists of four abstractions:

- An *endpoint* is used to reference the address space that contains a Java VM (Virtual Machine). An endpoint is a reference to a specific transport instance.

- A *channel* is the pathway between two address spaces. This channel is responsible for managing any connections from the client to the server and vice versa.

- A *connection* is an abstraction for transferring data (arguments and return values) between the client and server.

- The *transport* abstraction is responsible for setting up a channel between a local address space and a remote endpoint. The transport abstraction is also responsible for accepting incoming connections to the address space containing the abstraction.

The Transport layer sets up connections, manages existing connections, and handles remote objects residing in its address space. When the Transport layer receives a request from the client-side RRL, it locates the RMI server for the remote object that is being requested. Then the Transport layer establishes a socket connection to the server. Next, the Transport layer passes the established connection to the client-side RRL and adds a reference to the remote object to an internal table. At this point, the client is connected to the server.

The Transport layer monitors the "liveness" of the connection. If a significant amount of time passes with no activity on the connection, the Transport layer is responsible for shutting down the connection. The timeout period is 10 minutes.

An RMI Example

This section guides you through the steps for making, compiling, and running an RMI application. To create an application that is accessible to remote clients, there are a number of steps that you must follow:

1. Define interfaces for the remote classes.

2. Create and compile implementation classes for the remote classes.

3. Create stub and skeleton classes using the rmic command.

4. Create and compile a server application.

5. Start the RMI Registry and the server application.

6. Create and compile a client program to access the remote objects.

7. Test the client.

The sample program presented here models a simple credit card system. The server supports creating a new account, as well as performing transactions against an existing account. Because the intention of the example is to show you how to use RMI, there is no client-side user interface; the client simply makes a few hard-coded invocations.

Defining Interfaces for Remote Classes

The program uses two remote classes. The `CreditCardImpl` class maintains the username, balance, available credit, and personal ID signature number for a single credit card account. The `CreditManager` maintains a list of `Account` objects and creates new ones when necessary. The server-side application constructs a single instance of `CreditManagerImpl` and makes it available to remote clients.

Each of these classes must be described by an interface (`CreditCard` and `CreditManager`). The client-side stubs implement these interfaces. The stub classes are created in a later step by the `rmic` utility. The `rmic` has the following requirements:

- The interfaces must be public.
- The interfaces must extend the `Remote` interface.
- Each method must throw `RemoteException`.
- The stub and implementation code must reside in a package.

NOTE There are four trivial exception classes that are included on the CD-ROM but are not listed here. These classes extend `Exception` without adding new data or methods.

The definition of `CreditCard` is as follows:

```
package credit;

import credit.*;
import java.rmi.*;

public interface CreditCard extends java.rmi.Remote {

    /** This method returns a credit card's credit line. */
    public float getCreditLine() throws java.rmi.RemoteException;
```

```
/** This method allows a cardholder to pay all or some
    of a balance. Throws InvalidMoneyException if the
    money parameter is invalid. */
public void payTowardsBalance(float money) throws
    java.rmi.RemoteException, InvalidMoneyException;

/** This method allows the cardholder to make purchases
    against the line of credit. Throws CreditLineExceededException
    if the purchase exceeds available credit. */
public void makePurchase(float amount, int signature) throws
    java.rmi.RemoteException, InvalidSignatureException,
    CreditLineExceededException;

/** This method sets the card's personal ID signature. */
public void setSignature(int pin)throws java.rmi.RemoteException;
}
```

The structure of `CreditManager` is similar, although it defines only a single method:

```
package credit;

import credit.*;
import java.rmi.*;
import java.rmi.RemoteException;

public interface CreditManager extends java.rmi.Remote {

  /** This method finds an existing credit card for a given customer
      name. If the customer does not have an account, a new card will
      be "issued" with a random personal ID signature and a $5,000
      starting credit line. */
  public CreditCard findCreditAccount(String Customer) throws
    DuplicateAccountException, java.rmi.RemoteException;


  /** This method creates a new Credit Account with a random
      personal ID signature and a $5,000 starting credit line. */
  public CreditCard newCreditAccount(String newCustomer) throws
    java.rmi.RemoteException;
}
```

Creating and Compiling Implementation Classes

The implementation classes are server-side classes that implement the interfaces listed in the previous section.

The CreditCard interface that was defined earlier is implemented by the CreditCardImpl class. This class must implement all of the methods in the CreditCard interface, and it must extend Unicast-RemoteObject. The UnicastRemoteObject class defines the remote object as a *unicast* object, which means that it can handle only one client reference at a time. If more clients attempt to access the remote object, they will be queued up and will receive the object reference only when the current reference is given up. (To date, there is no support for multicast objects.)

Both interfaces and both classes declare that they belong to the credit package. All four sources should be compiled with the -d <*directoryname*> option to specify a destination directory. Within the destination directory, the compiler will automatically create a subdirectory called credit (if one does not already exist); the class files will be created in the credit subdirectory. The destination directory supplied to the -d option should be in the class path. An easy way to compile the interfaces and classes is to specify the current working directory as the destination directory, as follows:

```
javac -d . CreditCard.java
javac -d . CreditCardImpl.java
javac -d . CreditManager.java
javac -d . CreditManagerImpl.java
```

The following is the source code for the CreditCardImpl class.

```
package credit;

import java.rmi.*;
import java.rmi.server.*;
import java.io.Serializable;
```

```
/** This class is the remote object that will be referenced by the skeleton
    on the server side and the stub on the client side. */

public class CreditCardImpl
   extends UnicastRemoteObject
   implements CreditCard, Serializable
{
   private float currentBalance = 0;
   private float creditLine = 5000f;
   private int signature = 0;        // Like a pin number
   private String accountName;       // Name of owner

   /** Class constructor generates an initial pin.*/
   public CreditCardImpl(String customer) throws
   java.rmi.RemoteException, credit.DuplicateAccountException {
      accountName = customer;
      signature = (int)(Math.random() * 10000);
   }

   /** Returns credit line. */
   public float getCreditLine() throws java.rmi.RemoteException {
      return creditLine;
   }

   /** Pays off some debt. */
   public void payTowardsBalance(float money) throws
   java.rmi.RemoteException, credit.InvalidMoneyException {
      if (money <= 0) {
         throw new InvalidMoneyException ();
      } else {
         currentBalance -= money;
      }
   }

   /** Changes signature. */
   public void setSignature(int pin) throws java.rmi.RemoteException {
      signature = pin;
   }

   /** Makes a purchase. Makes sure enough credit is available,
       then increments balance and decrements available credit. */
   public void makePurchase(float amount, int signature) throws
   java.rmi.RemoteException, credit.InvalidSignatureException,
   credit.CreditLineExceededException {
```

```
        if (signature != this.signature) {
            throw new InvalidSignatureException();
        }
        if (currentBalance+amount > creditLine) {
            throw new CreditLineExceededException();
        } else {
            currentBalance += amount;
            creditLine -= amount;
        }
    }
}
```

The `CreditManagerImpl` class is responsible for creating and storing new accounts (as `CreditImpl` objects). This class uses a hashtable to store the account objects, keyed by owner name.

```
package credit;

import java.rmi.*;
import java.rmi.server.*;
import java.util.Hashtable;

public class CreditManagerImpl extends UnicastRemoteObject
implements CreditManager {
    private static transient Hashtable accounts = new Hashtable();

    /** This is the default class constructor that does nothing
        but implicitly call super(). */
    public CreditManagerImpl() throws RemoteException { }

    /** Creates a new account. Puts the customer name and the customer's
        credit card in the hashtable. */
    public CreditCard newCreditAccount(String customerName)
            throws java.rmi.RemoteException {
        CreditCardImpl newCard = null;
        try {
            newCard = new CreditCardImpl(customerName);
        } catch (DuplicateAccountException e) {
            return null;
        }
        accounts.put(customerName, newCard);
        return newCard;
    }
```

```
/** Searches the hashtable for an existing account. If there is
       no account for the customer name, one is created and
       added to the hashtable.
    Returns the account. */
 public CreditCard findCreditAccount(String customer)
        throws DuplicateAccountException, RemoteException {
     CreditCardImpl account = (CreditCardImpl)accounts.get(customer);
     if (account != null) {
        return account;
     }
     // Create new account. Add credit card to hashtable.
     account = new CreditCardImpl(customer);
     accounts.put(customer, account);
     return account;
   }
 }
```

Creating the Stub and Skeleton Classes

Once the implementation classes are compiled, the next step is to create the stub and skeleton class files that are used to access the implementation classes. The stub classes are used by the client code to communicate with the server skeleton code.

The rmic command automatically creates stub and skeleton code from the interface and implementation class definitions. The syntax of the command is:

```
rmic [options] package.interfaceImpl ...
```

For the example, the following command creates the stubs and skeletons for the CreditCard and CreditManager remote classes:

```
rmic -d . credit.CreditCardImpl credit.CreditManagerImpl
```

Note that the command requires specification of the package in which the class files reside; this is why all the source modules listed in the previous section declare that they belonged to the rmi.atm package.

The rmic command creates four class files in the credit package directory:

- CreditCardImpl_Skel.class
- CreditCardImpl_Stub.class
- CreditManagerImpl_Skel.class
- CreditManagerImpl_Stub.class

Now that the stubs and skeletons have been created, the next step is to create a server-side application that makes these classes available to clients for remote invocation.

Creating and Compiling the Server Application

Everything is now in place to create the server-side application. This is an application class called CardBank, whose main job is to construct an instance of CreditManager. Except for the line that calls the CreditManager constructor, all the rest of the CardBank code involves making the CreditManager object available to remote clients. The details of this process are explained after the following code listing.

```
package credit;

import java.util.*;
import java.rmi.*;
import java.rmi.RMISecurityManager;


public class CardBank {

    public static void main (String args[]) {
        //  Create and install a security manager.
        System.setSecurityManager(new RMISecurityManager());
```

```
try {
    // Create an instance of Credit Manager.
    System.out.println
        ("CreditManagerImpl: create a CreditManager");
    CreditManagerImpl cmi = new CreditManagerImpl();

    // Bind the object instance to the remote registry. Use the
    // static rebind() method to avoid conflicts.
    System.out.println("CreditManagerImpl: bind it to a name");
    Naming.rebind("cardManager", cmi);

    System.out.println("CreditManager is now ready");

} catch (Exception e) {
    System.out.println("An error occured");
    e.printStackTrace();
    System.out.println(e.getMessage());
}
    }
  }
```

By default, applications run without security managers. The set-SecurityManager() call enforces an RMI security manager.

The server "publishes" an object instance by binding a specified name to the instance and registering that name with the RMI Registry. There are two methods that allow an instance to be bound and registered:

```
public static void bind(String name, Remote obj)
    throws AlreadyBoundException, MalformedUrlException, UnknownHostException,
    RemoteException
```

```
public static void rebind(String name, Remote obj)
    throws MalformedUrlException, UnknownHostException, RemoteException
```

Notice that both methods are static and ask for a name to reference the object, as well as the actual remote object that is bound to the name. In the current example, the object name is cardManager; any reachable machine on the network can refer to this object by specifying the host machine and the object name.

The `name` argument required by both `bind()` and `rebind()` is a URL-like string. This string can be in this format :

protocol://host:port/bindingName

Here *protocol* should be `rmi`, *host* is the name of the RMI server, `port` is the port number on which the server should listen for requests, and *bindingName* is the exact name that should be used by a client when requesting access to the object. If just a name is given in the string, the default values are used. The defaults are `rmi` for the protocol, `localhost` for the server name, and `1099` for the port number.

Both `bind()` and `rebind()` associate a name with an object. They differ in their behavior when the name being bound has already been bound to an object. In this case, `bind()` will throw `AlreadyBound-Exception`, and `rebind()` will discard the old binding and enforce the new one.

Starting the RMI Registry and Server Application

The RMI Registry is an application that provides a simple naming lookup service. When the `AtmServer` calls `rebind()`, it is the Registry that maintains the binding. The Registry is an independent program, and it must be running before the server-side application is invoked. The program resides in the java/bin directory. It can be invoked by simply typing **rmiregistry** at the command line.

The following two command lines invoke the Registry and start up the card bank server:

rmiregistry

java credit.CardBank

The card bank application prints several status lines as it starts up the service. If there are no errors, you should see the following output:

```
CreditManagerImpl: create a CreditManager
CreditManagerImpl: bind it to a name
CreditManager is now ready
```

Once an object has been passed to the Registry, a client may request that the RMI Registry provide a reference to the remote object. The next section shows how this is done.

Creating and Compiling the Client Program

The `Shopper` application needs to find a `CreditManager` object on the remote server. The program assumes that the server name has been passed in as the first command-line argument. This name is used to create a URL-like string in this format:

```
rmi://<hostname>/atmManager
```

The string is passed to the static `lookup()` method of the `Naming` class. The `lookup()` call communicates with the server and returns a handle to the remote object that was constructed and registered in the previous step. (More accurately, what is returned is a handle to a stub that communicates with the remote object.)

The return type from `lookup()` is `Remote`, which is the parent of all stub interfaces. When the return value is cast to type `CreditManager`, the methods of `CreditManager` can be invoked on it.

The client expects two command-line arguments and an optional third. The first argument specifies the server. (For testing on a single machine, specify **localhost** for the server name.) The second argument is a string that provides an account name. The client program asks the server-side `CreditManager` object for a handle to the `CreditCard` object that represents this customer's account. (If the customer has no account yet, one will be created.) The initial random pin number is modified to something a user will find easier to remember. The client program then makes several purchases and one payment, reporting the available credit after each transaction. The following is the client code.

```
package credit;

import java.rmi.*;
import java.rmi.RMISecurityManager;

public class Shopper {

    public static void main(String args[]) {

        CreditManager cm = null;
        CreditCard account = null;

        // Check the command line.
        if (args.length < 2) {
            System.err.println("Usage:");
            System.err.println("java Shopper <server> <account name>");
            System.exit (1);
        }

        // Create and install a security manager.
        System.setSecurityManager(new RMISecurityManager());

        // Obtain reference to card manager.
        try {
            String url = new String ("//" + args[0] + "/cardManager");
            System.out.println ("Shopper: lookup cardManager, url = " + url);
            cm = (CreditManager)Naming.lookup(url);
        } catch (Exception e) {
            System.out.println("Error in getting card manager" + e);
        }

        // Get user's account.
        try {
            account = cm.findCreditAccount(args[1]);
            System.out.println ("Found account for " + args[1]);
        } catch (Exception e) {
            System.out.println("Error in getting account for " + args[1]);
        }

        // Do some transactions.
        try {
            System.out.println("Available credit is: "
                        + account.getCreditLine());
```

```
    System.out.println("Changing pin number for account");
    account.setSignature(1234);
    System.out.println("Buying a new watch for $100");
    account.makePurchase(100.00f, 1234);
    System.out.println("Available credit is now: " +
                account.getCreditLine());
    System.out.println("Buying a new pair of shoes for $160");
    account.makePurchase(160.00f, 1234);
    System.out.println("CardHolder: Paying off $136 of balance");
    account.payTowardsBalance(136.00f);
    System.out.println("Available credit is now: "+
                account.getCreditLine());
  } catch (Exception e) {
    System.out.println("Transaction error for " + args[1]);
  }

  System.exit(0);
 }
}
```

Testing the Client

The final step is to execute the client code. It can be run from any computer that has access to the server and to the supporting classes. Here is a sample session output on a Unix machine, with the remote service running on a host named sunbert (the first line is the invocation; the rest is output):

```
% java credit.Shopper sunbert pogo
Shopper: lookup cardManager, url = //sunbert/cardManager
Found account for pogo
Available credit is: 5000.0
Changing pin number for account
Buying a new watch for $100
Available credit is now: 4900.0
Buying a new pair of shoes for $160
CardHolder: Paying off $136 of balance
Available credit is now: 4740.0
```

After the client program has finished running, the remote objects are still alive. The execution shown here created a new account for the customer. A second invocation of the client will work with that account; the available credit numbers in the listing below reflect the current state of the account:

```
% java credit.Shopper sunbert pogo
Shopper: lookup cardManager, url = //sunbert/cardManager
Found account for pogo
Available credit is: 4740.0
Changing pin number for account
Buying a new watch for $100
Available credit is now: 4640.0
Buying a new pair of shoes for $160
CardHolder: Paying off $136 of balance
Available credit is now: 4480.0
```

Summary

Java's persistent object support provides a very useful facility for storing and reconstituting objects. This feature is valuable in its own right; moreover, it plays an essential role in RMI. Both features are moderately intricate, and successful programming (especially for RMI) involves a number of steps. However, the individual steps are not difficult. The sample code listed in this chapter and provided on the CD-ROM provides a template for development.

Sun introduced RPC (Remote Procedure Call) support in 1985. To this day, RPC is an essential building block of many distributed applications. It seems likely that RMI will play a vital role in distributed Java applications, where the distributed code will benefit from platform independence.

CHAPTER
TWENTY-THREE

JavaOS:
The Java Operating System

- JavaOS and the Network Computer

- The JavaOS architecture

- JavaStation as the Java Network Computer

- The HotJava Views interface

- Java-based embedded processing systems

- Java chips and microprocessors

In mid-1996, many leading computer manufacturers joined to announce the Network Computer Platform specification. The manufacturers included industry leaders such as IBM, Oracle, and Sun Microsystems. A core requirement of the Network Computer Platform specification was support for the Java VM (Virtual Machine) and Java classes. This means that the developers envision the future of the Network Computer system to be built around Java.

The first Network Computers developed from the platform specification had proprietary operating systems. Others used scaled-down versions of standard operating systems like OS9. The Sun Microsystems developers, the creators of Java, had greater plans for their version of the Network Computer. The JavaStation is the machine they developed, based on the platform specification, and JavaOS is the operating system it uses.

JavaOS (Java Operating System) is an operating system written mostly in the Java language, which incorporates the Java VM and classes. JavaOS shares the Java language's core precepts of portability and object-oriented design. JavaOS is small, portable, and efficient. These attributes make it ideal for Network Computers as well as other devices, such as embedded processors and appliances, that may need to connect to a network.

This chapter explains the Network Computer concept, the JavaOS architecture, the JavaStation and its HotJava Views interface, and embedded JavaOS. It also covers the picoJava I chip, which is designed for faster Java processing in computers and embedded devices.

Network Computers and JavaOS

The Network Computer Platform Specification is fairly Spartan. Peripheral devices and ports that people have come to expect on today's computers are not required; some of these devices are optional extras. Hard disk storage and floppy disk drives are not part of the base design of most Network Computers. JavaOS is designed for these minimally equipped computers, often called *thin clients*. JavaOS typically loads from the network to RAM or resides in ROM (preprogrammed in read-only memory) in the computer. This is in stark contrast to any of the current desktop operating systems, which typically require more than 50MB of hard disk space for the minimal installation.

The Network as the Computer System

With the growth of corporate networks and closed (or corporate) Internet sites called Intranets, the members of the corporate world are reexamining their computer systems. The computer departments are using distributed processing on a network, rather than centralized mainframe computers, for their information-processing systems. With the creation and endorsement of the Network Computer Platform, the computer industry is beginning to shift its focus to the importance of the network as a whole. The idiom "The network *is* the computer" implies that the power of the computer system does not reside in the hardware on the desktop computer, but rather on the network itself; the component parts and peripherals of the individual desktop computers become less important.

To make a network perform as a whole computer system, there needs to be some degree of continuity or compatibility among its functional *nodes,* or the network workstations. Supporting large networks is a daunting task when incompatibilities exist between network nodes.

Network managers now require many complex tools to keep track of the hardware and software configuration of machines attached to their network. The ideal network might incorporate some, or all, of the following attributes:

- Low-cost, compatible computers on every desk, with limited extras to keep track of

- Complete software compatibility, with all applications stored once on the network for easy tracking and maintenance

- Computers that support a language designed for network applications, which can be used for in-house developments

- Standard security systems built into the computer at the operating-system level

- Networking functionality at the core of the operating system, not just as an add-on package

Many of these requirements are achieved with the use of Java. The Java language has emerged as an ideal programming language for networking and to distribute applications over networks.

Figure 23.1 illustrates the different models of Java implementations, from browsers like Netscape Navigator to a Network Computer with JavaOS.

Notice that there is a layer of software between the Java VM and the operating system for the non-JavaOS platforms. This is called the *adapter* layer, and it contains the patches and extra functions needed by Java that are not supplied by the operating system.

IBM included the Java VM and Core API in its operating system with the release of OS/2 Version 4. Microsoft intends to provide an extension to Windows and NT that includes the Java VM. The Apple Macintosh operating system already follows this trend with the Mac OS Runtime for Java (MRJ). The direction of the development of desktop operating systems indicates the importance of Java and the Java VM to networking and the computer industry as a whole. This is also an indicator of the importance of JavaOS.

FIGURE 23.1

Java implementation models: Java with a browser, Java interpreter, and JavaOS

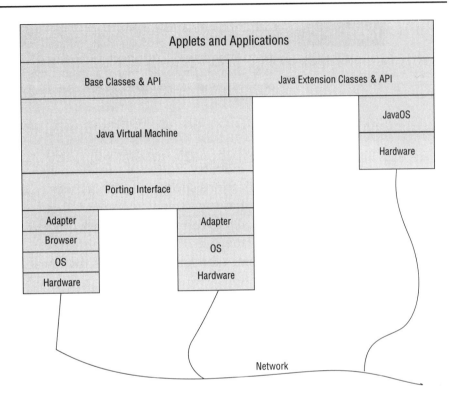

Running Java Applications and Applets on a Network Computer

A Network Computer with JavaOS will run Java applications and applets at the bytecode level. This means that software developers do not need to write different versions of their packages for different operating systems and computer platforms. Distribution of applications across a network is also simplified and more secure, because the application is centrally stored and downloaded by the Network Computers rather than requiring an individual copy to be stored on each computer that uses the application. The portability of the bytecode enables the same piece of Java software to run on any Network Computer, as well as on any conventional desktop computer attached to the network.

> **NOTE**
>
> The Core API is the same on JavaOS as it is on Netscape Navigator and any browser that implements the Java VM and classes (the internal architecture of JavaOS is described in the next section). This exact match provides the portability and platform independence unique to Java.

The focus on network computing has led to an interesting trend in the software industry: Software producers are releasing Java versions of their applications specifically for Network Computer use. Corel, for example, has rewritten its popular Office suite of applications in Java specifically to run from a network on JavaOS and Java-enabled computers. However, the picture is not all rosy. One shortcoming of Network Computers using JavaOS is that these computers can run only applications entirely written in Java. In other words, they cannot run anything that is not a Java application. That leaves a whole host of products and software unavailable to JavaOS users.

Computers with desktop operating systems will run Java programs with a Java interpreter, as well as many native applications written for that operating system. Desktop computers are more versatile, but they are also more expensive and harder to maintain.

There are many applications ideally suited for the Network Computer running JavaOS. The typical applications used in a corporate environment are e-mail, scheduling, word processing, spreadsheet, and database access. Java can support these applications very well, and as such, a JavaOS-based Network Computer is a very cost-effective solution. However, certain specialized applications are not suited to Java. For example, for applications like engineering design, image processing, and desktop publishing, dedicated workstations and personal computers work best. Processing power and raw speed are the main reasons that Java is not suitable for these applications. Other requirements like specialized peripherals, large memory usage, and special processors are not the norm for network computing, and these are not supported by the Java language or the Java OS.

JavaOS Architecture

JavaOS is built with several layers of software: the Kernel, the VM, device drivers, and the graphics unit. These layers are followed by the network support package (the `java.net` package), the Java windowing routines, and the Java classes, which make up the Core API.

A user interface, such as HotJava Views (described later in this chapter) or some other application, lays on top of the API. Figure 23.2 illustrates the structure and interdependence of the JavaOS layers. The following sections explain each of the layers and how they work together.

FIGURE 23.2

Layers of the JavaOS

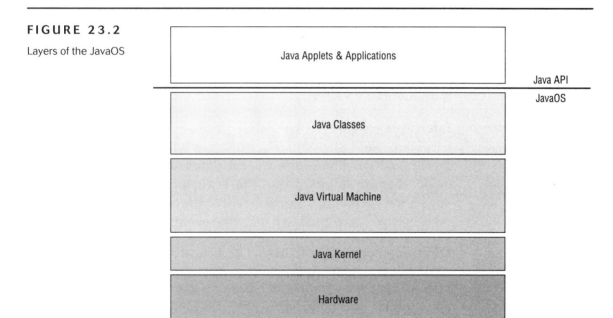

The JavaOS Kernel

The Kernel is at the core of JavaOS. It provides functions and routines to the Java VM. Because the Kernel interacts directly with the processor, and cannot use the Java VM, this layer must contain only machine code. The Kernel is written in assembler or a language such as C or C++, and is then compiled to machine code.

The functions of the Kernel interact directly with the processor and the computer hardware. The Java VM relies on the Kernel to control the hardware while it processes the API classes, drivers, and applications. The Kernel provides several sets of functions and components to the rest of the operating system:

Booting   The startup process for any computer when it is switched on or reset. Most of the boot process consists of testing hardware and initializing memory and devices as needed. This is a relatively fast process on a Network Computer because of its limited hardware and software. The boot process includes loading the operating system from the network into memory. The operating system can reside in ROM in the Network Computer. This provides the fastest boot process because it does not need to load JavaOS from the network into RAM.

Interrupts   Signals to the central processor indicating that some hardware needs attention. The processor will start a specific routine in the Kernel in response to each interrupt. An example of a device that causes interrupts is the keyboard. When you press a key on the keyboard, a signal is sent to the computer and the processor is interrupted to handle the event.

Direct memory access (DMA)   A piece of hardware that moves data between fast peripherals—for instance, between the network interface and the memory. The Kernel needs to initialize this section of the computer hardware. The routines necessary to move memory to and from peripheral devices using DMA are contained in the Kernel.

Memory management   Memory is allocated in Java when objects and variables are declared, and then recovered once they become redundant or go out of context. Routines in the Kernel handle the memory management or allocation and deallocation for the VM.

The VM does the object creation and garbage collection using these routines.

Threads   Java programs can run multiple processes simultaneously. Chapter 8 explains how to do this using threads, and what these threads are. The Kernel makes sure that the processor executes the threads in the correct order and that they start and end correctly.

Exceptions   The basic error-handling mechanism of Java is exceptions, as explained in Chapter 7. This is another part of the operating system that resides in the Kernel and requires special handling of the processor.

File system   The low-level code of the file system—such as reading or writing blocks of data, and opening and closing devices—is contained in the Kernel. The classes and methods in the Core API for file access use these routines.

The Java VM and JavaOS

Most of JavaOS is written in Java. In Figure 23.3, component parts of the operating system are drawn in different shades. The Kernel and Java VM are solid boxes, indicating that they are machine code and specific to the computer's processor. The gray boxes are written in Java and are therefore portable to any computer that has a Java VM.

You can see the important role the Java VM plays in all Java platforms, including JavaOS. The term *Virtual Machine* describes the function of this section of the Java platform. In effect, the Java VM emulates a computer processor. The instruction set for this virtual processor is Java bytecode. Each bytecode instruction is the same and has the same function on any computer running Java or JavaOS. Just as desktop operating systems are compiled to the machine code of their microprocessor, JavaOS is written in Java and compiled to bytecode. JavaOS runs on the underlying Java VM. The Java VM also ensures that the API and classes are consistent across all platforms. See Chapter 17 for a detailed discussion of the Java VM.

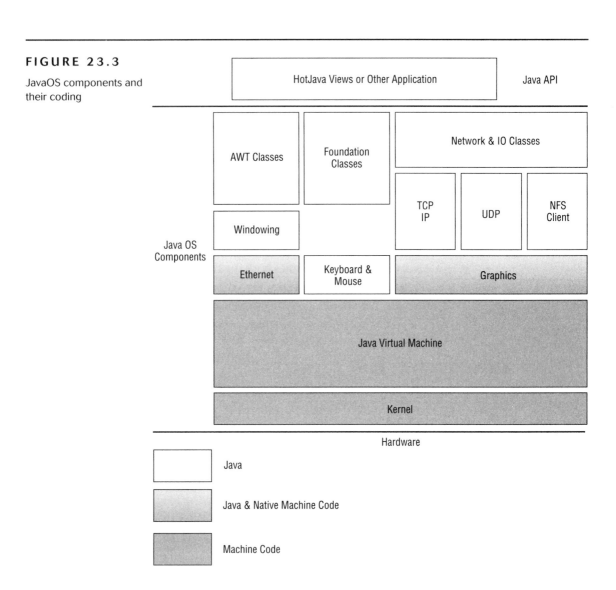

FIGURE 23.3

JavaOS components and their coding

Device Drivers and JavaOS

As explained in Chapter 15, in the discussion of I/O software layers, the device driver connects the operating system to hardware devices and provides users with the flexibility to add and change peripherals connected to their computers without requiring a new operating system. All desktop operating systems use device drivers to provide an easy way to configure and upgrade computers. For example, changing to a video interface card that has more colors or higher resolution is a matter of installing the device and loading the driver software. The new device driver either replaces the previous version or adds to the list of devices present in the machine.

All modern operating systems—Macintosh, Windows 95, NT, OS/2, and JavaOS—have device drivers. One big difference between JavaOS device drivers and those of the other operating systems is that the JavaOS device driver is not dependent on the processor that the computer uses; all the others do depend on the computer's processor.

JavaSoft wants the Java platform to be as portable as possible. In most operating systems, the device drivers are considered low-level code, and they are compiled to machine code, specific to the computer's processor. JavaSoft requires the device drivers to be written in Java, so the driver can be used on any computer running JavaOS.

Devices need to access memory, device ports, and handle interrupts when the hardware needs attention. JavaOS provides special classes to access memory, ports, and interrupts. These classes are not available to the standard (Core) API; they are available only to the device drivers.

To make the programming of device drivers easy and standard, JavaSoft is developing a device driver API. This new API will provide access to the special memory and interrupt classes. It will also outline the methods and function interfaces required to write device drivers.

The easier it is to implement device drivers and connect peripherals, the more likely a peripheral manufacturer will support a new computer platform like the Network Computer and JavaOS. This is a major advantage that JavaOS-based computers and the JavaStation have over other Network Computers: The peripheral manufacturer writes one device driver for *all* JavaOS-based computers. The other Network Computers will have their own specific methods of implementing device drivers, which will be processor-dependent.

> **NOTE**
>
> Other manufacturers have released machines similar to the JavaStation (which is described later in this chapter). These machines do not run JavaOS, but they do support the ability to run Java applets and applications. On the Java application and applet level, all the Network Computers are compatible. The non-JavaOS machines can run other non-Java software specific to their operating systems. This fact introduces incompatibility and discontinuity into the corporate network, and is therefore a disadvantage.

The Graphics Unit of JavaOS

The next layer of the operating system is the graphics and windowing package—or the graphics unit. This package makes up the nuts and bolts of functions used in the AWT classes.

It is essential that the graphics unit is optimized to perform the graphic operations as quickly and efficiently as possible. For this reason, many of the routines in this unit are *native methods*. That means that they are written in C, C++, or assembler, and then compiled to processor-specific machine code. The machine code is linked to Java bytecode as a native method. Some examples of routines that are optimized are the line-draw routines, the polygon-fill routines, and font rendering. Other sections of the graphics unit, where speed is less important, are written in Java.

Java Native Methods

In most Java programs, all the methods are implemented in the Java language. However, there may be situations in which you need to do something that the Java language cannot handle, such as interface with specialized hardware or a database driver. In these cases, you can declare a Java method and implement the function using the C, C++, or

Java Native Methods (Continued)

assembler language and compiler/linker specific to a platform. For example, in Windows, the native method is implemented as a dynamic-link library (DLL). This native object code library is loaded when the class containing the Java native method is instantiated. When a call is made to a Java native method, control is passed to the function in the native object code library that corresponds to this method. The native object function takes over, performs the function, and passes the control back to the Java program.

Native methods make a Java program nonportable and platform-dependent, so they should be used only when they are absolutely necessary. Here are some examples of when native methods might be required:

- To implement a common Java feature for a specific platform. For example, the JDBC-ODBC bridge methods (discussed in Chapter 18) need to interface with ODBC drivers native to each platform, which cannot be done with Java alone.

- For prototyping Java systems, especially for Intranet systems that interface with legacy programs. Rather than wait for a Java interface to become available for these systems, you can write the interface software components in C and implement them as native methods to communicate with the rest of the Java system.

- To support the Java platform in new hardware, such as intelligent cellular phones and network appliances. The specific device drivers for these devices can be written as objects in the Java language, with the device interface implemented as native methods in the micro-controller's C language.

- When the Java bytecode interpretation or JIT compiler are not fast enough, a method can be implemented as a native method in C or assembler for speed optimization.

Network Support Package for JavaOS

Because JavaOS is a network operating system, it must support the most popular network protocols as a minimum. In fact, the network-specific classes make up the largest block of the JavaOS code. All the network-support code is written in Java.

The following protocols for routing and transport are implemented:

- TCP/IP (Transmission Control Protocol / Internet Protocol)
- UDP (User Datagram Protocol)
- ICMP (Internet Control Messaging Protocol)

These are the standard communications protocols used on most networks, including the Internet and all Intranets. JavaOS uses the DNS (Domain Name Service) and NIS (Network Information Service) protocols to look up the different host names on the network and to deliver the user's password and username when logging on to that host.

JavaOS also supports SNMP (Simple Network Management Protocol), which enables the Network Computer to load information to and from a file server located on the network.

Like the device drivers, the network support package (java.net) is written in Java. No special implementation is required for different processors or computers. The TCP/IP performance is approximately twice as fast as the design specification requires, which makes it sufficient for Web browsing.

Windowing for JavaOS

Java supports a simple, memory-efficient windowing system. This system is used to create the overlapping window frames, buttons, and other screen items. The AWT classes in JavaOS are different from those used to develop programs with the JDK. This AWT is called "Tiny AWT" because it requires less functionality from the windowing and graphics package.

NOTE Critics of Java often cite performance and speed as its main drawback. You might expect poor performance from device drivers written in Java. Performance is most critical in the graphics and large data-transfer systems of the operating system. JavaSoft implemented the graphics unit using a mixture of Java and native methods to get maximum performance and still maintain some platform independence. Transfer of data to and from the network is currently rated at 500Kb per second peak (depending on the network connection method, of course). This is a respectable data-transfer rate for general desktop work, comparable to floppy disk-transfer speeds.

JavaStation: The Java and JavaOS Network Computer

To address the design of the ideal Network Computer, Sun Microsystems and JavaSoft joined forces to develop the *JavaStation*, which was released in December 1996. The JavaStation is not the first Network Computer on the market, nor the first Network Computer to support Java. The JavaStation is, however, the first Network Computer to implement JavaOS.

The following sections describe the JavaStation hardware, software, and HotJava Views user interface.

JavaStation Hardware

As explained, earlier in the chapter, the term *thin client* is a name given to network workstations with minimal peripherals and no local storage. The thin client uses the network server(s) for storage and access to peripherals as needed. For these reasons, this term applies to the Java-Station. For instance, the JavaStation has no local disk storage; files are stored on the network.

The following is an overview of the hardware specifications of the JavaStation, which is based on Sun Microsystems's processor:

- 100MHz microSPARC II processor
- 8MB RAM expandable to 64MB using standard 72-pin modules
- Optional flash ROM for JavaOS or loaded from the network
- 10/100-BaseT Fast Ethernet network interface
- PPP (Point-to-Point Protocol) and modem support
- PC-compatible, Super VGA-compatible video interface
- Accelerated graphics
- Standard PS-2 keyboard and mouse
- VGA monitor connection to use existing equipment

The JavaStation, shown in Figure 23.4, is primarily designed for connection to an existing Ethernet network and to provide immediate access to a company's Intranet.

NOTE As of this writing, the JavaSoft machine, without a video monitor, costs between $700 and $800.

FIGURE 23.4

The JavaStation

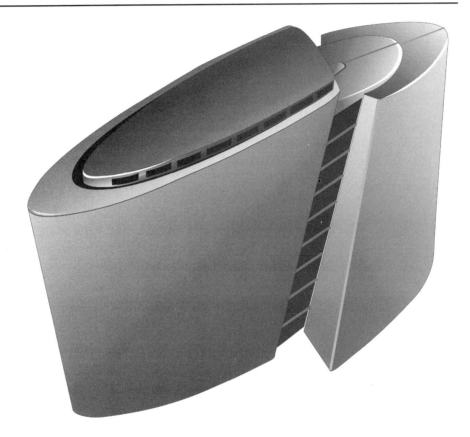

JavaStation Software and Software Support

Standard Java software, such as word processing and spreadsheet applications, is available for purchase from software vendors. Deploying and distributing this software is relatively easy; you just need to place the package in a common network area that all users can access. You do not need to install the application on each separate hard disk on each computer connected to the network. For example, Corel has implemented its popular WordPerfect word processor and Quattro Pro spreadsheet in Java. You could make these applications available to all network users, storing their individual settings in their private directories or areas on the network.

Many companies develop their own software for database access, order taking, analysis, reports, and other specialized applications. Often, a number of different versions are needed for the different hardware and operating system platforms on the network. If the programming language is Java, the program is compiled once and loaded on the network once. All users can load and run the application whenever and wherever it is needed. If all the applications are written in Java, it does not matter which platform a user has, as long as the program can use the Java VM. This means the developers no longer need to design a Mac version, a Windows 3.1 version, a Windows 95/NT version, and a Unix version. There could be one Java version for all platforms to use.

A large market for the Network Computer is in replacing dumb terminals that connect to mainframe and mini-computers. JavaStation can run terminal-emulator software that makes the Network Computer operate as if it were a terminal. This provides access to legacy software while the transition is made from centralized processing to distributed processing over the network. Meanwhile, the software development teams can work on developing Java versions of the programs that the terminals used. Eventually, the users can be converted from the terminal-emulation program to a more functional and easier-to-use Java application.

One of the largest tasks on a network is keeping track of software licenses. With workstations distributed across a network, each with its own hard disk, making sure all clients have current and compatible versions of programs can be difficult. But with the Network Computer, which loads all the programs and files from the network, this task becomes much easier. Network administrators can easily check the file server storage for version information, and they can configure the network so that all applications are loaded from the same place.

Java Desktop: HotJava Views

JavaOS does not contain a command-line interpreter or GUI like Windows or Macintosh systems; instead, it runs an application called HotJava Views to provide the user interface. HotJava Views is a suite of integrated applications, which includes all of the typical Desktop (or, in this case, Webtop) features: buttons, icons, mouse pointer, and other visual cues that you have come to expect from operating systems.

JavaSoft developed HotJava Views for the corporate environment, and designed it to be easy to use and administer by network managers. Settings in HotJava Views are saved on the network and relate to the user rather than to the Network Computer. No matter where the user logs on, all that user's settings will be restored, and HotJava Views will look exactly as he or she left it.

The Java GUI versus the PC Desktop

The Desktop environment for PCs is a metaphor for a work desk. The icons used for file folders, documents, and trash cans serve as symbols for the underlying file system and its functions. When the user opens a file or document in Windows, for instance, an overlapping window appears on the Desktop. The window represents or resembles a piece of paper. In contrast, HotJava Views interacts quite differently with the Network Computer. Part of that difference is reflected in the absence of a file system.

Java is an object-oriented language, and similarly JavaOS is an object-oriented operating system. This is in contrast to standard desktop operating systems that evolved from core file and disk operating systems. The equivalent of a file to JavaOS is an object, which contains data like a file, but also has methods to handle and access that data, as well as properties that describe and control the object. In a Desktop environment, you launch an application to process a file. With Java, the object has built-in methods to process the data and properties of the object.

HotJava Views uses this object-oriented approach to provide access to the data. For example, the Mail view is the "method" for interrogating and entering e-mail "objects," and the Calendar view is the method to manipulate the calendar-event objects. HotJava Views has no need for an equivalent to the Windows File Manager. The object-oriented approach is more consistent with JavaOS and the Java applications and applets that the Network Computer will run.

HotJava Views Components

HotJava Views consists of a number of productivity modules that are a requirement in most corporate offices. The suite includes e-mail, a contact database, a calendar and diary, and a HTML Web browser.

The integrated applications in the HotJava Views are called *views*; Java programs linked by the system administrator (or network manager) to a new button are called *views* or *applications*.

The left side of the HotJava Views screen contains the *selector bar*, which is the tool used to select between each of the different applications or views. These views and applications appear on the selector bar as icons or buttons. A single click launches the application or view. Here are brief descriptions of the views available in HotJava Views:

Calendar view   An appointment calendar and group scheduler. Naturally, the program displays calendars showing the dates and times of meetings and appointments. It is fully integrated with the e-mail view and the contact database (called NamesView). Figure 23.5 shows the Calendar view.

Names view   A view that provides access to the corporate and personal database of names and addresses. This view integrates with all the other views in the system. To send e-mail to a person from the database, simply click on the mail button in the Names view; to schedule an appointment, click on the calendar button. This view can also contain a URL for the person's home page or department home page.

FIGURE 23.5

The Calendar view in HotJava Views

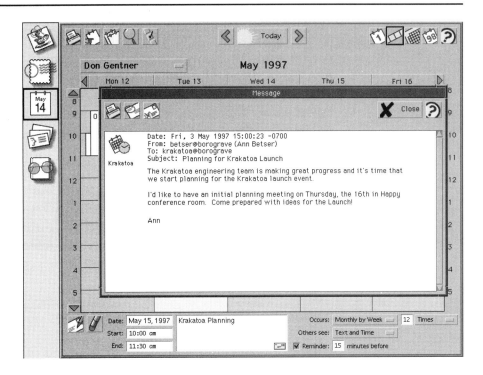

Mail view   A mail application, which allows appointments and live URLs to be attached. Names and addresses of mail senders and recipients can be stored in the integrated Names view. If a calendar appointment is attached to an e-mail message, the event can be dragged to the calendar and appears as a mail symbol located in the corner of the day-of-month display.

Web view   This view is an HTML browser that allows the user to open Web pages and run multiple Java applets. Because of the multi-tasking ability of Java, users can have multiple applets running simultaneously while they browse the Web or company Intranet.

TIP If the Web view supplied is not suitable, you can attach the standard HotJava Web browser to the selector instead. This provides more extensive Web access and more control to the administrator over access levels and rights.

Configurable Settings in HotJava Views

The system administrator can configure many aspects of the Webtop to suit his or her particular preferences and requirements. This is a key benefit of the Network Computer: Because all of the configuration settings are saved on the network, the settings are the same the next time the user logs in. Even if the user logs in from a different Network Computer, that user's Webtop will be just as he or she left it.

This is ideal if the Network Computer is replaced by a newer model or contains updated hardware. When the new unit is switched on and the user logs in, the old settings and configuration load from the network; minimal setup is required (real plug and play!).

Custom Desktops from Third Parties

HotJava Views is an application written in Java by JavaSoft. It provides an efficient and convenient interface and productivity suite for use with the Network Computer running JavaOS. However, there is no requirement for a JavaOS computer to use HotJava Views as the front end. If manufacturers or users want to write a different user interface program with a different type of Desktop, they certainly can.

Compared to other standard operating systems on the market, the ability to change the user interface could be perceived as a loose end. This "loose end" can be viewed as a benefit or a flaw in the JavaOS strategy. On the positive side, a corporation has the flexibility to design and implement its own Desktop and operating environment. On the negative side, there is no definitive JavaOS operator skills between different machines. Giving up strict standards in favor of flexibility can require additional training for new employees who used a different Desktop on another Network Computer.

Benefits of the JavaStation

Here is a summary of the advantages of the JavaStation:

- JavaOS is a multitasking operating system. The user can run multiple applications concurrently, increasing productivity and the ease of use of the JavaStation.

- Because JavaOS is a small operating system, and it can be stored in flash ROM, the JavaStation is a very fast booting computer. (How long do you wait for your computer to start up every morning?)

- Great effort has been expended to make sure that the Java VM is compatible and consistent on every platform and every computer. This fact makes the JavaStation very attractive to corporate clients who need this compatibility to build safe, secure, and reliable networks.

- Whether the user is running a Java application on a JavaStation, a PC, or a Macintosh, the results will be the same. This allows the company to supply low-cost JavaStations to those users who work on the network all the time, and PCs, PowerMacs, or workstation computers to those users who require the extra functionality and computing power.

JavaOS and Embedded Computing

Computers have now permeated our environment. Microprocessors are at the core of household items like video game systems, programmable thermostats, sewing machines, microwaves, and dimmer switches. Processors and computers incorporated into appliances or devices are called *embedded computers*.

A thermostat in the home requires very little computing power, memory, or peripherals. To use a Java-based embedded processing system in such a device would be overkill. However, a home-automation system, networked to control climate in multiple zones, a security system, fire detection, lighting, and perhaps a sprinkler system for the garden, would justify the use of an embedded Java computer.

Benefits of JavaOS for Embedded Computing

The embedded computing industry has had great interest in Java, and more recently, JavaOS and picoJava (described later in the chapter). The main reasons for this interest are as follows:

- JavaOS is a small, cost-efficient platform.

- Java is portable over multiple platforms.

- Java is standard, with very few variations.

- JavaOS can be tailored to suit an application.

NOTE   Java may not be the most efficient language in terms of execution speed, but it makes up for this in portability and reduced development and maintenance time. The main factor responsible for the poor performance is the bytecode interpretation. By using a Java chip, described in later in the chapter, or a Java-enhanced processor, this shortcoming can be eliminated.

JavaOS Cost Savings

A key issue in embedded computing is cost. Because Java is compact, fast, and efficient, it adds only a small overhead to the manufacturing costs of a device.

Component parts like ROM and RAM are kept to the minimum required to operate the device. A system incorporating JavaOS has certain minimum memory requirements. How small can JavaOS be made? An estimate of the essentials required is 512KB ROM for JavaOS and 128KB RAM for operating system workspace. More RAM for applications must be added to this minimum. This may sound like a lot of memory, but JavaOS is tiny compared with Windows 95, which requires at least 50MB of disk space and 8MB of RAM to operate.

Java Portability

When compiled to bytecode, a Java program will run with any processor that implements JavaOS. Sometimes, an embedded design requires a processor change—for speed, low power, cost, or some other reason. If Java is the programming language, engineers and programmers do not need to learn another set of processor instructions or architecture. As long as the new processor supports JavaOS, the software stays the same. This platform independence is one of the most attractive aspects of the language and underlying principles.

JavaOS Adaptability

The embedded version of JavaOS can be tailored to suit the application. For example, a data logger in a factory may have no display. The data logger connects to a network to transmit data from a piece of equipment to a central computer.

For this type of device, the AWT classes and the window and graphics subsystems are removed from JavaOS. More space is saved by removing the keyboard and mouse drivers. The network classes are necessary, because they allow the device to communicate with the network.

The Real-Time Kernel

The normal JavaOS Kernel, described earlier in this chapter, is designed for desktop use. With the desktop system, time is less critical than in industrial processing and machine control.

Control systems measure time in single microseconds rather than tens of milliseconds. The normal Java Kernel is unsuitable for this type of precision timing; instead, a *real-time Kernel* is required.

The real-time Kernel ensures that time-critical operations happen on time, and that interrupts are passed to the required process as soon as possible. For embedded Java applications, the Kernel is replaced with a real-time Java Kernel.

The picoJava I Design

For situations in which the performance of bytecode interpretation is too slow, Sun Microsystems has developed the JavaChip architecture and a microprocessor design called picoJava I. The picoJava I design basically implements the Java VM in silicon—executing the byte-codes directly in hardware. Other chip and processor manufacturers can license the design from Sun, and then produce their own Java chips under licensing arrangements. For example, Mitsubishi and Samsung have licensed the design and can therefore build their own versions of the Java microprocessor.

The following sections describe the picoJava I architecture, stack mechanisms, and performance.

The picoJava I Architecture

JavaOS running on a picoJava processor is reduced to the API classes, device drivers, and graphics and network packages. Without the Java VM component, JavaOS is smaller than with a conventional microprocessor. The API of a machine or device using the picoJava I processor and JavaOS is exactly the same as the API for any other platform with a Java VM.

The picoJava I design incorporates the many years of RISC design experience at Sun Microsystems. The architecture is relatively simple, and it is designed to be customizable for various applications.

Figure 23.6 shows a diagram of the processor function blocks. Note that the instruction cache and data cache can be configured from 0 to 16KB each, and the floating-point math unit can be omitted if the chip is configured for specific low-cost applications. The design includes an I/O bus and memory interface unit for connecting other peripherals that could be included in the same chip.

FIGURE 23.6

The architecture of the picoJava I processor

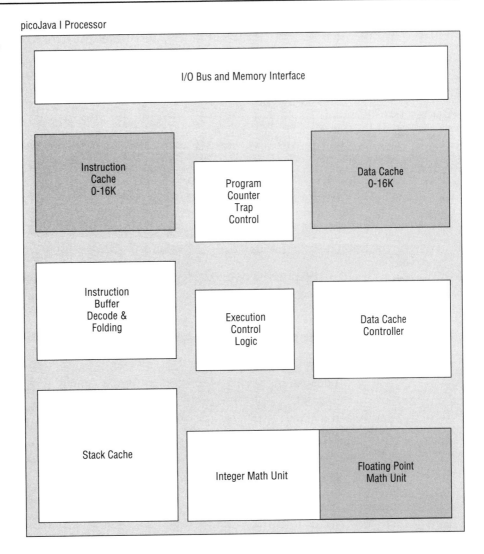

picoJava I Processor

Four-Stage Pipeline

Like most RISC processors, the picoJava I employs a pipeline execution unit. The pipeline consists of four stages: fetch, decode, execute, and write back. At any point in time, all the stages of the pipeline are operating on separate bytecodes. As the next bytecode instruction is fetched from memory, the current instruction is being examined by the decode pipeline stage. Concurrently, the previously decoded instruction is being executed and the results of the last execution are being written back to the stack. Figure 23.7 illustrates the simple four-stage pipeline

FIGURE 23.7

The picoJava I four-stage pipeline

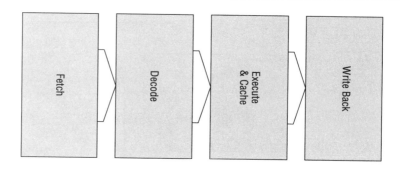

The pipeline is enhanced for the picoJava processor with support for method invocation, thread synchronization, and garbage collection.

The picoJava Stack Mechanism

Because the Java VM was designed as a stack machine, the efficiency of stack operations is critical. The Java platform makes extensive use of the stack and has none of the registers that are typical of general microprocessors. The picoJava processor has a very efficient and innovative stack mechanism. Some of the key features of this stack mechanism are described in the following sections.

Method Frame

When you call one of the methods from an object in Java, the processor creates what is called a *method frame*. This method frame is a packet of information that is saved on the stack, and its size varies depending on the number of local variables and parameters associated with the method.

Method frames contain parameters from the method call, local variables from the method, and the frame state. The frame state is the information required by the processor to set everything back to normal once a method is complete.

Dribbling

Several method frames can reside on the stack at any one time. The variable size of frames could cause the stack to overflow if too many methods were called in succession. To prevent overflow, the processor implements a background process that watches to see if the stack is getting too full.

When the stack fills past a certain level, the oldest information on the stack is removed and stored in the data cache, making room for new method frames. When room becomes available on the stack, the saved information is then replaced on the stack in the correct order. This system is called *dribbling*, referring to the way data dribbles from the bottom of the stack before an overflow can occur.

Folding

To accelerate operations using the stack, the picoJava I processor uses an innovative *folding* mechanism. In a typical stack operation, an instruction needs to access a data item that is not the next item to be popped off the stack. To access that item, a process moves the required item to the top of the stack, and then the instruction uses the data—two operations are required.

The picoJava I mechanism detects this type of operation and "folds" the two operations together. Effectively, the instruction just takes the data from where it resides in the stack. Sun Microsystems used simulations to evaluate the folding process and claims that the folding operation eliminates 60 percent of normal stack inefficiencies.

The Performance of the picoJava I Design

The reason for the creation of the picoJava processor design was to increase the performance of Java-based machines to comparable or better than current processor technologies. The benchmark tests performed by Sun compared the picoJava I with Intel 486 and Pentium processors with equal clock rates. These tests showed that picoJava I was 15 to 20 times the speed of the 486 running a Java interpreter and 5 times the speed of the Pentium running with a JIT (Just-In-Time) compiler.

Some chip manufacturers will implement Java accelerators for their processors. This will allow them to run their native code, for compatibility with legacy software and to provide a processor mode that executes Java bytecode. This kind of processor would be ideal for an operating system with built-in Java, such as OS/2.

Summary

JavaOS is a powerful and flexible operating system that is not tied to any specific processor or machine architecture. With built-in networking and Java's obvious association with the Internet, JavaOS is ideally positioned as the operating system for Network Computers. Sun Microsystems produce the JavaStation, the first Network Computer to implement JavaOS. Many more JavaOS-based computers are sure to follow.

One area of concern with Java, and therefore JavaOS, has been performance. Currently, it seems to be an issue only when comparisons are made with desktop computers running compiled code. With processors like picoJava I available, Java's performance will not be a concern.

The Java platform has not been around for long, so some skeptics are standing back and waiting to see if it will take off. However, as you have learned in this book, Java offers a powerful, object-oriented language, with built-in security, networking, and compatibility with almost any computer and operating system. Java and JavaOS have a bright future in the computer industry.

APPENDIX
A

JDK 1.1 Deprecated Methods

As part of the overhaul of the Java language from version 1.0.2 to 1.1, many methods and classes were altered, added, and eliminated. In order to retain compatibility with older versions of Java, old methods and objects were retained, but marked as *deprecated*. This status means that, although code that uses these methods will still compile and work, the compiler will generate warning messages. If your code uses deprecated methods, you should change them so that they will retain compatibility with future releases of Java. In addition, many of the new methods provide better implementations of certain features, making your Java programs faster and more efficient.

This appendix lists the deprecated methods and JDK (Java Development Kit) version 1.1 replacement methods, alphabetically by class. For more information about any particular deprecated method, consult the JDK documentation (available from JavaSoft's Web page: http://www .javasoft.com/products/jdk/1.1/docs/api/packages.html).

NOTE　Because of the constantly fluctuating nature of the Java Core API, this list cannot be entirely complete. It is intended as a quick reference for converting your code. To find a complete list of deprecated methods in your code, use the javac compiler with the -deprecation option, when the compiler warns you of such usage.

Deprecated Method	JDK 1.1 Replacement
Class: BorderLayout	
`public void addLayoutComponent` `(String name, Component comp)`	`addLayoutComponent(Component,` `Object)`
Class: ByteArrayOutputStream	
`public String toString(int hibyte)`	`toString(java.lang.String)`
Class: CardLayout	
`public void addLayoutComponent` `(Stringname, Component comp)`	`addLayoutComponent(Component,` `Object)`
Class: Character	
`public static boolean isJavaLetter` `(char ch)`	`isJavaIdentifierStart(char)`
`public static boolean` `isJavaLetterOrDigit(char ch)`	`isJavaIdentifierPart(char)`
`public static boolean` `isSpace(char ch)`	`isWhitespace(char)`
Class: CheckboxGroup	
`public Checkbox getCurrent()`	`getSelectedCheckbox()`
`public synchronized void setCurrent` `(Checkbox box)`	`setSelectedCheckbox(Checkbox)`
Class: Choice	
`public int countItems()`	`getItemCount()`
Class: ClassLoader	
`protected final Class defineClass` `(byte data[], int offset,` `int length)`	`defineClass(java.lang.String, byte[],` `int, int)`
Class: Component	
`public ComponentPeer getPeer()`	Programs should not directly manipulate peers.

Deprecated Method	JDK 1.1 Replacement
Class: Component	
public void enable()	setEnabled(boolean)
public void enable(boolean b)	setEnabled(boolean)
public void disable()	setEnabled(boolean)
public void show()	setVisible(boolean)
public void show(boolean b)	setVisible(boolean)
public void hide()	setVisible(boolean)
public Point location()	getLocation()
public void move(int x, int y)	setLocation(int, int)
public Dimension size()	getSize()
public void resize(int width, int height)	setSize(int, int)
public void resize(Dimension d)	setSize(Dimension)
public Rectangle bounds()	getBounds()
public void reshape(int x, int y, int width, int height)	setBounds(int, int, int, int)
public Dimension preferredSize()	getPreferredSize()
public Dimension minimumSize()	getMinimumSize()
public void layout()	doLayout()
public boolean inside (int x, int y)	contains(int, int)
public Component locate (int x, int y)	getComponentAt(int, int)
public void deliverEvent (Event e)	dispatchEvent (AWTEvent)
public boolean postEvent(Event e)	dispatchEvent(AWTEvent)
public boolean handleEvent (Event e)	processEvent (AWTEvent)

Deprecated Method	JDK 1.1 Replacement
Class: Component	
`public boolean mouseDown(Event evt, int x, int y)`	`processMouseEvent(MouseEvent)`
`public boolean mouseDrag (Event evt, int x, int y)`	`processMouseMotionEvent(MouseEvent)`
`public boolean mouseUp(Event evt, int x, int y)`	`processMouseEvent(MouseEvent)`
`public boolean mouseMove(Event evt, int x, int y)`	`processMouseMotionEvent(MouseEvent)`
`public boolean mouseEnter(Event evt, int x, int y)`	`processMouseEvent(MouseEvent)`
`public boolean mouseExit(Event evt, int x, int y)`	`processMouseEvent(MouseEvent)`
`public boolean keyDown(Event evt, int key)`	`processKeyEvent(KeyEvent)`
`public boolean keyUp(Event evt, int key)`	`processKeyEvent(KeyEvent)`
`public boolean action(Event evt, Object what)`	Should register this component as `Action-Listener` on component which fires action events.
`public boolean gotFocus(Event evt, Object what)`	`processFocusEvent(FocusEvent)`
`public boolean lostFocus(Event evt, Object what)`	`processFocusEvent(FocusEvent)`
`public void nextFocus()`	`transferFocus()`
Class: Container	
`public int countComponents()`	`getComponentCount()`
`public Insets insets()`	`getInsets()`
`public void layout()`	`doLayout()`
`public Dimension preferredSize()`	`getPreferredSize()`

Deprecated Method	JDK 1.1 Replacement
Class: Container	
`public Dimension minimumSize()`	`getMinimumSize()`
`public void deliverEvent(Event e)`	`dispatchEvent(AWTEvent e)`
`public Component locate` `(int x, int y)`	`getComponentAt(int, int)`
`void nextFocus(Component base)`	`transferFocus(Component)`
Class: DataInputStream	
`public final String readLine()` `throws IOException`	`BufferedReader.readLine()`
Class: Date	
`public Date (int year, int month, int date)`	See `Calendar`
`public Date (int year, int month, int date, int hrs, int min)`	See `Calendar`
`public Date (int year, int month, int date, int hrs, int min, int sec)`	See `Calendar`
`public Date (String s)`	See `DateFormat`
`public static long UTC(int year, int month, int date, int hrs, int min, int sec)`	See `Calendar`
`public static long parse(String s)`	See `DateFormat`
`public int getYear()`	See `Calendar`
`public void setYear(int year)`	See `Calendar`
`public int getMonth()`	See `Calendar`
`public void setMonth(int month)`	See `Calendar`
`public int getDate()`	See `Calendar`
`public void setDate(int date)`	See `Calendar`

Deprecated Method	JDK 1.1 Replacement
Class: Date	
`public int getDay()`	See `Calendar`
`public int getHours()`	See `Calendar`
`public void setHours(int hours)`	See `Calendar`
`public int getMinutes()`	See `Calendar`
`public void setMinutes(int minutes)`	See `Calendar`
`public int getSeconds()`	See `Calendar`
`public void setSeconds(int seconds)`	See `Calendar`
`public String toLocaleString()`	See `DateFormat`
`public String toGMTString()`	See `DateFormat`
`public int getTimezoneOffset()`	See `Calendar` and `TimeZone`
Class: EventListener	
Entire `sunw.util.EventListener` class	This is a compatibility type to allow Java Beans that were developed under JDK 1.0.2 to run correctly under JDK 1.1. The corresponding JDK 1.1 type is `java.util.EventListener`.
Class: EventObject	
Entire `sunw.util.EventObject` class	This is a compatibility type to allow Java Beans that were developed under JDK 1.0.2 to run correctly under JDK 1.1. The corresponding JDK 1.1 type is `java.util.EventObject`.
Class: Frame	
`public synchronized void setCursor (int cursorType)`	`Component.setCursor(Cursor)`
`public int getCursorType()`	`Component.setCursor(Cursor)` `Component.getCursor()`

Deprecated Method	JDK 1.1 Replacement
Class: Graphics	
`public Rectangle getClipRect()`	`getClipBounds()`
Class: KeyEvent	
`public KeyEvent(Component source, int id, long when, int modifiers, int keyCode)`	Do not use; will be removed in JDK 1.1.1.
Class: LineNumberInputStream	
Entire `java.io.LineNumber-InputStream` class	This class incorrectly assumes that bytes adequately represent characters. As of JDK 1.1, the preferred way to operate on character streams is via the new character-stream classes, which include a class for counting line numbers.
Class: List	
`public int countItems()`	`getItemCount()`
`public synchronized void clear()`	`removeAll()`
`public boolean isSelected (int index)`	`isIndexSelected(int)`
`public boolean allowsMultipleSelections()`	`isMultipleMode()`
`public synchronized void setMultipleSelections(boolean b)`	`setMultipleMode(boolean)`
`public Dimension preferredSize (int rows)`	`getPreferredSize(int)`
`public Dimension preferredSize()`	`getPreferredSize()`
`public Dimension minimumSize (int rows)`	`getMinimumSize(int)`
`public Dimension minimumSize()`	`getMinimumSize()`
`public synchronized void delItems(int start, int end)`	Not for public use in the future. This method is expected to be retained only as a package private method.

Deprecated Method	JDK 1.1 Replacement
Class: Menu	
`public int countItems()`	`getItemCount()`
Class: MenuBar	
`public int countMenus()`	`getMenuCount()`
Class: MenuComponent	
`public MenuComponentPeer getPeer()`	Programs should not directly manipulate peers.
Class: MenuItem	
`public synchronized void enable()`	`setEnabled(boolean)`
`public void enable(boolean b)`	`setEnabled(boolean)`
`public synchronized void disable()`	`setEnabled(boolean)`
Class: Polygon	
`public Rectangle getBoundingBox()`	`getBounds()`
`public boolean inside(int x, int y)`	`contains(int, int)`
Class: PrintStream	
Entire `java.io.PrintStream` class	The preferred way to print text is via the `PrintWriter` class.
Class: Rectangle	
`public void reshape(int x, int y, int width, int height)`	`setBounds(int, int, int, int)`
`public void move(int x, int y)`	`setLocation(int, int)`
`public void reSize(int width, int height)`	`setSize(int, int)`
`public boolean inside (int x, int y)`	`contains(int, int)`

Deprecated Method	JDK 1.1 Replacement
Class: Runtime	
`public InputStream getLocalizedInputStream (InputStream in)`	`BufferedReader(java.io.InputStream) InputStreamReader(java.io.InputStream)`
`public OutputStream getLocalizedOutputStream (OutputStream out)`	`BufferedWriter(java.io.OutputStream) OutputStreamWriter(java.io .OutputStream)PrintWriter (java.io.OutputStream)`
Class: Scrollbar	
`public int getVisible ()`	`getVisibleAmount()`
`public synchronized void setLineIncrement(int v)`	`setUnitIncrement(int)`
`public int getLineIncrement()`	`getUnitIncrement()`
`public synchronized void setPageIncrement(int v)`	`setBlockIncrement(int)`
`public int getPageIncrement()`	`getBlockIncrement()`
Class: ScrollPane	
`public void layout()`	`doLayout()`
Class: Serializable	
Entire `sunw.io.Serializable` class	This is a compatibility type to allow Java Beans that were developed under JDK 1.0.2 to run correctly under JDK 1.1. The corresponding JDK 1.1 type is `java.util.Serializable`.
Class: Socket	
`public Socket(String host, int port, boolean stream) throws IOException`	Use `DatagramSocket` instead for UDP transport.
`public Socket(InetAddress host, int port, boolean stream) throws IOException`	Use `DatagramSocket` instead for UDP transport.

Deprecated Method	JDK 1.1 Replacement
Class: StreamTokenizer	
`public StreamTokenizer` `(InputStream is)`	`StreamTokenizer(java.io.Reader)`
Class: String	
`public String(byte ascii[],` `int hibyte, int offset, int count)`	This method does not properly convert bytes into characters. As of JDK version 1.1, the preferred way to do this is via the `String` constructors that take a character-encoding name, or that use the default encoding.
`public String(byte ascii[],` `int hibyte)`	This method does not properly convert bytes into characters. As of JDK version 1.1, the preferred way to do this is via the `String` constructors that take a character-encoding name, or that use the platform's default encoding.

`public void getBytes(int srcBegin,`
`int srcEnd, byte dst[],`
`int dstBegin)`
	This method does not properly convert characters into bytes. As of JDK version 1.1, the preferred way to do this is via the `getBytes()` methods that take a character-encoding name, or that use the platform's default encoding.

Class: StringBufferInputStream	
Entire `java.io.StringBuffer-` `InputStream` class	This class does not properly convert characters into bytes. As of JDK 1.1, the preferred way to create a stream from a string is via the `StringReader` class.
Class: System	
`public static String getenv` `(String name)`	`getenv` is no longer supported. Use properties and `-D` instead.
Class: TextArea	
`public void insertText(String str,` `int pos)`	`insert(String, int)`
`public void appendText(String str)`	`append(String)`

Deprecated Method	JDK 1.1 Replacement
Class: TextArea	
`public void replaceText(String str, int start, int end)`	`replaceRange(String, int, int)`
`public Dimension preferredSize (int rows, int columns)`	`getPreferredSize(int, int)`
`public Dimension preferredSize()`	`getPreferredSize()`
`public Dimension minimumSize (int rows, int columns)`	`getMinimumSize(int, int)`
`public Dimension minimumSize()`	`getMinimumSize()`
Class: TextField	
`public void setEchoCharacter (char c)`	`setEchoChar(char)`
`public Dimension preferredSize (int columns)`	`getPreferredSize(int)`
`public Dimension preferredSize()`	`getPreferredSize()`
`public Dimension minimumSize (int columns)`	`getMinimumSize(int)`
`public Dimension minimumSize()`	`getMinimumSize()`
Class: Window	
`void nextFocus(Component base)`	`transferFocus(Component)`
`public boolean postEvent(Event e)`	`dispatchEvent(AWTEvent)`

A P P E N D I X
B

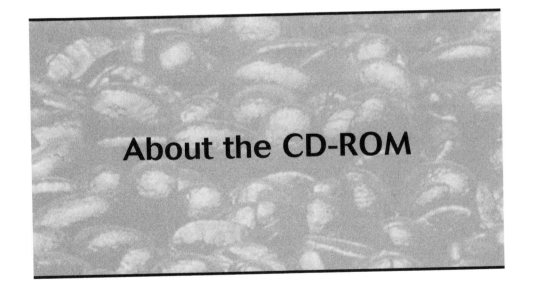

About the CD-ROM

The *Mastering Java 1.1, Second Edition* CD-ROM is designed for easy access to all source code and executable files from the book. It also contains versions of many of the most popular Java Integrated Development Environments (IDEs) and other third-party tools to use with, or as an alternative to, the Java Development Kit (JDK) 1.1.

Copying CD-ROM Files onto Your Hard Drive

To install the *Mastering Java 1.1, Second Edition* source code and executable files from the CD-ROM, click on the BookCode.exe file in the Mastering Java 1.1 folder. This program will automatically copy the files onto your C drive. Use Windows Explorer to copy the files to any other drive.

The Chapter folders contain three types of files:

- The .java files are the source code from the book.

- The .class files are the Java compiled code. These files can be run only from an HTML browser or a Java command line.

- The .html files run the Java applets via a Web browser.

When you use Windows Explorer to copy specific files to any drive, the files will be marked read-only. To deselect the read-only attribute, right-click on the files in Explorer, choose Properties, and click on the Read-Only checkbox.

Installing the Tools

The CD-ROM contains versions of many of the hottest Java tools available on the market today. Each third-party tool is located in its own folder; for example, Penumbra Software's Visual IDE, Mojo, is located in the Mojo folder, which contains the executable file to install the program. Some folders also contain readme files or software license agreements. The installation instructions may vary slightly, depending on the product. The following sections list the installation procedures by product. For more information, visit any of the Web sites listed below:

JDK 1.1 (JavaSoft)	http://www.javasoft.com
ED for Windows (Soft As It Gets)	http://www.getsoft.com
Jamba (AimTech)	http://www.aimtech.com
JetEffects (Peak Technologies)	http://www.peak-media.com.
Mojo (Penumbra)	http://www .penumbrasoftware.com
Vibe DE (Visix Software)	http://www.visix.com
Widgets (Connect! Quick)	http://www.connectcorp.com.

JDK 1.1

The JDK 1.1 is the full development package from Sun Microsystems. The version contained on this CD-ROM is the final release version 1.1 of the software and can be used for creating Java applets and applications.

To install the JDK, go to the Jdk folder and double-click on the jdk1_1-win32-x86.exe file. For updates or changes to the JDK, visit the JavaSoft Web site at http://www.javasoft.com.

ED for Windows

ED for Windows, from Soft As It Gets, was one of the first complete and comprehensive Java development environments to hit the market. ED's powerful editing capabilities make writing code a snap. Templates, smartype, autocorrection, and code completion can write code for you. The Java browser lets you see your complete class and method hierarchy at a glance. With ED's code-navigation features, you can move around your classes and methods at the touch of key.

To install the trial version of ED for Windows 3.71 available on the CD-ROM, go to the ED for Windows folder and double-click on the ed4w371t.zip file. This timed-out version will expire 45 days after it is installed onto your system.

For more information, visit the Soft As It Gets Web site at http://www.getsoft.com.

Jamba

Jamba, from Aimtech, is a new authoring software tool that enables Internet developers, creative professionals, and Webmasters to create interactive, media-rich Java applets and applications without programming or scripting. Built on industry-standard object-oriented software technology and Sun's Java, Jamba meets the growing demand for easy-to-use tools that enhance the interactivity of a company's Internet efforts.

To install the timed-out version of Jamba 1.1 from the CD-ROM, go to the Jamba folder and double-click on the jambatrl.exe file. Once installed, the timed-out version is valid for 30 days or 100 uses, whichever comes first.

For more information, visit the Jamba Web site at http://www.aimtech.com.

JetEffects

JetEffects, from Peak Technologies, is an easy-to-use Java animation tool for home and small-office Web page authors. JetEffects can be used sucessfully by novices and experts.

To install JetEffects, go to the JetEffects folder and double-click on the Jetfx.exe file. This trial version will expire 30 days after it is installed on your system.

For more information, visit the Peak Technologies Web site at http://www.peak-media.com.

Mojo

Penumbra's Mojo is a complete development environment for programmers using the Java language to create networking applets. Mojo consists of two primary components: a GUI Designer that provides a visual means for building Java applets and a Coder that organizes Java objects and gives the user direct access to all aspects of code. The Mojo Designer is designed for non-programmers who wish to enter the domain of Java programming with the smallest possible learning curve. Although the emphasis is on non-programmers, experienced programmers can also take advantage of Mojo's reuse of components and easy extensibility.

The CD-ROM contains the trial version of Mojo 2.0. To install the evaluation copy of Mojo, go to the Mojo folder and double-click on the setup.exe file. You will see a dialog box informing you that the trial version has already expired; however, only certain features, such as saving, have been disabled.

For more information or to download a more current demo version, visit the Mojo Web site at http://www.penumbrasoftware.com.

Vibe

Vibe DE, from Visix Software, is an intuitive integrated development and deployment environment for building Java applications. Vibe is comprised of a visual Java-specific IDE, which includes a compiler and debugger, an extensive set of class libraries, and ActiveX support. It also contains an enriched virtual machine (VM) for deploying production applications across Intranets.

The CD-ROM contains a demo/evaluation copy of Vibe DE 1.0. To install the demo copy, go to the Vibe folder and double-click on the vibedemo.exe file.

For more information, stop by the Visix Software Web site at http:// www.visix.com.

Widgets

Widgets, from Connect! Quick, is a library of sophisticated, prebuilt components for assembling commercial-quality Java applications. The product is written entirely in Java and has the same look, feel, and behavior in all Java-enabled environments, including Windows, Macintosh, and Unix.

To install the Widgets demo, go to the Widgets folder and double-click on the Widgets.exe file.

For more information, visit the Connect! Quick Web site at http://www.connectcorp.com.

APPENDIX

C

Glossary of Terms

A

abstract

Retaining the essential features of some thing, process, or structure. The opposite of concrete.

abstract class

A class that contains abstract methods. Abstract classes cannot be instantiated.

abstract function

A function that is declared but not implemented. Abstract functions are used to ensure that subclasses implement the function.

Abstract Window Toolkit (AWT)

The collection of Java classes that allows you to implement platform-independent (hence *abstract*) GUIs.

ActiveX

A set of technologies that use controls (formerly known as OCXs and VBXs) based on the Component Object Model (COM). COM is used throughout Microsoft's desktop applications for communication and automation. Integrating a Web browser with ActiveX controls extends the Microsoft desktop across the Internet.

additive colors

The set of primary colors (red, green, and blue) from which all other colors can be created by mixing.

API

See *Application Programming Interface.*

applet

A Java program that appears to be embedded in a Web document.

appletviewer

A JDK utility that displays only Java applets from HTML documents, as opposed to a Web browser, which shows applets embedded in Web documents.

Application Programming Interface (API)

A set of methods, functions, classes, or libraries provided by a language or operating system to help application developers write applications without needing to reinvent low-level functions. All of the standard Java packages combined form the Java Core API.

array

A group of variables of the same type that can be referenced by a common name. An array is an object with length as its public data member holding the size of the array. It can be initialized by a list of comma-separated expressions surrounded by curly braces.

atomic

Indivisible or uninterruptible. In the context of multithreading, an operation (statement, code block, or even an entire method) that cannot be interrupted. Code that accesses composite data structures shared with other threads usually must protect its critical sections by making them atomic.

autocommit

A method to turn off and on transaction processing. When autocommit is off, transactions can be undone using the `rollback()` method, or the database can be updated using the `commit()` method. When autocommit is on, transactions are automatically committed after each statement.

AWT

See *Abstract Window Toolkit.*

B

base class

The superclass from which each class in a set of classes inherits members.

BDK

See *Beans Development Kit*.

Beans Development Kit (BDK)

A JavaSoft tool that helps Java developers create reusable components (Beans) through the inclusion of introductory documentation, a tutorial, sample Beans, and a test container.

big-endian

An internal ordering of data bytes in memory. Big-endian ordering is also called *network ordering*. In the big-endian ordering, high bytes of a word are stored first in memory. RISC and Motorola processors use the big-endian byte ordering; Intel 80x86 processors use the little-endian byte ordering. In the little-endian ordering, the word will be stored as 0x34 0x12 in memory (the little end comes first).

black box

The concept of a functional entity whose internals are wholly irrelevant. A black box is characterized by the type of inputs it takes, the type of outputs produced, and the circumstances under which these outputs are generated (that is, the black box function).

blitting

To BLIT (Block Image Transfer). In graphical systems, the high-speed, rectangular copy operations often performed by dedicated accelerator hardware. Moving a window, scrolling a window's contents, and rendering text are examples of operations that rely heavily on blitting.

boolean

A variable that can assume only the values `true` or `false`. Booleans can be used to represent things that have a binary state, such as alive/dead, connected/disconnected, same/not the same, open/closed, and so on.

break statement

One of the flow-breaking statements. Without a label, control will be transferred to the statement just after the innermost enclosing loop or `switch` statement. With a label, control will be transferred to the enclosing statement or block of statements carrying the same label.

buffer

In the narrow sense, an amount of storage set aside to temporarily hold and/or accumulate some information, such as write and read disk buffers and frame buffers. In the wider sense, any decoupling system that desynchronizes two entities; that is, a system that lets the entities run at their own speeds or frequency.

bytecode verifier

Part of Java's security precautions, the bytecode verifier checks that the bytecodes can be executed safely by the Java Virtual Machine (VM).

bytecodes

Compiled Java code. Bytecodes are portable instructions that can be executed by any Java Virtual Machine (VM).

C

Call Level Interface (CLI)

An interface to perform SQL calls to databases. A CLI consists of method calls to the database that return values and result sets. The SQL statement is embedded in the calls. For example, the call `execute` takes the SQL string as a string parameter.

case clause

A part of a `switch` statement. The clause consists of the `case` keyword, followed by a constant expression, a colon, and one or more statements. See also *switch statement*.

casting

Explicitly coercing a value from one datatype to another.

CGI

See *Common Gateway Interface*.

class

A description of a specific kind of Java object, including the instructions that are particular to it.

class file

A binary file containing Java bytecodes. The Java compiler generates a class file from source code for each Java class.

class library

A collection of prefabricated classes that the programmer can use to build applications more rapidly. Java's class library is the Core API. In Java, these are also called *packages*.

class loader

The part of the Java Virtual Machine (VM) that fetches classes from the client file system or from across the network.

class variable

A variable within a class that is available for use by the class itself. Only one copy of the variable exists, and the class variable is unique to all instances of the class within the program.

CLI

See *Call Level Interface*.

client

An entity that relies on another (*server*) entity to accomplish some goal. Clients can be as simple as classes calling on other classes or (more frequently) client programs calling on server programs across a network.

client/server application model

An application model commonly employed in networked environments. The monolithic application program is split into two halves; one half running on the server machine, the other running on the client machines. The client/server model is used as a solution in multiuser systems where central resources must be shared/changed/consulted by many.

Common Gateway Interface (CGI)

A standard interface between Web servers and other server programs. The server programs are usually used to process database requests and generate HTML documents on the fly.

Common Object Request Broker Architecture (CORBA)

An Object Management Group (OMG) standard that defines an Interface Definition Language (IDL) that is vendor and language-neutral. The IDL is used to create a contract between a client and server implementation.

compiler

A utility that reads the commands in a source file, interprets each command, and creates a new file containing equivalent bytecodes (or in the case of a C compiler, creates a file with native machine code instructions).

concrete

Opposite of *abstract*.

conditional statement

A statement for selective execution of program segments, such as the `if` and `switch` statements.

constructor

A method that creates an instance of the class to which it belongs.

continue statement

One of the flow-breaking statements. Without a label, control will be transferred to the point immediately after the last statement in the enclosing loop body. With a label, control will be transferred to the end of the enclosing loop body carrying the same label.

convolve filter

A type of image-processing filter that combines the pixels located around a central pixel to form the new central pixel. Different weights are assigned to each neighbor in a 3 x 3 matrix. The resulting pixel is the weighted average of all pixels.

CORBA

See *Common Object Request Broker Architecture.*

critical section

In the context of multithreaded systems, any section of code that needs to take precautions to avoid corrupting data structures shared with other threads.

D

data hiding

The ability to hide data within a class. Any changes to the hidden data from outside the class, if permitted at all, must be via methods.

datagram

A type of packet that represents an entire communication. No connection or disconnection stages are needed to communicate by datagrams. It is analogous to sending a telegram.

datatype

The specific type of data stored in variables; for example, `int` variables hold whole numbers, `char` variables hold individual alphanumeric characters, and `String` variables hold groups of alphanumeric characters.

debugger

A utility that can monitor and suspend execution of a program so that the state of the running program can be examined.

decoupling

The avoidance of a direct link between two entities by inserting a third entity (an interface, a buffer, or a whole subsystem). Decoupling introduces an extra level of flexibility for the price of a slight reduction in performance. A hallmark of a well-designed software system is the loose coupling between its subsystems (achieved by a multitude of decoupling techniques).

default clause

An optional part of a `switch` statement. It consists of the `default` keyword, followed by a colon, and one or more statements. See also *switch statement.*

default constructor

A constructor that is automatically available to a class that does not define its own constructor.

deprecated methods

Methods that were supported in previous releases of the Java Development Kit (JDK) but are not the preferred ones in the 1.1 release. Future releases may drop the methods altogether.

design pattern

A reusable, standard approach to a design problem. This is different from algorithms in that design patterns address higher-level issues and usually describe solutions in structural/relationship terms.

destructor

A method that is called to delete an object from memory. Java does not support destructors directly.

dial-up connection

An Internet connection that needs to be established by having a leaf machine dial a modem connected to a host that is connected to the Internet 24 hours a day.

disassembler

A utility that displays the meaning of instructions in a compiled file. The Java disassembler (javap) shows what the Java Virtual Machine (VM) will do when it runs a class file of bytecodes.

DLL

See *dynamic link library*.

DNS

See *Domain Name System.*

do statements

One of the loop statements. The loop body is executed once, and then the conditional expression is evaluated. If it evaluates to true, the loop body is reexecuted and the conditional expression is retested. It will be repeated until the conditional expression evaluates to false.

documentation comment

A comment block that will be used by javadoc to create documentation.

Domain Name System (DNS)

A distributed Internet database that can resolve textual Internet addresses to their real numeric forms. The DNS is organized as a hierarchy with each node responsible for a subset of the Internet host address namespace (hence distributed database).

double buffering

In general, the use of two buffers to allow one buffer to be constructed while the other is being used. Double buffering is used in animation to display one animation frame while the next is being drawn off-screen. Double buffering can also be used in the context of I/O logic to decouple the algorithm's performance from the performance limits of the I/O device (called being *I/O-bound*).

dynamic link library (DLL)

An executable library module, usually in binary form as an external file, that will be loaded during the runtime of a program on an as-needed basis.

E

else clause

An optional clause for an if statement. If the conditional expression of an if statement is evaluated to false, the statement or block of statements of the else clause will be executed.

encapsulation

Embedding both data and code into a single entity.

event-driven programming

Programming that allows the user to control the sequence of operations that the application executes via a graphical user interface (GUI).

exception

An abnormal condition that disrupts normal program flow.

expression

A combination of terms that evaluates to a single data value.

F

File Transfer Protocol (FTP)

The Internet protocol that allows users to download publicly accessible files from any Internet machine that accepts FTP connections. FTP also allows users to transfer files from their machine to another machine on the Internet.

finalizer

A method that is called immediately before a class is garbage-collected.

flow-breaking statement

A statement for breaking the flow. These include `break`, `continue`, and `return` statements.

flow-control statement

A statement for flow control. These include conditional, loop, and flow-breaking statements.

flushing

Final writing of any output data left in a write buffer. Closing files and streams flush their data buffers automatically (this is one of the reasons to close files and streams).

for statements

One of the loop statements. The initialization part is executed, followed by the evaluation of the conditional expression. If the expression evaluates to `true`, the loop body is executed, followed by the execution of the increment part. This cycle is repeated if the conditional expression evaluates to `true`.

fractal

In graphics, a recursively self-similar structure of infinite complexity. Contradictory to their definition, fractals can often be generated by very simple, finite equations or algorithms.

frame

In the context of GUIs, the graphical outline of a window. In the context of data communications, another word for *packet*.

frame header

The collection of fields at the start of a frame (packet) that contain nonuser data necessary for the fluent and efficient operation of the protocol. A typical frame header field is the checksum field that allows a receiver to check whether received data arrived as sent.

frame rate

Frequency at which new images are displayed in animation sequences or film. Typical rates range from 24Hz to 60Hz. Rates are measured in frames per second (fps).

FTP

See *File Transfer Protocol*.

G

Gamelan

A comprehensive online source for Java tools and applets. Its URL is `http://www.gamelan.com`.

garbage collection

A feature of automatic memory management that discards unused blocks of memory, freeing the memory for new storage.

GIF

See *Graphics Interchange Format*.

graphical user interface (GUI)

The mouse-driven, iconic interface to modern computer operating systems. Also called *windows, icons, menus, and pointer (WIMP)* interface.

Graphics Interchange Format (GIF)

A standard format for storing compressed images.

GUI

See *graphical user interface*.

hashtable

A list-storing mechanism that uses key-value pairs; also a class in the `java.util` package.

HCI

See *human-computer interface*.

HTML

See *Hypertext Markup Language*.

HTTP

See *Hypertext Transfer Protocol*.

human-computer interface (HCI)

A broad concept comprising the physical and non-physical interaction between people and computers. Ergonomics is a physical facet of HCI. Graphical user interface (GUI) design is a (mainly) nonphysical aspect of HCI.

Hypertext Markup Language (HTML)

The language in which Web documents are written. Java applets appear embedded in HTML documents.

Hypertext Transfer Protocol (HTTP)

The application protocol used by the World Wide Web for requesting, transmitting, and receiving Web documents.

IAB

See *Internet Architecture Board*.

IDDE

See *Integrated Development and Debugging Environment*.

IDE

See *Integrated Development Environment*.

identifier

A name the programmer gives to a class, variable, or method. Identifiers have restrictions on leading characters.

IDL

See *Interface Definition Language*.

if statement

One of the two types of conditional statements. It consists of the `if` keyword, followed by a conditional expression enclosed in a pair of parentheses, and a statement (or block of statements) to be executed when the conditional expression evaluates to `true`. It may be followed by an optional `else` clause consisting of the `else` keyword and a statement (or block of statements) to be executed when the conditional expression evaluates to `false`.

image filtering

The process of altering (generally improving) a digital image. This can be as simple as changing a picture's overall brightness or as complicated as applying an optical correction to minimize a flaw in the physical optics of the device that made the picture (as was done with the Hubble telescope, for instance).

inheritance

The ability to write a class that inherits the member variables and member functions (or methods) of another class.

inner classes

Classes that are defined within other classes, much in the way methods are defined within those classes. Inner classes have the same scope and access as other variables and methods defined within the same class. Their existence is hidden from view behind the enclosing class.

instance

An instance of a class; in other words, an object.

instance variable

A variable within a class, a new copy of which is available for storage in each instance of that class. Each object of that class has its own copy of the instance variable. (This is as opposed to a class variable.)

instantiation

The process of creating an object instance of a class.

Integrated Development and Debugging Environment (IDDE)

The as an Integrated Development Environment (IDE), but with built-in debugging features; IDDE programs include Sun's Java WorkShop and Symantec's Café.

Integrated Development Environment (IDE)

A program that aids in application development by providing a graphical environment that combines all the tools required to write code.

interface

A formal set of method and constant declarations that must be defined by the classes that implement it.

Interface Definition Language (IDL)

A system that enables Java programs to communicate with CORBA (Common Object Request Broker Architecture) systems.

Internet Architecture Board (IAB)

One of the Internet standards bodies that applies the final technical review to any new proposed Internet standard (in the form of Request For Comments, or RFCs).

Internet Protocol (IP)

The core Internet protocol on which all other application-level Internet protocols build. Some of the counterintuitive characteristics of IP are that it does not guarantee delivery of data and that it can only transfer data in maximum 64KB chunks.

Internet Service Provider (ISP)

An organization (commercial or not) that allows users to hook up their machine to the Internet via a permanent or dial-up connection.

interpreter

A utility that reads the commands in a file, then interprets and executes each command one at a time.

introspection

A mechanism that allows classes to publish the operations and properties they support and a mechanism to support the discovery of such mechanisms.

IP

See *Internet Protocol*.

ISP

See *Internet Service Provider*.

J

Java Archive (JAR) file

Like a tar or zip file, a file that holds an aggregate of files. These may be signed by their creator to permit greater access to the user.

JavaBeans API

An API for the creation of reusable components. Through bridges, these Java objects can link with objects created in other languages, including ActiveX, OpenDoc, and several other industry standards. A Java "Bean" is a single reusable software component.

Java Core API

Java's class library. It contains core language features and functions for tasks such as networking, I/O, and graphics.

Java Database Connectivity (JDBC)

Defines a set of Java classes and methods to interface with databases.

Java Developers Kit (JDK)

The set of Java development tools distributed (for free) by Sun Microsystems. The JDK consists mainly of the Core API classes (including their source), a Java compiler (written in Java), and the Java Virtual Machine (VM) interpreter.

Java Electronic Commerce Framework (JECF)

A standard that provides support for Java applet-based shopping and other financial transactions.

Java Naming and Directory Interface (JNDI)

A Java API that provides naming and directory functionality.

Java Virtual Machine (VM)

The system that loads, verifies, and executes Java bytecodes.

JavaOS

An operating system written mostly in the Java language, which incorporates the Java Virtual Machine (VM) and classes.

JavaScript

A separate programming language loosely related to Java. JavaScript can be coded directly in an HTML document, which makes the JavaScript source code part of the document itself.

Java Server

A full-featured Web server program that can be extended via plug-in servlets.

JavaStation

The Network Computer developed by Sun Microsystems and JavaSoft, which used JavaOS (the Java operating system).

JDBC

See *Java Database Connectivity*.

JDK

See *Java Developers Kit*.

JECF

See *Java Electronic Commerce Framework*.

Jeeves

Early code name for a complete Web server written in Java. See *Java Server*.

JIT compiler

See *Just-In-Time (JIT) compiler*.

JNDI

See *Java Naming and Directory Interface*.

JPEG (Joint Photography Engineering Group) file

A compressed graphics file format. JPEG images may be compressed in a "lossy" fashion that sacrifices image detail for smaller image size, or in a "lossless" method, where information about the image is retained, but the file size increases accordingly.

Just-In-Time (JIT) compiler

A compiler that converts verified bytecodes to native processor instructions before execution and can significantly improve Java application performance.

keyword

A word that has a special meaning for the Java compiler, such as a datatype name or a program construct name.

LayoutManager

A Java class that handles preprogrammed layout styles for the graphical user interface (GUI) components.

literal

An actual value such as 35, or "Hello", as opposed to an identifier, which is a symbol for a value.

little-endian

An internal ordering of data bytes in memory. In the little-endian ordering, low bytes of the word are stored first in memory. In the big-endian ordering, high bytes of a word are stored first in memory.

RISC and Motorola processors use the big-endian byte ordering; Intel 80*x*86 processors use the little-endian byte ordering.

loop statement

A statement for the repeated execution of program segments. These include `for`, `while`, and `do` statements.

marshaling

The process of assembling and disassembling parameters to and from remote objects and methods is collectively called marshaling and unmarshaling the parameters.

MIME format

See *Multipurpose Internet Mail Extension*.

member

The generic term for data or code entities within a class.

member function

See *method*.

member variable

A variable that is part of a class.

message

A method call.

method

A function or routine that is part of a class. Also called a *member function*.

microJava

A medium-end Sun microchip that runs Java natively.

multidimensional array

An array of arrays. It can be nonrectangular. A multidimensional array can be initialized by grouping comma-separated expressions with nested curly braces.

multiple inheritance

The ability to write a class that inherits the member variables and methods (member functions) of more than one class. See also *inheritance*.

Multipurpose Internet Mail Extension (MIME) format

An extension to the standard Internet e-mail format to allow the inclusion (as file attachments) of content other than plain text. It is typically used for the newer multimedia types like audio/video clips, but is generally capable of handling any binary file format.

multithreading

The means to perform multiple tasks independent of each other.

N

namespace

A set of rules allowing the generation of valid names or labels. For example, the e-mail address syntax, US state number license plate format, and global telephone numbering systems define namespaces. Namespace also means the boundaries that can be accessed by a program. The operating system (or the Java Virtual Machine) defines the namespace for a program.

namespace partitioning

A set of rules to structure a namespace. The Java package namespace partitioning rules structure the namespace into a collection of non-overlapping trees.

native method

Code that is native to a specific processor. On Windows 95, native methods refer to code written specifically for Intel *x*86 processors.

nesting

The "Russian dolls" effect of repeatedly wrapping or layering entities around other entities. In graphical user interface (GUI) design, widgets are often nested in container widgets that themselves are nested in bigger containers and so on.

Netscape Plug-Ins

Netscape Communications has created a standard interface to extend its Navigator browser product line. Products adhering to the specification are called Netscape Plug-Ins.

Network Computer

A computer that meets the Network Computer Platform specification, which is designed based on the "network as the computer system" concept.

Network News Transfer Protocol (NNTP)

The Internet protocol behind the newsgroup reading programs. NNTP manages daily threads of discussion in some 15,000 "news" groups, such as comp.lang.java.programmer.

NNTP

See *Network News Transfer Protocol*.

null

A value that means *no object*, which can be held by an object variable.

#

object

A software "thing" that has characteristics (state) and behavior (methods).

object-oriented programming (OOP)

Programming that focuses on these independent objects and their relationships to other objects, rather than using a top-down, linear approach (as with traditional Pascal or C).

object pointer

In C++ and Delphi, an object variable that points to a specific memory location.

object variable

A name for an object. It may refer to an object or be null.

octet

Another term for the eight-bit byte. Used only in the data communications world.

ODBC

See *Open Database Connectivity*.

OOP

See *object-oriented programming*.

opcode

Short for operation code. It is an integer representing the code for an operation.

Open Database Connectivity (ODBC)

A specification for connecting databases; the ODBC is a C interface. ODBC is based on the X/Open SQL Command Level Interface (CLI).

overloaded functions

Functions defined multiple times, each definition having the same name but accepting different parameters, either in number or type. The compiler knows which function to call based on the parameters it is passed.

P

package

A collection of related classes.

packet

A unit of communication. A packet can contain mostly user data, or it can be a pure protocol management packet (that is, containing no user data whatsoever).

packet-switched

A type of web-structured (as opposed to star or ring-structured) data communications network that uses datagram packets as its building block packet type. Examples are the global X25 packet-switching network and the Internet.

parent class

See *superclass*.

persistence

The ability of a Java object to record its state so it can be reproduced in the future, perhaps in another environment.

persistent object stores

Database-independent, object-oriented storage systems for storing various types of objects, such as video, audio, and graphics.

picoJava

Low-end Sun Microsystems microchip that runs the Java language.

pipe

An abstract data connection between (typically) two processes or threads. Process A writes data to Process B via a pipe. Process B needs to read the data from the pipe to receive any data.

polymorphism

The ability of a single object to operate on many different types.

POP

See *Post Office Protocol.*

Post Office Protocol (POP)

The Internet protocol that handles e-mail collection.

properties

Describe attributes associated with a component in a graphical user interface (GUI), such as color, size, and the string to be used as a label.

protocol

The set of rules and the structures of legal packets that are used to provide some communication service between two computers. Common examples are TCP/IP, Z-Modem, Kermit, SLIP, PPP, X25, and IBM SNA.

RAD

See *Rapid Application Development.*

Rapid Application Development (RAD)

A kind of development tool that enables programmers to create sophisticated programs quickly.

reader

Similar to an input stream (used in I/O programming), but the basic unit of data is a Unicode character.

recursive

Self-calling. A recursive method calls itself repeatedly, either directly or indirectly.

registers

Known areas in a microprocessor for keeping small pieces of information like a pointer to the next instruction, the results of an addition, and so on. Usually, registers are in the microprocessor and can be accessed much faster than memory.

Remote Method Invocation (RMI)

The set of APIs for a Java program to call objects and methods that reside outside the current runtime environment or namespace.

rendering

Computer graphics jargon for drawing (used as both a verb and a noun).

request and response headers

Terms used to denote the ASCII-readable multiline headers of the HTTP protocol. The HTTP protocol consists of client (browser) requests followed by Web server (site) responses.

result set

The most common operations on a database are queries that return data. This data, which consists of many rows and columns, is called a result set.

return statement

One of the flow-breaking statements. It is used to return control to the caller from within a method or constructor. Before the control is passed back to the caller, all of the `finally` clauses of the enclosing `try` statements are executed, from the innermost `finally` clause to the outermost one.

RMI

See *Remote Method Invocation.*

root class

In general, any class that acts as the superclass for a subhierarchy. An entire inheritance hierarchy, like Java's, has a single absolute root class: class `Object`.

router

A device in a packet-switched network that can accept packets and decide to which of its many output ports it should forward the packet to bring the packet a step closer to its final destination.

S

schema

A description of data elements in a database and their relationships. Primarily used by database designers, developers, and administrators.

SecurityManager

A Java class that restricts access to files, the network, or other parts of the system for security purposes.

serialization

The process whereby an object records itself by writing out the values that describe its state. *Deserialization* is the process of restoring serialized objects.

server

An entity whose sole purpose is to serve clients (either sequentially or in parallel) by providing them with some kind of well-defined service, such as searching a database or accepting mail messages.

servlet

A mini server-side program, similar to an applet, defined in the Java Servlet API.

Servlet API

An API that makes it possible to create programs that can run within the context of a Java-enabled server.

signature

A method's unique profile, consisting of its name, argument list, and return type. If two methods with the same name have the slightest difference in their argument lists, they are considered totally unrelated as far as the compiler is concerned.

signed classes

Classes and applets that can be traced to the company who developed them. This is achieved by keeping a tamper-proof electronic signature in the .class file. The technology for this scheme is in development.

Simple Mail Transfer Protocol (SMTP)

The Internet protocol behind e-mail delivery. See also *Post Office Protocol (POP)*.

sink

The final destination for data moving through a stream.

SMTP

See *Simple Mail Transfer Protocol*.

socket

A software interface that connects an application to the network.

source file

A text file containing human-readable instructions. A Java source file is a text file written in the Java programming language.

stack

A list storing mechanism that uses the last-in, first-out (LIFO) metaphor. Also, a class in the `java.util` package.

state

An unambiguous, non-overlapping mode of "being;" for example, the binary states *on* and *off*.

stream

An abstract concept used in the context of I/O programming to represent a linear, sequential flow of bytes of input or output data. A program can read from *input streams* (that is, read the data a stream delivers to it), and write to *output streams* (that is, transfer data to a stream).

streaming

Term used to denote audio, video, and other Internet content that is distributed in real time and does not need to be downloaded.

subclass

A class that descends or inherits (*extends* in Java terminology) from a given class. Subclasses are more specialized than the classes they inherit from.

superclass

A class from which a given class inherits. This can be its immediate parent class or can be more levels away. Superclasses become more and more generic as you travel up the inheritance hierarchy, and for this reason, can often be abstract.

switch statement

A multiway selection statement. The integer expression is evaluated, and the first `case` clause whose constant expression evaluated to the same value is executed. The optional `default` clause is executed if there is no `case` clause matching the value. The `break` statement is usually used as the last statement of a `case` clause so that the control will not continue on to statements of the next `case` clause.

TCP

See *Transmission Control Protocol.*

TDS

See *Tubular Data Stream.*

telephony

Applications that combine telecommunications and multimedia computer technologies.

thread

A single flow of control within a program, similar to a process (or a running program), but easier to create and destroy than a process because less resource management is involved. Each thread must have its own resources, such as the program counter and the execution stack, as the context for execution. However, all threads in a program share many resources, such as memory space and opened files.

tokenizing

A common technique used to reduce the complexity of textual input.

transaction processing

A general term used in the context of databases to denote, among other things, consistency, recoverability, and data integrity of relational databases. A transaction consists of multiple SQL (Structured Query Language) commands that read and update databases.

Transmission Control Protocol (TCP)

The connection-oriented protocol built on top of the Internet Protocol (IP). TCP guarantees delivery of data and can handle arbitrary amounts of data.

Tubular Data Stream (TDS)

A type of data set from a database, usually relational, that has rows and columns of data. One important characteristic of TDS is that it has information about the data like the number of columns, the column titles, and so on.

UDP

See *User Datagram Protocol.*

Unicode

An International character-mapping scheme (see `http://www.stonehand.com/unicode.html` for more information).

Uniform Resource Locator (URL)

A string that identifies the location of a resource and the protocol used to access it.

unmarshaling

See *marshaling.*

untrusted applets

Applets downloaded from network whose source cannot be traced or trusted. These applets need to be verified before they are executed, because they could contain malicious virus programs.

URL

See *Uniform Resource Locator.*

User Datagram Protocol (UDP)

A protocol between Internet Protocol (IP) and Transmission Control Protocol (TCP). It allows IP-style datagrams to be sent to a port on a machine (instead of just a machine).

V

vector

A list-storing mechanism that continually resizes itself, as space allocation needs to be changed. Also, a class in the `java.util` package.

Virtual Machine

See *Java Vital Machine (VM).*

W

Web browser

A viewer program used by the client machine to display Web documents.

Web server

A network server that, upon request, transmits Web documents via HTTP (Hyptertext Transfer Protocol).

Web site

A set of Web documents belonging to a particular organization. A Web site may share a server machine with other sites or may extend across several machines.

while statements

One of the loop statements. The conditional expression is first evaluated. If it evaluates to `true`, the loop body is executed, and the conditional expression is reevaluated. It will cycle through the testing of the conditional expression and the execution of the loop body until the conditional expression evaluates to `false`.

widgets

From "window gadgets," a generic term for graphical user interface (GUI) elements like buttons, scrollbars, radio buttons, text input fields, and so on.

windows, icons, menus, and pointer (WIMP)

See *graphical user interface (GUI).*

World Wide Web (WWW)

A huge collection of interconnected hypertext documents on the Internet.

writer

Similar to an output stream (used in I/O programming), but the basic unit of data is a Unicode character.

INDEX

Note to the Reader: Throughout this index **boldfaced** page numbers indicate primary discussions of a topic. *Italicized* page numbers indicate illustrations.

B

C

D

E

F

G

H

J

N

O

S

U

V

W

X

Y

Z

Java™ Development Kit Version 1.1 Binary Code License

This binary code license ("License") contains rights and restrictions associated with use of the accompanying software and documentation ("Software"). Read the License carefully before installing the Software. By installing the Software you agree to the terms and conditions of this License.

1. Limited License Grant. Sun grants to you ("Licensee") a non-exclusive, non-transferable limited license to use the Software without fee for evaluation of the Software and for development of Java™ compatible applets and applications. Licensee may make one archival copy of the Software. Licensee may not re-distribute the Software in whole or in part, either separately or included with a product. Refer to the Java Runtime Environment Version 1.1 binary code license (http://www.javasoft.com/products/JDK/1.1/index.html) for the availability of runtime code which may be distributed with Java compatible applets and applications.

2. Java Platform Interface. Licensee may not modify the Java Platform Interface ("JPI", identified as classes contained within the "java" package or any subpackages of the "java" package), by creating additional classes within the JPI or otherwise causing the addition to or modification of the classes in the JPI. In the event that Licensee creates any Java-related API and distributes such API to others for applet or application development, Licensee must promptly publish an accurate specification for such API for free use by all developers of Java-based software.

3. Restrictions. Software is confidential copyrighted information of Sun and title to all copies is retained by Sun and/or its licensors. Licensee shall not modify, decompile, disassemble, decrypt, extract, or otherwise reverse engineer Software. Software may not be leased, assigned, or sublicensed, in whole or in part. **Software is not designed or intended for use in on-line control of aircraft, air traffic, aircraft navigation or aircraft communications; or in the design, construction, operation or maintenance of any nuclear facility. Licensee warrants that it will not use or redistribute the Software for such purposes.**

4. Trademarks and Logos. This License does not authorize Licensee to use any Sun name, trademark or logo. Licensee acknowledges that Sun owns the Java trademark and all Java-related trademarks, logos and icons including the Coffee Cup and Duke ("Java Marks") and agrees to: (i) to comply with the Java Trademark Guidelines at http://java.com/trademarks.html; (ii) not do anything harmful to or inconsistent with Sun's right in the Java Marks; and (iii) assist Sun in protecting those right, including assigning to Sun any rights acquired by Licensee in any Java Mark.

5. Disclaimer of Warranty. Software is provided "AS IS," without a warranty of any kind. ALL EXPRESS OR IMPLIED REPRESENTATIONS AND WARRANTIES, INCLUDING ANY IMPLIED WARRANTY OF MERCHANTABILITY, FITNESS FOR A PARTICULAR PURPOSE OR NON-INFRINGEMENT, ARE HEREBY EXCLUDED.

6. Limitations of Liability. SUN AND ITS LICENSORS SHALL NOT BE LIABLE FOR ANY DAMAGES SUFFERED BY LICENSEE OR ANY THIRD PARTY AS A RESULT OF USING OR DISTRIBUTING SOFTWARE. IN NO EVENT WILL SUN OR ITS LICENSORS BE LIABLE FOR ANY LOST REVENUE, PROFIT OR DATA, OR FOR DIRECT, INDIRECT, SPECIAL, CONSEQUENTIAL, INCIDENTAL OR PUNITIVE DAMAGES, HOWEVER CAUSED AND REGARDLESS OF THE THEORY OF LIABILITY, ARISING OUT OF THE USE OF OR INABILITY TO USE SOFTWARE, EVEN IF SUN HAS BEEN ADVISED OF THE POSSIBILITY OF SUCH DAMAGES.

7. Termination. Licensee may terminate this License at any time by destroying all copies of Software. This License will terminate immediately without notice from Sun if Licensee fails to comply with any provision of this License. Upon such termination, Licensee must destroy all copies of Software.

8. Export Regulations. Software, including technical data, is subject to U.S. export control laws, including the U.S. Export Administration Act and its associated regulations, and may be subject to export or import regulations in other countries. Licensee agrees to comply strictly with all such regulations and acknowledges that it has the responsibility to obtain licenses to export, re-export, or import Software. Software may not be downloaded, or otherwise exported or re-exported (i) into, or to a national or resident of, Cuba, Iraq, Iran, North Korea, Libya, Sudan, Syria or any country to which the U.S. has embargoed goods; or (ii) to anyone on the U.S. Treasury Department's list of Specially Designated Nations or the U.S. Commerce Department's Table of Denial Orders.

9. Restricted Rights. Use, duplication or disclosure by the United States government is subject to the restrictions as set forth in the Rights in Technical Data and Computer Software Clauses in DFARS 252.227-7013(c) (1) (ii) and FAR 52.227-19(c) (2) as applicable.

10. Governing Law. Any actions related to this License will be governed by California law and controlling U.S. federal law. No choice of law rules of any jurisdiction will apply.

11. Severability. If any of the above provisions are held to be in violation of applicable law, void, or unenforceable in any jurisdiction, then such provisions are herewith waived to the extent necessary for the License to be otherwise enforceable in such jurisdiction. However, if in Sun's opinion deletion of any provisions of the License by operation of this paragraph unreasonably compromises the rights or increase the liabilities of Sun or its licensors, Sun reserves the right to terminate the License and refund the fee paid by Licensee, if any, as Licensee's sole and exclusive remedy.

JDK1.1 BCL 2-9-97#

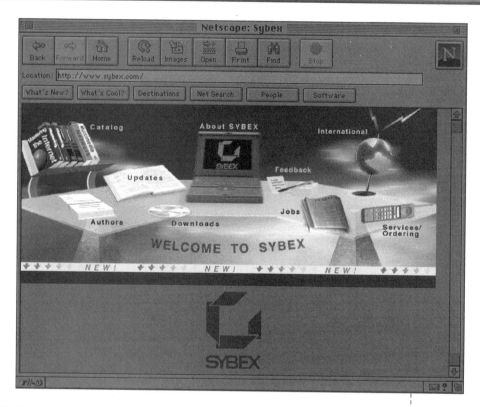

WHAT'S ON THE CD-ROM

This companion CD-ROM contains all the source code and executable files from the book, plus numerous cutting-edge Java Integrated Development Environments (IDEs) and third party tools to use with Java versions 1.0 and 1.1.

Products you will find on this CD include...

- **JDK 1.1**, the full development package from Sun Microsystems, Inc. for creating Java applications and applets.

- **Jamba 1.1**, a new authoring tool from Aimtech, enables Internet developers and Webmasters to create interactive, media-rich Java applets and applications without programming or scripting.

- **Mojo 2.0**, from Penumbra Software, is a complete development environment for creating networking applets. Mojo consists of a GUI Designer and a Coder.

- **ED for Windows 3.71**, from Soft As It Gets, is a complete Java development environment that offers powerful editing capabilities and code navigation features.

- **Widgets**™, from Connect! Quick, is a library of sophisticated, prebuilt components for assembling commercial-quality Java applications.

- **Vibe DE**, from Visix Software, is an intuitive integrated development and deployment environment for building Java applications. Vibe is comprised of a Java-specific IDE, which includes a compiler, debugger, and extensive set of class libraries, and ActiveX support.

- **JetEffects**, from Peak Technologies, is an easy-to-use Java animation tool for home and small-office Web page authors. JetEffects can be used by novices and experts.

The JDK Version 1.1 on this CD is the complete product from Sun Microsystems, Inc. The other products are fully functioning trial versions or demos that will time out after 20–45 days of use. Details about each product's capabilities, along with specific installation instructions, are located in Appendix B. Windows NT 3.51 does not support use of this CD-ROM. Windows NT 3.51 users can download all information available on this CD from the Sybex Web site: www.Sybex.com.